D1301118

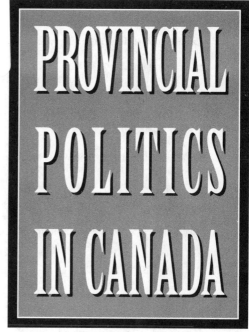

PROVINCIAL POLITICS IN CANADA

TOWARDS

THE TURN

OF THE

CENTURY

RAND DYCK

Laurentian University

PRENTICE HALL CANADA INC.
Scarborough, Ontario

Canadian Cataloguing in Publication Data

Dyck, Perry Rand, 1943–
    Provincial politics in Canada: towards the turn of the century

3rd ed.
Includes index.
ISBN 0-13-443391-2

1. Provincial governments – Canada.*
2. Canada – Politics and government – 1867–   .
I. Title

JL198.D92   1996   320.971   C95-930733-8

 © 1985, 1991, 1996 Prentice-Hall Canada Inc., Scarborough, Ontario
A Viacom Company

Prentice-Hall, Inc., Englewood Cliffs, New Jersey
Prentice-Hall International (UK) Limited, London
Prentice-Hall of Australia, Pty. Limited, Syndey
Prentice-Hall Hispanoamericana, S.A., Mexico City
Prentice-Hall of India Private Limited, New Delhi
Prentice-Hall of Japan, Inc., Tokyo
Simon & Schuster Asia Private Limited, Singapore
Editora Prentice-Hall do Brasil, Ltda., Rio de Janeiro

ISBN 0-13-443391-2

Acquisitions Editor: Patrick Ferrier
Editorial Assistant: Maria Tsombanelis
Production Editor: Avivah Wargon
Copy Editor: Therese Greenwood
Production Coordinator: Sharon Houston
Page Layout: B.J. Weckerle

Your comments on this book are welcome at **collegeinfo_pubcanada@prenhall.com**

1 2 3 4 5   RRD   99 98 97 96 95

Printed and bound in the USA.

Every reasonable effort has been made to obtain permissions for all material used in this edition.
If errors or omissions have occurred, they will be corrected in future editions provided written
notification has been received by the publisher.

To Joan, with even more love.

Contents

12. CONCLUSION   644

Preface

As in the two previous editions of this book, I have had the temerity to write about all 10 provinces myself. But, even more than before, I wish to acknowledge the hundreds of people who have assisted me by providing information. In preparing this edition I travelled across the country, wandered into legislatures and government offices of all kinds, collected documents, and talked to officials both in pre-arranged meetings and totally without warning. Wherever I went, officials were generous with their time and knowledge and invariably impressed me with their devotion to duty.

The second group of people without whom this edition would not have been possible are those who put it all together at Prentice Hall Canada: Pat Ferrier, Kelly Dickson, Pauline Peyton and Maria Tsombanelis, the copy editor Therese Greenwood, and especially Avivah Wargon.

I have also been fortunate in being able to call upon the assistance of several of my students at Laurentian University over the past few years, especially Troy Whetstone, Sam Bottomley, Michael Freeze, Dan Charbonneau, and Jamie Moon. Without their help the book could not have been completed on time. Also at Laurentian, Robert Wittmer demonstrated his wizardry at word processing, the library staff provided competent, sympathetic support, and our department secretary Doris Routhier again went well beyond the call of duty. Other friends and colleagues also provided encouragement. Rodney Marsh gave me free accommodation in Toronto. And my patient, forgiving, and badly neglected wife Joan put up with my long hours of intimacy with my computer.

Rand Dyck

INTRODUCTION

Canada is a decentralized federation of 10 distinctive provinces, each of considerable political and economic significance in its own right. This book examines each of the provinces as a "small world" or separate political system.[1] It also points out striking similarities and differences among the provinces, as well as exploring their relationships with the federal government. Each chapter begins with a semi-statistical account of geographic, economic, class, and demographic features of the province and an outline of its relationship with Ottawa. Attention then turns to the basic concerns of political science: the province's political culture, political parties, electoral system, pressure groups and mass media, and government institutions. A survey of its political evolution follows, with an emphasis on developments since 1970. A table of provincial election results and a list of provincial premiers round out each chapter. Those readers who desire more historical detail may choose to consult earlier editions of this book. Those who crave more interprovincial comparison will find such in the conclusion, as well as in the statistical tables in the appendix.

THE PROVINCES AND THE FEDERAL SYSTEM

This book is about provincial politics, but an initial word should be provided about how the provinces fit into the Canadian federal system. Federalism is characterized by a division of powers between a central government and provincial governments such that neither is subordinate to the other. This may not be an accurate description of the relationship in Canada in 1867, but it is certainly applicable today. At one time, the two levels of government functioned more or less independently—each within its own jurisdiction—but, especially since 1945, they have become closely intertwined in almost every field. Federal-provincial political and bureaucratic arrangements have become much more important than judicial interpretation of the division of powers between the two jurisdictions. Most remarkable are the financial arrangements in terms of both taxation

1

and expenditure. Since 1947, successive five-year agreements have co-ordinated many federal-provincial taxation powers as well as provided federal grants to the provinces. These may be conditional grants, where Ottawa typically pays 50 percent of the cost of a program if the province meets certain federal conditions; block grants, where the provinces are supposed to allocate funds to a specified field such as health care or post-secondary education, but without detailed federal supervision; or unconditional grants, where there are no restrictions on the provincial use of funds. By far the largest kind of unconditional grant consists of equalization payments, which the federal government pays to the "have-not" provinces. In fact, many provincial initiatives depend upon the availability of federal assistance. Such co-operation between the two levels of government is not always easily achieved and many federal-provincial conflicts are discussed in following chapters. It should be emphasized that intergovernmental co-ordination underlies a large proportion of the activity of both levels of government. As the two levels of government approach the turn of the century, however, provinces are becoming alarmed over reductions in federal grants and the off-loading of federal responsibilities, actions Ottawa is taking because of its emphasis on controlling the federal deficit. This becomes all the more contentious as the provinces are obsessed with their own deficits and debts.

If the post-Second World War period has been marked by increased federal-provincial interaction, many observers have also remarked on the growth in the powers and importance of the provinces. Hence the term "province-building," which has become a commonplace in recent years.[2] This concept is unfortunately somewhat vague and all-inclusive but is a convenient label to apply to a number of developments in many provinces. These include increases in provincial revenues and bureaucracies, and the creation of Crown corporations and central planning agencies. There is also a willingness as well as a capacity to intervene in the process of industrial development and diversification, a phenomenon often associated with the natural resource sector and identified with a particular class of entrepreneurs and state administrators. There is no doubt, however, that elements of province-building are more applicable to such provinces as Alberta and Quebec than to others. Similarly, certain aspects of the phenomenon, such as centralized planning, have a long history in some provinces, notably Saskatchewan. The concept should not be interpreted as a diminution of federal revenue and power—it preceded Ottawa's efforts to downsize its own operations —nor as an automatic increase in the degree of federal-provincial conflict. The provinces constitute worthy objects of study without denying the significance of the federal government, and without necessarily accepting the implications of the province-building concept in its fullest form.

SETTING

Each chapter begins with a section entitled "Setting." The first consideration here is geography and size, geographic features, regions, population distribution, and transportation links are examined. The second consideration involves a study of the provincial economy, beginning with a discussion of primary, secondary, and tertiary industries. The primary industries are agriculture, fishing, logging, and mining. While the number of employees in the primary sector may be relatively small and the revenue generated not always impressive, most of the secondary and tertiary industrial sectors in this country are based on primary industries. The importance of natural resources to the national economy has been a central tenet of Canadian political economy for generations, usually termed the "staples theory." This theory postulates that Canadian economic development has relied on resource exports—furs, fish, timber, wheat, minerals, and energy—rather than manufacturing. It argues that, internally, the Canadian economy remains underdeveloped and characterized by the dominance of one geographic region over another, while externally it is subject to the rise and decline of international markets, and usually dependent on a single foreign industrial power. The staples theory has often been more applicable to the provincial than the national level, for such resource industries fall largely within provincial jurisdiction. Where minerals, petroleum, or forests are involved, large companies have tended to develop close relations with the host provincial government, which has been anxious to see such resources exploited. In provinces where farming or fishing predominates, individual producers have had less influence on government and have often had to resist exploitation by the companies purchasing their produce. Due to the importance of resource development in provincial politics, considerable attention will be given to the resource base in each chapter. Mention will also be made of the electrical power situation because energy has become a significant issue in the past 20 years.

Secondary industry consists of processing and refining primary products and manufacturing finished goods, with the latter generally producing more revenue and employment than the former. Another component of the secondary sector is construction. The tertiary sector is commonly divided among transportation, communications, and utilities; trade; finance, insurance, and real estate; services; and public administration. While the Canadian economy has never relied heavily on manufacturing, attention in this "post-industrial" era is primarily focused on the tertiary or broader services sector.

The third part of the setting section of each chapter deals with the concept of class. It includes a discussion of the personal incomes of provincial residents, with reference to income disparities, unemployment, labour organizations, and the economic elite. It would not be difficult to apply an elite, class, or "political economy" analysis to provincial politics in Canada, but no such full-scale treatment is attempted here.[3]

The fourth section, on demography, includes a discussion of the ethnic, linguistic, and religious distribution of the population and the implications thereof. Despite some predictions that such social characteristics would decline in political significance over time, in many provinces ethnic origin, language, and religion remain near the top of the political agenda. These issues focus on services available to the francophone or anglophone minority in the province, the place of "other ethnics" (called "allophones" in Quebec), religious-minority schools, and, increasingly, the condition and aspirations of the aboriginal population.

The fifth aspect of the setting of each province is its relationship with the federal government. In a sense, the relationship of Ottawa vis-à-vis the provinces parallels the role of the United States as the main external factor in Canadian national politics. (That is not to say that the United States is not an important factor in the politics of every province, if for no other reason than it is where they often go to borrow money.)

Political science usually seeks to discover divisions or cleavages that engender political conflicts or issues, which in turn result in demands for government action. One of the main objectives of this text, therefore, is to determine the principal generators of political issues in each province. These may be ethnicity, language, religion, class, region, or gender, conflicts between rural and urban areas, competition among different industries, or conflicts among ideologies. Before the 1990s, such conflict was often over the *extension* of government action to support one interest or another. However, as we approach the turn of the century with an obsession with government debts and deficits, the issue is often framed in terms of which interests will *lose* support. It will also be seen that every province is preoccupied with economic development and unemployment. These issues lend themselves to controversy, including disagreement over the roles of the public and private sectors, competition among regions regarding the location of industry, and disputes over the short- and long-term implications in such areas as employment versus the environment. Consequently, there is usually no shortage of grist for the provincial political mill, and intraprovincial divisions are almost always compounded by conflicts between the province and the federal government.

POLITICAL CULTURE

The second part of each chapter deals with political culture, which can be defined as the sum total of the basic political values, beliefs, attitudes, orientations, and opinions of the people of the province. The realm of values and attitudes is a complex and subtle one and can be difficult to document.[4] However, one of the most accessible quantitative measures in this field, and one of great interest to political science, is that of voter turn-out. While it may be difficult to explain variations in this statistic, it is a crucial aspect of democracy and the most common form of political participation in Canada.

A second common numerical measure of provincial political culture has to do with how residents balance feelings of being citizens of the province with being citizens of the country. This is a measure of sentiment and support for the two political systems of which they are part. In a healthy federation, these loyalties should be in equilibrium—but that would hardly be expected in the Canada of the 1990s. *Maclean's,* a national news magazine, periodically publishes a Decima Research poll on this subject. The poll results for 1990 and 1994 are revealed in Table 1.1.

TABLE 1.1   **"Do you think of yourself as a Canadian first or as a citizen of your province?"**

	1990		1994	
	Canada	**Province**	**Canada**	**Province**
Quebec	44%	55%	45%	49%
Newfoundland	47%	53%	39%	57%
P.E.I.	57%	43%	50%	44%
Nova Scotia	63%	37%	69%	27%
Alberta	74%	24%	74%	16%
New Brunswick	75%	25%	64%	26%
British Columbia	83%	17%	76%	17%
Saskatchewan	83%	16%	82%	7%
Manitoba	84%	15%	77%	11%
Ontario	90%	9%	90%	9%
All Canada	73%	26%	72%	22%

Reproduced with permission of *Maclean's* magazine, 1 January 1990, and 3 January 1994.

While the author would like to measure all sorts of other political values and attitudes at the provincial level—efficacy, trust, ideology—the numbers are just not available. While national public opinion polls abound, especially at election time, they are federally oriented and sample sizes for individual provinces are not usually large enough to make meaningful observations at the sub-national level. Nevertheless, an attempt is made in the political culture part of each chapter to describe how the people of each province feel about themselves, what they consider to be the province's distinctive features, and to what extent they are committed to basic democratic values.

It is also desirable to categorize the provinces in terms of political sophistication or development. Leading political scientists have developed a variety of schemes for doing so. Gabriel Almond and Sydney Verba pioneered a classification combining attitudes toward a political system and patterns of political participation; Richard Simeon and David Elkins applied a somewhat similar approach to Canadian politics; and S.J.R. Noel concentrated on patterns of patronage.

Almond and Verba's classic study in 1963 developed a three-fold scheme by which to categorize political cultures.[5] A "parochial" political culture is one in which citizens are essentially unaware of the political system of which they are a part; in a "subject" political culture, citizens are aware of the political system, inform themselves about its operations, realize that it has some impact on their lives but undertake few initiatives to influence it. A "participant" political culture is one in which citizens are aware of the political system and actively attempt to influence it.

In 1980 Simeon and Elkins first explored degrees of trust or distrust toward provincial authorities and feelings of political efficacy or inefficacy—one's sense of being capable of influencing political events.[6] They then enlarged the model with such measurements of political involvement as voter turn-out, reading about and discussing politics, participating in election campaigns, and contacting public officials. Unfortunately, their statistics are over 20 years old.

Noel developed the concept of "clientelism" which deals with the practice of patronage and contains three stages of development.[7] In a primitive rural economy, more or less characteristic of the pre-Confederation period, a relationship developed between a local notable (the "patron") and his clients. In this first stage, the clients gave political support to the patron, who in return dispensed individual favours such as government jobs and contracts. He went to the provincial capital and bargained with other notables in the assembly or cabinet for a share of the public largesse. In the second stage, political parties made their appearance, and the patron-client relationship became less personal because of the involvement of political brokers or intermediaries. For example, government jobs and contracts began to be awarded on a partisan basis and thus, to a large extent, the party became the patron. In addition, the nature of the favours changed somewhat, taking the form of large contracts to build railways, canals, and other public works, benefitting not only the individual entrepreneurs involved but whole communities. This was the typical situation during the Confederation era and for some time afterwards. Finally, in the third stage, which is generally characteristic of the period since the Second World War, there was an enormous expansion of government activities and patronage could no longer be relied upon as a basis for staffing the public service. At this point, the entire patron-client relationship became bureaucratized. The bureaucracy emerged as the patron at the expense of the individual notable or the political party because the bureaucracy had the discretion to license, regulate, and inspect, and to distribute massive amounts of public funds through programs of grants, concessions, incentives, rebates, loans and services of every kind. To a large extent, these benefits favoured whole groups, communities, institutions, regions, or interests rather than individuals. Because this system was not guaranteed to produce results for politicians, they tried to retain parts of their power from the second stage. Thus, even when a province reached the third stage, vestiges of the two earlier periods remained. The more urbanized and industrialized the province, the more likely it is to have passed from the second to the third stage, although various regions within a province could be at different levels of development at the same time.

All of these approaches are useful in the following chapters. However, much more research must be conducted on provinces, individually and comparatively, before the subject of provincial political cultures can be satisfactorily analyzed.[8]

POLITICAL PARTIES

The first of the many aspects of political parties which interest political science concerns how many and what kind of parties make up the provincial party system. In this respect, John Wilson has proposed a three-stage model which relates the development of the party system to the concept of social class.[9] He argues that, shortly after 1900, the two parties of the 19th and early 20th centuries, the Liberals and Conservatives, found they had to contend with a newly enfranchised working class. The working-class phenomenon was of little importance in the four Atlantic provinces and Quebec prior to 1960, so that these provinces had what could still be considered a pre-industrial or non-polarized two-party system. In the absence of a strong working-class consciousness, the dominant divisions continued to be ethnic and religious ones. In political systems where the new class made more impact, one of two alternative kinds of party system emerged. In Ontario, the Cooperative Commonwealth Federation (CCF), which later became the New Democratic Party (NDP), gained significance as a new party representing the interests of the working class but until recently did not displace either traditional party. This left the province with a slightly polarized three-party system. In the western provinces, the new working-class (or farmer-class) party, the CCF/NDP, successfully displaced one of the traditional parties, at least for a time, resulting in a two-party system largely based on ideology or social class. At that time, Wilson predicted all provinces would move in this polarized two-party direction. However, as the following chapters show, this has not necessarily happened. In the western provinces in particular, the Liberal party has risen, Phoenix-like, from its ashes.

Wilson notes the relevance of the number of parties making up the provincial party system and their ideological orientation. Party systems can be classified in a variety of ways, including one-party dominant, two-party, three-party, and multi-party systems. One-party dominance occurs when parties are not evenly matched and do not alternate frequently in power. The degree of one-party dominance can be measured by the percentage of seats or popular vote held by the dominant party. It is appropriate to use this label where one party gained more than 70 percent of the seats or persistently attracted more than 50 percent of the vote. A two-party system, on the other hand, is one in which two parties capture the bulk of the vote between them, perhaps 90 percent, are relatively equal in strength, are separated by less than 10 percent of the popular vote, and regularly alternate power. At the parliamentary level, they share control of almost all of the seats. If each of three parties captured at least 20 or 25 percent of the popular vote, the system could be classified as three-party. This categorization would be even more apt if such a division of the vote resulted in a succession of governments of different political stripes and/or minority governments. Another designation might be "two plus" party system, in which an enduring but weak third party gained between 10 and 20 percent of the vote.

Whatever their merits, such definitions cannot be applied too rigidly. In the first place, the proportion of seats won by a party may not relate closely to its percentage of popular vote. What is classified as one-party dominant on the basis of number of seats could also be considered a two-party system in terms of proportion of popular vote. Another problem with such characterizations is that a province can move from one category to another without much warning. Furthermore, as Wilson points out, there are different kinds of two-party systems.[10] One type reflects a pre-industrial society in which few differences exist between parties, especially in class or ideology. On the other hand, perhaps after a transitional three-party period, a two-party system of another kind can emerge that is characterized by class and/or ideological differences. Thus, it is necessary to distinguish between polarized and non-polarized two-party systems.

Others have found it useful to concentrate on the origins of parties and to speak of parliamentary parties (Liberals and Conservatives), fragment parties which break away from the originals, and movement parties which can be populist (Social Credit) or socialist (CCF/NDP).[11] Various theories on the rise of third parties are referred to at the appropriate time.

Wilson's second point relates to party ideology and class support. Two main schools of thought co-exist in Canadian political science about the extent to which ideology motivates political activity and the degree of ideological difference among political parties. One school denies the existence of ideological variance, emphasizing the basic pragmatism or opportunism of all parties. It argues that once in power all parties are much the same, and/or that they are all captives of the corporate elite. Thus, much attention is focused on "broker" parties which are seen either as a pragmatic response to the needs of a diverse electorate in which economic, linguistic, ethnic, religious, and geographic interests are all relevant, or as a means for the economic elite to break down class lines.[12]

While no one would claim that there are profound ideological differences between federal Liberal and Conservative parties, a second school finds a difference of approach at the federal level, as well as a more significant ideological variation in the provinces, especially in the case of the NDP, Parti Québécois (PQ), and Social Credit.[13] Those who make such distinctions point out that the Liberal party has two main factions—business and reform liberalism. The two are slightly right and left of centre on an ideological scale, with inequality and individualism on the right and equality and collectivism on the left. The two forces may vary in balance from time to time, but they usually interact to put the Liberal party in the centre of the ideological spectrum. The NDP, on the other hand, is left of the Liberal party on both measures—equality and collectivism—although it too has a certain divergence of opinion as to how far left it should go. Being composed of a higher proportion of business liberals, the Conservatives are generally to the right of the Liberals on both the individualism and inequality scales. However, a minority stream within that party, the "progressive" wing, is slightly left of centre on the scales of equality and collectivism. This tension within the Conservative party also forces it toward the centre. Such a theoretical standpoint can be seen graphically below. Interesting provincial variations in the extent of ideological diversity are therefore to be expected and, where such diversity exists, it will presumably be accompanied by voting behaviour based on class.[14]

TABLE 1.2   Party Ideology in Canada

Collectivism	NDP	Liberals	Conservatives	Individualism
Equality	NDP	Liberals	Conservatives	Elitism

Related to the existence of ideological differences between parties is the issue of whether such differences are reflected in provincial government policies. To what extent are variations in provincial policies the result of party ideologies and to what extent do different parties pursue distinctive policies in government? This is a subject of great scholarly interest and too vast a field to treat in a comprehensive manner here. However, academic opinion is divided between those who argue that ideology makes little or no difference to government policies and those who argue it does. Within the Canadian provincial context, the debate usually focuses on whether CCF/NDP or Parti Québécois governments adopt distinctive policies.[15]

One reason for the generally negative results of these studies is the methodology employed: comparing provincial policies in terms of the relative amounts of spending in different areas such as health, welfare, education, and highways. This is a somewhat seductive but not entirely satisfactory approach, given the existence of variables such as federal contributions, different departmental structures, different patterns of provincial-municipal relations, and different distributions of funds within policy categories. More recent research, using subtler techniques, has usually indicated greater ideological differences between parties. J.A. McAllister found in 1984 that a left-wing partisan affiliation on the part of the government, as well as a poorer than average populace, was the best means of identifying a provincial government that taxed and spent to its limits.[16] Dale Poel analyzed 25 provincial policy innovations and found that 10 were pioneered in Saskatchewan, nine by the CCF/NDP.[17] William Chandler studied the influence of the CCF/NDP as an Opposition force and concluded that, in certain circumstances, the socialist threat had an identifiable impact on the spending patterns of governments, especially in the areas of health and social welfare.[18] Marsha Chandler examined the question with respect to natural resource policy, which is not based on expenditures and not subject to the homogenizing influence of federal conditional grants. She developed a four-category scheme of degrees of public intervention, from profits tax through gross royalties and super-royalties to public ownership, and found that left-wing parties (CCF/NDP and PQ) were more interventionist than others.[19] Similarly, she discovered CCF/NDP governments not only made more frequent use of Crown corporations, they did so with a different objective: for redistributive purposes rather than nationalistic reasons or to foster economic development.[20] Another group of Canadian political scientists also found that the provincial tax structure is made more progressive under governments of the left.[21]

Another aspect of political parties that requires discussion is that of party organization. On a theoretical level, it is common to distinguish between "mass" and "cadre" parties. A mass party has, or aspires to have, a large membership and gives significant power to its members. It chooses its leader at a convention or by a vote of party members and maintains some control over the leader afterwards. It is financed by membership fees and other small contributions from its members. It gives the membership a role in determining party policy. It also functions democratically, constitutionally, and throughout the year. In contrast, a cadre party is content to operate with a small local elite. It allows the parliamentary caucus to select the leader and then permits the leader to act without formal accountability. It depends financially on a relatively small number of very large contributions, usually from corporations. It gives the leader, cabinet, or caucus the power to formulate party policy. It also pays little attention to its constitution, is run by an elite group, and barely exists except at election time.

Another aspect of party organization in Canada concerns the relationship between federal and provincial parties. The Liberal, Conservative, and New Democratic parties all run a full slate of candidates in federal elections (even though the strength of their organizations varies considerably), but this does not occur at the provincial level. The Conservatives have no provincial party in Quebec, and not much of one in British Columbia. The recent resurrection of provincial Liberal parties in the western provinces has already been mentioned. The NDP may sometimes lack provincial candidates east of Ontario, especially in Quebec and P.E.I. The cause, or perhaps the consequence, of these gaps is the emergence of distinctive provincial parties, such as the Union Nationale and the Parti Québécois in Quebec, and Social Credit in British Columbia and Alberta. This phenomenon hampers the development of a symmetrical relationship of federal and provincial parties, and raises the question of what relations exist between the purely provincial parties and the three traditional ones at the national level. Another interesting issue is the relationship between the federal and provincial party organizations of the same name. D.V. Smiley has examined this relationship in terms of electoral dependence, party organization, party careers, finance, and ideology.[22] The author has argued elsewhere that the NDP is the most "integrated" of the three parties in question, the Conservatives the most "loosely linked confederal," while the Liberals have two distinctive kinds of federal-provincial relationships, one joint and the other split.[23] Some interesting federal-provincial alliances have also been formed, such as the close relationship between the Mulroney Conservatives and the Bourassa Liberals in Quebec in the late 1980s, and between the federal Tories and provincial Social Credit in B.C. in the 1970s and 1980s. Thus far, the federal Reform party has rebuffed suggestions that it should also enter provincial politics.

It is also interesting to examine the process by which parties choose their leaders. After a long period in which all parties chose their leaders at a party-delegate convention, provincial parties are now adopting a bewildering array of leadership-selection processes that generally involve giving all party members a direct vote on the leadership question, often via the telephone.

ELECTIONS

While most provinces now or will soon have orthodox "first-past-the-post" single-member systems—in which the candidate with the largest vote wins the constituency—they have experimented with a rich variety of electoral systems in the past. Most have used dual or multiple-member constituencies at one time or another, either in larger urban centres or in collective county ridings. In addition, some provinces have employed preferential voting schemes of one kind or another, in which voters had to rank candidates in order of preference rather than simply mark one or more Xs on the ballot. When it suited the purposes of the party in power, such systems were eliminated.

Another aspect of electoral systems is the degree to which each constituency has an equal number of voters or, conversely, the extent to which some areas are over-represented. There is no constitutional requirement that provincial electoral systems be equitable in this respect or paralleling the federal rule that constituency boundaries be redrawn every 10 years to reflect population growth and shifts. Consequently, gerrymandering—designing the constituency boundaries in the interests of the governing party or assigning an unrepresentative number of members to an area depending on its past voting record—has occurred in most provinces. This often coincided with an extreme over-representation of rural areas when it favoured the party in power. In many cases, this over-representation extended far beyond what was justifiable for large, sparsely populated rural or northern ridings. The federal government introduced the concept of an impartial redistribution commission in the 1960s, with rules limiting the disparity in the size of constituencies, and most provinces have since made improvements in this area. In many provinces where the redistribution of seats still appeared to be flawed, however, critics challenged the process in court. The courts have rendered several decisions on provincial redistribution procedures in relation to the democratic rights section of the Charter of Rights and Freedoms.

Another way to improve the fairness of the electoral system is by regulating campaign expenditures and contributions. Most provinces have experienced significant fund-raising scandals, and have taken appropriate steps to rectify this situation. Election finance legislation may involve limiting contributions and/or expenditures, disclosing contributions over a certain amount, providing tax credits, and subsidizing election expenses.[24] It is partly due to such reforms that the phenomenon of election-day "treating"—the offer of alcohol, cash, or other small inducement by a party or candidate in the hope of influencing votes—is increasingly a thing of the past.

Another interesting aspect of electoral systems is that of voting behaviour, some aspects of which have already been mentioned in terms of political culture. One main focus of Canadian research on this subject has been the extent to which citizens with common socio-economic characteristics vote in the same way. At the federal level, for example, regional patterns of party support are evident, and ethnic and religious groups have tended to identify with one party or another. The greatest controversy in the research concerns the role of social class: are voters conscious of their class and, if so, to what extent do voting patterns reflect such class consciousness? It is usually shown that the NDP gets the largest portion of its support from the working class, but more working-class votes go to other parties than to the NDP. In other words, class voting is not particularly evident in federal elections, although it is possible that it is more prominent at the provincial level. Somewhat like John Wilson, Jane Jenson classifies provincial party systems as traditional, transitional, or modern, in terms of the extent of class voting, and points out that class consciousness does not necessarily develop on its own. She argues that the "full mobilization of the electorate on the class cleavage requires a party that can interpret the world to the voters with an analysis explaining their conditions of life and politics." It often falls to intermediary organizations such as unions or co-operatives to alert their members to such an interpretation.[25]

The extent to which people vote consistently for the same party in federal and provincial elections is another aspect of electoral behaviour that bears examination. In some cases, of course, distinctive federal or provincial parties make such consistency impossible. But even in provinces where this is not the case, voter consistency is low. Expectations that people would vote for the same party in both federal and provincial elections are based on several assumptions: that voters would develop a party loyalty transcending federal and provincial elections; that parties of the same name would have similar ideological positions and equivalent organizational strength; and that issues at one level would affect results at the other. However, the federal and provincial wings of a party are often not well integrated, the degree of voters' party identification is usually low, and an ideological difference between federal and provincial levels of a party sometimes forces voters to switch to another party to be consistent. Since party leadership is a primary determinant of voting choice, there is even less reason to expect such congruence. In fact, recent Canadian voting behaviour has exhibited a high degree of volatility at every level.

Canadian federal-provincial voting patterns sometimes appear to be cyclical. Partly in response to the Trudeau Liberal regime in Ottawa, most provinces elected opposition Conservative governments during the 1970s. But, with the election of a Tory federal government in 1984, prospects for provincial Liberal parties seemed to improve immediately. In 1986, Ontario and Quebec elected Liberal provincial governments for the first time in many years. Since then, new Liberal governments have been elected in P.E.I., New Brunswick, Newfoundland, and Nova Scotia. Even more startling, the Liberal party elected significant numbers in Manitoba, Alberta, and B.C., provinces where that party had virtually disappeared. After the 1988 federal Conservative victory, NDP prospects improved in many provinces and it elected three provincial governments in 1990-91. It is too early to tell whether the federal Chrétien Liberal government, elected in 1993, will have the same negative impact on its provincial counterparts.

PRESSURE GROUPS AND THE MEDIA

No account of provincial politics would be complete without some mention of leading pressure groups and the mass media. The focus here is mainly on large, institutionalized groups with a continuing impact on the provincial scene. In one sense, provincial pressure groups are often branches of national groups, such as provincial chambers of commerce and the Canadian Chamber of Commerce. Even if such groups were previously organized at only one level of government, the era of co-operative federalism has encouraged them to operate in both federal and provincial arenas. In some cases, provincial branches such as teachers' federations, medical associations, and bar societies have more impact than their national counterparts. This is partly because such professional bodies have been granted powers of self-regulation in the province, giving them a powerful organizational tool lacking at the federal level. The politicization of the teaching and nursing professions is a striking aspect of recent Canadian provincial politics, and the medical profession has become increasingly combative. On the other hand, natural resource companies and the "property industry" have always been particularly active at the provincial level.

A further aspect of pressure group activity is the close association that often develops between a provincial government department and the groups it most affects, an association sometimes called a clientele or "symbiotic" relationship.[26] An example is found in the relationship between the provincial government and resource companies or mining, forestry, and petroleum associations, given that natural resources fall within provincial powers. Such groups may use their close relationship with provincial governments to influence the federal government, getting provincial governments to act or speak on behalf of the industry at the federal level.[27] It is not surprising that such groups may prefer to be regulated, taxed, and funded by hospitable provincial governments rather than by Ottawa, and that they occasionally seek to influence the constitutional division of powers in order to maximize provincial jurisdiction. As for the targets of their activity, pressure groups tend to concentrate attention on the bureaucracy and cabinet because of historic and continuing executive dominance in the provinces.

Finally, because the mass media transmit messages between governments and voters, often mould public opinion, and influence the authorities, the leading newspapers and broadcasting outlets in each province are identified.

GOVERNMENT INSTITUTIONS

The next section of each chapter deals with government institutions. This section is relatively short, not because such institutions are unimportant, but because they are essentially the same in all provinces. Based on the similarities discussed below, the related section in the following chapters highlights the most important and distinctive aspects of the governmental structure of each province.

Executive

The executive branch of government contains the non-political head of the province, the lieutenant-governor, and the political executive, the premier and cabinet. The position of lieutenant-governor today is largely symbolic and ceremonial, and most accounts of provincial government overlook it entirely.[28] In the beginning, however, lieutenant-governors had an important dual role. First, they were agents of the federal government with power to reserve provincial legislation for the consideration of the cabinet in Ottawa. Even though they are still appointed by the federal government, normally for a five-year term, they no longer perform this function because it is inconsistent with genuine federalism. Therefore, while the power of reservation has been exercised 70 times, it has been used only once since 1937, and, on that exceptional occasion, the action was roundly condemned.[29] Second, lieutenant-governors were representatives of the monarch and had equivalent powers of vetoing legislation, dismissing governments, and refusing requests to dissolve the legislature in order to call an election. Many of these powers have been used more frequently and more recently by lieutenant-governors than by the governor-general or the monarch herself. They have also been superseded by events such as the advance of democratic sentiment and the development of well-organized political parties. The five instances of a lieutenant-governor dismissing a government, the three refusals to grant a dissolution of the legislature, and the 28 occasions on which provincial legislation has been vetoed, all occurred in the early days of Confederation. None of these powers has been exercised since 1914.[30] A further responsibility is to ensure that there is always a government in office but this rarely requires personal initiative on the part of the lieutenant-governor because the largest party in the legislature almost always has a recognized leader who is the obvious person to form a government. Thus, apart from an emergency situation, lieutenant-governors are no longer expected to exercise personal discretion. They function as the monarch does, performing important ceremonial and social functions to relieve the premier of a heavy workload in these areas. They may also be able to exercise moral leadership for the province, and are available for confidential counsel to the premier should their advice be sought.

Acting officially as the Executive Council, a provincial cabinet typically sets priorities, decides how much money to raise and spend, and how to do so, determines policies, prepares legislation, oversees departmental administration, supervises the implementation of public programs, and issues regulations and makes order-in-council appointments, as authorized by statute.[31] Government operations have regularly expanded, especially in recent years, and the size of provincial cabinets has increased from a handful of ministers before 1900 to about 20 in most cases today. Premiers try to balance various interests when choosing their ministers. Matters such as region, religion and ethnicity are still important considerations, and ability alone is not always enough to secure a cabinet appointment. Since premiers usually select their ministers from elected members of the legislature, they are constrained in their choices by what the electorate has provided. In recent years, approximately three-quarters of legislators were university educated, one-half professionals, and one-third from business; ministers have shown the same or greater disproportions when compared to the general population.[32] The greatest disparities between population and membership in provincial cabinets and legislatures have been in terms of gender and working-class origins, although women are steadily increasing their representation.

As long as provincial governments were small and their activities limited, the full cabinet could make most decisions and do so in an informal manner. As governments grew and became more complicated, significant changes took place. These included the development of more formal procedures; the need for more solid information, planning and co-ordination; more efforts to control public expenditures; and the more frequent use of a cabinet committee system. All of these are sometimes considered marks of "province-building."

Some order was brought to federal cabinet procedures during the Second World War, and the activist CCF government in Saskatchewan recognized the need for cabinet re-organization in the 1940s. However, the reform of cabinet operations in other provinces did not begin until about 1970, when Manitoba and Ontario began reforms which coincided with similar developments in Ottawa. Thus, most provinces now have a Treasury Board (a cabinet committee which attempts to restrain departmental spending), and a planning and priorities committee chaired by the premier and focusing on these two key activities. To improve interdepartmental co-ordination, most provinces have cabinet committees in such policy areas as social and economic development, and procedures have been formalized so that most proposals proceed to one or more such committees before being considered by the full cabinet. In addition, a cabinet secretariat has emerged to provide procedural and secretarial assistance to the cabinet and cabinet committees, as well as expert advice to these groups and to the premier. Most provinces have also attempted to introduce various decision-making techniques to increase the degree of rationality of government operations. This means that advances made in recent years by provincial legislatures have been at least matched by improvements at the executive level. In fact, those provinces that have reformed the legislature most effectively (Ontario and Quebec) have also made the most extensive changes to the cabinet.

While some of these developments have detracted from the personal power of the premier, others have probably enhanced this position. Few premiers today would be allowed the capriciousness of a Joey Smallwood, a Maurice Duplessis, or a W.A.C. Bennett. But premiers retain certain powers, privileges, and prestige which continue to give them pre-eminence, even though their proposals must theoretically run the gauntlet of cabinet committees. Premiers select, shuffle, and remove ministers, and are increasingly the focus of both media and public attention during election campaigns. In addition, premiers have the privilege of consulting trusted advisors who are entirely outside the authorized channels. They are also first to learn the results of the latest government and party public opinion polls. Thus, while ministers are said to be individually responsible for their departments and collectively responsible for government policy, determined premiers can still make their presence felt throughout the government's operations. Indeed, it has been said that "provincial government is premier government,"[33] and the premier is probably relatively more powerful at the provincial level than the prime minister is in Ottawa.

Legislature

The provincial legislatures are the elected representatives of the people.[34] While five provinces possessed a two-house legislature after 1867, each province now has a single chamber.[35] For nearly 100 years after Confederation, Canadian provincial legislatures had little power and were characterized by a "debilitating subservience" to the executive.[36] The cabinet would make all significant decisions and call the legislature into session for a few weeks each year to pass legislation which the executive had prepared. That legislation provided ample opportunity for the cabinet to govern by issuing authoritative regulations and orders-in-council (edicts of the executive council, mostly involving appointments) between sessions of the assembly. The legislature had little scope to question or criticize, let alone contribute to the shape of government policies. In fact, short sessions, frequent one-party dominance, the absence of ideological issues, lack of resources for private members, and the higher ratio of ministers to backbenchers rendered provincial legislators even less significant in the policy-making process than their federal counterparts. Being a provincial legislator was a part-time responsibility and members went back to their "real" jobs after a short stint in the provincial capital. Before party lines hardened (and afterwards in the case of members of the government) the main year-round interest of legislators was in obtaining favours, such as jobs or contracts for their friends or constituents or public works and other services for their constituencies as a whole. As government business became more extensive and complicated, the executive branch—the cabinet and bureaucracy—expanded and private members of the legislature had even less input into policy development.

With this expansion in government activity, legislative sessions became longer, and members were deluged with requests to take up constituents' problems with the provincial bureaucracy. As these tasks consumed increasing amounts of their time, members began to demand clerical and administrative assistance. As the job of legislators continued to evolve into a full-time one, they sought better pay and a more meaningful say in the policy-making process.

The past 20 years have witnessed a revolutionary advance in the remuneration and services provided to members of provincial legislatures. Ontario led the way in the 1975-81 period, with Quebec close behind since 1976. These two provinces continue to be well ahead of the others in most respects, but the remaining eight have undergone significant changes.[37] In most provinces members now have legislative offices and secretaries or assistants, research staff, travel and accommodation allowances, extra pay for committee work when the legislature is not sitting, householder mass-mailing, telephone, and other privileges. These services are most generous in Ontario, and least extensive in the four Atlantic provinces. Members also now receive better salaries, usually comprised of a basic indemnity plus a tax-free allowance (which means their income is worth twice as much in taxable terms). As of 1994, the basic indemnities ranged from about $29,000 in Manitoba to over $60,000 in Quebec, while the tax-free allowances ranged from $9,000 in P.E.I. to over $19,000 in Alberta. In addition, between 40 percent and 80 percent of legislative members received supplementary indemnities because they held such offices as premier, cabinet minister, parliamentary assistant, opposition party leader, Speaker, deputy Speaker, house leader, or party whip. Legislative sessions have become longer and several approach 100 sitting days per year. In addition, committee meetings sometimes take up almost as much time and, when not on duty in the provincial capital, legislators must meet with constituents at home. Even with the creation of provincial ombudsmen and the appointment of members' assistants, most provincial legislators have a heavy "caseload," and an increasing number regard being a provincial legislator as a full-time job.

In terms of procedure, all provincial legislatures now have an oral question period, although many are of recent origin. Ontario and Quebec principally use standing committees to consider legislation clause by clause and to examine the spending estimates of government departments. Other provinces are moving in this direction, but still depend largely on the committee of the whole (or supply) to conduct these functions. Some legislatures also appoint special or select committees from time to time and permit them to investigate issues and make recommendations before the government has finalized its approach to a problem. Most provinces now have an independent auditor to review government spending and report abuses to the legislature, and this report is investigated by a public accounts committee chaired by an Opposition member. However, only a few provinces (Quebec and Saskatchewan) provide for an effective review of regulations issued by the executive.

The recent transformation in Canadian provincial legislatures essentially means that private members can now do a better job in the areas of criticizing, questioning, and informing the cabinet. Cabinets continue to make the crucial decisions, however, and legislatures are not much closer to being involved directly in the decision-making process. There is much room for legislators who are not in the cabinet to play a more significant part in government, and for provincial cabinets to take their suggestions more seriously.

For a time, the increased importance of legislatures could be linked to the decline in the use of the plebiscite or referendum. Between 1900 and 1934 more than 40 provincial referendums took place, mostly on the subject of liquor. Well over half took place in the western provinces, a reflection of their tradition of direct democracy.[38] Newfoundland and Quebec engaged in crucial constitutional referendums in 1948 and 1980 respectively and, in the 1990s, the referendum gained new popularity. Quebec, Alberta, and British Columbia passed legislation to make a referendum compulsory on constitutional amendments and, in the end, residents of all provinces voted on the major constitutional amendments contained in the 1993 Charlottetown Accord. Quebec's 1995 referendum on whether to remain in Canada may perhaps be considered the most important of all.

Bureaucracy

The provincial bureaucracy, or public service, consists of government employees whose function is to advise the cabinet on its decisions and implement its programs.[39] In its first role, the public service is asked for information and advice before the cabinet decides to initiate any new policy, program or law. At this early stage, the bureaucracy may originate the request for action or may be the vehicle by which pressure groups transmit demands to the cabinet. Once the cabinet decides to proceed and determines the general direction it wishes to take, it again turns to the bureaucracy. In its second role, that branch of government, with its concentration of technical information and experience, must flesh out the new initiative in the policy formulation stage and draft a new statute if necessary. After the cabinet and legislature have given official approval to a new policy, program, or law, the bureaucracy is responsible for its implemention. In addition to providing services, enforcing rules, collecting taxes, and engaging in other administrative activities, the public service must draft regulations which contain the detailed substance of the law in question. This may involve consultation with relevant pressure groups. Thus, the modern bureaucracy is no mere neutral agent in providing advice to and administering policies established by the cabinet. It is a power to be reckoned with in its own right.

The functions of provincial governments were minimal until well into the 20th century and the number of government departments was small. No particular qualifications were required for public employment, and provinces could afford to operate on the "spoils system." Under this system, a wholesale turnover of public employees occurred whenever the government changed and each new government sought to reward its own friends. As in many other areas, the CCF government of Saskatchewan in the 1940s pioneered the first modern provincial public service in Canada, emphasizing expertise, permanence, and impartiality. Several other provinces established a civil service commission quite early, but none operated effectively because politicians could not restrain themselves from making partisan appointments.[40] Eventually, of course, politicians in all provinces recognized the need for permanent experts to respond to a larger population, increased demands, and a changing philosophy of public responsibility.[41] Ontario and Quebec were the next to develop a modern bureaucracy, in the early 1960s, and the other provinces followed suit later in that decade or in the early 1970s.

Between 1945 and 1971, the size of the provincial public service in Canada increased by more than 400 percent, and the expansion continued at least until about 1990. This increase is seen in larger departments (especially education and health), a greater number of government departments in each province, and new central agencies such as cabinet secretariats, treasury boards, and public service commissions. Each province also has every imaginable kind of semi-independent agency, board, or commission, operating outside the ordinary departmental structure.[42] These typically include a human rights commission, a workers' compensation board, a labour relations board, a social assistance appeal board, a variety of marketing boards, a liquor commission and liquor licensing board, and a public utilities commission. Most provinces have also established a range of Crown corporations, such as public hydro commissions, and government ventures in the natural resources field.

It should be noted, however, that privatization of some provincial Crown corporations and other government functions, as well as the implementation of severe restraint programs in the 1980s and 1990s, have ended the pattern of growth or reduced the size of government in most provinces.[43] Such retrenchment has had implications for the provincial public sector in its widest sense, including teachers, professors, and hospital and municipal employees.

Following Saskatchewan's lead, provinces have extended collective bargaining rights to public servants, although a few provinces still deny them (or some of them) the right to strike. However, virtually all provinces placed selective restraints on collective bargaining rights in the 1970s and 1980s, and even more in the 1990s, when provincial cabinets became unanimously concerned about debts and deficits.

Another aspect of the provincial bureaucracy is its relationship to the federal government. Regardless of constitutional jurisdiction, the two levels of government have each created departments in almost every policy field and, during the era of co-operative federalism, the federal and provincial bureaucracies usually worked closely together. Even if relations were less co-operative in the period between 1966 and 1984, frequent federal-provincial interaction continued. Indeed, it was partly due to the need to negotiate constructively with federal officials that provinces strengthened their bureaucracies during this period.

The enormous size and influence of the provincial public service naturally raises questions of responsibility and responsiveness. For example, some doubt exists as to whether the political executive can maintain control over the bureaucracy given the cabinet's reliance on public service expertise. Several of the legislative and cabinet reforms mentioned earlier were at least partly directed towards this objective. The issue of responsiveness to the public raises concerns about government secrecy—the public's right to know—and accessibility and citizen involvement. Most provinces now have freedom of information laws. Provincial departments have often developed close ties to particular pressure groups, but this leaves doubt as to their openness to less-organized and less-powerful interests. One traditional means for governments to seek the views of the public is the royal commission. Most provinces are also becoming proficient at the more modern technique of conducting public opinion polls.

Judiciary

While provincial legislatures, cabinets, and bureaucracies may regularly interact with their federal counterparts, they do so on a basis of legal equality. The relationship between the provincial and federal judiciaries, however, is somewhat different. There are three main aspects to the inferiority of provincial courts: their decisions may be subject to appeal to the Supreme Court of Canada; they must utilize the federal criminal code; and county, district, and Superior court judges are appointed by the federal government. On the other hand, the provincial attorney general is responsible for prosecuting most criminal offenses, and provinces determine the structure of their own courts. The judiciary essentially engages in interpreting the law in cases of dispute between private parties, between an individual or company and the government, or between governments. It renders an authoritative judgment, based on law, to settle such disputes. To perform this function, each province has established a complex structure of courts which until recently contained three distinct levels. At the bottom are the "provincial courts" including small claims courts, family courts, and those handling minor criminal offenses. The provincial cabinet appoints judges at this level. In recent years the element of partisanship in their selection has been reduced somewhat, and the qualifications for appointment raised. At the intermediate level, there were county and district courts, which generally heard more serious cases. At the top, the Supreme Court of the province is usually divided into a Trial division, comprised of individual judges, and an Appeal division, in which a panel of judges considers appeals from other courts. All provinces have now abolished county and district courts, effectively amalgamating them with their Supreme Courts. Although the structure differs little from province to province, the names given to the courts vary. Courts will play an increasingly important part in the political process in the future because of their power to overturn legislation they rule contrary to the Canadian Charter of Rights and Freedoms.

Municipal Government

Although this book focuses mainly on the provincial level, a word should be added about municipal government because the two are closely connected. The province determines the structures, responsibilities, and financial powers of municipal governments. Despite this discretion, and a great deal of minor variation, a fairly common pattern of local governments has emerged in Canada. They are typically classified as cities, towns, villages, townships, and rural municipalities, to which may be added upper-tier metropolitan governments, regional municipalities, and counties.

As cities grew rapidly after the Second World War, a conglomeration of independent suburbs sprang up around a central core in the largest urban centres, presenting serious obstacles to co-ordination and planning. Canadian provinces have been reasonably successful in dealing with this issue, however, either by amalgamating all surrounding towns into a single large municipal unit or by setting up a two-tier structure, on which all area municipalities are represented, to assume responsibility for metropolitan problems.

Generally speaking, local governments are responsible for such services to property as streets, sidewalks, water, sewers, garbage, and fire protection, as well as recreation and libraries, and, in larger centres, police. There is more variation among the provinces in the provision of such services to people as health, welfare, and housing. In some cases these responsibilities are assumed by the province rather than the municipality, or they are sometimes shared. Even greater diversity among the provinces exists with regard to the jurisdiction and financing of local school boards. The most significant of these distinctive features is outlined in the following chapters, but such variations make it difficult to compare the provinces in terms of the size of their budgets or bureaucracy.

POLITICAL EVOLUTION

Although all the provinces have fascinating pasts spanning several centuries, our examination of the political histories of each usually begins with the year that province joined Confederation. From that date until about 1970, this book contains only the highlights of each province's development, although somewhat more detailed accounts are provided in earlier editions of this book. Here, each chapter emphasizes political developments in the last three decades of the 20th century. A new generation of younger premiers emerged in the early 1970s; the 1980s saw a move toward privatization, deregulation, and fiscal restraint; and, as we approach the turn of the century, provincial governments are exhibiting an overwhelming concern with debts and deficits.

Each chapter ends with a short conclusion highlighting the province's most distinctive political features, a list of provincial premiers from the date of joining Confederation, and a table of recent provincial election results, usually from about 1920 onward. Party lines were not usually solidified much before this time, election returns for many provinces are incomplete for the earlier period, and major realignments took place after the First World War in the aftermath of conscription and coalition government in Ottawa. The election results were compiled from the official reports of the chief electoral officer. As for public documents, I have listed only those that are important, relevant, and distinctive. In each province, certain other public documents are also indispensable—the budgets, estimates, and public accounts, departmental annual reports, chief electoral officers' reports, and royal commission reports—which should not be ignored.

The concluding chapter attempts to draw some comparative generalizations which transcend the previous emphasis on the distinctiveness of the individual provinces.

THE NORTH

Besides its 10 provinces, Canada has two northern territories: the Yukon and the Northwest Territories. They have been excluded from this volume for two reasons: they have not yet attained provincial status, and the text is already of sufficient length. Nevertheless, a word about them should be added.

The Yukon had a 1991 census population of 27,797, of which about 23 percent were aboriginal, mostly Indians. Because the territory has virtually no Inuit, the remainder of the population is non-Native. The Yukon is the more constitutionally developed of the two territories with an assembly of 17 members and an executive council, or cabinet, of five chaired by a "government leader" similar to a provincial premier. A federally appointed commissioner has been instructed since 1979 to operate as a lieutenant-governor and to take the advice of the ministry. The Yukon has gradually developed a party system, and the results of the 1992 election were as follows: Yukon Party (formerly Progressive

Conservative), seven; NDP, six; and others, four. The leader of the Yukon Party, John Ostashek, took over as government leader.

The Northwest Territories had a population of 57,649 in 1991. Its residents consist of 60 percent aboriginal—35 percent Inuit, 16 percent Dene (Indians), and six percent Métis—and about 40 percent non-Native. The federally appointed commissioner has slightly more power than the Yukon commissioner, and the government leader somewhat less. A Native commissioner was appointed for the first time in 1989. The assembly consists of 24 members who are elected as independents. Lacking a party system, they vote among themselves for the positions of government leader and seven additional ministers. Without the discipline imposed by a party system, the assembly operates on the basis of consensus, being characterized by shifting coalitions more akin to a municipal council than a provincial legislature.

Ottawa has delegated most of the powers possessed by the provinces to the two territories, but without any similar constitutional protection. Territorial bureaucracies are increasingly supplanting the authority of the federal Department of Indian Affairs and Northern Development.

Beyond the issue of increasing autonomy for the public governments of the two northern territories are questions of Native land claims and aboriginal self-government. Four comprehensive Native land claims have been under discussion for many years: the Inuvialuit in the Mackenzie River delta, the Dene in the Mackenzie Valley, the Inuit in the eastern Arctic, and the Council of Yukon Indians in the Yukon. The Inuvialuit claim was settled in 1984, and the Dene and CYI claims are close to settlement. The biggest problem was that of the eastern Inuit, who wanted the NWT split into two separate territories so that they would predominate in the eastern portion, Nunavut. A boundary division was ratified in a plebiscite in 1992 and a land claim agreement signed in 1993, the same year that the Nunavut Act was passed. Division of the NWT into two separate territories is to be established on April 1, 1999. While Nunavut will represent a general correlation between an aboriginal land claim and an aboriginal government, in other parts of the Arctic, aboriginal self-governments are being negotiated separately from land claims and within the public territorial governments. For example, 14 First Nations are pursuing aboriginal self-government within the Yukon territory.

The northern territories will increasingly resemble provinces in the future but it will be many years before they are accorded full provincial status.

A NOTE ON THE NUMBERS

First, to avoid being bogged down in endnotes, I have not noted many of the statistics included in the tables in the appendix. Second, in some tables, the numbers do not add up to the exact total given or 100 percent. This is due to rounding, sometimes by the author, and sometimes by the source, usually

Statistics Canada. Third, the notation "adapted by author" is included to absolve anyone else of responsibility for any errors in my manipulations of the figures, usually by adding percentages.

For statistics on the size of cities, the difference between the size of the actual municipal corporation and the larger labour market area (what Statistics Canada calls census metropolitan area) is noted where this is significant. Generally speaking, statistics in this section refer to labour market areas unless otherwise noted.

For figures on the provincial labour force, I have referred to the 1991 census, although many alternative sources exist. In any such categorization, the "government" entry is slightly misleading because many of those employed in "services," such as educational and health services, are actually employed by government or work in the broader public sector. While the "government" entry is narrowly defined, it does include federal and municipal government employees, not just provincial ones. For up-to-date figures on the composition of provincial gross domestic products, I have used the Conference Board of Canada. Again, there are many alternative sources with considerably different results. I have used Statistics Canada figures for union membership but Canadian Labour Congress figures for membership of provincial federations of labour.

Statistics Canada and other sources provide a variety of tables on per capita personal income and income distribution. Because these differ to some extent, I have included 1991 census figures on family incomes and more recent Statistics Canada figures on per capita income.

Unlike previous editions, this one omits tables on Ethnic Origin. This is because an increasing number of Canadians are of mixed ethnic origins—and an increasing number actually call themselves "Canadians." However desirable this may be in other ways, it makes census statistics on ethnic origin almost useless. For statistics on mother tongue and home language, the problem is minor. The numbers of those with two mother tongues have been divided in half, and the numbers of those with three mother tongues have been divided into thirds.

There is not much disagreement over the amount of federal transfers to the provinces, nor over the proportion of provincial revenue received from Ottawa. I have also included federal transfers to municipalities, persons, and businesses. I have omitted any calculation of how much the federal government spends in each province in total, especially in comparison to how much it raises in each province in revenues. Many attempts have been made to come up with such figures, especially in the light of Quebec's referendum on sovereignty, but there is no consensus on this question.

It is almost as difficult to obtain solid figures on the size of the provincial public service. I have used Statistics Canada figures which single out those who work in departments, ministries and agencies, those who work in government business enterprises, and then those who work in the wider public sector. Even Statistics Canada warns us not to use these figures for inter-provincial comparisons. The wider public sector is difficult to define, as not all provinces include the same types of employees, and the division of responsibility between provincial and municipal governments varies from province to province.

Finally, although provincial public finances are of great interest as we approach the turn of the century, there are many problems in using statistics on expenditures, revenues, deficits, and debts. Finance ministers have often been widely off when estimating these figures in their budgets, sometimes deliberately so. It is also difficult to know whether to include Crown corporations in such figures, especially when dealing with provincial government debts. In general, I have omitted Crown corporations from such calculations, and, rather than relying on raw provincial budgets, I have used Statistics Canada's Financial Management System, which presents such statistics in a uniform format.

ENDNOTES

1. It is thus constructed on the theoretical framework of the political system as developed by David Easton. "Small World" is David Elkins' and Richard Simeon's term, see Elkins and Simeon, eds., *Small Worlds: Provinces and Parties in Canadian Political Life* (Toronto: Methuen, 1980).

2. R.A. Young, Philippe Faucher, and André Blais, "The Concept of Province-Building: A Critique," *Canadian Journal of Political Science* (December 1984); E.R. Black and A.C. Cairns, "A Different Perspective on Canadian Federalism," *Canadian Public Administration* (1966); Garth Stevenson, *Unfulfilled Union* (Toronto: Gage, 3rd ed. 1989); and the conclusion to Elkins and Simeon, *Small Worlds*. Recent books on Canadian federalism include R.D. Olling and M.W. Westmacott, eds. *Perspectives on Canadian Federalism* (Scarborough: Prentice-Hall Canada, 1988), and Garth Stevenson, ed., *Federalism in Canada* (Toronto: McClelland and Stewart, 1989).

3. Although I have not taken such an explicit approach, I have tried to include enough material in this vein for those who choose to adopt it. Brownsey and Howlett take such an approach with mixed results in *The Provincial State* (Mississauga: Copp Clark Pitman, 1992). See also such sources as Patricia Marchak, "Canadian Political Economy," *Canadian Review of Sociology and Anthropology* (22:5, 1985); Wallace Clement and Glen Williams, eds., *The New Canadian Political Economy* (Montreal: McGill-Queen's University Press, 1989); Leo Panitch, "Elites, Classes, and Power in Canada," in Michael Whittington and Glen Williams, eds., *Canadian Politics in the 1990s* (Scarborough: Nelson Canada, 1995); Robert Brym, ed., *Regionalism in Canada* (Toronto: Irwin, 1986); and Wallace Clement and Daniel Drache, eds., *A Practical Guide to Canadian Political Economy* (Toronto: Lorimer, 1978), along with their New Guide, 1985.

4. John Wilson argues persuasively that it makes sense to talk about 10 provincial political cultures in "The Canadian Political Cultures: Towards a Redefinition of the Nature of the Canadian Political Systems," *Canadian Journal of Political Science* (September 1974).

5. Gabriel Almond and Sydney Verba, *The Civic Culture* (Princeton: Princeton University Press, 1963).

6. Richard Simeon and David Elkins, "Provincial Political Cultures in Canada," in *Small Worlds*.

7. S.J.R. Noel, "Leadership and Clientelism," in David Bellamy, Jon Pammett, and Donald C. Rowat, eds., *The Provincial Political Systems: Comparative Essays* (Toronto: Methuen, 1976).

8. I would have included more material on this subject from various national election studies but for the devastating critique by Nelson Wiseman, "The Use, Misuse and Abuse of the National Election Studies," *Journal of Canadian Studies* (Spring 1986). He argues that the provincial samples which make up the national sample are too small to reach definitive conclusions about individual provinces.

9. Wilson, "The Canadian Political Cultures." I have taken some liberties with his original proposal and updated it.

10. Ibid., p. 449.

11. Conrad Winn and John McMenemy, *Political Parties in Canada* (Toronto: McGraw-Hill Ryerson, 1976).

12. Kevin Edwards, "Political Parties: Limits on Policy-Making by Social Democratic Parties," in Donald C. Rowat, ed., *Provincial Policy-Making: Comparative Essays* (Ottawa: Carleton University, 1981), p. 97. Many analysts from the political economy and/or neo-Marxist schools take this approach. Some of their work is listed in endnote 3.

13. The most complete treatment along these lines is William Christian and Colin Campbell, *Canadian Political Ideologies* (Toronto: McGraw-Hill Ryerson, 2nd ed. 1983) and their third edition in 1989. Several authors have predicted greater ideological diversity at the provincial level.

14. Although there is no necessary relationship between class-based voting behaviour and distinctive party ideologies, and they deserve separate treatment, the two usually go together. A party with a left-wing ideology would expect to be supported by lower-class voters, while a right-wing party would anticipate upper-class support.

15. Several studies at the cross-national level have found that countries governed by social democratic regimes have higher degrees of welfare state development than those that have experienced fewer years of social democratic rule, despite comparable levels of socio-economic development. See Andrew Sharpe, "A Quantitative Analysis of the Development of the Welfare State in Canada, 1926-1982," *Canadian Political Science Association* (June 1984). The counter-argument is usually made in terms of levels of socio-economic development being more significant than party ideology.

16. J.A. McAllister, "Fiscal Capacity and Tax Effort: Explaining Public Expenditures in the 10 Canadian Provinces," *Canadian Political Science Association* (June 1984), p. 35.

17. Dale Poel, "The Diffusion of Legislation among the Canadian Provinces: A Statistical Analysis," in *Canadian Journal of Political Science* (December 1976).

18. William Chandler, "Canadian Socialism and Policy Impact: Contagion from the Left?", in *Canadian Journal of Political Science* (December 1977).

19. M.A. Chandler, "The Politics of Provincial Resource Policy," in Michael Atkinson and Marsha Chandler, eds., *The Politics of Canadian Public Policy* (Toronto: University of Toronto Press, 1983).

20. M.A. Chandler, "State Enterprise and Partisanship in Provincial Politics," *Canadian Journal of Political Science* (December 1982).

21. André Blais, Helene Gaboury, and Kenneth McRoberts, "Do Political Parties Affect the Progressivity of Personal Income Tax?" Canadian Political Science Association (June 1987).

22. D.V. Smiley, *Canada in Question: Federalism in the Eighties* (Toronto: McGraw-Hill Ryerson, 3rd ed. 1980), pp. 121-122.

23. Rand Dyck, "Relations Between Federal and Provincial Parties," in Alain Gagnon and Brian Tanguay, eds., *Canadian Parties in Transition* (Scarborough: Nelson Canada, 1989).

24. J. Patrick Boyer, *Money and Message* (Toronto: Butterworths, 1983); the Ontario Commission on Election Finances used to publish such comparative studies on this subject as *A Comparative Study of Election Finance Legislation 1988.*

25. Jane Jenson, "Party Systems," in Bellamy, et al., *The Provincial Political Systems*, p. 124; see also M.J. Brodie and Jane Jenson, *Crisis, Challenge and Change: Party and Class in Canada* (Toronto: Methuen, 1980), ch. 1, and their second edition (Carleton University Press, 1988); also Jon Pammett, "Class Voting and Class Consciousness in Canada," in *Canadian Review of Sociology and Anthropology* 24:2, 1987.

26. Robert Presthus, *Elite Accommodation in Canadian Politics* (Toronto: Macmillan, 1973), p. 91.

27. See, for example, M.W. Bucovetsky, "The Mining Industry and the Great Tax Reform Debate," in Paul Pross, ed., *Pressure Group Behaviour in Canadian Politics* (Toronto: McGraw-Hill Ryerson, 1975).

28. Sources on the position of lieutenant-governor include Bellamy, Pammett, and Rowat, *The Provincial Political Systems*, ch. 20; Rowat, *Provincial Government and Politics: Comparative Essays* (Ottawa: Carleton University, 2nd ed. 1973), ch. 5; and J.T. Saywell, *The Office of Lieutenant-Governor* (Toronto: University of Toronto Press, 1957).

29. The Constitution also permits the federal cabinet to bypass the lieutenant-governor and directly disallow provincial legislation. Although the power of disallowance has been used on 112 occasions, the last in 1943, this power is not appropriate in a true federation.

30. Twenty-seven of these vetoes, in fact, were on the advice or with the concurrence of the provincial government.

31. While members of the federal Privy Council retain the title "Honourable" for life, those of the provincial executive council lose the title when they lose the position. Otherwise, there is a theoretical parallel between the Privy Council advising the governor-general and the executive council advising the lieutenant-governor.

32. Allan Kornberg, et al., eds., *Representative Democracy in the Canadian Provinces* (Scarborough: Prentice Hall Canada, 1982), p. 174.

33. Walter Young and Terry Morley, "The Premier and the Cabinet," in Morley et al., eds., *The Reins of Power* (Vancouver: Douglas and McIntyre), p. 54; Leslie Pal and David Taras, eds., *Prime Ministers and Premiers* (Scarborough: Prentice Hall Canada, 1988).

34. The best general source on provincial legislatures is Gary Levy and Graham White, eds., *Provincial and Territorial Legislatures in Canada* (Toronto: University of Toronto Press, 1989). See also R. J. Fleming's *Canadian Legislatures 1992*, (Agincourt: Global Press, 1992).

35. The member is called an MLA (Member of the Legislative Assembly) in most provinces; in Ontario, MPP (Member of the Provincial Parliament); in Quebec, MNA (Member of the National Assembly); and in Newfoundland, MHA (Member of the House of Assembly).

36. Michael Atkinson and Graham White, "The Development of Provincial Legislatures," in H.D. Clarke, et al., eds., *Parliament, Policy and Representation* (Toronto: Methuen, 1980), p. 255.

37. Atkinson and White speak of provincial legislatures moving toward a "transformative" model—possessing an independent capacity to transform proposals into laws. They argue that three factors are necessary for this development: professionalization of members' careers, a growth in legislative resources, and more effective committee systems. They suggest several catalysts for such a development, including legislative size (the larger the legislature, the greater the emphasis on policy, specialization, effective criticism, and alternative proposals); minority government (which forces the government to pay more attention to the legislature, and which engenders more bargaining and an increased importance of committees); and the presence in the legislature of the NDP (which puts more emphasis on policy rather than arguing over government incompetence). Ontario and Quebec have obviously moved farthest toward the transformative model, the four western provinces are in an intermediate position, and the four Atlantic provinces are least advanced in this direction.

38. Agar Adamson, "We Were Here Before: The Referendum in Canadian Experience," *Policy Options* (March 1980); Richard Théoret, "Provincial Plebiscites," in Rowat, *Provincial Policy-Making*.

39. Useful sources on the subject of provincial bureaucracies include J.E. Hodgetts and O.P. Dwivedi, eds., *Provincial Governments as Employers* (Montreal: McGill-Queen's University Press, 1974) and A.R. Vining and R. Botterell, "An Overview of the Origins, Growth, Size and Functions of Provincial Crown Corporations," in J.R.S. Prichard, *Crown Corporations in Canada: the Calculus of Instrument Choice* (Toronto: Butterworths, 1983).

40. J.E. Hodgetts and O.P. Dwivedi, "Administration and Personnel," in Bellamy et al., *The Provincial Political Systems*, p. 14.

41. Hodgetts and Dwivedi, *Provincial Governments as Employers*, p. 14.

42. Two up-to-date sources on provincial government structures are the annual editions of *Corpus Almanac and Canadian Sourcebook* published by Southam Information and Technology Group, Don Mills, Ont., and *Canadian Almanac and Directory* published by Canadian Almanac and Directory Publishing Co., Toronto, Ont.

43. On the subjects of privatization and restraint, see L.R. Jones, "Financial Restraint Management and Budget Control in Canadian Provincial Governments," *Canadian Public Administration* (Summer 1986), and "Coping with Revenue and Expenditure Restraints in the Provincial Government Context," *Canadian Public Administration* (Winter 1986); M.A. Molot, "The Provinces and Privatization: Are the Provinces Really Getting Out of Business?" Canadian Political Science Association (June 1987); Herschel Hardin, *The Privatization Putsch* (Halifax: Institute for Research on Public Policy, 1989); and J.M. Pitsula and Ken Rasmussen, *Privatizing a Province* (Vancouver: New Star Books, 1990).

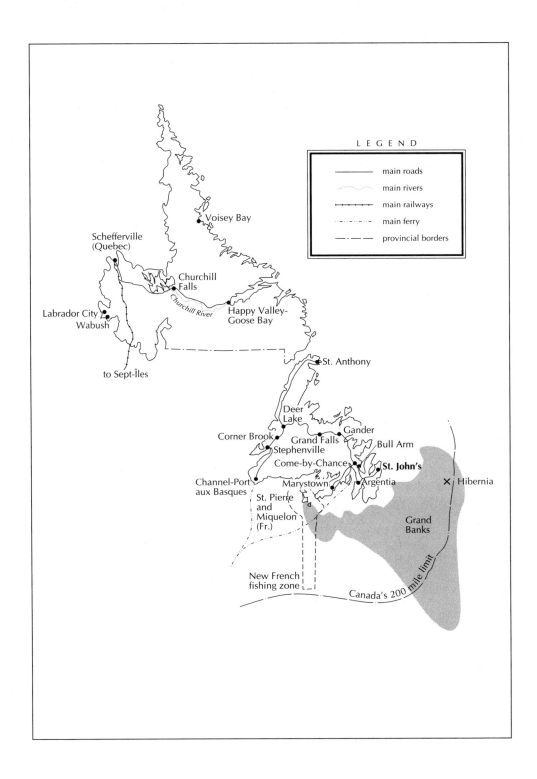

LEGEND

——————	main roads
∼∼∼∼∼	main rivers
—+—+—+—	main railways
—··—··—	main ferry
—·—·—·—	provincial borders

Voisey Bay

Schefferville
(Quebec)

Churchill
Falls

Churchill River

Labrador City
Wabush

Happy Valley-
Goose Bay

to Sept-Îles

St. Anthony

Deer
Lake

Gander

Corner Brook

Grand Falls

Bull Arm

Stephenville

Come-by-Chance

St. John's

Channel-Port
aux Basques

Marystown

Argentia

× Hibernia

St. Pierre
and
Miquelon
(Fr.)

Grand
Banks

New French
fishing zone

Canada's 200 mile limit

CHAPTER 2

NEWFOUNDLAND

Newfoundland is Canada's youngest province, having joined Confederation in 1949. This union largely came about through the efforts of Joey Smallwood, who persuaded his fellow Newfoundlanders to give up their independence in favour of the benefits they would automatically receive as Canadians. His arguments gained credibility because Newfoundland was well behind the Canadian norm in social and economic development. Since then the province's progress in these respects has been astounding, but it continues to be the poorest in Canada. As Newfoundland approaches the turn of the century, its historic raison-d'être, the fishing industry, has all but collapsed, although the province has hopes that a newer product of the sea—offshore petroleum—will compensate to some extent. Economic realities continue to underlie much of its political activity, both internally and in its relations with Ottawa.

SETTING

Geography

The province consists of two distinct but equally rocky parts: the triangular-shaped island of Newfoundland, an extension of the Appalachians; and the Labrador region, part of the Canadian Shield, attached to eastern Quebec.[1] The total province is 404,520 square kilometres in area, about one-quarter represented by the island portion. The two parts are separated by the Strait of Belle Isle, 18 kilometres wide at its narrowest point and crossed by ferry except in the winter months.

Besides this basic geographic division, several regions can be identified on the island of Newfoundland: the Avalon Peninsula, on which the capital, St. John's, is located; the central region and northeast coast; the Burin Peninsula and south coast; and the western region, a long narrow strip from

Port-aux-Basques in the southwest corner to St. Anthony in the north, with Corner Brook located about midway. The island portion of the province is famous across Canada for being one half-hour behind Atlantic Time, although Labrador shares a time zone with the Maritime provinces.

Newfoundland had a 1991 census population of 568,474 (and 579,500 by January 1995), of which about 95 percent resided on the island, leaving about five percent in Labrador. St. John's is the only large city. The city proper boasts about 95,770 residents with 171,860 living in the metropolitan region (including adjacent Mount Pearl with 23,689 residents). In many ways the province is divided between this metropolis, the core of political and economic power, and the periphery or hinterland. Corner Brook on the west coast is the only other city, with a population of 33,790. Smaller urban centres on the island include Grand Falls-Windsor (25,285) and Gander (11,053). The two largest settlements in Labrador are Labrador City in the extreme west along the Quebec border (11,392) and Happy Valley-Goose Bay on the Hamilton Inlet. Hundreds of outports dot the 17,540 kilometres of provincial coastline, settlements that, until recently, were virtually isolated and provided a strong sense of localism in the province. Officially, Newfoundland is the most urbanized of the Atlantic provinces at 53.6 percent, but this figure is somewhat misleading because of the dominance of St. John's.

Given its isolated geographical position, Newfoundland puts a premium on transportation. Airports at Gander on the island and Goose Bay in Labrador became famous during wartime, and as refuelling stations for transatlantic flights, but are less important now. Other NATO countries use Canadian Forces Base Goose Bay as a training base. While low-level military flights have upset the native Innu, the province and the town of Happy Valley-Goose Bay are pushing for an expansion of such flights. They want to maximize the economic advantages of the operation and claim that environmental assessment reports support their stand that the flights have no adverse effect on the aboriginal residents or the environment. Air transport continues to be a vital means of travel within the province, especially between the island and Labrador, and St. John's is the 10th busiest airport in the country in terms of cargo. Likewise, the ferry services from Sydney, N.S., year-round to Port-aux-Basques and, in the summer, to Argentia, are vital lifelines to Newfoundland. The Trans-Canada Highway, which crosses the province from St. John's to Port-aux-Basques, functions as Newfoundland's spinal cord. It has been of particular importance since the parallel narrow-gauge railway line was closed by Ottawa in 1988, in return for which the province received $800 million. Some of this money, as well as other federal grants, have been used to maintain, upgrade, widen, and expand the highway, but Islanders are not entirely content with the resulting heavy truck and bus traffic.

Economy

Newfoundland's economy is based on three primary industries: fishing, mining, and forestry. All are export industries, leaving the province vulnerable to international tastes, recession and competition, as well as unfavourable exchange rates. Overall, its gross domestic product constitutes about 1.4 percent of the national total.

Fishing has been the foundation of the province for centuries and, even though the industry was devastated in the early 1990s, among the primary industries it still provides employment for the largest number of residents. Northern cod has been the predominant catch, with smaller volumes of other cod, capelin, crab, lobster, shrimp, scallops, and salmon. Fishing was the historic mainstay of over 700 rural communities along the coast of both the island portion and Labrador, with the Grand Banks to the southeast of the island being particularly productive. The industry was rarely very profitable for individual fishermen, however, for they faced no end of problems.[2] Even when the fish were plentiful, the international demand was often poor and the price low; increasing mechanization meant borrowing money, often at high rates of interest; and a high value of the Canadian dollar discouraged exports.

Newfoundland claims to be the only province whose most important industry is beyond its control. It has never been satisfied with the manner in which Ottawa has exercised federal constitutional jurisdiction in this field. Newfoundland has regularly complained about Ottawa's minimal consultation with the province on common problems, its lack of backbone in enforcing Canadian fishing rights and negotiating with the foreign countries involved, and the generally low priority which the External Affairs Department has given to fishing issues. In the spring of 1995, federal Fisheries Minister Brian Tobin was more aggressive in taking on Spain and the European Union in a fight over allocations of the turbot catch.

The state of crisis which characterizes the Newfoundland fishery in the 1990s is discussed in detail in Inset 2.1. After many years of not imposing sufficiently low fishing quotas, Ottawa has banned virtually all cod fishing and enacted strict quotas for other groundfish for the foreseeable future. Although the pelagic and shellfish parts of the industry continue to operate in a normal fashion, the groundfish ban has left huge numbers of Newfoundland fishermen and fish processing plant workers unemployed. In general terms, the entire industry now accounts for less than half of the employment and value in Newfoundland that it did in the late 1980s. Displaced fishermen and plant workers have to depend on special federal income support programs to survive, although in some cases at a higher level than they did before. The federal government is seeking to reduce the size of the workforce in the industry by encouraging early retirements and training for other jobs. Ottawa expects those who insist on remaining in the industry to seek upgrading and training in the hope of developing a smaller, more professional workforce.

INSET 2.1 The Atlantic Fisheries Crisis

Unlike previous downturns in the Atlantic fishing industry, the current crisis is largely a problem of supply. The many experts who have addressed the problem have not agreed on a single cause for the sudden drop in fish stocks. Rather, it seems a number of factors is responsible. Foreign overfishing is usually thought to be the single most important cause. Europeans in particular took staggering volumes of fish over the 1958-73 period, and the stocks fell dramatically. European fishermen tended to take everything they caught in small-mesh nets, not leaving younger fish to grow and reproduce. But Canadian fishermen are also to blame to some extent. They sometimes overfished and under-reported their catches and dumped smaller dead fish overboard. Cheating on quotas was tempting when enforcement was lax and when they were facing large interest payments on money borrowed to buy equipment. Most authorities also believe that, since the ban on the full-scale seal hunt in the early 1980s, the huge population of seals is part of the problem. The animals are staying in the area longer than they used to and eating anything available. The decline of capelin, on which the cod normally feed, has also contributed. Some scientists argue that a cooling of ocean temperatures has made it less conducive for fish to reproduce, while others claim that changing ocean currents and levels of salinity are affecting the migration patterns of the fish. Some of these same scientists, formerly optimistic the stocks would rebuild themselves, employed flawed models and methodologies and seriously overestimated the fisheries biomass. Finally, the politicians, more interested in the voters than in fish, did not respond quickly enough when the scientists finally discovered the severity of the problem.

The initial quota cuts of 1988 were followed by reductions in 1989, 1990, and 1991, usually announced in December for the following fishing season. But in 1992, Ottawa made two extraordinary cuts, one in February and one in July. The July 1992 decision involved an immediate two-year shutdown of the northern cod fishery on the east coast of Newfoundland, with a separate announcement relating to capelin and commercial salmon. Further quota cuts in December 1992 and August 1993 were followed in December 1993 when the new Fisheries Minister, Brian Tobin, suspended the whole East Coast cod industry indefinitely—except for the area off southwestern Nova Scotia—and cut quotas for other species of groundfish. By this time, an estimated 40,000 fishermen and fish plant workers had been laid off. Further cuts followed in 1994. The reduction in quantity and value of fish landed can be seen in Tables 2.1 and 2.2.

Ottawa accompanied these tragic announcements with the creation of income support programs for those affected. Such packages, however, contained provisions for restructuring and downsizing the industry and for economic diversification. The three principal announcements of this nature came in May 1990, July 1992, and April 1994. In May 1990, then federal Fisheries Minister John Crosbie announced a five-year $580-million aid package for the East Coast fishery called the Atlantic Fisheries Adjustment Program. It involved rebuilding fish stocks, increased research, better surveillance and enforcement, increased fines, income support, and economic diversification. Then, in July 1992, Crosbie came up with an $800-million income support and retraining package for about 25,000 fishermen and plant workers who would be laid off by that point. It was called the Northern Cod Adjustment and Recovery Program (NCARP) or, colloquially, "the package." Finally, in the spring of 1994, the Liberal Fisheries Minister, Brian Tobin, unveiled an extension and expansion of Crosbie's program. Called The Atlantic Groundfish Strategy (TAGS), it was partly based on the 1993 report of the Cashin Task Force Report, appointed in March 1992 to advise on compensation. The 1994 package offered six percent less support (an average of about $282 per week per individual), was more stringent regarding eligibility, and required recipients to upgrade their education or work on government-sponsored projects.

TABLE 2.1   Volume of Atlantic Fish Catch by Province and Species, 1988 and 1993 (tonnes)

	Newfoundland		Nova Scotia		PEI		New Brunswick	
	1988	1993	1988	1993	1988	1993	1988	1993
Cod	298,960	32,531	126,627	33,697	4,264	817	9,971	869
All Groundfish	390,445	91,794	252,761	161,822	10,650	7,580	19,145	5,574
All Pelagics	117,519	75,051	128,799	103,556	13,071	10,944	92,169	82,606
Lobster	2,502	2,222	17,008	17,855	9,546	8,794	6,940	7,631
All Shellfish	32,987	58,658	94,495	119,282	13,233	14,462	22,893	27,030
Total	540,951	226,688	476,055	400,930	36,954	32,986	134,207	115,483

TABLE 2.2   Value of Atlantic Fish Catch by Province and Species, 1988 and 1993 (thousands of dollars)

	Newfoundland		Nova Scotia		PEI		New Brunswick	
	1988	1993	1988	1993	1988	1993	1988	1993
Cod	153,887	18,422	80,523	36,282	1,670	668	4,467	1,017
All Groundfish	188,705	42,954	159,558	126,655	3,949	2,974	8,685	3,182
All Pelagics	37,612	20,075	29,975	37,718	3,466	2,794	15,996	12,219
Lobster	14,206	17,149	127,277	155,842	48,922	50,976	41,259	44,828
All Shellfish	70,897	105,554	222,766	302,771	54,281	59,646	83,664	87,347
Total	297,855	171,935	413,777	470,362	61,700	65,414	108,655	103,118

Source: Department of Fisheries and Oceans, *Canadian Fisheries Landings, 1987-1988 (Preliminary)*, Vol. 10, No. 12 and *Canadian Fisheries Landings,* December 1993, Vol. 15, No. 4 (Ottawa: Department of Fisheries and Oceans, 1994), used with permission.

It is generally assumed that most fishermen over 50 will opt for early retirement; those between 30 and 50 will probably want to stay in the industry; and those under 30 will seek opportunities for training and retraining in other fields. Not all of them will adopt a serious approach to the compulsory upgrading and retraining programs. Authorities also feel that about 50 percent of the labour force in both harvesting and processing fish must be eliminated. Thus, even if research and an improved system of fisheries management are successful in rebuilding the stocks, the industry must be restructured with the objective of a smaller, professionalized workforce, as the Cashin Report recommended.

It should be added that the pelagic and shellfish industries are largely unaffected, but this is of little consolation to Newfoundland. Neither is the fact that, for fish plants normally processing domestic groundfish, some work is being provided by processing imported fish caught by Russians.

Other Industries

Even before these disastrous developments, mining was the province's second primary industry, generating more provincial revenue than fishing. It is dominated by the iron ore deposits in western Labrador at Wabush and Labrador City. These have been developed by Wabush Mines and the Iron Ore Company of Canada and are so far removed from St. John's that they might be said to be psychologically located in Quebec, especially given the rail links to Sept-Iles, Que., and the Wabush refining plant in Point Noire, Que. Newfoundland is the leading Canadian producer of iron ore but this mineral is particularly susceptible to variations in U.S. demand and import regulations. Serious layoffs occurred in the early 1980s. The closing of the Iron Ore Co.'s Schefferville operation in Quebec also resulted in many Labrador workers losing their jobs. Several other mines have closed due to the exhaustion of the supply (asbestos, zinc and copper). However, other minerals found on the island include gypsum (at Flat Bay, owned by Domtar), peat (at 10 locations of which the largest is Bishop's Falls), gold (at Hope Brook, owned by Royal Oak Mines), and construction materials such as slate, limestone, granite, and cement, especially at Trinity Bay. In the spring of 1995, a huge deposit of nickel, copper, and cobalt was discovered at Voisey Bay on the northeastern coast of Labrador.

Much excitement has also been generated over the past several years by the discovery of petroleum off the provincial coast. The most promising oil find is at Hibernia, 320 kilometres southeast of the island. Although no actual production is anticipated until 1997, the exploration and construction associated with it has been an important contributor to the Newfoundland economy. For example, the province benefits from repair and maintenance services to oil rigs, especially in the Marystown shipyard on the south coast. Much of the construction and assembly of the Hibernia project between 1991 and 1996 is taking place around Bull Arm. More detail on the Hibernia development is provided in Inset 2.2.

INSET 2.2 The Hibernia Project

Once the federal and Newfoundland governments agreed on joint jurisdiction over the development of offshore petroleum in 1985, the Hibernia deal was signed in 1988. It was refined in 1990, and renegotiated in 1992. The final participants and their share of the costs are: Mobil Oil, 33.125 percent, Chevron Oil, 26,875 percent, Petro-Canada, 25 percent, the Government of Canada, 8.5 percent, and Murphy Oil, 6.5 percent. An earlier partner, Gulf Oil, pulled out of the project in 1992. The project is expected to cost about $5 billion to construct with about $2.7 billion coming from Ottawa in the form of cash and loan guarantees.

The field is located on the eastern edge of the Grand Banks, and some disruption of commercial fishing is expected. Its sponsors anticipate that the field will produce about 100,000 barrels of oil per day over a period of about 20 years starting in 1997, for a total of about 600 million barrels, about 12 percent of total Canadian production. The oil will probably have to be refined in the United States because of its waxy consistency. At mid-1990s international oil prices, it would not cover its production costs.

The oil will be produced from a fixed concrete platform placed in the middle of the field, as illustrated in Figure 2.2. A Gravity Base Structure (GBS) 106 metres in diameter and 111 metres high sits on the ocean floor in water 80 metres deep. This round structure has 16 "teeth" designed to absorb the impact of icebergs. The base extends five metres above the water and four shafts extend 26 metres higher to support the production platform or "topsides." This consists of five super modules (process, wellhead, mud, utility, and service-living quarters) and seven smaller modules (helideck, two drilling derricks, two lifeboat stations, a piperack and a flare boom). The living quarters will house 280 people.

It is expected that 83 development wells will be drilled from the production platform, with the oil stored in the GBS, which has a capacity of 1.3 million barrels. The oil will then be pumped from the GBS to crude oil transport tankers via the offshore loading system.

The GBS is being built at Bull Arm in Newfoundland. One of the super modules is also being constructed there, while two each are being made in Korea and Italy. Four of the seven smaller modules will also be locally produced. All parts should be finished by 1996, in which case the topsides will be attached to the GBS and the whole structure towed out to its intended location. Hibernia is providing an average of about 2,000 construction jobs per year until 1996, and should require a workforce of about 1,000 in production. When a shipyard in Marystown, Newfoundland, could not complete the work on two drilling modules in late 1994, Quebec objected to their transfer to New Brunswick to be finished.

Although both the federal and provincial governments have provided generous financial incentives, neither will receive much money in return. It is hoped, however, that this project will lead to the development of other nearby fields—Terra Nova, Hebran, and Whiterose—and eventually to local refining.

FIGURE 2.1   Sketch of the Hibernia Platform

Source: Hibernia Management and Development Company Ltd.

The province's third primary industry is forestry. Although long-term leases to major companies resulted in a lack of reforestation in the past, recent changes in the leasing system and developments in silviculture, tree care and forest management have made the province increasingly optimistic about its long-term wood supply. About one-third of the timber cut is used as firewood; about 60 percent takes the form of pulpwood converted into newsprint; and the rest is cut into lumber. The province possesses some 1,500 small sawmills and three paper mills: the Kruger mill in Corner Brook, and two Abitibi-Price mills, one at Grand Falls and one at Stephenville. In the case of the Stephenville plant, a modern linerboard operation was converted to paper production. The other two plants, built in 1905 and 1923 respectively, have undergone badly needed modernization with help from Atlantic Canada Opportunities Agency. But all three plants must keep pace with environmental standards, efficient competitors, and the contemporary emphasis on recycling. The mills frequently shut down all or part of operations due to lack of demand or need of repair. In 1994, Abitibi-Price laid off 100 workers at Grand Falls and Kruger had to shut down one of four paper machines in Corner Brook because of a shortage of cash, with those employees it retained accepting wage concessions.

TABLE 2.3   Newfoundland 1991 Labour Force and Estimated 1995 Gross Domestic Product by Industry

Industry	1991 Labour Force		Est. 1995 GDP ($ millions)	
Agriculture	2,170	0.8%	22	0.3%
Fishing	11,335	4.4%	79	1.1%
Forestry	3,575	1.4%	71	1.0%
Mining	4,495	1.7%	275	3.9%
TOTAL PRIMARY	21,575	8.3%	447	6.3%
Manufacturing	34,945	13.5%	429	6.1%
Construction	18,155	7.0%	773	10.9%
TOTAL SECONDARY	53,100	20.5%	1,202	17.0%
Transportation, communications & utilities	19,725	7.7%	1,032	14.6%
Trade	44,505	17.2%	845	11.9%
Finance, insurance & real estate	7,335	2.8%	1,148	16.2%
Services	80,455	31.1%	1,695	23.9%
Government	31,845	12.3%	714	10.1%
TOTAL TERTIARY	183,865	71.1%	5,434	76.7%
TOTAL ALL INDUSTRIES	258,540		7,084	

Source: Reproduced by authority of the Minister of Industry, 1995; Statistics Canada, *1991 Census,* cat. nos. 93-326 and 95-302; and Conference Board of Canada, *Provincial Outlook, Economic Forecast* (Ottawa: Summer 1994), Vol. 9, No. 2. Adapted by author.

The province has little in the way of agriculture, largely because glaciers carried most of the soil out to sea. Farming consists of small holdings close to urban centres and supplements fishing and forestry activities, providing marginal economic benefit for much of the rural population. In 1991, Newfoundland had 725 farms, with an average size of 161 acres, both census figures being the lowest in the country. The principal agricultural output consists of dairy products, poultry, and eggs. In spite of this limited production, the province has set up marketing boards for milk, eggs, chicken, and hogs.

Turning to electric power, although the Churchill Falls hydro development in Labrador is one of the largest single electricity producers in the country, according to the 1968 agreement with Quebec only 10 percent of its production is available to the province. Moreover, no cable exists to carry the electricity to the island. Newfoundland must sell the other 90 percent to Quebec, which resells it at an enormous profit to the United States. Newfoundland calculates it loses some $800 million annually from this deal, a situation that causes it much anguish. It hopes to some day develop the Lower Churchill so that some of the electricity generated can be exported on its own terms or transmitted to the island. That part of the province currently depends on a combination of small hydro plants or imported oil to generate electricity. These plants are mostly operated by Newfoundland and Labrador Hydro, a Crown corporation, which then sells the electricity to the privately owned Newfoundland Light and Power Ltd. for distribution. In a very controversial move, Premier Wells put the Crown corporation up for sale in 1993 to help finance day-to-day government operations.

The province's manufacturing industry ranks ninth in the country and consists almost entirely of fish processing plants and newsprint production. Small amounts of other food and beverages, as well as chemical, mineral, and wood products round out this sector. As mentioned previously, the fish processing industry experienced serious difficulties during the early 1980s and many plants closed or operated at levels far below capacity. Nevertheless, the province has put much effort into the field of marine technology, based on research institutes at Memorial University and the Institute of Fisheries and Marine Technology.

The service sector is the largest employer in the province and tourism is of increasing significance. Among the attractions the province offers are the historic Viking settlement at l'Anse aux Meadows and the splendid landlocked fjords of Gros Morne National Park, both UNESCO World Heritage Sites; fishing and hunting; watching whales, icebergs, and seabirds (especially puffins); skiing facilities at Marble Mountain and White Hills; spectacular coastal scenery; and unique hospitality, folklore, and colourful characters.

Government provides relatively more employment in Newfoundland than elsewhere, with those employed by the province greatly exceeding those working for other levels of government. If school teachers are included, the total labour force of all three levels of government approaches 50,000 people.

Class

By most standards, Newfoundland is the poorest province in Canada. Even before the collapse of the fishing industry, it had the highest official unemployment rate—usually at least 15, sometimes more than 20 percent, and probably much higher. Thus the province has always depended heavily on unemployment insurance, both for long-term and seasonal unemployment. A landmark of social policy in the province occurred in 1957 when UI coverage was extended to fishermen. Now, as mentioned previously, those unemployed as a result of the recent bans on groundfish have been eligible for special federal compensation programs. Perhaps the best way of categorizing classes in Newfoundland is that used by the Royal Commission on Employment and Unemployment: the wealthy, the regularly employed, the seasonally employed, and the non-employed.[3]

Even many full-time jobs are not well paid. The median family income in 1991 was $35,184, with 23.4 percent of families living on less than $20,000 and 12 percent over $70,000. In 1992, the per capita income was $17,227. Newfoundland also has the lowest average level of educational attainment in the country, the largest proportion with less than Grade 9, and the smallest proportion with university degrees.

Organized labour is of some significance in the province. In total, 92,100 paid workers were unionized in 1991 which, at 53 percent, gives Newfoundland the highest unionization rate in the country. The largest union, at least until recently, was the fishermen and fish plant workers' union, now called the Fishermen, Food and Allied Workers. It grew in strength under the outspoken leadership of Richard Cashin, and joined the Canadian Auto Workers in 1988. Other important private sector unions are the CEP (Communications, Energy, and Paperworkers Union of Canada) and the UFCW (United Food and Commercial Workers Union), while the largest public service unions are NAPE (the Newfoundland Association of Public Employees) and CUPE (the Canadian Union of Public Employees). The Newfoundland Federation of Labour has a membership of about 65,000 and, with the help of this base, the NDP has occasionally won federal and provincial seats.

Contrary to the image of poverty which Newfoundland often engenders, however, the province has its share of rich residents, including many members of the legislature. Newfoundland contains several wealthy old merchant families including the Lundrigans of Corner Brook, and the Collingwoods, Pratts, and Crosbies of St. John's.[4] The Crosbies once owned 36 firms including merchant ships, trucking operations, hotels, cocktail bars, newspapers, and insurance companies. But while the nationally recognized John Crosbie was enjoying a successful, high-profile career in provincial and federal politics, his brother Andrew lost most of the family assets in the first half of the 1980s. The empire, now run by Tim of the next generation, has dwindled to a few real estate developments. The Lundrigan fortune has also collapsed. More recent business successes include broadcaster Geoff Stirling, Vic Young of FPI, Harry Steele who runs Newfoundland Capital Corp. from its headquarters in Nova Scotia, David Mercer of Fortis Inc., which owns Newfoundland Light and Power, and Craig Dobbin owner of CHC Helicopters and a prominent developer.

Some have taken a neo-Marxist approach to recent Newfoundland politics but it is probably more realistic to emphasize the independent influence of political and economic elites.[5]

Demography

Over 90 percent of Newfoundland's population is of British heritage, comprising the descendants of original settlers from the west of England and from Ireland. Those of French descent are a distant second, and the proportion of other ethnic groups is miniscule. Most of the French have been assimilated, however, so that about 99 percent of residents share English as their mother tongue and use it as their home language. Thus the many French and even Portuguese place names are relics of a distant past, left by fishermen who landed but did not stay. Along the Quebec-Labrador border some French-language schools pre-dated the Charter of Rights and Freedoms but, more recently, a French-language school has been established in Mainland and another is planned for St. John's. Newfoundland has the highest proportion of residents born in the province (93 percent) and the lowest born outside of Canada (1.5 percent). The Innu and Inuit of Labrador, who number about 13,000 and constitute 2.3 percent of the population, are virtually the only aboriginals remaining. In addition to their protests over low-flying aircraft, they made headlines in the early 1990s because of deplorable living conditions, especially those at Davis Inlet. This small hamlet's high level of suicides and substance abuse alarmed the whole country.

TABLE 2.4   Newfoundland Mother Tongue and Home Language, 1991

	Mother Tongue	Home Language
English	98.6%	99.2%
French	0.5%	0.2%
Other	0.9%	0.5%

Source: Reproduced by authority of the Minister of Industry, 1995, Statistics Canada, *1991 Census*, cat. no. 93-317, adapted by author.

This apparent ethnic and linguistic homogeneity is complicated by the interesting distribution of religious affiliations in the province. There are three main religious groups: Catholics (37 percent), Anglicans (26 percent), and United

Church (17 percent), with those of British ancestry being Protestants and those of Irish, Roman Catholics. The Salvation Army, Pentecostals, and Seventh Day Adventists are also prominent, while Newfoundland has the lowest proportion of residents with no organized religion.

Religion has played an important and unusual role in provincial affairs. Each of the main affiliations originally established its own school system and some out-port communities once had as many as three or four tiny schools. Since 1968, the Anglican, United Church, and Salvation Army have integrated their schools. But many separate Roman Catholic schools remain, in addition to those operated by the Pentecostals and Seventh Day Adventists. All of the various denominational schools fell under the general supervision of the Department of Education. In 1992-93, 16 integrated school districts operated 287 schools with an enrollment of 67,635; the Roman Catholic system had nine school districts with 168 schools and 47,545 students enrolled; the Pentecostals had 40 schools with 6,289 students, while the Seventh Day Adventists had six schools with 303 students.

Two-thirds of the members of each school board must be elected by popular vote of those adhering to the denomination involved but the relevant churches can appoint the other third. Roman Catholic, integrated, and Pentecostal educational councils advise the Department. In 1992 the Royal Commission on Education recommended an end to the denominational system along with a continuing emphasis on morals and values.[6] The government accepted this recommendation but Catholic and Pentecostal opposition delayed its implementation. In mid-1994, a determined Premier Clyde Wells announced that it would be done, moving to replace the 27 religious school boards with 10 secular ones.

Another unorthodox feature of Newfoundland until 1975 was that representation in the Assembly was based on religious denomination. But the equitable distribution of government positions and other spoils among the various religious groups has largely kept religious cleavages "out of politics."[7] Richard Gwyn adds that this principle extended to cabinets, civil service positions, contracts, judicial appointments, knighthoods and even Rhodes scholarships.

TABLE 2.5   Religion in Newfoundland, 1991

Protestant		343,960 (61.0%)
Anglican	147,520 (26.2%)	
United Church	97,395 (17.3%)	
Salvation Army	44,490 (7.9%)	
Pentecostal	40,125 (7.1%)	
Other Protestant	14,430 (2.6%)	
Roman Catholic		208,900 (37.0%)
Other and None		11,075 (2.0%)

Source: Reproduced by authority of the Minister of Industry, 1995, Statistics Canada, *1991 Census*, cat. no. 93-319, adapted by author.

The government of Newfoundland has been spared the French-English eth-nic politics of some other provinces, but the division between the English-Protestant and Irish-Catholic groups, reinforced by their general geographic segregation in the western and eastern parts of the island respectively, is still prominent. This division is reinforced by a historic conflict between rich St. John's merchants and the poor outport fishermen, as well as by an assortment of local and regional demands. Such conflicts often involve competition among the three main primary industries and are intensified by the scarce economic resources available. This scarcity is another reason Newfoundland politics is dominated by federal-provincial conflicts.

Federal-Provincial Relations

Although Joey Smallwood had a warm relationship with Ottawa for most of the period from 1949 to 1972, fundamental intergovernmental battles have often overshadowed Newfoundland's internal political issues when the federal Conservatives were in power. In 1959, two disputes erupted between Prime Minister John Diefenbaker and Premier Smallwood. One concerned the amount that Canada was committed to pay Newfoundland under the 1949 Terms of Union; the other centred on sending RCMP reinforcements to the province in connection with a loggers' strike. In addition, there was continuing disagree-ment over the extent of federal commitment to railway service in the province, an argument that peaked with the cancellation of the "Newfie Bullet" passenger train in 1969. The province has regularly demanded it be granted concurrent jurisdiction over the off-shore fishing industry in order to have more control over this vital component of the economy. It has also been locked in a simmer-ing conflict with Quebec over Churchill Falls hydro production and has sought federal assistance to help resolve this dispute. The province has also requested the federal government grant a right-of-way through Quebec which would allow Newfoundland to export electricity from the proposed Lower Churchill power development. With the Conservatives in power provincially after 1972, a protracted struggle occurred between the Peckford and Trudeau governments regarding jurisdiction of the off-shore oil industry.

With the election of the Mulroney government, federal-Newfoundland rela-tions improved dramatically. The federal Progressive Conservatives first negotiat-ed the Atlantic Accord with Peckford to ease his general concerns about the offshore oil industry. They followed this up with a specific agreement on the development of Hibernia. Peckford was an enthusiastic supporter of the federal free trade and Meech Lake initiatives. He only differed from his partisan col-leagues in Ottawa on such fishery issues as granting a factory freezer trawler licence to National Sea Products of Nova Scotia, and the federal government's failure to take a hard line with France in rival claims to the fishing territory south of the province. With the arrival of Liberal premier Clyde Wells in 1989, the federal government faced a fatal obstacle on the Meech Lake issue, although

Wells supported the Charlottetown Accord based on the earlier document. Nevertheless, Wells and Mulroney went ahead with the final Hibernia agreement and Tory and Liberal governments in Ottawa responded in 1992 and 1994 respectively to the fisheries crisis with assistance packages.

The Newfoundland government receives a greater proportion of its revenues from Ottawa than any other province—about 45 percent in 1992. In that year, the federal government transferred $1,500 million to the provincial government and $35 million to municipalities, in addition to the $1,940 million and $285 million it transferred to persons and businesses respectively.

POLITICAL CULTURE

Newfoundland shares some values and attitudes with its fellow Atlantic provinces but its political culture is in many ways unique,[8] a result of its longer experience as a British colony and as an independent dominion prior to joining Confederation. The province possesses an identity more distinct than any other except Quebec. Besides its own myths, heroes, and historical accomplishments, this identity includes a feeling of toughness, independence, and resilience. There is also a strong "sense of place," a localism more extreme than in the other Atlantic provinces and based on the isolation of its outports.[9] This is complemented by a feeling of insularity derived from the isolation of the island, the absence of immigration, and the dominance of a single industry. At least until recently, Newfoundlanders also made a virtue of the non-materialistic values inherited from their English and Irish ancestors, and cherished the concept of an oral society, rich in folklore, storytellers, and eloquent public speakers. Other traditional values included the importance of family and community and the dominant role of the churches. Thus, the province's political culture also possessed a "sectarian-factional" character created by geographic, economic, ethnic, and religious conflicts.[10] Given the prominence of the ethnic and religious divisions, no realignment took place on the basis of economic class, even though the exploitation of the outport fishermen by St. John's merchants was a blatant reality. This was partly because fishermen viewed themselves as independent producers rather than exploited workers, and partly because the church, religious schools, and religious-ethnic organizations were the main agents of political socialization.[11]

A related feature was the weakness of the democratic spirit on the island.[12] The willingness to revert to colonial status in 1934 is perhaps only slightly more remarkable than the dominance that Newfoundlanders permitted Joey Smallwood to exercise for 20 years after joining Confederation. This domination by a single leader also raises questions about patronage and corruption, both of which are more prominent and persistent than in most other Canadian jurisdictions.[13] Smallwood practised a consistent policy of rewarding friends and punishing enemies. Not only were contracts and appointments awarded on a partisan basis, he made many such decisions personally. Firms conducting business with the government were required to contribute generously to the Liberal party, ministers and friends travelled and entertained themselves at public expense, and blatant conflict of interest situations involving cabinet ministers were condoned.[14] Much of this can be related to the "marginal work world" of the province, where poverty and unemployment force individuals and communities to place a high premium on government favours.[15] The province could also be classified as being in the first stage of "clientelism"—the reliance of the supplicant on the handouts of the local notable-politician—and, during the Smallwood period, the fount of all beneficence was the premier himself. He was available in person, often answering his own telephone, always ready to interrupt his work to try to respond to individuals or delegations. It is sometimes argued that this kind of hand-out mentality and feeling of dependence developed after Confederation, sapping residents' earlier initiative and feisty spirit.[16]

There is no doubt that the conservatism of provincial values has declined since 1949. A growing secularization has occurred permitting, among other things, integrated schools. Ethnic identities do not appear to be as strong today as in the past. Transportation and communication improvements have ended the isolation of many outports and lifestyles have been dramatically altered, especially by exposure to television. The vote for Confederation in 1949, as narrow as it was, constituted a decision to integrate "into the more prosperous, dynamic and competitive system of North American industrial capitalism" with its consumer culture and liberal values.[17]

What of Newfoundlanders' attitudes toward Canada? While support for Confederation was barely over the 50 percent mark in 1949, it is probably safe to say that, after receiving millions of dollars worth of such federal aid as family allowances, old age pensions, unemployment insurance, and the Trans-Canada Highway, and with Smallwood singing Canada's praises (as well as his own), the degree of support increased considerably. During the Peckford era, however, Newfoundland demonstrated a much more aggressive attitude toward the federal government. This stemmed from the fact that, while it had the highest rate of both unemployment and poverty in the country, it also had more cause for optimism about the future than its Atlantic neighbours. On issue after issue—fisheries, offshore oil, and hydro development—Newfoundlanders saw the federal government as an obstacle to prosperity and developed a "new nationalism." Newfoundlanders then appeared to support Clyde Wells when he helped veto the Meech Lake Accord. In the 1990 *Maclean's* survey, Newfoundland ranked second to Quebec in primary loyalty to province (53 percent) and secondary loyalty to Canada (47 percent). And, in 1994, it was even more provincially oriented than Quebec.

When Newfoundland is compared with other provinces in terms of degree of political participation, efficacy, and trust, it generally ranks near the bottom.[18] As seen in Table 2.6, voter turnout in federal elections is in the 60 percent range, consistently the lowest in the country. It has been higher in most provincial elections since 1971 and now averages about 78 percent.[19]

TABLE 2.6 **Newfoundland Voter Turnout Rate in Recent Federal and Provincial Elections**

Federal Elections		Provincial Elections	
1974	57%	1975	73%
1979	60%	1979	73%
1980	59%	1982	78%
1984	65%	1985	78%
1988	67%	1989	81%
1993	55%	1993	86%
Average	60.5%	Average	78%

Source: *Reports of the Chief Electoral Officer,* calculations by author.

POLITICAL PARTIES

Party System

Between 1949 and 1989, Newfoundland experienced two long periods of one-party dominance headed by two forceful personalities, Joey Smallwood (Liberal) and Brian Peckford (Conservative). As Figure 2.1 shows, the governing party regularly received 60 percent of the popular vote. As Table 2.7 shows, between them the Liberals and Conservatives gained over 90 percent of the popular vote and about 97 percent of the seats. Such figures suggest a two-party system characterized by a single period of dominance by each party, rather than a regular rotation in office. The replacement of the Liberals by the Conservatives in 1971-72 was rooted in the emergence of a more sophisticated electorate wanting a more modern government. Such periods of one-party dominance have been closely related to positive or negative relations with the federal government (either strategy could be useful) and the end of the Tory dominance in 1989 can be attributed to federal as well as internal factors. The NDP has struggled on the sidelines, showing some signs of life in the mid-1980s, but almost disappearing in the 1989 election. Newfoundland has also had several fragment parties, such as the United Newfoundland Party, which temporarily broke away from the Conservatives, and a Liberal Reform group which twice separated from the Liberals. In fact, more politicians have crossed the floor in Newfoundland than in any other province. Many Liberals were former Conservatives, just as many

Conservatives, including Brian Peckford, John Crosbie, and Premier Tom Rideout, were former Liberals. This degree of movement is reminiscent of earlier periods in Canadian politics when party loyalties were not well established. It also reflects the importance of personality and the lack of ideological focus in the two parties themselves. It is not likely to happen so frequently in the future.

TABLE 2.7   Party Support in Newfoundland, 1970–1995

	Years in Office	Average Percentage of Vote	Percentage of Seats
Liberals	8 (32%)	41.0	38.3
Conservatives	17 (68%)	50.1	58.6
Combined	25 (100%)	91.1	96.9

Source: *Reports of the Chief Electoral Officer,* calculations by author.

FIGURE 2.2   Percentage of Vote by Party in Newfoundland Elections, 1970–1995

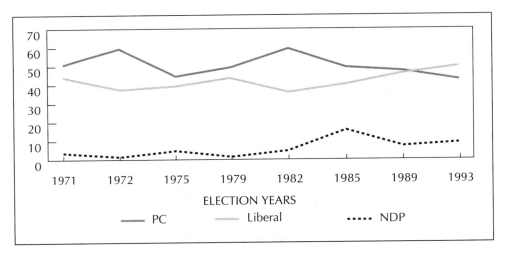

Party Organization

In terms of party organization, the striking lack of such in the case of Smallwood's Liberals deserves comment. Since Smallwood selected all candidates for both provincial and federal elections, and since each election campaign was essentially a referendum on his leadership, there was little need for local constituency associations.[20] The Smallwood Liberals could probably best be termed a classic "cadre" party, comprised of local notables who distributed government patronage and headed a local ad hoc election committee.[21] Only in preparation for the 1969 leadership convention did Smallwood encourage the establishment of constituency associations. Furthermore, no provincial party convention was held between 1949 and 1969 because there was no need to review the party leadership or contribute to government policy. This lack of a constitutional provision for leadership review eventually backfired, resulting in challenges to Smallwood's leadership within the party after he failed to follow through on his promises to retire. Since the end of the Smallwood era both parties have developed more orthodox local and provincial organizations.

Federal-Provincial Party Links

Joey Smallwood established unusually intimate links with the federal Liberal government from 1949 to 1957 and again from 1963 to 1972. When Newfoundland entered Confederation it received, as custom demanded, a representative in the federal cabinet. A few years later, J.W. Pickersgill's desire to enter politics conveniently coincided with Smallwood's desire to have him assume that cabinet position. Pickersgill developed a warm relationship with the premier, to their mutual political benefit, and, being an ex-Manitoban, he would not challenge Smallwood's authority within Newfoundland. Smallwood's only serious dispute with his Ottawa brethren came in 1959, when the federal party was not impressed with his anti-union actions in the International Woodworkers of America strike. Similarly, relations were generally harmonious between the federal and provincial Conservative administrations during Joe Clark's brief tenure as prime minister. Relations were even closer with the Brian Mulroney regime after 1984. On the other hand, Diefenbaker's decisions on the RCMP reinforcements and federal financial obligations under the Terms of Union caused a breach between the federal and Newfoundland Conservative parties.

Party Leadership

Leadership has been a crucial factor in Newfoundland politics.[22] First, there was Joey Smallwood, the folksy, eloquent, charismatic, entertaining populist (some would say demagogue), who dominated the province for 23 years. His was a guided democracy, paternalistic and autocratic, and he did what he felt necessary to bring Newfoundland out of its backward state. Obsessed with building mammoth economic development projects, Smallwood's "dreams were his greatest downfall."[23] He signed deals that would come back to haunt his successors, gave away cash the province sorely lacked, guaranteed the borrowings of unreliable, if not swindling, American entrepreneurs, and forfeited much of the province's resource base. Smallwood was held in high affection both within and beyond the province when he first took office, but gradually lost this popularity, especially among politicians, as he grew older. He became increasingly authoritarian, impulsive, and vindictive, growing farther and farther away from his grass roots' origins, and instilling a climate of cynicism and fear.[24]

Frank Moores was a much less striking leader. His tenure was characterized primarily by a more modern, technological, and managerial orientation. A great deal of overdue administrative reform took place during his premiership and he reduced the corruption associated with the Smallwood years.

In contrast, the province's third post-Confederation premier, Brian Peckford, originally a high school English teacher, was another very powerful personality. He developed the reputation of an aggressive, abrasive streetfighter, and a strong defender of provincial rights. During his term, most political issues had an intergovernmental orientation. Peckford emphasized provincial self-reliance and self-determination based on control of its own natural resources.[25] He appeared unafraid to challenge Pierre Trudeau, his particular adversary, or anyone else whom he felt stood in his way. After the Supreme Court decision on Churchill Falls, however, Peckford adopted a more restrained approach.

Clyde Wells proved himself to be, especially in his opposition to Meech Lake, an urbane version of Brian Peckford. Unlike Peckford, Wells was not obsessed with provincial autonomy. Indeed, his main concern was that Ottawa remain strong enough to help provinces such as his. Both in his views and in his style—tenacity, sophistication, and autocratic tendencies—many saw a political reincarnation of Pierre Trudeau.

Clyde Wells won the Liberal mantle in 1987 at a traditional leadership convention.[26] The same method was used to elect Lynn Verge as the Progressive Conservative leader in 1995, while NDP leader Jack Harris was elected by acclamation.

Party Ideology

The Liberal and Conservative parties have never been divided by ideology in Newfoundland; indeed, both have been exceedingly pragmatic and all-inclusive. While Smallwood periodically labelled himself a "socialist," for example, he catered to fishermen on the one hand and, increasingly, to international financiers on the other. Instead, provincial parties can be distinguished by their leadership, sources of support, and relations with the federal government. Even the change of government in 1972 represented more of a difference in style than substance.

In 1979, Peckford represented the embodiment of a new middle class that wished to engage in province-building and take control of its destiny. He asserted provincial control of resource development, pushed for local servicing and manufacturing through forward and backward linkages and maximized the involvement of local business.[27] Though a Liberal, economic circumstances forced Clyde Wells to take many conservative-minded initiatives including the privatization of government economic enterprises.

ELECTIONS

Electoral System

Newfoundland has an orthodox Canadian electoral system with single-member constituencies based on the general principle of representation by population. Until 1975, however, it had a peculiar system in which constituency boundaries were drawn on the basis of the religious distribution in the province.[28]

Another striking feature of the early electoral system was the heavy over-representation of rural areas. This could be justified in part by the sparseness of the outport population, but it also conveniently served the interests of the Liberal party. Because Smallwood had greatest appeal to fishermen, the Liberals gained more seats than they deserved. Smallwood claimed that rural over-representation was legitimate because it

> was recognized throughout the world that the people of the countryside, what we call the outports, are socially sounder than the people of the cities and urban areas...the great yeomanry, the great peasantry, the great farming class, the great countryside class, the great outport class...are socially and politically the soundest people of any country.[29]

An independent redistribution procedure was not introduced until 1973-74, at which time it served the Conservatives to do so. The situation is now more equitable, with a second impartial redistribution carried out in 1979, and a third in 1984. A new act passed in 1992 provided for a 1993 redistribution which would reduce the legislature to a maximum of 46 seats. It was too late, however, to take effect for the election of that year. Thus, representation disparities in the 1993 election, as seen in Table 2.8, show that about 10 years after the previous redistribution only 71 percent of constituencies fell within the plus or minus 25 percent range, while the other 29 percent varied enormously. The new rules no longer guarantee Labrador four seats, but more or less ensured that aboriginals living there would constitute one constituency.

TABLE 2.8   Representational Disparities in 1993 Election

Mean no. of voters per constituency	8,660
Largest constituency (Mount Pearl)	13,108 (+91.6% of mean)
Smallest constituency (Torngat Mountains)	1,468 (-83% of mean)
Average variation from mean	21.6%
Constituencies within ±10%	32.7%
Constituencies within ±25%	71.2%

Reports of the Chief Electoral Officer, calculations by author.

Elections in the Smallwood period were characterized by promises of reward for constituencies that returned a Liberal member and threats of punishment for those that did not.[30] Election-day "treating" has also been common in the province. New legislation in this field was finally enacted in 1992. It limited contributions ($2,500 for individuals and $10,000 for unions and corporations) with disclosure of contributors over $100. It restricted the advertising period to 21 days and put ceilings on both candidate and party expenditures. Candidates receiving at least 15 percent of the vote would be reimbursed about one-third of their expenditures. Contributors would receive a tax credit similar to federal legislation, 75 percent up to $100 and declining thereafter.

Voting Behaviour

An important early influence on voting in Newfoundland was the voter's attitude toward union with Canada. Supporters of Confederation usually voted Liberal, while opponents opted for the Conservatives. This division coincided to a large extent with place of residence, as urbanites and those in Avalon Peninsula voted Conservative, while outport and western residents supported the Liberals. Similarly, merchants voted Tory, fishermen Liberal. Residence and occupation were reinforced by religion, probably the strongest factor of all, as Protestants tended to vote Liberal, and Roman Catholics, Conservative. This particular pattern persists even in the absence of recent religious issues and is an interesting reversal of the pattern established in the rest of the country.

The province's economic situation might be expected to give rise to greater class-consciousness and support for a more radical alternative like the NDP. However, a number of factors have mitigated against such a development, including pure habit, the fishermen's deference toward the more affluent, the influence of the churches, geographic isolation of communities, and the small proportion of industrial workers. Added to this could be the observed tendency of the indigent to prefer the status quo to the risk of losing the little they have. In addition, a dominant sentiment in the province favours rallying behind a leader who will get immediate benefits or a better long-range deal from Ottawa. Newfoundlanders have always been persuaded that enormous prosperity is just around the corner and that the incumbent authorities will shortly make it appear.[31] Nevertheless, a growing middle class was the backbone of Conservative support after 1970 and, at least for a time in the 1980s, it seemed that an awakened class consciousness of the fishermen and fish plant workers might translate into NDP support. To some extent, this support evaporated in 1989.

While Smallwood was premier, the electorate voted Liberal consistently at both levels of government. Starting in 1968, the province switched to support the Conservatives in federal and provincial elections, although the federal Liberals fared better than their provincial counterparts and sometimes took a majority of Newfoundland seats. By the late 1980s, the province was once again supporting the Liberals at both levels.

PRESSURE GROUPS AND THE MEDIA

Pressure Groups

Economic and religious pressure groups were most evident in the pre-Confederation period. The St. John's merchants usually had de facto control of the government and the fishermen had an effective counterforce for a time in the form of William Coaker's Fishermen's Protective Union. In addition to the local merchants, several international businessmen and companies have been very influential since 1949, and the Canadian Manufacturers' Association has a division in the province called the Newfoundland Manufacturers' Association. The Roman Catholic, Anglican, and United churches were the leading religious groups; they have been joined since Confederation by the Salvation Army, Pentecostals, and Seventh Day Adventists. Opposition to a secular school system and the coverup of child sexual abuse at the Catholic-run Mount Cashel orphanage are evidence of the continuing influence of the Roman Catholic Church in particular.

TABLE 2.9   Leading Newfoundland Pressure Groups

Peak Business	Newfoundland Manufacturers' Association
	Newfoundland and Labrador Employers' Council
Industrial	Fisheries Association of Newfoundland and Labrador
	Canadian Sealers Association
	Newfoundland and Labrador Construction Association
	Independent Fish Producers Association
Labour	Newfoundland and Labrador Federation of Labour
	Newfoundland Association of Public Employees
Agriculture	Newfoundland and Labrador Federation of Agriculture
Professional	Law Society of Newfoundland
	Newfoundland and Labrador Medical Association
	Newfoundland Teachers' Association
	Newfoundland Dental Association
	Newfoundland Nurses' Union
Institutional	Newfoundland and Labrador Federation of Municipalities
	Newfoundland School Trustees Association
	Newfoundland Hospital and Nursing Home Association
Environmental	Newfoundland and Labrador Wildlife Federation
Public Interest	Community Services Council

After the demise of the FPU in the 1920s, fishermen were not effectively organized until Richard Cashin resurrected the fishermen's union as a strong force representing processing plant workers, trawler crews, and inshore fishermen. Forest and pulp and paper mill workers were weakened after Smallwood outlawed their local of the International Woodworkers of America. The premier tried to create reverse pressure groups under his control among fishermen and forest workers but without much success.[32] The Newfoundland Federation of

Labour constitutes an umbrella group in the labour field. After the advances in post-Confederation education, the Newfoundland Teachers' Association has become prominent, as have the Newfoundland and Labrador Nurses' Union and a variety of citizen groups. The increase in the number of interest groups since 1970 reflects the increasing diversity and modernity of Newfoundland society.[33]

The Media

Thomson Newspaper Ltd.'s *Evening Telegram* in St. John's is the leading daily newspaper with a circulation of about 41,000.[34] Thomson also publishes the *Western Star* in Corner Brook with a circulation of about 12,000. An anti-establishment weekly, *The Sunday Express*, has been converted to a bland weekly *Express*. Both the Canadian Broadcasting Corporation and CTV have television stations in St. John's, while the province is also served by several CBC radio stations and an array of private radio broadcasters.

GOVERNMENT INSTITUTIONS

As a British colony, Newfoundland underwent a constitutional development similar to that of its Maritime sister colonies before 1867 and its Canadian neighbour afterwards. A British-appointed governor began to share power with appointed executive and legislative councils and, after an assembly was created, the executive council developed into a cabinet on the principle of responsible government. In 1934, however, Newfoundland reverted to a kind of colonial status as complete executive and legislative power was given to a six-man government commission appointed by the British government. Thus, with Newfoundland's entry into Confederation, the province's governmental institutions were created anew.

Executive

After 1949, the lieutenant-governor was appointed by Ottawa in place of the governor-general previously sent from London. None of the appointees after 1949 caused controversy by interfering in the operation of responsible government, and a confused constitutional situation in 1971-72 was resolved before the lieutenant-governor had to act on his own initiative. Partly because of strong British ties, and partly because of Newfoundland's relatively small size, the lieutenant-governor is a more visible presence than in most provinces. It is the only place in Canada where the lieutenant-governor's daily itinerary (Government House Calendar) is published in the newspaper in the same manner as that of the royal family in London.

While Joey Smallwood was premier, from 1949 to 1972, the cabinet operated under his control and little thought was given to cabinet procedure. When power changed hands in Newfoundland, several other provinces, notably Ontario, were in the process of restructuring their executive operations. Thus, the new premier, Frank Moores, set up the Committee on Government Administration and Productivity in 1972 and, upon the presentation of its report, made several changes in executive procedures. To a large extent these were based on the Ontario cabinet committee model and remain unchanged: a planning and priorities committee chaired by the premier, a treasury board chaired by the minister of finance, resource policy and social policy committees, and a committee on routine matters.

Clyde Wells reduced the size of the cabinet to 14 members, and premiers have always balanced religious and regional interests in their choice of ministers. The main cabinet support mechanism is the executive council office, within which a cabinet secretariat prepares material for cabinet and cabinet committees, an intergovernmental affairs secretariat is kept busy with federal-provincial problems, and another group looks after protocol and the lieutenant-governor. The premier's office, with a staff of 15 or 20, handles public relations and the premier's constituency problems.

Legislature

Newfoundland was created with a single-chamber legislature, as no one saw a need to resurrect the old upper house, the Legislative Council. The House of Assembly now has 52 single-member seats[35] and sits for an average of nearly 80 days per year. It is located in the modern Confederation Building in St. John's and recently moved from the 10th to the first floor. In a departure from procedure in most provincial legislatures, the government party sits to the left of the Speaker.

The legislature has three substantive standing committees, government services, resource, and social services, each chaired by a government member with a vice-chair from the Opposition. The public accounts committee has an Opposition chair. The committee on standing orders is the only one containing cabinet ministers. Bills can go to standing committees or committee of the whole, or both, after second reading. During the Wells regime, the legislature has experienced an active use of closure, that is, the cutting off of debate by the government.

Newfoundland paid its private members a basic indemnity of about $36,000 in 1994 along with a non-taxable allowance of about $18,000. It has also provided members of the House with research and administrative support.

Bureaucracy

Newfoundland employs about 12,500 people in government departments and agencies, another 2,600 in government business enterprises (half of them in

Newfoundland Hydro), and 13,400 more in the wider public sector. Although a civil service act was passed in 1926, neither it nor its successor, adopted in 1947, was a barrier to partisan appointments. As a result, the provincial public service remained very small and poorly qualified right up to 1970. For example, as in the other Atlantic provinces, the Newfoundland bureaucracy was not equal to the task of evaluating the claims of "fast-talking promoters" who, in the 1950s and 1960s, exploited the province's desperation to modernize.[36] Since Smallwood's departure, however, the patronage situation has improved considerably. The province now possesses a skilled, modern bureaucracy[37] with a new management system, and a strong cabinet secretariat.

Newfoundland introduced collective bargaining for its civil service in 1970. These employees, with the exception of those in managerial positions and essential services, now have the right to strike, although the definition of essential services became controversial during Peckford's premiership. The province passed an ombudsman act in 1970 but did not appoint an ombudsman until 1975—perhaps because Smallwood preferred to act in this capacity himself.

Premier Wells revamped and reduced the departmental structure when first elected in 1989. In 1993 he transformed the Department of Development into the Department of Industry, Trade and Technology, with a central role in implementing the province's strategic economic plan. His 13 government departments in the mid-1990s can be seen in Table 2.10.

TABLE 2.10   Newfoundland Government Departments, 1994

Education and Training
Employment and Labour Relations
Environment
Finance and Treasury Board
Fisheries, Forestry and Agriculture
Health
Industry, Trade and Technology
Justice
Natural Resources
Municipal and Provincial Affairs
Social Services
Tourism, Culture and Recreation
Works, Services and Transportation

In addition to the regular government departments, Newfoundland has an array of semi-independent agencies, boards, commissions, and Crown corporations, the most important of which are listed in Table 2.11. One of the most interesting is the Royal Newfoundland Constabulary, a provincial police force which operates in St. John's, Corner Brook, and Labrador West (the RCMP polices the rest of the province). Two economic advisory agencies exist, including the Economic Recovery Commission. Newfoundland and Labrador Hydro, a Crown corporation established in 1975, produces most of the province's electricity. A subsidiary, Churchill Falls (Labrador) Corporation, was formed when the province assumed control of that project. It also has a 51 percent interest in the Lower Churchill Development Corporation, with the remaining 49 percent held by the Government of Canada. After 1993, Wells tried to privatize Newfoundland Hydro, along with Newfoundland and Labrador Computer Services and parts of Newfoundland and Labrador Housing Corporation.

TABLE 2.11   Leading Newfoundland Agencies, Boards, Commissions and Crown Corporations

Crown Corporations:	Churchill Falls (Labrador) Corp. Ltd.
	Lower Churchill Development Corp.
	Newfoundland and Labrador Hydro
	Newfoundland Liquor Corporation
	Newfoundland and Labrador Housing Corporation
Agencies, Boards and Commissions:	Advisory Council on the Status of Women
	Advisory Council on the Economy
	Commissioners of Public Utilities
	Economic Recovery Commission
	Enterprise Newfoundland and Labrador Development Corporation
	Fisheries Loan Board
	Human Rights Commission
	Medical Care Commission
	Social Assistance Appeal Board
	Workers' Compensation Commission

Judiciary

The Newfoundland Supreme Court consists of appeal and trial divisions, below which are provincial district courts and a unified family court. Confederation introduced Newfoundland to a new criminal code but the civil law was not greatly affected.[38]

Municipal Government

When Newfoundland entered Confederation, it had only 20 organized municipalities. Services that municipal governments usually performed, such as sewage disposal and transportation, were performed by the sea, and others such as social services by churches, private charities, family, friends, corporations, or the province. The population was clustered in isolated settlements. It had a long tradition of self-help and was intensely hostile toward provincial intervention and the imposition of local taxation.[39] Residents eventually realized the deficiencies in their situation as provincial grants and subsidies began to encourage municipal organization. The obsessive fear of property taxation remains in many communities, however, and only about 70 percent levy such a tax.[40]

Today there are three cities (St. John's, Corner Brook, and Mount Pearl), numerous towns, community councils, and local service districts. Municipalities now provide such services as roads, water, sewage systems, and fire protection, but do not provide social services. There is a tradition of strong administrative support at the local level in the form of town or city managers. Municipalities are encouraged to be more self-sufficient than in the past and amalgamations and/or new regional councils are anticipated later in the 1990s. A proposed metropolitan structure for St. John's and Mount Pearl has yet to be established.

POLITICAL EVOLUTION

To 1949

Given that Newfoundland entered Confederation much later than the other provinces, brief mention should be made of its development over the preceding 100 years.[41] Although called "Britain's oldest colony," it was for centuries used only as a fishing base and naval training ground. Settlement was discouraged if not forbidden. In 1832 the colony was granted a representative assembly and in 1855 the principle of responsible government was recognized.

Newfoundland was only marginally involved in the 1867 Confederation scheme, although it sent representatives to the Quebec Conference and the governor attempted to encourage a union. Newfoundland's geographic separation, the irrelevance of such issues as railways, Fenian raiders, and possible American invasion, its strong national pride, and its tendency to look eastward to Britain rather than westward to Canada, were all factors discouraging any move towards joining in Confederation. Provision was made in the British North America Act for both Newfoundland and Prince Edward Island to join at a later date but the election of an anti-Confederation government in Newfoundland in 1869 put an end to that issue for many years.[42] As in the other provinces, railway politics became the next prominent issue in Newfoundland. A railway from St. John's to Port-aux-Basques was completed in 1896 by a private firm to which the government made generous concessions.

The period after 1908 witnessed the dramatic rise of William F. Coaker's Fishermen's Protective Union.[43] Although the Newfoundland fishermen were poor and exploited by both large and small merchants, little effort had been made to improve their lot. Coaker trekked tirelessly from one village to another, setting up a union local in each community, and establishing a co-operative buying system so that fishermen were no longer at the mercy of local merchants. By 1911 the union had more than 12,500 members in 116 locals. Many of these workers had developed a sense of class consciousness, a feeling of solidarity, and a pride in their work. This set the stage for political action in the election of 1913 in which the FPU party elected eight members. Coaker, even in opposition, dominated the assembly for several years.

Shortly after that election came the outbreak of the First World War. Because it was a British colony, Newfoundland was automatically committed to the British war effort and originally raised troops by voluntary means. Also, paralleling developments in Canada, a coalition government was formed and a decision made to impose conscription in the latter stages of the war. (In addition, Newfoundland tried to prohibit the sale of alcohol, but this law proved to be as unenforceable there as in Canadian provinces with similar measures.)

Following the war, Newfoundland descended from wartime prosperity into serious economic difficulty. Pre-war and wartime government borrowing was compounded by annual post-war deficits. In 1923, a scandal of large proportions involved Prime Minister Richard Squires and his minister of Agriculture and Mines. They were found to be engaged in rampant patronage and corruption, misappropriation of funds, and graft in the liquor control department, which was active in bootlegging rather than prohibiting liquor. Added to these problems was the fact that the government was forced to assume full responsibility for the railway's past debts and continuing deficits.

In the late 1920s, the province repealed prohibition, and extended the franchise to women. In 1927, the judicial committee of the privy council confirmed that Labrador belonged to Newfoundland rather than Quebec, thus ending another longstanding dispute between Newfoundland and Canada. Party lines were still fluid, defections were common, and each government seemed more corrupt than the last.

In the early 1930s Newfoundland was battered by the world-wide impact of the Great Depression. By 1931, for example, the country's debt had reached about $100 million and interest payments consumed some 65 percent of current revenues. At first, help came from Britain, Imperial Oil, Canadian commercial banks operating in Newfoundland, and the Canadian government itself. Further British and Canadian loans were forthcoming only on the condition that a commission be appointed to examine the country's future and finances. This commission reported in 1933 and the British government immediately acted on its recommendations. Newfoundland would surrender its responsible government status until such time as it might become self-supporting again. The assembly, legislative council, and cabinet were all suspended. Authority was placed in the hands of the governor and a six-member commission appointed by the British government which had three members from Britain and three from Newfoundland. The residents seemed unconcerned about this retrograde step, apparently because the financial crisis and the repetition of scandals left them anxious for a rest from party politics.

The period of commission government, 1934-1949, has been called a "benevolent dictatorship."[44] It was marked by a competent bureaucracy backed by financial assistance from Britain, but also by frequent conflict among commission members and an absence of innovative policy. The commission's lack of contact with the constituency led to a riot in 1935, and the number of people on government relief continued to climb until 1938-39. Public opposition to the commission increased until the outbreak of the Second World War brought new prosperity. This prosperity was founded on an agreement that gave the United States three military bases on the island, bringing thousands of American servicemen to Newfoundland. Other contributing factors were the establishment of several new Canadian-built bases, and increased prices for fish.[45] By 1942, a budget surplus allowed the government to improve public services.

The new post-war British government decided that a national convention of 45 representatives should be elected to make recommendations regarding possible forms of future government. Those recommendations would be submitted to the people of Newfoundland in a referendum. Among the candidates elected was Joseph R. Smallwood, who had been born in the outport of Gambo in 1900 but grew up in St. John's. As part of his earlier, largely unsuccessful, attempts to gain a livelihood, Smallwood had been a journalist, a union organizer, a broadcaster, a defeated candidate in 1932, and, most recently, a pig farmer in Gander. His daily 15-minute radio program called "The Barrelman," composed of local history, folklore, and anecdote, was one of his more successful ventures. About 1945 he had been struck by the conviction that the best future course for Newfoundland was to become part of Canada.[46]

Smallwood had made the acquaintance of J.W. Pickersgill, principal secretary to the Canadian prime minister, and they became close allies on the Confederation project. Once the convention began, it was apparent that those favouring Confederation were in a minority. However, because the proceedings were broadcast on radio, Smallwood made good use of his experience in this field by speaking directly to the thousands of radio listeners. This was an important element in the decision to send delegates to Ottawa where negotiations took place between June and September 1947. In November the terms of a proposed union between Newfoundland and Canada were tabled at the convention. But, by the time it dissolved in January 1948, the convention had voted to recommend only two alternatives be put on the ballot—responsible government as it existed before 1934, and a continuation of government by the commission. After much pressure from the pro-Confederation forces, however, the British government agreed that Confederation with Canada should be a third option and the referendum was scheduled for June.

By this time, each side had established an organization for the campaign— the Confederate Association and the Responsible Government League. A third group tried to generate support for economic union with the United States but that alternative was not officially available. Smallwood was effectively the leader of the Confederate group and drove himself to exhaustion by writing, organizing, speaking, and travelling from one community to another in a manner reminiscent of union organizer William Coaker. Among the advantages that Confederation would confer on Newfoundland, he emphasized, were family allowances, old age pensions, and federal public works. His efforts were financed in part by the Liberal Party of Canada and he was not above promising senatorships and other post-Confederation positions in return for contributions. But many Newfoundlanders continued to feel ill will toward Canada, reinforced by the fear of higher taxation, and preferred the idea of independence. Thus, despite Smallwood's energy and ability, and the Confederate Association's superior campaign, the results of the referendum were as follows:

Responsible Government	69,400	44.5%
Confederation	64,066	41.1%
Commission Government	22,311	14.3%

The British government wanted a clear majority decision of over 50 percent of voters, so a second ballot was ordered for July. In this run-off poll, religious division became a central focus as the Roman Catholic archbishop led a strong anti-Confederation campaign. Members of the Protestant Orange Order naturally countered with support for the Confederation forces. In the end, with Roman Catholics, St. John's merchants, and professionals generally opposed to Confederation, and with Protestants and fishermen in favour, the results of the second ballot were as follows:

Confederation	78,323	52.3%
Responsible Government	71,344	47.4%

The Canadian and British governments indicated satisfaction with the Newfoundland decision and more negotiations took place in Ottawa between October and December 1948, producing the final Terms of Union of Newfoundland with Canada. These were submitted to the Canadian parliament and the British parliament amended the British North America Act to permit the annexation of Newfoundland to Canada. In addition to the extension of Canadian citizenship, social services, and many Canadian statutes to Newfoundland, the new province was granted seven MPs, six senators, and, by convention, a cabinet minister. Special provisions in the Terms of Union related to denominational schools, permission to sell margarine (later allowed in the rest of Canada by decision of the Supreme Court), the continuation of provincial fishery laws in the province for five years, and the guarantee of a vehicular ferry service. In the financial sphere, because Newfoundland gave up its right to levy customs and excise duties, transitional grants were provided which started at $6.5 million per year and decreased over 12 years to $350,000. This was in addition to other federal subsidies and Canadian assumption of Newfoundland's external debt. Term 29 also promised that, within eight years, a royal commission would be appointed study whether additional financial assistance was required. Once Confederation was safely on track, Smallwood devoted his efforts to ensuring he would be the first provincial premier.

1949–1969[47]

On March 31, 1949, Newfoundland was united with Canada. On April 1, Joey Smallwood was sworn in as premier. On April 30, he was chosen leader of the provincial Liberal party and soon led his forces to an overwhelming election victory. Smallwood's party was essentially his own creation, as he shrewdly converted his Confederate Association into the provincial branch of the Liberal Party of Canada. By default, those opposed to Confederation became the Progressive Conservative party.

The new province was socially and economically far behind most others. It had a high illiteracy rate, a rather primitive denominational school system, and no degree-granting post-secondary institutions. Electricity was rare, and overland travel from one major centre to another was almost impossible because there were few roads, except on the Avalon Peninsula. The only large industry consisted of paper mills at Corner Brook and Grand Falls, the companies involved having been given most of the province's best timber. Local sawmills and a handful of small mining operations were the other primary sector alternatives to the fishing industry. Fishing was mostly confined to individual and family seasonal in-shore efforts, with the catch laid out to dry and then sold as salt cod. Fishermen exchanged their produce for credit with the local merchant in a semi-feudal relationship called the "truck system."

Smallwood assumed the premiership undaunted by the unfavourable prospects. He inherited a minimal administrative apparatus from the former commission government and so set up new government departments, including one for economic development. Some of his early initiatives included bank loans for co-operatives and fisheries, public utilities, hydroelectric commissions, workmen's compensation, slum clearance, and fisheries accident insurance legislation. He established Memorial University in 1949, which at first served to produce new teachers for the province's schools. At the same time, federal social benefits such as family allowances and old age pensions suddenly provided purchasing power for Newfoundlanders, many of whom had rarely seen cash. Smallwood took as much personal credit as he could for these federal transfer payments and built on them to develop a "comprehensive provincial social welfare system."[48]

But the premier also wanted to promote the economic development of the province, and sought to diversify its historic reliance on the fishery—which was soon to shift to frozen fish processing—in the direction of secondary industry. To this end he devised a three-fold strategy: to improve the education system; to build extensive roads; and, with the manpower and infrastructure in place, to attract outside industry to Newfoundland.

The quest for industrialization prompted Smallwood to appoint as his economic advisor the urbane and inscrutable Latvian economist, Alfred Valdmanis. The two travelled around Europe in search of interested entrepreneurs, and several small industries were established with the generous financial assistance of the provincial government. In 1954, after more trips abroad in search of developers, Valdmanis was convicted of defrauding the government of $200,000 and sentenced to four years hard labour.[49]

In 1953, Smallwood initiated a program of "centralization." Under this program a small sum of money was offered to each household in tiny outport communities if all residents agreed to relocate to larger centres. The rationale was that Newfoundland's dispersed population made it difficult to provide services and to attract industries that would serve as alternatives to the fishery. In 1954, Smallwood promoted a regional integration of schools and encouraged attendance with a high school bursary system. In the same year, the Newfoundland and Labrador Power Commission was created to administer the rural electrification program, which extended electricity to rural parts of the province. The largest initiative of this period was the deal to develop the iron ore of western Labrador. After a search for investors, Smallwood granted John C. Doyle of Canadian Javelin the exploration and development rights to 2,400 square kilometres of Labrador, and later guaranteed a bond issue of $16.5 million, a staggering amount for that province, to get the Wabush mines project started.

It was after 1953 and the loss of Valdmanis that Smallwood began his relationship with the new Newfoundland representative in the federal cabinet, J.W. Pickersgill. The partnership proved so fruitful that by 1956 Smallwood could announce the extension of unemployment insurance to the province's fishermen. The next few years saw a continuation of the building program—schools, roads, and hospitals—but there was little new economic development, and the traditional fishing industry stagnated. To make matters worse, the federal Liberals were defeated in 1957 and Smallwood could not expect to forge a close association with the Diefenbaker Conservatives, especially as he continued to ensure the province sent mostly Liberal representatives to Ottawa. During this time, the other Atlantic provinces were revelling in the solicitude of the new federal regime. Newfoundland did gain substantially in such areas as rural electrification, vocational schools, highway construction, and an additional $7.5 million in Atlantic provinces adjustment grants.

Newfoundland experienced two traumatic intergovernmental battles in 1959. The first involved a long and bitter strike by the International Woodworkers of America against the owner of the Grand Falls pulp and paper mill and surrounding forests. Despite his former career in labour organization and his claims that he represented the "toiling masses," Smallwood intervened with a masterful use of propaganda. He accused the "foreign" union of lawlessness, and

invited its members to join a new local, government-sponsored union. The puni-
tive anti-labour legislation he introduced went far beyond outlawing the IWA,
and five days later a riot occurred in which a constable was killed. A request to
Ottawa for RCMP reinforcements had been accepted by federal Minister of
Justice Davie Fulton, but the full cabinet overruled him on the grounds that the
mounties would be used to break the strike. This decision prompted the resignation of the RCMP commissioner.[50]

The two sides were still arguing about the legality of the federal decision on
this issue when another dispute arose. A federal royal commission had been
established in 1957, as per Term 29 of the Terms of Union, to review the
province's financial position and recommend whether further financial assistance
was required. Smallwood was unhappy at its recommendation, issued in 1958,
that Newfoundland be given an additional $6.6 million in 1957 and $8 million in
perpetuity from 1961. He had expected $15 million annually, the figure recom-
mended by a provincial royal commission, and was stunned by the Diefenbaker
government's decision to end the annual grant of $8 million in 1962.[51] The
provincial Conservative party was badly split by the issues of the strike and the
grants, and some members left to form a United Newfoundland Party.

Over the next few years, several construction projects were completed,
including the Confederation Building (1960), the new campus of Memorial
University (1961), and new vocational high schools. Smallwood welcomed the
return of the federal Liberals to office in 1963 with Pickersgill becoming the
province's representative in the Pearson cabinet, and the province benefited
from federal largesse as never before. The Pearson government was persuaded to
pay 90 percent of the cost of completing the Trans-Canada Highway in
Newfoundland, and finally, in 1965, a paved road extended from St. John's to
Port-aux-Basques. Other federal funds were directed towards a new fisheries aid
scheme, rural post offices, and improved ferry terminals. At the province's
request, a 12-mile off-shore fishing limit was established and the National
Harbours Board assumed responsibility for the St. John's harbour.[52] In 1967, the
new summertime car ferry system began operation between Sydney, N.S., and
Argentia. Also during this time, Harry Steele's Eastern Provincial Airways, with
its head office in Gander, grew with provincial government support and became
the major airline of the Atlantic region. The unique College of Fisheries,
Navigation, Marine Engineering, and Electronics opened its doors. An expanded
"resettlement" program began with federal assistance and, in total, some 200
settlements disappeared. Considerable activity also occurred in Labrador. The
Wabush iron ore mine went into production and a second mine owned by the
Iron Ore Company of Canada began operating in Labrador City.

But a project of even greater magnitude was being negotiated, the proposed
development of a hydroelectric project at Hamilton Falls (renamed Churchill
Falls in 1965 in honour of Winston Churchill). Protracted discussions ensued
because of the conflicting interests of Newfoundland, Quebec, and the various
companies involved. At the height of the difficult negotiations, Smallwood

began the practice of referring to the province as the government of Newfoundland *and Labrador,* just in case Quebec needed a reminder. The various sides finally reached an agreement in 1968. The development company, BRIN-CO, naturally insisted on maximizing its profits, and Quebec Hydro could only be expected to buy the power produced at a rock-bottom price. After an alternative Atlantic transmission route had been rejected as too expensive, Newfoundland was forced to accept the other parties' conditions. The province could only use 10 percent of the energy produced and would receive about $15 million a year in cash from the export of the other 90 percent. Even at the time, some doubts were expressed as to whether the 40-year deal with a 25-year option was of much value or fairness to Newfoundland. Furthermore, no practical plan existed for transmitting power from Labrador to the island where, it was hoped, it would be a catalyst for economic expansion.[53]

Another dramatic but short-lived innovation was Smallwood's program of providing living allowances and free tuition for students at Memorial University, as well as at trade and vocational schools. At the same time, much of the elementary and secondary education system was integrated.

By 1968, Smallwood's world began to fall apart. It was a period of great economic difficulty and labour unrest. The fisheries were in a state of crisis as the price of frozen fish fell suddenly, prompting the closing of two large fish plants. The provincial budget was severe, increasing most taxes, cutting social services—including the recently established program of assistance to university students—and raising the provincial debt. More and more people, both inside the cabinet and among the general public, were tiring of Smallwood's increasingly autocratic style, his vanity, his choice of friends, and his government's widespread patronage and corruption.[54] Two ministers, John Crosbie and Clyde Wells, resigned from the cabinet over Smallwood's plans to have an oil refinery constructed by John Shaheen at Come-by-Chance. This ice-free harbour tucked into the south coast of the island was deep enough to handle tankers in excess of 200,000 tonnes. Shaheen proposed to build an oil refinery which would be the base of a petrochemical industry in the province. As usual, however, the developer invested little of his own money, with $150 million guaranteed by the province.

These immediate causes of Smallwood's declining popularity were compounded by several long-term economic and demographic factors. For all the premier's efforts and grand designs, the economy had remained troubled. The fishing and forestry industries were volatile and increasingly mechanized. Many of the new manufacturing industries had faltered, and the province derived little return from its iron ore and hydroelectric resources in Labrador. Jobs had been created in the construction industry, largely based on federal funding, or in service industries. But, when the construction boom ended, the base of the economy was still small.[55] The resettlement program had not succeeded because more often than not there were no jobs in the larger centres. The closure of American defence bases aggravated the unemployment problem. Smallwood's base of support dwindled as the outport population shrank, the literacy rate rose, and Memorial University produced more graduates.

In 1969, Smallwood devised yet another "megaproject," a linerboard (cardboard) mill to be built by John C. Doyle in Stephenville, where an American base had closed. Again, the province guaranteed over $60 million for the project, and both the minister and deputy minister of Finance resigned. Smallwood increased taxes again and continued to mention his imminent retirement. He organized party constituency associations for the first time in preparation for election campaigns under a less charismatic successor and called a leadership convention for November. Ex-minister John Crosbie became the leading contender but, because Smallwood could not countenance that prospect, he ran to succeed himself. After packing the delegate-selection meetings, he emerged triumphant. This unexpected resolution of the leadership issue prompted much political movement in the province over the next two years. Crosbie and three colleagues first sat as independent Liberals and then as the Liberal Reform group, while Tom Burgess founded his own Labrador Party.

The Conservatives chose Frank Moores as their leader in 1970, but Crosbie tended to overshadow Moores in Opposition, both before and after joining the Conservative ranks. Smallwood continued to rely on the Newfoundland representative in the federal Trudeau cabinet, at this time Donald Jamieson, to provide assistance for every imaginable purpose. Such assistance came increasingly from the Department of Regional Economic Expansion (DREE). Another important federal initiative was the creation of the Salt Fish Corporation, a marketing board similar to the Canadian Wheat Board, to help stabilize the cod industry.

Faced with several strikes in the summer of 1971, especially a violent fishermen's strike in Burgeo, and with the Opposition gaining momentum, Smallwood delayed the election until the last possible moment. The results of the October election were a dramatic repudiation of the 22-year-old Smallwood regime, and yet were also indecisive. While the Conservatives won 52 percent of the popular vote to the Liberals' 44 percent, the Tories were only one seat ahead, 21-20, with the remaining seat won by Tom Burgess in Labrador. In this confused situation, Smallwood called another Liberal leadership convention for February 1972 but raised much controversy by remaining in office in the interim. Some felt that the lieutenant-governor should have had him removed but, when it appeared that the Conservatives would maintain their lead, Smallwood resigned in January and Moores took over as premier. The leadership convention was won by Smallwood's young former assistant and Health minister, Edward Roberts.

The 1970s[56]

Three themes dominated Frank Moores' seven years as premier: administrative reform, including a decline in the incidence of patronage and corruption; the salvaging of Smallwood's megaprojects; and coping with such local economic problems as strikes and the troubled fishing industry. Moores began, however, by calling another election for March 1972, immediately after presenting his speech from the throne. The issue was a new development and industrialization policy designed to replace the "misguided" Smallwood approach in which enormous financial gains were made by American promoters but little long-term benefit accrued to the province. While the new premier was of the merchant class, he was an unusual Conservative for Newfoundland in that he was a Protestant from outside St. John's. This background may have contributed to the expansion of Conservative support to all parts of the province in 1972, no longer concentrated in urban and Roman Catholic areas.

After the election, the Moores government's first major decision was to purchase the linerboard mill at Stephenville. Innumerable irregularities had been revealed by an inquiry into the deal between Smallwood and Doyle. Another royal commission discovered that Smallwood, his former deputy Minister of Economic Development, O.L. Vardy, and businessman Arthur Lundrigan were behind a scheme to rent buildings to the Newfoundland Liquor Commission at large profits. Even worse, they used the buildings as collateral for a loan to buy BRINCO stock at the very time Smallwood and Doyle were negotiating with its principals over the Churchill Falls contract.

Another early initiative of the Moores government was the establishment of a more efficient, rational, and businesslike decision-making apparatus in the provincial executive. He introduced a cabinet committee system and reorganized the departmental structure. Moores reformed the Liquor Commission, passed a public tendering act, created a new rural development agency which sought to develop local resources on a smaller scale, and cancelled the resettlement program. Later, in the same vein, the Moores government established Newfoundland and Labrador Hydro, the Newfoundland and Labrador Development Corporation, and reformed municipal government in the province.

Over the next few years, the government directed much of its energy toward the three large projects inherited from Smallwood. The Stephenville linerboard plant, for example, continued to lose money. Meanwhile, its developer, John C. Doyle, was arrested for fraud after having previously skipped bail in the U.S. to avoid a prison sentence for breaching securities regulations. In 1974, the provincial government bought the Churchill Falls (Labrador) Corporation from BRINCO. This move was designed to give the province a stronger position should it try to renegotiate the contract with Quebec or seek more control over developing the Lower Churchill sites. The oil refinery in Come by Chance began production in 1973 with a lavish official opening. Construction began of a second refinery, three times larger than the first, for which the province loaned developer Shaheen almost $80 million. A year later, after the price of crude oil skyrocketed, the new plan was scaled down. By 1975, following the revelation of design problems and mismanagement, the project was experiencing serious difficulties.

Three positive developments also occurred in this period. In the fishing industry, the Food, Fish and Allied Workers Union and trawler companies agreed that crew members would receive wages rather than be regarded as co-adventurers paid based on the volume of the catch. The government unveiled a new forestry management policy under which it would increase taxes and improve conservation guidelines. Almost every aspect of the provincial economy benefited to some extent from the General Development Agreement signed with Ottawa in 1974.

Still faced with many economic problems, the Moores government might not have survived the next election were it not for divisions within the opposition Liberal party. Edward Roberts faced a leadership convention in October 1974 and, even though he had previously been Smallwood's protégé, the "premier emeritus" decided to re-enter the fray against him. With help from the federal wing of the party under Donald Jamieson, Roberts narrowly hung on to the job. Smallwood promptly created a new Liberal Reform Party which split the opposition vote in the September 1975 election. Moores continued in power with a reduced majority of 30 seats, compared with 16 for Roberts and four for Smallwood. The former premier later made peace with his Liberal colleagues and resigned from the legislature in 1977. He died in 1991.

Moores remained premier until 1979 and during that time economic conditions generally began to improve. For example, after the government decided in 1977 to close down the linerboard mill at Stephenville because it required an annual subsidy of $30 million, Abitibi-Price bought the mill and converted it to pulp and paper production. In January 1977, the federal government established a 200-mile off-shore economic zone in which Canadians had control of the fishing industry, a policy long demanded by Newfoundland. This act was accompanied by other federal fishing initiatives such as the introduction of new fish stock management techniques and the enforcement of more reasonable foreign fishing quotas. The 1979 test results of Mobil Oil's Hibernia well off the southeast coast of the island were the first strong indicators of commercial oil possibilities. On the other hand, the oil refinery at Come by Chance closed down, becoming the largest bankruptcy in Canadian history. Also, Newfoundlanders finally began to appreciate the magnitude of the power and revenue the province had lost at Churchill Falls. Quebec refused to allow Newfoundland to recall some of the Churchill Falls power for its own use or to raise the price. Thus, Newfoundland continued to be stalled in its efforts to develop the Lower Churchill project, although a new federal-provincial corporation had been created in 1978 for this purpose.

Frank Moores decided to return to the business world after seven years as premier and called a leadership convention for March 1979. The prize was won rather easily by Moores' young, abrasive and dynamic minister of Mines and Energy, Brian Peckford.[57] He called an election for June 1979. The Liberals hurriedly installed former External Affairs Minister Donald Jamieson as their provincial leader, but to no avail.

The 1980s[58]

During Brian Peckford's premiership, Newfoundland politics was concerned largely with three intergovernmental issues: fishing, hydroelectricity, and offshore oil. The province was virtually powerless to exploit its vast resources in these areas and used every political and judicial technique in the fight to gain some control over its destiny.[59]

In 1980, the province developed a detailed proposal for concurrent jurisdiction over fisheries, part of the general constitutional discussions of that period. The industry nearly collapsed in 1982, with processing plants fed by the offshore trawler fleet being the hardest hit. The federal government responded with the appointment of the Kirby Task Force which reported in February 1984. As a result, Fishery Products International was created from seven ailing firms operating in the province. It was a huge vertically integrated enterprise with trawlers, processing plants, and a work force of thousands of fishermen and plant workers. Ownership was primarily shared among the Canadian government (60 percent), the Newfoundland government (25 percent), and the Bank of Nova Scotia (12 percent). Later in the decade the federal and provincial governments divested themselves of shares in the company as part of the privatization theory popular at the time.

Peckford tackled the Churchill Falls issue more aggressively than his predecessors. That the contract price was 3.6 mills per kilowatt hour, when the power was now worth 30 to 40 mills as a result of the energy crisis and inflation, was an "unconscionable inequity," Peckford said, estimating that the province was losing several hundred million dollars annually on the deal.[60] Thus, in 1979 the province passed the Water Rights Reversion Act which would have allowed Newfoundland to rescind the water rights originally granted to the Churchill Falls Corporation in 1961. The legislation, a means of forcing Quebec to renegotiate the contract, was upheld by the Newfoundland Supreme Court in 1982 but overturned by the Supreme Court of Canada two years later. In 1984 both courts ruled against Newfoundland on the validity of the province's other efforts to obtain a larger share of the power generated at Churchill Falls.

While Peckford was seeking political redress, Quebec was intransigent—blithely signing a 13-year, $6-billion deal in 1982 to supply power to New York state—and would only consider renegotiation if it were tied to boundary adjustments and the transfer of territory to Quebec from Newfoundland.[61] Failing a resolution of the Upper Churchill Falls dispute, Peckford wanted the federal government to pass legislation permitting Newfoundland to "wheel" power from the Lower Churchill projects through Hydro-Quebec transmission lines to the United States, analogous to oil and gas pipelines in other provinces. Ottawa created a right-of-way across Quebec for the transmission of electrical power from Labrador to the United States, but Newfoundland later abandoned this idea.

Peckford's most protracted and successful battle was with the federal government over ownership of the off-shore oil and gas reserves.[62] Since both governments claimed jurisdiction, the increasing number of companies wanting to drill had to obtain permits from Ottawa and St. John's. The federal government suggested putting aside the ownership issue to concentrate on management and revenue-sharing, but demanded a majority voice on any joint-management authority. The province argued that the territory in question had been part of Newfoundland before 1949 and had been brought with it when Newfoundland joined Canada. The province thus sought to distinguish itself from other coastal provinces and place itself in a situation analogous to that of Alberta, where oil and gas were below ground rather than below water. Peckford was insistent that Newfoundland receive the lion's share of the benefits of development and that the pace of development allow traditional values to be maintained. The province had so much riding on this industry that it could not allow the federal government a majority on the joint management board.[63] Instead, it proposed equal federal and provincial representation, with an independent chairperson. The other main stumbling blocks appeared to be the share of revenue each level of government would receive, Newfoundland's demand that the deal be constitutionalized to guarantee its permanence, and the effect of oil revenues on the level of provincial equalization payments.

When an off-shore oil rig, the Ocean Ranger, capsized and sank in a storm in February 1982, claiming 84 lives, the two levels of government appointed separate royal commissions to investigate the tragedy. Reason eventually prevailed and the commissions combined, although the two governments later issued contradictory orders to oil rigs about putting back to port in the case of poor weather conditions and iceberg threats. Also in February 1982, in connection with an unrelated issue, the premier asked the Newfoundland Supreme Court to rule on the off-shore ownership question.

Then, to gain more clout in his negotiations with Ottawa, Peckford called a snap election for April 1982. After the establishment of an arts council and the adoption of a new provincial flag provided symbolic support for his "new nationalism," he hoped that a strong showing would force the federal government to respond to his proposals. But, although Peckford was returned with an overwhelming majority and defeated both the Liberal and NDP leaders, he found Ottawa no more agreeable than it had been prior to the election.

In May 1982, Prime Minister Pierre Trudeau sent the issue of the ownership of the Hibernia field to the Supreme Court of Canada while political negotiations continued. In February 1983, the Newfoundland Supreme Court rendered its decision in favour of federal jurisdiction over the entire off-shore. This was confirmed by the Supreme Court of Canada in March of 1984 in a 6-0 decision in favour of federal ownership of Hibernia. The court reasoned that the off-shore rights arose from international law and, even if Newfoundland had possession of them in 1949, it did not as a province. It was strictly a question of external sovereignty. Peckford then responded that the question should be seen in moral, not legal, terms and that a province as poor as Newfoundland should be able to control and benefit from the riches off its coast.

With the election of the federal Progressive Conservatives in September 1984, however, Peckford gained new hope. The Atlantic Accord, signed on February 11, 1985, established the seven-member Canada-Newfoundland Offshore Petroleum Board with three federal and three provincial appointees and an independent chairperson. In spite of the Supreme Court decision, the accord granted Newfoundland the right to collect revenues from under-sea resources in the same manner as under-land resources, and the right to make decisions about off-shore development except in cases concerning national security. Ottawa would contribute 75 percent of a five-year, $300-million Offshore Development Fund. The province expected to expand its industrial base, increase employment, and optimize spinoff activity in the local economy. The agreement also provided for an orderly phase-down of equalization payments as resource revenues increased.

Meanwhile, the provincial income tax, at 60 percent of the federal tax, was the highest in the country, as was the 12 percent sales tax. Peckford announced a tough austerity program in February 1984 which froze provincial public sector wages for a two-year period beyond the expiry of existing contracts. Other demoralizing news came when Harry Steele relocated his Eastern Provincial Airways from Gander to Halifax and subsequently sold it to Canadian Pacific. Newfoundland politics became even more interesting with the election of Leo Barry as the new leader of the provincial Liberal party, three years after he had resigned from the Peckford cabinet. From the fall of 1984 onward, added political heat was provided by labour and the NDP. In a September by-election, party leader Peter Fenwick became the first NDP member of the provincial legislature. Shortly afterwards, ex-Liberal Richard Cashin and his fishermen's union affiliated with the NDP, and two government labour bills raised the ire of all unions in the province. The first widened the definition of essential services, denying the right to strike to a larger group in the public service. The second retroactively amended the Labour Standards Act relating to severance pay, partly to cement the sale of the Corner Brook paper mill, which was rescued from closure at the last minute by Kruger Inc. of Montreal. This activity on the labour front led to the establishment of an anti-government Coalition of Equality.

On a more positive note for the government, the converted Abitibi-Price Stephenville paper mill reopened in 1981, as did the fluorspar mine at St. Lawrence and the asbestos mine at Baie Verte (albeit, in the latter case, with a reduced labour force and not for long). Along with a new 1984 General Development Agreement providing nearly $500 million in federal funds over 10 years for a variety of cost-shared projects, Newfoundland received $24 million from Ottawa for the fisheries. The province added a Grade 12 to a reorganized high school program, appointed a royal commission on employment in January 1985, and gave Petro-Canada control of the refinery in Come by Chance.

In the wake of the long-awaited Hibernia agreement, two opposition Liberal members crossed the floor and Peckford called an election for April. He emphasized that the new Tory connection in Ottawa could be expected to provide additional benefits to the province as indeed occurred during the campaign, with Newfoundland receiving $180 million in grants due to the active participation of John Crosbie. Lacking the foil of Pierre Trudeau, however, Peckford was uncharacteristically subdued and was dogged in the campaign by teachers and other public sector workers whom he had alienated with wage freezes and other legislation. Thus, in spite of the Atlantic Accord, the Conservatives were returned with a reduced majority. Barry's Liberals and Fenwick's New Democrats both registered significant increases in popular support.

Between 1985 and his resignation in 1989, Peckford experienced more failures than successes. On the positive side, the Come by Chance oil refinery was sold in 1986 to an American company that immediately set to work to return it to a refining capacity of 100,000 barrels per day. The somewhat mysterious company imports crude oil from North Sea sources and sells its refined product on the American market. And, while the federal government discontinued subsidizing rail freight in the province and the Canadian National subsidiary was closed, Ottawa gave Newfoundland $800 million in compensation, primarily to improve the highway system. A new megaproject in the province, enthusiastically supported by the Peckford government, was a high-tech greenhouse that used a special covering and a soil-less hydroponic technique to grow cucumbers. The innovation was the inspiration of a respectable Calgary businessman, Philip Sprung, although his first cucumber-growing facility in that city had failed. After a somewhat optimistic start, the greenhouse experienced a massive cucumber crop failure in 1988 and, because the provincial government had given the plant almost $20 million in cash and loan guarantees, the minister of Agriculture resigned. This infatuation with megaprojects continued even in the wake of the 1986 House Royal Commission on Employment and Unemployment (*Building on Our Strengths*) which recommended small-scale development instead. Because the revised Hibernia agreement of 1988 was not economically viable as an energy project, federal and provincial governments justified it as a regional development project that could create jobs.[64] In legal matters, the Supreme Court of Canada put an end to the province's hope of overturning the Churchill Falls contract with Quebec. The government's labour legislation precipitated much public service unrest, and the NDP leader, Peter Fenwick, was jailed for two months for defying a court injunction against picketing during what the legislation deemed an illegal strike. The Liberal caucus revolted against Leo Barry in 1987, and a leadership convention replaced him with another St. John's lawyer, Clyde Wells.

When Peckford decided to resign as premier in 1989 he was succeeded by his Fisheries Minister Thomas Rideout. Peter Fenwick took this opportunity to resign as provincial NDP leader and was replaced by Cle Newhook. Since the previous election had been in 1985, Rideout decided to call another for April 20 before bringing the legislature back into session. His election campaign began to flounder, however, as the new Liberal leader, Clyde Wells, suddenly made an impact.

Rideout's task was not helped by his Tory colleagues in Ottawa. During the campaign, the federal Progressive Conservative government cut back unemployment insurance again and came to an agreement with France to send their off-shore boundary dispute to binding arbitration by a five-member international tribunal. Unfortunately, in order to gain such agreement, Canada had to give France access to an increased quota of northern cod within Canadian waters.

The 1990s

Clyde Wells ended 17 years of provincial Tory rule (and Rideout's 47-day premiership) when the Liberals won 31 seats to the Progressive Conservatives' 21, although the popular vote was slightly in the Tories' favour. Wells himself was defeated but quickly gained a seat when an obliging backbencher resigned and the opposition parties chose not to contest the resulting by-election. Wells was 51 and had served in Smallwood's cabinet before resigning to resume his law career. He came across as an attractive, intelligent, and articulate leader. He also appeared stubborn and self-righteous.[65] Among his early actions was the elimination of eight government departments along with their deputy ministers and the withdrawal of government support for the greenhouse project. That project went into receivership, was sold to private interests for $1, and later closed. Wells also inherited the judicial inquiry into sexual abuse by the Christian Brothers, a lay order, at the Mount Cashel orphanage. This inquiry shed light on many aspects of Newfoundland society, especially the prominence of the Roman Catholic Church with regard to the police and the government. The inquiry revealed that, during the period in question, police failed to investigate allegations thoroughly, and government ministers were not informed.

Wells' first years in office were also dominated by the Meech Lake Accord, the fishing crisis, and Hibernia. He became one of the most effective foes of the Meech Lake Accord, which was designed to bring Quebec back into the Canadian constitutional fold. First he had the Newfoundland legislature rescind its previous approval and, ultimately, he refused to allow the legislature to vote on an amended resolution. In particular, he objected to the possibility that Quebec might obtain additional powers through judicial interpretation of the distinct society clause, as well as to weakening the federal government's spending power.

The groundfish crisis of the 1990s has been detailed in Inset 2.1. The problem of supply was complicated by the dispute which erupted between Canada and France over that country's islands of St. Pierre and Miquelon. Both countries declared 200-mile economic zones that overlapped in some of the best fishing grounds south of Newfoundland. In June 1992, an international tribunal gave France a 24-nautical mile corridor around the islands and a narrow 10 1/2-mile corridor 200 miles south. It was a compromise for both countries. Three years later, Canada's "turbot war" with Spain resulted in a compromise that was generally in Canada's favour.

In 1992, the Wells government published a strategic economic plan calling for better education and training, a more favourable investment climate for business, economic diversification, and an emphasis on tourism, energy, and manufacturing. But the government soon admitted that the deteriorating economic situation in the province would impede the complete implementation of the plan. It hoped that a new economic development agency, Enterprise Newfoundland and Labrador, would spur economic development, and that the new Economic Recovery Commmission headed by Dr. Douglas House would come up with new ideas. The 1992 Royal Commission on Education recommended far-reaching changes to the province's education system including a longer school year, more emphasis on basics, and a devolution of authority from churches to parents.

Not surprisingly, the Wells government budgets became increasingly severe. In 1991, for example, some 2,600 public servants lost their jobs, including large numbers of teachers and nurses, as the government closed 360 hospital beds. It also imposed a one-year freeze on the wages of those who remained. In 1992, Wells cancelled public sector compensation contracts, and imposed a further one-year freeze on salaries. But circumstances required a mini-budget at the end of the year which revealed an obsession with the province's credit rating and credit rating agencies. Departments were directed to freeze or cut expenditures, and the possibility of privatizing certain Crown corporations was raised. The government repeatedly raised personal income and other taxes but cut corporate income and business taxes. The 1993 budget, with its reduction of $70 million in the public sector compensation package, had public servants, especially teachers, up in arms. Wells used their protests as a pretence to call the May 1993 election. By this time, the Conservatives had chosen Len Simms as their new leader. The NDP named Jack Harris, who had entered the legislature in a 1990 by-election. A new elections act regulated party finances for the first time. Because over half of the province's public sector workers had voted in favour of strike action, Wells asked voters whether they wanted the government or the public servants and teachers to run the province. Despite the economic hardships of the last four years and promises of more restraint to come, the electorate responded to Wells' call, with the Liberals collecting 35 seats, the Progressive Conservatives, 16, and the NDP, one.

After the election, the teachers and nurses agreed to cuts to pension plan contributions in return for job protection. But the province's finances did not improve. The 1994 budget required another $50-million cut in total public sector compensation costs, along with a $30-million cut in program spending and a $20-million increase in additional taxes. The government changed student grants to loans and closed 50 acute care hospital beds. Such retrenchment meant the loss of 800 teaching jobs over the following few years, led to another confrontation with provincial teachers, and culminated in a month-long strike which ended just in time to salvage the school year. Other public servants accepted their sacrifice of

millions of dollars in remuneration more willingly. At the same time, the government continued to decrease corporate taxes and remove regulations that bothered business. "Promote business investment" became the government's
dominant theme and the budget provided a 10-year tax holiday and minimal regulation for new and expanding businesses that met certain criteria. On the other
hand, unlike so many other provinces, Newfoundland rejected government casinos as a source of revenue. Table 2.12 illustrates the annual deficit situation of
the province between 1990–91 and 1994–95. With more spending cuts and an
increase in revenues, the government hoped to balance the 1995–96 budget.

TABLE 2.12   **Government of Newfoundland Finances, 1990/91–1994/95
($ millions)**

	1990/91	1991/92	1992/93	1993/94	1994/95
Total revenues	$3,182.9	$3,289.9	$3,417.1	$3,355.6	$3,481.6
Debt charges	551.0	592.3	558.9	537.2	561.6
Total expenditures	3,413.1	3,563.6	3,643.8	3,539.7	3,632.0
Deficit	230.2	273.7	226.7	184.1	150.4

Source: Reproduced by authority of the Minister of Industry, 1995; Statistics Canada, *Public Sector
Finance, 1994-95*, Financial Management System, cat. no. 68-212 (March 1995). Adapted by author.

Another seemingly intractible problem, not directly related to funding, is
that of the Innu residents of Davis Inlet. Having been moved to that isolated
island off the Labrador coast against their will in 1967, and having suffered
through high rates of suicide, assault, and substance abuse, they were relunctant
to trust the federal and provincial governments which attempted to move them
again. Seventeen troubled youth were sent to an Alberta treatment centre for six
months of intensive therapy, which seemed to have little effect. Also, to protest
against the flooding of their land for the Churchill Falls development in the
1970s, the Innu removed their electricity meters in 1992. Moreover, finding the
government's definition of justice did not correspond with their own, they ran
the local judge out of town in December 1993 and blocked the airstrip for nearly
a year so that he and his RCMP associates could not return.

CONCLUSION

For 40 years the Liberals and Progressive Conservatives governed Newfoundland
primarily by being friends or foes of the party in power in Ottawa. Premier Clyde
Wells now continues a third phase of this pattern. In the 1990s, the Liberal and
Conservative parties appeared to become more evenly balanced and the NDP has

the potential to transform the province into a two-and-one-half party system. Besides the overriding problem of unemployment, the government must await the answers to three questions. First, what effect will the Hibernia project have on the province's economy? Second, will the fishing industry ever become profitable? Third, will there ever be a resolution of the Churchill Falls hydroelectric dispute between Newfoundland and Quebec? The province also hoped that the Voisey Bay mineral discovery would somewhat offset the significance of those questions.

TABLE 2.13   Newfoundland Provincial Election Results Since 1949

Year	Liberal		Progressive Conservative		CCF/NDP		Other	
	Seats	Popular Vote	Seats	Popular Vote	Seats	Popular Vote	Seats	Popular Vote
1949	22	70%	5	28%			1	2%
1951	24	69%	4	30%				
1956	32	67%	4	32%				
1959	31	58%	3	25%	–	7%	2	10%*
1962	34	59%	7	36%	–	4%	1	1%*
1966	39	60%	3	33%	–	2%		
1971	20	44%	21	51%	–	2%	1	3%**
1972	9	38%	33	60%	–	0%		
1975	16	37%	30	45%	–	4%	5	13%***
1979	19	41%	33	50%	–	8%		
1982	8	35%	44	61%	–	4%		
1985	15	37%	36	49%	1	14%		
1989	31	47%	21	48%	–	4%		
1993	35	49%	16	42%	1	7%		

* United Newfoundland Party
** New Labrador Party
*** Liberal Reform Party

TABLE 2.14   Premiers of Newfoundland Since 1949

Premier	Party	Year Elected
Joey Smallwood	Liberal	1949
Frank Moores	Progressive Conservative	1972
Brian Peckford	Progressive Conservative	1979
Tom Rideout	Progressive Conservative	1989
Clyde Wells	Liberal	1989

ENDNOTES

1. Gary McManus and Clifford Wood, *Atlas of Newfoundland and Labrador* (St. John's: Memorial University, 1991).

2. Ministry of Supply and Services Canada, *Charting a New Course: Towards the Fishery of the Future* [Cashin Report] (Ottawa: Fisheries and Oceans, 1993); Fisheries Resource Conservation Council, *1991 Conservation Requirements for Atlantic Groundfish* (Ottawa: Fisheries and Oceans, 1993); Pol Chantraine, *The Last Cod-fish: Life and Death of the Newfoundland Way of Life* (Montreal: Davies, 1993).

3. Government of Newfoundland, *Royal Commission on Employment and Unemployment* (St. John's: Queen's Printer 1986).

4. Peter Newman, *The Canadian Establishment* (Toronto: Seal Books, Rev. ed., 1979), pp. 248-252. Newman also mentions the Ayres, Hickmans, Outerbridges, Bells, Monroes, and Lakes. Richard Gwyn, *Smallwood, the Unlikely Revolutionary* (Toronto: McClelland and Stewart, Rev. ed., 1972), p. 101, adds other old St. John's merchant families: Baird, Bowring, Cashin, Goodridge, Harvey, Joy, MacPherson, and Winter. See also Michael Harris, *Rare Ambition: the Crosbies of Newfoundland* (Toronto: Viking, 1992).

5. J.D. House, "The Mouse That Roars: New Directions in Canadian Political Economy —the Case of Newfoundland," in R.J. Brym, ed., *Regionalism in Canada* (Toronto: Irwin, 1986); Valerie Summers, "Newfoundland: Resource Politics and Regime Change in the Federal Era, 1949-1991," in Keith Brownsey and Michael Howlett, eds., *The Provincial State* (Mississauga: Copp Clark Pitman, 1992).

6. Government of Newfoundland. *Royal Commission on Education* (St. John's: Queen's Printer 1992).

7. Gwyn, *Smallwood*, p. 107.

8. Among the sources on this subject are S.J.R. Noel, *Politics in Newfoundland* (Toronto: University of Toronto Press, 1971); David Bellamy, "The Atlantic Provinces," in David Bellamy et al., *The Provincial Political Systems* (Toronto: Methuen, 1976); Gwyn, *Smallwood*; and James Overton, "A Newfoundland Culture?" Canadian Political Science Association (May 1985). See also Barbara Fairbairn, "Peckford, Particularism and Natural Resources: the New Radicalism of the Government of Newfoundland," *Occasional Papers*, Institute of Canadian Studies (Ottawa: Carleton University, 1982); and F.L. Jackson, *Newfoundland in Canada* (St. John's: Cuff, 1984).

9. Gwyn, *Smallwood*, p. 62. Some of the myths of hardiness are discussed in Peter Neary, "Democracy in Newfoundland: A Comment," in *Journal of Canadian Studies* (February 1969), p. 43.

10. Noel, *Politics in Newfoundland*, p. 275.

11. *Ibid.*, p. 22. In "Democracy in Newfoundland," Neary adds that class consciousness was retarded by such nationalistic sentiment as wartime sacrifice.

12. In particular, see Neary, "Democracy in Newfoundland." He attributes this weakness in part to the dominant and authoritarian churches and the absence of local government as a democratic training ground.

13. Jeffrey Simpson, *Spoils of Power* (Toronto: Collins, 1988).

14. *Ibid.*, pp. 236-7. Smallwood accepted "all the gifts that contractors and suppliers

offered" in building his own home, but on the understanding that he would donate it to the province after his death to be used as a premier's residence, p. 231. Neary, "Democracy in Newfoundland," p. 41, says that because the churches were so involved with the state, especially in education, they turned a blind eye to patronage and corruption.

15. Richard Apostle and Paul Pross, "Marginality and Political Culture: A New Approach to Political Culture in Atlantic Canada," Canadian Political Science Association (May 1981).

16. G.A. Rawlyk and Tom Wien, "The Newfoundland Elite," in G.A. Rawlyk, ed., *The Atlantic Provinces and the Problems of Confederation* (St. John's: Breakwater, 1979), p. 372.

17. Noel, *Politics in Newfoundland,* p. 263; Raymond Blake, *Canadians at Last: Canada Integrates Newfoundland as a Province* (Toronto: University of Toronto Press, 1994).

18. See the studies by David J. Elkins and Richard Simeon in Elkins and Simeon, eds., *Small Worlds: Provinces and Parties in Canadian Political Life* (Toronto: Methuen, 1980); and Marsha Chandler and William Chandler, *Public Policy and Provincial Politics* (Toronto: McGraw-Hill Ryerson, 1979), pp. 77-83.

19. The turnout rate for 1993 is difficult to determine because they did not do a proper enumeration. This may have made the average unreliable.

20. Joseph Wearing, *The L-Shaped Party: The Liberal Party of Canada, 1958-1980* (Toronto: McGraw-Hill Ryerson), p. 87.

21. Noel, *Politics in Newfoundland,* p. 284; Gwyn, *Smallwood,* p. 289.

22. Jennifer Smith, "Ruling Small Worlds: Political Leadership in Atlantic Canada," in Leslie Pal and David Taras, eds., *Prime Ministers and Premiers* (Scarborough: Prentice Hall Canada, 1988).

23. Ralph Matthews, "The Smallwood Legacy: The Development of Underdevelopment in Newfoundland 1949-1972," *Journal of Canadian Studies* (Winter 1978-79), p. 28.

24. Gwyn, *Smallwood,* pp. 233-5. The premier also attended all sittings of the House and dominated debate: McCorquodale, "Newfoundland," in Martin Robin, ed., *Canadian Provincial Politics* (Scarborough: Prentice Hall Canada, 1989), p. 147. Thus, new Liberal leader Ed Roberts' dilemma in the 1972 campaign was whether to stick with Smallwood to attract his traditional supporters or distance himself so as not to offend Smallwood's detractors.

25. Fairbairn, "Peckford, Particularism and Natural Resources."

26. Mark Graesser, "Leadership Crises in an Opposition Party: The Liberal Party of Newfoundland," in Kenneth Carty et al., eds., *Leaders and Parties in Canadian Politics: Experiences of the Provinces* (Toronto: Harcourt Brace Jovanovich, 1992).

27. Ibid.; Lawrence F. Felt; "Fish and Oil: Federal and Provincial Responses to Resource Development in Newfoundland," Canadian Political Science Association (May 1981); J.D. House, "Premier Peckford, Petroleum Policy, and Popular Politics in Newfoundland and Labrador," *Journal of Canadian Studies* (Summer 1982).

28. G.O. Rothney, "The Denominational Basis of Representation in the Newfoundland Assembly, 1919-1962," *Canadian Journal of Economics and Political Science* (November

1962). Rothney makes the point that this practice tended to make people conscious of religious differences which had no political significance. By placing restrictions on the choice of candidates, it reduced the quality of the Assembly and the government, p. 570.

29. Parzival Copes, "The Fishermen's Vote in Newfoundland," in *Canadian Journal of Political Science* (December 1970), p. 590. Copes adds that, as long as Smallwood could count on the electoral support of fishermen, the premier could afford to risk the antagonism of labour and other interests, p. 598.

30. Neary, "Democracy in Newfoundland," p. 44.

31. Noel, *Politics in Newfoundland*, p. 276.

32. These were classic cases of "reverse" pressure groups, set up by government to be controlled. In this case, the same man served for a time as president of one and secretary of the other. Copes, "The Fisherman's Vote in Newfoundland," pp. 586-7.

33. *Canadian Annual Review of Politics and Public Affairs*, (Toronto: University of Toronto Press, 1971), p. 221; (1973), p. 208.

34. *Canadian Advertising Rates and Data*, August 1994.

35. This evolution since 1949 was as follows:
    1949-1956:   28
    1956-1962:   36
    1962-1975:   42
    1975-1979:   51
    1979-present: 52
    See Susan McCorquodale, "Newfoundland: Personality, Party, and Politics," in G. Levy and G. White, eds., *Provincial and Territorial Legislatures in Canada* (Toronto: University of Toronto Press, 1989).

36. Thorburn, *Planning and the Economy* (Toronto: Canadian Institute for Economic Policy, 1984), p. 151.

37. Susan McCorquodale, "Aspects of the Administrative State in Newfoundland," Canadian Political Science Association (1988).

38. R.I. McAllister, ed., *Newfoundland and Labrador, The First Fifteen Years of Confederation* (St. John's: Dicks & Co., 1965), p. 18.

39. Peter Boswell, "Recent Structural Changes in Newfoundland Local Government," Canadian Political Science Association (June 1984), p. 12. "There are many stories of government employees going into communities during this period to encourage the establishment of municipal government, only to be verbally and physically attacked by the citizens, and to have their vehicles damaged or burned."

40. Because people feared losing their homes if they were unable to pay their property taxes, the law was amended to the effect that a municipality could not sell a house for payment of back taxes as long as its owner lived in it.

41. The best general accounts of this period are Noel, *Politics in Newfoundland*, and F.W. Rowe, *A History of Newfoundland and Labrador* (Toronto: McGraw-Hill Ryerson, 1980).

42. H.B. Mayo, "Newfoundland and Confederation in the Eighteen-Sixties," in *Canadian Historical Review* (June 1948); and Terry Campbell and G.A. Rawlyk, "The Historical

Framework of Newfoundland and Confederation," in Rawlyk, ed., *The Atlantic Provinces and the Problems of Confederation.*

43. Noel, *Politics in Newfoundland*, ch. 7.

44. H.B. Mayo, "Newfoundland's Entry into the Dominion," *Canadian Journal of Economics and Political Science* (November 1949), p. 508; Noel, *Politics in Newfoundland*, ch. 15; Peter Neary, *Newfoundland in the North American World, 1929-1949* (Kingston: McGill-Queen's University Press, 1988).

45. Cardoulis, John, A *Friendly Invasion: the American Military in Newfoundland, 1940-1990* (St. John's: Breakwater, 1990).

46. Gwyn, *Smallwood*, pp. 76-78.

47. The best sources on this period include Gwyn, *Smallwood*; F.W. Rowe, *The Smallwood Era* (Toronto: McGraw-Hill Ryerson, 1985); Joseph R. Smallwood, *I Chose Canada* (Toronto: MacMillan, 1973); Harold Horwood, *Joey: The Life and Times of Joey Smallwood* (Toronto: Stoddart, 1989); annual accounts in the *Canadian Annual Review* from 1960 onward, articles by Neary and Matthews cited below, and Susan McCorquodale, "Newfoundland," in Martin Robin, ed., *Canadian Provincial Politics* (Scarborough: Prentice Hall Canada, 1978).

48. Peter Neary, "Party Politics in Newfoundland, 1949-71: a Survey and Analysis," in *Journal of Canadian Studies* (November 1971), p. 6.

49. One of Smallwood's most distinguished ministers, Dr. H.L. Pottle, resigned and wrote a critical book about the premier's operations called *Newfoundland: Dawn Without Light* (St. John's: Breakwater, 1979). See other early colleagues' views in books by Horwood and Rowe.

50. Smallwood's Newfoundland Brotherhood of Woods Workers did not last long, and by the end of the 1960s a bona fide union had made the gains struck for in 1959.

51. Gwyn, *Smallwood*, p. 186, calls this the most acrimonious dispute between the federal government and any province in the 1945-60 period. In 1961 Diefenbaker agreed to extend the period for five years after 1962, and in 1965 the Pearson government decided to pay it in perpetuity, *ibid.*, pp. 196-7.

52. Gwyn says that Pickersgill stretched the letter of every act and statute to make Newfoundland Ottawa's favourite province, *ibid.*, p. 282.

53. Philip Mathias, *Forced Growth* (Toronto: James Lewis and Samuel, 1971), ch. 3.

54. Gwyn, *Smallwood*, pp. 233-7.

55. Peter Neary, "Politics in Newfoundland: the End of the Smallwood Era," in *Journal of Canadian Studies* (February 1972), p. 11; Matthews, "The Smallwood Legacy."

56. The best source on this period is the annual account on Newfoundland and Labrador by L.H. Harris in the *Canadian Annual Review of Politics and Public Affairs.* (Toronto: University of Toronto Press).

57. *Ibid.*, 1979, p. 388. On the whole 1977-79 period see Robert Paine, *Ayatollahs and Turkey Trots: Political Rhetoric in the New Newfoundland* (St. John's: Breakwater, 1981).

58. The best sources on this period are the annual accounts in the *Canadian Annual Review of Politics and Public Affairs* and provincial publications dealing with the era's three main issues .

59. Premier Peckford expressed his frustration at this situation as follows: "In the past few years I've been criticized as the premier of Newfoundland of being too forceful, too single-minded, too passionate in my representation of the rights of Newfoundland as we perceive them to be. I admit that that may have often appeared to be the case. But...we have lived with deprivation for over 400 years and Newfoundlanders live every day knowing that the solution to our problems is very close at hand. So close and yet so far." Notes for an address to the Moncton Rotary Club, April 16, 1984, pp. 8-9. See also D.J. Savoie, "The Atlantic Region: the Politics of Dependency," in R.D. Olling and M.W. Westmacott, eds., *Perspectives on Canadian Federalism* (Scarborough: Prentice Hall Canada, 1988), p. 299; and Brian Peckford, *The Past in the Present* (St. John's: Cuff Publications, 1983).

60. Government of Newfoundland, *Discussion Paper on Major Bilateral Issues* (St. John's: Queen's Printer, May 1980), p. 18.

61. *Canadian Annual Review of Politics and Public Affairs,* (Toronto: University of Toronto Press, 1981), p. 451.

62. Sources on this issue include the following Government of Newfoundland documents: "A Framework for Agreement, Canada-Newfoundland Offshore Mineral Resources Negotiations" (St. John's: Queen's Printer November 1981); "A Proposal for Settlement, Canada-Newfoundland Offshore Negotiations" (St. John's, January 1982); and "Analysis of the Compromise Proposal of the Government of Newfoundland and Labrador in the 1981-82 Offshore Resource Negotiations" (St. John's, March 1982).

63. For example, "the creation of employment opportunities, reduction in the high level of unemployment, stimulation of technologically advanced exports, provision of revenues to improve the quality of social services and to invest in our renewable resources such as the forestry and the fishery," *Discussion Paper on Major Bilateral Issues*, pp. 23-4.

64. On the Newfoundland offshore oil industry, see J.D. House, *The Challenge of Oil: Newfoundland's Quest for Controlled Development* (St. John's: Memorial University Institute of Social and Economic Research, 1985); David Baugh, "A Province in Search of a Country: The Atlantic Accord and the Canada-Newfoundland Offshore Board," Canadian Political Science Association (Winter, 1988); and Brian O'Neill, "The Sinking of the Ocean Ranger, 1982: The Politics of a Resource Tragedy," in Gary Burrill and Ian McKay, eds., *People, Resources, and Power.* (Fredericton: Acadiensis Press, 1987).

65. Claire Hoy, *Clyde Wells: A Political Biography* (Toronto: Stoddart, 1992). He has also been called "a pompous autocrat."

READINGS

Blake, Raymond. *Canadians at Last: Canada Integrates Newfoundland as a Province.* Toronto: University of Toronto Press, 1994.

Burrill, Gary, and Ian McKay, eds. *People, Resources, and Power.* Fredericton: Acadiensis Press, 1987.

Canadian Annual Review of Politics and Public Affairs. Toronto: University of Toronto Press, annual.

Chantraine, Pol. *The Last Cod-fish: Life and Death of the Newfoundland Way of Life.* Montreal: Davies, 1993.

Government of Newfoundland. *The Economy.* St. John's: Cabinet Secretariat, annual.

Horwood, Harold. *Joey: The Life and Times of Joey Smallwood.* Toronto: Stoddart, 1989.

Hoy, Claire. *Clyde Wells: A Political Biography.* Toronto: Stoddart, 1992.

Summers, Valerie. "Newfoundland: Resource Politics and Regime Change in the Federal Era, 1949-1991." In Keith Brownsey and Michael Howlett, eds. *The Provincial State.* Mississauga: Copp Clark Pitman, 1992.

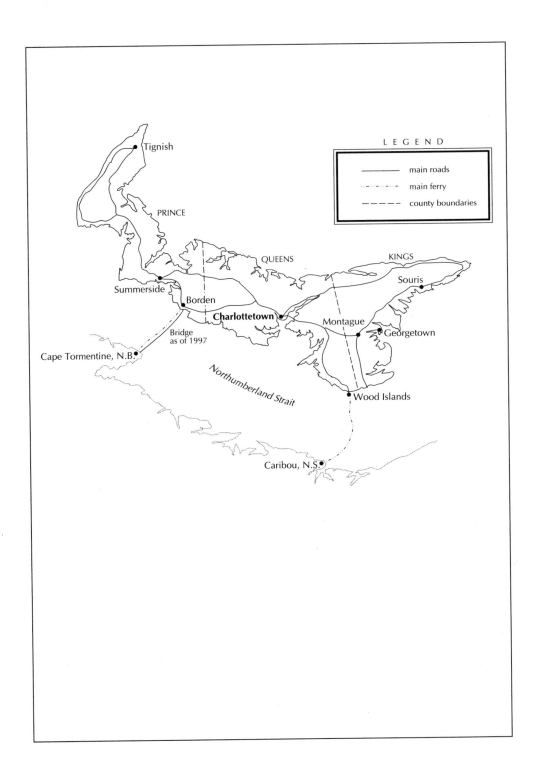

PRINCE EDWARD ISLAND

The most striking aspect of politics in Prince Edward Island is that the province has all the paraphernalia of a major political system—lieutenant-governor, premier, cabinet, legislature, several government departments, a Supreme Court, and a system of municipal government—for a population of only 130,000, roughly equivalent to that of a medium-sized Canadian city. This situation has tended to politicize almost all aspects of Island life, and the result, some suggest, is that important matters like economic development have been overshadowed by such petty political intricacies as appointments, contracts, and local public works.[1] The province has always been heavily dependent on federal government funding and this federal link also looms large in its political affairs. With the scheduled completion in 1997 of the "fixed link," a bridge joining P.E.I. to New Brunswick, the province is expected to shed some of its parochialism and to become much more oriented towards the outside world.

SETTING

Geography

Prince Edward Island is Canada's smallest province: 5,660 square kilometres in area and 224 kilometres long from tip to tip. Its small size has naturally given rise to concern about land use and ownership, an issue as heated today as at the time of Confederation. The Island has always had a problem with non-resident owners, now in particular with regard to ownership of shoreline. It is also worried about corporate ownership of farmland and about keeping such land in agricultural production. The 1990 *Royal Commission on the Land* revealed the province had almost 10,000 non-resident property owners who collectively possessed nearly 150,000 acres of land.[2]

The main divisions within the province are not physiographic but political. It is divided into three historic counties: Prince, Queens, and Kings, with 1991 census populations of 43,241, 67,196, and 19,328 respectively. The county divisions have featured prominently in the distribution of seats in the legislature and in cabinet representation. On the other hand, school boards cross county boundaries, and the new system of electing members to the legislature will probably result in a decline of county consciousness.

The province had 129,765 residents in 1991, which increased to 135,500 by January 1995. The central Queens County contains Charlottetown, the provincial capital. That city is the largest centre but, with a population of about 15,400 (57,472 in the metropolitan area), it is small for a provincial capital. Summerside, in Prince County, with a city population of 7,474 and with 15,237 in the labour market area, is the only other urban settlement of significant size. About 60 percent of the population is considered rural by Statistics Canada, making P.E.I. the most rural province in the country, although only eight percent of its inhabitants are actually employed in agriculture.

The Island has always had a natural preoccupation with the question of transportation, both between the Island and the mainland and within the province itself. A steamship ferry link to New Brunswick was a condition of P.E.I.'s entry into Confederation, and a Canadian National ferry connects Borden, P.E.I. to Cape Tormentine, N.B. The many daily crossings take about an hour and ice-breaking ferries maintain the service throughout the winter. A privately owned but subsidized summer ferry also operates between Wood Islands and Caribou, N.S. With the advent of air service, the ferry system was rendered slightly less vital. However, the prospect of a causeway to New Brunswick created much excitement in the 1960s, as did the concept of a "fixed link" in the 1980s and 1990s. Finally, in 1993, the federal and provincial governments signed a deal with Strait Crossing Development Inc. to construct a bridge between the Island and New Brunswick across the Northumberland Strait to replace the ferry service. Construction of the 13-kilometre structure began in 1994 with a scheduled completion date of 1997.

Within the province, a comprehensive network of roads and a railway (the latter also part of the Confederation settlement) have both been prominent political issues. As in Newfoundland, the railway was recently closed by Ottawa.

Economy

Prince Edward Island constitutes about 0.3 percent of the national gross domestic product, and farming, fishing, and tourism are the cornerstones of the Island's economy. This economy is rendered volatile in the first two cases by their heavy dependence on externally determined commodity prices, and all three are seasonal in nature.[3] P.E.I. has the second-highest reliance on primary sector employment and the lowest proportion of tertiary employment in the country.

Agriculture is the leading primary industry with potatoes the single most important crop. Indeed, despite P.E.I.'s small size, its famous red soil produces more potatoes than any other province. Much of the production is exported to other provinces, especially Ontario, and much to other countries, notably the United States. Unfortunately, incomes from this source vary widely from year to year because of disease, poor weather, variable demand, and erratic prices, a situation Island farmers share with western Canadian wheat farmers. The industry was the subject of a royal commission study in 1987 and, for several years afterwards, the United States accused the province of exporting seed potatoes containing the PVYn virus, a virus that threatens other crops but doesn't affect humans. With this issue resolved by 1994, prospects for the industry looked brighter in the second half of the decade.

Dairy farming, cattle, and hogs are also important, while grain, vegetables, fruit, poultry, and tobacco round out the agricultural sector. Farmers have traditionally belonged to the P.E.I. Federation of Agriculture, but the more militant National Farmers Union has also established an active branch on the Island. The number of farms on the Island has dropped dramatically and their size increased (2,361 farms in 1991 with an average size of 271 acres), and the growth of corporate farming has caused serious concern. The province has experienced a series of plebiscites among farmers on the issue of potato marketing, pitting owners of small- and medium-sized potato farms, usually members of the NFU, against larger farmers, represented by the Federation of Agriculture. Other institutional players in the industry include the Potato Marketing Board, the P.E.I. Potato Producers' Association, the Potato Dealers' Association, and the Processors' Council.[4] In addition to potatoes, provincial marketing boards operate in most of the other sectors of agriculture.

Fishing is the second most important primary industry. It is predominantly an inshore industry and, because lobster is the most significant catch, P.E.I. was not seriously affected by the bans on groundfish imposed by the federal government in the early 1990s. P.E.I. fishermen lack collective bargaining rights and are not affluent but their dependence on lucrative lobsters, which rank second to potatoes as the province's leading export, sustains the fishing industry. Oysters, mussels, and crab are also plentiful in adjacent waters, and natural stocks are increasingly supplemented with those produced through aquaculture.

Logging is just beginning to re-emerge as a significant industry in the form of some 50 sawmills, but mining is of little consequence.

The provision of electricity on the Island has become a serious problem in the past 20 years. Since the province had neither fossil fuels nor hydroelectric power, it relied on oil-generated electricity, the price of which escalated sharply after 1973. P.E.I. now imports almost all of its electricity via undersea cable from New Brunswick and continues to pay the highest rates in the country. It has left this utility in private hands, the Maritime Electric Company Ltd., and in the early 1990s the government proposed selling the company to New Brunswick Power Corp., the main source of its product. Instead, a Newfoundland company, Fortis Inc., took effective control of the company, subject to a good deal of government regulation aimed at reducing electricity costs in P.E.I.

The province's manufacturing industry is not well-developed and is mostly connected to the processing of fish and farm products—for example, the production of french fries. McCain's and the Irving-owned Cavendish Farms both operate plants in P.E.I. in addition to those in their native New Brunswick. The Atlantic Veterinary College and the Food Technology Centre are active in research and development in the food processing field. However, the Island's distance from markets and the high cost of electricity are impediments to further industrialization.

TABLE 3.1   Prince Edward Island 1991 Labour Force and Estimated 1995 Gross Domestic Product by Industry

Industry	1991 Labour Force		Est. 1995 GDP ($ millions)	
Agriculture	5,535	8.2%	150	8.1%
Fishing	3,800	5.6%	32	1.7%
Forestry	425	0.6%	—	—
Mining	205	0.3%	—	—
TOTAL PRIMARY	9,965	14.7%	182	9.8%
Manufacturing	7,040	10.4%	135	7.3%
Construction	4,445	6.6%	141	7.6%
TOTAL SECONDARY	11,485	17.0%	276	14.9%
Transportation, communications and utilities	4,565	6.8%	217	11.7%
Trade	10,030	14.9%	196	10.5%
Finance, insurance and real estate	2,010	3.0%	281	15.1%
Services	21,305	31.6%	502	27.0%
Government	8,105	12.0%	207	11.1%
TOTAL TERTIARY	46,015	68.3%	1,403	75.5%
TOTAL ALL INDUSTRIES	67,465		1,861	

Source: Reproduced by authority of the Minister of Industry, 1995, Statistics Canada, *1991 Census,* cat. nos. 93-326 and 95-309; and Conference Board of Canada, *Provincial Outlook, Economic Forecast* (Ottawa: Summer 1994), Vol. 9, No. 2. Adapted by author.

Service industries employ over 68 percent of the labour force and, within the tertiary sector, tourism is most significant to the provincial economy. Indeed, Prince Edward Island depends on tourism more than any other province. Tourist attractions include those based on the fictional character Anne of Green Gables, Cavendish and other beaches, golf courses, the Confederation Centre, and the Island's rustic charm. The heirs of Lucy Maud Montgomery, the creator of *Anne of Green Gables,* and the province recently agreed to transfer ownership of the

Anne trademarks to a new joint licensing authority. Fishing and tourism have been combined in the "lobster supper," now a P.E.I. tradition. Government employment and expenditures also play a disproportionate role in the P.E.I. economy. Besides over 10,000 provincial and municipal public servants, the 3,600 employees of the Government of Canada represent a relatively large federal presence in the province.

Class

By most standards, Prince Edward Island is Canada's second-poorest province. Its per capita income in 1992 was $17,915. According to the 1991 census, 17.5 percent of families had incomes under $20,000, while 12.2 percent received over $70,000, for a median family income of $37,486. In the early 1990s, the province's unemployment rate rose to the level of 17 to 18 percent. This high overall unemployment rate combined with the seasonal or part-time employment of a large proportion of the population to place a heavy reliance on unemployment insurance benefits as a source of income. The union movement on the Island is weak, the P.E.I. Federation of Labour having about 15,000 members in 1994. Three years earlier, 13,200 Islanders (about 33 percent of paid workers) were unionized. The largest private sector unions are the United Food and Commercial Workers and the Canadian Auto Workers, but more significant are the PEIUPSE (P.E.I. Union of Public Sector Employees), CUPE (Canadian Union of Public Employees), and the Public Service Alliance of Canada (PSAC) in the public sector. Provincial government workers were never very militant but their unions sprang to life in 1994 with protests, advertising campaigns, and withdrawals of voluntary services, as a result of government retrenchment and wage rollback programs.

It is simple for academics to apply a class-based political economy approach to Prince Edward Island, emphasizing economic inequalities, class divisions, and the dependence of potato farmers and fishermen on dealers who buy their products. Many of the province's farmers and fishermen feel as powerless in this relationship as Newfoundland's outport fishermen have in their dependence upon merchants. Small farm operators have never considered themselves in control of the potato marketing process, nor have many fishermen believed they were adequately compensated for their labour.[5]

On the other hand, some Island residents enjoy high incomes. In addition to some "old money" families in agriculture and other traditional industries, the province is starting to see wealth being created in new fields. Two examples include Regis Duffy of the Diagnostic Chemicals company and Allan Scales of Island Fertilizer, not to mention the corporate invasion of the McCain and Irving families from New Brunswick. Cavendish Farms in particular never neglects to seek P.E.I. subsidization of its new facilities.

Demography

Prince Edward Islanders are overwhelmingly of British (especially Scottish) descent, and English is the mother tongue for over 94 percent of the population. This means, among other things, that Island politics has experienced little in the way of ethnic cleavages. Over the past 30 years, however, a slight renaissance has occurred among the province's Acadians, who are of French ancestry. French is the mother tongue of less than five percent of the population and just over two percent use it at home. The province has two French-language schools with an independent French school board, and has made marginal efforts in other ways to serve the Acadian community. P.E.I. has both the smallest number of residents of aboriginal origin (1,880) and the smallest proportion (1.5 percent) in the country. Other ethnic groups are negligible, for nearly 80 percent of provincial residents were born on the Island and just over three percent were born outside Canada.

TABLE 3.2   Prince Edward Island Mother Tongue and Home Language, 1991

	Mother Tongue	Home Language
English	94.2%	97.3%
French	4.5%	2.3%
Other	1.2%	0.3%

Source: Reproduced by authority of the Minister of Industry, 1995, Statistics Canada, *1991 Census,* cat. no. 93-317. Adapted by author.

The population is almost equally divided between Protestants and Roman Catholics, a division with significant consequences for provincial affairs. Certain political issues have had a religious basis or connection, such as the question of establishing a Roman Catholic separate school system in 1876, the certification of Roman Catholic teachers in 1957, and the 1969 creation of the University of Prince Edward Island from the Catholic St. Dunstan's and the Protestant Prince of Wales College. Provincial politicians have generally tried to keep religion "out of politics," however, by ensuring the equitable distribution of government handouts and appointments in back-room "gentlemen's agreements."[6] Furthermore, party preferences have not usually coincided with religious affiliation. With a general decline in religiosity and increasing intermarriage, religion is expected to be a less important factor in Island politics in the future. Indeed, the abolition of dual-member ridings in which the two religious groups could be balanced may signal the end of religion's role in the province's affairs.

TABLE 3.3   Religion in Prince Edward Island, 1991

Protestant		62,000 (48.3%)
United Church	25,995 (20.3%)	
Presbyterian	10,990 (8.5%)	
Anglican	6,690 (5.2%)	
Baptist	5,315 (4.1%)	
Other Protestant	13,010 (10.2%)	
Roman Catholic		60,635 (47.3%)
Other and None		5,465 (4.3%)

Source: Reproduced by authority of the Minister of Industry, 1995, Statistics Canada, *1991 Census*, cat. no. 93-319. Adapted by author.

Competition among these economic, geographic, and social divisions—Catholic and Protestant, rich and poor, labour and management, rural and urban, Federation of Agriculture and NFU, and the three counties, as well as different industries—contributes to many of the Island's political issues. However, the authorities usually have little difficulty dealing with such issues except in terms of the general scarcity of public funds. The balance of interests between groups means that no division constitutes such an enormous schism that it commands overwhelming governmental attention.

Federal-Provincial Relations

Good relations between the province and the federal government have always been high on the Island's political agenda. The province depends on federal transfers more than any other except Newfoundland, about 41 percent in 1992. In addition to the $299 million transferred to the province and $4 million to municipalities, in 1992 Ottawa paid out $433 million to persons and $73 million to businesses on the Island.[7] Individual Islanders also rely heavily on federal payments such as unemployment insurance. Specific demands for federal assistance include improved transportation and communications with the mainland, a political issue since 1873, and the province's comprehensive development plan of the 1970s. Issues in the 1980s included financial assistance for the Atlantic Veterinary College, the transfer of the federal Department of Veterans Affairs to Charlottetown, and demands for federal subsidization of electricity rates. However, Ottawa's endorsement of a fixed link to New Brunswick did not save the seats of Tory MPs in the 1988 federal election. The announced closing of the Canadian Forces base in Summerside in 1989 also helped Joe Ghiz's Liberals win two provincial elections. Prior to the 1992 Canadian Forces Base Summerside crisis, the Island was spared the federal-provincial hostility that has characterized such relations in many other provinces and, apart from that issue, the Ghiz government had good relations with the Mulroney Conservatives. P.E.I. is simply too small to challenge Ottawa. It prefers to rely on pleading and persuasion, and usually makes sure it elects a government of the same party label as the one in office federally.[8] Parties have regularly campaigned on this precise theme, of being best able to co-operate with the federal government, and voters have consciously responded, "attempting to retain a partisan congruence between the two levels of government."[9] The 1986-93 experience of electing a provincial government and federal MPs in opposition to the party in power in Ottawa is therefore quite unusual.

In general, especially with declining federal contributions, P.E.I. looks less and less to Ottawa to be its saviour, and is therefore less obsessed with getting on side in a partisan sense. As far as the fixed link is concerned, that was largely a federal initiative which left Island opinion seriously divided.

POLITICAL CULTURE

Until the 1960s, the Island's political culture was dominated by the "myth of the garden."[10] This myth embodied the concept of a society of independent farmers, "protected from the world in an unspoiled pastoral setting." It incorporated such values as traditionalism, conservatism, and community, a parochialism which bordered on the xenophobic, and the sanctity of the family farm. Such an inward-looking orientation may explain why Prince Edward Islanders have the third highest rate of loyalty to their province (43 to 44 percent) and the third-lowest rate of loyalty to Canada (50 to 57 percent).

Over the last 35 years or so, the garden has been somewhat transformed and opinion has become divided between those still adhering to the garden mentality and those advocating modernization and industrialization. As recently as 1984, for example, a legislative committee on the quality of life exhibited "a noticeable tone of fundamental conservatism,"[11] but the 1986 rejection of the Litton plant because of its militaristic purposes may have been the last victory of the traditionalists. Those advocating change and development are gaining ground and, while many politicians remain tied to primary industries and reluctant to abandon the "Island way of life," young people are challenging traditional assumptions and demanding modern jobs. Education has improved, mobility has increased and, as the economy has diversified, agriculture has lost its predominance. Cavendish Farms' ultra-modern potato storage facility and the world-class Crowbush Cove golf complex are evidence of such a change, and the fixed link will clearly set the province in the direction of further modernization and development.

As in most other provinces, the primacy of political parties and politicians is being displaced by interest groups, bureaucrats, and the media. Political patronage is still alive and well, however, partly because the government is such a major factor in the economy. Appointments to government boards and the courts continue to be made on a partisan basis. But even in this aspect of the

P.E.I. political culture, bureaucrats are increasingly replacing politicians as the main dispensers of favours.[12]

In comparative studies of provincial political cultures, P.E.I. is usually placed in the same category as its Maritime neighbours, "underdeveloped." The paradox of high political involvement but low political trust and efficacy is perhaps more marked on the Island than anywhere else.[13] As seen in Table 3.4, residents generally have a voting turnout rate in both provincial and federal elections of over 80 percent, the highest in the country. This paradox is partly explained by the fact that Islanders are intensely partisan and view politics as a source of entertainment or personal benefit, but have low expectations of overall positive results.[14]

TABLE 3.4   P.E.I. Voter Turnout Rate in Recent Federal and Provincial Elections

Federal Elections		Provincial Elections	
1974	80%	1974	82%
1979	81%	1978	86%
1980	79%	1982	78%
1984	85%	1986	88%
1988	85%	1989	83%
1993	73%	1993	81%
Average	80.5%	Average	83.0%

Source: Reports of the federal and provincial chief electoral officers, calculations by author.

POLITICAL PARTIES

Party System

Throughout its entire post-Confederation history, Prince Edward Island has been characterized by a two-party system. The two major parties, the Liberals and the Conservatives, have divided the popular vote in almost equal proportions, have regularly alternated in office, and have never permitted any other parties, including the Progressives (farmers) or the CCF/NDP, to take root. Table 3.5 and Figure 3.1 indicate the continuation of this pattern over the 1970-1995 period, with two turnovers in 25 years. With the Liberals and Conservatives gaining an average of almost 97 percent of the total vote between them, other parties are hardly worth mentioning. However, with the Liberals averaging 52.3 percent of the vote and the Progressive Conservatives, 44.5 percent, an average difference in popular support of 11.5 percent, and with the Liberals holding office for over twice as long in the post-1970 period, it is a two-party system verging on one-party dominance.

TABLE 3.5   Party Support in P.E.I., 1970-1995

	Years in Office		Average Percentage of Vote	Percentage of Seats
Liberals	17	(68%)	52.3	68.0
Conservatives	8	(32%)	44.5	32.0
Combined	25	(100%)	96.8	100.0

Source: Reports of the chief electoral officer, calculations by author.

FIGURE 3.1   Percentage of Vote by Party in P.E.I. Elections, 1970-95

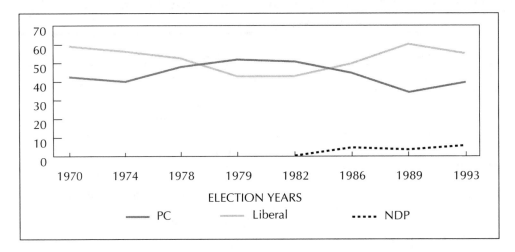

Party Organization

While Prince Edward Island continues to possess a classic traditional or preindustrial two-party system, it also has a more elaborate party organization than other provinces. Parties are organized right down to the poll level. But, now that parties are replacing delegate nomination meetings with all-member votes, the poll organizations have become mostly an election apparatus. In the small context of Island politics, especially in more traditional times, parties were usually able to establish the political preference of almost every voter. This was particularly vital prior to 1963 when the transportation of voters to the polls on election day was a major and rewarding undertaking, as many voters were eligible to vote in more than one location. Identifying and getting out the vote remains important, however, given the small margin of victory in many contests.

Federal-Provincial Party Links

The relationship between the federal and provincial wings of the P.E.I. Liberal and Conservative parties is generally close and congenial. The parties can hardly afford it to be otherwise, if for no other reason than federal issues are often prominent in provincial campaigns. Moreover, the province has usually had the foresight to elect MPs of the party which forms the federal government ("as P.E.I. goes, so goes the nation"). Because of the province's size, this foresight has not necessarily guaranteed representation in the federal cabinet.

Party Leadership

Island politics have rarely been dominated by a single leader for any length of time.[15] The two premiers with the longest service were Walter Jones, 10 years, and Alex Campbell, 12 years. Even when a particular party stayed in office for some time, it usually changed leaders regularly, as holders of the office used it as a stepping stone. If the leadership factor is not as important in P.E.I. as elsewhere, it may explain why the Island has had three of the oldest leaders of any province: Walter Jones retired at 75, Walter Shaw at 78, and Angus MacLean at 67. All three were viewed as dependable, grandfatherly figures, and all were well educated. Jones was probably the most colourful and domineering premier in the Island's history, with a background of an ex-Progressive, a professor of agriculture, and a highly successful farmer. He was full of ideas and took on a large part of the government operation himself. On the other hand, the premier who served between Shaw and MacLean, Alex Campbell, was a young, photogenic, urban lawyer. The son of another highly respected premier, Thane Campbell, he intensified the modernization efforts of his predecessor Shaw, winning an unprecedented four provincial elections. Joe Ghiz was also unusual in his Lebanese background and in his dynamic, eloquent style. The businesslike Catherine Callbeck was the first woman to be elected premier in any province.

The P.E.I. Conservatives were among the first provincial parties to depart from the delegate convention method of choosing a leader. Patricia Mella was elected leader in 1990 by all card-carrying Tories in the province. (Perhaps only in Prince Edward Island would it be possible for all party members across the province to attend the convention personally.) On the other hand, when Catherine Callbeck was selected as Liberal leader in 1993, the process was particularly undemocratic. Each party poll captain was authorized to decide how to choose five delegates—by appointment, election, or drawing names from a hat.

Party Ideology

All analyses have concluded that ideology has played and continues to play little part in Island politics,[16] so it is safe to say that the province has a non-polarized two-party system. For a time in the 1970s there may have been a somewhat different approach, with the Liberals promoting more government and the Conservatives less, but since the controversies surrounding the development plan have subsided, such a distinction is less clear.

ELECTIONS

Electoral System

P.E.I.'s system of dual-member constituencies began in 1893 and remained unique in the country. However, this distinctive feature is scheduled for removal in the provincial election expected in 1997. There were many peculiarities to this system.[17] For example, property owners could vote for both an assemblyman and a councillor, while those without property could only vote for the assemblyman. Property owners could also vote in every constituency in which they held property. Thus, in an extreme case, a husband and wife with strategically placed real estate could command 60 votes between them. This strange and somewhat undemocratic system was not changed until 1963, when the preferential treatment of property owners was discontinued and everyone was limited to two votes. One of the most important reasons for retaining the dual-member system for so long was to allow both parties to nominate one Protestant and one Roman Catholic candidate in most constituencies so that candidates for the assemblyman and councillor positions were distributed by religion. Given the balance in the religious distribution of the population, this was done in an effort to keep controversial religious issues out of the political spotlight.

TABLE 3.6   **Representational Disparities in 1993 Election**

Mean no. of voters per constituency	5,759	
Largest constituency (Fifth Queens)	12,681	(+120.2% of mean)
Smallest constituency (Fifth Kings)	1,995	(-65.4% of mean)
Average variation from mean	54.0%	
Constituencies within ±40% of the mean	25.0%	
Constituencies beyond ±60% of the mean	37.5%	
Average Constituency by county: Kings	2,789	
Queens	7,990	
Prince	6,054	

Source: Report of the chief electoral officer, calculated by author.

Prior to 1966, each of the three counties had an equal number of seats, after which Prince and Kings had 10 each and Queens 12. Since the size of the population (or electorate) of the three counties was considerably different, this system represented a stark departure from the principle of representation by population. It also indicated the rigidity of existing riding boundaries and how deeply the concept of county equality was ingrained in the Island's culture. Besides the general inequity of the electoral system, there was a serious over-representation of rural areas. But even the 1966 granting of two more seats to the more urbanized Queens county proved to be controversial.

Table 3.6 describes the representational disparities in the 1993 election and shows why the system had to be modernized, with a new 27-single-member arrangement adopted in 1994 for the following election. This change was the culmination of events which began with Donald MacKinnon's court challenge of the old system on the basis of its departure from the principle of representation by population. In 1993, the largest constituency was 120 percent above the provincial mean, while the smallest was 65 percent below the mean. The P.E.I. Supreme Court agreed with MacKinnon and suggested a maximum population variance of plus or minus 10 percent of the mean.[18] The government appointed an election boundaries commission whose 1994 report recommended a legislature of 30 seats in which county boundaries would be ignored in designing constituencies. Their population would have to be within plus or minus 15 percent of the provincial mean. The bill which was eventually passed was a compromise introduced by Liberal backbencher Ross Young and was the subject of a rare free vote. It provided for 27 single-member ridings, allowed plus or minus 25 percent variance of the mean, and revived county rivalries by giving Prince, Queens and Kings nine, 13 and five members respectively. The idea of establishing a special Acadian seat was considered but rejected. No thought was given to special aboriginal representation. Charlottetown authorities were unhappy with the increase in the variance because a closer adherence to the principle of representation by population would have given the capital city more seats. But, even with these imperfections, the 1994 legislation was a significant reform.

Several other aspects of the electoral system should be noted. The secret ballot was not introduced until 1915 and no voters' list existed until 1966. Election day treating was rampant, with the distribution of $5 bills or bottles of rum, shoes, clothing, lawn mowers, paved driveways, or even bathrooms, persisting longer than in most other provinces.[19] Largely a thing of the past, such practices were extensions of the acquisitive nature of Island politics which is still evident between elections. Frank MacKinnon emphasizes this intimate aspect of the province where "the paving of an extra mile of road, the giving of some benefit to a family, or the recognition of the services of a party worker ... can easily become important issues in a tiny constituency."[20]

A new election expenses act was passed in 1983 and proclaimed two years later. It imposed ceilings on both party and candidate spending, required disclosure of the names of those contributing over $250, and reimbursed some expenses of candidates who gained at least 15 percent of the vote. It also provided annual funding to parties having at least two members in the legislature.

During the 1993 campaign, many people became alarmed at the extent of third-party advertising. The government subsequently set up a legislative committee which recommended regulation in this area, as well as such amendments as including annual funding to any party fielding candidates in at least 60 percent of the seats and gaining at least five percent of the popular vote. These criteria would benefit the NDP, deliberately excluded from such benefits in the past.

Another casualty of modernization is the local public meeting, "characterized by a great deal of good-natured heckling, drinking, and fighting, [where] candidates of both parties did their best to outshout their opponents, and the audience itself."[21] Now individual parties have separate rallies, and various interest groups, such as women or farmers, sponsor meetings and invite all candidates to come and answer questions.

Voting Behaviour

It is difficult to analyze voting behaviour in P.E.I. in terms of such group preferences as ethnic, religious, or urban-rural divisions. Parties take such pains to balance their tickets between Protestants and Roman Catholics that religious affiliation is not a sound indicator of party preference. In addition, the homogeneous ethnic background of the population eliminates ethnicity as a factor which might affect voting behaviour. The province is so traditional and lacking in class consciousness that voters cannot be divided on that basis, and only slight regional party preferences, based on county of residence, can be established. Until recently, most Islanders identified strongly with one party or the other and supported it consistently in federal and provincial elections. This is now less true, especially in urban areas. With two ballots to cast until 1993, most residents voted consistently and the two successful candidates in each riding usually belonged to the same party. Given the small margins of victory, however, splits did occasionally occur, including three in 1986, two in 1989, and one in 1993.

PRESSURE GROUPS AND THE MEDIA

Pressure Groups

Prince Edward Island was once so heavily dependent on agriculture that it was said that the provincial Federation of Agriculture could get anything it wanted from the government. This is no longer the case, especially with farmers split between that organization and the National Farmers Union, to say nothing of the P.E.I. Potato Producers Association and the Potato Dealers Association. With a somewhat diversified economy, there is now a wide array of organized interests seeking to influence the government, as revealed in Table 3.7. These include the Tourism Industry Association, the P.E.I. Fishermen's Association, the P.E.I. Federation of Labour, and the churches. In recent years, several ad hoc public interest groups have become very active. These include the Friends of the Island, who opposed the fixed link and took the federal government to court over the issue, and the Island Nature Trust, a conservation group which tries to protect natural areas and which has had some success over developers. The women's movement has also become important, and the Social Action Commission has been prominent on social issues.

TABLE 3.7   Leading P.E.I. Pressure Groups

Peak Business	Canadian Manufacturers' Association (P.E.I. branch)
Industrial	Construction Association of P.E.I.
	P.E.I. Roadbuilders Association
	P.E.I. Shellfish Association
	P.E.I. Truckers Association
	Tourism Industry Association of P.E.I.
	P.E.I. Potato Dealers Association
	P.E.I. Potato Producers Association
	P.E.I. Fishermen's Association
Labour	P.E.I. Federation of Labour
Agriculture	P.E.I. Federation of Agriculture
	National Farmers Union
Professional	P.E.I. Nurses Union
	P.E.I. Teachers Federation
Ethnic	Native Council of P.E.I.
Institutional	Federation of P.E.I. Municipalities
Environmental	Island Nature Trust
Public Interest	Social Action Commission
	Friends of the Island

The Media

For many years an exciting rivalry existed between the two Charlottetown daily newspapers, with the *Patriot* supporting the Liberals and the *Guardian,* the Conservatives. Modernization in the form of Thomson Newspapers Ltd. brought an end to this. The amalgamated operation *Guardian and Patriot* produces morning and evening clones with a collective circulation of nearly 26,000.[22] Newspaper baron Conrad Black owns the other daily newspaper in the province, the *Summerside Journal Pioneer,* with a circulation of about 10,700. Among the weekly papers is *La Voix Acadienne.* In addition to several local radio stations and reception of offshore television stations, the Canadian Broadcasting Corporation has a radio and a television station in Charlottetown.

GOVERNMENT INSTITUTIONS

As mentioned earlier, Prince Edward Island has the usual complement of provincial governmental institutions,[23] even if they are of questionable necessity given the small population and territory they serve. Islanders have been wise enough, however, to operate these institutions with less formality than that found in most other provinces. Cabinet solidarity, for example, has not always been taken seriously, some officials serve the cabinet and legislature simultaneously and, for a time, the cabinet also served as a divorce court.[24]

Executive

The position of lieutenant-governor is probably more significant in P.E.I. than elsewhere, for this appointee is expected to be the focus of social life in the province and may be called upon to officiate at any event, at any place, at any time.

In 1993 Premier Catherine Callbeck reduced the size of the cabinet to 10 from 11 members. About one-third of the members of the Assembly still sit in the cabinet and a majority of members on the government side may be ministers. The premier attempts to balance regional, religious, urban, and rural interests when selecting the cabinet and sometimes includes an Acadian. The premier often assumes one or more departmental portfolios and ministers may be in charge of more than one department or combined departments. (On occasion, difficulties have arisen when the small government caucus contained no lawyer to be attorney-general.) Within the small confines of the Island, ministers personally exercise more detailed supervision of their ministries than is possible in larger provinces.

Cabinet procedures were streamlined in the early 1970s, mainly as a result of the Comprehensive Development Plan, discussed in detail below. Because the cabinet is so small the need for cabinet committees is not great, but the province has a management board chaired by the provincial treasurer, and a community consultative committee, the latter also containing government MLAs. There is a premier's office of about 10 officials, and an executive council office (including policy and intergovernmental affairs units) of between 15 and 20.

Legislature[25]

The P.E.I. legislature is the country's smallest (even the municipal councils of Montreal and Metropolitan Toronto are larger). The legislature elected in 1993 consisted of representatives of 16 two-member constituencies for a total of 32 members. The next election transforms the legislature into 27 single-member constituencies.

P.E.I. entered Confederation in 1873 with a two-chamber legislature consisting of a Legislative Council as well as a Legislative Assembly. However, unlike other bicameral provinces, P.E.I. provided for popular election of members to both bodies. The franchise for the council was more restrictive than for the assembly. While the province soon recognized it was over-governed, the council twice saved itself from extinction by vetoing a bill designed with that objective. A disagreement between the two houses sparked the final abolition of the upper house in 1893. The two chambers were technically merged into one, with each constituency electing two members, one called the councillor, the other, the assemblyman.

Other unusual features of the P.E.I. legislature are that, as in Newfoundland, the government members sit to the left of the Speaker, the opposition to the right, and the lack of a Hansard, a record of legislative debates. In 1983, however, the province began to transcribe and print a record of its Question Period. If television stations wish to tape or broadcast legislative proceedings, they must bring their own equipment into the chamber.

The legislature appoints 10 or so standing committees which generally correspond to government departments. A cabinet minister usually sits on each committee except public accounts, the only committee chaired by an Opposition member. Bills and estimates are both examined in the committee of the whole. Members are expected to "think locally" and bring results back to their ridings. They are constantly pressed to find enough work to qualify individual constituents for unemployment insurance.

Not surprisingly, the financial allowance for private members ($32,000) is lower than in other provinces. MLAs have no support services except a telephone calling card and a $9,700 tax-free expense allowance, cut to $9,000 in 1994. An independent commission makes binding recommendations on members' pay. At the same time, members tend not to regard their legislative work as a full-time job because the legislature meets only about 25 days per year.

The ratio of ministers to private members is so high that there is even less opportunity for independent action and effective criticism than in other provinces. The P.E.I. legislature is thus not perceived by its members or observers as the arena where political issues are debated and resolved. For example, the fixed link was never debated there at all. Instead, and especially when the government has an overwhelming majority, all real debate occurs in the cabinet and government caucus, and the legislature merely serves as a rubber stamp. Premier Callbeck's backbenchers have complained that government decisions were not even *announced* in the Liberal caucus. Recognizing that it operated under the dominance of the cabinet, the legislature set up a committee in 1994 to recommend changes which would transform it into a more powerful institution.

Bureaucracy

Prince Edward Island employs about 3,200 people in government departments and agencies, another 300 in government business enterprises, and nearly 4,000 in the wider public sector. It was one of the last provinces to move away from the patronage system in the appointment of public servants and did not establish a civil service commission until 1963. Its provincial public service was notoriously weak until recently, although significant improvements began in the early 1970s, largely inspired by the development plan. The province has a bureaucracy based on merit and party patronage is now mostly confined to work on highway construction and maintenance and casual government employment. Despite Liberal Joe Ghiz's promises to the contrary, however, several Progressive Conservative supporters were dismissed after the 1986 Liberal election victory. About 50 such cases were taken to the Human Rights Commission or to the courts.

In 1993, Premier Callbeck began her term in office by streamlining government operations, downsizing the number of government departments to eight. The departmental structure in 1994 is illustrated in Table 3.8.

TABLE 3.8   P.E.I. Government Departments, 1994

Agriculture, Fisheries and Forestry
Economic Development and Tourism
Education and Human Resources
Environmental Resources
Health and Social Services
Provincial Affairs and Attorney General
Provincial Treasury
Transportation and Public Works

TABLE 3.9   Leading P.E.I. Agencies, Boards, Commissions and Crown Corporations

Crown Corporations	Enterprise P.E.I.
	P.E.I. Grain Elevators Corporation
	P.E.I. Housing Corporation
	P.E.I. Liquor Control Commission
Agencies, Boards, and Commissions	P.E.I. Energy Corporation
	P.E.I. Lotteries Commission
	P.E.I. Lending Agency
	P.E.I. Human Rights Commission
	Workers' Compensation Board
	P.E.I. Agricultural Development Corporation
	P.E.I. Advisory Council on the Status of Women
	Regulatory and Appeals Commission
	Hospital and Health Services Commission

In addition to the eight departments, the province has a host of several semi-independent agencies, boards, commissions and Crown corporations, some of which are listed in Table 3.9. Cabinet appointments to such boards are often made on a patronage basis. P.E.I. is the only province without an ombudsman, apparently a reflection of the belief that any complaints citizens may have with public servants can be settled face to face.

Judiciary

Since its reform in 1975, the judicial system consists of three provincial courts, one for each county, and the Supreme Court. Retiring premiers and attorneys general are regularly appointed to these judicial positions. Indeed, when it was smaller, the Supreme Court was at times composed entirely of ex-premiers.[26] A more recent reform divided the Supreme Court into trial and appeal divisions, containing three and five judges respectively. In 1994, judges were unhappy that the principle of judicial independence did not insulate them from the 7.5 percent rollback of public servant salaries. They went to count to challenge their inclusion.

Municipal Government

Municipal government in Prince Edward Island is rudimentary, given that almost everything can be handled provincially. P.E.I. has one of the most centralized provincial-municipal relationships in the country. Charlottetown has recently grown through amalgamations and, in the same way, Summerside has become the province's second city. These cities and the province's seven towns each have a mayor and council, but these officials have a narrow range of responsibilities. There is virtually no municipal organization in the villages or rural areas, and the two recently reformed school boards (two English and one French) have limited power.

POLITICAL EVOLUTION

1873-1969

From the mid-1860s to the mid-1870s, Prince Edward Island's history centred on the question of Confederation. Although it hosted the Charlottetown Conference in 1864, P.E.I. at first rejected the idea of joining Canada because it did not see any advantages in the scheme. The immediate pre-Confederation period, in fact, is often called the Island's "Golden Age"—its most prosperous period. By 1873, however, P.E.I. was persuaded to reconsider because the federal government was agreeable to three basic commitments: to assume the provincial railway debt and complete the project; to guarantee a steamship ferry link to the mainland; and to help the province buy out its absentee landlords with a loan of $800,000. Given that the railway had virtually bankrupted the colony, and the absentee landlord issue had plagued it for nearly a century, Confederation was a temptation that could hardly be resisted.[27] The period until 1960 or so was one of limited government, when little was expected of provincial authorities and much of their time was devoted to "appointments, contracts and local public works."[28] Such political activity is often called the "politics of acquisition."[29]

The first main issue in the post-Confederation period was the separate school question. A temporary coalition of Liberal and Conservative Protestants formed the government and passed legislation which ostensibly removed religious teaching from the single public school system. However, informal arrangements developed which largely satisfied both groups, including Catholics attending one public school and Protestants another, or the alternation of teachers along religious lines.[30] After 1879 the two parties were well established and a fairly regular rotation of Liberal and Conservative governments occurred. Indeed, the two parties' only company in the legislature were the Patrons of Industry in 1896 and the Progressives in 1923.

Shortly before 1920, the introduction of the automobile put the question of roads and highways near the top of the political agenda, and there it has remained, just as in other provinces. "Highway politics" enabled governments to "curry voters, repay political obligations and stimulate employment," just as "railway politics" had done some 50 years earlier.[31] Initial hostility to automobiles led to a 1908 law banning their use on Island roads. The vehicles were later restricted to three days of use a week, or required to have someone on foot precede them carrying a warning flag. This penchant for the status quo was also evident in the 1922 legislation which prohibited any non-resident from canvassing or campaigning in a provincial election.

In 1906, P.E.I. became the first province to enact Prohibition and this issue remained a factor in Island politics for more than 40 years. By 1931, the province was beginning to feel the effects of the Great Depression and the Liberals went down to defeat. But, when economic conditions continued to worsen over the next four years, the new Conservative government was literally wiped out. Islanders were so incensed with the Conservative performance that the Liberals won all 30 seats in 1935, although the Tories received 42 percent of the popular vote. The Liberals went on to win five consecutive elections in 1939, 1943, 1947, 1951, and 1955. The CCF ran candidates between 1943 and 1951 but gained few votes and soon withdrew.[32]

The Liberals took advantage of increased prosperity and ran a competent, progressive administration under Thane Campbell from 1936 to 1943, during which time he laid the foundation for the tourism industry. When Campbell retired to the provincial Supreme Court, he was succeeded by the flamboyant Walter Jones, father of many new initiatives. Two memorable events of this period were the final repeal of Prohibition, and the Canada Packers strike of

1947. In the former case, the lieutenant-governor vetoed the 1945 bill which sought to end the long official dry spell, and thus prolonged it for another three years.[33] In the Canada Packers strike, Jones took over the plant and had replacement labour cross the picket lines to keep the operation running.[34] Jones almost resembled Newfoundland's Joey Smallwood in claiming credit for federal funds in the form of old age pensions, the Trans-Canada Highway, and a new ferry. When he retired in 1953, he was succeeded by Alexander Matheson. The new premier vigorously promoted rural electrification in order to improve the lot of the farm community.

Many of the issues that arose in this early period related to the federal government and improving the ferry service was an almost constant theme.[35] Repeated protests to Ottawa over inadequate summer and non-existent winter service led to the construction of new boats and ice-breaking mechanisms. In 1917 the ferry began to carry railway cars, and in the 1930s it started transporting motor vehicles, including trucks. P.E.I. premiers also made regular pilgrimages to Ottawa to protest the effects of federal economic policies on the Island, and to demand financial compensation of various sorts.[36] Another concern centred on the province's declining representation in the House of Commons. Initially six, the number of P.E.I. MPs gradually dropped until 1915 when it was successful in its argument that no province should have fewer MPs than it had senators. Henceforth, P.E.I. was guaranteed a House of Commons contingent of four.

The election of the Conservatives under Walter Shaw in 1959 constituted a significant change in direction in the political evolution of the province. Similar to Quebec, P.E.I. began in 1960 to embrace the forces of modernization. It is only since then that the size of the population began to rise again after 80 years of stagnation or decline.[37] Shaw's election followed in the wake of the Diefenbaker landslide at the federal level and seemed to suggest that Islanders, as usual, wanted to get on the winning side. Among the Tories' specific promises in 1959 was the construction of a causeway to provide a permanent link to the mainland, an issue that would remain prominent for a decade. The new federal Progressive Conservative government greatly increased its grants to the provinces and Shaw was only too happy to line up for the Island's share. He was also concerned with the question of economic diversification, and created a new department of tourism. After the 1962 election, Shaw eliminated the preferential franchise for property owners, modernized liquor laws, and established a civil service commission. Meanwhile, the Liberals took office in Ottawa.

Since both parties had committed themselves to a causeway in the 1963, planning proceeded on this project and construction started just prior to the 1965 federal election. The other main issue of this period was the Georgetown project. This was to consist of Garden Gulf Foods, which would process fish and vegetables, and Bathurst Marine, which would build fishing boats. It was an exciting prospect and the Shaw government was willing to provide cash and other concessions to aid its development.[38]

However, the viability of the operation became an issue in the 1966 election, which pitted the 78-year-old premier against the new 32-year-old Liberal leader, Alex Campbell. On election night the parties were tied, each having won 15 seats in the new 32-member house. The death of one candidate before election day had caused the vote for the two members in the riding of First Kings to be deferred and that campaign is a chapter of Island history unto itself. Great ingenuity was used by both sides to swing the riding their way, and much of the activity involved asphalt. "If it moves, pension it; if it doesn't move, pave it," was said to be the approach used, and many stories were told about paving machines crashing into each other in a single driveway or about signs being erected saying "Please do not pave my lawn." In the end, the Liberals won both seats and Campbell became premier.

The pace of modernization increased with the election of the Campbell government, although its early years were dominated by the causeway and Georgetown issues. The federal government began to worry about the cost of the causeway project in 1967 and decided to reassess its commitment. In 1969 the project was cancelled, even though a considerable sum had been spent on completing the approach roads. By that time, both Bathurst Marine and Garden Gulf Foods had closed in bankruptcy after having received some $10 million in provincial public funds. A royal commission placed much of the blame on the Shaw government, and especially its fisheries minister, but the general lesson learned was not specific only to P.E.I.: small provinces lacked the personnel and other resources to deal with large developments and questionable promoters.[39] Garden Gulf Foods was later purchased by the Nickerson interests and renamed Georgetown Seafoods. It was ultimately shut down, although the shipyard continued to limp along under provincial ownership. The government later sold it to the Irving family for $1, and its prospects improved in the 1990s with the construction of the fixed link.

The 1970s

The 1970s were dominated by another large project that had been brewing within the federal and provincial bureaucracies: the Comprehensive Development Plan. The plan was unquestionably the most expensive and controversial undertaking to that point in the province's history. When it finally wound down, it had at least allowed the province to keep pace with developments elsewhere in the country. Its objectives were extremely general and ambitious—to strengthen and rationalize the provincial economy, improve public services, increase production, restructure the agriculture and fisheries industries, enhance education, training, and management, and develop new markets for Island products. In short, it involved an "all-embracing program of social and economic change."[40] The plan was to run for 15 years and depended primarily on an infusion of federal funds and outside expertise to be combined with increased provincial spending. It was a forerunner of the General Development Agreement scheme which Ottawa later signed with other provinces.

Given this broad scope, almost all provincial government activity over the following 10 to 15 years related to the plan, and almost every action generated controversy. At the heart of the problem was its management system.[41] The federal government was so sceptical of the competence of the provincial public service that it insisted on the creation of a new Department of Development, staffed almost entirely by imported experts. These experts had daily clashes with the provincial administration and the extensive network of channels and contacts it had established. Islanders felt that a group of highly educated officials, ignorant of local circumstances, had moved in and taken over. Some doubted whether even the premier and cabinet continued to have any control. The other side of the story, of course, was that the provincial public service was still weak, having just emerged from the patronage system, and one clear result of the plan was the strengthened managerial capacity of the Island government in terms of both the cabinet and the bureaucracy.

As for the plan's effects on other areas, the results appear mixed. A general criticism was that too much federal funding was directed toward social services and consumption rather than long-term industrial development or production. Schemes to increase the size of Island farms to improve productivity had the negative effect of reducing the number of family farms and encouraging vertical integration and corporate farming such as that practised by Cavendish Farms. The consolidation of tiny schools into larger, more modern institutions with a wider range of offerings was probably inevitable and certainly well intended, and its origins actually pre-dated the plan. However, it resulted in an impersonal educational atmosphere, and destroyed small communities whose heart had been the local school.[42] The upgrading and expansion of tourism facilities, designed to improve the economy by increasing tourist spending, also brought congestion, noise, and some attractions which offended Islanders' sense of propriety.[43] Similarly, the introduction of large shopping malls for the convenience of consumers put small local operations out of business, and some of the new manufacturing firms enticed by the industrial parks and malls closed down because they were unable to compete with similar firms in central Canada. In most of these situations an almost irreconcilable conflict arose between the rationality of the planners and the traditional Island way of life.

The elections of 1970 and 1974 focused largely on the advantages and disadvantages of the plan and Premier Campbell defended it successfully. The 1972 session also saw the passage of a law requiring cabinet approval of non-resident purchases of land of over 10 acres or over five chains, or 100 metres, of shoreline. This was challenged in the courts by two Americans, but the law was given the blessing of the Supreme Court of Canada in 1975. Another divisive issue extending over the 1972-74 period was whether the National Farmers Union should be designated the bargaining agent for P.E.I. potato producers. In 1975, a new Human Rights Commission was created and the court structure reformed. Not surprisingly, energy became an important issue from this time onward, especially because of the Island's reliance on electricity generated from oil. P.E.I. signed a long-term agreement with New Brunswick for two submarine power cables between the provinces, a move which would reduce the Island's dependence on oil and increase the supply, if not lower the price, of electricity. These became operative in 1977.

Two elections followed in quick succession in 1978 and 1979. In 1976, Angus MacLean had returned from a career in federal politics to take over the leadership of the provincial Conservatives. With his emphasis on a "rural renaissance," he came close to defeating the Liberals in April 1978.[44] Alex Campbell decided to resign as premier (later moving, predictably, to the provincial Supreme Court) and was succeeded by his finance minister, Bennett Campbell (no relation). Excluding the speaker, this move gave the parties an equal number of seats in the legislature, made its work unpredictable, and necessitated another election in April 1979. This time, with a Progressive Conservative regime in Ottawa and after 13 years of Campbell Liberalism, MacLean's Conservatives were successful. Bennett Campbell resigned in turn, later succeeding Dan McDonald as P.E.I.'s representative in the federal cabinet and as Minister of Veterans Affairs, while work progressed on McDonald's previously announced plan to move that federal department to Charlottetown. The Liberals chose Joe Ghiz, a Harvard-trained Charlottetown lawyer, as his successor.

The 1980s

The MacLean government shifted emphasis to the traditional industries of agriculture and fishing, and encouraged related secondary industry. MacLean was also interested in tourism and a revival of the forest industry. In addition, the government paid $100,000 to withdraw from the Point Lepreau nuclear project in New Brunswick, placed a moratorium on the construction of more shopping malls, and faced such new issues as minority language education rights and doctors opting out of the government's medical insurance program. Then, after serving only two and one-half years as premier, MacLean resigned in November 1981, to be succeeded by Health and Social Services Minister James Lee.

The new government faced a number of problems. The last phase of the Comprehensive Development Plan was signed but the federal government stopped paying the salaries of 200 officials involved. A public inquiry was established to study the problem of high electricity rates and, in an effort to stem the tide of modernization, Lee restricted corporate ownership of land to 3,000 acres. There were also problems in the potato industry, and trouble erupted in the construction of the Hilton Hotel and Convention Centre in downtown Charlottetown.

The two new leaders squared off in the 1982 election, with Ghiz appearing to be a much more dynamic speaker than Lee. The Lee government ran on its record, preached economic restraint, and was criticized for doing nothing new. The Liberals had many innovative proposals which were promptly dubbed financially irresponsible. Rather unusually, the Liberals did not emphasize the advantages of partisan alignment with the Liberal federal government; instead, they tried to distance themselves from their Ottawa counterparts. In other respects, however, it was a typical P.E.I. election. Familiar charges arose that the Highways Department had provided gravel for private roads during the campaign, but Lee's Conservatives were re-elected.

After the election, Lee showed himself to be less rurally oriented than his predecessor and "Blending Tradition and Innovation" was the title of his 1984 development strategy. Lee signed a new five-year, $120-million Economic Regional Development Agreement with the federal Liberals and, a year later, an agreement on electricity with the new Progressive Conservative government in Ottawa. Federal grants would allow P.E.I. to pay off the debt it owed for the underwater cable from New Brunswick, as well as to reduce rates to industrial and residential users by about 20 percent. In spite of the agreement, electricity rates remained the highest in the country and a legal battle over them continued with New Brunswick. The overly ambitious Hilton-Dale Prince Edward hotel-convention centre complex went into receivership. Mary Jane Irving of Cavendish Farms, who already owned in excess of the provincial limit of 3,000 acres, sought to buy more land for her potato and french fry operations. Meanwhile, the Island's representative in the federal cabinet, Tom McMillan, revived the idea of a fixed crossing between P.E.I. and New Brunswick. Because the federal government was subsidizing the ferry service to the tune of about $40 million annually, he argued, a tunnel, or combination of tunnel, bridge, and causeway, would ultimately save money.

With the economy improving somewhat, Lee called an election for April 1986. He sought to exploit the federal Progressive Conservative connection by promising the construction of a Litton Systems Canada Ltd. radar components plant in the province. Such an economic asset would ordinarily have been welcomed but the military aspect of the project raised controversy among more traditional residents.

When the votes were counted, the Liberals had defeated the Progressive Conservatives and Premier Lee had lost his own seat. This outcome was based on several factors, including Joe Ghiz's superior rhetoric, opposition to the proposed Litton plant, and a disillusionment with the two-year-old federal Progressive Conservative regime, which cut unemployment insurance and increased park fees and ferry rates. Lee was also seen as insensitive to women's issues and had links to the Dale family involved in the Prince Edward Hotel fiasco.

For some time after the election, the biggest issue on the Island was the proposed building of a fixed link to the mainland. With the federal government promoting the idea, the cautious Premier Ghiz called a provincial referendum on the question in January 1988. The result, 33,229 in favour and 22,472 opposed, gave the project further impetus, although technical, financial, and environmental questions remained. Seven construction companies submitted bids to the federal government, which eventually opted for a bridge rather than a tunnel. Construction was scheduled to start in 1989 at a cost of about $1 billion. However, immediately following the 1988 federal election, in which P.E.I. elected a slate of Liberals, Ottawa delayed the project to have an independent panel of experts review its environmental impact. Fishermen and environmentalists still preferred the idea of a tunnel, or no link at all, to a bridge. Meanwhile, the P.E.I. railroad, including its ferry link to New Brunswick, was closed, putting added pressure on the province's highways.

Another major issue at this time was the fate of the potato industry. The government accepted the Royal Commission on Potatoes recommendation in 1987 that the Potato Marketing Board be replaced with a new marketing commission consisting only of producers. In 1988 the government purchased one of the province's largest potato dealers with the objective of reselling shares to independent producers. It also bought Gemini Foods of Toronto, a potato broker, to ensure P.E.I.'s produce made its way to the Ontario market. Gemini was privatized in 1989 after the government fired its chief executive, who successfully sued for wrongful dismissal.

In other developments in the late 1980s, the ill-fated Prince Edward Hotel was first taken over by the province and then sold to CP Hotels at a huge loss to federal and Island governments. In 1988, in another effort to reduce power costs, P.E.I. signed a tripartite agreement which would supply Quebec-generated electricity to the province via New Brunswick. The province's precious, limited land base continued to cause concern, especially because of the actions of speculators and sales to foreigners. The government set up a royal commission on land use and ownership in 1988, strengthened land use controls, and increased taxes on non-resident property owners.

In addition to federal cutbacks in regional development and unemployment insurance programs, the province was particularly incensed by Michael Wilson's May 1989 budget which earmarked Canadian Forces Base Summerside for closure in 1992. This closure would directly eliminate 1,300 jobs in a community of about 8,000, a major blow both to Summerside and to the province. To the embarrassment of the Tories, Premier Ghiz chose this moment to call an election. He claimed that his 1986 mandate had been fulfilled, including the implementation of a drug plan for seniors and dental care for children. The Liberals emphasized leadership and road construction in a slick campaign dominated by Ghiz's rhetoric. The Tories ran a low-key campaign under their new leader, a folksy, quiet ex-MP, Mel Gass, who pointed out 10 reasons not to vote Liberal, including unemployment and the exodus of young people from the province.

The Liberals won a landslide victory, 30 of 32 seats. The Tories elected the remaining two members, but Gass did not gain a seat. After the election, two New Brunswick potato interests, Cavendish Farms and McCain's, came into conflict over french fry plants in the Summerside area. Cavendish expanded its plant with the help of public funds, and McCain's constructed a new one. Next, a local industrial development corporation took over the assets of the military base, transforming it into an industrial park. With financial incentives from the provincial budget, it became a major aerospace centre where such companies as Craig Dobbin's CHC Helicopter Corp. of Newfoundland maintain and repair aircraft. Finally, Prime Minister Brian Mulroney announced that the Goods and Services Tax would have its administrative centre in Summerside and Ottawa built a major facility for that purpose.

The 1990s

Like other provincial governments in the 1990s, the P.E.I. legislature has been concerned above all with deficits and the provincial debt. But the distinctive feature of P.E.I. in this decade is the construction of its fixed link to the mainland (Inset 3.1).

INSET 3.1 The Northumberland Strait Bridge

The Northumberland Strait bridge, expected to cost its private developers about $800 million, was finally given the green light in 1993 after years of controversy and environmental objections. Strait Crossing, a consortium of French, U.S. and Canadian companies, is to operate the bridge for 35 years upon its scheduled completion in 1997, and then turn it over to the federal government. In the meantime, the consortium would receive an annual federal subsidy of $42 million, the current cost of the ferry service, in addition to charging tolls of about $18 million per year. Construction began in 1994, with plans calling for a 13-kilometre bridge composed of 65 concrete and steel spans supported by concrete piers sitting on the ocean floor, previously dredged for a stable footing. The spans, 250 metres long, provide for one lane in each direction, with shoulders on each side, making it 11 metres from guardrail to guardrail. The bridge will stand about 40 metres above the water, except for a raised section of 51 metres to allow large ships to pass underneath.

Some 70 percent of the materials and services will be procured in the Atlantic region, and the developer also committed to constructing a new, expanded Hillsborough Bridge outside Charlottetown. The developers estimated the construction phase would involve 1,000 direct jobs, and operations beginning after 1997, some 50 to 60 jobs. A workforce adjustment package is to be provided for the 600 or so displaced ferry workers and, in case dredging for piers disturbed the scallop and lobster grounds, a $10-million compensation fund was established for the affected fishermen. A Federal Court decision required that a constitutional amendment be passed to the effect that the bridge replaces the 1873 obligation on Ottawa to provide a steamship service to the Island.[45]

As for the other traditional issue in P.E.I., that of ownership of its land base, the Royal Commission on Land reported its finding in October 1990. Its primary objectives were to preserve farmland and discourage non-resident ownership. It recommended farmland be frozen in its current use so that it could not be sold for any other purpose. It criticized successive governments for their routine exemption of individual applications to exceed the maximum non-resident ownership restrictions, especially with respect to shoreline property. It also endorsed higher taxes for non-residents than for P.E.I. residents. The report did not take kindly to Irving interests' request to expand their holdings to 8,000 acres. The province's double taxation of non-residents (by means of giving residents a rebate on their property taxes) was subsequently upheld by the P.E.I. Supreme Court.

In the early 1990s, the provincial deficit mushroomed to $76 million in 1992-93 from $54 million in 1991-92 and $14 million in 1990-91. Such deficits were routinely well in excess of original budget predictions. Except for corporate income taxes—which were slashed in 1992, especially for the Summerside area—taxes were raised or broadened over this period, but without reducing the deficit.

The provincial government of the early 1990s was also preoccupied with the national constitutional problem. As soon as that issue was unsuccessfully resolved in October 1992 with the popular defeat of the Charlottetown Accord, Premier Joe Ghiz announced his intention to resign. He was lauded for his contributions to the constitutional discussions, as well as for representing the province with distinction in federal-provincial affairs. On internal issues, however, his retirement announcement brought criticism of the high unemployment rate, the rising deficit, political patronage, botched government initiatives in potato marketing, and indecision on issues like land use and the fixed link. He was soon appointed dean of the Dalhousie University Law School in Halifax, and later, to the P.E.I. Supreme Court.

Catherine Callbeck became Liberal leader and premier in January 1993. She came from a teaching and business background, had served in the provincial cabinet in the 1970s as minister of health and, after a 10-year hiatus, represented the Island in the House of Commons from 1988 to the time of her accession to the premiership. She was usually described as a bland and uninspiring speaker. Her actions, however, spoke volumes. She immediately reduced the of number of government departments from 13 to eight, and the cabinet from 11 to 10. Then, determined to address the $352 million accumulated provincial debt, her government brought in a tough 1993 budget with a promise to balance the budget by 1996. After this preparation, Callbeck called an election, the first in Canadian history in which the two major parties were both led by women. It was a quiet campaign in which the new premier made two main promises: to improve the education curriculum and to help small business. Results were virtually unchanged: the Liberals won 31 seats, while the Conservatives elected only their leader, Pat Mella.

Because the 1993-94 deficit ballooned to $69 million, as seen in Table 3.10, the government devoted even more attention to its finances in 1994. The speech from the throne emphasized deficit reduction, education and training, and economic development. The budget imposed a wage rollback of 7.5 percent on provincial public servants making over $28,000, and 3.75 percent for those under $28,000. After much discord with the public service, the government appointed a royal commission to examine all aspects of government-union relations. When the government announced plans to reduce the generosity of the MLAs' pension plan, former premier Joe Ghiz threatened to challenge that move in the courts. The budget also significantly reduced welfare benefits. In 1995, the treasurer forecast a balanced budget with further spending cuts, but not as drastic as those of the year before. The province's serenity was wracked instead by a pipe-bomb explosion that damaged the historic legislative building.

TABLE 3.10   Government of Prince Edward Island Finances, 1990/91–1994/95 (millions)

	1990/91	1991/92	1992/93	1993/94	1994/95
Total revenues	$729.8	$740.4	$747.9	$782.5	$808.4
Debt charges	86.8	94.0	101.1	121.5	125.8
Total expenditures	743.5	794.7	824.1	850.8	830.3
Deficit	13.7	54.3	76.2	68.3	21.9

Source: Reproduced by authority of the Minister of Industry, 1995, Statistics Canada, *Public Sector Finance, 1994–95*, Financial Management System, cat. no. 68-212 (March 1995). Adapted by author.

CONCLUSION

Prince Edward Island has carried on for over a century in its traditional, small-scale way with a stable party system and a fairly balanced economy. Despite prohibitive electricity rates, high unemployment, and low per capita income, the pre-industrial two-party system is well entrenched. Neither the New Democratic Party, class consciousness, nor ideology seems likely to upset this system. Instead, through balancing religious and regional interests, maintaining an intimate relationship with the grassroots, and encouraging close ties to the federal parties, the provincial Liberal and Conservative parties have continued to monopolize Island politics. Notwithstanding the absence of significant differences between them, the electorate continues to turn out in record numbers to demonstrate its support for one or the other. However, many bureaucratic and procedural changes have taken place in recent years and, as P.E.I. approaches the turn of the century, and the bridge to the mainland is completed, the province is expected to experience other modernizing influences.

TABLE 3.11   Prince Edward Island Provincial Election Results Since 1923

Year	Liberals		Conservatives		NDP	
	Seats	Popular Vote	Seats	Popular Vote	Seats	Popular Vote
1923	5	44%	25	52%	—	—
1927	24	53%	6	47%	—	—
1931	12	48%	18	52%	—	—
1935	30	58%	—	42%	—	—
1939	27	53%	3	47%	—	—
1943	20	51%	10	46%	—	—
1947	24	50%	6	46%	—	—
1951	24	52%	6	47%	—	—
1955	27	55%	3	45%	—	—
1959	8	49%	22	51%	—	—
1962	11	49%	19	51%	—	—
1966	17	51%	15	49%	—	—
1970	27	58%	5	42%	—	—
1974	26	54%	6	40%	—	—
1978	17	51%	15	48%	—	—
1979	11	45%	21	53%	—	—
1982	11	45%	21	52%	—	—
1986	21	50%	11	46%	—	4%
1989	30	61%	2	36%	—	3%
1993	31	54%	1	39%	—	5%

TABLE 3.12   Premiers of Prince Edward Island Since 1873

Premier	Party	Year Elected
J.C. Pope	Conservative	1873
L.C. Owen	Conservative	1873
L.H. Davies	Coalition	1876
W.W. Sullivan	Conservative	1879
Neil MacLeod	Conservative	1889
Frederick Peters	Liberal	1891
A.B. Warburton	Liberal	1897
Donald Farquharson	Liberal	1898
Arthur Peters	Liberal	1901
F.L. Haszard	Liberal	1908
James Palmer	Liberal	1911
J.A. Mathieson	Conservative	1911
A.E. Arsenault	Conservative	1917

TABLE 3.12 continued

J.H. Bell	Liberal	1919
J.D. Stewart	Conservative	1923
A.C. Saunders	Liberal	1927
W.M. Lea	Liberal	1930
J.D. Stewart	Conservative	1931
W.J.P. MacMillan	Conservative	1933
W.M. Lea	Liberal	1935
T.A. Campbell	Liberal	1936
Walter Jones	Liberal	1943
A.W. Matheson	Liberal	1953
Walter Shaw	Conservative	1959
Alex Campbell	Liberal	1966
Bennett Campbell	Liberal	1978
Angus MacLean	Conservative	1979
James Lee	Conservative	1981
Joe Ghiz	Liberal	1986
Catherine Callbeck	Liberal	1993

ENDNOTES

1. This is the general theme of Frank MacKinnon in his chapter on Prince Edward Island in Martin Robin, ed., *Canadian Provincial Politics* (Scarborough: Prentice Hall Canada, 2nd ed. 1978).

2. Government of P.E.I., *The Royal Commission on the Land* (Charlottetown: Queen's Printer, 1990).

3. Government of P.E.I., *The P.E.I. Economy: Challenges and Opportunities in the 1990s*, Charlottetown Policy and Planning Division, (Charlottetown: P.E.I. Department of Industry, June 1991), and Atlantic Provinces Economic Council, *Atlantic Report* (Halifax: April 1994).

4. Marie Burge, "The Political Education of Bud the Spud: Producers and Plebiscites on Prince Edward Island," in Gary Burrill and Ian McKay, eds., *People, Resources, and Power* (Fredericton: Acadiensis Press, 1987); and Grace Skogstad, "State Autonomy and Provincial Policy-Making: Potato Marketing in New Brunswick and P.E.I.," *Canadian Journal of Political Science* (September 1987).

5. Burrill and McKay, *People, Resources, and Power;* David Milne, "Politics in a Beleaguered Garden," in Keith Brownsey and Michael Howlett, eds., *The Provincial State* (Mississauga: Copp Clark Pitman, 1992).

6. Wayne MacKinnon, *The Life of the Party* (Summerside: Williams and Crue, 1973), pp. 60, 76; and M.R. Clark, "Island Politics," in F.W.P. Bolger, ed., *Canada's Smallest Province* (Charlottetown: P.E.I. Centennial Commission, 1973), p. 300. Lieutenant-governors, senators and judges have also been rotated.

7. At times the federal share of provincial government revenues has reached the two-thirds mark.

8. This phenomenon has been widely noted but the fullest discussion is Ian Stewart, "Friends at Court: An Analysis of Prince Edward Island Provincial Elections," *Canadian Journal of Political Science* (March 1986).

9. Stewart, "Friends at Court."

10. David Milne, "Politics in a Beleaguered Garden," and J.M. Bumsted, "The Only Island There Is: The Writing of Prince Edward Island History," in Verner Smitheram, David Milne, and Satadal Dasgupta, eds., *The Garden Transformed, Prince Edward Island 1945-1980* (Charlottetown: Ragweed Press, 1982).

11. *Canadian Annual Review of Politics and Public Affairs,* (Toronto: University of Toronto Press, 1984), p. 227.

12. S.J.R. Noel, "Leadership and Clientelism," in David Bellamy et al, eds., *The Provincial Political Systems* (Toronto: Methuen, 1976); A.F. Macdonald, *The Politics of Acquisition: A Study of Corruption in Prince Edward Island,* unpublished MA thesis, Queen's University, April 1979; and Jeffrey Simpson, *Spoils of Power* (Toronto: Collins, 1988).

13. Richard Simeon and David Elkins, "Regional Political Cultures in Canada," in Elkins and Simeon, eds., *Small Worlds: Provinces and Parties in Canadian Political Life* (Toronto: Methuen, 1980); M.A. Chandler and W. Chandler, *Public Policy and Provincial Politics* (Toronto: McGraw-Hill Ryerson, 1979), pp. 74-84; and Harold Clarke et al., *Political Choice in Canada* (Toronto: McGraw-Hill Ryerson, 1980), p.31.

14. Frank MacKinnon uses the phrases "grand time," "great sport," and "fun" to describe Island politics in his article in Robin, *Canadian Provincial Politics.* The acquisitive aspect is also examined in Richard Apostle and Paul Pross, "Marginality and Political Culture: A New Approach to Political Culture in Atlantic Canada," Canadian Political Science Association (1981).

15. Jennifer Smith, "Ruling Small Worlds: Political Leadership in Atlantic Canada," in Leslie Pal and David Taras, eds., *Prime Ministers and Premiers* (Scarborough: Prentice Hall Canada, 1988).

16. Frank MacKinnon, *The Government of Prince Edward Island* (Toronto: University of Toronto Press, 1951); Wayne MacKinnon, *The Life of the Party,* p. 82.

17. M.R. Clark, "Island Politics," in Bolger, *Canada's Smallest Province,* pp. 295-312.

18. *Re MacKinnon and the Government of Prince Edward Island* [1993] 101 D.L.R. (4th) 362.

19. Milne, "Politics in the Beleaguered Garden," in Smitheram et al., *The Garden Transformed,* p. 60.

20. Frank MacKinnon in Robin, *Canadian Provincial Politics,* p. 227.

21. Wayne MacKinnon, *The Life of the Party,* p. 125.

22. *Canadian Advertising Rates and Data,* August 1994.

23. The best historical source on this subject is the work of Frank MacKinnon, including *The Government of Prince Edward Island,* and his article in Robin, *Canadian Provincial Politics.*

24. Frank MacKinnon, *The Government of Prince Edward Island,* pp. 186-194 and 262-266. As recently as 1976 and 1977, there were public disagreements within the cabinet. See the *Canadian Annual Review* (Toronto: University of Toronto Press, 1976), p. 256, and for 1977, p. 201.

25. Ian Stewart, "Prince Edward Island: 'A damned queer parliament'," in Gary Levy and Graham White, eds., *Provincial and Territorial Legislatures in Canada* (Toronto: University of Toronto Press, 1989).

26. Frank MacKinnon, *The Government of Prince Edward Island*, p. 179.

27. F.W.P. Bolger, *Prince Edward Island and Confederation, 1863-1873* (Charlottetown: St. Dunstan's University Press, 1964); his article in *Canada's Smallest Province;* and Frank MacKinnon's chapter 6 in *The Government of Prince Edward Island.*

28. Clark, "Island Politics," in Bolger, *Canada's Smallest Province*, p. 318.

29. Frank MacKinnon in Robin, *Canadian Provincial Politics*, p. 230; Macdonald, *The Politics of Acquisition.*

30. Errol Sharpe, *A People's History of Prince Edward Island* (Toronto: Steel Rail Publishing, 1976), p. 134. L.B. Sellick, *My Island Home* (Windsor, N.S.: Lancelot Press, 1973) goes even further, mentioning the rotation, on a religious basis, of bank managers on the Island, p. 40.

31. Wayne MacKinnon, *The Life of the Party*, p. 84.

32. Andrew Robb, "Third Party Experience on the Island," in Smitheram et al., *The Garden Transformed.*

33. The next lieutenant-governor approved the bill. Lieutenant-governors also withheld assent from two religious bills—one incorporating the Orange Order in 1880 and the other establishing the United Church on the Island in 1924. Frank MacKinnon, *The Government of Prince Edward Island*, pp. 154-155.

34. David Milne, "Politics in a Beleaguered Garden," in Smitheram et al., *The Garden Transformed*, p.43; Sharpe, *A People's History of Prince Edward Island*, ch. 23.

35. Mary K. Cullen, "The Transportation Issue, 1873-1973," in Bolger, *Canada's Smallest Province.*

36. F.L. Driscoll, "The Island and the Dominion," in Bolger, *Canada's Smallest Province.*

37. The population in 1961 was below that of 1881.

38. Philip Mathias, *Forced Growth* (Toronto: James Lewis and Samuel, 1971), ch. 2.

39. The royal commission said that "Ministers of the Crown should call upon their Departmental staff for assistance and guidance in matters which are within the knowledge of such officials. And, when such officials are lacking in expertise with respect to any matter, resort should be had to outside sources. But in no case should policy be determined solely on the opinion of project promoters or experts retained by them, whose interests may be in conflict with those of Government." Quoted by Mathias, *Forced Growth*, p. 28.

40. Frank MacKinnon in *Canadian Annual Review*, (1969), p. 154; H.G. Thorburn, *Planning and the Economy* (Toronto: Canadian Institute for Economic Policy, 1984).

41. Donald Nemetz, "Managing Development," in Smitheram et al., *The Garden Transformed.*

42. Verner Smitheram, "Development and Debate over School Consolidation," in Smitheram et al., *The Garden Transformed.*

43. For example, "Kitten" waitresses at the Brudenell tourist complex. When the "F-word" was used on stage at the Confederation Centre in a play about Elvis Presley, the head of the board, now known as Premier Catherine Callbeck, resigned.

44. Milne, "Politics in a Beleaguered Garden," in Smitheram et al., *The Garden Transformed*, pp. 41, 67-69.

45. For a negative perspective, see Lorraine Begley, ed., *Crossing that Bridge: a Critical Look at the PEI Fixed Link* (Charlottetown: Ragweed Press, 1993).

READINGS

Canadian Annual Review of Politics and Public Affairs. Toronto: University of Toronto Press, annual.

Milne, David. "Politics in a Beleaguered Garden." Keith Brownsey and Michael Howlett, eds. *The Provincial State*. Mississauga: Copp Clark Pitman, 1992.

P.E.I. Department of Finance. *Annual Statistical Review*.

Smitheram, Verner, David Milne, and Satadal Dasgupta, eds. *The Garden Transformed, Prince Edward Island, 1945-1980*. Charlottetown: Ragweed Press, 1982.

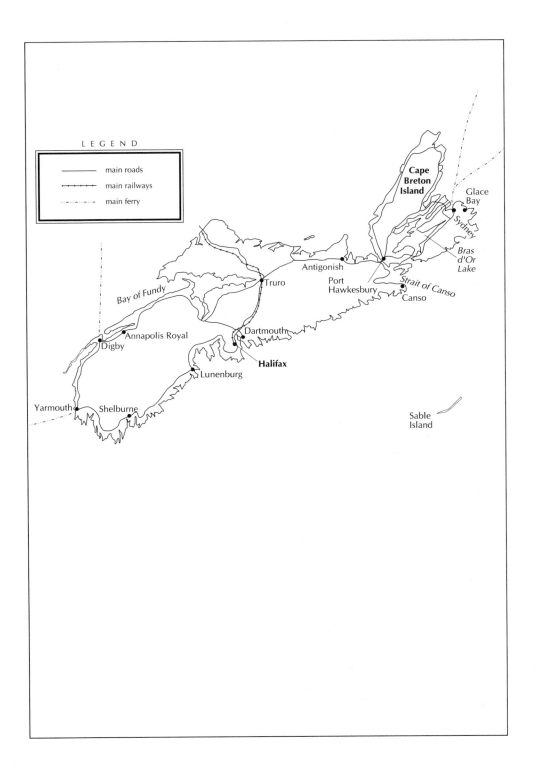

LEGEND

main roads
main railways
main ferry

Cape Breton Island

Glace Bay

Sydney

Bras d'Or Lake

Antigonish

Strait of Canso

Port Hawkesbury

Canso

Truro

Bay of Fundy

Dartmouth

Annapolis Royal

Halifax

Digby

Lunenburg

Yarmouth

Shelburne

Sable Island

CHAPTER 4

NOVA SCOTIA

Nova Scotia tends to regard itself, and is also seen by outsiders, as the most prosperous and progressive Atlantic province. Although Nova Scotia could not be considered affluent, it has been spared the degree of economic turmoil experienced by some of its neighbours, and its political life has been generally calm.[1] In fact, Nova Scotian politics have been so placid in recent years that in many respects the province has lost its position of political leadership and policy innovation in Atlantic Canada. The government elected in 1993 is trying to regain that position.

SETTING

Geography

Nova Scotia is part of the Appalachian region and consists of two geographic parts: a mainland portion forming a peninsula linked to New Brunswick by the narrow Chignecto Isthmus, and Cape Breton Island to the northeast. Cape Breton constitutes about 20 percent of the province's total area of 55,500 square kilometres, the whole being some 580 kilometres long and averaging 130 kilometres across. A causeway linking the Island to the mainland was constructed in 1955.

This geographic division results in two distinct regions: the mainland and Cape Breton. The mainland is further broken down into four regions: the Annapolis Valley along the Bay of Fundy in the northwest, the southwest coast, the Northumberland-Pictou area in the northeast, and the Halifax-Dartmouth metropolitan area. Officially, the province is composed of 18 counties, four of which are on Cape Breton.

Nova Scotia's population was 899,942 according to the 1991 census (rising to 938,300 by January 1995), making it the most populous Atlantic province. The inhabitants are grouped into two major urban concentrations. The city of Halifax had a 1991 population of 114,455, and the city of Dartmouth 67,798, but the combined metropolitan area of about 320,500 constitutes over one-third of the total provincial population. Halifax-Dartmouth is a cosmopolitan public sector community which is distinct from, and clearly dominates, the surrounding hinterland. The Sydney labour market area, including Glace Bay, North Sydney, and Sydney Mines at the eastern end of Cape Breton, provides an opposite pole of influence, with a combined population of about 116,100. Thus, nearly 20 percent of the province's population live on Cape Breton, while nearly half of Nova Scotians live in communities of less than 5,000, mostly dotted along the coast. Statistics Canada designates 53.5 percent of the province's population as urban.

The principal Nova Scotia highways link Halifax to Sydney as well as paralleling the coastline around the province. Passenger and freight trains as well as the Trans-Canada Highway cross the Chignecto Isthmus to connect Nova Scotia to New Brunswick and beyond, but other passenger trains have been discontinued. Ferries run between Sydney and Argentia and Port-aux-Basques, Nfld., Caribou and Wood Islands, P.E.I., and Digby and Saint John, N.B. as well as Yarmouth and the U.S. state of Maine. The province has many air links, with Halifax International Airport being the seventh busiest in Canada in terms of both passengers and cargo. Halifax also ranks seventh in the country as a port. It was a pioneer in the containerization method of shipping and transport, in which goods are transported in huge boxcarlike containers instead of smaller boxes, and now has four container berths, a new Canadian National inter-modal terminal for transferring goods between ships and trucks and trains, and an up-to-date shipyard and drydock. Dartmouth also has a large two-berth autoport for the import and export of automobiles. Point Tupper in the Canso Strait can accommodate large crude oil supertankers and, in addition, the area on either side of the causeway has attracted heavy industry and serves as a supply base for offshore petroleum developments. Sydney is the third main deep-water port.

Economy

Nova Scotia has the most even balance of the four primary industries of any Atlantic province. Agriculture, fishing, mining, and forestry all contribute substantially to its gross domestic product. It is also balanced among primary, secondary, and tertiary sectors, and constitutes 2.6 percent of the national gross domestic product.

Fishing has been an integral part of the province's history and continues to be one of its most valuable primary industries. It is the centre of activity in many smaller coastal communities, and is especially important in the southwest region which, in addition to its rich inshore stock, has proximity to Georges Bank. The province's main catches are lobster, scallops, cod, haddock, pollock, crab, and herring. Nova Scotia fishermen may be employers, employees, or self-employed. Although fishing has been a troubled industry in many respects, it improved in 1977 when Canada's offshore management zone was extended to 200 miles.

Overly optimistic expansion and heavy borrowing, however, led to increased problems in the early 1980s. Especially in terms of the vertically integrated National Sea Products, which owned everything from fishing boats to processing plants, the restructuring of the industry brought renewed prosperity in the mid-1980s, but declining fish stocks triggered another crisis at the end of the decade. As indicated previously in Inset 2.1, the federal government gradually but drastically tightened the noose on the Atlantic groundfish industry between 1988 and 1993, with bans on fishing almost all species, especially cod. Although not affected in the same drastic way as Newfoundland, Nova Scotia certainly suffered and large numbers of fishermen and processing plant workers lost their jobs. Nova Scotia was cushioned from the bans, however, because they exempted the southwest corner of the province and also because of its greater dependence on shellfish.

Agriculture accounts for almost as much employment and total value of production as fishing, and is concentrated in the fertile Annapolis Valley and Northumberland regions. The province had nearly 4,000 farms in 1991, most of them family operated, with an average size of 247 acres. They principally produce dairy products, poultry, eggs, cattle, hogs, and three main fruit crops: apples, blueberries, and strawberries. Some of these products are sold in their natural state by their own marketing boards, while others contribute to the processing industry.

Mining accounts for the least employment among the primary industries, but sometimes the largest value. Coal is the leading mineral, and is concentrated in the Sydney region of Cape Breton, with other fields in the Pictou and Cumberland areas of the mainland. Coal nearly disappeared as a valuable commodity until the energy crisis of the mid-1970s precipitated a reduced dependence on imported oil as a source of electricity and a larger proportion of power began to be produced using coal. Nova Scotia stands fourth among the provinces in the value and quantity of coal production, but several mines closed in the early 1990s, leaving only two operating in Cape Breton. The explosion at the Westray coal mine on the mainland in 1992 killed 26 miners, confirming that, while the region's coal was of excellent quality, it was dangerous to produce. Moreover, with the privatization of N.S. Power, that company is under less pressure to use Nova Scotian coal. Other minerals found in sizeable quantities include gypsum (about three-quarters of the Canadian total), tin (Rio Algom's mine at Yarmouth being the largest in North America), and lead.

In the early 1980s, the province was excited by oil and gas exploration off Sable Island, with the Venture gas field find appearing the most promising. Further exploration did not produce the hoped-for results, however, and drilling stopped for several years. It resumed in the 1990s with less optimistic expectations, and the exploration process alone contributed significantly to the provincial economy. Offshore gas will probably be developed some day but, in the meantime, oil began to flow from the nearby Cohasset-Panuke field in 1992. It is

produced by a combination of British-based Lasmo Co. and the Crown corporation, N.S. Resources. It is expected to have a life-span of five years, and puts
Nova Scotia in competition with Manitoba as the fourth-largest petroleum producing province.

   Forestry is the last of the four main primary industries, and in most aspects
of it Nova Scotia ranks sixth in the country. Over 80 percent of the provincial
land area is covered by forest, but three-quarters of forest land is held by many
small owners who have been less conscientious about good forest management
than the government has on the remaining 25 per cent. While the supply of
wood is substantial, with a significant production of lumber, even more important is the pulp and paper industry. Nova Scotia was a leading shipbuilder in the
days of wooden sailing ships, but the industry declined with the coming of steam
and steel. The threat of the spruce budworm which kills trees and the controversy over whether or not to spray the forest with insecticides subsided by the
mid-1990s.

   In total, these primary industries employ about seven percent of the Nova
Scotian labour force—one of the lowest proportions in the country. As for the

TABLE 4.1   **Nova Scotia 1991 Labour Force and Estimated 1995 Gross
Domestic Product by Industry**

Industry	1991 Labour Force		Est. 1995 GDP ($ millions)	
Agriculture	9,595	2.2%	177	1.3%
Fishing	9,955	2.3%	184	1.4%
Forestry	5,375	1.2%	95	0.7%
Mining	5,150	1.2%	201	1.5%
TOTAL PRIMARY	30,075	6.9%	657	4.8%
Manufacturing	51,805	11.8%	1,627	11.9%
Construction	29,290	6.7%	751	5.5%
TOTAL SECONDARY	81,095	18.5%	2,378	17.4%
Transportation, communications and utilities	32,630	7.4%	1,401	10.3%
Trade	77,790	17.7%	1,799	13.2%
Finance, insurance and real estate	19,365	4.4%	2,367	17.4%
Services	145,560	33.1%	3,357	24.6%
Government	53,325	12.1%	1,670	12.3%
TOTAL TERTIARY	328,670	74.7%	10,594	77.8%
TOTAL ALL INDUSTRIES	439,840		13,629	

Source: Reproduced by authority of the Minister of Industry, 1995, Statistics Canada, *1991 Census*,
cat. nos. 93-326 and 95-313, and Conference Board of Canada, *Provincial Outlook, Economic Forecast*
(Ottawa: Summer 1994), Vol. 9, No. 2.

generation of electricity, the province relies mostly on a combination of coal (three-quarters) and imported oil (one-quarter). Among the generating stations on Cape Breton using local coal are those at Lingan, Point Tupper, and Glace Bay, while the newest coal-fired plant at Point Aconi has generated much controversy over experimental technology which has not avoided either air or water pollution. The main hydro plant is at Wreck Cove. A potential new energy source is the Annapolis Tidal Power Project. The Bay of Fundy has the highest tides in the world and, if the pilot project at Annapolis Royal had succeeded, the province hoped to construct larger tidal power installations in the area. Unfortunately several problems arose, including flooding, siltation, and land erosion caused by a raising of the water levels. The project still operates, almost as a tourist attraction, but there are no expansion plans.

Manufacturing in Nova Scotia is built upon the primary industries to a large extent, especially food and beverages and paper products. The largest manufacturing plants include the Sydney Steel plant; Stora, Bowater Mersey, and Scott pulp and paper mills; and fish and agricultural processing plants, especially the National Sea Products operation in Lunenburg, Clearwater Fine Foods, Oxford Frozen Foods (Oxford), and Seafreez Foods (Canso). Other manufacturing includes Stanfield's underwear (Truro), petroleum refining, Trenton railway cars (New Glasgow), the Volvo assembly plant (Halifax), and aerospace plants—IMP, Pratt and Whitney, and Litton Systems. The single largest manufacturer is Michelin tire, which has three plants in the province (Granton, Bridgewater, and Cambridge) with a total workforce of nearly 4,000. These are accompanied by a great variety of smaller manufacturing industries, many located in the 40 industrial parks established in recent years. Overall, the province ranks relatively high in the development of its manufacturing sector.

As for services, Halifax is the financial, service, educational, and medical centre of the Atlantic region. Most major financial institutions have their regional headquarters there, and it houses several universities including Dalhousie and St. Mary's. The province has a flourishing tourist industry, and among the leading attractions are the restored Fortress of Louisbourg and the spectacular Cabot Trail on Cape Breton, the many scenic, historical and cultural delights of Halifax, the fabled Peggy's Cove, and sailing, wind surfing, canoeing, fishing and swimming.

In addition to regular federal, provincial, and municipal government operations, Halifax is home to the headquarters of the Maritime Command of the Canadian Armed Forces, helping to give Nova Scotia the highest per capita defence establishment and the highest per capita federal government presence of any province. In numerical terms, there are about 66,000 government employees divided almost equally between provincial and municipal levels, and nearly 40,000 federal employees in Nova Scotia. Unfortunately, this heavy reliance on government makes it difficult for the province to extract itself from recession when both levels of government are retrenching expenditures.

Class

This balanced industrial structure leaves Nova Scotia with the highest per capita income of the Atlantic provinces. In the early 1990s, it was even ahead of Saskatchewan, at $18,680 in 1992. Nova Scotia actually outranks all provinces except Ontario, Alberta and British Columbia in its average level of educational attainment. The 1991 census indicated that the median family income in Nova Scotia was $38,997, with 19 percent of families living on less than $20,000 and 14 percent receiving over $70,000. The province relies heavily on unemployment insurance benefits, although not to the same extent as Newfoundland and P.E.I. Nova Scotia normally has a slightly lower unemployment rate than the rest of the region (rising from 10 to 15 percent over the first half of the 1990s), and most fishermen and forest workers depend on UI to some extent in the winter months. Many fishermen are also part-time farmers and part-time foresters, eking out a living as best they can.[2] As the federal fishing restrictions of the early 1990s began to encroach on Nova Scotia, many of its full-time fishermen lost their jobs and were eligible for various income support, upgrading, and retraining programs.

The union movement in Nova Scotia was historically stronger than in the other Atlantic provinces, especially among steelworkers and mineworkers. This sometimes translated into political activity in terms of strikes and party preferences. Such support as the CCF/NDP have received, for example, has traditionally been on Cape Breton. There is no strong fishermen's union as in Newfoundland; it is mostly fish plant workers who are unionized in Nova Scotia, and successful independent fishermen can actually come to oppose unions. Nowadays organized labour is not so strong, and the overall rate of unionization among paid workers is the second lowest in the country, only 31 percent. The Nova Scotia Federation of Labour has a membership of some 70,000 out of a unionized labour force of 100,000. Nearly one-quarter of union members are in government unions—the Nova Scotia Government Employees Union (NSGEU), CUPE (Canadian Union of Public Employees), and PSAC (Public Service Alliance of Canada)—but the Communications, Energy and Paperworkers (CEP) and Canadian Auto Workers (CAW) are large in the private sector.

Nova Scotia boasts some very affluent native families, including the Sobeys (supermarkets, energy, and property development), the Jodreys (power, pulp and paper, insurance, Extendicare, and Crownx), and the Olands (brewing).[3] The Sobeys and Jodreys jointly control Halifax Developments Ltd., which owns a major share of National Sea Products. Other rich and/or powerful business figures include J. Gogan, head of Sobey's Empire Company Ltd., John Risley (Clearwater Fine Foods), Thomas Hall (Stora), Henry Demore (National Sea Products), Kenneth Rowe (IMP Group), I. Dewar (Maritime Telephone and Telegraph), Louis Comeau (N.S. Power), and Ralph Medjuck.

While academics have little difficulty applying a class analysis to much of Nova Scotian life, residents themselves have given little support to class-based movements.[4] Many of the farmers, fishermen, and foresters temper their proletarian consciousness with the "strong mythology of independence and individualism" of small producers.[5]

Demography

Over 70 percent of Nova Scotians are of British background (largely Scottish and Irish); 93.6 percent have English as their mother tongue, and 96.3 percent use English in the home. Mention should be made of the revival of the Scottish-based Gaelic tradition on Cape Breton in recent years. The Acadian element is second largest, at about 10 percent, but French is the mother tongue of only 4.1 percent of Nova Scotians and only 2.5 percent speak it at home. Nova Scotia has a greater proportion of other ethnic and racial groups than its neighbours, including Germans, Dutch, Native Peoples, and Blacks. To some extent the different groups are located in separate sections of the province: Acadians in the Annapolis Valley from which they were originally expelled, Germans in Lunenburg, Irish in Truro, Scots in Pictou and Northumberland, and Yorkshiremen in the west. A large contingent of United Empire Loyalists arrived in 1783 and settled in the Shelburne region.

The political significance of the divisions between those of English, Irish, and Scottish descent has declined over time, and the overwhelming British heritage has meant that ethnic politics have not been prominent. Certain issues have affected the interests of the Acadian minority, such as the reorganization of school boards, which raised the questions of a loss of local control over education, and of what proportion of French should be taught in Acadian schools.[6] Certain French schools in Acadian parts of the province predated the Charter of Rights and Freedoms, although they do not satisfy the Supreme Court's requirements regarding francophone control of such schools. Several anglophone school boards have established French schools, and the province set up one French-language school board to serve the metropolitan Halifax region.

The deplorable condition of many Blacks in the province has also attracted much recent attention. They have suffered from blatant discrimination in law and policy since arriving after the War of 1812. In the hope of improving their lot, the government informally granted them a seat in the legislature in the 1992 redistribution. Nova Scotia has over 20,000 people of aboriginal origin (2.5 percent of the population), mostly Micmacs (sometimes spelled Mi'kmaq), and discrimination against them has also been rampant. This was most tragically exemplified by the case of Donald Marshall, a native person who spent over 10 years in jail for a murder he did not commit.

The province regularly loses more residents to emigration than it gains through immigration or inter-provincial migration. Nova Scotia often complains that its greatest export is "brains." In 1991, about 80 percent of Nova Scotians were born in the province, and over 95 percent were born in the country.

TABLE 4.2 Nova Scotia Mother Tongue and Home Language, 1991

	Mother Tongue	Home Language
English	93.6%	96.3%
French	4.1%	2.5%
Other	2.3%	1.2%

Source: Reproduced by authority of the Minister of Industry, 1995, Statistics Canada, *1991 Census,* cat. no. 93-317, adapted by author.

Over half of the population is Protestant (54.1 percent), with large contingents of United Church, Anglicans, and Baptists. Thirty-seven percent are Roman Catholics, and this sizeable minority has been a factor of some importance in the political life of the province. For example, while not as rigid as P.E.I. in this respect, there is an expectation that certain offices will alternate between Catholics and Protestants and, in some cases, a religious balance among candidates is prescribed.[7] The question of separate schools is the political issue most commonly linked to religion in the other provinces, but this was resolved in Nova Scotia prior to Confederation. In 1865, Premier Charles Tupper refused to allow Catholics a separate school system, but permitted an unofficial arrangement of "local elasticity" whereby certain public schools were staffed with Catholic teachers and could engage in religious instruction after regular hours. Although such religious divisions are of decreasing significance, public schools may still be designated informally as either Catholic or Protestant.

TABLE 4.3 Religion in Nova Scotia, 1991

Protestant		482,180 (54.2%)
United Church	153,040 (17.2%)	
Anglican	128,375 (14.4%)	
Baptist	98,490 (11.1%)	
Presbyterian	31,225 (3.5%)	
Other Protestant	71,050 (8.0%)	
Roman Catholic		331,340 (37.2%)
Other and None		77,430 (8.7%)

Source: Reproduced by authority of the Minister of Industry, 1995, Statistics Canada, *1991 Census,* cat. no. 93-319, adapted by author.

Generally speaking, internal ethnic, religious, or class divisions have not constituted serious political issues in the province, although each has arisen from time to time. Cape Breton, on the other hand, has regularly posed political problems, both as a geographic region and as a distinct and usually depressed economy dominated by its steel plant and coal mines. It has a history of corporate carpetbaggers taking advantage of government grants, subsidies, and loans. The government has also had its hands full propping up industry in other parts of the province, coping with the high cost of energy, and trying to satisfy a variety of demands with limited funds. Efforts to attract industry to Nova Scotia have been intense, sometimes controversial and, in two cases at least, nothing short of disastrous.[8] Governing Nova Scotia, then, has consisted of responding to conflicting demands, mostly of a sectional or occupational nature, easily balancing religious interests, and promoting economic development in a society largely unconscious of class cleavages.[9]

Federal-Provincial Relations

The federal connection has often been a political issue in the province, especially in the early period, and, like Quebec, Nova Scotia did not hesitate to use the threat of secession to make its point. Over the years the province has been in the forefront of the Maritime Rights movement, being concerned largely with the effects of the national tariff on local industry. In more recent times, there has been less conflict, but much federal-provincial negotiation occurred over the coal and steel industries, the fate of the heavy water plants, attracting alternative industry to Cape Breton, and the development of offshore petroleum. This subdued tone of debate reflects Nova Scotia's heavy reliance on the federal government for equalization payments and assistance in economic development programs.[10] Although not quite to the extent of Newfoundland and P.E.I., a substantial proportion of provincial revenue comes from Ottawa—over 37 percent in 1992. In addition to the $1,637 million it gave to the province and $90 million to municipalities, Ottawa transferred $2,337 million to individuals and $181 million to businesses. In the 1980s, the provincial Progressive Conservative government supported the Canada-U.S. Free Trade Agreement and the Meech Lake Accord without much hesitation. Federal-provincial issues in the 1990s include the closure of federal armed forces bases, the fisheries compensation package, the cleanup of Halifax harbour, highways, the removal of interprovincial trade barriers, and the reform of social programs.

POLITICAL CULTURE

Nova Scotia's political culture has a variety of dimensions. Similar to Prince Edward Islanders, Nova Scotians have possessed a parochialism which historically took the form of antipathy towards outsiders, especially Upper Canadians, and towards Confederation.[11] In fact, opposition to Ottawa was probably stronger than in P.E.I. for, while islanders always demanded more from the federal government, Ottawa had at least helped P.E.I. solve its basic pre-Confederation problems. Nova Scotians, however, often felt that Confederation was the source, not the solution, of their difficulties. P.E.I.'s golden age ended before it joined Confederation in 1873, and Nova Scotia's undoubtedly would also have ended had the province delayed its entry.[12] But in 1867 Nova Scotia was still experiencing its greatest prosperity, causing the province to develop an attitude of paranoia when an economic decline began shortly afterwards.

In more recent times, this attitude has mellowed somewhat. Since the election of the Diefenbaker government in 1957, it appears that the province's concerns have been taken more seriously by Ottawa, with the result that most Nova Scotians now possess a healthy balance of loyalty to province and country. There is still a very strong provincial identity, but it is no longer based on hostility to Canada.[13] Several *Maclean's* surveys have shown that only one-third of Nova Scotians feel loyalty first to the province, compared to two-thirds who felt themselves to be Canadians first.

In another sense, Nova Scotia possesses many values considered common to the Atlantic region including tradition, caution, parochialism, cynicism, and conservatism.[14] The population has been fairly static over the post-Confederation period, and not many new ideas have gained acceptance among Nova Scotians. Residents generally prefer the status quo, which coincides with the high value placed on family, community, smallness, and a simple lifestyle. The addition of a significant group of United Empire Loyalists may well have reinforced such values as hierarchy, elitism, and conservatism, and an admiration for things British. Some observers have gone so far as to characterize Nova Scotia as having a "subject" political culture. They point to the deferential nature of much political activity, the apparent predilection for "father figures" in provincial leaders, and feelings of economic dependency and loss of confidence.[15] "Subject-participant" might be a more accurate designation, however, given the high participation rate. Because it is the leader of the Atlantic provinces in most respects, one could expect a greater degree of political sophistication and morality in Nova Scotia, but this does not appear to be the case. For example, legislation with regard to freedom of information and election expenses have been less substantial than one would expect, and ample evidence of political patronage and corruption can be found.[16]

One rather unusual strain of the province's culture is the co-operative movement, often called the Antigonish Movement because it originated at St. Francis Xavier University in Antigonish. With the inspiration of two priests, M.M. Coady and J.J. Tompkins, many co-operative organizations were formed, especially in the 1920s and 1930s. Such organizations included marketing and producers' co-operatives, retail stores, co-operative housing projects, and credit unions. The movement is usually seen as a great benefit to the hard-pressed farmers, miners, and fishermen, but in some ways it reinforced traditional values such as the sanctity of small communities. It could also be seen as siphoning off discontent that might otherwise have taken a more overtly political direction. In any case, a new attitude of self-reliance appears to be emerging in Cape Breton.

Finally, the participatory aspect of the province's political culture can be examined. Nova Scotians are highly involved in political activity and, while the voter turnout rate cannot match P.E.I.'s extraordinary record, it is still in the 73 to 75 percent range for both provincial and federal elections. In one study, Nova Scotia was found to have the highest composite participation score of all provinces.[17] Thus there is no contradiction in the Nova Scotia political culture— high participation coincides with a feeling of effectiveness, a sense of political efficacy, distinguishing the province somewhat from its Atlantic neighbours.

TABLE 4.4   **Nova Scotia Voter Turnout Rate in Recent Federal and Provincial Elections**

Federal Elections		Provincial Elections	
1974	74%	1974	78%
1979	75%	1978	78%
1980	72%	1981	74%
1984	75%	1984	68%
1988	75%	1988	76%
1993	65%	1993	75%
Average	72.7%	Average	74.8%

Source: *Reports of the Chief Electoral Officer*, calculations by author.

POLITICAL PARTIES

Party System

There is no question that Nova Scotia is best characterized as having had a Liberal one-party dominant system from 1867 to 1956. During this period there were only two short Conservative deviations from Liberal rule, and third parties had only brief success. While the Conservatives were ousted as the official Opposition in 1920 and 1945, they regularly won a sizeable share of the popular vote. Since 1920 they have rarely fallen below 40 percent and never under 34 percent. Since 1956, both Liberals and Conservatives have formed governments, but, until 1993, the Tories had occupied the government benches for all but eight years. Furthermore, Liberal support reached an all-time low in the 1981-84 period, hardly over 30 percent. An additional complication has been the steady rise in New Democratic Party support, which in the last five elections exceeded the height of Co-operative Commonwealth Federation strength in 1945, and is greater in Nova Scotia than in any other Atlantic province. It is probably most accurate to speak of Conservative party dominance, at least from 1956 to 1988, because the Conservatives generally had a substantial margin over the Liberals in terms of both seats and popular vote. With the revival and election of the Liberals in 1988 and 1993 respectively, however, and with the NDP maintaining about 15 percent of the popular vote, the 1990s would seem to be best classified as a two-and-one-half or two-plus party system.

TABLE 4.5   Party Support in Nova Scotia, 1970-95

	Years in Office		Average Percentage of Vote	Percentage of Seats
Liberals	10	(40%)	40.4	43.2
Conservatives	15	(60%)	43.4	50.9
Combined	25	(100%)	83.8	94.1
NDP	—	—	14.7	5.1

Source: *Reports of the Chief Electoral Officer,* calculations by author.

FIGURE 4.1   Percentage of Vote by Party in Nova Scotia Elections, 1970-1993

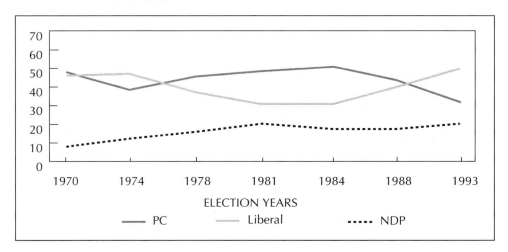

Federal-Provincial Party Links

A distinctive feature of federal-provincial party links is the number of Nova Scotia politicians who achieved success in the federal arena: Charles Tupper, Joseph Howe, John Thompson, W.S. Fielding, Robert Borden, Angus L. Macdonald, Robert Stanfield, and Allan MacEachen. The dominant province in the Atlantic region, Nova Scotia is the only one to have laid claim to federal party leadership. Native sons John Thompson, Charles Tupper, Robert Borden, and Robert Stanfield all led the national Conservative party, with the first three also serving as prime minister. The fact that most Nova Scotians who succeeded in the federal arena were Tories reflects another interesting feature of federal-provincial relations: until 1956, at least, the most able Conservatives sought federal office, while the better Liberals tended to remain in provincial politics.

Relations have generally been good between the federal and provincial wings of each party (for example, the Diefenbaker-Stanfield, Trudeau-Regan, Mulroney-Buchanan, and Chrétien-Savage governments have strong links). In the mid-1960s, however, the federal Liberals sought to strengthen the provincial party by replacing its leader Earl Urquhart with Gerald Regan, and were somewhat disappointed that Allan MacEachen did not do more to strengthen the party machine in the entire province rather than only in his constituency.[18] Even so, special mention should be made of "Godfather" MacEachen, who was the province's representative in the federal Liberal cabinet for more than 20 years and participated in most decisions involving the two levels of government over that period. He took particular interest in his own area—Cape Breton and the eastern part of the mainland—and was thus intimately connected to federal-provincial discussions of the coal, steel, and heavy water industries. The later presence of former premier Gerald Regan in the federal Liberal ranks gave the province two representatives in the subsequent Trudeau and Turner cabinets, while Brian Mulroney also found room for two Nova Scotians when forming his new, larger government in 1984. Senator Lowell Murray became an influential minister after 1986 and, in 1993, David Dingwall appeared to inherit the Liberal "MacEachen" tradition by becoming a strong Cape Breton representative in the Chrétien cabinet.

Party Leadership

Leadership has obviously been a major factor in Nova Scotia's politics, partly the result of the relative absence of ideological or societal cleavages.[19] Five party leaders (W.S. Fielding, G.H. Murray, Angus L. Macdonald, Robert Stanfield, and John Buchanan) served long terms as premier. In many cases, a father-figure relationship characterized their leaderships, perhaps a reflection of a deferential provincial political culture. Most were also strong defenders of provincial autonomy, and in this way were reacting to another aspect of the province's mentality. Macdonald and Stanfield shared many leadership qualities including intellectualism, pragmatism, paternalism, and elitism,[20] yet they also differed in many respects. Macdonald had risen from an impoverished background in his native Cape Breton, was of Catholic-Gaelic descent, and was an eloquent public speaker. Stanfield hailed from an affluent WASP Truro family and was publicly inarticulate. In spite of his lack of eloquence, Stanfield transformed the politics, and perhaps the economy, of the province. More recently, John Buchanan sailed through 12 years as premier as a populist and highly popular, if somewhat lightweight, leader. He was a consummate politician who knew how "to work a room." During that period, however, the province lost its position of policy leadership and gained an unsavoury reputation for patronage and corruption, and the premier eventually left office under a cloud of controversy. John Savage, a Welsh-born physician, took over at the age of 60. He presented the no-nonsense image of someone determined to take charge after the long period of lassitude under Buchanan. He was initially preoccupied with paring down the deficit and reforming the province's administrative apparatus. Although he had been Mayor of Dartmouth, he was new to provincial politics, and was seen as somewhat aloof, especially when compared to Buchanan.

Party leaders in Nova Scotia have normally been selected at traditional leadership conventions but, when the Liberals decided to replace Vince MacLean in 1992, they gave each party member the option of attending the convention in person (at a cost of $45) or voting via the telephone (for $25). Out of a membership of nearly 17,000, only 7,450 registered and the bulk chose to vote from home. A first in Canadian history, the computerized telephone voting system malfunctioned on the initial try. A second attempt two weeks later was successful, and Savage was chosen on the second ballot. If the more traditional convention method had been used the result might have been different, for seniors, neophytes, and Cape Bretoners would have been less likely to travel to Halifax. Moreover, it seems that one person abused the process by "buying" 232 personal identification numbers.[21]

The contemporary Liberals are very open about leadership review. In 1994, many disgruntled residents bought a $5 Liberal membership in order to vote against Savage at the party's fall convention. When over 2,000 unionized construction workers did so, party officials decided to cancel the meeting and reschedule the vote to June 1995. In contrast to the ultra-democratic Liberals, Terry Donahoe was chosen as leader by the Conservative caucus.

Party Ideology

The leading student of Nova Scotian politics, Murray Beck, was never able to detect any ideological differences between the Liberal and Conservative parties in the province.[22] Nova Scotia's traditional, conservative values have led both parties to be pragmatic and expedient, relying on patronage—which has often played a large part in road construction—and established family ties for success. Stanfield epitomized this pragmatic, non-ideological approach by using an activist government to encourage private investment. He was the quintessential "red Tory," not adverse to government intervention. Subsequent leaders have called for less government but, once in office, both Regan's Liberals and Buchanan's Tories steadily increased their scope and influence. Thus, no matter how one designates the Nova Scotia party system in terms of numbers, it is essentially non-polarized. The NDP has had mixed feelings about concentrating its attention on the working class, and limited success in extending the ideological range of public debate. Nevertheless, the NDP chips away at the traditional, non-ideological system, even though its leadership is now primarily composed of members of the middle class rather than the working class. Many writers have contributed to a class-based political economy interpretation of Nova Scotia, emphasizing the role of large corporations and their links to government, but this approach has not translated into popular acceptance or concern.

ELECTIONS

Electoral System

The only peculiarity of the early Nova Scotia electoral system was that it contained mostly two-member ridings and a handful with three, four, or five representatives. In such cases, parties usually found it advantageous to nominate both Catholic and Protestant candidates, at least in areas where the two religious groups were evenly divided. The multiple-member constituencies were mostly eliminated in 1933; the few remaining two-member ridings were abolished in 1981. Since the move to single-member constituencies, parties have sometimes informally agreed on which should have Catholic and Protestant candidates.

Representation by county and by population have been widely accepted. While rural areas have been over-represented, Nova Scotia has never had a serious problem with gerrymandering, even though redistribution was originally conducted by an assembly committee dominated by the government. Nova Scotia undertook its first independent redistribution of riding boundaries in 1992, under the guidance of a commission headed by political scientist Ronald Landes.[23] In designing constituency boundaries, the commission did not adopt a specific maximum variation from the provincial mean but, at the time of its work, 45 of the 52 ridings were within plus or minus 15 percent. In an effort to "encourage but not guarantee" minority representation in the legislature, three constituencies in Acadian areas were deliberately left smaller by population than the others. Similarly, the constituency of Preston was created in the area just outside Dartmouth, where the greatest concentration of black Nova Scotians lived. While it was impossible to make the riding small enough so that it contained a black majority, it was kept to about half the size of the provincial mean to encourage the election of a black representative. The commission was also mandated to establish an aboriginal (Mi'kmaq) seat, but had to report before the aboriginals, who have since demanded two seats, agreed on how to do so. In five cases, county boundaries had to be crossed to create equitably sized constituencies. The legislature retained the right to alter the commission's map, but accepted it virtually unchanged.

TABLE 4.6   Representational Disparities in the 1993 Election

Mean no. of voters per constituency	12,582
Largest constituency (Halifax Bedford Basin)	16,230 (+29% of mean)
Smallest constituency (Preston)	5,910 (-53% of mean)
Average variation from mean	13.2%
Constituencies within ± 10%	48.1%
Constituencies within ± 25%	88.5%
Constituencies beyond ± 50%	1.9%

Source: *Reports of the Chief Electoral Officer,* calculated by author.

Like other Atlantic provinces, the role of "treating" on election day was more pronounced in Nova Scotia than in the more "moral" provinces from Ontario to the West. The Liberals were embarrassed as recently as 1988, when five party workers were convicted of buying votes with cash and liquor, although no evidence of treating emerged in 1993. Nova Scotia was, however, a pioneer in election expenses legislation, with a law passed as early as 1969. The law included limits on party and candidate spending, a tax credit for contributions, and public reimbursement of some expenditures. But today Nova Scotia is behind most other provinces in that it neither limits the amount of contributions nor requires disclosure of the names of contributors, and abuses in these areas continue.

Voting Behaviour

In general, no great ethnic, religious, or class antagonisms have been evident in Nova Scotians' voting behaviour, as both the Liberals and Conservatives have tried to cater to all interests. Until 1956, Roman Catholics (whether of French, Irish, or Scottish descent) primarily supported the Liberals but, as noted, both parties ran Catholic candidates in Roman Catholic dominated areas. Liberals also received the bulk of the low income vote until 1956. The class dimension has been most evident on Cape Breton where, after 1938, working-class voters sometimes followed their unions' lead and supported CCF or NDP candidates. Two reasons have been suggested for the relative weakness of this support. First, most workers in the coal mines and steel mills have now become either federal or provincial public servants: "the heart of the industrial proletariat has also become one component of the public sector." Second, while many isolated strikes have occurred in the province, this "exceptional local level militancy [has been] coupled with a general absence of a wider trade union consciousness."[24] Since the split in the NDP in the early 1980s, the party has fared poorly in Cape Breton but better in urban middle-class "intellectual" Halifax ridings.

Prior to 1956, Nova Scotians exhibited a tendency to elect Liberals provincially and Conservatives federally. Whatever the cause of this phenomenon, such a balance has not applied since Stanfield and Diefenbaker transformed traditional provincial and federal voting patterns, and 1988 saw a rise in Liberal support at both levels. The strong family tradition of voting either Liberal or Conservative should also be noted, although this pattern was somewhat transformed by Stanfield, as he broadened the Conservative appeal to include Roman Catholics and the working class. It has also declined in the more sophisticated Halifax-Dartmouth region. After Stanfield's premiership, it became harder to detect any group preferences in voting behaviour, except perhaps the Acadian-Liberal connection, and a disposition of Cape Bretoners to vote Liberal while their rural counterparts on the mainland voted Conservative.

PRESSURE GROUPS AND THE MEDIA

Pressure Groups

Being a more diversified society than its neighbours, Nova Scotia possesses a wider range of pressure groups. Business pressure groups include the Nova Scotia division of the Canadian Manufacturers' Association, but corporations also lobby on their own and in industrial groups. The Nova Scotia fishing industry is fractured into many different organizations depending on species caught, location, and size of operations, and the distinction between employers and employees is not always clear. Such divisions have weakened the influence of the industry in dealing with federal and provincial governments. The Nova Scotia federations of agriculture and labour represent the respective interests of farmers and workers. On the professional front, the Medical Society of Nova Scotia, the Nova Scotia Dental Association, the Nova Scotia Teachers' Union and the Nova Scotia Nurses' Union are all active. Ethnic pressure groups include the Black United Front, the Fédération Acadienne de la Nouvelle Ecosse, and the Native Council of Nova Scotia. Municipalities and school boards also have their respective groups, and many others enter or exit the political arena as issues dictate.

The Media

In the coverage of Nova Scotia provincial politics, the independently owned *Halifax Chronicle-Herald* (formerly the *Halifax Herald*), has always been influential. The *Mail-Star* is a clone of the *Chronicle-Herald*, and they have a combined province-wide circulation of nearly 150,000. The independent *Daily News* serves the metropolitan Halifax area, while Thomson Newspaper Ltd.'s *Cape Breton Post* covers the eastern end of the province. A complete list of daily newspapers is provided in Table 4.8. The Canadian Broadcasting Corporation and CTV networks have television stations in Halifax. CBC radio operates out of Halifax and Sydney (with a French station in Halifax as well), and the usual array of private radio stations serve local areas of the province.

TABLE 4.7   Leading Nova Scotia Pressure Groups

Industrial	Chamber of Mineral Resources of Nova Scotia
	Seafood Producers of Nova Scotia
	Tourism Industry Association of Nova Scotia
	Nova Scotia Home Builders Association
	Nova Scotia Roadbuilders Association
	Construction Association of Nova Scotia
Labour	Nova Scotia Federation of Labour
	Nova Scotia Government Employees Union
Agriculture	Nova Scotia Federation of Agriculture
Professional	Medical Society of Nova Scotia
	Nova Scotia Dental Association
	Nova Scotia Teachers' Union
	Nova Scotia Nurses' Union
Ethnic	Fédération Acadienne de la Nouvelle Ecosse
	Native Council of Nova Scotia
	Black United Front
Institutional	Union of Nova Scotia Municipalities
	Nova Scotia School Boards Association
	Nova Scotia Association of Health Organizations
Environmental	Nova Scotia Environmental Alliance
Public Interest	People Against Casinos in Nova Scotia
	Nova Scotia Civil Liberties Association

TABLE 4.8   Daily Newspapers in Nova Scotia, 1994

	Circulation	Chain Affiliation
Halifax Chronicle-Herald	97,298	None
Halifax Mail-Star	50,437	None
Daily News	23,538	None
New Glasgow Evening News	11,162	Thomson Newspapers Ltd.
Sydney *Cape Breton Post*	31,968	Thomson Newspapers Ltd.
Truro Daily News	9,045	Thomson Newspapers Ltd.

Source: *Canadian Advertising Rates and Data* (August 1994).

GOVERNMENT INSTITUTIONS

Nova Scotia is historically famous as the place where the principle of responsible government was first recognized in 1848. Having established that principle, its political institutions have since functioned in an orthodox way.

Executive

As in other small-sized provinces, the lieutenant-governor is expected to engage in a substantial amount of entertaining, but has rarely used the discretionary power of vetoing or reserving bills. In fact, faced with long-serving premiers, lieutenant-governors have had little influence.[25]

In constructing their cabinets, premiers have had little difficulty balancing the different interests of the province's five regions. Some attention has also been given to Catholic representation, which usually results in the appointment of an Acadian to the cabinet. The province has never had difficulty maintaining cabinet solidarity, because a number of premiers have been in office so long they easily acquired dominance over cabinet colleagues.

Nova Scotia was rather slow to reform cabinet operations but, since the late 1970s, it has had a cabinet committee system. John Savage reduced the size of the cabinet to 17 members, after an historic high of 22 under John Buchanan. In 1994, his four cabinet committees were economic recovery, human resources, government services, and priority and planning (chaired by the minister of Finance). Support is provided by a partisan premier's office with a staff of 10 to 15, and the executive council office. The ECO, which handles cabinet documents, minutes, and briefings, is headed by the clerk, who is recognized as the chief bureaucrat. Attached to it are the intergovernmental affairs, youth, aboriginal affairs, and francophone affairs secretariats, as well as the priorities and planning secretariat of about 20 to 25 people who support the Priority and Planning committee of cabinet.

Legislature

Nova Scotia entered Confederation with a two-chamber legislature, a legislative council as well as a legislative assembly. In the context of a small province with financial difficulties and in an increasingly democratic age, the appointed council was generally seen as superfluous and anachronistic. For a variety of reasons, however, it was not abolished until 1928. The council was more or less ignored except in the rare instance of a Conservative victory in the assembly, when its Liberal majority became an effective check on the government. The council vetoed a bill providing for its abolition on more than one occasion, and attempted to stave off extinction by agreeing to a diminution of its powers in 1925 and a 10-year term for newly appointed members. Finally the judicial committee of the Privy Council ruled that the members of the Legislative Council served at the pleasure of the Crown and could therefore be removed by the government. It also asserted that there was no limit to the number of councillors who could be appointed. Armed with that newly discovered authority, the government ensured that the abolition bill would pass through a combination of appointments and dismissals. Since 1928, the province has had a unicameral legislature.[26]

The legislative chamber, the oldest and smallest in Canada, currently has 52 seats, having experienced a gradual expansion from 38 at the time of Confederation.[27] Quite often the government majorities in the legislature have been overwhelming, causing Opposition criticism to be rather ineffective.[28] Legislative sessions are often short, averaging 55 days per year, but the Savage government passed a law requiring two sittings annually and, at the same time, reforming the MLA pension plan. Members' allowances are among the lowest in the country (about $30,000 in indemnity and $15,000 in non-taxable allowance in 1994), and research and administrative support is scarce. Although some improvements have been made in recent years, the residual government dominance is surprising for the "leader" of the Atlantic provinces: the attorney general chairs the law amendments committee, which examines most public bills, and ministers routinely sit on or chair other legislative committees. The public accounts committee is chaired by an Opposition member, however, while the estimates are scrutinized in committee of the whole. This committee also considers bills after they go to the law amendments or private and local bills committee. Other committees include community services, human resources, economic development, resources, veterans affairs, and internal affairs, which is chaired by the premier.

Nova Scotia was the site of an unusual 1992-93 court case stemming from the Speaker's ruling that members of the news media could not use hand-held cameras in the galleries of the assembly. The media argued that this was a violation of their charter right guaranteeing freedom of the press, but the Supreme Court of Canada held that the Speaker had the right, on the basis of parliamentary privilege, to exclude persons if it was necessary for the assembly to proceed in an orderly and efficient fashion.[29] In the meantime, however, a video taping system was developed with the approval of the members.

Bureaucracy

Nova Scotia employs 11,600 people in regular government departments and agencies, another 7,000 in government business enterprises, and 19,000 more in the wider public sector. Although Nova Scotia adopted a civil service commission in 1935 to keep patronage out of the provincial bureaucracy, the agency did not function as intended. The widespread turnover of public servants which occurred whenever power changed hands did not decline until after the Second World War, and it took the Conservative victory of 1956 to ensure continuity of service within the bureaucracy. Thus the province had a rather weak public service until the 1960s, when an increased emphasis on planning, rationality, and the need to engage in sophisticated economic development analysis with the federal government required considerable improvement in the quality of public servants.[30] Since then parties have rewarded their friends in two ways: government appointments and contracts.[31] The province has a strong tradition of awarding government supporters with contracts for such things as road work and stocking the liquor stores.[32] As recently as 1988, Premier Buchanan stated publicly that, other things being equal, government posts would be awarded to friends of the government.[33] However, such unsavory practices eventually forced him from office in 1990. When John Savage took over in 1993, he sacked nine of 21 deputy ministers, but otherwise did not undertake mass firings. This restraint made him unpopular with many of his own Liberals, however, especially rural highway superintendents and foremen. Party pressure eventually forced him to lay off 160 highway supervisors hired by the Tories, and replace them through the civil service process. Savage created a human resources department to remove partisanship from public service hiring, and set out to "re-engineer" the whole structure of government. He established a system of management audits of departments to improve efficiency, effectiveness, and accountability. New buzzwords included "downsizing," "empowerment," and "privatization," and some former Conservative appointees lost their jobs as a result.

TABLE 4.9   Nova Scotia Government Departments, 1994

Agriculture and Marketing
Community Services
Economic Development and Tourism
Education
Environment
Finance
Fisheries
Health
Housing and Consumer Affairs
Human Resources
Justice
Labour
Municipal Affairs
Natural Resources
Supply and Services
Transportation and Communications

Regular departments are supplemented by an array of agencies, boards, commissions, and Crown corporations. The latter includes Nova Scotia Resources Ltd., the Tidal Power Corporation, and the Sydney Steel Corporation (SYSCO). Nova Scotia Power Corporation was privatized in 1992, and the province has had an ombudsman since 1971. Otherwise, Nova Scotia's agencies, boards, and commissions are typical of other provinces.

TABLE 4.10   Leading Nova Scotia Agencies, Boards, Commissions and Crown Corporations

Crown Corporations	Nova Scotia Liquor Corporation
	Nova Scotia Resources Ltd.
	Tidal Power Corporation
	Sydney Steel Corporation (SYSCO)
Agencies, Boards and Commissions	Farm Loan Board
	Fisheries Loan Board
	Nova Scotia Police Commission
	Nova Scotia Utility and Review Board
	Labour Relations Board
	Advisory Council on the Status of Women
	Human Resources Commission
	Liquor License Board
	Municipal Finance Corporation
	Workers' Compensation Board
	Residential Tenancies Board
	Nova Scotia Lottery Commission

Judiciary

The Nova Scotia judicial system consists of provincial courts, family courts, the Supreme Court, and the Court of Appeal. Nova Scotia was the last province to retain its intermediate county and district courts, but passed legislation to abolish them in 1992.

Municipal Government

Nova Scotia was slow to adopt municipal government because of the public's fear of increased taxation, but a fully developed system of local government now exists.[34] Of the 18 counties, 12 operate as rural municipalities, and the other six are each divided into two rural municipalities. In addition, there are 39 towns and three cities (Halifax, Dartmouth, and Sydney), which operate independently of the counties which surround them.

In 1971, the Graham Royal Commission on Education, Public Services, and Provincial-Municipal Relations was appointed. Its recommendations were so comprehensive that few direct results ensued, especially in relation to its main proposal that responsibility for all "general" services be shifted to the provincial government, leaving municipalities only with "local" service responsibilities. Some centralization occurred during the subsequent years, and a metropolitan structure for Halifax-Dartmouth was established with responsibilities restricted to transit and solid waste disposal.

With municipal government in desperate need of reform and pressure coming from the Union of Nova Scotia Municipalities, the government established a Task Force on Local Government in 1991. Its report the following recommended two types of reforms: structural and boundary changes at the local level, and changes in the division of responsibilities between the province and the municipalities. A one-tier regional government was the task force's preferred form of local government restructuring. It also recommended that most cost-shared programs be terminated and that the province take over full responsibility for social services, justice, and health, leaving municipalities with police and roads.

In 1993, the government established one-person municipal reform commissions for Industrial Cape Breton (Cape Breton County) and the Halifax Metropolitan Area (Halifax County). These both recommended one-tier regional governments, incorporating the proposed division of responsibilities. Later in the year, the new Savage government issued a discussion paper on the exchange of services between the province and municipalities, proposing the province take over welfare in exchange for municipalities assuming more responsibility for police and roads. The proposals were to be implemented in April 1995, leaving municipal government in Nova Scotia in the mid-1990s in a state of flux.

Major reforms of school administration were made previously, some linked to the Graham report. Legislation increased the provincial funding of local education costs. After 1978, the proportion of elected members of school boards increased until today they are all elected. In 1982, the 85 local school boards were replaced by 22 district school boards, with increased provincial funding. Unlike the situation in some provinces where school boards can dictate how much funding local municipalities must provide them, Nova Scotia's school boards are funded according to a provincially determined formula.

POLITICAL EVOLUTION

1867-1969[35]

Nova Scotia had a long and exciting history as a colony before Confederation, including the adoption of the principle of responsible government. In 1867, as in Newfoundland in 1949, a deep division of opinion developed about becoming part of Canada. In both cases, such conflict provided the foundation of the early party system; unlike Newfoundland, however, those Nova Scotians in favour of Confederation were Conservatives, while those opposed became Liberals. Also unlike Newfoundland, Nova Scotians did not have the opportunity to vote on the issue. By the time they elected an anti-Confederate government in November 1867, it was too late to stop union with Canada. Although the issue did not divide the parties for very long, periodic outbreaks of separatist sentiment continued; and it was partly this lingering resentment that was responsible for the almost continuous election of Liberal governments from 1867 to 1956.

The Liberals governed Nova Scotia for 43 consecutive years, 1882 to 1925, the longest period of continuous party rule in Canada.

The period immediately prior to Confederation had been one of great prosperity, dependent on reciprocity, shipbuilding, merchant marine, and lucrative customs duties. It was also a time in which the province was more or less in charge of its own affairs.[36] The brilliant orator, newspaper editor, and pre-Confederation premier, Joseph Howe, became the leader of the first post-Confederation regional protest. Howe immediately attempted to obtain "repeal" of Confederation from the British government but, when that failed, he sought "better terms" from Ottawa and even accepted a post in Prime Minister John A. Macdonald's federal cabinet. The Nova Scotia government gradually abandoned its anti-Confederate focus and label, and developed into the provincial wing of the national Liberal party.

Murray Beck explains the long Liberal domination in terms of favourable historical circumstances, good organization, and able leadership, factors of particular importance when differences in party philosophy were so slight.[37] Nova Scotia's first major post-Confederation premier, W.S. Fielding, was admired for such qualities as ability, integrity, a forceful personality, and an impressive speaking style, but his initial claim to fame was that he led the second secessionist movement in the province. In 1886 he threatened to secede if the federal government would not ameliorate the province's financial position.[38] When John A. Macdonald refused, Fielding introduced a repeal resolution which sought the British parliament's permission to withdraw from Confederation.

Fielding left for Ottawa in 1896 to take over as finance minister in the Laurier cabinet, the second Nova Scotia secessionist leader to become a federal cabinet minister. His successor, George Murray, served continuously for the next 27 years, the longest premiership in Canadian history. Murray was not particularly innovative, refusing any initiative that had not previously proved itself successful in Ontario. His longevity as premier could be attributed to certain agreeable personal traits and obvious political skills—affability, moderation, caution, and expediency—plus good organization, the adroit use of patronage, and the relatively low expectations people had of government at that time.

Given this long period of rather stagnant and uninspired leadership, the election of 11 Farmer-Labour candidates in 1920 is not surprising, especially considering that similar developments were occurring in many other provinces and at the federal level at about the same time. This radical protest was the result of dissatisfaction with the long-serving provincial Liberals, and the fact that provincial Conservatives were tainted with their federal Union Government connection, the latter being unpopular among labour and farmer groups for adopting conscription. It was also related to a period of general economic decline which affected farmers and workers in particular. Just as the protest parties were becoming established in 1919-20, however, Murray called an election, pre-empting the possibility of further advances. The Farmer and Labour members who were elected formed a coalition Opposition and forced the Conservatives into a position even more ignominious than usual. The two groups had difficulty working together, however, and the political side of both movements declined.[39]

Murray's retirement in 1923 set the stage for a second brief Conservative government in Nova Scotia after 1925. It took up the cause of "Maritime rights," the first time that cause had been embraced by the Conservatives.[40] Ably assisted by the *Halifax Herald*, the government demanded genuine financial concessions from Ottawa in taxation, trade, freight rates, and fisheries. A number of positive achievements characterized their first few years in office, including abolition of the legislative council, administrative reform, the establishment of teachers' pensions, and allowances for widowed mothers. Once again, however, the Conservatives had the misfortune of being in office during a depression, this time the Great Depression. The public was therefore inclined to believe the Liberal charge that the two phenomena, the election of the Conservatives and the Depression, coincided, and chose the Liberals again in 1933.

Thus began part one of the 16-year tenure of Angus L. Macdonald.[41] Part of Macdonald's success depended on his early policy initiatives: free school books, pavement of roads (with an eye on the tourist industry as well as local and political utility), proclamation of the old age pensions act, and passage of labour legislation. No less than four royal commissions—three federal and one provincial—examined the problems of federal-provincial financial relations in the 1920s and 1930s. Macdonald was credited with the province's growing post-Depression prosperity, and increasing revenues allowed him room for innovations; but the reverence in which he was held was mainly due to his personal attributes. Macdonald rose from humble Catholic Gaelic origins in Cape Breton to achieve international scholarly acclaim, and later lectured at the Dalhousie University Law School. He combined a poetic imagination with sound practicality and good judgment. Blessed with an engaging, magnetic personality in private, he was an impressive orator whose speeches revealed a fine literary touch. He was the idol of the newspapers, and his mastery of the new medium of radio added to his revered status.

After having been returned to office in 1937, an election in which the CCF entered the race for the first time, Macdonald took the unusual step of joining the federal Liberal wartime cabinet as Minister of National Defence for Naval Services, leaving the province in the hands of A.S. MacMillan. The latter was the opposite of Macdonald in many respects—uneducated, controversial, crude, and relatively old. He had been a successful Highways minister, however, during a period when road paving was a principal issue, and he was responsible for rural electrification. MacMillan led the party to victory in the 1941 election; and the CCF (having been endorsed by District 26 of the United Mine Workers in 1938), elected its first three members of the legislature. Macdonald returned to Nova Scotia in 1945, and was persuaded to become premier again, serving until his death in 1954.

In the 1945 election, the Liberals campaigned under the slogan "All's well with Angus L," and the Conservatives were shut out. The two-seat CCF formed the opposition although they had a smaller share of the popular vote than the Tories. Macdonald's popularity gradually declined in his second stint as premier, partly due to his growing conservativism, the loss of cabinet competence, and patronage problems in the Highways department.[42] Two of his last decisions were to build a bridge between Halifax and Dartmouth, a structure which now bears his name, and to link his native Cape Breton to the mainland with a causeway.

Macdonald was briefly succeeded as Liberal leader by a Catholic, Harold Connolly, but the party soon chose Protestant Henry Hicks, who had been one of Macdonald's most impressive ministers. Unfortunately, the convention which elected Hicks was split along religious lines and he had difficulty retaining the traditional Catholic Liberal vote. In the two years before the next election he improved the provincial educational system (at the expense of higher municipal taxes), and removed some of the patronage which had taken root in the government.[43]

Just after the Tory party had been annihilated by Macdonald in the election of 1945, Robert Stanfield was chosen to head its committee on policy and organization, and became party leader in 1948. Although part of the wealthy Truro underwear manufacturing family, he was a hard-working, unprepossessing sort who had excelled at Harvard, just as Macdonald before him. The party's prospects at that time could hardly have been bleaker but, in his methodical, plodding way, Stanfield gradually brought it back to life. Stanfield trekked tirelessly from one community to another, and provided a solid Opposition performance in the legislature, exposing scandal and calling for economic development. Dalton Camp began to advise him on strategy and personal deportment as early as 1953, and Tory prospects increased immeasurably with the death of Macdonald and the subsequent religious division within the Liberal party. The surprising Conservative victory in 1956 was very much engineered by Stanfield himself. He had established a strong party organization, emphasized policy with a series of position papers on several provincial issues, and promised to pave a lot of roads.

Stanfield initially assumed the Education and Provincial Treasurer portfolios as well as the premiership, and two of his early priorities were improving the education system and road construction.[44] He provided increased provincial funding, expedited the consolidation of rural primary schools, established comprehensive secondary schools, and extended French-language education to the end of Grade 12. Stanfield removed some of the worst aspects of party patronage in government appointments and contracts and, respecting the jurisdiction of the civil service commission, dismissed only the highly partisan employees who had been engaged in government road work.[45] During his tenure, the province entered the federal-provincial hospital insurance scheme and began to gear up for medicare, and established a human rights commission. Provincial grants increased under the politically compatible Diefenbaker regime, and Stanfield fought for more money when the federal Liberals returned to office in 1963.

Stanfield's main claim to fame, however, was in the field of economic development. He was determined to raise the province's standard of living and improve employment opportunities, convinced that, rather than simply relying on market forces, the government would be required to assume a more active role. Having improved the roads and the educational system, he sought to attract outside investment via Industrial Estates Ltd. (IEL). This agency, with Frank Sobey its first president, operated at arm's length from the government. Industrial Estates had much early success; some of its largest projects were a heavy water plant, a Clairtone Sound factory, Volvo and Toyota assembly plants in Dartmouth and Sydney respectively, and eventually three Michelin tire plants.[46] Another project was the National Sea Products plant in Lunenburg, exemplifying an expanding fishing industry which in turn stimulated the building of boats. Industrial Estates also brought in many smaller operations, offering cash grants for equipment, lease-back facilities, and other inducements. Stanfield was hailed as the founder of the "New Nova Scotia," and his every move was roundly applauded by the *Halifax Chronicle-Herald*.[47]

By 1967 Stanfield had led his Progressive Conservatives to four consecutive victories in the province. Stanfield had stressed policy positions in 1956 and had an increasingly successful record to emphasize in the subsequent campaigns. But, as with Angus L. Macdonald before him, it was to a large extent the Stanfield image that became the key to these electoral successes. It has been said that as time went on he converted "position" issues into "style" issues.[48] Although at first sight his image seemed rather negative—he appeared to be slow, inarticulate, and unphotogenic—other aspects of his style began to prevail. Of these, the most frequently mentioned were his honesty and integrity, his believability and dependability, and his slow, sober, astute, and unostentatious approach to government business. In his own way, in both word and action, Stanfield also revived Nova Scotians' self-respect.[49]

Immediately after the 1967 victory, a vacancy occurred in the federal Conservative leadership, and Stanfield was eventually persuaded to enter the race by Dalton Camp and others (sometimes referred to as the "Maritime Mafia"). After Stanfield's victory, G.I. "Ike" Smith, a fellow Truro lawyer who had been his close colleague for many years, took over the premiership and finished Stanfield's final term. Smith was probably a more able leader than he seemed, but was plagued with many problems which were not of his own making.

First, Dominion Steel and Coal (DOSCO), controlled by Hawker-Siddeley, announced in 1965 that it was about to close its Cape Breton coal mines. Since the federal government had been supporting the industry for many years, Ottawa decided in 1967 to nationalize the mines in a new Crown corporation, the Cape Breton Development Corporation (DEVCO).

The strategy it adopted was to phase out the mines over a 15-year period, although some might be rehabilitated in the meantime. The company was also mandated to attract new industry to the region to replace the closed mines. In the first few years of DEVCO's operation, mines were closed but little success was achieved in establishing alternative employment. Then, unexpectedly, the OPEC increase in the price of oil made coal more competitive as a generator of electricity, and new mines were opened.[50]

In 1967, DOSCO announced the imminent closure of another major enterprise, the Sydney Steel plant. In this case the industry was regarded as a provincial responsibility; thus, after much anguish, and in a move paralleling the federal nationalization of the coal mines, the Smith government decided to buy the steel mill, hoping for federal assistance. Although the first few years looked promising, the Sydney Steel Corporation (SYSCO) has been in deep trouble ever since, and has continued to be a major drain on both federal and provincial governments.

Whereas DEVCO enjoyed some long-term success and SYSCO some initial promise, two other projects were utterly disastrous: the Glace Bay Heavy Water plant and the Clairtone Sound operation at Stellarton.[51] These developments were attracted to the province by Industrial Estates in the mid-1960s when Stanfield was still premier, but it was not until the Smith regime that the problems associated with these projects reached scandalous proportions.

Clairtone had been established by Torontonian Peter Munk, and was expected to produce high-quality stereos and colour television sets. The company received much assistance from Industrial Estates Ltd. in addition to other federal, provincial, and municipal favours. Unfortunately, a series of problems—escalating production costs, cheaper imported competition, management and labour disagreements—eventually forced IEL to assume control of the company. Before long it closed Clairtone completely, at a total cost to the province of $20 million.

The Glace Bay operation was an even more expensive proposition. As Atomic Energy of Canada Ltd. needed heavy water for its Candu nuclear reactors, a "shrewd, smooth-talking" American, Jerome Spevack, set up a company, Deuterium of Canada Ltd. to provide it.[52] Intense pressure on the federal cabinet from Nova Scotia and its federal minister, Allan MacEachen, resulted in a government decision to locate the plant in Glace Bay, utilizing Cape Breton coal, but only on the condition that the company become Canadian. Thus the Nova Scotia government was forced to become the majority shareholder. The project underwent an even wider array of difficulties than the Clairtone plant, and required repeated refurbishing. Nova Scotia taxpayers contributed over $130 million to the project, to say nothing of later federal expenditures. Nevertheless, another heavy water plant was built in Port Hawkesbury by Canadian General Electric.

Premier Smith did have some successes. He made a favourable impression at a number of constitutional conferences, appointed the first Acadian to head a major government department (and the first Catholic minister of Education), enacted an innovative election expenses act, and strengthened human rights legislation after complaints from the Black community. Other developments, some of which were begun while Stanfield was premier, came to fruition, such as a government medical insurance program and the Michelin and Toyota plants. Smith's record of achievement was mixed, but not respectable enough to secure re-election.[53]

The 1970s

Following the 1970 election, the vigorous, tenacious, and loquacious Liberal leader, Gerald Regan, formed a minority Liberal government (with the two NDP seats constituting the balance of power). Before long, by-election victories provided him with a sufficient majority to carry on for a normal four-year term.[54]

Regan, though a Liberal, bore many similarities to Newfoundland's new Conservative premier, Frank Moores. They were both young, modern, technocratic, and businesslike. Regan engaged in similar modernization and reform efforts, especially within the government itself. The new premier restructured departments, created new Departments of Development and the Environment, appointed an ombudsman, and established the Graham royal commission on municipal government.

Energy was a pivotal issue, especially because the province's electricity was produced mostly from increasingly expensive imported oil, and the new government took several initiatives in this area. Regan spoke glowingly of developing offshore oil and natural gas on Sable Island, initiated exploration there, and promoted the development of Fundy tidal power. In a particularly ambitious vein, the Regan government embarked on the creation of a single public power system in the province. To this end, the Nova Scotia Power Commission took over the privately owned Nova Scotia Light and Power Company, and the new entity was renamed the Nova Scotia Power Corporation. Nevertheless, electricity costs rose several times—with one increase alone of 56 percent.

Other problems facing the Regan government were rising unemployment, inflation, and frequent labour disputes in the public sector. More of the earlier Conservative economic development projects, such as the Toyota assembly plant, collapsed. The federal government loaned $75 million to Atomic Energy of Canada Ltd. to rehabilitate the Glace Bay heavy water plant, which had been sitting idle and rusting for some time. The plant eventually passed from provincial to federal ownership.

On the positive side, the government provided free drugs for old age pensioners and free dental care for some school children, established an advisory council on the status of women, and formulated the country's first freedom of information act. It also streamlined rules in the legislature, introduced collective bargaining for fishermen and public servants, and redistributed legislative seats.

Federal money helped out in some cases, such as DREE (Department of Regional Economic Expansion) grants for tourism and forestry.

On the other side of the House, the leadership of the Conservative party changed hands in 1971 when the 38-year-old former Minister of Fisheries and Public Works, John Buchanan, succeeded the ailing Ike Smith. Buchanan immediately set to work to rebuild the Conservative party although, over the next several years, recurrent doubts were expressed about his abilities. He continued as Tory leader even after he lost the 1974 election, gradually gaining the favourable image of a man who had come out of the Cape Breton steel mills and retained some feeling for the "little people." By 1978, for a number of reasons, Nova Scotians were willing to give him a chance to govern. They suffered from high energy costs and a poor economy; they were upset at the temporary closure of the Halifax shipyard and the interminable difficulties at SYSCO (Sydney Steel Co.); they were dissatisfied with the response of the federal Liberal government to their repeated pleas for assistance; and they were fed up with the Regan government's unfulfilled promises of prosperity. Voters no doubt also responded to Buchanan's commitment to freeze power rates and taxes for four years. After leading the Opposition for two years, Regan returned to federal politics, and was rewarded with a seat in the Trudeau cabinet.

The 1980s

The 1980s began with both the Liberals and NDP changing leaders. The Liberals chose the former Development minister, Sandy Cameron. The NDP selected Alexa McDonough, who became one of the country's first female party leaders. McDonough's father, Lloyd Shaw, was a long-time back-room powerhouse in the party, and she was a social worker. About this time, a bizarre division erupted in the NDP—a conflict resulting in the expulsion from the caucus and the party of a Cape Breton MLA, Paul MacEwan. Four factors apparently combined to create internecine turmoil: MacEwan's peculiar personality; a division of opinion on the relationship between the caucus and the party organization; a geographic problem, with the caucus all coming from Cape Breton and the party hierarchy largely resident in Halifax; and an ideological split with the Cape Breton members focusing on the working class and the mainland members trying to broaden the party's appeal to the middle class.[55] MacEwan first sat as an Independent, went on to establish a Cape Breton Labour Party, and later served as a Liberal, ending up as Speaker of the Assembly.

Among the items on Buchanan's agenda, the Sydney Steel Corporation continued to be a major headache. After much federal-provincial argument, an agreement on a revitalization plan was announced in 1981. Another controversial issue was the "Michelin Tire" bill. This Buchanan initiative, brought forward in anticipation of the construction of a third Michelin tire plant, required unions to organize in all of the operations of such a company, rather than just one, effectively guaranteeing no union in the new plant. Then, after 100 years of debate and with federal assistance, a start was made on the Annapolis Tidal Project. As the prospects for offshore petroleum increased, Buchanan created Nova Scotia Resources Ltd., a Crown corporation which could act in partnership with other firms in any such developments.

In the 1981 election, the Liberals sunk to their lowest level ever. The NDP increased its popular vote and elected its new leader in Halifax, won its first seat on the mainland, but it lost its two remaining Cape Breton seats. Paul MacEwan split the working-class vote on the island, but managed to retain his own seat.

Over the next three years, Buchanan achieved several successes. First, he negotiated an agreement with the federal government on offshore development. The complex document, signed in March 1982, essentially provided that the two governments set aside the ownership issue and establish a joint development board on which Ottawa had a majority; Nova Scotia would receive the maximum federal aid available to provinces until it became a "have" province, and received an advance of $200 million for the development of new facilities.[56] This package, which Brian Peckford found unacceptable to Newfoundland, sparked much exploration around Sable Island. Second, renewed federal interest in the fishing industry, coupled with increased funding for facilities, sparked new hope for that sector of the economy. In the wake of the Kirby report, *Navigating Troubled Waters,* the Nova Scotia fishery was reorganized in a manner somewhat similar to that which had occurred in Newfoundland. In this case, National Sea Products Ltd. (NSP) became the dominant firm. The federal and provincial governments each bought some preferred shares, but the company remained in private hands.

On the other hand, Buchanan faced a number of problems. SYSCO suffered from strikes, shutdowns, and charges of air pollution, but then won a temporary reprieve with a large order of CN rails. The province's dispute with the United States over the international boundary in the area of the rich Georges Bank fishing ground was referred to the International Court of Justice. Its 1984 decision awarded most of the territory in question to the U.S., but Nova Scotia retained ownership of some of the more lucrative scallop grounds.[57] A strange new problem was that, after difficult beginnings, the two heavy water plants on Cape Breton were now producing surplus heavy water, given the poor sales of Candu reactors. As long as Allan MacEachen was in the federal cabinet, however, Ottawa continued to maintain the plants by stockpiling their output, although the Trudeau government did Nova Scotia no favour by moving the headquarters of the naval reserve from Halifax to Quebec City. Serious subterranean pressure problems developed in the offshore Venture gas project, and increasing doubts were expressed about the commercial viability of the field. Meanwhile, power rates continued to rise dramatically.

Nevertheless, the Buchanan government maintained its popularity, while the Liberals were troubled by the conviction of two party officials, including a senator, for conspiring to peddle influence during the Regan regime. In the wake of the Mulroney landslide victory, Buchanan called another election for November 1984, after only a three-year interval. Having defended his offshore agreement with the Trudeau Liberals, Buchanan now claimed to require a new mandate to negotiate a better deal with the Mulroney government. Buchanan used a media blitz approach, campaigning on the basis of optimism and leadership, puzzling observers with his remark that "elections should not be fought on issues." The Liberals' message was overshadowed by Sandy Cameron's charges that the attorney general had halted an RCMP investigation of alleged expense account irregularities on the part of two ministers and one Tory backbencher. Under the articulate Alexa McDonough, the NDP tried to champion the average Nova Scotian looking for a fairer deal, and criticized the government's social service cutbacks. In the end, Cameron suffered from an image problem, especially in urban areas, and lost his seat. The NDP gained two new mainland seats, for a total of three, did quite well in urban areas, but lost support in Cape Breton.

Following the election, Nova Scotia's economy remained somewhat troubled. An explosion in the Mobil Oil underwater Venture gas well caused much difficulty, and even after the hole was plugged the well's quality of gas was of questionable commercial value. The phasing out of the federal Petroleum Incentive Program (PIP) grants and the exodus of drilling rigs at the end of 1985 made the future of the industry unpredictable. And all was bleak in Glace Bay. In addition to a mine fire, the Highland Fisheries plant burned down and, in the 1985 budget, the federal government announced the closure of the two Cape Breton heavy water plants. SYSCO, the area's other major source of employment, was also suffering a lack of orders. These factors combined to raise the local unemployment rate to over 50 percent. In response to these many problems, the federal government established Enterprise Cape Breton in an attempt to lure outside entrepreneurs to the island with even sweeter incentives than usual. At least at first, the response seemed fairly positive. The modernization program for the Sydney Steel Corporation, first announced in 1981, was re-announced in 1987, when Ottawa and the province agreed to provide another $150 million for an electric arc furnace. This new technology, implemented in 1989, would allow SYSCO to continue operations, but with a severely reduced work force. It was also designed to reduce the health hazards associated with the older coke ovens.

In other economic developments in the late 1980s, the Litton plant which P.E.I. rejected was constructed near Halifax with a $5.8 million provincial loan, and National Sea Products enjoyed a profitable period until 1988. Michelin Tire promised to modernize its three plants, with federal and provincial government assistance, and to add 600 jobs. On the other hand, the Annapolis River tidal power station was not expanded, primarily because of fear of environmental damage and the decline in the international price for oil. This low price was also the main reason drilling for gas or oil off Nova Scotia was virtually abandoned.

After three attempts, Bob White announced that the Canadian Auto Workers were giving up trying to unionize the workers at Michelin Tire. He did take credit, however, for forcing the company to improve wages, pensions, and work hours in order to pre-empt the union's membership drive.

On the political side, this period was plagued by government scandal. Culture and Recreation Minister Billy Joe MacLean was convicted of forging ministerial expense account claims. When he refused to resign, a bill was passed to expel him from the legislature, but he ran as an Independent in a by-election to succeed himself and was re-elected. Backbencher Greg MacIsaac was convicted of similar fraud charges and sentenced to jail. Edmund Morris, the social services minister, was convicted of violating the Freedom of Information Act after he retaliated against a critical client by making public details of the woman's confidential social services file. Deputy Premier Roland Thornhill resigned after it was revealed that four banks had agreed to write off some $140,000 in personal loans in 1980 and after allegations that the attorney general's department had interfered with an RCMP criminal investigation into the matter. In 1988, however, he returned to the cabinet. Next, a former law partner of the premier, Ralph Medjuck, was awarded an untendered $48-million contract to lease office space to the government. These scandals emerged against the backdrop of the Marshall inquiry. Donald Marshall, a Micmac Indian, was convicted of murder and served nearly 11 years in jail for a crime he did not commit. The inquiry's hearings and its 1990 report revealed that, far beyond the Marshall case, incompetence, racism, and coverups pervaded the province's police forces and its judicial system, and the actions of almost every attorney general since 1970 were questioned. In the 1989-90 period, Buchanan's government repeatedly fought against Dr. Henry Morgentaler's attempts to establish an abortion clinic in the province, but the latter was ultimately successful in the courts.

Despite his practice of going to the polls every three years, Buchanan waited a full four years before he set the next provincial election for September 1988. His government's scandals had made any earlier date inopportune; indeed, the election took place during a recess in the Marshall inquiry. No one expected an easy Conservative victory, although Buchanan was called "Teflon John" because he retained his enormous personal popularity regardless of the unsavory behaviour surrounding him. This charming, folksy style, as well as a relatively buoyant economy on the mainland, were his main assets. Not surprisingly, Buchanan unveiled an ethics package in the middle of the campaign. The Tory slogan, "The Issue is Leadership," exploited Buchanan's popularity in contrast to that of the new Liberal leader, Vince MacLean. The election resulted in a fourth straight victory for Buchanan's Tories, but with a reduced majority.

The biggest issue in Nova Scotia after the election was the fishing industry's dramatic decline, which resulted in many plant closures and layoffs. This was primarily due to two factors: the federal government's restriction of catches due to the shortage of fish, and a strong Canadian dollar which increased the price of exports. The first two major shutdowns were the Clearwater Fine Foods plant in Port Mouton and the NSP plant in Lockeport. Later, NSP announced production would also be reduced or curtailed at other plants, then sold its Canso plant to Seafreez Foods, which would catch capelin to sell to the Soviet Union. The company also planned to diversify its production to include microwaveable chicken and fishburgers.

The 1990s

The early 1990s witnessed the collapse of the Buchanan Conservatives, the election of the Liberals in spite of their leadership crisis, and a period of grim economic news. For example, the province proposed a $436-million coal-fired electrical power plant at Point Aconi on Cape Breton, but ran into a wall of environmental protest. When Ottawa refused to participate in an environmental assessment of the project, the province forged ahead, ignoring claims the plant would cause air and water pollution, endanger wildlife, and cause other disruptions. The 1990 budget raised almost every tax in the province while cutting such services as education.

In the wake of the Royal Commission on the Donald Marshall Jr. Prosecution, the province made a formal apology to the wrongly convicted Donald Marshall and granted him and his family $700,000 compensation. The inquiry also prompted the police to reopen the Roland Thornhill case and Attorney General Tom McInnis to clean up his department. Then the premier himself fell into disrepute. Former Deputy Minister of Government Services Michael Zareski testified before the public accounts committee that Buchanan had interfered in department operations to the benefit of the premier's friends. Zareski accused him of dispensing coveted office leases to Ralph Medjuck, purchasing $50,000 worth of electronic toilet-seat-cover dispensers from another friend, and granting at least $50,000 to confidant Mark Cleary as a surcharge for restoration work on the legislative building. The premier may also have received unauthorized benefits from the public purse. The RCMP announced it would investigate these allegations, and Health Minister David Nantes later resigned after trying to discredit Zareski by releasing confidential medical information. The accumulation of such charges forced the popular and previously untainted John Buchanan to resign as premier in mid-1990, accepting a seat in the Senate as a reward for his faithful service to the prime minister. Housing Minister Roger Bacon was sworn in temporarily as Buchanan's successor, and a traditional Conservative leadership convention in February 1991 chose Industry Minister Donald Cameron to pick up the pieces.

By most accounts, the popular Cameron performed well during his two-year term as premier, beginning to bring order out of the chaos he had inherited. To distance himself from the Buchanan years, Cameron sold the cars and airplane which had been at the premier's disposal, trimmed the cabinet from 22 to 17, and consolidated several departments. He then brought in a wide-ranging reform package which included conflict of interest and party finance legislation, an independent redistribution of constituency boundaries, and reform of the Human Rights Act by adding sexual orientation as a grounds for discrimination. With its tough approach to the government deficit, his 1991 budget broke collective agreements by freezing public sector wages for two years, and eliminated 300 government jobs. Given the fragile Tory majority in the Assembly, the budget passed only with the Speaker's vote. The 1992 budget was chiefly concerned with tax breaks for business. Cameron also announced that the government planned to sell two Crown corporations, Nova Scotia Power Corporation and SYSCO, although only the former was privatized at the time. After the collapse of the Meech Lake Accord, Cameron appointed a committee headed by recent arrival, Eric Kierans, to advise on constitutional reform.

Although Cameron was establishing a clean-cut image and was raising Conservative standings in the polls, two 1992 developments eclipsed his efforts. First, more revelations surfaced about his predecessor's finances. While the conflict of interest commissioner dismissed charges against Buchanan on a technicality, and the RCMP dropped criminal charges for lack of conclusive evidence, two of Buchanan's friends were charged as a result of the Zareski allegations. Moreover, it became clear that Buchanan had received about $1 million from various party trust funds while he was premier—about $300,000 to pay off debts, and about $40,000 annually to augment his $97,000 salary.[58]

Second, Cameron's reputation was damaged by his involvement in the Westray coal mine affair. On May 9, 1992, 26 miners died when they were trapped underground by a coal dust explosion triggered by a methane gas fire. The $140-million mine, owned by Curragh Inc. of Toronto and located in Cameron's constituency, had been funded by a $12-million loan from the province and an $85-million loan guarantee from Ottawa. Curragh had made generous contributions to both federal and provincial Conservative parties, had hired professional lobbyists in Ottawa, and had both Buchanan and Cameron seek the support of the federal Conservative government on its behalf. When the mine had to be abandoned (with 11 bodies unrecovered), the cost to the taxpayers was almost $100 million.[59] Blame was laid on inadequate mine inspections by provincial officials as well as the company's numerous violations of safety regulations. Charges of manslaughter and criminal negligence causing death were eventually laid against the owner and two senior managers, but dismissed on a technicality. The government also set up a judicial inquiry into the accident, but this was derailed on the constitutional grounds that such an inquiry might jeopardize the defendants' rights in a criminal trial.

Meanwhile, the Liberals had problems of their own. Vince MacLean, the Cape Breton teacher who never managed to win the confidence of the party elite in Halifax, was found to be receiving some $46,000 annually from Liberal party trust funds to supplement his salary. Moreover, some of these funds had

originally been raised during the Regan regime by "toll-gating" liquor companies, contributing funds to the party in power in return for having its brands
sold in government liquor stores. MacLean survived a Liberal party leadership
review in February 1992 with only 52 percent of the vote. Then, facing a caucus
revolt, he resigned.[60]

The Liberals decided on a precedent-setting method of choosing their new
leader, the "televote." After a telephone vote on June 6, 1992, was aborted
because of a Maritime Telegraph and Telephone technological breakdown, two
weeks later the contest came down to a second ballot between Dartmouth
mayor John Savage and farmer Donald Downe, neither members of the
Assembly. Savage was the victor and soon worked his party back to a lead in the
polls, and then to power, when Cameron finally called the election for May 25,
1993. Although he retained his seat, Cameron immediately resigned from it and
from the party leadership. The Tory caucus chose Terry Donahoe as leader of the
Opposition.

Savage's new cabinet included the first Black elected to the Assembly,
Wayne Adams from Preston. Bernie Boudreau, who had led calls for an inquiry
into the Westray mine disaster, became minister of Finance. The 1993 budget
concentrated on the fact that the deficit and provincial debt were much larger
than forecast. Savage broke his election promise not to raise taxes, increased the
sales tax to 11 percent and introduced a surtax on higher incomes. Public servants were encouraged to take early retirement and forced to take five days off
without pay (equal to a two-percent salary rollback), leading to protests outside
the legislature. In spite of such measures, Moody's Bond Rating Service downgraded the province's credit rating. A "Blueprint For Recovery," a four-year plan
to improve the fiscal situation of the province, accompanied the budget, singling
out health and education for major cuts.

Once again, in the 1994 budget, the government curbed public sector wages
with a three-percent wage roll-back and a three-year salary freeze (for those
earning over $25,000). Led by the teachers, public sector unions formed the
Coalition for Fair Collective Bargaining and threatened a province-wide strike.
But when the Nova Scotia Government Employees Union voted against an illegal walkout, the idea fizzled and parties returned to the bargaining table.
Teachers ultimately voted to accept the contract, including its early retirement
package, because without it even more of them would have lost their jobs.
Nurses were particularly upset about the elimination of hundreds of beds and
sometimes entire rural hospitals. In total, over 700 jobs were eliminated in the
public services, while doctors' fees and salaries were rolled back. A document
tabled with the 1994 budget outlined how the government planned to achieve
fiscal recovery and economic renewal through expenditure control. A three-percent reduction in net program spending in 1994-95 and 1995-96 and two percent in each of the following two years would turn the current account deficit
into a current account surplus. On the other hand, certain business taxes were
lifted, and the government planned to increase its revenues with two casinos,

one in Halifax and one in Sydney. This suggestion, however, aroused much public opposition.

TABLE 4.11   Government of Nova Scotia Finances, 1990/91–1994/95 (millions)

	1990/91	1991/92	1992/93	1993/94	1994/95
Total revenues	$4,310.2	$4,336.9	$4,417.9	$4,439.9	$4,542.0
Debt charges	756.0	805.6	873.5	939.7	1,018.3
Total expenditures	4,617.1	4,860.4	4,988.1	5,074.1	5,196.5
Deficit	306.9	523.5	570.2	634.2	654.5

Source: Reproduced by authority of the Minister of Industry, 1995, Statistics Canada, *Public Sector Finance, 1994–95*, Financial Management System, cat. no. 68-212 (March 1995). Adapted by author.

Other early concerns of the Savage government included anti-smoking and revised freedom of information legislation, and the controversial "Steen" bill dealing with sensitive labour issues. The government prohibited the sale of tobacco in vending machines and to persons under 19 years of age, but it was reluctantly forced to lower cigarette taxes due to federal anti-smuggling initiatives and related action in New Brunswick. The Steen bill reversed a court decision and forced union and non-union labour to work at the same construction site. It prompted much protest, especially when 400 unionists stormed the legislature in April 1994, punched the premier, and forced the session to close just as the budget was about to be read. The angry unionized construction workers vowed to join the Liberal party so they could vote against Savage's leadership but, as noted earlier, when about 2,000 did so, the leadership review was postponed. The premier's popularity among party members otherwise increased when he loosened his stand on patronage appointments. Savage dealt with aboriginals on a nation-to-nation basis, introduced new metropolitan governments in Halifax-Dartmouth and Sydney, and reformed the provincial-municipal division of responsibilities. Environmental and workers' compensation legislation were slated for review, and Nova Scotians anticipated some degree of consolidation among their many universities. As in several other provinces, the government also undertook a radical reform of the health care system. Legislation created four regional health boards to determine the number and type of hospitals needed in each region and the method of paying doctors. These boards supervised community health boards, which emphasized prevention and community health centres in place of expensive acute-care hospitals. By mid-1994, the closure of three rural hospitals was announced and services reduced at 29 others.

Other grim economic news in the mid-1990s included tighter federal fishing quotas and a revised income assistance plan, Ottawa's decision to close armed forces bases, including Cornwallis in the Annapolis Valley, and Ultramar's decision to sell its oil refinery despite earlier promises to keep it open until 1997. The provincial government decided it would be too costly to reopen the Westray mine, but looked for a developer for the nearby strip mine. The $387-million cleanup of Halifax harbour was stalled because the three levels of government could not find sufficient money.

On the other hand, the government found $15.4 million to keep the Stora Forest Industries pulp mill alive in Port Hawkesbury, and Halifax-Dartmouth Industries remained afloat, along with its contract to build 12 navy minesweepers, when bought by Irving Shipbuilding of New Brunswick. Although the Sydney steel plant suffered a fire and explosion, it appeared that Chinese interests were prepared to buy it. By this time SYSCO operated with state-of-the art technology, but had difficulty selling to the U.S. market. The U.S. put tariffs on such imports because it felt Canadian prices were artificially low due to government subsidies. The Chinese market was welcome, unless the new owners' intention was to dismantle the plant and take it to Asia. Another encouraging sign was that David Dingwall, Nova Scotia's representative in the federal cabinet, was delivering "Dingwall Dollars" in a manner reminiscent of Allan MacEachen. He may, however, have gone too far when he diverted funds from improving the Trans-Canada highway to a road in his own constituency.

In 1995, the Minister of Finance predicted a balanced budget by 1997-98, contingent on further spending cuts, especially in health care. The 1995 budget provided modest tax breaks for business, imposed a premium of about $200 for the provincial prescription drug plan, and contained a list of 71 public ventures that the government hoped to privatize.

CONCLUSION

While a Conservative government was entrenched between 1978 and 1993, Premier John Buchanan ultimately resigned in disrepute, unlike such highly respected longtime premiers as Angus L. Macdonald and Robert Stanfield. Problems in the fishing industry and Cape Breton continue to require inspired leadership on the part of both Halifax and Ottawa. But, in spite of these and other difficulties, a dynamic new government is determined to turn around the desperate public finances of the province and return Nova Scotia to a position of regional leadership.

TABLE 4.12　Nova Scotia Provincial Election Results Since 1920

Year	Liberals		Conservatives		CCF/NDP		Other	
	Seats	Popular Vote	Seats	Popular Vote	Seats	Popular Vote	Seats	Popular Vote
1920	29	44%	3	23%			11	31%*
1925	3	36%	40	61%				
1928	20	48%	23	51%				
1933	22	53%	8	46%				
1937	25	53%	5	46%				
1941	23	53%	4	40%	3	7%		
1945	28	53%	0	34%	2	14%		
1949	28	51%	7	39%	2	10%		
1953	23	49%	12	43%	2	7%		
1956	18	48%	24	49%	1	3%		
1960	15	43%	27	48%	1	9%		
1963	4	40%	39	56%	0	4%		
1967	6	42%	40	53%	0	5%		
1970	24	46%	20	47%	2	7%		
1974	31	48%	12	39%	3	13%		
1978	17	38%	31	46%	4	15%		
1981	13	31%	37	47%	1	18%	1	4%**
1984	6	31%	42	51%	3	16%	1	2%**
1988	21	40%	28	43%	2	16%	1	1%**
1993	40	49%	9	31%	3	18%	—	2%

*Farmer-Labour
**Cape Breton Labour Party

TABLE 4.13　Premiers of Nova Scotia Since 1867

Premier	Party	Year Elected
Hiram Blanchard	Confederate (Conservative)	1867
William Annand	Anti-Confederate (Liberal)	1867
P.C. Hill	Liberal	1875
S.D. Holmes	Conservative	1878
J.S.D. Thompson	Conservative	1882
W.T. Pipes	Liberal	1882
W.S. Fielding	Liberal	1884
G.H. Murray	Liberal	1896
E.H. Armstrong	Liberal	1923
E.N. Rhodes	Conservative	1925
C.S. Harrington	Conservative	1930
Angus L. Macdonald	Liberal	1933
A.S. MacMillan	Liberal	1940

TABLE 4.13 continued

Premier	Party	Year Elected
Angus L. Macdonald	Liberal	1945
Harold Connolly	Liberal	1954
Henry Hicks	Liberal	1954
Robert Stanfield	Conservative	1956
G.I. Smith	Conservative	1967
Gerald Regan	Liberal	1970
John Buchanan	Conservative	1978
Roger Bacon	Conservative	1990
Donald Cameron	Conservative	1991
John Savage	Liberal	1993

ENDNOTES

1. Just as Frank MacKinnon has been the leading authority on P.E.I. for a generation, J. Murray Beck has been the standard source on Nova Scotia. Both *The Government of Nova Scotia* (Toronto: University of Toronto Press, 1957) and his article "Nova Scotia, Tradition and Conservatism," in Martin Robin, ed., *Canadian Provincial Politics* (Scarborough: Prentice Hall Canada, 1978), emphasize the conservative, traditional nature of Nova Scotian politics.

2. Julia McMahon, "The New Forest in Nova Scotia," and Aaron Schneider, "Underdeveloping Nova Scotia's Forests and the Role of Corporate Counter-Intelligence," both in Gary Burrill and Ian McKay, eds., *People, Resources, and Power* (Fredericton: Acadiensis Press, 1987).

3. Peter C. Newman, *The Canadian Establishment* (Toronto: Seal Books, [Rev. ed.] 1979), pp. 234-241; *Debrett's Illustrated Guide to the Canadian Establishment* (Toronto: Methuen, 1983). See also Eleanor O'Donnell, "Leading the Way: An Unauthorized Guide to the Sobeys Empire," in Burrill and McKay, eds., *People, Resources, and Power.*

4. L. Gene Barrett, "Underdevelopment and Social Movements in the Nova Scotia Fishing Industry to 1938," and R.J. Sacouman, "Underdevelopment and the Structural Origins of Antigonish Movement Co-operatives in Eastern Nova Scotia," both in Brym and Sacouman, *Underdevelopment and Social Movements in Atlantic Canada* (Toronto: New Hogtown Press, 1979); Gene Barrett, "The State and Capital in the Fishing Industry: the Case of Nova Scotia," Canadian Political Science Association (May 1981); Anthony Thomson, "Nova Scotia Labour in the 1980s: Response to the Crisis," Canadian Political Science Association (June 1984); and Burrill and McKay, eds., *People, Resources, and Power* are some of such class-based analyses.

5. Rick Williams, "Inshore Fishermen, Unionisation, and the Struggle against Underdevelopment Today," in Brym and Sacouman, *Underdevelopment and Social Movements in Atlantic Canada*, p. 173.

6. Harley d'Entremont, "Acadians and Local Political Power in Nova Scotia," Canadian Political Science Association (June 1983).

7. Beck, *The Government of Nova Scotia*, p. 254.

8. See the discussion below on the heavy water plant at Glace Bay and the Clairtone Sound fiasco.

9. Beck asserts that most elections have hinged on the management of the day-to-day business of government, "Nova Scotia," in Robin, ed., *Canadian Provincial Politics*, p. 175; on the absence of cleavages, p. 200.

10. James P. Bickerton, *Nova Scotia, Ottawa, and the Politics of Regional Development* (Toronto: University of Toronto Press, 1990).

11. G.A. Rawlyk, "Nova Scotia Regional Protest, 1867-1967," in *Queen's Quarterly* (Spring 1968), pp. 105-108.

12. Beck, *The Government of Nova Scotia*, p. 327.

13. *Ibid.*, p. 342; G.A. Rawlyk and Mary-Pat MacKinnon, "The Nova Scotia Elite," in G.A. Rawlyk, ed., *The Atlantic Provinces and the Problems of Confederation* (Halifax: Breakwater Press, 1979), pp. 347-352.

14. David Bellamy, "The Atlantic Provinces," in David Bellamy et al., eds., *The Provincial Political Systems* (Toronto: Methuen, 1976); Beck, "Nova Scotia," in Robin, ed., *Canadian Provincial Politics*, p. 180.

15. Beck, "Nova Scotia," in Robin, ed., *Canadian Provincial Politics*, p. 200; Peter Aucoin, "The Stanfield Era: A Political Analysis," *Dalhousie Review* (Autumn 1967), p. 408.

16. Jeffrey Simpson, *Spoils of Power* (Toronto: Collins, 1988). See also Stephen Tomblin "Assessing the Politics of Reform in Nova Scotia and New Brunswick," Canadian Political Science Association (May 1990).

17. Marsha Chandler and William Chandler, *Public Policy and Provincial Politics* (Toronto: McGraw-Hill Ryerson, 1979), pp. 77-83. This view is not shared by Richard Simeon and David Elkins, "Provincial Political Cultures in Canada," in Elkins and Simeon, eds., *Small Worlds: Provinces and Parties in Canadian Political Life* (Toronto: Methuen, 1980), ch. 2.

18. Joseph Wearing, *The L-Shaped Party: The Liberal Party of Canada, 1958-1980* (Toronto: McGraw-Hill Ryerson, 1981), pp. 93-95.

19. Jennifer Smith, "Ruling Small Worlds: Political Leadership in Atlantic Canada," in Leslie Pal and David Taras, eds., *Prime Ministers and Premiers* (Scarborough: Prentice Hall Canada, 1988).

20. Geoffrey Stevens, *Stanfield* (Toronto: McClelland and Stewart, 1973), p. 101.

21. Bill Cross, "Direct Election of Party Leaders: Provincial Experiences and Lessons Learned," Canadian Political Science Association (1994).

22. Beck, *The Government of Nova Scotia*, pp. 156-157, and "Nova Scotia," in Robin, ed., *Canadian Provincial Politics*, pp. 179-180. Beck makes the point that they not only failed to maintain consistently different positions on ideological issues, but actually exchanged positions without apology. On the other hand, Stevens argues in *Stanfield* that Stanfield was more progressive than Macdonald.

23. Provincial Electoral Boundaries Commission, *Effective Political Representation in Nova Scotia* (Halifax, March 1992).

24. Anthony Thomson, "Nova Scotia Labour in the 1980s: Response to the Crisis," Canadian Political Science Association (June 1984), p. 24.

25. Beck, *The Government of Nova Scotia,* p. 179. Early in the province's history there were six vetoes by the lieutenant-governor, but none in recent times.

26. *Ibid.,* ch. 15.

27. Except for the reduction between 1933 and 1949:

    1867-1916:   38
    1916-1933:   43
    1933-1949:   30
    1949-1956:   37
    1956-1967:   43
    1967-1978:   46
    1978-present: 52

28. On the Nova Scotia legislature, see Agar Adamson, "Nova Scotia: The Wisdom of Their Ancestors is its Foundation," in Gary Levy and Graham White, eds., *Provincial and Territorial Legislatures in Canada* (Toronto: University of Toronto Press, 1989).

29. *New Brunswick Broadcasting Co. v. Nova Scotia (Speaker of the House of Assembly)* [1993] 1 SCR, p. 403.

30. H.G. Thorburn, *Planning and the Economy* (Toronto: Canadian Institute for Economic Policy, 1984), p. 144.

31. Simpson, *Spoils of Power.*

32. J. Murray Beck, "An Atlantic Region Political Culture: A Chimera," in D.J. Bercuson and P.A. Buckner, eds., *Eastern and Western Perspectives* (Toronto: University of Toronto Press, 1981), p. 149.

33. The 1988 *Canadian Annual Review of Politics and Public Affairs* (Toronto: University of Toronto Press). See also P.J. Smith and M.W. Conley, "Empty Harbours, Empty Dreams: The Democratic Socialist Tradition in Atlantic Canada," in J.W. Brennan, ed., *Building the Co-operative Commonwealth: Essays on the Democratic Socialist Tradition in Canada* (Regina: Canadian Plains Research Centre, 1984), p. 248.

34. D.H. Higgins, "Approaches to Local Government Reorganization: Continuities and Discontinuities," Canadian Political Science Association (June 1983), and Lorraine Eden, "Provincial-Municipal Equalization in the Maritime Provinces," *Canadian Public Administration* (Winter 1987).

35. This section is largely based on Beck, *The Government of Nova Scotia,* and his articles in Robin, ed., *Canadian Provincial Politics;* and G.A. Rawlyk, "Nova Scotia Regional Protest, 1867-1967," in *Queen's Quarterly* (Spring 1968). See also J. Murray Beck's *Politics of Nova Scotia,* Vols. 1 and 2 (Tantallon: Four East Publications, 1985).

36. See Beck, *The Government of Nova Scotia,* ch. 10; Rawlyk, "Nova Scotia Regional Protest"; Paul MacEwan, *Confederation and the Maritimes* (Windsor, N.S.: Lancelot Press, 1976); and K.G. Pryke, *Nova Scotia and Confederation* (Toronto: University of Toronto Press, 1979).

37. Beck, *The Government of Nova Scotia,* p. 158.

38. Rawlyk, "Nova Scotia Regional Protest," pp. 115-119. See also C.P. McLennan, "Nova Scotia's Post-Confederation Leaders," *Dalhousie Review* (October 1946).

39. G.A. Rawlyk, "The Farmer-Labour Movement and the Failure of Socialism in Nova Scotia," in Laurier Lapierre, ed., *Essays on the Left* (Toronto: McClelland and Stewart, 1971).

40. Rawlyk, "Nova Scotia Regional Protest," pp. 119-122; E.R. Forbes, *The Maritime Rights Movement, 1919-1927* (Montreal: McGill-Queen's University Press, 1979).

41. The account of Angus L. Macdonald is largely based on W.J. Hawkins, *The Life and Times of Angus L.* (Windsor, N.S.: Lancelot Press, 1969). See also Jennifer Smith, "The Political Liberalism of Angus L. Macdonald," Canadian Political Science Association (May 1990).

42. Hawkins, *The Life and Times of Angus L.*, chs. 14, 16, 17.

43. Stevens, *Stanfield*, p. 101.

44. This account is based on Stevens' book; an annual account of Nova Scotia politics in *The Canadian Annual Review*, beginning in 1960; Beck, *Politics of Nova Scotia*, Vol. 2, Ch. 10 and 11; and Dalton Camp, *Gentlemen, Players and Politicians* (Toronto: McClelland and Stewart, 1970), ch. 25.

45. Simpson, *Spoils of Power*.

46. The Michelin plant was a coup because Quebec was also bidding for it and felt a French company should naturally locate in Quebec.

47. Stevens, *Stanfield*, p. 134.

48. Peter Aucoin, "The Stanfield Era," p. 403.

49. Stevens, *Stanfield*, pp. 139-40.

50. Roy George, "Cape Breton Development Corporation," in Allan Tupper and G.B. Doern, eds., *Public Corporations and Public Policy in Canada* (Montreal: Institute for Research on Public Policy, 1981); and Allan Tupper, "Public Enterprise as Social Welfare: the Case of the Cape Breton Development Corporation," in *Canadian Public Administration* (Autumn 1978). On SYSCO, see Alexander Bruce, "Blood, Sweat and Steel," *Canadian Business* (October 1989).

51. Stevens, *Stanfield*, ch. 8; Philip Mathias, *Forced Growth* (Toronto: James Lewis and Samuel, 1971); R.E. George, *The Life and Times of Industrial Estates Limited* (Halifax: Dalhousie University Institute of Public Affairs, 1974); and Garth Hopkins, *Clairtone* (Toronto: McClelland and Stewart, 1978). Generally speaking, these authors distribute the blame among IEL, Stanfield, bad management, labour problems, inadequate engineering, and poor markets. With a little bit of luck, however, these plans might have succeeded. Mathias makes the point that public officials, desperate for development but incapable of judging its merits, placed too much trust in unknown entrepreneurs. Some say that Stanfield and his cohorts were dazzled by the glamour of these two future-oriented industries, but others credit him with pioneering the IEL approach and point out that some failures were to be expected.

52. Stevens, *Stanfield*, p. 147.

53. Peter Aucoin, "The 1970 Nova Scotia Provincial Election: Some Observations on Recent Party Performance and Electoral Support," in *Journal of Canadian Studies* (1972), p. 30. See also Beck, *Politics of Nova Scotia*, Vol. 2, Ch. 12.

54. John Hawkins, *Recollections of the Regan Years: a Political Memoir.* (Hantsport: Lancelot Press, 1990).

55. Peter S. MacIntosh, *The Politics of Discord: Turmoil in the Nova Scotia New Democratic Party 1968-80,* unpublished MA thesis, Dalhousie University, 1982.

56. *Canada-Nova Scotia Agreement on Offshore Oil and Gas Resource Management and Revenue Sharing* (March 1982). On the early Buchanan era, see Beck, *Politics of Nova Scotia,* Vol. 2, Ch. 13.

57. Douglas Day, "Maritime Boundaries, Jurisdictional Disputes, and Offshore Hydrocarbon Exploration in Eastern Canada," *Journal of Canadian Studies* (Fall 1988).

58. Donald Ripley, *Bag Man: a Life in Nova Scotia Politics* (Toronto: Key Porter Books, 1993).

59. Shaun Comish, *The Westray Tragedy: a Miner's Story* (Toronto: Fernwood, 1993); Stevie Cameron, *On the Take: Crime, Corruption and Greed in the Mulroney Years* (Toronto: Macfarlane Walter & Ross, 1994).

60. Agar Adamson et al., "Pressing the Right Buttons: the Nova Scotia Liberals and Tele-Democracy," Canadian Political Science Association (1993).

READINGS

Beck, J. Murray. *Politics of Nova Scotia.* Vol. 2, 1896-1988. Tantallon: Four East Publications, 1988.

Bickerton, James P. *Nova Scotia, Ottawa and the Politics of Regional Development.* Toronto: University of Toronto Press, 1990.

Brym, R.J., and R.J. Sacouman, eds. *Underdevelopment and Social Movements in Atlantic Canada.* Toronto: New Hogtown Press, 1979.

Burrill, Gary, and Ian Mackay, eds., *People Resources and Power.* Fredericton: Acadiensis Press. 1987.

Canadian Annual Review of Politics and Public Affairs. Toronto: University of Toronto Press, annual.

Hawkins, John. *Recollections of the Regan Years: a Political Memoir.* Hantsport: Lancelot Press, 1990.

Nova Scotia Department of Economic Development. *Nova Scotia Statistical Review.* Halifax: Annual.

Rawlyk, G.A. "Nova Scotia Regional Protest, 1867-1967." *Queen's Quarterly.* (Spring 1968).

Starr, Richard. "Blood on the Coal." *Canadian Forum.* May 1993.

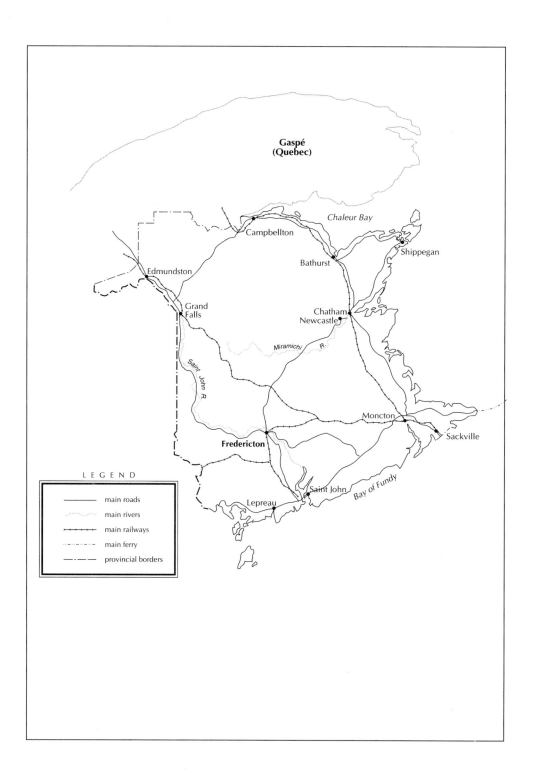

**Gaspé
(Quebec)**

Chaleur Bay

Campbellton

Shippegan

Bathurst

Edmundston

Grand
Falls

Chatham
Newcastle

Miramichi R.

Saint John R.

Moncton

Sackville

Fredericton

Saint John

Lepreau

Bay of Fundy

L E G E N D

—— main roads

····· main rivers

—+—+— main railways

—··—··— main ferry

—··—··— provincial borders

NEW BRUNSWICK

New Brunswick's most distinctive feature is the relative balance that exists between its English- and French-speaking populations. This is all the more note-worthy because, generally speaking, the two cultures have lived "together, yet apart, in mutual respect and tolerance."[1] New Brunswick resembles its Maritime neighbours in adhering to conservative values, although it did experience a "quiet revolution" in the 1960s which modernized its social services. It also shares the Atlantic provinces' problems in the realm of economic development but, under the dynamic leadership of Frank McKenna, in recent years has prob-ably achieved greater success than its neighbours.

SETTING

Geography

With an area of 73,437 square kilometres, New Brunswick is almost square-shaped, the length being 322 kilometres, and the width, 242 kilometres. Part of the Appalachian region, about 85 percent of the province, is covered by forest, especially in the mountainous north. Some agricultural land exists along the Saint John River and in the southern part of the province. The topography has not created strong geographic divisions in the province, but historically entrenched county identities persist. New Brunswick is also characterized by a clear socio-economic division demarcated by an imaginary line drawn diagonally from northwest to southeast. The north, northwest, and northeast are largely Acadian, Roman Catholic, and relatively poor, while the south and southwest are primarily Anglophone, Protestant, and more prosperous.

New Brunswick had a population of 723,900 in 1991, which increased to 760,600 by January 1995. Saint John, on the southern coast, is the largest city and the province's industrial nerve-centre, with a population of 124,981; Moncton, in the southeast and straddling the diagonal division mentioned, has

106,503 residents; while Fredericton, the capital, is the third largest city at 71,869. The other two leading urban centres are Bathurst and Edmunston, while some of the Campbellton labour market area spills over into Quebec. About 52.3 percent of the province's population is categorized as rural, making it second only to P.E.I.

Railways and highways cross the province, linking Nova Scotia and P.E.I. to Quebec but, in the area of transportation, the Port of Saint John is particularly important. It is the sixth busiest port in Canada, and is also the site of a drydock for ship repairs and the ship-building facilities owned by the Irving family.

Economy

The New Brunswick economy constitutes about two percent of the national gross domestic product, with a relative balance among primary, secondary, and tertiary sectors.[2] The province is currently placing great emphasis on communications and technology within the services sector.

Forestry has traditionally been New Brunswick's leading primary industry, both in terms of value and employment. Lumber, pulp, paper, newsprint, shingles, plywood, particleboard, and other forest products are all significant contributors to the provincial economy. Industry leaders include Irving, Noranda of Toronto, Repap Enterprises of Montreal, and Stone Consolidated, which collectively own about 20 percent of the province's forest land; the Crown owns about 50 percent, and the remainder is in the hands of private woodlot owners. Half of the province's single-industry communities are wood-based, and wood is a key component of the industrial base of all urban centres except Fredericton and Moncton. New Brunswick ranks fourth among the provinces in most aspects of forestry, but first on a per capita basis: it is estimated that one in seven jobs in New Brunswick is directly or indirectly based on forestry, including one-third of all employment in the manufacturing sector.

In the 1970s and 1980s, many observers became concerned about the long-term prospects of the forest industry. This was partly a result of the threat posed by the spruce budworm invasion, and partly a lack of reforestation, although the Irvings took good care of their own forest lands. There may be a shortage of quality sawlogs in the near future, but reforestation, silviculture, and forest management efforts have improved the long-term supply. In this area, and in the modernization of pulp and paper mills, the province has depended heavily on federal financial assistance.

Agriculture employs the second largest number of people among primary industries, and the most important crop is potatoes. Fortunately for New Brunswick, it was essentially spared the potato virus controversy that plagued P.E.I. for several years. McCain Foods dominates the potato industry, owning much of the land, supplying seed, fertilizer, and farm equipment, and extending credit to the diminishing number of small farmers. Although such control contributes to the company's profits, it is also based on McCain's need for specific types of potatoes for its various markets. Potato marketing arrangements, now controlled by the New Brunswick Potato Agency, have repeatedly been a heated political issue.[3] Dairy products, poultry and eggs, and livestock are other leading agricultural industries. In 1991, New Brunswick had 3,252 farms with an average size of 285 acres. Agriculture is the basis for much further processing, including the potato chip, juice, and frozen food sectors, all of which are dominated by McCain's.

Mining is a third prominent and diversified industry. In the primary sector alone it ranks second in terms of contribution to gross domestic product. Zinc, of which New Brunswick is the leading Canadian producer, is by far the province's most important mineral. After that come lead, in which it ranks third in Canada, silver, second, and peat moss, first. The province is also Canada's fifth-largest producer of both copper and coal. Much of the mining is centred in the northeastern part of the province around Bathurst, where Noranda's Brunswick Mining and Smelting has the world's largest underground zinc mine. The coal at Minto finds a ready market at New Brunswick Power, and two potash mines are in production in the south.

Finally, there is a substantial fishing industry along the east coast in the Bay of Chaleur and the Bay of Fundy in the south. Although cod was part of its industry, New Brunswick was not seriously affected by the recent federal fishing bans because it depends on lobster, crab, scallops, and herring more than on groundfish. Aquaculture is a growing industry, and the value of farmed salmon in the Bay of Fundy is increasing rapidly.

Electricity in New Brunswick is produced from hydro, coal, oil, gas, and diesel plants, as well as the Atlantic provinces' only CANDU nuclear reactor at Point Lepreau, west of Saint John. The world-wide energy crisis of the 1970s prompted New Brunswick to reduce its dependence on foreign oil and increase its use of domestic coal to generate electricity. Its power rates are lower than those of other Atlantic provinces. New Brunswick generates about 60 percent of its electricity from thermal sources, mostly coal, less than 20 percent from nuclear sources, and about 25 percent from hydro power. While it imports electricity from Quebec, it also exports it to P.E.I. and the United States. At one time, the government proposed building a second nuclear plant, but the decline in export demands put an end to that idea; the new $1-billion plant at Belledune is fired by coal.

New Brunswick competes with Nova Scotia for sixth place in terms of the total value of its manufacturing output. The leading manufacturing shipments include paper and allied industries, food and beverages, wood products, mineral, metal, and chemical products, printing and publishing, oil refining, and shipbuilding. Paper and paperboard, refined oil, pulp, and food and beverages are its main exports.

TABLE 5.1   **New Brunswick 1991 Labour Force and 1995 Estimated Gross Domestic Product by Industry**

Industry	1991 Labour Force		Est. 1995 GDP ($ millions)	
Agriculture	7,870	2.3%	134	1.2%
Fishing	4,765	1.4%	44	0.4%
Forestry	8,475	2.4%	277	2.5%
Mining	4,545	1.3%	203	1.8%
TOTAL PRIMARY	25,655	7.4%	658	5.9%
Manufacturing	47,575	13.7%	1,728	15.5%
Construction	24,240	7.0%	789	7.1%
TOTAL SECONDARY	71,815	20.7%	2,517	22.6%
Transportation, communications and utilities	28,405	8.1%	1,775	15.9%
Trade	59,990	17.2%	1,205	10.8%
Finance, insurance and real estate	12,975	3.8%	1,560	14.0%
Services	113,025	32.4%	2,402	21.6%
Government	35,835	10.3%	1,025	9.2%
TOTAL TERTIARY	250,230	71.8%	7,967	71.5%
TOTAL ALL INDUSTRIES	347,700		11,141	

Source: Reproduced by authority of the Minister of Industry, 1995, Statistics Canada, *1991 Census*, cat. nos. 93-326 and 95-320; and Conference Board of Canada, *Provincial Outlook, Economic Forecast* (Ottawa: Summer 1994), Vol. 9, No. 2.

In the 1990s, New Brunswick has attempted to become a leader in the telecommunications field. This initiative was motivated by the fact that such an industry is insensitive to distance, overcoming what has been one of the province's traditional disadvantages. The strategy is based on an intimate relationship between the government and the privately owned telephone company in the province, NBTel, which invested heavily in state-of-the-art telecommunications technology. With this selling point, the government has attracted many communications firms anxious to take advantage of the province's lower costs, bilingualism, and quiet quality of life. Such new arrivals include Purolator Courier, Canada Post, United Parcel Service, Unitel Communications, Livingstone International, Canada Trust, Federal Express, Unisys Canada, CAMDEV Ltd., CP Express and Transport, Business-to-Business TM Inc., CAMCO, and Meditrust Pharmacy. To bolster such efforts, New Brunswick became the first province to appoint a Minister of State for the Electronic Information Highway.

Government is relatively important to the New Brunswick economy and includes about 20,000 federal, 50,000 provincial, and 6,000 municipal employees. Although New Brunswick has the highest per capita proportion of provincial employees of any province, it also has the lowest proportion of municipal employees.

Class

New Brunswick is generally classified behind Nova Scotia and ahead of P.E.I. and Newfoundland in terms of per capita income ($17,724 in 1992). In 1991, 20.9 percent of its families had an income of less than $20,000, while 12.7 percent received more than $70,000, for a median family income of $37,152. New Brunswick's average level of education is the second lowest in the country in terms of average years of schooling and percentage of residents with a university degree.

Unemployment is chronically high, usually over 12 percent, and much of the population depends on unemployment insurance for at least seasonal support. Many, especially on the northern and eastern coasts, are part-time farmers, fishermen, labourers, and small woodlot owners. There are 95,000 unionized workers in the province, giving it a relatively high rate of 36.8 percent of paid workers, but organized labour has never acquired much solidarity or political consciousness. The New Brunswick Federation of Labour has a membership of about 50,000, including CUPE (Canadian Union of Public Employees) and PSAC (Public Service Alliance of Canada) in the public sector, and three major private sector unions—the Communication, Energy and Paperworkers, the Steelworkers, and the United Food and Commercial Workers.

New Brunswick has produced a number of very wealthy and powerful citizens over the years such as Sir James Dunn, Lord Beaverbrook (formerly Max Aiken), and Lady Beaverbrook (formerly Lady Dunn). All three have been honoured with buildings, scholarships, and other memorials. The McCain family made its fortune in potatoes and related ventures, and now owns an array of enterprises including the Florenceville plants which produce its well-known French fries, pizza, frozen vegetables, and desserts. McCain's is the world's largest producer of frozen French fries and one of the largest frozen food processors.[4] In recent years, the company has been embroiled in a prolonged familial and legal feud between the two major players, brothers Wallace and Harrison McCain.

The Irving family, however, is by far the most wealthy and powerful force in New Brunswick. K.C. Irving's empire began with a single car dealership, logically extended to gas stations, and grew by leaps and bounds, one industry leading to the acquisition of another. The Irving companies are private and family owned, so it is difficult to gain information about them and to ascertain the full extent of the holdings. The Irving operations, based in Saint John, include at least the following vertically integrated interests: 3,000 gas stations, real estate and construction, hardware, trucking, bus lines, bus construction, veneer, shipping, fishing, shipbuilding and repair, oil refining, fuel oil and propane distribution, two million acres of forest, a major pulp mill, saw mills, and, to top it off, a virtual media monopoly which includes all of the English-language daily newspapers in the province plus, until recently, radio and TV stations.[5] All told, it is estimated that about one in 12 residents is employed by Irving. Any government of New Brunswick must obviously contend with such an economic power, and over the years Irving has wrung untold concessions out of provincial and municipal governments. K.C. Irving died in 1992, but controversy over the erection of a monument in the Saint John Loyalist cemetery in his honour has kept him in the public eye.

The Irvings and McCains can be distinguished in that the former have a wide range of interests in a narrow geographic area. Having saturated the local market, however, the Irvings are expanding into Maine and other northeastern U.S. states, as well as into central Canada. The McCains, on the other hand, have a narrow product line but a wide geographic span. Other major corporations operating in the province are Noranda (forestry and mining), Repap Enterprises, Potash Corp. of Saskatchewan, NBTel (headed by T.C. Bird), G.E. Barbour (canned foods), Ganongs (chocolates), Olands (brewing and transportation), Connors Brothers (fish), Lantic Sugar, and Fundy Cablevision. The most prominent francophone institution in the private sector is the Assomption Mutelle-Vie insurance company headed by Michel Bastarache.

Given the McCains' tight grip on the farming industry and the Irving family's influence on almost all sectors of the economy, one might expect a more ideological orientation to New Brunswick politics. The lack of such a deep class cleavage can be explained in part by the Irving media monopoly which maximizes the family's political influence while minimizing critical coverage of the empire. The continued exploitation of potato farmers is also due to their apparent "ingrained individualism," which inhibits collective organization, and to their division by language, distance and size.[6] While average household incomes are highest in anglophone counties, lower in mixed English-French counties, and lowest in French counties, in the interaction between class and ethnicity, it is class that usually gets overlooked.

Demography

New Brunswick is distinctive as the province with the closest English-French balance in the country. Slightly over half of its residents are of British background, and nearly 40 percent are of French descent. In this context, the Acadians are more capable of resisting assimilation in New Brunswick than are French-speaking minorities in other provinces, and New Brunswick has the second-lowest "language transfer rate" in the country. French is the mother tongue of 33.6 percent of the population, and 31.2 percent speak French at home. It is thus convenient to view the Acadians as comprising between one-third and two-fifths of the New Brunswick population.

To a large extent the different ethnic groups have settled in separate regions of the province. As noted earlier, the French and English are roughly divided by an imaginary diagonal line or arc drawn from northwest to southeast.[7] The three main Acadian concentrations are in the northwest, northeast, and southeast corners of the province, the "French" counties being Gloucester, Kent, and "La Republique du Madawaska." Restigouche, Victoria, and Westmoreland (containing Moncton) are "mixed" English and French. The English population consists primarily of Loyalist descendants, in the southwest part of the province, Yorkshiremen, and a large number of Irish in Saint John, Moncton, Restigouche, and the Miramichi river basin.[8]

TABLE 5.2   New Brunswick Mother Tongue and Home Language, 1991

	Mother Tongue	Home Language
English	65.1%	68.2%
French	33.6%	31.2%
Other	1.3%	0.7%

Source: Reproduced by authority of the Minister of Industry, 1995, Statistics Canada, *1991 Census,* cat. no. 93-317, adapted by author.

Given the French-English balance, ethnic politics have been fairly prominent in New Brunswick, especially in recent years.[9] In the 19th century the Acadians were concerned with the adoption of a national flag and patron saint and, in the early 20th century, they often fought with the Irish within the Roman Catholic Church over such matters as the appointment of bishops. Traditional concerns also included language, education, and cultural survival. The Acadian community was strengthened by a certain amount of economic power in the form of co-operatives—the Fédération des Caisses Populaires Acadiennes (credit unions) and the Assomption Mutuelle-Vie, an insurance company which supported many Acadian ventures. But it has only been since about 1960, with the considerable improvement of their educational system, that Acadians have made their influence felt politically. The Parti Acadien, formed in 1971, at first sought to promote Acadian interests in traditional areas but soon came to embody the notion of a separate province. In 1973 the Société des Acadiens du Nouveau-Brunswick was established as a distinctive New Brunswick pressure group. It demanded "the creation of institutional structures that recognize the ethnic duality" of the province, indicating the Acadians' reduced support for ad hoc solutions and the elite accommodation of the past. After the Robichaud official languages act was passed in 1969, the Hatfield government brought in Bill 88, the Act Recognizing the Equality of the Two Official Linguistic Communities in New Brunswick in 1982. At the same time, Premier Richard Hatfield committed the province to official bilingualism in the new Constitution. He also created unilingual French and English school districts and minority language school boards. Then, in 1993, the Canadian Constitution was further amended to strengthen the equality of the two groups in New Brunswick. The New Brunswick approach to its ethnic duality could be labelled "separate but equal" as opposed to "integrated bilingualism." Generally speaking, the move to official bilingualism in the province has been smooth, displeasing only a few extremists on either side, and receiving the support of both Liberal and Conservative parties.

New Brunswick has relatively few residents of any other origins, mother tongues, or home languages. Nearly 83 percent of New Brunswickers were born in the province, while nearly 97 percent were born in Canada. Its aboriginal population is only about 13,000, the second-smallest proportion in the country.

Given its Acadian and Irish elements, it is not surprising that the province's population is more than one-half Roman Catholic, 54 percent compared with 40.1 percent Protestant in 1991. The latter category includes an unusually large number of Baptists in addition to those belonging to the United and Anglican churches. The issue of separate schools was settled in New Brunswick in an informal manner somewhat similar to that which occurred in Nova Scotia and Prince Edward Island. Officially there is a single public school system, but schools have tended to be either Catholic or Protestant at the local level. This arrangement served the province fairly well for many years, but the recent consolidation of schools has sometimes disturbed long-standing practice in this regard. There are a few private religious schools, and cross-border shopping has led to some relaxation of restrictions on commercial activity on Sunday. Generally speaking, however, religion is probably less prominent in New Brunswick politics than in P.E.I. or Nova Scotia; it is complicated, and often overshadowed, by ethnic politics.

TABLE 5.3   Religion in New Brunswick, 1991

Roman Catholic		386,580 (54.0%)
Protestant		287,435 (40.1%)
Baptist	80,935 (11.3%)	
United Church	75,570 (10.5%)	
Anglican	61,245 (8.5%)	
Other Protestant	69,685 (9.7%)	
Other and None		42,480 (5.9%)

Source: Reproduced by authority of the Minister of Industry, 1995, Statistics Canada, *1991 Census*, cat. no. 93-319, adapted by author.

Thus, the New Brunswick government faces a clearly divided population: Acadian Roman Catholics on one side and English Protestants on the other, with region coinciding with ethnicity and religion. This social division is intensified by economics, for the Acadian population has suffered considerable economic difficulty, while the English, especially in Saint John, generally prosper. These regional economic problems have preoccupied successive New Brunswick governments, and the ethnic-religious factors have only complicated matters.[10] While this ethnic-religious-geographic-economic division is the central aspect of political life, it does not detract from New Brunswick's basic stability in the same way similar divisions affect Northern Ireland, for example. This is partly because the cleavages overlap to some extent—over one-quarter of the "English" population is Roman Catholic, and there are both English and French elites. The province's stability is also due in part to the tradition of co-operation or accommodation to which the leadership of both groups is committed.[11]

Federal-Provincial Relations

New Brunswick's vulnerable economy has led it to rely heavily on the federal government. The province enjoyed great prosperity in the days of wooden sailing ships, preferential trade with Britain, and reciprocity with the United States, but suffered a post-Confederation economic decline. Confederation deprived the province of customs duty revenues, and the railway link to Upper Canada was of little benefit. It merely established a colonial relationship that saw New Brunswick exchange raw materials for imported manufactured goods. The province has demanded federal assistance for every imaginable purpose and project since 1867, but has never received what it considers its fair share. In recent years, the most prominent forms of assistance have been equalization payments, a variety of conditional grants, and grants from the Department of Regional Economic (or Industrial) Expansion and the Atlantic Canada Opportunities Agency. During the last 20 years, virtually no economic development has occurred without federal aid.[12] In 1992, the federal share of provincial government revenues was 35.5 percent, the fourth highest in Canada. Ottawa transferred $1,405 million to the province and $47 million to municipalities, as well as $1,975 million to individuals and $226 million to businesses. New Brunswick has been quite successful in its negotiations with Ottawa, but is so dependent that, unlike the governments of Nova Scotia and Newfoundland, it has rarely challenged or threatened the federal government.

In recent years, the province has benefited from federal funding of bilingualism, for the more bilingual Ottawa can make New Brunswick, the less distinctive Quebec can claim to be. The federal government literally pushes New Brunswick onto the world francophone stage, such as in La Francophonie, an organization comprised of the world's francophone countries. The province also has reason to be grateful for federal frigate contracts, but continues to press for more funds to upgrade the Trans-Canada Highway. Although a Liberal, Premier Frank McKenna supported the Canada-U.S. Free Trade Agreement. But after replacing

Richard Hatfield, who signed the Meech Lake Accord on behalf of the province, McKenna dragged his feet for three years, contributing to that agreement's demise.

POLITICAL CULTURE

New Brunswick's unique combination of French and English ethnic groups complicates any discussion of its political culture. To some extent, though, their values and attitudes are similar, emphasizing conservatism, tradition, history, and the status quo.[13]

The United Empire Loyalists added their distinctive traits—Toryism, elitism, hierarchy, a penchant for the monarchy and things British, as well as their Protestantism to this common culture.[14] However, not all "English" in the province are of Loyalist stock, and some have a more egalitarian, democratic frame of mind. The Acadians, at least until recently, adhered to the beliefs of traditional Catholicism, giving primacy to church and family. As mentioned, they demonstrated a political passivity until about 1960. Acadians differ from French-Canadians in Quebec in that their identity is focused on their expulsion from the region in 1755 and their subsequent "martyrdom and survival."[15] Given their physical and political separation from the Québécois, the Acadians have also developed a certain distinctiveness of dialect and culture. Like other Maritimers, New Brunswickers have strong partisan loyalties, even in the virtual absence of ideological differences between the parties. There is also a certain parochialism in New Brunswick which often limits horizons to the local community.

New Brunswickers generally demonstrate an even balance of loyalties between province and country. In the 1990 and 1994 *Maclean's* magazine surveys, about one-quarter indicated a primary loyalty to the province, while between 65 and 75 percent expressed a first loyalty to Canada. There may be occasional resentment toward Upper Canadians or Ottawa, but the deeply held feeling of economic vulnerability and dependence leads the province to favour a strong federal government. Indeed, the "marginal work world" which characterizes New Brunswick may well be a central aspect of its political culture. It could explain, for example, why patronage and corruption appear to be so widely accepted in New Brunswick. In the context of economic marginalism and a strong tradition of parochialism, various forms of government aid are often pursued vigorously. Fewer patronage appointments are now made, but partisanship appeared to be prevalent in government contracts until the end of the Hatfield era, given the numerous kickback charges levied against his government. At the same time, the use of patronage politics, while a necessary means of survival, "diminishes political life in the eyes of the very people who depend upon it."[16] Nevertheless, recent legislation to change the system has left some government members unhappy; the province has moved so far into the third stage of clientelism that the bureaucracy has displaced elected politicians in the distribution of government benefits. Perhaps the mark of a truly modern public service was Premier Frank McKenna's decision after his 1987 election not to replace the thousands of casual employees on the provincial payroll.[17]

Without the political activism of Prince Edward Island or the high levels of efficacy of Nova Scotia, New Brunswick is more consistently a "subject" or "disaffected" political culture.[18] Some studies have shown that New Brunswickers demonstrate less political trust, efficacy, and interest, and more cynicism, than other Canadians, and rank among the lowest in composite score.[19] However, the average turnout in federal and provincial elections is about 73 percent and 80 percent respectively. A positive side of the predominant deference to social and political elites is that leaders can engage in elite accommodation to minimize divisive ethnic and religious issues.[20]

TABLE 5.4   New Brunswick Voter Turnout in Recent Federal and Provincial Elections.

Federal Elections		Provincial Elections	
1974	71%	1970	81%
1979	74%	1974	77%
1980	71%	1978	76%
1984	77%	1982	82%
1988	76%	1987	82%
1993	70%	1991	80%
Average	73.2%	Average	79.7%

Source: *Reports of the Chief Electoral Officer,* calculations by author.

POLITICAL PARTIES

Party System

Prior to 1987, when the Liberals won every seat in the legislature, New Brunswick possessed Canada's most perfect and durable two-party system. The Liberals and Conservatives alternated in power at regular intervals, most commonly after serving two terms each. Other parties have rarely been represented in the legislature and, especially since 1960, the two old-line parties usually split the vote almost evenly. On the other hand, the New Democratic Party has attracted an average of over seven percent of the vote since 1970, and the Confederation of Regions party formed the official Opposition after the 1991 election.

The two major parties began by using the names "Government" and "Opposition," and the modern party system was slow to develop. At first, parties were mostly composed of local representatives ("loose fish") seeking patronage for their constituencies, and party discipline was rare. It took some time for each group to restrict itself to "Liberals" or "Conservatives," and it was not until 1935 and 1944 respectively that the modern party labels were officially adopted. Federalism and parochialism appear to have retarded such a practice. "Liberal" and "Conservative" were federal party labels, whereas each provincial party wished to appeal to those of all federal persuasions. The avoidance of the federal labels also reflected a certain anti-Dominion sentiment.[21] Moreover, "the established traditions of localism, logrolling and patronage were firmly entrenched — and party discipline was not allowed to interfere."[22] In fact, even the use of a common party election manifesto was delayed in New Brunswick, suggesting that each provincial party was largely a "coalition of county parties."[23] Certainly in the early years, the poll, parish, and county organizations were more significant than the provincial party association.

TABLE 5.5   Party Support in New Brunswick, 1970-1995

	Years in Office	Average Percentage of Vote	Percentage of Seats
Conservatives	17 (68%)	39.2%	39.1%
Liberals	8 (32%)	48.0%	58.0%
Combined	25 (100%)	87.2%	97.1%
NDP	– –	7.3%	0.6%

Source: *Reports of the Chief Electoral Officer,* calculations by author.

FIGURE 5.1   Percentage of Vote by Party in New Brunswick Elections, 1970-95

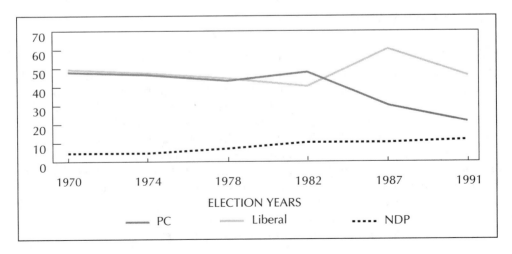

Federal-Provincial Party Links

Relations have generally been cordial between the federal and provincial wings of the two major parties in New Brunswick.[24] Long before provincial parties officially adopted the Liberal and Conservative labels, they were working closely with their Ottawa counterparts. Many ex-premiers went on to become federal ministers, and several, such as Andrew Blair and J.D. Hazen, continued to influence provincial party affairs.[25] New Brunswick has normally been awarded one minister in the federal cabinet but, after the time of Samuel Tilley, this representative has rarely been given an important post or exercised much influence. The province has usually divided its federal MPs fairly evenly between the two major parties—Liberals in the north and Conservatives in the south—but has almost always given the party which formed the national government a larger share.[26] In addition, the provincial government has usually been of the same political stripe as the federal and, even when different, the relationships were often good, such as those which existed between Richard Hatfield and Pierre Trudeau or Frank McKenna and Brian Mulroney.

Party Leadership

New Brunswick had 23 premiers between 1867 and 1960, serving for an average of only four years in office.[27] Except for Andrew Blair who occupied the post for 13 years and John McNair for 12, most left little mark, even though they were powerful figures in a province where deference to authority is a prominent value. Parties in New Brunswick have rarely bothered with leadership review mechanisms, giving party leaders the freedom to set policies, choose candidates, and otherwise exert complete control.[28]

Louis Robichaud, premier during the 1960s, had more fire and passion in his policies and his public oratory than most of his predecessors. Undoubtedly he made the most dramatic changes to the province up to that time. Many, but not all, of these were connected to his Equal Opportunity Program, as he fearlessly confronted the forces of "tradition, parochialism, intolerance, industrial power, and ethnic and economic disparity."[29] Richard Hatfield's long success, on the other hand, was in many ways a conundrum. He and his government were plagued by charges of scandal and corruption, he had a reputation for taking long absences from the province to enjoy the good life abroad, and once even admitted he was "neither articulate nor efficient." Yet Hatfield cheerfully carried on, moderate, intellectual, and sophisticated, basking in immense popularity until his abrupt political demise. It has been said that Hatfield possessed "an almost mystical comprehension of what New Brunswick is all about. He has an intuitive understanding of what New Brunswickers will and won't accept."[30] His record was progressively pragmatic, he handled the bilingualism issue skilfully and, as with other successful premiers, he specialized in paving roads. Frank McKenna is Hatfield's opposite in many ways, especially in personal deportment.

McKenna's social and economic reforms, which defy ideological categorization, have attracted much attention and are likely to be models for the rest of the country. In addition to his reputation for far-sightedness, McKenna is a "detail man" who takes a "hands-on" approach to every project in which the government has an interest. "King Frank" completely dominates the political scene.

All of the current party leaders in New Brunswick were elected at conventional leadership conventions. This includes the Confederation of Regions leader, although his tenure has been challenged in court by dissident party members.

Party Ideology

Politics in New Brunswick has been dominated by pragmatism and, as in the other Maritime provinces, there are no consistent ideological differences between the Liberals and Conservatives.[31] Parties draw up election manifestos which are remarkably similar to each other as well as to platforms of the past. The poor economy has always been an excuse for not implementing election promises. Members and governments usually run on their records, and the challengers regularly charge them with patronage and corruption, but often with little effect. It could be argued that such charges have at least kept divisive cultural issues out of the limelight, and permitted a healthy bipartisan consensus on them.[32]

The Robichaud Program for Equal Opportunity was the only significant ideological departure from the status quo and, because of the province's pragmatic and conservative past, the program appeared more radical than it really was. In trying to match the standards of other provinces, the program fell within the "equality of opportunity" doctrine usually associated with modern liberalism. It is a mark of New Brunswick pragmatism, however, that Hatfield continued to pursue the policy, as far as finances would permit. Such pragmatism was also reflected in Hatfield's approach to bilingualism, an issue which had more divisive, ideological overtones in other provinces. The CCF and later the NDP received some credit for raising progressive alternatives in the province, despite limited numbers.[33] The temporary takeover of the NDP in the early 1970s by the ultra-left-wing Waffle Movement provided some observers with amusement when even orthodox NDP policies had difficulty finding an audience among New Brunswick's electorate.

ELECTIONS

Electoral System

Today New Brunswick has an orthodox single-member electoral system, but it experienced some peculiarities in the past. Until 1974, most counties elected two, three, four, or five members. This permitted the parties to balance the ticket among various ethnic and religious groups, and quite rigid conventions developed in this connection.[34] Until 1967, New Brunswick was unique in its lack of an official ballot. Instead, each party prepared its own ballot and, at the polling booth, voters selected a party ballot, either voting for all of the party's candidates or deleting some names and adding others. Alternatively, voters used a blank piece of paper and wrote down the names of their selections. This archaic system, combined with the multi-member ridings, was responsible for uncertainty surrounding election results as recently as 1963.

As in other provinces, the percentage of popular vote which parties attract does not always correspond to their percentage of seats. Moreover, on at least one occasion, the party with the lower percentage of popular support actually formed the government. This was partly because the province never had an independent redistribution of seats, and some counties were over-represented.

Table 5.6 reveals the considerable representational disparities in the 1991 New Brunswick election. The realization of these disparities prompted the government to set up an impartial commission which reported its findings in 1993. The commission decided to reduce the number of constituencies to 55, with a provincial mean of 9,411 and an allowable variation of plus or minus 25 percent. In fact, all but one riding, Fundy Isles, were well within 20 percent. The commission also felt that county lines were no longer reflective of the social, economic and cultural reality of present-day New Brunswick, and gave them little notice. While it was directed to provide for aboriginal representation, the commission decided such representation should await aboriginal request.[35]

TABLE 5.6   Representational Disparities in 1991 Election

Mean no. of voters per constituency	8,924
Largest constituency (Petitcodiac)	19,930 (+123.3% of mean)
Smallest constituency (Queens North)	4,064 (-54.5% of mean)
Average variation from mean	31.7%
Constituencies within ± 10% (5 out of 58)	8.6%
Constituencies within ± 25% (25 out of 58)	43.1%

Source: *Reports of the Chief Electoral Officer,* calculations by author.

Election-day treating seems to have survived longer than in most provinces, with $2 bills, a bottle of rum, or a box of chocolates the favourite inducements.[36] (Chocolates were common in the political activity of the Ganong family.) However, New Brunswick has modernized election financing. Legislation limits political contributions ($9,000 per year), imposes a ceiling on party and candidate spending, gives tax credits to contributors and requires the disclosure of their names, and provides partial reimbursement to candidates and an annual allowance to parties. The province was early in its recruitment of central Canadian advertising agencies to help run party campaigns, the most famous being Dalton Camp, a New Brunswick native whose services were used by provincial Tories as early as 1952.[37]

Voting Behaviour

One New Brunswick observer has asserted that "regions, traditions, families, prejudices, feuds, favours, finances, faiths, taboos, tongues, old political slights and patronage, class distinctions ... all are part of the voting pattern."[38] In general terms, the Acadian, Catholic, poor northeast has usually voted solidly Liberal, while the English, Protestant, prosperous southwest has been mostly Conservative. This is so even though both parties tailor their slate of candidates to the demographics of each county. The battle has usually been most fierce in the mixed and English counties. Thus New Brunswick has exhibited all the signs of a traditional, pre-industrial, or underdeveloped party system where parties and voters are divided by language and religion. This general principle still exists although, while Richard Hatfield was leader of the Conservatives, his party made significant inroads into Acadian Liberal territory. This was clearly a response to his policies with respect to such issues as bilingualism. Little evidence of class voting exists in the province, except as it is intermingled with ethnic, religious, and regional factors.

PRESSURE GROUPS AND THE MEDIA

Pressure Groups

The Irving empire, including the Irving media monopoly, is undoubtedly the most powerful group in the New Brunswick political system. Several other family firms, including McCain's, are also influential. On the corporate side, the forestry industry is well organized, with such groups as the New Brunswick Forest Products Association, and the New Brunswick Federation of Woodlot Owners. Other business groups include various construction interests and the Tourism Industry Association. The Atlantic Provinces Chamber of Commerce has an office in Moncton serving all four provinces, while the New Brunswick division of the Canadian Manufacturers' Association also has its office in that city. In the farming sector, New Brunswick has the Federation of Agriculture and, in labour, the Federation of Labour. Francophone and aboriginal groups each have a number of pressure groups, and the New Brunswick Association of English-speaking Canadians has organized to oppose the Acadian interest. Such professions as doctors, lawyers, teachers, and nurses all have organizations, as do such institutions as cities, school trustees, and hospitals. What is particularly striking about pressure groups in New Brunswick is that in many cases they have separated into two linguistic entities which work together when common interests override linguistic ones.

TABLE 5.7   Leading New Brunswick Pressure Groups

Industrial	New Brunswick Forest Products Association
	Canadian Forestry Association of New Brunswick
	Federation of Woodlot Owners
	Tourism Industry Association of New Brunswick
	Construction Association of New Brunswick
	New Brunswick Home Builders' Association
	Road Builders' Association of New Brunswick
Labour	New Brunswick Federation of Labour
	New Brunswick Public Employees' Association
Agriculture	New Brunswick Federation of Agriculture
	New Brunswick Potato Council
Professional	New Brunswick Medical Society
	New Brunswick Teachers Federation
	Law Society of New Brunswick
Institutional	Cities of New Brunswick Association
	New Brunswick School Trustees' Association
	New Brunswick Healthcare Association
Ethnic	Société nationale de l'Acadie
	Société des acadiens et acadiennes du Nouveau-Brunswick
	Union of New Brunswick Indians
	Aboriginal Peoples' Council
Environmental	New Brunswick Wildlife Federation
Public Interest	Dialogue New Brunswick
	New Brunswick Civil Liberties Association

The Media

L'Acadie Nouvelle, published in Caraquet, is the only alternative daily newspaper to Irving's *Fredericton Daily Gleaner, Moncton Times-Transcript, Saint John Telegraph-Journal,* and its clone, the *Times-Globe.* Despite the fact that Irving has a monopoly of English daily newspapers in the province, it had a charge of violating federal competition laws overturned on appeal. The Irving monopoly has prompted questions about how comprehensively it covers Irving's other operations, such as Saint John air pollution caused by an Irving oil refinery and pulp mill. The Canadian Broadcasting Corporation used to be without a full-fledged television station in New Brunswick, but recently bought the Irving station in Saint John. It also has three English radio stations of its own in the province, while its French wing, Radio Canada, has one radio and one television station in Moncton. There are also many private radio stations, a few owned by Irving.

TABLE 5.8   Daily Newspapers in New Brunswick, 1994

Newspaper	Circulation	Ownership
L'Acadie Nouvelle	18,099	Independent
Fredericton Daily Gleaner	30,974	Irving
Moncton Times-Transcript	43,843	Irving
Saint John Telegraph-Journal	24,816	Irving
Saint John Times-Globe	32,014	Irving

Source: *Canadian Advertising Rates and Data* (August 1994).

GOVERNMENT INSTITUTIONS

New Brunswick's political institutions demonstrate peculiarities primarily in the sphere of official bilingualism, provincial-municipal relations, and in the one-party legislature between 1987 and 1991.

Executive

The position of lieutenant-governor has not been controversial in New Brunswick. Given the lack of strong party lines and frequent turnover of premiers in the first 15 years after Confederation, however, the governor tended to oversee the premier.[39]

Given the varied demographic context of the province, premiers have naturally tried to balance ethnic, religious, and geographic factors when making cabinet selections. Only 14 percent of ministers from 1900 to 1959 were Acadians, however, so that group has only recently been proportionately represented— sometimes constituting over 50 percent under Robichaud or given such important portfolios as Finance or Education under Hatfield and McKenna.[40] In that earlier period, only 30 percent of ministers were Roman Catholics, indicating another element of disproportion. Thus, it seems that a proper balance of county representation was often given priority.

When Richard Hatfield became premier in 1970, he introduced a cabinet committee system[41] paralleling similar developments in Ottawa, Ontario, and some other provinces. However, in a sense, New Brunswick pioneered the "envelope system," whereby the policy making and budgeting processes are closely integrated.[42] Frank McKenna, who reduced his cabinet to 20 from 24 members, chairs the policy and priorities committee of his cabinet. The other main committee is board of management, for which the Finance Department acts as a secretariat. Other ad hoc committees are appointed from time to time. The premier is supported by a partisan premier's office, with a staff of about 20, while the executive council office, with about 40 career public servants headed by the Clerk, provides a secretariat to the cabinet and cabinet committees.

Legislature

New Brunswick entered Confederation in 1867 with a bicameral legislature, a legislative council as well as a legislative assembly. Like P.E.I. and Nova Scotia, the province quickly realized that the upper house was an expensive and unnecessary appendage to the governmental process. It was abolished in 1892, 10 years after the present (two-chamber) building was constructed. The ingenious device used in this instance, because the legislative council could veto any bill aimed at eliminating itself, was to wait until attrition had reduced its numbers to such a level that the appointment of a group of abolitionists would carry the day.[43]

The legislative assembly originally had 40 seats, and by 1967 had gradually increased to 58.[44] However, the number is to decline to 55 after the election expected in 1995. Acadians originally had to speak English in the legislature but, since 1967, the chamber has operated on a bilingual basis with simultaneous interpretation. There is a Hansard, but the official, edited version takes some time to appear because everything requires translation. New Brunswick legislative sessions are still brief, an average of about 35 days, but members attend to committee work during recesses and most legislators now regard their positions as "full-time." Members' indemnities have increased substantially to about $36,000 with a $14,000 tax-free allowance in 1994. Recent legislation provided for constituency office allowances for MLAs. With the election of 58 Liberals and no opposition members between 1987 and 1991, legislative operations had to be altered somewhat; for example, there was no Opposition member to chair the public accounts committee.[45] But, even after 1991, the justice minister chaired the law amendments committee, and ministers sat on many of the seven standing committees. Committee of the whole and committee of supply are used to examine bills and estimates respectively, and government arrogance was clearly evident when, in 1993, it forced the committee of the whole to consider 48 of 49 public bills at one time, although more than half had been introduced only two days earlier.[46]

Bureaucracy

New Brunswick employs about 11,000 people in departments and agencies, another 5,000 in government business enterprises, and a further 34,000 in the wider public sector. New Brunswick created a civil service commission in 1938 and strengthened it in 1943, but that guaranteed neither a skilled nor a nonpartisan provincial bureaucracy. In fact, it was charged that the Liberals had adopted the commission to protect their partisan appointments. In other words, the civil service commission protected incumbent civil servants, but because new governments still appointed their own supporters as casuals, game wardens, court clerks, and supervisors, foremen and even labourers in road construction, the bureaucracy grew to almost twice its authorized size.[47] Consequently, New

Brunswick has more bureaucrats per 1,000 residents than any other province, although this is also related to the centralized nature of provincial-municipal relations. Turnover among high-level public officials was reduced as a result of government changes after 1952, but there was still substantial patronage in evidence at lower levels. Somewhat ironically, the government amended the Civil Service Act in 1992 to allow public servants more political rights, a move strongly suggested by the Supreme Court of Canada.

One indication of the bureaucracy's weakness in the early 1960s was Premier Robichaud's reliance on royal commissions to investigate public problems. The provincial civil service was greatly expanded and strengthened in that decade, especially in connection with the Program of Equal Opportunity. More Acadians were hired and a large number of professional public servants came to the province from other jurisdictions, such as Saskatchewan. Since then, such administrative expertise has been essential, particularly in negotiations with the federal government over General Development Agreement and Economic and Regional Development Agreement projects. Also, public servants now have the right to strike.

TABLE 5.9   New Brunswick Government Departments, 1994

Advanced Education and Labour
Agriculture
Economic Development and Tourism
Education
Environment
Finance
Fisheries and Aquaculture
Health and Community Services
Human Resources Development
Justice
Mines and Energy
Municipalities, Culture and Housing
Natural Resources and Energy
Solicitor General
Supply and Services
Transportation

In addition to government departments, the province has a large array of semi-independent agencies, boards, commissions, and Crown corporations. The New Brunswick Power Corp. provides electricity to the province, and such agencies include N.B. Coal Ltd., an array of agricultural and forestry marketing boards, and a public utilities board, to name a few. As mentioned, although NBTel is a private company it works closely with the government, especially with the Minister of State for the Electronic Information Highway.

TABLE 5.10   Leading New Brunswick Agencies, Boards, Commissions and Crown Corporations

Crown Corporations:	New Brunswick Housing Corporation
	New Brunswick Liquor Control Commission
	New Brunswick Coal Ltd.
	New Brunswick Electric Power Commission
Agencies, Boards and Commissions:	Advisory Council on the Status of Women
	Human Rights Commission
	Lotteries Commission of New Brunswick
	New Brunswick Industrial Development Board
	New Brunswick Public Utilities Board
	Workers' Compensation Board

Judiciary

The highest echelon of the province's judicial system is the Supreme Court of New Brunswick, which is made up of the Court of Queen's Bench and the Court of Appeal. The provincial courts service lower-level cases.

Municipal Government

Municipal government in New Brunswick consists of cities, towns, and villages. Until the system was reformed in the mid-1960s, the province also possessed county units in rural areas and a complicated array of local school boards, made up mostly of appointed members. The Equal Opportunity Program of 1966-67 profoundly altered the operation of municipal government in the province. These reforms made New Brunswick unique in the degree to which "municipal" services were assumed by the province, and New Brunswick property owners probably enjoy the lowest property tax rates in the country. The 40 percent of the population living in rural areas is divided into 291 unincorporated local service districts administered directly from Fredericton. As in many other provinces, the number of local school boards was reduced about one-third in 1992. A decision was also made to amalgamate the towns of Newcastle and Chatham into the city of Miramichi on January 1, 1995.

POLITICAL EVOLUTION

1867-1969[48]

Although political parties in New Brunswick were slow to develop into their modern, disciplined form, eight different regimes can be identified in the 1867-1969 period. Four "Conservative" periods alternated with four "Liberal" ones, the longest being the 25-year Liberal rule between 1883 and 1908. It would be misleading to view the early period in terms of a modern two-party system, however, because party discipline was weak, governments were often coalitions of Liberals and Conservatives, and they used the labels "Government" and "Opposition."

After the Samuel Tilley government actively engaged in Confederation discussions in the 1864-65 period, an anti-Confederation provincial government was elected in 1865. With the machinations of the lieutenant-governor, the support of the British government, and financial assistance from Upper Canada, however, the Confederationalists continued their fight. This forced the premier, Albert Smith, to resign, and an election was called for 1866. The threat of a Fenian raid and provincial financial problems helped the Confederationalists win, and New Brunswick became one of the original partners in Confederation. Tilley then moved on to Ottawa and, by 1870, Confederation was no longer a contentious issue.

The next major controversy to emerge was that of separate schools. The King government brought in the Common Schools Act of 1871 which established a single public school system and prohibited religious instruction. This issue was the main focus of the 1874 election, dividing Roman Catholics from Protestants and Acadians from anglophones. Almost immediately thereafter, two people were killed in the "Caraquet riots," an outbreak of violence between English Protestant constables and Acadians. New Brunswick ultimately decided that Catholic students could be taught religion after regular school hours and, in Catholic areas, schools could be rented from the Church, which would provide teachers.[49] This difficult issue was resolved by 1876, when two Roman Catholics were added to the cabinet.

The second regime, from 1883 to 1908, encompassed six elections. Andrew Blair served as premier for the first 13 years and established the all-party coalition which continued successfully after his departure. While Blair's party and subsequent governments were composed of both Conservatives and Liberals, he imposed an unprecedented sense of discipline. Some legislative members were still primarily interested in gaining patronage for their constituencies, but they now had to demonstrate loyalty to the government in return for such favours.[50] In 1890 Blair issued the first government election manifesto and, as time went on, pressure mounted for the Government party to call itself "Liberal" and for the Opposition to don the "Conservative" label. Blair was hailed in 1890 for giving all men the right to vote regardless of income or property, and the abolition of the legislative council in 1892. The (Liberal) Government was favoured with increased Acadian support after Wilfrid Laurier became the first French-Canadian to lead a national party, and Premier Blair joined his Nova Scotian counterpart, W.S. Fielding, in the federal Laurier cabinet in 1896.

In 1908, John Douglas Hazen was elected to lead a new government. He was associated with the federal Conservative party, but continued to seek a broad coalition within the province. James Kidd Flemming, a spellbinding speaker and an immensely popular figure, won a landslide victory in 1912 on the issue of constructing a railway line along the Saint John river valley. After the Opposition charged him with demanding campaign funds from the railway contractors, however, Flemming resigned. By 1917, continued charges of provincial government corruption, combined with the unpopularity of conscription at the federal level, caused the defeat of the government after nine years and two terms in office.[51]

The Liberals were re-elected in the 1920 election, but it was marked, as in many other provinces, by the entry of farmer and labour candidates. Eight United Farmers and four Independents were elected. Premier Walter Foster had several accomplishments to his credit, particularly the establishment of the Health Department, the New Brunswick Electric Power Commission, and a modern highway system. After Foster resigned in 1923, Peter J. Veniot became the first Acadian premier, although he had been anglicized by his Nova Scotia upbringing. Veniot exploited anti-conscriptionist feelings in the Acadian community and, as minister of public works, was responsible for the massive road building program. As premier, he was primarily concerned with the development of electric power under the auspices of a new government commission. The Grand Falls power project was a prominent issue in the 1925 election, with the government committed to public development.

The new (Conservative) premier, John B.M. Baxter, sold the Grand Falls power project to an American firm,[52] relaxed the liquor laws, and paved many roads. However, his attempt to establish bilingual schools was rejected and, in the subsequent absence of provincial legislation on the subject, it was left to be resolved at the local school district level. Baxter was also a leader of the Maritime Rights Movement, which demanded better treatment of the Maritime provinces from Ottawa, and to which the federal government responded with the Duncan and White royal commissions. In 1933, L.P.D. Tilley, son of the father of confederation Sir Leonard Tilley, became premier, and coped with the effects of the Great Depression as well as could be expected. But, in 1935, like many of its sister Conservative regimes of the era, the Tilley government was defeated in these difficult economic circumstances.[53]

Since the Conservative government had come to be associated with the hardships of the Depression, the Liberals enjoyed a lengthy rule, from 1935 to 1952. Allison Dysart won the first two elections for the Liberals in this period, while John McNair successfully led the party through the other two. Dysart was a Roman Catholic premier, a rarity in New Brunswick. He initiated job creation projects in road and bridge construction and highway paving, and also sponsored the Civil Service Act of 1938 which sought to reduce patronage in government employment. McNair succeeded him in 1940 and served for 12 years, winning re-election in 1944 and 1948. The 1944 campaign was remarkable in that it was the first time the Opposition party explicitly used a party label

(Progressive Conservative), the name adopted by the federal party shortly before.[54] It also marked the most intense Co-operative Commonwealth Federation effort in the province, although the new party failed to attract much support.[55] McNair's government was activist in many respects; two of its most enduring accomplishments were the rural electrification program and a consolidated school system in rural areas.

Several issues contributed to the Liberal defeat in 1952, including the imposition of a four-percent retail sales tax. McNair sought to make an issue of the unionization of New Brunswick Electric Power Commission employees, but the union was moved by the Conservative leader's appeal to delay their strike and subsequently supported that party. This rather strange alliance hurt the CCF as well as the Liberals and, in the end, the Conservatives won a majority of seats, even though the Liberals remained slightly ahead in terms of popular vote. Hugh John Flemming, son of a previous premier, ruled until 1960. He expanded the power commission, notably with the construction of the Beechwood Hydro Electric dam on the upper Saint John river. This $200-million undertaking was the largest of its kind in the province's history. Flemming was also instrumental in obtaining increased federal funding (especially after the national Conservative victory in 1957), such as the Atlantic Provinces Adjustment Grants. In 1960 he introduced a new social assistance act which finally abandoned the anachronistic social welfare system based on the Elizabethan Poor Law, involving local almshouses and overseers of the poor. Later, as federal minister of Forestry, Flemming continued to assist the province's economic development with the Atlantic Development Board and the Agricultural Rehabilitation and Development Act (ARDA).

The Conservatives were generally expected to win the 1960 election, their strategy being to emphasize their close association with the Diefenbaker government. However, they were narrowly defeated by the Liberals and their new leader, Louis Robichaud. The decisive factor seems to have been Robichaud's promise to abolish hospital insurance premiums (the annual premium of $50 being prohibitive for many families), and to absorb the cost of the program from general government revenues. He had also worked hard to rebuild the Liberal party organization after assuming control in 1958.

Robichaud thus became the first Acadian to be elected to the premiership (Veniot having taken office in mid-term), and Liberal support was concentrated in the Acadian sector.[56] He had risen from poverty to study economics and political science under Father Georges-Henri Lévesque at Université Laval in Quebec before articling as a lawyer in Bathurst. He soon won the Liberal leadership and became premier at only 34. Robichaud possessed a dynamic, charismatic personality,[57] and was imbued with infectious energy and enthusiasm. He quickly acquired the affectionate nickname of "Little Louis" ("P'tit Louis" in French).

The next 10 years would witness the most revolutionary changes to have occurred in New Brunswick in a century, but Robichaud's first few years in office were comparatively quiet. Royal commissions were established on higher education, liquor laws, and provincial-municipal relations. Several new industrial developments took shape including the vast Brunswick Mining and Smelting complex at Belledune, north of Bathurst. On both of these projects, the Liberals encountered opposition from industrial magnate K.C. Irving, who had supported Robichaud in the 1960 election. After battling with Irving for control of the Belledune complex, the government asked Noranda to intervene and administer the smelter's operation. The government constructed roads and bridges and abolished insurance premiums, but at the price of creating a provincial government deficit.

In the 1963 election campaign, Robichaud proposed another major hydro development, the dam at Mactaquac, and pledged that all New Brunswickers, regardless of which region they resided in, would have "equal opportunities" for employment, income, and human betterment.[58]

The next four years were very active. First, the government overhauled the higher education system, creating the Université de Moncton in 1963 and expanding the University of New Brunswick in Fredericton and Mount Allison in Sackville. Second, the $110-million Mactaquac hydro development began operating in early 1964. Third, the New Brunswick Development Corporation was established with the goal of establishing new industry in the province. Many new operations appeared, mostly in the mining and forest industries—fertilizer plants, new mines, smelters and concentrators, and pulp and paper mills. Unfortunately, most of these new plants later experienced difficulties. Some closed permanently and others temporarily, revealing the civil service's inability to adequately assess the viability of projects and the lack of an overall strategy of economic development.

Overshadowing all else in the 1964-67 period, however, was the Program for Equal Opportunity, which stemmed from the Byrne Royal Commission on Finance and Municipal Taxation in New Brunswick. The commission reported in February 1964 that local government in New Brunswick was in very poor condition, with great disparities in municipal services from one region to another. Educational opportunity in particular had to be equalized.[59] Byrne recommended that the province assume responsibility for four general services—education, welfare, health, and the administration of justice, a revolutionary proposal.[60] The government agreed that minimum standards of service and opportunity for all New Brunswickers should be provided regardless of the financial resources of their municipality. Henceforth, under its Program for Equal Opportunity, the four major services would be financed and administered by the province.

In education, the province established a uniform salary scale for teachers—although local school boards continued to be responsible for hiring—and built many new central, consolidated schools. For the first time, it fully recognized the right to a complete French-language education for Acadians.[61] The result was a genuine equality of opportunity for all students in all regions. Provincial assumption of social welfare costs and programs was probably the second-most significant aspect of the plan, because the province's welfare system was still rather archaic. The province also took control of the health field, except for the ownership of hospitals. A more gradual evolution took place in the realm of justice, but the province aimed to assume full responsibility, upgrading jail and court facilities and appointing full-time Crown prosecutors and sheriffs.

Immense administrative problems arose in centralizing these four major functions in Fredericton. The provincial public service had not been particularly strong and may have been incapable of administering such an innovative program had it not been for an influx of civil servants from Saskatchewan who had dealt with similar programs under the CCF government. The Saskatchewan civil servants had either been fired by, or were fleeing from, the new Liberal government of Ross Thatcher.[62] Thus much of the administrative talent necessary for the operation of the program came from outside the province.

The province also reformed municipal government; county councils were abolished, leaving no municipal structures in rural areas except for advisory local service district committees. Cities, towns, and new villages were responsible for providing services associated with property. The province took over assessment and tax collection, paid needy municipalities an equalization grant, and established a uniform property tax rate, to which the locally determined municipal services and supplementary school rates were added. Municipalities were otherwise not allowed to levy local taxes; age-old poll taxes and taxes on other forms of property, including livestock and household goods, were abolished.[63]

Under the new system, property taxes decreased for many residents, and services improved for most, which meant the province needed additional sources of revenue. The government's initial response was to double the retail sales tax to six percent and impose an income tax surcharge. The province was fortunate that the federal government was implementing the Canada Assistance Plan at this time, so that much of the funding for better services, especially in the welfare field, came from Ottawa. Later, Department of Regional Economic Expansion agreements with the federal government also assisted the poorer areas of the province, and the federal medicare program helped finance increased health costs. Thus federal funding assisted in the implementation of the Equal Opportunity Program.

The program was so pervasive that it provoked tremendous opposition. Part of this was a natural and restrained resentment among higher income earners, urban residents, and businesses, whose overall tax burden increased. Perhaps the most vociferous opponents were companies, especially the firms constituting the industrial empire of K.C. Irving, that had earlier persuaded municipalities or the province to grant them various kinds of tax concessions. Irving himself emerged from his traditional seclusion to denounce the program at the legislature, and his media outlets fulminated against it with all their monopoly might.[64] The most vitriolic critic was the *Fredericton Gleaner*, recently acquired by

Irving. Robichaud responded to the tax concessions issue by promising a "fair and equitable" settlement, but the controversy raged until the government agreed that existing tax concessions would be honoured until their expiry, but no new ones would be granted.

The opposition took an even uglier tone with the charge that the object of the entire Equal Opportunity Program was to "rob Peter to pay Pierre." While it was true that more wealth existed in the English southwest and greater poverty in the Acadian northeast, there were also many poor rural "English" areas. The allegation roused such emotion that threats were made on the Acadian premier's life. The *Gleaner* also lambasted the program for the concentration of power and patronage that would be placed in the premier's hands. The Robichaud government was fortunate, however, in that it faced a relatively weak Conservative Opposition in the period from 1964 to 1966.

With the legislative framework of Equal Opportunity in place (entailing some 130 pieces of legislation), attention turned to administrative implementation in early 1967. Other Robichaud initiatives included adding six seats in anticipation of the next election, and developing a uniform official ballot listing the party affiliation of candidates. The government also appointed an ombudsman, following close on the heels of a similar initiative in Alberta.

In 1966, the Progressive Conservatives chose the flamboyant Charles Van Horne as their new leader. Van Horne had once served as executive assistant to K.C. Irving and then as a Tory MP from 1955 to 1960, when he established a reputation as a maverick. Since then, he had been "wheeling and dealing" in a variety of areas, most recently selling real estate in California. He was a bilingual Catholic, his mother was French, and he was popular in the Acadian community where the Conservatives had always been weak.

The September 1967 election has been called the "toughest, dirtiest election in Canadian provincial politics for at least 25 years,"[65] pitting Robichaud and the Program for Equal Opportunity against Charlie Van Horne and K.C. Irving. Some were impressed that Van Horne's criticisms emphasized non-ethnic aspects of the plan,[66] while the exhausted premier challenged Irving to run for election if he wished to control the province. Surprisingly, the results were virtually unchanged from 1963. The Opposition leader even lost his own seat, as the Acadian areas voted solidly for Robichaud.

The major initiative of the next three years was the New Brunswick Official Languages Act, which Robichaud introduced in 1968 and which more or less coincided with similar developments in Ottawa. The act stipulated that services in schools, courts, the legislature, the public service, and government agencies be available in both English and French. Most services had previously been offered only in English. Only isolated extremist opposition was expressed at the time, and credit is usually given to the two Conservative leaders, Van Horne and Richard Hatfield, for not allowing it to become a bitter, partisan issue. Van Horne had attempted to present a motion on this question in the legislature even before the government's bill was introduced. Although it was largely a statement of principle, and not all of its provisions were immediately implemented, the legislation, in combination with the Program for Equal Opportunity, allowed Acadians to be integrated into the mainstream of provincial life.

These were hard times for both the government and private enterprise. The government raised taxes, postponed the implementation of medicare, and took over and then closed coal mines. Frequent labour disputes erupted, farmers and fisherman experienced difficulty, the spruce budworm appeared, and the Saint John River became increasingly polluted. Granting the public service collective bargaining rights fostered a rivalry between the Canadian Union of Public Employees and the New Brunswick Public Employees' Association, and the National Farmers Union came to the aid of potato farmers by rejecting a new potato industry act. On the other hand, the Bathurst-Newcastle and Saint John areas were generally prosperous, and some industrial expansion occurred, including a new $14-million Irving oil terminal.

In this "continued public ferment over a wide variety of issues,"[67] Robichaud called an election for October 1970. It was a quiet campaign, partly because the entire country was consumed by the FLQ crisis simultaneously occurring in Quebec, but there was sufficient dissatisfaction to bring the Liberals down.

The 1970s[68]

The Conservatives won a narrow victory under their new leader, Richard Hatfield, but he went on to serve as premier longer than any of his predecessors in New Brunswick or any of his contemporaries in other provinces. His political longevity was due in part to continued disruption within the provincial Liberal party and problems over its leadership, but Hatfield became a colourful and skilful politician in his own right. His long-standing concern for the welfare of the Acadian population and generally progressive legislative program contributed significantly to his success. Hatfield's political career would collapse in the 1980s but, during the 1970s, he was not seriously challenged.

In its first few years, the Hatfield government was most closely identified with one particular project, the Bricklin car. Malcolm Bricklin was a dashing young American who had designed a new car that appeared to exemplify the "playboy" lifestyle. Hatfield bought the idea for a half-million dollars and generous loan guarantees. Bricklin repeatedly returned to the premier for additional funds, until the province had contributed $10 million in addition to $3 million in federal financing. By 1974, a number of Bricklin cars had actually been produced, and Hatfield proudly used one on the campaign trail in that year's election. A few days after Hatfield was re-elected, however, it was revealed that the project was in deep trouble. After receiving an additional $8.7 million in 1975, the company went into receivership. The Bricklin is now a fine museum piece, and a testament to desperate and gullible premiers.[69]

Hatfield was more successful in his relations with the Acadian community. He helped consolidate their progress through his administration of the Equal Opportunity Program and implementation of the official languages act, and increased their influence in the cabinet. His sympathetic approach paid dividends in the 1974 election when the Conservatives made significant inroads into Acadian territory. At the same time, however, bilingualism was being opposed by Leonard Jones, the mayor of Moncton. He clashed repeatedly with Moncton university students on the issue, and later unsuccessfully challenged the constitutionality of both the federal and provincial official languages acts in the courts. Robert Stanfield subsequently refused to accept Jones as a Conservative candidate in the federal election of 1974, but he ran and won as an Independent.

Hatfield responded to the increased Acadian support by establishing French-language trials and a French-language law school at the Université de Moncton. Even so, Acadians continued to campaign for more power and services, led by the French daily, L'Évangeline, and the Parti Acadien. Hatfield took much of the steam out of the separatist Acadian cause with Bill 88, which provided both English and French communities with distinct cultural and social institutions. The bill promised cultural equality in such areas as hospitals, community colleges, the civil service, and the courts, while a companion bill established two autonomous unilingual school systems.

Hatfield ran an activist government which established a legal aid plan, constructed hospitals, created new departments, and changed succession duties. The latter apparently prompted K.C. Irving to move to the Bahamas and later Bermuda, leaving his companies in the hands of his three sons. The government set up a new Crown corporation, the New Brunswick Forest Authority, to manage and control crown woodlands, and transformed the electoral system into 58 single-member constituencies. In response to the wave of layoffs and shutdowns later in the decade, Hatfield introduced an employment termination act and, reacting to charges of scandal, authored a new election funding law. Other significant legislative developments included a new Crown lands and forest act, which gave renewed hope to the future of the forest industry; reform of the family law system; and a pioneering right to information act.

Robichaud's former minister of Finance, lawyer Robert Higgins, succeeded him as Liberal leader in 1971, and generally provided a thoughtful, low-key opposition. The provincial NDP—which in 1971 had adopted the Waffle Manifesto, the left-wing platform of the dissident Waffle wing of the party, and had been temporarily expelled from the national party—the quasi-separatist Parti Acadien, and another group opposed to bilingualism also ran candidates in the 1974 election, but none gained much support. Incidents of government patronage and impropriety involving Tourism Minister Charlie Van Horne and other ministers surfaced from time to time, but most were not exploited by the

Opposition. Indeed, the Liberal leader admitted his reluctance to do so for fear that past Liberal indiscretions would be unearthed in retaliation. Higgins did, however, reveal Tory "toll-gating" practices in the liquor business, where political contributions were extracted from liquor companies in return for stocking their brands in government liquor stores.[70] He also accused the provincial justice department of interfering in the Royal Canadian Mounted Police investigation of the kickback charge. Despite overwhelming supporting evidence, only one party official was charged.[71] Hatfield appointed a judicial commission to investigate the allegations of political interference and, in 1978, the commission's report cleared the government of this charge. Higgins took the honourable course and resigned as leader of the Liberal party, later becoming a county court judge. A Liberal convention selected Joseph Daigle, a former judge, as its new leader.

Daigle made some strong attacks on the government's patronage and kickback practices in the 1978 election, and succeeded in coming within two seats of the victorious Conservatives. After the election, Hatfield cleverly chose a Liberal, Robert McCready, as Speaker of the legislature. The government experienced some tense moments wondering if it would survive, until McCready crossed the floor to become a Conservative. Hatfield was doubly blessed with dissatisfaction within the Liberal ranks concerning the performance of their leader. Eventually, the caucus revolted against Daigle in November 1981, in spite of his strong showing three years before.

Two of the most important economic issues of the decade related to the spruce budworm and the Point Lepreau nuclear plant. While the invasion of the voracious budworm represented a threat to the province's forestry industry, many objected strenuously to the spraying of insecticides, linking them to Reye's Syndrome, a condition which predominantly afflicts young children, causing brain swelling and leading to neurological damage or convulsions, coma and death. Great controversy emerged as to whether to spray or not to spray. The government chose to spray, but several plane crashes as well as spraying in the wrong area occurred, mainly because the spray fleet consisted of planes left over from the Second World War.[72] After the 1978 election, it was revealed that the Lepreau nuclear project was seriously over budget. It had been plagued with problems throughout its construction—leaks, mechanical breakdowns, and labour disruptions—which placed it two years behind schedule. Other Atlantic provinces had considered becoming part of the project but later backed off, leaving Hatfield to hope he might recover some of the costs by exporting surplus electricity to the United States.

Other economic problems also developed: shutdowns and layoffs continued in lumber and paper mills and other industries, while Moncton lost two major employers, the Canadian National shops and Eaton's catalogue. Labour problems also occurred, including strikes in the public and private sectors. Meanwhile, the government itself was faced with financial difficulties and responded with cutbacks in many programs—schools, hospitals, and social services—to the extent that Hatfield was charged with dismantling Robichaud's Equal Opportunity Program. The Irving shipyards thrived, but only with federal subsidies, and the promising start of a potash mining industry was achieved at the expense of extremely generous government concessions.

The 1980s

The 1980s saw Richard Hatfield at his height as a national statesman, but also at his nadir when his party was wiped out of the legislature in 1987. The first few years of the decade were dominated by constitutional matters, and Hatfield increasingly attempted to divert attention from his government's economic and political problems by involving himself in the national unity debate. After participating in the 1980 Quebec referendum campaign, Hatfield supported the Trudeau Liberals' constitutional initiatives, even ensuring his province became officially bilingual in the 1982 Canadian Constitution.

On the internal legislative front, the government brought forward a new occupational health and safety bill and a compulsory seat belt law, and, as promised in the 1982 election campaign, created more kindergartens. Due to the difficult financial situation, however, Hatfield was twice forced to raise the retail sales and personal income taxes, limit public employee salary increases, and impose tuition fees at community colleges. The province became more dependent than ever on such federal handouts as development agreements.

After having dumped Daigle in 1991, the Liberals chose Doug Young, the leading conspirator against him, as their new leader. He was a bilingual anglophone from the Acadian part of the province, and waged an aggressive campaign against Hatfield in the 1982 election. However, Hatfield increased his majority to 39 seats, while the NDP elected its first member in the province. Hatfield thus became the longest-serving premier of the province, while Young resigned as Liberal leader and was replaced on an acting basis by Ray Frenette. The provincial media situation changed with the demise of *L'Évangeline* in September 1982, although a new French-language daily, *L'Acadie Nouvelle* began to publish in July 1984. On the other hand, the CRTC renewed the Irving TV licence in the province despite its policy to end cross-media ownership.

Hatfield's political fortunes went downhill after 1982. First, he was charged with possession of marijuana after the substance was discovered in his suitcase during the Royal Tour of Queen Elizabeth and Prince Philip to celebrate the province's bicentennial. Although he was found not guilty, several unanswered questions remained about how the police investigation and trial were conducted.[73] Immediately afterwards, Hatfield also denied allegations that he had passed out cocaine to college students in his home in 1981. At the same time, he was criticized for his extravagant expense account, which included regular weekend trips to New York City at the province's expense. These incidents placed his cabinet and caucus colleagues in an awkward position, but he vowed to lead the party into the next election. Meanwhile, Prime Minister Brian Mulroney appointed two of Hatfield's key ministers to the Senate, including J.M. Simard, Hatfield's Acadian lieutenant who had been instrumental in the Tory breakthrough in francophone areas.[74]

These problems culminated in the question of reviewing Hatfield's leadership at the party's annual meeting in November 1985. Since the provincial Progressive Conservative constitution had no leadership review mechanism, party dissidents organized in advance to attempt to add such a clause. Hatfield loyalists staged their own campaign, and the premier fought back with a cabinet shuffle and a government reorganization which included a reduction in the number of departments and a cut in the size of the civil service. The meeting was in the secure control of Hatfield supporters, and delegates turned down the proposed amendment to the constitution to provide for a vote on a leadership convention.

Meanwhile, French-English relations in the province were deteriorating, including controversy over the decision to fly the Acadian flag on public buildings. At this point, the government established a committee to hold public hearings on the two-year-old Poirier-Bastarache report, *Towards Equality of Official Languages in New Brunswick*. The report had found little real bilingualism in the central administration in Fredericton and made 96 recommendations to improve the situation. It primarily urged a dual system be adopted whereby every government department and agency would be divided into French and English sections. The 1984-85 public hearings revealed a profound difference of opinion on the question of bilingualism in the province and, in their early outings, committee members were met with insults and pelted with eggs. Since very few of the English population spoke French, any extension of French-language services was seen as a threat to English employment opportunities. Also, any expansion of bilingualism at the municipal level or in the education system was expected to entail an increase in taxes.[75] In this charged situation, not surprisingly, a new pressure group, the New Brunswick Association of English-speaking Canadians, was formed to oppose any changes. Hatfield attempted to defuse the bilingualism issue by rejecting the recommendations of the advisory committee.

By the beginning of 1986, if not earlier, all signs pointed towards Hatfield's defeat. Given these indications and additional revelations about his legal bills and travel expenses, Hatfield postponed the election until October 1987, but no one anticipated the voters' dramatic repudiation of his regime. In the meantime, the Liberals had chosen a new leader, Chatham lawyer Frank McKenna, over acting leader Ray Frenette. McKenna was young and relatively new to the legislature, but had an attractive, dynamic image. With a turnout rate of 82 percent, New Brunswickers swept Hatfield from office, giving the Liberals 60 percent of the vote, the Tories, only 28 percent, and the NDP, 10 percent. Even more remarkably, the Liberals won all 58 seats in the legislature, an accomplishment achieved only once before in Canadian history, in P.E.I. in 1935. Hatfield accepted personal responsibility for the election debacle and resigned immediately. He had retained relatively greater support in French parts of the province and, upon his departure from office, was credited with significantly improving the lot of New Brunswick's Acadians. Despite his personal spending habits and other problems, he had modernized the province in almost every field. Brian Mulroney appointed him to the Senate in 1990 and he died of brain cancer a year later.

Many wondered how the legislature would function with no official Opposition, and indeed the Liberals' first few years in power were tame. Liberal backbenchers were reluctant to ask critical questions during question period, but did present petitions on behalf of their constituents. McKenna made minor concessions to the other parties, however, including a grant of office and meeting space and minimal funding, the privilege of taking notes in the gallery, the use of expanded research services in the legislative library, and the opportunity to appear as witnesses before legislative committees. A new estimates committee gave opposition parties and the public an opportunity to question government spending.[76] In early 1989, the opposition parties were granted the further privilege of submitting written questions to the clerk of the legislature for the immediate and spontaneous reply of the ministry at the end of the daily question period. New NDP leader Elizabeth Weir was much more active than new Tory leader Barbara Baird-Filliter in making use of these opportunities and criticizing the government.

McKenna's governing style was a dramatic contrast to that of his predecessor. He put in long hours at the office, had the legislature meet at 8:30 a.m., and insisted on belt-tightening at every turn, symbolically selling the government plane that had so often transported Hatfield to New York City. The government's main priorities were job creation and deficit reduction; it therefore introduced a variety of incentives for business and made cuts in health, education, and social services. Good prices for forest products and minerals ensured a relatively prosperous provincial economy, the spruce budworm problem declined, and the $45 million Repap Enterprises Inc. coated-paper mill opened at Newcastle.

Specific government initiatives included legislation to outlaw police strikes and send such disputes to binding arbitration; replacing a provincial highway patrol, begun by Hatfield in the early 1980s, with the RCMP; a pay equity law for the public service and expansion of French language services; a legislative task force unearthed deplorable housing conditions in many parts of the province; and a hydro deal with Quebec. His only political problem occurred at N.B. Power Corporation, where the minister in charge resigned after revelations of untendered contracts and other questionable practices.

The government supported the federal Conservatives on free trade, against the wishes of the federal Liberal leader. New Brunswick subsequently won the $3.5 billion federal government contract to construct six more navy frigates (for a total of nine) in Saint John. It also signed a new five-year Economic and Regional Development Agreement in 1989 involving $100 million in federal funds. All this did not seem to soften McKenna's opposition to the Meech Lake Accord, however, as he became the first of three premiers to renege on his predecessor's initial approval. McKenna later tried to repair the damage and play peacemaker with a "parallel accord" which would respond to northern, native, and women's concerns, oblige the federal government to promote minority language rights in all provinces, and make clear that the Quebec distinct society clause did not supersede the Charter of Rights. After it was too late, in mid-1990, McKenna announced that he could live with the accord. In its wake, he set up a nine-member constitutional commission.

The 1990s

During the first half of the 1990s, the McKenna government established a reputation for innovative social policy, futuristic economic thinking, and restraint in public spending. One of the few economic problems was a long strike at Bathurst Mining and Smelting during 1990 and 1991.

McKenna put his monopoly of legislative seats on the line in an election in September 1991. The Tories had chosen Dennis Cochrane as their leader just three months before, but that party was still reeling from the Hatfield legacy, the indifferent leadership of Barbara Baird-Filliter, and the exodus of members opposed to bilingualism, who were joining the Confederation of Regions (CoR) party. McKenna was easily re-elected, while the Conservatives and CoR were almost tied in popular vote (at 21 percent), though the latter won eight seats to the former's three. The NDP elected its leader, Elizabeth Weir. The CoR leader, however, lost in his constituency, so Danny Cameron was chosen to lead the party in the legislature. Two of his brightest MLAs later challenged his leadership and left the caucus to sit as Independents.

McKenna's concern about the government deficit only increased in the 1990s. Over the 1990-93 period, he cut nearly 2,000 public service jobs, mostly by attrition, closed hospital beds, and eliminated or amalgamated government agencies. Within the public service, he emphasized rationalization, restructuring, privatization, and voluntary unpaid time off. Although he considered user fees to reduce medicare costs, he ultimately resisted this idea. Instead, patients were sent statements showing how much their "free" medical services had cost.[77]

The 1991 budget included a surtax on high incomes, and broke collective agreements by imposing a one-year freeze on public service salaries. When the freeze was repeated in the 1992 budget, it provoked an illegal public service strike which closed government offices, hospitals, and schools. Eventually the two sides agreed to a one-percent salary increase in 1992 and two-percent in 1993. The 1993 budget raised and extended taxes and cut such programs as the seniors' drug plan. That year McKenna also passed a law requiring the government to produce a balanced budget for operating expenses over a four-year period. In 1994, McKenna slashed another 600 government positions and added

**TABLE 5.11   Government of New Brunswick Finances,
1990/91–1994/95 (millions)**

	1990/91	1991/92	1992/93	1993/94	1994/95
Total revenues	$3,968.3	$4,009.4	$4,207.1	$4,333.1	$4,469.2
Debt charges	581.1	634.5	657.7	785.0	791.9
Total expenditures	4,128.4	4,345.9	4,522.4	4,550.4	4,519.6
Deficit	160.1	336.5	315.3	217.3	50.4

Source: Reproduced by authority of the Minister of Industry, 1995, Statistics Canada, *Public Sector Finance, 1994–95,* Financial Management System, cat. no. 68-212 (March 1995). Adapted by author.

another pay freeze. By eliminating 400 more jobs and cutting other expenditures, the 1995 budget was finally balanced. Table 5.10 provides basic information on the 1990 to 1994 budgets.

McKenna was also doing his utmost to attract new businesses to the province. He succeeded in getting well over a dozen firms to set up "back office" or other communications branches in New Brunswick—telemarketing, billing, data processing, telephone orders, and market research. Most settled in Moncton to take advantage of the city's bilingualism, but some also went to Fredericton and Saint John. New Brunswick's unemployment rate fell below that of Nova Scotia, and some attributed the drop to the efforts of the premier and the government.

The third main thrust of the McKenna strategy was reform of social policy. In this respect, too, it had a conservative approach. The royal commission on education found the education system needed more money, more emphasis on such basics as math, science and language skills, more testing, and more teaching days per year. McKenna immediately began to implement these ideas, but saw the situation in a broader light. Education, social assistance, and unemployment insurance were linked, and he wanted to use education and training to reduce the reliance on unemployment insurance and welfare. Over 100 literacy centres were established for upgrading purposes. Federal-provincial pilot projects were also set up to provide those on income assistance programs with income supplements for transportation, child care, and other factors that would make it easier to find employment. Alternatively, three-year N.B. Works training programs were designed specifically for such long-term social assistance recipients as single mothers. The N.B. Jobs Corps provided income for people aged 50 to 65 who chose to work on such community projects as planting trees or cleaning up beaches. McKenna insisted that, through the discipline of work or training, people could increase their dignity and self-esteem. In 1995, the government announced that welfare benefits, already the lowest in the country, would be reduced if recipients refused an offer of training or a job.

The mid-1990s saw several other interesting developments. Dr. Henry Morgentaler opened an abortion clinic in Fredericton and ran into the usual hassles of being denied authority to practice and funding under the province's public medical insurance plan. The federal government closed Canadian Forces Base Chatham, while the province shut down Kingsclear, a young offenders facility rife with physical and sexual abuse. A new institution was scheduled for construction in the Miramichi, where it was expected to offset the effects of the closure of the military base. The government also announced that most liquor outlets would be privatized, and Wallace McCain left to take over Maple Leaf Foods. Perhaps most interesting, charismatic former Mulroney minister Bernard Valcourt took over the Conservative party leadership.

CONCLUSION

Following the long period of Hatfield Conservatism in New Brunswick, the McKenna Liberals have gained a stranglehold on power. The presence of the Confederation of Regions party has hindered the Conservatives' rebuilding efforts. Barring unforeseen circumstances, such as Frank McKenna moving on to the national political scene, it appears that New Brunswick is destined for a protracted period of Liberalism. This is not only due to weakness and divisions on the part of the Opposition. It is also because McKenna is one of the ablest premiers in office in the 1990s. His far-sighted and energetic performance has given New Brunswick residents renewed hope that a small remote province might have a bright future after all.

TABLE 5.12   New Brunswick Provincial Election Results Since 1920

Year	Liberals		Conservatives		CCF/NDP		Other	
	Seats	Popular Vote	Seats	Popular Vote	Seats	Popular Vote	Seats	Popular Vote
1920	24	46%	13	27%	9	20%	2	7%
1925	11	45%	37	53%	—	2%		
1930	17	48%	31	52%				
1935	43	60%	5	40%				
1939	29	55%	19	45%				
1944	37	48%	11	40%	—	13%		
1948	47	58%	5	31%	—	6%	—	5%
1952	16	49%	36	49%	—	1%		
1956	15	46%	37	52%	—	2%		
1960	31	53%	21	46%				
1963	32	51%	20	48%				
1967	32	53%	26	47%				
1970	25	49%	33	48%	—	3%		

TABLE 5.12 continued

Year	Liberals		Conservatives		CCF/NDP		Other	
	Seats	Popular Vote	Seats	Popular Vote	Seats	Popular Vote	Seats	Popular Vote
1974	27	47%	31	47%	—	3%	—	3%**
1978	28	44%	30	44%	—	7%	—	5%**
1982	18	41%	39	47%	1	10%	—	1%**
1987	58	60%	—	28%	—	10%	—	2%
1991	46	47%	3	21%	1	11%	8	21%***

*   United Farmers
**   Parti Acadien
*** Confederation of Regions

TABLE 5.13   Premiers of New Brunswick Since 1867

Premier	Party	Year Elected
Andrew Wetmore	(Conservative)	1867
George King	(Conservative)	1870
George Hatheway	(Conservative)	1871
George King	(Conservative)	1872
James Fraser	(Conservative)	1878
Daniel Hanington	(Conservative)	1882
Andrew Blair	(Liberal)	1883
James Mitchell	(Liberal)	1896
Henry Emmerson	(Liberal)	1897
Lemuel Tweedie	(Liberal)	1900
William Pugsley	(Liberal)	1907
Clifford Robinson	(Liberal)	1907
John Douglas Hazen	(Conservative)	1908
James Kidd Flemming	(Conservative)	1911
George Clarke	(Conservative)	1914
James Murray	(Conservative)	1917
Walter Foster	(Liberal)	1917
Peter Veniot	(Liberal)	1923
John B.M. Baxter	(Conservative)	1925
Charles Richards	(Conservative)	1931
Leonard Tilley	(Conservative)	1933
Allison Dysart	Liberal	1935
John McNair	Liberal	1940
Hugh John Flemming	Progressive Conservative	1952
Louis Robichaud	Liberal	1960
Richard Hatfield	Progressive Conservative	1970
Frank McKenna	Liberal	1987

ENDNOTES

1. Hugh G. Thorburn, *Politics in New Brunswick* (Toronto: University of Toronto Press, 1961), p. 186.

2. New Brunswick Department of Finance, *New Brunswick Economy,* 1994.

3. Tom Murphy, "Potato Capitalism: McCain and Industrial Farming in New Brunswick," and Darrell McLaughlin, "From Self-Reliance to Dependence to Struggle: Agribusiness and the Politics of Potatoes in New Brunswick," in Gary Burrill and Ian McKay, eds., *People, Resources, and Power* (Fredericton: Acadiensis Press, 1987); and Grace Skogstad, "State Autonomy and Provincial Policy-Making: Potato Marketing in New Brunswick and Prince Edward Island," *Canadian Journal of Political Science* (September 1987).

4. Murphy, "Potato Capitalism," and McLaughlin, "From Self-Reliance to Dependence," in Burrill and McKay, eds., *People, Resources, and Power.*

5. Russell Hunt and Robert Campbell, *K.C. Irving: The Art of the Industrialist* (Toronto: McClelland and Stewart, 1973), who say: "Irving's domination of his province was almost total," p. 115. His son once claimed that, at least until 1967, Irving had never lost an election, p. 121. "Surely no individual in any single Canadian province had ever held so much raw economic power," writes J.E. Belliveau, *Little Louis and the Giant KC.* (Hantsport, N.S.: Lancelot Press, 1980), p. 15. See also John DeMont, *Citizens Irving: K.C. Irving and his Legacy.* (Toronto: Doubleday, 1991), and Douglas How and Ralph Costello, *K.C.: The Biography of K.C. Irving* (Toronto: Key Porter Books, 1994).

6. Skogstad, "State Autonomy and Provincial Policy-making," p. 508; McLaughlin, "From Self-Reliance to Dependence," p. 32; Hugh Mellon, "The Politics of Reform," in Keith Brownsey and Michael Howlett, eds., *The Provincial State* (Mississauga: Copp Clark Pitman, 1992).

7. Edmund A. Aunger, *In Search of Political Stability: a Comparative Study of New Brunswick and Northern Ireland* (Montreal: McGill-Queen's University Press, 1981), p. 20.

8. Thorburn, *Politics in New Brunswick,* p. 4.

9. Emery Fanjoy, "Language and Politics in New Brunswick," *Canadian Parliamentary Review* (Summer 1990); Harley d'Entremont, "Reflections on Recent Manifestations of Acadian Nationalism," Département de science politique, Université de Moncton, 1981; Harley d'Entremont, Phillippe Doucet, and Jean-Guy Finn, "Acadian Neo-Nationalism and Political Power," Département de science politique, Université de Moncton; and Doucet and Finn, "Elements de reforme du système électoral du Nouveau-Brunswick," *Journal of Canadian Studies* (Winter 1983-84).

10. On this subject, Thorburn writes: "...there is a complex of dispersive influences: the North Shore rivals the South Shore; the St. John drainage basin competes with the Miramichi; the forest economy is challenged by agriculture, fishing, manufacturing, and now mining; the French population claims its rights from the English; Catholics expand their influence at the expense of Protestants. The result is great variety but little homogeneity—watchful rivalry but no unity of purpose," see Thorburn, *Politics in New Brunswick,* p. 50.

11. Edmund Aunger has written a fascinating comparison of politics in New Brunswick and Northern Ireland, contrasting the political stability of the former with the instability of the latter.

12. Donald J. Savoie, *Federal-Provincial Collaboration: the Canada-New Brunswick General Development Agreement* (Montreal: McGill-Queen's University Press, 1981), and "The General Development Agreement Approach and the Bureaucratization of Provincial Governments in the Atlantic Provinces," in *Canadian Public Administration* (Spring 1981).

13. Thorburn, *Politics in New Brunswick*, p. 83. P.J. Fitzpatrick uses the words "parochial, stagnant and anachronistic" in "New Brunswick, The Politics of Pragmatism," in Martin Robin, ed., *Canadian Provincial Politics* (Scarborough: Prentice Hall Canada, 1978), p. 120.

14. David Bellamy, "The Atlantic Provinces," in David Bellamy et al., eds., *The Provincial Political Systems* (Toronto: Methuen, 1976); Aunger attributes deference to the Loyalists, as well as economic underdevelopment and clientelism, *In Search of Political Stability*, p. 165.

15. Thorburn, *Politics in New Brunswick*, p. 21. See also d'Entremont, "Reflections on Recent Manifestations," and d'Entremont, Doucet, and Finn, "Acadian Neo-Nationalism."

16. The "marginal work world" concept is used in Richard Apostle and Paul Pross, "Marginality and Political Culture: A New Approach to Political Culture in Atlantic Canada," Canadian Political Science Association, 1981. A somewhat contrary thesis is that "during the past three decades, there has been an erosion of the conditions on which patronage politics was based. One of the most significant factors in this erosion has been the growth and influence of the mass media." See Mark Pedersen, *The Transition From Patronage to Media Politics and Its Impact on New Brunswick Political Parties*, unpublished MA thesis, Queen's University, 1982, p. 1.

17. Jeffrey Simpson, *Spoils of Power* (Toronto: Collins, 1988).

18. For example, David J. Elkins and Richard Simeon, eds., *Small Worlds: Provinces and Parties in Canadian Political Life* (Toronto: Methuen, 1980).

19. Marsha Chandler and William Chandler, *Public Policy and Provincial Politics* (Toronto: McGraw-Hill Ryerson, 1979), pp. 77-83; Stephen Ullman, "Political Disaffection in the Province of New Brunswick: Manifestations and Sources," *American Review of Canadian Studies* (Summer 1990).

20. Aunger, *The Search For Stability*, pp. 165-66.

21. Calvin A. Woodward, *The History of New Brunswick Provincial Election Campaigns and Platforms, 1866-1974* (Micromedia, 1976), pp. 2-6.

22. Thorburn, *Politics in New Brunswick*, p. 13.

23. Della M.M. Stanley, *Louis Robichaud, a Decade of Power* (Halifax: Nimbus Publishing, 1984), p. 39.

24. For the Liberal case, see Joseph Wearing, *The L-Shaped Party* (Toronto: McGraw-Hill Ryerson, 1981), pp. 89-96.

25. Arthur T. Doyle, *The Premiers of New Brunswick* (Fredericton: Brunswick Press, 1983), pp. 18, 34.

26. Thorburn, *Politics in New Brunswick,* p. 183, states: "the province has been on the winning side whenever this could be divined with any accuracy before the election."

27. Doyle, *The Premiers of New Brunswick,* pp. vii-xii. See also Jennifer Smith, "Ruling Small Worlds: Political Leadership in Atlantic Canada," in Leslie Pal and David Taras, eds., *Prime Ministers and Premiers* (Scarborough: Prentice Hall Canada 1988).

28. The Liberals did away with a leadership review mechanism in their constitution, while the Conservatives have never had one, rejecting the idea in 1985.

29. Stanley, *Louis Robichaud,* pp. 221-25.

30. Val Sears, "Richard Hatfield: A Matter of Style," *The Toronto Star,* 27 October 1984, p. 5, quoting *Moncton Times-Journalist* reporter Don Hoyt.

31. Thorburn, *Politics in New Brunswick,* p. 181, states: "The two dominant parties stand for traditions, principles, attitudes, and prejudices which resemble one another very closely. Consequently a change of government involves no striking change of policy —mainly a change of personalities in the cabinet and some shifts in the distribution of patronage."

32. Aunger, *In Search of Stability,* p. 152.

33. Thorburn, *Politics in New Brunswick,* p. 104.

34. Aunger, *In Search of Political Stability,* pp. 48, 62, 67, and 75.

35. The Representation and Electoral District Boundaries Commission, *A New Electoral Map for New Brunswick* (Fredericton, 1993).

36. Fitzpatrick, "New Brunswick, The Politics of Pragmatism," in Robin, *Canadian Provincial Politics,* p. 134.

37. Dalton Camp, *Gentlemen, Players and Politicians* (Toronto: McClelland and Stewart, 1970); Thorburn, *Politics in New Brunswick,* p. 122.

38. Belliveau, *Little Louis and the Giant KC,* p. 37.

39. John T. Saywell, *The Office of Lieutenant-Governor* (Toronto: University of Toronto Press, 1957), pp. 38, 221.

40. Thorburn, *Politics in New Brunswick,* p. 205; Aunger feels Acadians were fairly represented in the cabinet at least since 1948, *In Search of Political Stability,* p. 119.

41. Paul C. Leger, "The Cabinet Committee System of Policy-making and Resource Allocation in the Government of New Brunswick," in *Canadian Public Administration* (Spring 1983). Reports surfaced that the premier himself was frequently absent from cabinet and caucus meetings.

42. Hugh G. Thorburn, *Planning and the Economy* (Toronto: Canadian Institute for Economic Policy, 1984), p. 147.

43. G. William Kitchin, "The Abolition of Upper Chambers," in Donald C. Rowat, ed., *Provincial Government and Politics: Comparative Essays* (Ottawa: Department of Political Science, Carleton University, 1972), pp. 68-71.

44. 1867-1874: 40   1912-1948: 48
     1874-1895: 41   1948-1967: 52
     1895-1912: 46   1967-1995: 58
                             1995-   55

     See David Peterson, "New Brunswick: A bilingual assembly for a bilingual province," in Gary Levy and Graham White, eds., *Provincial and Territorial Legislatures in Canada* (Toronto: University of Toronto Press, 1989).

45. Agar Adamson, "Digging Democracy Out from Under McKenna's Landslide," *Parliamentary Government* (1988, No. 1).

46. New Brunswick Legislative Assembly, *Legislative Activities, 1993* (Fredericton, 1993).

47. Thorburn, *Politics in New Brunswick,* pp. 161-4; Simpson, *Spoils of Power,* ch. 9; and Starr, *Richard Hatfield.* Hatfield and even McKenna have been quoted as saying that patronage is a fact of political life in the province, and Dalton Camp echoes the "marginal work world" theorists in saying that patronage, which is "a matter of political favour and partisan right, is often a matter of survival as well," in Camp, *Gentlemen, Players and Politicians,* p. 20. Aunger also discusses this in *In Search of Political Stability,* p. 151.

48. In the absence of a good general post-Confederation history of New Brunswick, the most valuable sources here are Woodward, *The History of New Brunswick Provincial Election Campaigns and Platforms,* and Doyle, *The Premiers of New Brunswick.*

49. Doyle, *The Premiers,* pp. 5-6; Woodward, *New Brunswick Provincial Election Campaigns,* p. 12; George King is usually regarded as one of the "great premiers" of the province and later served on the New Brunswick and Canadian Supreme Courts. Aunger outlines the compromise on p. 137 of *In Search of Stability.*

50. Woodward, *New Brunswick Provincial Election Campaigns,* pp. 20-21. Doyle describes Blair as handsome, distinguished, strikingly impressive, and an excellent debater, p. 14.

51. Arthur T. Doyle, *Front Benches & Back Rooms* (Omega Publications, 1976), ch. 4; Aunger, *In Search of Political Stability,* p. 150.

52. Woodward, *New Brunswick Provincial Election Campaigns,* p. 53.

53. Ibid., p. 56.

54. Ibid., p. 62.

55. Ibid., p. 64. The CCF ran one candidate in 1939, 41 in 1944, and 20 in 1948, with the following percentages of popular vote: one, 13, and six percent respectively. Part of the reason for such low support were such outrageous allegations as that it was totalitarian and stood for a socialist dictatorship, etc.

56. The description of this well-documented decade is based on Stanley, *Louis Robichaud, A Decade of Power;* Belliveau, *Little Louis and the Giant KC;* Hunt and Campbell, *K.C Irving: The Art of the Industrialist;* and Richard Wilbur's annual account of New Brunswick in John Saywell, ed., *The Canadian Annual Review* (Toronto: University of Toronto Press).

57. He has been described as colourful, peppery, ebullient, flamboyant, a bundle of dynamite, a chunky ball of energy, a passionate reformer, and possessed of dramatic flair. Others have used such terms as short, slick, sweaty, hard-drinking and feisty. Another popular promise in 1960 was to bring back the moose hunt. Belliveau, *Little Louis and the Giant KC,* p. 42.

58. Woodward, *New Brunswick Provincial Election Campaigns,* p. 79.

59. The best analysis of the Program for Equal Opportunity is contained in R.R. Krueger, "The Provincial-Municipal Government Revolution in New Brunswick," in *Canadian Public Administration* (Spring 1970), pp. 51-99. R.A. Young looks back in "Remembering Equal Opportunity: Clearing the Undergrowth in New Brunswick," *Canadian Public Administration* (Spring 1987).

60. Interestingly enough, John Graham, the author of the royal commission report on the same subject in Nova Scotia (with the same basic thrust) was also a consultant to the Byrne royal commission.

61. Stanley, *Louis Robichaud,* p. 181.

62. Ibid., p. 92; interviews with New Brunswick officials.

63. As Krueger describes it, "the municipal taxation situation in New Brunswick was indeed in bad shape. There was a jungle of assessment and tax laws; the decentralized assessment procedures led to a great variety of interpretations of existing laws: there were serious tax inequities across the province and even within municipalities; and almost one-third of all taxes were in arrears. Moreover, at a time when there was growing concern about economic disparities within the province, the municipal taxes were highest in the economically depressed areas where the people could least afford to pay them," p. 67.

64. Hunt and Campbell, *K.C. Irving: The Art of the Industrialist,* ch. 5.

65. Belliveau, *Little Louis and the Giant KC,* p. 97, quoting Walter Stewart in the *Toronto Star.*

66. Peter Leslie, "The Role of Political Parties in Promoting the Interests of Ethnic Minorities," in *Canadian Journal of Political Science* (1969) emphasizes, as does Aunger, the maturity of party leaders in avoiding inflammatory issues.

67. *Canadian Annual Review,* 1970, p. 253.

68. The best sources on this period are Richard Starr, *Richard Hatfield, the Seventeen Year Saga* (Halifax: Formac Publishing, (1987); Michel Cormier and Achille Michaud, *Richard Hatfield: Power and Disobedience* (Fredericton: Goose Lane Editions, 1992); Nancy Southam, ed., *Remembering Richard: An Informal Portrait of Richard Hatfield* (Halifax: Formac, 1993); and the annual account in the *Canadian Annual Review of Politics and Public Affairs.*

69. Starr, *Richard Hatfield,* ch. 6.

70. Ibid.

71. Simpson, *Spoils of Power.*

72. *Canadian Annual Review* (Toronto: University of Toronto Press, 1976), p. 224. See also Bruce Livesey, "The Political Economy of Pesticide and Herbicide Testing in New Brunswick," in Burrill and McKay, eds., *People, Resources, and Power.*

73. While many observers had no trouble believing that the marijuana could have belonged to Hatfield, one claim is that it was planted there by a jealous ex-lover. See Donald Ripley, *Bag Man: A Life in Nova Scotia Politics* (Toronto: Key Porter Books, 1993).

74. Starr, *Richard Hatfield.*

75. Aunger, *In Search of Stability,* p. 68.

76. Adamson, "Digging Democracy out from Under McKenna's Landslide."

77. Merle MacIsaac, "Faith, Hope and Hold the Charity," *Canadian Business Magazine* (December 1992).

READINGS

Burrill, Gary, and Ian McKay, eds. *People, Resources, and Power.* Fredericton: Acadiensis Press, 1987.

Canadian Annual Review of Politics and Public Affairs. Toronto: University of Toronto Press, annual.

Cormier, Michel, and Achille Michaud. *Richard Hatfield: Power and Disobedience.* Fredericton: Goose Lane Editions, 1992.

DeMont, John. *Citizens Irving: K.C. Irving and his Legacy.* Toronto: Doubleday, 1991.

How, Douglas, and Ralph Costello, *K.C.: The Biography of K.C. Irving.* Toronto: Key Porter Books, 1994.

Mellon, Hugh. "The Politics of Reform." Keith Brownsey and Michael Howlett, eds. *The Provincial State.* Mississauga: Copp Clark Pitman, 1992.

New Brunswick Department of Finance. *The New Brunswick Economy.*

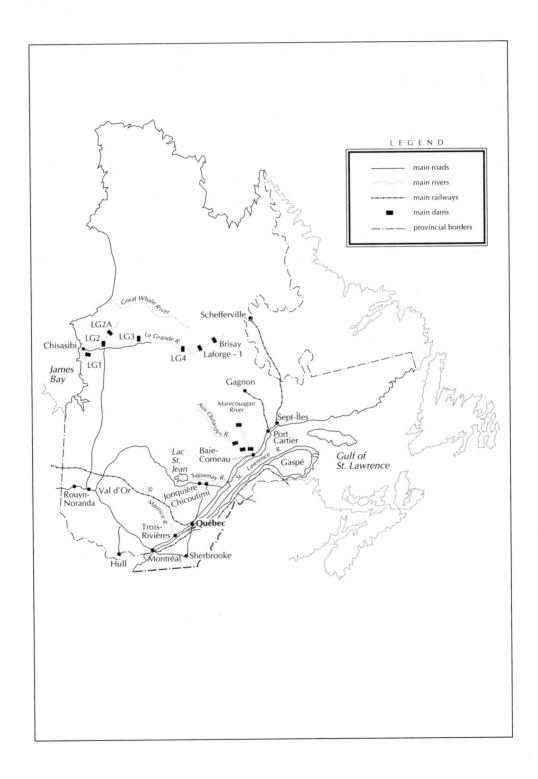

LEGEND

——	main roads
〜〜	main rivers
+++	main railways
■	main dams
–·–·–	provincial borders

Great Whale River

Schefferville

LG2A

LG2   LG3   La Grande R.

Chisasibi

LG1   LG4   Brisay
Laforge - 1

James
Bay

Gagnon

Manicouagan
River

Aux Outardes R.

Sept-Îles

Port
Cartier

Lac
St.
Jean

Baie-
Comeau

St. Lawrence R.

Gaspé

Gulf of
St. Lawrence

Saguenay R.

Rouyn-
Noranda   Val d'Or

Jonquière
Chicoutimi

St. Maurice R.

Trois-
Rivières

Québec

Hull   Montréal   Sherbrooke

QUEBEC

Quebec is Canada's most distinctive province, essentially because the majority of its inhabitants are of French descent. It has had a long history as a distinctive social and cultural entity, to which the role of the Roman Catholic Church was historically central, and it has been preoccupied with preserving its unique values and way of life. The French language is now more predominant than ever, and plays an important part in the province's vibrant culture. Thus, Quebec considers itself to be a "distinct society"—in some sense even a nation—and in recent years has widely entertained the idea of becoming a sovereign state. There is no province in which federal-provincial relations have been more significant, and much attention is focused on this question. However, given the province's unusual characteristics, internal political developments have also been of great interest. In this respect, 1960 is the great dividing line between the old, backward, authoritarian, inward-looking and church-dominated Quebec society, and the modern, progressive, self-confident, outgoing, secular Quebec of today. The province underwent a "Quiet Revolution" in the 1960s which transformed it almost beyond recognition. The rejection of the Charlottetown Constitutional Accord in 1992, and the election of the separatist Parti Québécois in 1994, set the stage for the 1995 referendum on Quebec sovereignty.

SETTING

Geography

Quebec has an area of 1,540,700 square kilometres, making it considerably larger than Ontario, and extends farther north than any other province. Quebec is comprised mostly of the Canadian Shield, but the fertile St. Lawrence lowlands are located along that river, and the Gaspé and southeastern part of the province are part of the Appalachian region. The St. Lawrence has been central to all aspects of the province's development for centuries, but there are a number of other powerful rivers—the Saguenay, Manicouagan, Aux Outardes, St. Maurice, and La Grande—which provide the basis for the province's hydroelectric power. The province is usually divided into 10 regions, of which Montreal and Quebec City (and their surroundings) are most well known. The others are the Eastern Townships (or Estrie), centred around Sherbrooke in the southeast; the Bas-Saint-Laurent and Gaspé Peninsula (Gaspésie); Côte-Nord, the rugged north bank of the St. Lawrence; the Saguenay-Lac St. Jean region that includes Chicoutimi-Jonquière; Mauricie surrounds the St. Maurice River and Trois-Rivières; Outaouais extends north from Hull; Abitibi-Timiscamingue in the northwest; and New Quebec in the north. There is intense rivalry between the cities of Quebec and Montreal, extending from political and economic power to tourism and hockey, and considerable competition among the other regions. They each have their own economic interests, are somewhat remote from each other, and are all in need of government assistance. A general cleavage between urban and rural forces can also be detected.

The province's transportation system includes ports along the St. Lawrence River and Seaway, especially Port-Cartier, Sept-Iles, Montreal, and Quebec, which rank second to fifth in the country. Montreal is a deep-water port with container facilities, and is the headquarters of both Canadian Pacific and Canadian National railways, as well as Air Canada. Montreal's Dorval Airport is the third-busiest in the country in terms of passengers and sixth in cargo, whereas Mirabel is third in cargo but sixth in passengers. A railway connects Sept-Îles, on the St. Lawrence, to the iron mines of Schefferville and Labrador, and another runs north from Port Cartier. Highways run along both sides of the St. Lawrence, and connect New Brunswick to Ontario.

According to the 1991 census, the province's population was 6,895,963, or 25.3 percent of the Canadian total. The figure had risen to 7,300,000 by January, 1995. The Montreal metropolitan area is the largest urban concentration with some 3,127,242 inhabitants, or close to one-half of the population of the province. This includes the city of Montreal at 1,017,666, the city of Laval (314,398) and many surrounding municipalities. Montreal has always dominated the province economically and culturally, even though the provincial capital is Quebec City. That is the second-largest community, with a population of 645,550 in the labour market area, and is also the location of major insurance companies, a port, and some manufacturing. Only four other centres have populations which exceed 100,000: Hull (226,957); Chicoutimi-Jonquière (160,928); Sherbrooke (139,194); and Trois-Rivières (136,303). Overall, Quebec is the fourth most urbanized province, at 77.6 percent.

Economy

The Quebec economy is based on vast natural resources—mining, forestry, agriculture, and hydroelectric power—although it is increasingly expanding into secondary and tertiary sectors. Talk of separation or sovereignty often leads to questions about the Quebec economy and its ability to sustain an independent country. Many different answers have been offered.

Despite the limited amount of arable land, Quebec's most important primary industry is agriculture, and the province is the fourth-largest agricultural producer in the country after Ontario, Alberta, and Saskatchewan. Since 1978 the province's supply of agricultural land has been carefully controlled. In 1991, it had 38,076 census farms with an average size of 223 acres. These small strip farms specialize in dairy products and hogs (in both of which it leads the country), as well as poultry and eggs (second), and cattle (fourth). Crops are less important, but include vegetables, corn, nursery products, potatoes, and fruit, along with maple products. The province hosts a large number of agricultural marketing boards, and agriculture also contributes to the food and beverage sector of manufacturing.

The second most valuable primary industry is mining, in which it ranks fifth in comparison with other provinces. Quebec's two main minerals are gold and iron ore, in both of which it ranks second in the country; next come copper and asbestos, in which it is third and first respectively. Until company president Brian Mulroney closed the Iron Ore Co. of Canada operations at Schefferville in 1983, it was the leading source of iron ore within the province. The town remains alive as a commercial centre for surrounding aboriginal communities, but Quebec Cartier Mining now produces Quebec's iron. The entire industry was hard hit in the early 1980s and the town of Gagnon was also abandoned. For about 25 years the province owned Sidbec, privatized in 1994, which produces about 70 percent of Quebec's steel. Then, between 1978 and 1982, the provincial government nationalized two major firms in the asbestos industry with the creation of the Société Nationale de l'Amiante (SNA). Asbestos was also one of the province's leading exports, but it is no longer in such great demand. Zinc, peat, and silver are also extracted. Quebec is a major producer and exporter of aluminum, and contains plants owned by most of the world's largest aluminum firms including Alcan Aluminum, Reynolds, and Pechiney. In this case, however, the raw material, bauxite, is imported, and production in Quebec is based on abundant hydroelectric power, of which the conversion process requires a great deal. The province also specializes in such structural materials as stone, cement, sand, gravel, and limestone.

Forestry is the province's third most valuable primary industry and, in this respect, it is second in the nation to British Columbia. Almost half the province is covered by commercial forest, most of it on public land. While B.C. produces more lumber, Quebec is ahead in wood pulp, newsprint, and other paper and paperboard. Pulp and paper is the largest part of the forestry industry, and newsprint is the province's leading export. Major companies involved include Domtar Inc. and Donohue Inc., which are largely controlled by the Quebec government, as well as Consolidated Bathurst Inc., Kruger, Scott Paper, and E.B. Eddy. Pulp and paper facilities were recently modernized. Quebec has also battled the spruce budworm, and much concern has been expressed about reforestation efforts.

There is also a considerable commercial fishing industry in the St. Lawrence River and Gulf, and around the Gaspé. Cod, herring, lobster, shrimp, and crab are the leading catches, along with ocean perch, halibut, and mackerel. The industry provides employment for many fishermen and fish processing plant workers.

Hydroelectricity is in some ways the province's most valuable resource, and Quebec slightly outranks Ontario in its production. After the nationalization of the remaining private firms in 1963, Hydro-Quebec expanded its operations enormously and is now one of the largest electricity utilities in North America. The St. Lawrence river used to be the main site of hydroelectric dams but, in the past 25 years, development of the northern rivers has occurred at a breathtaking pace. The Manic complex in northeastern Quebec on the Manicouagan and Aux Outardes rivers consists of seven power stations. Quebec exports a good deal of electricity, especially to the United States and Ontario and, as noted in earlier chapters, buys a huge amount of power from Newfoundland and resells it at a large profit. As of 1994, Quebec had 54 hydroelectric and 30 thermal generating stations. The former provided about 92 percent of the province's electricity, while the latter included one nuclear plant, one oil, three gas-turbine, and several diesel units. Electricity is seen as the key to Quebec's economic progress, as it is cheaper and more abundant than almost anywhere else (see Inset 6.1). The province actively seeks industries which use large quantities of electricity, especially in the form of electrochemistry and electrometallurgy, such as in the production of aluminum.

INSET 6.1 The James Bay Hydroelectric Project

Since the dawn of the Quiet Revolution, political leaders in Quebec have seen the production of hydroelectricity as the province's single most important asset. Their first concern was to get it into francophone hands, where it could serve as a symbol of francophone competence and a catalyst for high-level francophone employment. In the early 1960s, the simplest way of achieving francophone control of the industry was by means of a Crown corporation, Hydro-Québec, but René Lévesque foresaw how such a state-owned enterprise could be used by the government to foster desirable economic development. The Liberal and Union Nationale governments of the 1960s built many dams, especially on the Manicouagan and Aux Outardes rivers, and signed the deal to buy electricity from Churchill Falls in Labrador.

When Robert Bourassa came on the scene in 1970, he was obsessed with the idea of expanding the production of hydroelectricity as the backbone of the Quebec economy. During his first term as premier, 1970-76, he began construction of the first phase of the James Bay project, which involved diverting five rivers into La Grande

Rivière in northern Quebec at a cost of some $14 billion. This massive development involved negotiating an agreement with the resident Crees under which they received cash and territorial rights for giving up land for the project. An agreement was signed by the federal and provincial governments and aboriginal peoples in 1975. The latter received exclusive use of 13,700 square kilometres of land and an additional 450,000 square kilometres of exclusive hunting, fishing, and trapping rights, along with $225 million in cash, in return for surrendering their claim to the rest of the territory. At the time, most observers were impressed with the fairness of the agreement but, in retrospect, many are less enthusiastic. The environmental damage was much greater than expected, and an unanticipated chemical reaction between water and rock in the flooded land caused the mercury poisoning of fish and the Natives who ate them.

The Parti Québécois government from 1976 to 1985 completed the construction of phase one of the La Grande project, which consisted of four major dams: LG-2, LG-2A, LG-3, and LG-4. Bourassa returned to office in 1985 with even more grandiose plans for hydroelectric development. Phase two of the La Grande project involved three more major generating stations, LG-1, Laforge 1, and Brisay, and construction started immediately.

In addition to the two phases of La Grande, Bourassa had two other megaprojects in mind. First, the Great Whale (Grande Baleine) project to the north of La Grande would entail spending over $13 billion to build three main generating stations (GB1, GB2, and GB3) to produce about 3,000 megawatts of electricity. It would also divert five rivers into the Great Whale and flood a substantial area, including 1,500 square kilometres of land. After 10 years of experience with La Grande, the Cree of the area, along with environmentalists largely outside Quebec, immediately mounted a sustained protest. After a great deal of haggling, including court cases and threats of unilateral action by the two levels of government and the Cree, in early 1992 a federal-provincial-aboriginal environmental review was agreed upon. Meanwhile, Matthew Coon-Come, grand chief of the James Bay Cree, went to the United Nations and New York State (where he found an ally in Robert Kennedy Jr.) to outline how the project would affect his people. The Cree even took out a $40,000 (US) ad in the leading American newspaper, the *New York Times*. They did, however, sign a deal with Hydro to finish the La Grande project and received some $125 million in compensation. Bourassa put Great Whale on hold in August 1991 when New York state asked for time to think about renewing its $17-billion contract. In March 1992, New York told Quebec that it would not renew. The state cancelled another $5-billion contract in 1993, the year Hydro-Québec released a $400-million, 30-volume feasibility study on the Great Whale project. Although Hydro started to encourage conservation of energy, nothing happened until two years later, when new Premier Parizeau "shelved the project for the foreseeable future."

Bourassa and Hydro-Québec had also planned an 8,400 megawatt Nottaway-Broadback-Rupert (NBR) project to the south of La Grande, which would have affected many more Cree. Because it was planned as the final part of the monumental project, its development became more unlikely with the suspension of Great Whale. Figure 6.1 indicates the sites of those dams constructed as part of the La Grande project, as well as those planned as part of Great Whale and NBR.

FIGURE 6.1   Map of the James Bay Hydroelectric Project

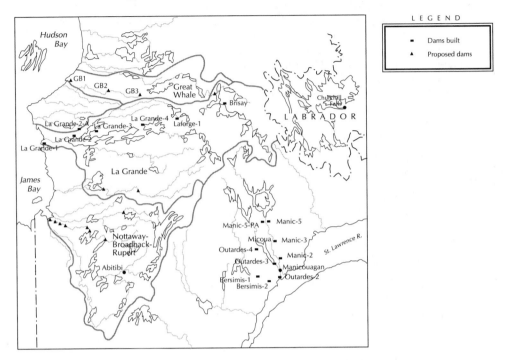

Quebec's annual manufacturing output has the second-largest value in the country, but is less than half that of Ontario. Leading segments of the manufacturing industry are primary metals and metal fabricating, food and beverages, clothing and textiles, aeronautics, paper and allied products, machinery and electrical products, transportation equipment, wood and furniture, pharmaceuticals, chemicals and chemical products, and petroleum refining and petrochemicals. To some extent, high-tech industries are displacing the traditional reliance on textiles, clothing, leather, footwear, and furniture. Quebec's most dynamic manufacturing firm is probably Bombardier Inc., which began with the invention of the snowmobile. The company now also produces subway cars and railway products, and owns Canadair, which received the maintenance contract for the military's CF-18 fighter planes as well as other federal defence contracts. Bombardier has also become a multi-national corporation with Irish, French, and American acquisitions, including the U.S. Lear jet. While much resource processing and refining is carried out in various hinterland locations, 70 percent of the more sophisticated manufacturing industries are located in the Montreal region. Among the leading manufactured exports are motor vehicles, and airplane engines and parts. General Motors of Canada has a plant at Ste-Thérèse, and Hyundai Auto Canada Inc. at Bromont.

TABLE 6.1   Quebec 1991 Labour Force and Estimated 1995 Gross Domestic Product by Industry

Industry	1991 Labour Force		Est. 1995 GDP ($ millions)	
Agriculture	84,755	2.5%	1,893	1.5%
Fishing	4,185	0.1%	61	—
Logging	25,410	0.7%	862	0.7%
Mining	23,495	0.7%	1,083	0.9%
TOTAL PRIMARY	137,845	4.0%	3,899	3.1%
Manufacturing	609,910	17.7%	26,108	21.0%
Construction	208,100	6.0%	6,866	5.5%
TOTAL SECONDARY	818,010	23.7%	32,974	26.5%
Transportation, Communications and Utilities	252,405	7.3%	15,807	12.7%
Trade	601,260	17.5%	16,078	12.9%
Finance, Insurance and Real Estate	191,600	5.6%	19,576	15.7%
Services	1,184,670	34.4%	27,697	22.2%
Government	255,025	7.4%	8,417	6.8%
TOTAL TERTIARY	2,484,960	72.2%	87,575	70.3%
TOTAL ALL INDUSTRIES	3,440,810		124,448	

Source: Reproduced by authority of the Minister of Industry, 1995, Statistics Canada, *1991 Census,* cat. nos. 93-326 and 95-326, and Conference Board of Canada, *Provincial Outlook, Economic Forecast* (Ottawa: Summer 1994), Vol. 9, No. 2.

TABLE 6.2   Manufacturing in Quebec, 1990

Sector	Workers	Salaries and Wages (millions of dollars)	Value of Shipments (millions of dollars)
Clothing	58,794	$1,099.4	$4,519.8
Food and beverages	53,947	1,579.6	22,298.0
Transportation equipment	41,044	1,480.5	6,753.3
Paper and paper products	40,227	1,615.9	7,845.7
Fabricated metals	37,954	1,074.9	4,355.4
Electronics and electrical products	35,687	1,203.2	5,267.4
Printing and publishing	34,683	1,074.2	3,758.7
Wood	30,320	755.3	3,549.8
Primary metals	27,579	1,194.2	6,401.1
Primary textiles and textiles	27,171	685.7	3,363.6
Other sectors	125,135	3,664.0	12,718.6
Total	512,541	$15,426.9	$80,831.1

Source: Reproduced by authority of the Minister of Industry, 1995, Statistics Canada, *Manufacturing Industries of Canada,* cat. no. 31-203 (Ottawa: March 1994), adapted by author.

As in other provinces, the service industry accounts for the greatest employment. Montreal is the centre of French-Canadian services—including culture, production-oriented services, world-class engineering consultants—and trade. Quebec also has a thriving tourist industry which is largely based on the province's cultural distinctiveness, history, natural beauty, and ski resorts.

The financial sector has witnessed the relocation of some chartered banks and insurance companies to Toronto. However, three main banks still maintain headquarters in the province (Bank of Montreal, Royal Bank, and the Banque Nationale); the Montreal Stock Exchange remains active, as do several insurance firms. The pervasiveness of the credit union movement in the province is unique. These "caisses populaires" are grouped into federations and collectively operate as the Mouvement Desjardins, a financial power to be reckoned with (in 1994 its assets rose to $80 from $60 billion with its takeover of the Laurentian Group Corporation). Another important financial institution is the Caisse de Dépôt et Placement. It manages the Quebec Pension Plan and other pension plans and, in the process, holds an interest in many firms for total assets of $48 billion in 1994. The Caisse has invested in many Quebec companies to strengthen them and the economy in general, as well as to encourage greater French-Canadian management and control of the provincial economy. Its beneficiaries are legion and include Provigo, Vidéotron, Cascades, Domtar, Donohue, Univa, Quebecor, and the National Bank. Quebec has obviously developed a strong, indigenous and increasingly francophone financial base in recent years.

Government is also a large factor in the province, with about 667,000 employees. The federal government employs some 112,699 Quebecers, many living in Hull, while the province has a workforce of 335,285, and municipalities another 218,838.

Because its per capita income is below the Canadian average, Quebec is considered to be a "have-not" province and receives huge annual federal equalization payments. The explanation for Quebec's lack of prosperity, given its abundant natural resources, is a complicated one. Apart from hydroelectric power, its resources are unremarkable in quantity or value and many of its operations, whether farming or manufacturing, are small scale. The absence of coal and the relatively late discovery of iron inhibited the development of a steel industry, while automobile manufacturing became centred in Ontario, partly due to that province's proximity to U.S. parent plants. In recent years, there has been little demand for some of its core output, especially iron ore and refined petroleum. Other obstacles to prosperity until 1960 included the high birth rate and a poorly trained labour force. Other factors have been labour-intensive industries, seasonal jobs, reliance on imported technology, the vulnerability of its exports to international market fluctuations, and foreign competition for imports. Quebec claims that federal tariff and transportation policies have discriminated against the province, and have been at best of greater if not exclusive benefit to Ontario. Until recently, another important factor was the discouragement of Québécois entrepreneurship, as the Catholic church stressed spiritual rather than material values. Finally, non-Quebec officers of foreign firms were primarily interested in profits and had little interest in developing the province or advancing French-Canadian employees.

Class

Within the province the usual income disparities exist. In 1991, 18.1 percent of families received under $20,000; 16.8 percent made over $70,000, and the median family income was $41,051. In 1992, the per capita personal income was $20,648, the fourth highest in the country. The average level of education in the province is rising, but unemployment is traditionally high, rising to 13 percent in 1992-93.

Organized labour was historically weak in Quebec but is now much stronger, with some 1,095,500 union members, or 40.6 percent of the province's paid workers, the second-highest proportion in the country. The largest unions are in the public sector—the teachers' union (Centrale de l'Enseignement du Québec or CEQ), the Fédération des affaires sociales, the Fonctionnaires provinciaux du Québec, the Canadian Union of Public Employees, and the Public Service Alliance of Canada. Large private sector unions include the United Food and Commercial Workers, the Steelworkers, and the Communications, Energy and Paperworkers unions. There are two main central labour organizations: the Quebec Federation of Labour (Fédération des travailleurs du Québec or FTQ) is associated with the Canadian Labour Congress and has about 400,000 members; and the Confédération des syndicats nationaux (CSN), which operates almost exclusively in Quebec with about 175,000 members. Such divisions and rivalries, compounded by the CSN dissidents' Centrale des Syndicats Démocratiques (CSD) probably do not help the cause of the working class although, since 1972, the FTQ, the CSN, and the CEQ have formed a common front to bargain for public sector workers. Two more recent features of the union movement in Quebec are worthy of mention. First, the Fonds de Solidarité, a fund set up by the FTQ in 1983, channels workers' savings into an investment fund to buy into companies that might otherwise close. Second, all three of the major labour organizations now support Quebec independence.

The migration to Toronto of several corporations and establishment figures deprived the Quebec economic elite of many members with a national perspective, but they have been progressively replaced by a new francophone bourgeoisie. Anglophones in charge of Canada-wide companies with headquarters in Quebec include Hollis Harris (Air Canada), Purdy Crawford (Imasco), Matthew Barrett (Bank of Montreal), Lynton (Red) Wilson (BCE Inc.), John McLennan (Bell Canada), John Cleghorn (Royal Bank), David Caplan (Pratt and Whitney Canada Inc.), William Stinson (Canadian Pacific), Chuck Hantho (Dominion Textile Inc.), George Petty (Repap Enterprises Inc.), Edgar Bronfman (The

Seagram Company), and James Doughan (Stone-Consolidated Inc.). An Italian porcelain company recently bought the historic but insolvent retailer, Henry Birk and Sons. One of the first francophone economic stars was Paul Desmarais, originally of Sudbury, who heads Power Corporation and whose interests include Great West Life and *La Presse* and other newspapers. Another was the de Gaspé de Beaubien family which controls Télémédia Inc. More recent additions include Jacques Bougie (Alcan Aluminum), Raymond Garneau (Industrial-Alliance Life Insurance), Paul Gagné (Avenor Inc., formerly CP Forest), Henri-Paul Rousseau (Laurentian Bank), Pierre Lessard (Métro-Richelieu Inc.), Claude Béland and Humberto Santos (Mouvement Desjardins), André Bérard (National Bank of Canada), Robert Gratton (Power Financial Corp.), Alain Ferland (Ultramar Canada Inc.), Laurent Beaudoin (Bombardier Inc.), Richard Drouin (Hydro-Québec), Paul Tellier (CN), Jean-Claude Delorme (Caisse de Dépôt), Pierre Desjardins (Domtar Inc.), André Caillé (Gaz Métropolitain Inc.), Pierre Péladeau (Quebecor Inc.), Pierre Mignault (Provigo Inc.), Guy Saint-Pierre (SNC-Lavalin Group Inc.), Charles Sirois (Teleglobe Inc.), Bertin Nadeau (Unigesco Inc.), Jean Coutu (pharmacies), André Chagnon (Le Groupe Vidéotron), Jean-Pierre Deschênes (Coopérative Fédérée de Québec), and Bernard Lemaire (Cascades Inc. pulp and paper). The creation of a strong francophone private sector in the province was one of the principal long-run effects of the Quiet Revolution. It means that French Canadians now control a substantial portion of the Quebec economy[1]—they are no longer merely "hewers of wood and drawers of water."

Demography

Quebec is the only province with a francophone majority. In the 1991 census, French was the mother tongue of 82.2 percent of the population, English, 9.7 percent, and others, 8.1 percent, with the non-French-speaking groups concentrated in Montreal. Some 83 percent spoke French at home, compared with 11.2 percent English, and 5.8 some other language. Thus, the assimilation of francophones into the English-language population does not appear to be marked. Indeed, the figures suggest that many members of other ethnic groups have adopted French as their home language. In total, 87.3 percent of Quebecers were born in the province, four percent come from elsewhere in Canada, and 8.7 percent from abroad.

The French-English cleavage has been at the heart of Quebec politics for centuries, and never more so than in the past 35 years.[2] While the francophone group always held a large majority in the legislature, cabinet, and bureaucracy, and was in no danger of losing power, it had three main preoccupations. First, because Quebec was the only province in which the French constituted a majority and because they were a minority at the federal level, the province felt a special responsibility to protect the "French fact" by maximizing provincial jurisdiction under the Constitution. Hence, many federal-provincial disputes erupted, with Ottawa representing an anglophone majority and Quebec, a francophone one. Second, the advent of the birth control pill in the 1960s put an end to the "revanche des berceux" (revenge of the cradle) and the Quebec birth rate, which had been the highest in the country, suddenly plummeted. The Quebec government began to worry about the future of the province's French character, particularly in Montreal. In the 1960s, population growth was caused largely by immigration, but many new immigrants assimilated into the English-speaking community. Third, English remained the language of big business in Quebec, and the corporate structure was so dominated by foreign or Anglo-Canadian firms that French-Canadians were denied opportunity to rise in corporate ranks, giving the province a "cultural division of labour."[3] Successive Quebec governments faced the dilemma of either welcoming extra-provincial companies to create jobs, or risking their exodus by requiring them to operate in French. Until about 1960, the former strategy was adopted but, especially since 1970, the Bourassa and Lévesque governments attempted to make French the working language of the province, even at higher management levels in the private sector, and tried to force immigrants to integrate with the French community. Some of the provisions of Bill 22 (1974) and Bill 101 (1977), Bourassa's and Lévesque's respective language laws, attracted vehement opposition, especially those aspects related to the restricted availability of English-language schools, the prohibition of non-French store signs in the province, and the limited use of English in the justice system. A substantial portion of the anglophone population left the province in the wake of such language legislation. Despite the attempt to recruit francophone immigrants, they constitute only about one-third of all immigrants to Quebec.

TABLE 6.3   Quebec Mother Tongue and Home Language, 1991

	Mother Tongue	Home Language
English	9.7%	11.2%
French	82.2%	83.0%
Other	8.1%	5.8%

Source: Reproduced by authority of the Minister of Industry, 1995, Statistics Canada, *1991 Census*, cat. no. 93-317, adapted by author.

Quebec had 137,615 people of aboriginal ancestry in the 1991 census, or two percent of the population. Native peoples in the province were largely ignored until the James Bay hydroelectric project disrupted their lives. A settlement was eventually hammered out in 1975 in connection with phase one of the project. In 1983, the Lévesque government adopted 15 principles with respect to aboriginal peoples in Quebec, and this formed the basis of a 1985 leg-islative resolution which, among other things, guaranteed aboriginal nations the right to self-government within Quebec.[4] The subsequent Bourassa government was less sympathetic to aboriginal peoples, ran into much opposition from the Cree and Inuit when it unveiled the second phase of the James Bay project, and faced a legal attack against the original settlement. Premier Jacques Parizeau put aboriginal affairs under his personal supervision in 1994, but many observers speculate on the role of aboriginal peoples in Quebec if the government decides to separate.

TABLE 6.4   Religion in Quebec, 1991

Roman Catholic			5,861,205	(86.1%)
Protestant			398,725	(5.9%)
Anglican	96,065	(1.4%)		
United Church	62,030	(0.9%)		
Jehovah Witness	33,420	(0.5%)		
Presbyterian	28,955	(0.4%)		
Baptist	27,505	(0.4%)		
Other Protestant	150,750	(2.2%)		
Jewish			97,735	(1.4%)
Eastern Non-Christian			97,550	(1.4%)
Eastern Orthodox			89,285	(1.3%)
Other (3,000) and None (262,800)			265,800	(3.9%)

Source: Reproduced by authority of the Minister of Industry, 1995, Statistics Canada, *1991 Census*, cat. no. 93-319, adapted by author.

With an overwhelming francophone majority, it is not surprising that more than 86 percent of the population is Catholic, although a large proportion are not devout in their observances. That leaves only 5.9 percent Protestants, mostly Anglican and United Church, while Jews constitute 1.4 percent, non-believers, 3.9 percent, and Jehovah Witnesses, 0.5 percent. Just as certain English-language rights in Quebec were guaranteed in the British North America Act, so the Protestant separate school system was constitutionally protected. The con-centration of the English-Protestant group in Montreal gave them some clout, and their school system has generated considerable political conflict over the years. There was also intense hostility between the Roman Catholic Church and both the Jehovah Witness sect and "atheistic" Communists. For generations after 1867, a cleavage existed within the Catholic community between those upholding the traditional role of the Church (the ultramontanes) and those representing the forces of increased secularization. It is safe to say that after the Quiet Revolution the latter won out. In 1993, the Supreme Court of Canada upheld the province's Bill 107, which changed the base of the school system to language from religion, as long as constitutional rights guaranteed in 1867 were respected.

Federal-Provincial Relations

In addition to Quebec's sometimes difficult internal regional, ethnic, and religious divisions, the degree of interdependence between federal and provincial governments cannot be overemphasized. More than any other province, Quebec has been influenced by political conflicts with Ottawa, although relations during the early years were relatively calm. Conservative regimes coexisted in Ottawa and Quebec City until 1896, followed by federal and provincial Liberal governments for most of the period until the 1930s. Quebec's financial dependence on Ottawa and its recognition of the federal government's role in protecting French minorities in other provinces also contributed to the tranquility of relations. The early exception was the Mercier government, elected largely as a result of the execution of Louis Riel, which took a generally anti-federal approach. Further conflict arose in connection with the Boer War, and school and language legislation in the Prairie provinces around the turn of the century. Then, during the First World War, the Gouin government vigorously opposed conscription.

In the 1920s and early 1930s there were no such dramatic battles, although Premier Louis-Alexandre Taschereau (1920-1936) challenged Ottawa on several issues, including jurisdictional conflicts over fisheries, broadcasting, taxation, and natural resources. In 1936 Quebec became the last province to join the federal-provincial old age pensions scheme, and in 1927 it had not been impressed with Ottawa's lukewarm defence of its claim to Labrador. Among Taschereau's provincially oriented demands was the "compact theory" of confederation, which contended that no changes to the British North America Act could be made without unanimous provincial consent. Quebec also operated more independently of Ottawa under Taschereau, partly because the province had its own tax resources and partly because Mackenzie King left federal matters in the province in the hands of his French-Canadian lieutenant, Ernest Lapointe. After 1936, Premier Maurice Duplessis intensified opposition to the federal government, particularly with respect to the Second World War. He was a leading opponent of conscription and a principal spokesman for the view that Canada had no international obligations. He fought against the centralization of taxing powers in Ottawa both during and after the war, and on both constitutional and ideological grounds objected to such federal social programs as unemployment insurance, family allowances, and old age security. Duplessis later opposed such shared-cost programs as hospital insurance, the Trans-Canada Highway, and block grants to universities as invasions of provincial jurisdiction, but did not exercise the provincial powers he claimed. He was also unhappy with what he considered to be Ottawa's lack of vigour in fighting communism. Because he so ably represented the French-Canadian viewpoint on conscription and the war effort, Duplessis was generally able to retain popular support for his other stances, however much they disadvantaged most Quebec residents. It was a classic case of blocking reformist urges within the province by focusing the electorate's attention on external events.

In the 1960s, even though three of the six years of the Lesage administration coincided with the Pearson Liberal regime in Ottawa, relations between the provincial and federal governments remained tense. Premier Jean Lesage never stopped demanding more federal funding, the right to opt out of joint programs, and the relaxation of federal funding conditions. In contrast to the Union Nationale period, Quebec now wanted not only to keep Ottawa out, but to develop its own plans in the health and welfare fields. Lesage demanded a larger share of such direct taxes as personal and corporate income taxes, and a more generous equalization formula. Lester B. Pearson agreed to these demands in an effort to defuse the separatist threat. Quebec vetoed the Fulton-Favreau Formula, an amending procedure for the BNA Act, after having previously supported it. It also insisted on having its own pension plan, which was superior in concept to Ottawa's.[5]

Quebec participation in international francophone affairs was the main bone of contention between the federal and Quebec governments during the Johnson-Bertrand period (1966-70), although Daniel Johnson also wanted much more domestic power for the province. Robert Bourassa set out to demonstrate that federalism could be profitable for Quebec and was more concerned about internal autonomy, fighting successfully for greater provincial control over family allowances and immigration, and unsuccessfully for power over communications.

After 1976 intergovernmental relations reached their nadir in the propaganda battle between Ottawa and the Parti Québécois. The PQ never tired of pointing out faults in the federal system and ways in which Quebec was being discriminated against by federal policies. In the statistical wars which erupted, the two sides argued over whether the province gained or lost after the calculation of both federal taxation and spending in Quebec.

It was particularly difficult for the Trudeau government to press for its vision of a bilingual Canada when René Lévesque was making Quebec increasingly unilingual. During the 1981-82 constitutional negotiations (primarily designed to respond to the Québécois after they rejected sovereignty-association in the 1980 referendum), Quebec co-operated with fellow autonomy-minded provinces by undertaking court challenges and lobbying in England. Ultimately an accord was struck which reflected the Trudeau approach, and only Quebec refused to sign it.

Prime Minister Brian Mulroney was determined to end Quebec's constitutional alienation, and initially succeeded in persuading the other premiers to agree to Bourassa's demands in the Meech Lake Accord. The Quebec premier unexpectedly became an ally of the Canada-U.S. free trade agreement as well. Newfoundland and Manitoba later rejected the accord, and Quebec took a more nationalistic turn. The Quebec Liberal party's Allaire report recommended a wholesale decentralization of powers from Ottawa, while the legislature's Bélanger-Campeau report insisted on a referendum on sovereignty by the fall of

1992. Instead, a referendum was held on the Charlottetown Accord, and the latter was rejected in Quebec as well as in several other provinces. This led to the 1995 referendum on sovereignty.

One hotly debated issue with regard to separatism is whether Ottawa raises more funds from Quebec than it spends, or vice versa. Despite many efforts, often with political motives, to calculate this balance sheet, no consensus has been achieved. What can be said is that Ottawa provided 18.9 percent of the provincial government's revenue in 1992 (some $7.5 billion), and transferred $156 million to municipalities, $13,708 million to persons, and $1,227 million to businesses in Quebec.

POLITICAL CULTURE[6]

Like so much else in Quebec, any discussion of political culture must distinguish between the pre- and post-1960 periods. Before the Quiet Revolution, the Quebec political culture was generally traditional, conservative, patronage-oriented, authoritarian, backward, rural, corrupt, and heavily influenced by the Roman Catholic Church. Over the past 35 years or so, however, it has become progressive—if not radical—urban, democratic, modern, secularized, and bureaucratized. Even the only feature apparently common to the two periods, the importance of nationalism, has changed in nature. Rather than nationalism of survival (survivance) largely based on the church, and after a catching-up phase (rattrapage), it became one of expansion and growth (épanouissement) which is outward-looking and aggressive. But this nationalism, one stream of which promotes becoming a sovereign state, is now referred to as "market nationalism" because it is associated with the new business class, the rising francophone entrepreneurial elite.

The nationalism of survival was based on an intense determination to maintain the province's French-Canadian and Catholic distinctiveness in the midst of the overwhelming English-speaking, and largely Protestant, North American environment. The Church was even more dominant in Quebec than other Catholic communities largely because of "its close association with the struggle for cultural survival." Its influence extended beyond strictly religious matters to all aspects of "intellectual, professional, economic and social life."[7] The province's self-image, as extolled by such historians as Lionel Groulx, promoted the superiority of a rural, religious, spiritual, family-oriented, isolated, defensive, simple, and unsophisticated French way of life.

Pierre Trudeau among others has suggested that, before 1960, Quebec was a distinct political subculture, less committed to democracy than the rest of the country.[8] He wrote of the authoritarian background—absolute monarchy, seigneurial system, and hierarchical and omnipresent church—and argued that French-Canadians could hardly be blamed for their lack of attachment to the democratic ideal when they were a permanent minority always forced to defend themselves. French Canadians tolerated the anti-democratic laws and practices of the Duplessis government and trusted that their high birthrate, antagonism toward Ottawa, faith in religious leaders, and isolation from outside forces—their fortress mentality—would protect their distinct language, culture, and religion.

However, the forces of modernization, urbanization, and secularization had become explosive by the time Duplessis died in 1959. In 1960, the Liberal party was able to respond to such pent-up pressures in the form of the Quiet Revolution.[9] During the next six years the province was totally transformed; one of the main characteristics of the period was the rapid expansion of the provincial state. At the same time, another group of French-Canadians became concerned about the increasingly nationalistic stances of the Lesage government and sought to establish a strong francophone presence in Ottawa to act as a counterbalance. Jean Marchand, Gérard Pelletier, and Pierre Trudeau led this movement, and soon became prominent in the Pearson administration. This federally oriented group pressed for more French-Canadian power and bilingualism in the federal bureaucracy and cabinet, and federal support for francophone minorities in other provinces. Thus, since 1965 there have been two intense appeals to French-Canadian nationalism and two strategies to promote the French fact, one centred on Quebec, and the other focused on Ottawa and opposed to the development of special status, autonomy, or independence for the province.[10] Oddly enough, as Louis Balthazar writes, the majority of Quebecers never accepted the version of nationalism proposed by either of their most venerated political leaders, Lévesque or Trudeau.[11] Most want to remain in Canada but be recognized in the Constitution as a distinct society.

Quebecers have been divided in their respective loyalties to province and country; some have defined themselves as Québécois with little or no attachment to Canada, while others view themselves as a distinct group within the larger Canadian federation. The majority of the population probably occupies a somewhat confused and ambivalent position in between, but several studies have shown that, as a whole, French-Canadian Quebecers have a weaker degree of attachment to their country than most Canadians. In contrast, English-speaking Quebecers are usually among the most nationalistic Canadians.[12] When *Maclean's* magazine asked Quebecers whether they thought of themselves first as Canadians or citizens of their province, the provincialists took precedence: 55 to 44 percent in 1990, and 49 to 45 percent in 1994. The first acid test of such sentiments was the 1980 referendum on the sovereignty-association issue. While the question itself was vaguely worded, the results could be interpreted as indicating that at least 60 percent of Quebecers rejected separatism and, at most, 40 percent supported it. The PQ's defeat in the referendum and the simultaneous downturn in the economy ushered in a new era in Quebec. The wind was knocked out of separatist sails and attention shifted from politics to economics.

With the province's French character secured, cultural and linguistic concerns were replaced by an emphasis on business and, in this more fragmented and less obsessed atmosphere, even the vibrancy of artistic life declined. Linguistic and constitutional issues resurfaced in the late 1980s, however, in the form of the Meech Lake Accord and Bill 178. The rejection of the accord by other provinces provided the base for a more self-confident separatist movement in the 1990s.

Francophone Quebecers have made tremendous advances in all aspects of their provincial life, such as the number of francophones in key posts in Ottawa and the rest of the country. For these reasons, French-Canadian Quebecers have a strong democratic commitment (with the exception of their rejection of minority anglophone rights), and Quebec is now one of the most developed provinces. In many respects, such as in electoral legislation, Quebec operates more democratically than the others; it has also progressed from being the weakest to one of the strongest provinces in terms of the ability of its public service and its politicians' self-restraint in patronage.[13]

In studies conducted in the late 1960s and early 1970s, francophone Quebecers registered low levels of trust, efficacy, and political interest, and were categorized as "disaffected" at generally higher levels than Atlantic Canadians.[14] Anglophone Quebecers, on the other hand, demonstrated high levels of such behaviour. Today the situation might well be reversed, because in the post-1970 period the English-speaking community has been under siege in terms of language legislation. Quebecers have a relatively low-to-medium ranking in electoral turnout at the federal level (73 percent) and a very high rate in provincial elections (81 percent). On the other hand, Quebec had the highest voter turnout of any province in both the 1992 referendum and the 1993 federal election.

TABLE 6.5 **Quebec Voter Turnout in Recent Federal and Provincial Elections.**

Federal Elections		Provincial Elections	
1974	67%	1973	80%
1979	76%	1976	85%
1980	68%	1981	83%
1984	76%	1985	76%
1988	75%	1989	81%
1993	77%	1994	82%
Average	73.2%	Average	81.2%

Source: *Reports of the Chief Electoral Officer*, calculations by author.

POLITICAL PARTIES

Party System[15]

Quebec has had a series of two-party systems: the Conservatives and Liberals until 1936; the Liberals and Union Nationale until about 1970; and, since 1976, the Liberals and Parti Québécois. However, there were long stretches of one-party dominance during these periods: the Conservatives dominated until 1897, the Liberals from 1897 to 1936, and the Union Nationale from 1944 to 1960. Since then a more regular rotation has taken place, reflecting the province's increased political fermentation. The first half of the 1970s was a period of transition during which the Créditistes rose and fell and the Union Nationale dropped out of serious contention.[16] The mid-1980s witnessed a rupture within the Parti Québécois over the independence issue, but by 1990 it had re-united as a clearly separatist party and defeated the Liberals four years later. The Equality Party entered the fray in 1989 but withered away by 1994. A more sovereignty-minded group broke away from the Liberals and elected its leader, Mario Dumont, under the Parti Action Démocratique label.

TABLE 6.6   Party Support in Quebec, 1970-1995

	Years in Office	**Average Percentage of Vote**	**Percentage of Seats**
Liberals	15	47.2%	58.4%
Parti Québécois	10	38.1%	35.6%
Combined	25	85.3%	94.0%

Source: *Reports of the Chief Electoral Officer,* calculations by author.

FIGURE 6.2   Percentage of Vote by Party in Quebec Elections, 1970-1994

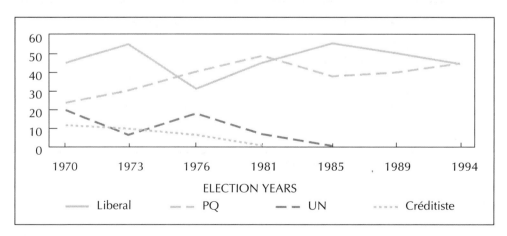

Party Organization

Until the Quiet Revolution, parties in Quebec were less democratic than elsewhere, and fell into the classic cadre category. For example, Duplessis singlehandedly controlled the Union Nationale, and it did not start to build official party structures until 1965. The Liberal party consisted of two chief organizers (for separate Montreal and Quebec regions), constituency organizers, poll captains, and fund-raisers, but until the 1950s there was no "party" with a constitution, memberships, or provincial or constituency associations.[17] Both the Union Nationale and the Liberal party were essentially patronage and electoral organizations. Since 1967, however, the Parti Québécois has aspired to operate very much in the mass party tradition, emphasizing mass membership campaigns (resulting in a party membership of 300,000 in 1980) and mass fund-raising, and giving a significant voice to rank and file members at frequent policy-making conventions. René Lévesque never felt comfortable with such structures and tried to downplay their authority,[18] but he was usually able to obtain his preferred policy stands, and the policy variations on sovereignty-association were inspired by his reading of public opinion. Despite the presence of many genuine separatists in the party, he maintained a version of sovereignty-association from at least 1967 and, when a 1981 PQ convention rejected the economic association aspect of his policy, he managed to reverse it with a hastily concocted party referendum. The frequency and significance of policy discussion by the rank and file of the PQ was unusual, and the PQ was the first party in Canada to choose its leader by a vote among all party members when it replaced René Lévesque in 1985.[19] To a large extent, the Liberal party has been forced to follow suit in terms of memberships, finance, and policy-making and, while more elitist than the PQ, it operates more democratically than most of its sister parties in other provinces. Both parties have headquarters in Montreal, but the PQ has more elaborate and active regional organizations, as well as stricter rules about voting at nomination meetings.

Until the Quiet Revolution, Quebec was at least as corrupt and patronage-ridden as any other province (English-Canadian commentators often rank Quebec lowest in this respect, but it was probably no worse than the Maritimes).[20] Dependence on the politician- or premier-patron was great, whether for individual jobs and contracts or collective public works such as roads.[21] Quebec's economic underdevelopment was similar to that of the Atlantic provinces where political favours were sought to compensate for the lack of economic benefits, but the Quebec case was complicated by the linguistic situation.[22] English control of the economic system in Quebec made francophones even more reliant on the goodwill of politicians. One of the basic reasons for a significant decline in patronage and corruption since 1960 has been the enhanced economic opportunity available within the province. Reforms adopted by the Lesage government were reinforced by those implemented by the PQ before patronage practices were finally brought to an end.

Federal-Provincial Party Links[23]

Surprisingly in light of later developments, federal-Quebec party relations were very close until about 1935 as the fortunes of both levels of government rose and fell together. This changed somewhat after the provincial Liberals were defeated, the Quebec Conservatives were transformed into the Union Nationale, and Duplessis became preoccupied with internal affairs. However, local "non-aggression" pacts were concluded in the late 1940s between Union Nationale MLAs and federal Liberal MPs, and Duplessis and St. Laurent became more friendly in the early 1950s much to the chagrin of the provincial Liberal leadership.[24] After a falling out (over the non-aggression pacts among other things), Duplessis was so determined to defeat the federal Liberals that he pulled out all the stops in favour of the Diefenbaker Conservatives in 1957-58 with the remarkable result that Quebec elected 50 Progressive Conservative federal members.

After 1935, the provincial Liberal party was in disarray and had to be resurrected by the federal party. This was most apparent in the 1939 campaign when the federal organization not only provided the election issue (conscription), but also took control of the provincial party, making the Godbout government a client of Ottawa.[25] When St. Laurent later warmed to Duplessis, the provincial party had no choice but to become independent. Relations improved in the late 1950s and early 1960s, but soured after Liberals were elected to office at both levels of government. Separate federal and provincial Quebec Liberal parties were created in 1964 (although they shared many activists and supporters), and Lesage was only persuaded to support the federal Liberals in the last days of the 1965 campaign.[26] Relations were slightly better during the first Bourassa period, but the constitutional proposals of Trudeau and Claude Ryan later revealed profound differences, and the federal party did not hesitate to intervene in the referendum campaign on its own terms. While Lévesque discouraged the creation of a federal PQ organization just as Mulroney did the establishment of a provincial Progressive Conservative party in Quebec, Bourassa tried to maintain good relations with both federal parties. He soon fell under the charm of Brian Mulroney, however, and supported free trade in response to Meech Lake, attracting the hostility of most federal Liberals. The Quebec wing of the NDP has had a troubled relationship with the national party, and provincial NDP activity has been minimal. In 1989 the provincial party cut ties with the federal NDP, with little effect. By 1990, the pattern of federal-provincial party relations in Quebec was quite confused. Since then, with the federal Bloc Québécois in the picture and the demise of the federal Conservatives in the province, Quebec has developed more symmetrical federal-provincial party links.

Party Leadership[27]

Quebec politics have been characterized by a series of dominant leaders: Honoré Mercier, Lomer Gouin, L.-A.Taschereau, Maurice Duplessis, Jean Lesage, René

Lévesque, Robert Bourassa, and Jacques Parizeau. This is likely a consequence of the role of nationalism in Quebec politics, and the electorate's need to focus on the leader as a defender against the threat of English Canada.[28] Duplessis was a virtual dictator who governed in an authoritarian manner, while Lesage and Lévesque were pre-eminent leaders of a strong team. Quite a contrast existed between Lesage's attractive urbanity and Lévesque's harried, chain-smoking, populist image, but all three left an indelible mark on Quebec. In spite of the PQ's abhorrence of many of Duplessis' methods, that party erected a statue of Duplessis which the Liberals and the Union Nationale had kept hidden in various government basements. Although the early PQ had many outstanding members, it was described as "a heterogeneous mixture of political currents, linked together by the common goal of independence, and the prestige of René Lévesque."[29] The strong personalities of Lévesque and Pierre Trudeau were in part what inspired Quebecers to support them simultaneously. Lévesque was so much the incarnation of the Quebec people, in fact, that he maintained his popularity after losing the referendum and the constitutional battle, becoming an ordinary provincial premier struggling with difficult political and economic questions.[30] Robert Bourassa also deserves mention for his remarkable political longevity. Originally selected in 1970 in the wave of new, young, technocratic premiers—Ed Schreyer, Frank Moores, Allan Blakeney, Peter Lougheed—and despite his unpopular six-year record, in 1983 the Liberals again selected him to give the province more stable economic direction (but only after he had spent some time in purgatory and had relentlessly worked his way back). In his second coming, he was more at ease and more respected, although he was never regarded with great affection until after he resigned for health reasons in 1994. Bourassa was the quintessence of prudence, ambiguity, equivocation, and calculation. His internationally educated successor, Daniel Johnson Jr., was usually considered to be rigid, bland, and boring, although he came to life as premier and leader of the Opposition. Jacques Parizeau then took firm command of the PQ and, like Lévesque before him, recast it in his own image. Parizeau, who developed an English accent at the London School of Economics, was generally seen as stuffy, pompous, and aristocratic. No one, however, opposed Jacques Parizeau when he replaced Pierre Marc Johnson.

Party Ideology

Two lines of party ideology can be identified in Quebec: the extent of governmental intervention, and the national question (the issue of provincial autonomy). These have respectively been called the "internal" and "external" ideologies of the various parties.[31] In the second category the Union Nationale was consistently more provincialist than the Liberals, as Duplessis desperately attempted to prevent any federal intervention in such joint programs as hospital insurance and the Trans-Canada Highway. This approach culminated in Daniel Johnson's call for equality or independence in the 1960s. The cause of independence provided the PQ with its core of militants and supporters, but surveys consistently indicated that not all who voted for the PQ supported such a stance.[32] The PQ first promoted provincial sovereignty in the early 1970s, then, a continued economic association with Canada in the 1980 referendum, maximum short-run decentralization in the mid-1980s, and back again to a fairly clear-cut sovereignty under Parizeau in the 1990s. Parizeau reverted to a form of sovereignty-association, however, just prior to the 1995 referendum.

As for the Liberals, Bourassa was often pictured as a puppet of Ottawa in his first term as premier, but his success in achieving greater autonomy has probably been underestimated. The resurrected Bourassa, with Mulroney's help, tried desperately to get significant constitutional change adopted in the Meech Lake Accord. He took a much more autonomist stand after the death of that accord, but fellow Quebecers apparently did not feel he went far enough when they rejected the Charlottetown Accord in 1992.

As for internal ideology, strong social democratic sentiments were delayed until their growth became integral to national consciousness. All parties shifted to the left after the outbreak of the Quiet Revolution when the quest for provincial autonomy was coupled with the assumption of a strong interventionist provincial state.[33] The Liberals under Lesage were more left-wing than the Union Nationale in the 1960s, and passed an array of progressive legislation which generally matched that of other provinces and, occasionally, was more advanced.[34] The Johnson-Bertrand period was comparatively more conservative, and the Bourassa Liberals probably fell somewhere in between the conservatism of the Union Nationale and the left-wing stance of the Lesage Liberals. All three governments wanted to see the Quebec economy developed by Quebecers and were almost indistinguishable in creating economic development agencies. Bourassa added the monumental James Bay Development Corporation to Johnson's SOQUIP, Rexfor, and Radio-Québec, which were built on the foundation of Lesage's Hydro-Québec, Société Générale de Financement, Caisse de Dépôt, SOQUEM, and Sidbec. The Parti Québécois contained diverse ideological streams—left-wing and right-wing nationalists and more moderate technocrats—but generally carried out a social democratic program. Some of its measures transcended those of the NDP but many were in the same ideological grain or slightly less radical, such as the nationalization of the Asbestos Corporation and partial nationalization of automobile insurance.[35] Although it lacked the link with organized labour which characterizes the NDP, the PQ took many significant pro-labour initiatives during its first few years in office. The party was increasingly interventionist during its first term but, in the 1980s, the poor economy and generally conservative mood both in the province and in the country as a whole caused a marked shift toward the right. In its second mandate the PQ rolled back public sector wages and resorted to back-to-work legislation on several occasions.[36] The size of the deficit became an increasing concern, Parizeau's budgets were generally conservative throughout, and the party promoted the new pro-business "market nationalism." After Pierre Marc Johnson replaced Lévesque as leader, the PQ's ideology bore a suspicious similarity to that of his father's Union Nationale. The Ryan and new Bourassa Liberals also occupied a blurred internal ideological position, but Bourassa's second cabinet included prominent business people and his government generally supported private-sector solutions. It is probably safe to say that, while both the PQ and Liberals have moved to the right of their earlier positions, they are still moderately progressive and there is little difference in their internal ideological positions.[37] Brian Tanguay argues that "the poor, the marginal, and the powerless are now effectively disenfranchised, as both of the major parties seem eager to sacrifice their needs to the new gods of competitiveness and globalization."[38]

In reviewing the overall ideology of the province, it can be said that the private sector was predominant before 1960, after which the Quiet Revolution had a basic étatiste orientation. During the latter period, much attention centred on the status of the new middle class and of labour, especially in the public sector. During the 1980s, however, the francophone private sector emerged as the dominant force in Quebec society.

ELECTIONS

Electoral System

Quebec has always had a fairly orthodox single-member electoral system, but it has been more controversial than in most other provinces. One anomaly was Section 80 of the original British North America Act which protected a number of English-majority ridings, permitting them to be changed or abolished only with the approval of the members concerned. Even though they lost population and became largely French in character, these constituencies remained intact until the early 1970s. Then, there was the extraordinary gerrymandering and electoral corruption of the Taschereau and Duplessis governments, when election-day activity exhibited unprecedented levels of misrepresentation, intimidation, and even violence. In 1944 and 1966 the Liberals lost despite having an advantage in the popular vote, partly because of persistent rural over-representation. In the 1970-76 period the Parti Québécois won few seats in relation to its large popular vote, a possibility in the first-past-the-post system even if seats are properly distributed. This led the PQ to seriously consider adopting a proportional representation system. Although it came close to doing so, the party probably lost some of its enthusiasm after beginning to benefit from the existing electoral system. Quebec has had impartial redistributions since the mid-1960s, but the protected seats and rural over-representation were not removed until a decade later. Constituency boundaries are now revised immediately after each election by a three-member commission which is generally constrained by a 25 percent rule.

TABLE 6.7   Representational Disparities in 1994 Election

Mean no. of voters per constituency	39,148
Largest constituency (Chauveau)	54,351 (+38.8% of the mean)
Smallest constituency (Îles de la Madeleine)	10,682 (-72.7% of the mean)
Average variation from mean	13.5%
Constituencies within ± 10% (56 of 125)	44.8%
Constituencies within ± 25% (111 of 125)	88.8%

Reports of the Chief Electoral Officer, calculations by author.

Quebec has a permanent voters list with annual enumeration and provision for pre-election revisions but, prior to the 1995 referendum, Premier Parizeau announced reform of this system to enhance his prospects. Quebec is more generous than other provinces in allowing residents who are out of the province to vote.

The province's record in election finance in the form of kickbacks and natural resource concessions was so abysmal that in 1963 the Lesage government became the first in any province to clean up this aspect of political life.[39] The original legislation contained a disclosure clause, spending ceilings for parties and candidates, and reimbursement of a large portion of the expenditures of candidates who received at least 20 percent of the vote. During the Bourassa regime there were further allegations of scandal, however, so the PQ government quickly tightened the regulations. In 1977 it imposed a maximum of $3,000 on contributions and allowed only registered voters (that is, only individuals, not corporations or unions) to make donations; it also introduced a tax credit scheme. Quebec thus effectively limits both the raising and spending of election funds, and is unique in allowing only individual contributions. It remains one of the few provinces to provide an annual grant to parties, even in non-election years, to help with routine operations.[40]

Voting Behaviour

The Quebec electorate is surely the most polled in Canada, resulting in many (often contradictory) studies of its voting behaviour.[41] In terms of social background, a fairly clear-cut distinction existed between the supporters of the two parties in the 1960s. The Liberals attracted urban dwellers, the middle to upper class, the well-educated, and the majority of non-francophones. In fact, the "new middle class" made up of teachers, technocrats, public servants, and other professionals, was the backbone of Liberal party support in that period. The Union Nationale captured the support of rural voters, those with relatively lower incomes and levels of educational attainment, and proportionally more voters of French origin. These groups temporarily divided their support between the Union Nationale and Créditistes in the early 1970s. The Parti Québécois was first supported by students and members of the new middle class inheriting this vanguard from the Quiet Revolution Liberals in 1970.[42] By 1973 the PQ had extended its appeal to the urban working class and by 1976 to rural areas. The PQ alienated much of organized labour (by reducing public sector salaries) and many other groups in the mid-1980s, and was reduced to its original militantly nationalistic support. The Liberal party picked up the pieces by default and added to its already substantial support by non-francophone groups, more affluent urban residents, and those more oriented to the private sector. Non-francophones abandoned the Liberal party in 1989 but came back in 1994, while the PQ retrieved much of its earlier support in those two campaigns, its appeal generally declining with the age of the voter and increasing with level of education. Recent Quebec voting behaviour has thus been influenced by a combination of ethnic, age, and class considerations. Men are more likely than women to vote PQ, and some regional and rural-urban distinctions are also evident.

One of the most striking aspects of Quebec electoral behaviour is the disparity between federal and provincial election results. After lending consistent support to federal and provincial Conservatives until about 1900 and to federal and provincial Liberals from then until 1935, Quebec voters began to elect starkly different parties at the two levels of government. From 1936 to 1960, they elected an anti-Liberal Union Nationale government provincially, followed by a solid slate of federal Liberal MPs. More consistency emerged from 1939-1944 and from 1960-1966 but, since then, and especially between 1976 and 1993, there has been the same discrepancy between electing federal Liberals and provincial Péquistes, or, in 1984-89, federal Conservatives and provincial Liberals. Given that Trudeau and Lévesque embraced opposite strategies of enhancing French-Canadian influence, this pattern of voting can perhaps be explained by Quebec voters feeling more secure in electing the strongest defender of their interests at each level regardless of party,[43] or in voting for the most charismatic leaders. In the Mulroney-Bourassa period, the only thing that divided the two leaders was their party label, so the federal-provincial discrepancy was based more on appearances than reality. The difference in federal and provincial election results can also be explained in part by variations in voter turnout, along with a high rate of rejected ballots in federal elections in the province. The 1993 and 1994 elections witnessed much greater consistency: Liberal-Liberal and BQ-PQ.

PRESSURE GROUPS AND THE MEDIA

Pressure Groups

Pressure groups have always played an important role in Quebec politics. Prior to the 1960s, most were church-sponsored farmer, labour, youth, caisse populaire, and other co-operative groups, which provided much support to the government. Since the Quiet Revolution, secularized but still nationalistic pressure groups have been integrated into the province's general policy-making process to an unusual degree.[44] Many business groups operate in the province, including the Conseil du patronat du Québec, the Quebec Manufacturers' Association, and the provincial and Montreal Chambres de commerce (the latter now incorporating the Montreal Board of Trade). More specialized organizations include those representing the manufacturing, pulp and paper, forest, steel, metal, and textile industries.[45] The main labour groups are the Fédération des travailleurs du Québec, the Centrale de l'enseignement du Québec, and the Confédération des syndicats nationaux. Labour has become much more militant in recent years, first opposing the Bourassa regime and lending strong support to the PQ, and more recently challenging the Lévesque and second Bourassa governments. The Union des producteurs agricoles and the Coopérative fédérée de Québec are the main agricultural groups. The Société Saint-Jean Baptiste has been a vehemently nationalistic organization, and the Alliance Quebec was recently formed to defend English-language rights in the province. Municipal groups include the Quebec Union of Municipalities. Two of the most notable lobbying efforts in the province were those mounted against the PQ's 1977 auto insurance legislation by the insurance industry and the bar association, Barreau du Québec, and that carried out by General Dynamics Corp. over the nationalization of the asbestos industry.[46] Many of these groups have a distinct status within national, federal organizations, but the Girl Guides recently broke away from its national organization because the latter did not want men involved.

There is a corporatist flavour to Quebec society and politics not found in the other provinces. It is seen most clearly in the "concertation" process in which regular tripartite economic summit meetings are held among peak business and labour associations, along with government. The overriding objective of protecting and promoting the French character of the province provides a special incentive for these three groups to come to agreements.

TABLE 6.8   Leading Quebec Pressure Groups

Peak Business	Conseil du patronat du Québec
	Mouvement Desjardins
	Quebec Manufacturers' Association
	Chambre de commerce du Québec
Industrial	Association des industries forestières du Québec
	Association forestière québecoise Inc.
	Association minière du Québec
	Canadian Pulp and Paper Association
	Association de la construction du Québec
Labour	Fédération des travailleurs du Québec
	Confédération des syndicats nationaux
	Centrale des syndicats démocratiques

TABLE 6.8 continued

Agriculture	Union des producteurs agricoles
	Coopérative fédérée du Québec
Professional	Centrale de l'enseignement du Québec
	Corporation professionnelle des médecins du Québec
	Association médicale du Québec
	Quebec Federation of Nurses
Ethnic	Société Saint-Jean Baptiste
	Mouvement Québec français
	Alliance Quebec
	Grand Council of the Crees of Quebec
Religious	Assemblée des évêques du Québec
	Quebec Association of Protestant School Boards
Institutional	Association des hôpitaux du Québec
	Union des municipalités du Québec
	Fédération des commissions scolaires du Québec
Environmental	Fédération québecoise de la faune
	Union québécoise pour la conservation de la nature
	Société pour vaincre la pollution
Public Interest	Ligue des droits et libertés

The Media

The media have also played an influential role in Quebec politics. The often financially troubled *Le Devoir*, put on a more secure foundation in the early 1990s when a number of organizations contributed to a large trust fund, has had great impact in intellectual circles, while Paul Desmarais' *La Presse* and Conrad Black's *Le Soleil* are more populist newspapers. Even more populist are Pierre Péladeau's tabloids, *Le Journal de Montréal* and *Le Journal de Québec*. The major English-language newspaper is the *Gazette;* the demise of the *Montreal Star* in 1979 and an English-language tabloid in 1989 symbolized the decline of the anglophone minority. The PQ government expressed concern in 1995 that 10 of the province's 11 daily newspapers were owned by three men. The provincial government owns its own educational television network, Radio-Québec. The French network of the Canadian Broadcasting Corporation, Radio-Canada, is largely a Quebec network and consists of 10 owned or affiliated radio stations and two owned and several affiliated television stations. English-language CBC has two radio and two TV stations. The French equivalent of CTV is TVA, centred on Télé-Métropole in Montreal and comprising nine other private stations, while a second private French network is the eight-station Télévision Quatre Saisons. The Canadian Radio-television and Telecommunications Commission has imposed minimum quotas on the amount of French music played on Quebec radio.

TABLE 6.9   Daily Newspapers in Quebec, 1994

	Circulation	Chain Affiliation
Le Devoir (Montreal)	28,537	Independent
Le Journal de Montréal	283,310	Péladeau
Le Journal de Québec	103,655	Péladeau
Le Nouvelliste (Trois-Rivières)	51,430	Desmarais
La Presse (Montreal)	186,785	Desmarais
Le Quotidien (Chicoutimi)	30,950	Desmarais
Le Soleil (Québec)	97,526	Black
La Tribune (Sherbrooke)	34,961	Desmarais
La Voie de l'Est (Granby)	15,404	Desmarais
Montreal Gazette	154,096	Southam
Sherbrooke Record	5,428	Péladeau

Source: *Canadian Advertising Rates and Data* (August 1994).

GOVERNMENT INSTITUTIONS[47]

Given the province's francophone majority, Quebec's political institutions have many distinctive features. In particular, some of the more "British" aspects of the institutions have been replaced with French or French-Canadian touches.

Executive

Recent Quebec governments have not had much use for the Queen's representative, the lieutenant-governor, and the PQ does its best to ignore him completely.[48] In 1959 and 1960, after the deaths of premiers Duplessis and Sauvé, the Union Nationale cabinet and caucus quickly recommended successors to the deceased party leaders, removing any danger of leaving the decision to the lieutenant-governor.[49]

The premier, called the "premier ministre," occupies a special role in Quebec. Because Quebec is a distinct society, the premier must be both a political leader and a societal leader. "Quebec premiers cannot escape the fact that more is expected of them than basic management of a provincial government or the winning of an election."[50] Given this exalted role, the premier has a larger supporting staff than in other provinces, divided between the premier's office and the Ministère du Conseil Exécutif. The head of the premier's office, the chief of staff or directeur de cabinet, has figured prominently in successive governments. The Department of the Executive Council under the Secrétaire général du Conseil exécutif, the chief public servant, supports the cabinet as well as the premier. This organization provides logistical assistance and policy advice to the cabinet and its committees—a secretariat for each committee—and contains several secretariats which report to the premier, including, in the case of Parizeau, family, youth, aboriginal peoples, regional development, status of women, con-certation, Quebec City, Greater Montreal, administrative reform, and intergov-ernmental affairs. Thus the executive council office is larger than any other provincial cabinet office.

Between 1989 and 1994, Bourassa's cabinet consisted of 29 or 30 members, including a number of junior ministers (ministres d'état), compared to Johnson's 21 and Parizeau's 19. Premiers have been concerned with balancing regional interests and, at least until 1976, ensuring appropriate ethnic and religious rep-resentation. In the early years, the anglophone population was over-represented in the cabinet, but has recently been under-represented. Especially since 1960, representatives of various nationalistic and ideological positions have been included and their solidarity has been constantly strained. Much of the cabinet's work is conducted in committees structured liked those of several other provinces. The "inner cabinet" worked particularly well in the early years of the Lévesque regime, when its members were charged with developing government position papers and co-ordinating policy. After 1985, Bourassa had no such inner group but relied on six standing committees: treasury, legislation, social and cultural affairs, regional development and the environment, economic development, and Greater Montreal. Parizeau's government began operations with four cabinet committees: priorities, treasury, legislation, and Greater Montreal. In addition to his cabinet ministers, Parizeau appointed 14 caucus members as regional representatives to transmit local concerns to the cabinet and to sell sovereignty in their parts of the province.

Legislature

The Quebec legislature, now called the National Assembly, contains 125 mem-bers all of whom are elected from single-member constituencies using the first-past-the-post system.[51] The Quebec legislature originally had two chambers, the elected legislative assembly and the appointed 24-member Legislative Council. While other bicameral provinces eliminated their upper houses by 1928, Quebec did not do so until 1968. Attempts to abolish it had been made as early as 1878, when there were conflicts between the Council and the Assembly, but such early moves were vetoed by the Council. The Lesage government tried to cir-cumvent this veto by seeking an amendment to the BNA Act from the British parliament, but no action was taken. The upper chamber was a good source of patronage, served to protect minority interests, and gave the province a certain added "national" stature, but it became another victim of the Quiet Revolution. It was left to the Union Nationale regime of Daniel Johnson to abolish the council by paying the councillors an annual pension equal to the amount of their salary.[52]

The National Assembly functions in a manner similar to other provincial leg-islatures, but Quebec has been more willing to deviate from British terminology and usages. Thus, after the lieutenant-governor welcomes the members back, the throne speech is replaced by the premier's inaugural address (discours inaugural). The Speaker is called "le Président" and wears no robes; the committee on the budget and administration replaces public accounts; and, perhaps most significantly, some bills are sent to committee after first reading rather than after being approved in principle at the second reading stage, as is the British tradition. This means that most of the work of the assembly—including debate on the principle of bills—is conducted in standing committees, of which there are now eight. Five of the committees are chaired by members from the government side and three from the opposition, while ministers only sit on committees examining their bills. These functional, specialized committees, which have both staff and research assistants, parallel government departments; committee work on estimates and legislation makes the position of MNA a full-time one.

The legislature normally has two sittings in each calendar year and, in the 1990-93 period, averaged about 78 days per annum. As of 1994, Quebec had the highest basic renumeration of any provincial legislature—$63,469 in taxable indemnity and $11,203 in non-taxable expense allowance. Other services and facilities for MNAs (committee allowances, accommodation and travel allowances, offices, staff, telephone calls, caucus services, and support services in the constituency) rank with those of Ontario as the best in the country.[53] An official record of legislative proceedings has been available since 1964 (and of committees since 1965), and television was introduced in the chamber in 1978.

Bureaucracy

Quebec employs about 69,000 people in departments and agencies, another 36,000 in government business enterprises, and a further 225,000 in the wider public sector. Prior to 1960, Quebec's public service was small and weak, primarily consisting of "thousands of clerks."[54] In 1943, a civil service commission was established to end rampant patronage but, after the government changed hands in 1944, the commission did not function for 16 years. Reviving that body was a small part of the dramatic transformation which has occurred in the Quebec public service since the early 1960s. It has expanded enormously, recruiting thousands of university graduates from many fields. Two indications of the bureaucracy's improvement were its work on the Quebec Pension Plan in the mid-1960s which proved superior to that of its federal counterparts, and its adoption of the Planning, Programming and Budgeting System (PPBS) management technique in the early 1970s, shortly after Ontario adopted the system. Today the Quebec public service is large, highly educated and well trained; it is often an innovative political force, and is sometimes called the heart of the new middle class. Although political patronage is largely a thing of the past, the provincial auditor has recently faulted the Quebec bureaucracy for "bureaucratic patronage," the hiring of civil servants' friends. The public service was granted collective bargaining rights in 1965 and several serious strikes have since occurred, although only in the recession years of 1982-85 did the government abandon its generous treatment of this group. Since 1979, Quebec has also had an ombudsman (protecteur du citoyen) to oversee administrative behaviour. Once the arena of outrageous party patronage, government contracts over $10,000 must now be awarded to the lowest bidder in a public tendering process.

TABLE 6.10   Quebec Government Departments, 1994

Affaires intergouvernementales canadiennes
Affaires internationales, immigration et communautés culturelles
Affaires municipales
Agriculture, des pêcheries et de l'alimentation
Conseil du trésor
Culture et communications
Education
Emplois
Environnement et de la faune
Finances et revenue
Industrie, du commerce, de la science et de la technologie
Justice
Ressources naturelles
Santé et des services sociaux
Sécurité publique
Sécurité du revenue
Transports

In addition to the regular government departments, there is a large array of administrative agencies. The increase in the number of such semi-independent agencies has been phenomenal and clearly demonstrates the enormity of the provincial state: 34 in the 1960s, 64 in the 1970s, and at least 37 more in the 1980s.[55] Many of these parallel similar semi-independent bodies in other provinces, such as the Quebec Municipal Commission, the Quebec Agricultural Marketing Board, the public service, liquor, and human rights commissions, and the Council on the Status of Women. Like Ontario, there is a provincial police force (Sûreté du Québec), a Quebec police commission and, as in most other provinces, an industrial development corporation. However, Quebec's administrative agencies in the linguistic and cultural fields are distinctive. Several agencies are concerned with promoting and protecting the French language—Conseil de la langue française, Office de la langue française, Commission d'appel de francisation des entreprises, and Commission d'appel sur la langue d'enseignement. There are three general agencies dealing with culture including the

Société de développement des industries culturelles (SODIC) and three dealing specifically with film, books, and educational television.

The Quebec government has been actively involved in the economic life of the province since 1960, primarily in the form of Crown corporations or state-owned enterprises (SOEs). Besides the giant Crown corporation Hydro-Québec and its subsidiary, the James Bay Development Corporation, there was Sidbec (the government-owned steel-making operation), the Asbestos Corporation (Société nationale de l'amiante), and the government automobile insurance corporation (Régie de l'assurance automobile du Québec). The government has also become involved in the food industry (SOQUIA, Société québécoise d'initiatives agro-alimentaires), mineral exploration (SOQUEM, Société québécoise d'exploration minière), forestry (REXFOR), and petroleum (SOQUIP, Société québécoise d'initiatives pétrolières). There is also the Société générale de financement (SGF), a holding company for many of the government's industrial operations, and the Caisse de dépôt et placement, the agency which manages the funds collected by the Quebec Pension Plan and numerous other large pension and insurance funds in the province.

TABLE 6.11   Quebec Agencies, Boards, Commissions and Crown Corporations, 1994

Crown Corporations:	Caisse de dépôt et placement
	Hydro-Québec
	Radio-Québec
	Régie de l'assurance automobile du Québec
	Société de développement industriel (SDI)
	Société d'énergie de la baie James
	Société de radio-télévision du Québec (Radio-Québec)
	Société de récupération, d'exploitation et de développement Forestiers du Québec (REXFOR)
	Société d'habitation du Québec
	Société générale de financement
	Société générale des industries culturelles
	Société québécoise d'exploration minière (SOQUEM)
	Société québécoise d'initiatives agro-alimentaires (SOQUIA)
	Société québécoise d'initiatives pétrolières (SOQUIP)
Agencies, Boards, and Commissions:	Commission de protection de la langue française
	Commission des droits de la personne
	Commission municipale du Québec
	Conseil de la langue française
	Conseil du statut de la femme
	Office de la langue française
	Régie du logement du Québec
	Sûreté du Québec

The caisse currently has assets of nearly $40 billion with substantial equity holdings in a number of Canada's major corporations inside and outside Quebec, including Inco Ltd., Canadian Pacific, Alcan, John Labatt, Thomson, Seagram, Laidlaw, Bombardier, American Barrick, Cambridge Shopping Centres, and most of the chartered banks.[56] It is clearly more than just a state-owned trust company, and has become an important instrument of provincial economic policy. In 1981, for example, the caisse along with SGF took controlling interest in Domtar, and was also influential in the creation of Provigo Inc. The caisse joined forces with SGF to buy a portion of Noranda, with Socanav to gain control of Steinberg's, and with SOQUIP to take over Gaz Métropolitain.

The growth in the provincial state came to an end in 1986 when the primacy of the private sector was asserted by the Bourassa government's three task forces: the Gobeil report on government reorganization, the Fortier report on the privatization of SOEs, and the Scowen report on deregulation. By 1995, the following agencies had been privatized or abolished: Raffinerie du Sucre, Québécair, Madelipêche and other fishing operations, Société nationale de l'amiante, Donohue Inc. and other forestry operations, and Sidbec.

Judiciary

The Court of Appeal, with 16 judges, stands at the apex of the Quebec court system and generally makes decisions in banks of three judges. The Superior Court consists of about 130 judges who make decisions individually and possess the functions of district and county courts. The court of Quebec is the lowest level and, in 1988, incorporated three previously independent bodies, the provincial court, the court of the sessions of the peace, and the youth court. It contains some 155 judges who deal with small claims and other civil matters and less serious criminal cases. Montreal, Quebec City and Laval also have municipal courts. What is most distinctive about the Quebec judicial system is that the civil code is the basis of civil law in the province. The Quiet Revolution sparked a comprehensive revision of the code and a massive overhaul was passed in 1991.

Municipal Government

Municipal government has been complex and fragmented, with a vast array of local categories, most very small: cities, towns, villages, parishes, townships, united townships, and counties. The latter were upper-tier authorities performing certain functions for parishes, villages, and unorganized territory. In 1979, counties were replaced with upper-tier regional municipalities with the main function of preparing and implementing a regional land use development plan.[57] Montreal and Quebec possess two-tier urban communities analogous to Metropolitan Toronto, while Hull and Chicoutimi have similar regional structures.

POLITICAL EVOLUTION

To 1867[58]

Quebec politics in the post-Confederation period cannot be fully understood without a brief account of developments before 1867. It was in this period that the habitants established a distinctive cultural identity, that the francophone collectivity's determination to survive was consolidated, and that English Canada was forced to accept the federal reality of Canadian society.[59]

The British capture of the colony of New France in 1759 established the basis of Quebec's development over the next two centuries. First, most of the upper-class—economic and political—returned to France, leaving the Roman Catholic clergy and the seigneurs as the only French elite. English-speaking entrepreneurs replaced the French economic elite. A francophone petite bourgeoisie emerged (small businessmen, merchants, and professionals), and the rural and urban working class remained predominantly French. Second, the primacy of the English language and the Church of England gradually eroded until the French were permitted to use their own language, even in the business of government. Freedom to worship and the Roman Catholic Church's right to tithe were also recognized. The Quebec Act of 1774 provided for a legislative council to which many French-Canadians were appointed, and for a judicial system that reflected both English criminal and French civil law. Third, an interdependent relationship developed between English political authorities and the French clergy. The conquest reinforced the French-Canadian determination to preserve and defend their distinctiveness and led francophones to view the Church as the guardian of their language and culture. It also essentially severed ties between Quebec and France, so that Quebec was largely unaffected by the French Revolution, Quebec's clergy being determined to insulate the province from the liberal democratic ideas of that event.

The Constitutional Act of 1791 divided Upper and Lower Canada (Ontario and Quebec) into two separate British colonies, each with a governor, an appointed executive and legislative council, and an elected assembly. The assembly in Lower Canada was primarily composed of French-Canadian representatives, but they were understandably frustrated, given their larger numbers, because the principle of responsible government had not yet been established and the anglophone executive could overrule the elected members. This led to the rebellions of 1837-38 in which several rebels or "patriotes" were killed. A rebellion also occurred in Upper Canada, even though it lacked the ethnic complications of the Quebec uprising. The British government sent Lord Durham to investigate the causes of the rebellions and he found conflict between the assembly and the other organs of government, as well as "two nations warring in the bosom of a single state" in Lower Canada. Among his well-known recommendations were a union of the two colonies and the exclusive use of English in government. This would assist the assimilation of francophones, in his view the only practical solution to the unrest. He also recommended responsible government to break the deadlock between the executive and legislative councils and the assembly.

The British government implemented Durham's recommendations with limited success. The two parts of the united colony, Canada East (Quebec) and Canada West (Ontario), were granted equal representation in the assembly, but this did not lead to the assimilation of the French. Rather, they demanded the use of their language in the new government. In fact, a "double majority" principle emerged under which a bill had to receive the support of a majority of each section to be passed, and most governments were headed by English and French co-leaders. While the principle of responsible government was established, the situation moved increasingly in the direction of political deadlock between the two linguistic and geographic sectors.

Federalism in the form of Confederation was the solution to these problems. Ontario and Quebec would be separate provinces with a large degree of autonomy in linguistic, cultural, legal, and religious matters. Quebec would retain its civil law system, and provincial jurisdiction would include property and civil rights, health and welfare, municipal institutions, public lands, local works, education, and the administration of justice. The new government in Ottawa would deal with issues which transcended such divisions: trade and commerce, defence, banking, and criminal law. Quebec entered Confederation with a two-party system, the Liberals, composed of radical Rouge elements as well as moderates, and the Conservatives, a coalition of the English and French bourgeoisie dominated by George-Étienne Cartier. The Rouges' radicalism was evident in its advocacy of democracy and the separation of Church and state, particularly in the educational system, and it was consequently condemned by the Church. Many francophones were opposed to Confederation, fearing that provincial powers were too confined, language rights too narrow, and that the province would be overwhelmed by the anglophone majority in Ottawa.

1867-1960[60]

The federal and provincial Conservative parties dominated Quebec politics for the first 30 years of Confederation. A close relationship existed between federal and provincial governments; John A. Macdonald was generally sensitive to francophone opinion; and within Quebec, a francophone majority coexisted with an over-represented anglophone minority. Despite the party's success, however, no predominant Conservative premier emerged in this period.

Pierre-Joseph Chauveau became Quebec's first premier, winning a large majority in the 1867 election, and remaining until 1873. To a large extent, however, Macdonald's Quebec lieutenant in the federal cabinet, Cartier, also ran the province. He emphasized religious tolerance and a limited role for the Church, ethnic partnership, and a moderate degree of government involvement, especially in infrastructure development.[61] Like the rest of Canada, Quebec had a preoccupation with the construction of railways, and the government advanced great sums to private companies for this purpose.

By 1873 ideological, regional, and personal tensions within the Conservative party forced Chauveau's resignation and he was replaced by Gédéon Ouimet. The ideological conflict primarily centred on the ultramontagne group, who espoused the view that the Church should have primacy over the state in public affairs. Specifically, the ultramontagne Conservatives believed that Quebec society should be organized according to Catholic principles, the Church controlling Quebec's main institutions and politicians deferring to bishops in formulating legislation or determining the extent of government activity.[62] Ouimet was forced to resign due to a land-transfer scandal in 1874.

Quebec's third premier was Charles Boucher de Boucherville, another Conservative, but one who sat in the Legislative Council. While he was heralded for his electoral reforms (including the secret ballot and a uniform election day), he has since been criticized for abolishing the Department of Public Instruction under pressure from the Quebec Roman Catholic bishops. Education became the responsibility of the Council of Public Instruction, which had both Catholic and Protestant committees, and the two religious groups henceforth controlled the province's education system. In 1878, the newly appointed Liberal lieutenant-governor, Luc Letellier de Saint-Just, exploited another railway controversy to dismiss de Boucherville and install the province's first Liberal government under Henri-G. Joly.[63] He was defeated when the new provincial Conservative leader, J.-Adolphe Chapleau, persuaded a number of Liberal Assembly members to cross the floor, and Chapleau became premier in 1879. A year after winning the 1881 election, Chapleau decided to move to the federal level, switching places with federal minister J.-Alfred Mousseau. Mousseau resigned in 1884 under pressure from the ultramontagne group, and made way for John James Ross, who sat in the Legislative Council.

The hanging of Louis Riel in Regina in 1885 was the beginning of the end of the Conservative party in Quebec. Liberal leader Honoré Mercier formed the Parti National in an effort to provide a unified Quebec front against the federal Conservative decision to execute Riel, and some Conservatives joined his group. Mercier became premier in 1887, the same year another French-Canadian, Wilfrid Laurier, took over as national leader of the Liberal party. Two of Laurier's most notable early accomplishments were a speech distinguishing British moderate liberalism from French revolutionary liberalism, and his persuading the Roman Catholic Church to withdraw its opposition to the Liberal party, now more moderate than the former Rouge faction.

Mercier was probably the most prominent of the early Quebec premiers, although he was only in office for four years. The Riel affair appeared to demonstrate the lack of French-Canadian influence in Ottawa, and Mercier was the first Quebec premier to demand greater autonomy from the federal government.

In this regard, he convened an interprovincial conference in 1887 attended by five other dissatisfied premiers. Mercier pursued an activist economic policy, extending railways to the Lac St. Jean region, and building roads and bridges through the province. He also emphasized the development of agriculture and forestry, and created the Department of Agriculture and Colonization.

One problem that had been unresolved since 1759 was the matter of compensating the Jesuits for the expropriation of their estates. Since the Roman Catholic hierarchy believed that not all the money should go to the Jesuits, Mercier set aside $400,000 and asked the pope to distribute it among the Jesuits and other Catholic institutions. Even though $60,000 was made available for English-Protestant post-secondary education, many regarded this sum as inadequate, and the intervention of the pope raised Protestant hackles throughout the country. In Quebec, however, this sympathetic treatment of Church relations by Mercier, a pre-Riel Liberal, helped till the soil of legitimacy for Laurier and the federal Liberal party.

Mercier's rule was brought to an abrupt halt in 1891 when a scandal was revealed in connection with the Baie des Chaleurs railway.[64] It was unclear whether Mercier was personally aware of the situation, but the lieutenant-governor dismissed him and for the second time asked de Boucherville to form a government. The economic situation in the mid-1890s proved unfavourable to the provincial Conservatives, and the federal party collapsed after the death of John A. Macdonald.

The federal Liberals swept to victory across the country in 1896, and former Quebec premier Joly was made a minister in the Laurier cabinet. Laurier's strength in his own province was somewhat surprising because the bishops still generally supported the Conservatives.[65] In particular they opposed Laurier's stand on the Manitoba School Question of whether the federal government should intervene to protect the Roman Catholic separate school system in Manitoba when the Protestant majority there abolished it. Laurier favoured leaving the matter to federal-provincial negotiation, rather than have Ottawa impose a solution. But Quebecers in general, including some of the lower clergy, enthusiastically supported this urbane, bilingual fellow francophone, and the provincial Liberals rode his coat-tails to power in 1897. There followed a period of nearly 40 years of uninterrupted Liberal rule in the province (the third longest tenure of any party anywhere), dominated by two men, Lomer Gouin (1905-1920) and L.-A. Taschereau (1920-1936).[66]

The first premier of this period was F.-G. Marchand who died in 1900. His efforts to reform the educational system with a public Department of Education were naturally opposed by the bishops and, after the intervention of the Vatican and Laurier and its defeat in the Legislative Council, the plan was abandoned.[67] The Minister of Lands, S.-N. Parent presided over new natural resource development which provided employment and enriched the public treasury. Parent succeeded Marchand as premier and served for five years. On two occasions, in

1900 and 1904, he called a provincial election in the immediate aftermath of a federal election, and benefited from his association with Laurier.

Parent was charged with being corrupt, autocratic, and too pro-business, and in 1905 he was forced to resign due to a deep split within the Liberal Party. The leader of the dissident group, Lomer Gouin, a lawyer and the son-in-law of Mercier, served as premier for the next 15 years. Gouin was considered a radical for favouring educational reform, and a nationalist who had challenged Laurier on increased federal subsidies to Quebec. On the other hand, he proved to be a cautious, fiscally conservative leader, with a talent for compromise, and it was a generally prosperous, stable era, at least until the outbreak of the First World War.

During this period, legislation was passed which required that pulpwood cut on public lands be processed into pulp or paper before being exported, a regulation that had a positive effect on the growth of the pulp and paper industry. Another leading activity of the early 1900s was road building, a key factor in economic development. Gouin was also intensely interested in educational reform, but he was restrained by the clergy, and the Quebec school system remained backward in many respects. He was able to introduce one significant public innovation, however, a system of vocational and technical education including the Ecole des Hautes Etudes Commerciales. In addition, women were granted access to a classical college education, and the Université de Montréal was raised to full university status. In 1906 the Quebec Cooperative Syndicates Act was passed, which encouraged the expansion of the caisse populaire movement founded by Alphonse Desjardins and actively supported by the Church. Gouin's 1909 Workmen's Compensation Act predated Ontario's, but was less effective.

In the 1908 election, Gouin was opposed by the articulate Nationalist, Henri Bourassa, who had previously resigned his House of Commons seat over Canadian participation in the Boer War. His two main themes were anti-imperialism in foreign policy and cultural dualism throughout Canada. In 1910, Bourassa went on to found the daily newspaper *Le Devoir*. In 1912, the provincial electoral process was slightly improved with the adoption of full male suffrage and the abolition of plural voting.

Gouin supported the Canadian war effort after 1914, but was adamantly opposed to conscription. Naturally enough, the proportion of volunteers for military duty from Quebec was much smaller than from other provinces. After the federal Conservatives initiated compulsory military service in 1917, violence erupted in the streets of Montreal, and the nationalist movement switched to support the Liberals, especially in light of the Ontario Conservatives' treatment of French-language educational rights with Regulation 17 restricting French-language education to the lowest grades in Ontario. The situation worsened in the spring of 1918, when a conscription-inspired riot occurred in Quebec City, and the federal Conservative government sent in the army, resulting in four deaths and many injuries. What little federal Conservative support was left in the province after Riel's execution was lost by the end of the war.

Although still held in high esteem, Gouin resigned in 1920, later serving for a time as Minister of Justice in Mackenzie King's federal cabinet. He was succeeded by Louis-Alexandre Taschereau, a lawyer-businessman and scion of a prominent Quebec family, who remained premier for 16 years. Even more than Gouin, Taschereau put a premium on industrialization, and this change of administration marked the real beginning of urban, industrial Quebec. For the first time, for example, the 1921 census revealed a majority of urban residents in the province.

Even though this policy of industrialization was not popular with the Church, the Conservatives, or the Nationalists, all of whom called for more emphasis on agriculture, it was largely unavoidable. The Liberals advocated rapid resource exploitation and manufacturing, not only as the route to prosperity but also as a source of employment. Existing farms had been subdivided as much as possible among successive generations of large families and most of the province's good agricultural land was already under cultivation, leading to an exodus of rural young people to urban areas as well as to the United States. Taschereau's development policy meant relying on outsiders, since little domestic capital was available for investment.

The Liberals took every opportunity to attract British, American and English-Canadian capitalists to the province by extolling its abundant natural resources, its hydroelectric potential, its docile and hardworking labour force, and the government's sympathetic attitude toward private enterprise.[68] Land grants, tax exemptions, and other concessions were common, taxes were kept low, and social and labour legislation was weak. Thus, a number of large power companies established generating stations on the Saguenay, Ottawa, and St. Lawrence rivers. Two of the main users of such power were pulp and paper mills and aluminum smelters, especially the Alcan smelter built at Arvida in 1924. The mining industry also expanded during the 1920s, and enjoyed little or no government regulation. Manufacturing was undertaken in such fields as shoes, clothing, textiles, tobacco, iron and steel, newsprint and other paper products, and chemicals, while new industries included electrical appliances, petroleum refining, sugar, brewing and distilling, automobiles, pharmaceuticals, rubber, and machinery. The entire economic picture was dominated by non-resident, capital-intensive monopolies, in which English-speaking, non-Quebec management controlled the large unorganized francophone work force. Relations between the government and the corporations were so close that ministers often sat on corporate boards of directors.[69]

Two of Taschereau's other early initiatives were the passage of a public charities act and the creation of a liquor commission. Although the Church was still largely responsible for health and welfare services, legislation in 1921 divided the costs among the institution, the municipality, and the provincial government. Unlike the other provinces, Quebec did not adopt prohibition in the 1920 period. In its place, the Quebec Liquor Commission was given a monopoly on the sale of liquor and wine.

The Conservative leader, Arthur Sauvé, dissociated himself from the federal party in the early 1920s and resigned in 1929, to be succeeded by the colourful mayor of Montreal, Camillien Houde. But, even with the Depression and the popularity of the federal Conservatives in the province in 1930, the Liberals were not endangered. They benefited from the federal party's defence of French-Canadian interests, as well as from extensive patronage, gerrymandering, and rural over-representation in the legislature. Roadwork continued to be a key to success, since it provided construction and supplies contracts for friends of the government, jobs for workers, and could be promised in return for a specific constituency's support. The Liberals won again in 1931, and when several defeated Conservatives challenged Liberal victors on the basis of fraudulent practices on election day, the Liberals enacted a law which retroactively removed such cases from the jurisdiction of the courts.[70]

As the strength of the rural parish declined, the Church tried to control various economic and social groups in the province, especially labour and farm organizations. If it could not halt the industrialization process, the Church could at least direct the union movement so that it did not fall into the secular and materialistic hands of international unionism. Thus, in 1921, the Catholic trade union movement was established in the form of the Confédération des travailleurs catholiques du Canada (CTCC). In the wake of the national Progressive movement, which only marginally touched Quebec, a farmer's organization called the Union catholique des cultivateurs, was founded in 1924. The Church was also connected to the caisses populaires, the farmers' co-operative, the Coopérative fédérée, and to the youth movement, called Association catholique de la jeunesse canadienne-française.

What finally brought the long Liberal regime to an end was the coalescing of forces opposed to the party's industrialization policies.[71] Opposition centred on nationalist intellectuals and the Church. Together they organized back-to-the-land and colonization movements and encouraged the growth of French-Canadian businesses. But it was only in the early 1930s, after the population suffered from widespread unemployment and destitution caused by the Great Depression, that such nationalist opposition became effective. One reform group headed by Paul Gouin (son of the former premier), and calling itself L'Action libérale nationale (ALN), was established within the Liberal party. Gouin's group of young, left-wing Liberals was greatly influenced by the nationalist critique of Taschereau's record, and opposed both his conservative policies and his authoritarian control. Just prior to the 1935 provincial election, the group left the Liberals to establish their own party. They adopted a comprehensive program, including agricultural, labour, industrial, commercial, economic, financial, political, administrative, electoral, fiscal, and judicial reforms.[72] In the meantime, the

Conservatives chose Maurice Duplessis, a lawyer from Trois-Rivières, as their new leader in 1931. About two weeks prior to the election, the ALN and Conservative leaders formed a coalition called the Union Nationale Duplessis-Gouin. To this mutually advantageous arrangement the Conservatives contributed practical political experience and financial resources, while the ALN brought with it a comprehensive reform platform, new personnel, and new popular support.[73] This combination was so successful that it won 42 seats compared with 48 for the Taschereau Liberals, who had resorted to all their usual electoral abuses—election-day treating, manipulation of voters' lists, impersonation of voters, lost ballot boxes, and intimidation.[74]

Duplessis demonstrated his mastery of parliamentary procedure when the legislature met in 1936. His main weapon was the public accounts committee which had been dormant for many years. Duplessis unveiled to the committee a sordid picture of government abuses of every kind. Taschereau himself was revealed to be one of the leading practitioners of nepotism, with 45 relatives on the public payroll. Other relatives and friends of the government were beneficiaries of rampant patronage handouts, and public servants received improper gifts and took scandalous advantage of their position. Most of the province's newspapers had also been bought off with large government printing contracts and sales of government advertising. The public reaction was so intense that Taschereau resigned, and the "clean" Adelard Godbout, Minister of Agriculture, succeeded him. Godbout decided on an early election in order to dissociate himself from the previous regime.

In the 1936 campaign both parties embraced a much more progressive set of policies. Godbout was naturally more concerned about agriculture than his predecessor, attempting to appeal to the over-represented rural vote. Gouin quit the Union Nationale partnership with Duplessis just prior to the election, but the other members of the ALN remained, so that the coalition ostensibly continued intact. The UN won an overwhelming victory.

The Union Nationale governed Quebec for the following 25 years, except for a brief stint in Opposition between 1939 and 1944.[75] Duplessis was premier until his death in 1959, and the government was quickly defeated thereafter. At first glance Duplessis' longevity is puzzling, given that he promptly repudiated most of the original party platform and that his tenure could hardly be differentiated from that of Taschereau. The explanation can be found in the Quebec electorate's concern for federal rather than provincial policies, for Duplessis provided vehement opposition to Ottawa. In particular, he fanned the flames of nationalist sentiment in connection with the Second World War, eliciting the traditional fear of domination by the English-Canadian majority. Other factors in his longevity were the lack of a strong democratic spirit in the province and the electorate's fear of expressing dissent.[76]

It soon became clear that Duplessis had no intention of fulfilling his stated commitment to implement the ALN program, and the subsequent departure of the rest of the ALN leadership left no internal constraints on his leadership. He thereupon espoused the same economic liberalism as Taschereau: an emphasis on industrialization through non-resident capitalists, a minimal role for the provincial state, and a reliance on the Church in areas of health, education, and welfare. Measures enacted in the 1936-39 period included a prohibition on cabinet ministers becoming members of corporate boards of directors, labour legislation, which gave the government the authority to set hours, wages, or other working conditions in any industry, limited assistance for destitute mothers and the blind, and a general cleaning out of Liberal nepotism in the public service. Duplessis' infamous padlock law, passed in 1937, allowed him, as attorney general, to padlock any building deemed to be used for the propagation of communism or bolshevism—as he chose to define them. Only in the agricultural sector did Duplessis fulfil his promises: he established agricultural credit, schools, roads, colonization, and other benefits. Such attention was undoubtedly based on the premier's genuine desire to promote this sector of the economy, as well as to benefit from the rural over-representation in the legislature. On the other hand, Duplessis' extravagance had doubled the provincial debt in three years, and his personal weakness for alcohol and sex was similar to that of Mitch Hepburn in Ontario.[77]

Duplessis abruptly called the 1939 Quebec election almost immediately after the declaration of war. It was a tactic to demonstrate Quebecers' opposition to an extensive role in the conflict and conscription; it may also have been his only hope for re-election after abandoning his 1936 electoral program.[78] Duplessis ostensibly opposed the invocation of the War Measures Act which he claimed would be used to encroach on provincial jurisdiction. It was a clever move, but Duplessis was up against another masterful strategist in the prime minister. Mackenzie King was upset that his carefully balanced approach to the war had been challenged; he sent his Quebec ministers into the provincial campaign with the message that they would resign if Duplessis were victorious. That would have left an all-anglophone federal cabinet, which would be sure to enact conscription. King proved the better man in this confrontation, and the Liberals returned to power under Godbout.

The Liberal period from the end of 1939 to August 1944 was overshadowed largely by national and international developments. Among several notable Godbout initiatives, however, were the establishment of a civil service commission; the enfranchisement of women in provincial elections in 1940, long after other provinces; the nationalization of the Montreal Light, Heat and Power Company, constituting the beginning of Hydro-Québec; compulsory education to age 14, which the Church had previously obstructed; free textbooks; and more progressive labour legislation, including a general minimum wage and a superior council of labour.

Because he did not oppose federal social and economic initiatives such as unemployment insurance, family allowances, and centralization of taxation powers, Godbout was branded as a creature of the federal Liberal party.[79] Then, in 1942, King held a national plebiscite to release the prime minister from his commitment to not impose conscription, a plebiscite which was approved nationally with the exception of Quebec.[80] That led to legislation allowing the federal cabinet to send conscripts overseas—"conscription if necessary but not necessarily conscription." Montreal mayor and former Conservative leader Houde was interned for counselling people to disobey the compulsory registration, King gradually lost most of his Quebec ministers, and Godbout became increasingly vulnerable. Conscription was virtually the only issue in the 1944 provincial election, in spite of Godbout's attempts to emphasize provincial concerns. The two main parties were joined by the Bloc Populaire, led by André Laurendeau, which was opposed to the war and conscription, but otherwise advocated a program of economic and social reform. The Union Nationale captured 48 seats (37 percent), the Liberals 37 (40 percent), and the Bloc Populaire 4 (15 percent). In the same month as the election, some 16,000 Canadian conscripts were sent overseas, but few saw the front lines before the war was over.

Except on a personal level (where his conduct became more circumspect after he developed diabetes), Duplessis carried on after 1944 where he had left off in 1939. The war itself had advanced the process of industrialization in Quebec, especially because of the demand for mineral, forest, and manufactured products and the pace of development quickened in the post-war period. This was largely due to Duplessis' policy of encouraging natural resource exploitation and manufacturing expansion by non-residents, who received considerable assistance from the state. He was not troubled by the anglophone dominance of the Quebec economy and had warm personal relations with many English corporate leaders. He gave pulp and paper companies generous leases of Crown lands, mining companies paid minimal royalties, and tax exemptions abounded. It was in this period, for example, that American companies began to develop the iron ore resources of Nouveau-Québec on very generous terms and built a railway through Labrador from Sept-Iles to Schefferville.[81] Despite such support of industrialization, Duplessis continued to favour the agricultural sector and spoke of the rural classes in the same glowing terms as Smallwood would later refer to his outport fishermen.[82] He provided loans, drainage, schools and colleges, and extensions of rural electrification, and a minimum wage for forestry workers.

This period was also marked by great expansion of the trade union movement. The increasing dynamism of even the CTCC worried Duplessis because an obedient labour force had been a key factor in the province's industrial expansion. In 1949, he brought in a labour code which, among other things, prohibited unions from having officers who belonged to any Communist or related organization. Another tactic which Duplessis used to repress the union movement was to send the provincial police into any town experiencing a strike. The most famous such incidents were the asbestos strike of 1949 and the strike in

Murdochville in 1957. In spite of this anti-union approach, Duplessis continued to be supported by much of the urban working class and even some labour leaders. Workers liked the Union Nationale's nationalistic stance, and Duplessis himself had cultivated the image of a man of the people.[83]

Duplessis' conservative social policy was based his alliance with the Church, which still demanded its monopoly in the fields of health, education, and welfare, and with corporate elites, who wanted to keep taxes low. This view was also supported by many conservative intellectuals of the time, such as those who wrote the ultra-nationalistic Tremblay Report in 1954. This royal commission report was "nothing less than an examination in depth of the philosophical and moral basis of French-Canadian society," continuing to emphasize the primacy of the Church, the limited role of the state, and the superiority of the rural way of life.[84]

Since French-Canadian cultural survival was considered dependent on Quebec provincial autonomy, Duplessis strongly opposed post-war federal reconstruction proposals based on Keynesian economics. These involved Ottawa controlling the main sources of taxation and the expansion of federal social programs. Although it was too late to do anything about unemployment insurance and family allowances, Duplessis fought against a federal hospital insurance scheme, criticized the old age security legislation, refused to allow Quebec universities to accept federal grants, and rejected other federal conditional grants. Quebec consequently lost an estimated $82 million in federal funds in 1959-60 alone. In 1954, he imposed a unique provincial personal income tax which forced the federal government to respond by lowering its rates within Quebec. His biographer claims Duplessis' greatest contribution to Quebec was that "he wrenched from Ottawa the fiscal and jurisdictional powers necessary to the autonomy of the province," although Duplessis made little use of such powers once acquired.[85]

Patronage, corruption, violations of parliamentary procedure, and electoral abuses also contributed to Duplessis' longevity.[86] Duplessis exploited Quebecers' ignorance of proper parliamentary practice by allowing many departments and agencies to spend huge sums in excess of authorized amounts. He ran the legislature with an iron hand and both the Speaker and his ministers were completely at his command for 15 years.[87] Like Taschereau, with whom he later became very close, Duplessis continued to buy off the press with printing and advertising contracts and gifts to editors and reporters. Duplessis' relationship with the anglophone press was at least as close as with the French, and it was said that nothing derogatory was ever printed about him except in *Le Devoir*.[88]

The Union Nationale "worked hard to maintain a close identification with local communities" and municipal officials, and tried to secure the support of key individuals in every community by offering them jobs, appointments, or contracts, in the hope that they would enlist support for the party among their respective followers.[89] The party also attracted as many "ordinary" individuals as possible through the distribution of part-time jobs on roads or other government projects. Collectively, municipalities, school districts, constituencies, and religious institutions were given grants and other favours on the condition that they support the government. Religious authorities made it known that Duplessis had been generous in his assistance. Duplessis' leadership displayed a classic pattern of patron-client reciprocal relationships—both individual and collective—in which government favours and rewards were granted in return for electoral support.[90]

On election day, votes were bought with hams, sacks of potatoes, bags of flour, nylon stockings, or shoes, and the party freely dispensed liquor for two or three weeks prior to the election. Such beneficence required a huge election fund, largely comprised of kickbacks from corporations doing business with the government and those fortunate enough to receive a liquor licence. Manipulation of the voters' list and a range of other election-day abuses were practised.

"Le chef" was in complete control of the government, the legislature, the party, and the election machine.[91] He was overbearing, paternalistic, encouraged sycophancy, and possessed amazing energy and a staggering knowledge of the province's laws and people. His gregariousness, "ebullient mind," magnetic eyes, biting wit, and repartee were conspicuous and, while he could be forgiving and magnanimous on occasion, he was often cruel, vindictive, and a dangerous adversary. At times it pleased him to be pitiless, perpetuating fear and ensuring that his generosity would never be taken for granted.[92]

During the 1950s, opposition to Duplessis' leadership gradually increased. Radical nationalism resurfaced in various guises, including *Le Devoir*, while the asbestos strike of 1949 raised the consciousness of many labour leaders and intellectuals such as Jean Marchand, Gérard Pelletier, and Pierre Trudeau.[93] Until 1949, the Church and Duplessis were generally close—indeed, he claimed that the "bishops eat out of my hand." But after the asbestos strike, the bishops issued a pro-labour pastoral letter, and sections of the Church moved into opposition and inspired reform. Academic-religious protest was centred in the faculty of social science at l'Université Laval, headed by Rev. Georges-Henri Lévesque. A wholly secular opposition group, including Trudeau and Pelletier, published a magazine, *Cité Libre*, which challenged not only the Union Nationale government, the Church, the federal Liberal party, and the conservative-nationalist intellectuals, but also the entire nationalistic approach.[94] Trudeau was among those denied university appointments because of the government's interference.

Such opposition could only be fully effective, however, if it were concentrated in an alternative political party. Godbout led the Liberals to a disastrous showing in the 1948 election and then resigned in favour of Georges Lapalme in 1950. Lapalme initiated a vigorous organizational drive and also began to modernize party policy, incorporating the demands of most of the disparate opposition groups. When the Diefenbaker Conservatives assumed office in 1957, a generally warm relationship with Duplessis ensued. But such co-operation nec-essarily blunted Duplessis' anti-Ottawa position. Lapalme resigned as provincial Liberal leader in 1958, to be was succeeded by Jean Lesage who until 1957 had served as Minister of Northern Affairs and Natural Resources in the federal St. Laurent government. Lesage expanded upon earlier Liberal promises of reform, compiling a comprehensive program for the 1960 election.

Duplessis died in September 1959 on a trip to Schefferville. The obvious suc-cessor was his Minister of Youth and Social Welfare, Paul Sauvé, son of the for-mer Conservative leader, Arthur Sauvé. Despite having been close to Duplessis, Sauvé immediately unleashed forces of fundamental reform in almost every aspect of government policy and practice, one specific accomplishment being an agreement with Diefenbaker on university grants. Sauvé consequently received an enthusiastic response in the rest of the country, but died suddenly in January 1960, just three months into the job. This time the party was divided on the leadership question, and Antonio Barrette, the Minister of Labour, emerged as a compromise candidate. But many Quebecers were attracted by the Liberal promises of policy reforms, and the electorate finally seemed concerned about electoral corruption. Jean Lesage led his Liberals to victory in the 1960 election, and the Quiet Revolution had begun.

The 1960s[95]

The Quiet Revolution consisted of dramatic changes in the attitudes, values, and behaviour of French-Canadian Quebecers, and an enormous expansion in the role of the provincial state. The latter was in response to the frustrated demands of Quebec society which erupted under intellectual and middle-class leadership following the death of Maurice Duplessis. Indeed, the Lesage government was pushed by the momentum of events to move much farther and faster than it ever intended. While Lesage was clearly the leader of the modernization team, he had several influential, individualistic, and interventionist ministers, especial-ly René Lévesque, Paul Gérin-Lajoie, and later Eric Kierans, Pierre Laporte, and Claude Wagner, collectively referred to as the "équipe du tonnerre" (thunder team), and many capable advisers such as Claude Morin, Arthur Tremblay, Claude Castonguay, and Jacques Parizeau.

There were several aspects to the ideological transformation encompassed by the Quiet Revolution.[96] In one sense it was a refutation of French-Canada's tra-ditional identity as an agrarian, anti-industrial society, coupled with a strong desire to see social and economic development in Quebec keep pace with the rest of the continent. This coincided with a new spirit of French-Canadian confi-dence. In addition, the attention of most of the movement's leaders centred on Quebec; "French Canadians" became "Québécois," less attention was directed towards their brethren in other provinces, and they were less concerned with influencing Ottawa. Indeed, after the election of John Diefenbaker in 1957, francophone Quebecers felt a profound alienation from the federal scene.[97] All of these changes culminated in a new attitude toward the state: the provincial state—the Quebec government staffed by competent Québécois—would be the principal engine of social and economic development.

Upon taking office in early July 1960, Lesage made several key appointments, but refused to overturn as many Union Nationale appointments as his supporters demanded. The early agenda was a heavy one indeed. Lesage created several new ministries, including the Ministry of Cultural Affairs; he unveiled a comprehensive highway plan which emphasized ultra-modern autoroute construction; and he took steps to introduce a hansard. The Lesage government reformed agricultural programs, partly as a result of entering the Agricultural Rehabilitation and Rural Development Act agreement with Ottawa, and increased funding under the Quebec Farm Credit Act. It transformed the educational system: expanded free education, extended compulsory school attendance, introduced a school allowance, and replaced discretionary ministerial decisions on funding to school commissions with statutory grants. Universities also received more funding, and a royal commission on education was established under Monseigneur Alphonse-Marie Parent of Université Laval. In 1961, Lesage established a treasury board and a new economic council, and began redistributing electoral boundaries. He quickly informed the federal government that Quebec would join the national hospital insurance and Trans-Canada Highway programs, and all departments, especially the Ministries of Public Works and Roads, were instructed to award contracts on the basis of public tenders and to end patronage.[98]

René Lévesque and Paul Gérin-Lajoie were the most aggressive cabinet ministers. As Minister of Natural Resources, Lévesque had officials investigate the viability of nationalizing private power companies and subsequently began a personal campaign on the issue, even though this was not part of the 1960 party platform. The main objective of nationalization would be to provide the government with an important tool of economic planning and development. In addition, service could be expanded and equalized, federal taxes avoided, and rates to consumers lowered. There was an equally important symbolic motive: this key aspect of economic activity would be controlled by French-Canadians, a striking confirmation of their economic emancipation. A sceptical Lesage was finally convinced of the merits of the nationalization plan, and he called an election for November 1962 as a kind of referendum on the question. "Maîtres chez nous" (Masters in our own house) was the party slogan.[99]

Barrette had been forced out of the Union Nationale leadership shortly after the 1960 defeat, and in September 1961 was succeeded by Daniel Johnson, chosen at a rare party convention. The separatist Rassemblement pour l'Indépendance Nationale (RIN), which had been formed in October 1960 after the publication of Marcel Chaput's book, *Why I Am a Separatist*, also entered the election contest. The Liberals increased their support and, while they had emphasized the hydro nationalization issue, studies indicated that their support was based largely on Lesage's leadership image and a general feeling of satisfaction with the government.[100]

With this mandate, the government proceeded with Lévesque's nationalization plans. Sufficient funds were borrowed from Americans to make an acceptable offer to the shareholders, and other private, co-operative, or municipal power authorities were taken over with little difficulty. By 1966, Hydro-Québec had become a monumental French-Canadian operation, and the Manic I dam had also begun production. On the other hand, Quebec and Newfoundland had not reached a settlement regarding the Churchill Falls development in Labrador.[101]

The other dominant cabinet minister, Paul Gérin-Lajoie, had been granted the Youth portfolio, and as such was responsible for the limited government role in education. With the advice of Arthur Tremblay, however, he began to expand his jurisdiction in a manner similar to Lévesque. In its report in April 1963, the Parent royal commission recommended a department of education be established and, after much consultation with the Church hierarchy, Lesage introduced Bill 60 with a view towards implementing Parent's recommendation. With the cabinet deeply divided, Gérin-Lajoie sought public support in a public speaking tour across the province and became Quebec's first Minister of Education in 1964. Although the Church had insisted on Catholic and Protestant associate deputy ministers and denominational advisory committees, these only had power over purely religious aspects of the school system.

Several other significant educational reforms occurred during this period. Local responsibility was centralized through the creation of regional school commissions, new regional composite schools replaced smaller local ones, and the classical colleges were phased out so that after 11 years of elementary and secondary education, students would proceed to one of the new CEGEPs (Collèges d'Enseignement Général et Professional). There they would take two years of pre-university courses or three years of technical training. Quebec suddenly began producing graduates in science, engineering, technology, commerce, political science, economics, and public administration, rather than the four main earlier products of the classical colleges, doctors, lawyers, notaries, and priests.

The third major initiative of the Lesage government was the Quebec Pension Plan. Although the new Liberal Pearson government in Ottawa was committed to introducing a national contributory pension plan, Quebec preferred to run its own plan on a different principle. The federal scheme was based on the pay-as-you-go approach, whereas Quebec preferred a funded plan, in order to accumulate a large pool of capital for public investment. After much federal-provincial conflict, Pearson decided to meld the Canada Pension Plan with that of Quebec,[102] and secret negotiations resulted in an alignment of the two to ensure compatibility and mobility between them. Lesage established the Caisse de Dépôt et Placement to invest the funds provided under the provincial plan.

In health and welfare fields, the government either took over church-related institutions or subjected them to increasing control. The federal-provincial hospital insurance scheme ensured much provincial regulation, for example, and the government became more directly involved in providing its own welfare programs. In 1965, two of the most dynamic economic ministers, René Lévesque and Eric Kierans, were transferred to Social Welfare and Health respectively, in order to restructure those sectors of government operations. The other distinguishing aspect of health and welfare policy was the province's decision to "opt out" of federal-provincial joint programs such as the Canada Assistance Plan. However, in order to retain federal compensation, it had to maintain equivalent programs.

The Lesage government was also concerned with improving the quality of the French language in Quebec and promoting the province's culture. The Office de la langue française attempted to purify the language by preparing and distributing lists of correct words and expressions, many of which were intended to replace the growing number of anglicisms then in popular use. Another creation in the cultural field was the Quebec Arts Council.

Electoral reform was also on the agenda. By 1966, electoral boundaries had been redistributed, including 11 new seats in the Montreal area, but rural over-representation continued. Quebec's election law was transformed from the worst to the best in the country when the province pioneered election expense reform by setting a ceiling on party and candidate spending, and providing public reimbursement of some expenditures for candidates and parties. Party labels were also added to the ballot, and the voting age was reduced to 18.

The government succeeded in reforming the entire provincial judicial system, and in 1960 the first woman was elected to the Quebec legislature, Marie-Claire Kirkland-Casgrain, who became the first female cabinet minister two years later. Municipal government was not substantially changed in this period, except for the creation of the City of Laval on the Ile-Jésus adjacent to Montreal. The province also assisted Montreal with some of the city's "megaprojects" such as expressway construction, the Métro subway system, and preparations for Expo 67.

The Lesage government was concerned with economic development as well as social and political change. Beyond the major accomplishment of hydro nationalization, this involved stimulating economic growth and increasing French-Canadian control. The creation of the Caisse de Dépôt and its purchase of shares in private companies was central in both respects. The government also created an economic development agency, SGF, whose first ventures were in support of small French-Canadian secondary industries such as Marine Industries in Sorel. SGF was also behind the Société de Montage Automobile, which was to assemble such French cars as Renault and Peugeot in Quebec. A plant was built in St. Bruno and operations began in 1965, but it later closed. More ambitious was the plan to establish an integrated steel plant, Sidbec, which would be the base of heavy industry in the province. However, it was not until 1968, after Lesage's defeat, that Sidbec assumed control of the Dosco Ltd. plant at Contrecoeur and began production. Such SGF enterprises were not highly profitable, but neither were they as disastrous as in several other provinces. As Minister of Natural Resources, Lévesque pushed for a government-owned mining company and was successful in having SOQUEM created in 1965. The agriculture industry was strengthened with a new agriculture faculty at Laval, new institutes of agricultural technology, the appointment of a royal commission, and major pieces of legislation which were designed to modernize the industry and improve marketing.

As a result of all these social and economic initiatives, the Quebec public sector expanded enormously between 1960 and 1966. The size of the civil service rose by 43 percent and other public agencies increased by 93 percent; six new ministries and 21 new government bodies were created, including consultative councils, regulatory bodies, public enterprises, and administrative tribunals.[103] Lesage realized that he would need to develop a skilled, non-partisan public service in order to achieve his objectives, and recruited university faculty and new university graduates, especially in the social sciences. He introduced collective bargaining in the public service in 1964 along with the right to strike. A series of strikes immediately occurred at the Liquor Commission, Hydro-Québec, hospitals, and schools, as workers insisted on improved wages and working conditions after being liberated from the restrictions of the Duplessis regime.

All this expansion entailed a large increase in government spending, a situation complicated by Lesage's 1960 promise to maintain provincial tax levels. The provincial and national economies were both relatively buoyant in the mid-1960s, and some new taxes were imposed, local levies increased, and considerable sums borrowed. Lesage also put intense pressure on Ottawa to increase its financial contributions to the province, arguing that Quebec's needs took priority over those of Ottawa. Quebec also wanted Ottawa to remove any conditions attached to such monies. With the compliance of the Pearson government, "opting out" became the operative phrase in federal-provincial financial relations. By 1966, Quebec had withdrawn from 29 of 45 shared-cost programs, and was allowed to keep 47 percent of personal income tax revenues in the province. Quebec was also successful in having the equalization formula changed in its favour.

The only constitutional issue of the period was the federal-provincial agreement on an amending formula, the Fulton-Favreau Formula. After indicating his approval, Lesage reacted to nationalist opposition in the province and decided that he could not accept it. On the other hand, he resurrected the Provincial Premiers' Conference in 1960, a group which has continued to meet annually ever since. Of even greater significance, however, was Quebec's new relationship with France. It was during this period that Quebec and France "discovered" each other, and several ministerial contacts were established, including meetings between Lesage and Charles de Gaulle. These relations soon bothered the federal government because France appeared to treat Quebec as a sovereign state. Ever the diplomat, Prime Minister Lester B. Pearson's solution was an umbrella agreement (accord-cadre) between Canada and France, under which provinces could make detailed arrangements with that country.

Much of the academic analysis of the Quiet Revolution centres on the concept of the "new middle class," especially insofar as this class emerged in the public sector.[104] Throwing off the yoke of the Church, these new public officials could design and expand social services as they saw fit, especially with increased public funding. Moreover, as a result of opting out, the province also extricated itself from most federal influence. Thus "the new middle class could use nationalism to legitimize its own aspirations."[105] The provincial bureaucracy also grew in fields where the Church had not been dominant, as the new class of bureaucrats applied their specialized knowledge to the demands of urban and industrial growth. The newly nationalized Hydro-Québec in particular became an important symbol of French-Canadian managerial competence, while other crown corporations also provided new opportunities. Given that upward mobility in the English-dominated private sector was still difficult, this class saw "that their personal and collective mobility was closely linked to the expansion of the Quebec state."[106] Outside of government, the new middle class could also be seen in the co-operative movement, especially the Desjardins organization, and in the francophone private sector, such as Bombardier, the Quebec banks, and trust companies.[107]

Given the magnitude of the transformation in Quebec society which occurred over a mere six-year period, many were stunned at the Lesage government's defeat in 1966. While the Liberals won 47 percent of the vote compared with 41 percent for the Union Nationale, this represented a loss of nine percent for the Liberals from 1962. Continued rural over-representation accounted for the Union Nationale's gain of 56 seats to Lesage's 50, because Johnson had strategically concentrated his efforts in rural areas. However, it has also been said that the Liberals moved too far, too fast, without adequate explanation for the bulk of the population. On the other hand, that separatist parties gained eight percent of the vote in 1966 suggests that the Liberals had not kept pace with the nationalistic revolutionary momentum. Liberal abstentions and defections were probably also influenced by the discontinuance of patronage[108] and discontent with Lesage in regard to his "politique de grandeur."

The Union Nationale regime between 1966 and 1970 lacked the clear-cut focus of the preceding administration.[109] In some respects it continued to implement Lesage initiatives, but the pace of modernization generally slowed. With regard to intergovernmental affairs, Johnson was even more nationalistic than Lesage had been, but in a more theoretical and less practical way; thus fewer changes occurred in federal-provincial relations than earlier in the decade. However, Johnson was a more concrete threat to the federal government because he sought a broader role on the international stage. The period of Union Nationale rule was also somewhat unfocused due to Daniel Johnson's death from a heart attack in September 1968, the day before he was to open the Manic 5 dam (since renamed for him). His more moderate successor, Jean-Jacques Bertrand, did not possess Johnson's vigour or vision.

Among Liberal initiatives carried through by the Johnson government were the post-secondary education reforms, including the creation of some 30 CEGEPs, as well as the multi-campus Université du Québec, and increasing student aid. Sidbec became operational in 1968 as a purely public enterprise, hydro dams continued to be constructed, and a deal on the Churchill Falls project was finally concluded—one that Newfoundland still regrets. In addition, with federal and provincial support, Mayor Drapeau's Expo 67 was a resounding success.

Other Union Nationale innovations included the reactivation of Radio-Québec as an educational broadcasting agency, and the province's entry into the national medicare scheme. It created new upper-tier municipal structures in Montreal, Quebec, and the Hull region; SOQUIP and REXFOR, public agencies in the petroleum and forestry fields; and a Ministry of Communications to promote the French language. Considerable controversy erupted in the matter of encouraging immigrant children to learn French rather than English, especially among Italians in the Montreal suburb of St. Léonard. At this point, the government appointed a royal commission on the language situation, with Denis Gendron as chairman. Other innovations included the creation of the Société d'Habitation du Québec, the establishment of provincial family allowances, and the enfranchisement of reserve Indians in provincial elections. Some observers found that expansions in government operations in this period were more the result of bureaucratic influence—from Claude Morin, Arthur Tremblay, and Jacques Parizeau, for example—than the intention of the party and cabinet.[110]

Even these limited initiatives required an increase in the sales tax from six to eight percent. But, in general, the rate of increase in government employment and government expenditure declined from the previous period. Such a containment of public sector expansion reflected the Union Nationale's rural electoral base. The government faced much labour unrest, resorting several times to back-to-work legislation.

In the area of federal-provincial relations Johnson stood by his 1965 book, *Égalité ou Indépendance*, and advocated greater autonomy for Quebec as the homeland of the French-Canadian nation. This viewpoint was expressed at the Confederation for Tomorrow Conference convened by Premier Robarts in Toronto in 1967, and at the federal-provincial constitutional conference called by Pearson in February 1968.[111] While Johnson was more nationalistic than Lesage, the Union Nationale was not anxious to expand provincial government activities in areas of joint occupation with Ottawa.[112] By this time, the federal government position toward decentralization had hardened as a result of the influence of Pierre Trudeau (among others) and Johnson gained nothing of substance in this respect during this period.

In international affairs, on the other hand, Johnson reorganized the Department of Federal-Provincial Relations as the Department of Intergovernmental Affairs, and established a new Department of Immigration. Quebec now demanded a greater role on the world scene, and sought to deal with foreign countries in matters of provincial jurisdiction. In particular, Quebec wished to attend international conferences of francophone states on education and culture, and to sign international agreements related to these areas. On several occasions, Quebec and Canadian delegations to international conventions fought over representation, seating, display of flags, and other symbols.

One striking event was the triumphal procession of French President Charles de Gaulle from Quebec City to Montreal in July 1967, culminating in his famous cry at the Montreal City Hall, "Vive le Québec libre." De Gaulle's actions were termed "unacceptable" by Ottawa and he was forced to leave the country without meeting federal authorities.[113]

During this period, there were even more significant developments on the Opposition side of the National Assembly. The Lesage government had been increasingly autonomist in its last days of office, and an internal debate developed about this question. The conflict continued after its defeat, and in September 1967, René Lévesque asserted that "Quebec should become a sovereign state."[114] At the party conference in October, Eric Kierans and Jean Lesage argued for federalism, albeit with a special status and increased powers for Quebec and, after much procedural wrangling, Lévesque announced his resignation, and walked away with about 100 of his supporters. Lévesque lost no time in creating the Mouvement Souveraineté-Association (MSA). The other two separatist groups already in the picture were the RN (Ralliement National) and the RIN (Rassemblement pour l'Indépendance Nationale), but ideological differences and varied formulas of separatism kept them distinct. In October 1968, Lévesque transformed the MSA into the Parti Québécois, and shortly thereafter completed a union with the RN and RIN.[115] Earlier that year, Pearson called the first of a series of constitutional conferences and Pierre Trudeau became prime minister. Violence in this period escalated and, at the St. Jean Baptiste Day parade in Montreal on the day before the 1968 federal election, RIN members pelted Trudeau with bottles.

The 1970s[116]

The 1970s in Quebec began with a new Liberal premier, but six years later the Parti Québécois came to power. The decade ended with the defeat of the first PQ referendum on Quebec sovereignty.

When Jean Lesage retired, a convention in 1970 chose 37-year-old Robert Bourassa as the new Liberal leader. Well-educated—Montreal, Harvard, and

Oxford universities—and an experienced economist, Bourassa was first elected to the legislature in 1966 and quickly advanced to the position of finance critic. Shortly after becoming Liberal leader, he was faced with the April 1970 election campaign.

Many francophones had grown disenchanted with the Union Nationale government's failure to continue the modernizing process of the Quiet Revolution, its unwillingness to take a strong stand in promoting the French culture and language within Quebec, and its lack of concern for organized labour. Some of the discontented moved toward separatism as a solution to all problems, especially given the hard line Ottawa took against further concessions to the province. Because this was the first outing of the Parti Québécois, Bourassa concentrated on campaigning against separatism. As a response to the poor economy, he promised to use his expertise to create 100,000 new jobs annually. The Parti Québécois ran on an explicit separatist platform which had gained credibility with the conversion of Jacques Parizeau but was damaged by the "Brinks Affair." A *Montreal Gazette* photograph showed eight Brinks trucks crossing the border into Ontario loaded with Quebec securities whose value might be threatened by a PQ victory. The Créditistes also entered provincial politics in January 1970 under a new provincial leader, Camille Samson, applying Social Credit solutions to rural discontent. The election results demonstrated a peculiar disparity between the percentage of popular vote each party won when compared with their number of seats. The Liberals were victorious with 72 seats based on 45 percent of the vote, while the Union Nationale was reduced to 17 seats and 20 percent of the vote. The Créditistes captured 11 percent of the vote for 13 seats, while the PQ actually came second in terms of the popular vote with 23 percent, but were fourth in seats with just seven. Party leader René Lévesque was not elected.

Bourassa called the next election for October 1973 while social and economic conditions were favourable and before support for the PQ could grow. The Liberal campaign focused on Bourassa—a builder, a competent technocrat—and "a new plan for action." Bourassa cited his accomplishments and stressed the disastrous consequences of a PQ victory. His external ideology was based on decentralized federalism and cultural sovereignty for Quebec. Lévesque emphasized political sovereignty as the only solution to the province's many problems and, in an attempt to counter Bourassa's charges and to reassure voters it was economically safe to elect the PQ, a model first-year budget was proposed. This served mainly to provide the other parties with more ammunition, especially given the PQ's assumption of a 9.5 percent increase in economic growth. The 1973 results were a Liberal landslide: 102 seats (55 percent of the vote) to six for the PQ (30 percent) and two for the Créditistes (10 percent). Once again, René Lévesque was defeated in his own riding.[117]

Robert Bourassa's administration was socially progressive but economically conservative, and somewhat responsive to demands for language reform. In intergovernmental relations, he applied pressure for more provincial autonomy, but generally sought close relations with the federal Liberal government, practising "profitable federalism," (le fédéralisme rentable). Bourassa's apparent conservatism can perhaps best be explained by his obsession with attracting American investment in order to create jobs; such investment would not be encouraged by radical economic or linguistic legislation, or by threats of separation.[118]

Soon after the 1970 election, Bourassa was confronted with an escalation of violence which peaked with the October Crisis. This involved the Front de Libération du Québec's kidnapping of British trade commissioner James Cross and provincial Labour Minister Pierre Laporte.[119] It is still not clear whether the Trudeau cabinet really believed it was necessary to invoke the War Measures Act for the first time in the absence of war to contend with this small band of terrorists, or whether it deliberately engaged in overkill. Some 400 people with peaceful nationalist or separatist notions were jailed without charges being laid, and the public generally supported this authoritarian action. While the FLQ crisis made the federal government appear strong, it revealed Bourassa's government as weak. In the end, Cross was released, Laporte was murdered, and several FLQ members were jailed or sent into exile in Cuba.

Another major controversial development during this period was Bourassa's announcement in 1971 of the massive $6-billion James Bay hydroelectric project (see Inset 6.1). Controversy also emerged concerning the government's relations with the province's unions. The three main labour groups, the Fédération des travailleurs du Québec, the Confédération des syndicats nationaux, and the Teachers' Federation (CEQ), formed a common front in 1971 to negotiate for public sector employees. They called a general strike after negotiations had failed, but the government legislated 200,000 strikers back to work. In May, the three union leaders, Louis Laberge, Marcel Pépin, and Yvon Charbonneau, were sentenced to a year in jail for encouraging workers to disobey injunctions. Other labour problems included a strike-demonstration-riot at *La Presse* in 1971, and violence and sabotage at the James Bay LG-2 site in March 1974. A commission under Judge Robert Cliche, a once-prominent Quebec New Democrat, and including a young lawyer named Brian Mulroney, was appointed to investigate violence and corruption in the construction unions. Legislation followed which put the unions under trusteeship and outlawed anyone with a criminal record from union office. On four other occasions back-to-work laws were passed.

In June 1971, after three years of intense discussion, the federal and provincial first ministers tentatively approved the Victoria Charter as a first step toward constitutional change. Bourassa returned to Quebec to face a strong nationalistic opposition to the charter, led by Claude Ryan of *Le Devoir*. Like Lesage on the Fulton-Favreau Formula, he reneged on his promised support—a course of action which exacerbated his reputation for weakness. Bourassa justified his stance by claiming that the charter did not guarantee provincial autonomy in social policy. More positively, the province reached an agreement with the federal government on family allowances in 1973 which permitted Quebec to operate a distinctive scheme in this field. Quebec also obtained significant federal concessions in sharing jurisdiction over immigration. On the other hand, Bourassa's most nationalistic minister, Jean-Paul L'Allier, fought for more provincial control over communications with little success.

The Gendron royal commission recommended in 1972 that French be made the official and working language of Quebec and, in 1974, Bourassa enacted legislation favouring the French language. Among the provisions of Bill 22, French became the official language of Quebec and in many spheres was given preferential status over English, although the latter could often be used as well; a knowledge of French became compulsory in some professions; immigrant children were tested on their knowledge of English and, if it was insufficient, were sent to French-language schools; government contracts were drawn up in French; and many internal corporate documents such as labour-management contracts had to be in that language. While the anglophone and immigrant communities were understandably upset, many francophones felt the law did not go far enough. The federal Liberal government was also concerned because it was trying to persuade the rest of the country to become more bilingual, not less.

Intense emotions were also aroused by the issue of whether pilots flying in Quebec could use French in speaking to air traffic controllers.[120] In June 1976, the federal government was faced with walkouts of both controllers and pilots, which created a chaotic situation at Quebec's airports. The francophones involved formed les Gens de l'Air, and the federal government set up a committee to study the question. Transport Minister Otto Lang endorsed its recommendation that English be used over Quebec for safety reasons, federal Environment Minister Jean Marchand resigned, and the Quebec National Assembly unanimously passed a resolution supporting les Gens de l'Air. When later tests showed that safety could be guaranteed, the Clark government restored bilingualism to Quebec skies. The whole affair greatly benefited the Parti Québécois, which had led the fight for the use of French, because the problem could be interpreted as discriminating against francophones and demonstrating their powerlessness in Ottawa—just as the party always claimed.

Other initiatives of the Bourassa government included the 1975 passage of Quebec's own charter of rights, the Charte des Droits et Libertés de la Personne. In the social field, its main contributions were the comprehensive and centralized health insurance and social services programs established by Social Affairs Minister Claude Castonguay, based on his own royal commission. Other legislative initiatives included legal aid, consumer and environmental protection, and compensation for the victims of crime. The government created a permanent voters' list, introduced innovative party election finance legislation, reformed legislative procedures and, as part of its job-creation strategy, established the Société de Développement Industriel du Québec, an agency to lend money to businesses when no one else would.

In party affairs during this period, public servants Claude Morin and Louis Bernard and writer Pierre Vallières joined Parti Québécois ranks. The PQ experienced many internal difficulties throughout the 1970-76 period, trying to function as a mass party, struggling with policy divisions, and geographically split between a small caucus in Quebec and its leader in Montreal. Lévesque persistently opposed proposals to restrict the status of the English language in the province. Of greater significance was the party's 1974 decision to dilute its approach to separation. Claude Morin was one of the leading advocates of "étapisme," or separation by steps. The party debated this issue throughout 1974 and eventually changed its strategy: following the election of a PQ government, a referendum would be held on the issue of separation prior to an actual declaration of sovereignty. In other words, a vote for a PQ government was no longer an automatic vote for separation. This gradual approach upset some of the more militant PQ activists, but was favoured by many voters who saw the PQ as heir to the Quiet Revolution in advocating continued modernization through the auspices of the state, greater public involvement in the economy, more radical language policy, and greater sympathy for organized labour.[121]

As in 1973, Bourassa called the 1976 election long before his mandate expired in the hope of pre-empting the PQ. But as the campaign unfolded, Liberal party prospects declined. The results can be explained by a combination of anti-Liberal sentiment and such incentives for voting PQ as the fact that the independence issue was not the main determinant of voter support.[122]

Although Quebec had experienced many worse governments than Bourassa's, the electorate had many complaints.[123] There had been much labour unrest, recent school, hospital, and other public service disruptions were fresh in the minds of voters on election day, and a Hydro strike occurred during the campaign. Bourassa's attempts to find a middle ground on labour disputes alienated both sides and, "by promising to regulate strikes in the public sector in the future, the Liberal party was skirting the real issue: its own past management of labour conflicts."[124] The premier's compromise on the language legislation issue also satisfied no one. Many non-francophones deserted the Liberals because Bill 22 was too repressive, but francophones bolted to the PQ because the legislation did not go far enough. A third cause of dissatisfaction was the frequent revelation of patronage and corruption. Most of the incidents were not major in themselves but, taken as a whole, they offered an unsavory picture. Bourassa also suffered on the economic front. The province's rate of inflation and unemployment did not say much for his vaunted economic expertise, and the recently completed Olympic Games had caused a huge debt. (The roof of the Olympic stadium continues to be a political issue 20 years later.[125]) The overall image of weak leadership created by these issues was probably the decisive factor in reducing the Liberal vote by 20 percent over a three-year period. Such an image was substantiated by the open contempt with which Bourassa was viewed by his fellow Liberals in Ottawa, and was not aided by the "vanity" issue, including allegations that Bourassa's hairdresser was never far from his side. The "fear machine was put into high gear" in the media as the Liberal party and its supporters portrayed the disastrous consequences of a PQ victory.[126]

It was now safe to vote PQ, however, because separatism could later be rejected in the referendum. Many other reasons existed for supporting Lévesque: the PQ boasted a strong, honest, popular leader ("un vrai chef") together with able colleagues, a set of progressive social and economic policies, a determination to strengthen the position of the French language in the province and, at least until the referendum, an intention of seeking maximum provincial autonomy within the existing federal structure. Even Claude Ryan at *Le Devoir* supported the PQ.[127]

Although the election of the PQ caused great unease in many quarters, both inside and outside Quebec, Lévesque immediately went out of his way to be reassuring.[128] Indeed, it was never entirely clear whether the premier himself really wanted independence, and he consistently acted as a counterweight to those in the party who did. As head of a mass party, however, he had to repeatedly persuade the majority of the membership to his point of view. For nearly four years Lévesque concentrated on providing "good government" rather than a separatist government, and he discovered that many of his objectives could be accomplished within the existing federal system.

The PQ cabinet was the best educated, federal or provincial, in Canadian history. About half of its members had taught at university and more than half had done graduate studies in France, England, or the United States (though none in English Canada).[129] Most had a public sector background—ex-civil servants, teachers, labour lawyers, or journalists—and, while ranging somewhat over the ideological and nationalist spectrums, they generally favoured a strong interventionist state. The structure of the early cabinet was also striking—a two-tier arrangement adapted from the post-1971 Ontario experience by chief adviser Louis Bernard. A priorities committee engaged in planning and co-ordinating functions, and five of the senior ministers were relieved of routine departmental responsibilities and charged with developing plans in broad policy areas. Among the most prominent ministers were: Camille Laurin (Cultural Development), Bernard Landry (Economic Development), Jacques Parizeau (Finance), and Claude Morin (Intergovernmental Affairs). For the first time in Quebec history, no anglophones were included in the cabinet, although this omission was later rectified. Long after its defeat, the PQ suffered considerable embarrassment when it was revealed that Claude Morin was also working for the Royal Canadian Mounted Police.

Undoubtedly the most significant piece of legislation passed by the PQ government was Bill 101, the Charter of the French Language. It was largely the work of Camille Laurin who, as a psychiatrist, saw the bill in psychotherapeutic terms. His aim was to end the economic inferiority of French-speaking Quebecers, promote the assimilation of immigrants with the francophone community, and create a "symbolic affirmation of Quebec as a French-speaking place."[130] He used Bourassa's Bill 22 as a starting point, but moved beyond it in several ways.[131] First, the bill established the fundamental right of every Quebecer to use French in the workplace. This applied to the public service, with an important extension to local public institutions, but also to the private sector. Every firm with more than 50 employees was required to prepare a francization program covering such things as French communications with employees (manuals, catalogues, contracts, firm names, product labels, advertising notices, and signs), and ensuring a satisfactory knowledge of the language among management. The bill was initially intended to promote francophones, but it was amended to refer to anyone who could speak French. In order to assimilate immigrant children, the only ones who could go to an English school were those with a parent who had attended an English school in Quebec. The symbolic aspects of the law included a provision that all signs be in French only, intended to give the province a French appearance (un visage français). It challenged section 133 of the British North America Act by restricting the use of English in the courts to individuals (not corporations), and by making French the official language of the legislature and the provincial law. Laurin toured the province, defending his proposals with great passion, Cartesian logic, and rigidity. One effect was that French became the working language of the province, as companies began to operate increasingly in French and opened more managerial positions to francophone candidates. However, many firms (most notably Sun Life Assurance in 1978) moved all or part of their operations out of the province, while other anglophones emigrated voluntarily. The constitutionality of the legislation was challenged, and the restrictions on the use of English in the courts and in provincial laws were overturned, requiring the government to pass English versions of its post-1977 French-only laws. Later, when the new national Charter of Rights guaranteed minority language education in all provinces, those clauses were thrown out as well, even though Quebec had not signed the Charter. Later still, the sign provisions were challenged in the Supreme Court. While much of the non-French population in Quebec adapted to the new state of affairs, many specific incidents of conflict arose; these centred on the issue of signs, professionals failing French tests, and children being denied access to English schools. The bill was strictly enforced by the Office de la langue française, and prompted angry reaction against bilingualism in the rest of the country. Interesting attempts have been made to apply a class analysis to the legislation; it appears that the middle-class "word merchants" (teachers, journalists, academics, public servants, labour and co-operative officials) would benefit most from the bill's enactment.[132]

The 1976-81 period witnessed an array of significant social and economic reforms which many saw as a continuation of the Quiet Revolution. These reforms generally reflected a social democratic perspective that occasionally extended beyond that of contemporary NDP regimes in other provinces. The PQ strengthened already progressive legislation on election finance with a prohibition on all campaign contributions except those from individuals.[133] Its other advanced social measures included youth protection act, family law reforms, consumer protection and class-action legislation, a day-care program, a move toward a guaranteed annual income in the form of work income supplements, and action on handicapped rights. In addition, the province provided free prescription drugs for those over 65 and free dental care for children. It is an amazing commentary on the rapid modernization of attitudes in Quebec that it became the first province to allow Dr. Henry Morgentaler to operate abortion clinics, and to ban discrimination against homosexuals in its bill of rights. The PQ also passed several pieces of labour legislation: an anti-scab law which prohibited the use of replacement workers and provided other protection to striking workers, occupational health and safety legislation, and labour code reforms which gave Quebec the highest minimum wage in the country.[134] The Quebec Anti-Inflation Board was abolished; and fines imposed on 7,000 strikers in the 1975-76 period were cancelled. In spite of all these moves, the PQ had great trouble in its negotiations with public sector employees. There were several strikes, legal and illegal, among hospital workers, teachers, and hydro workers, and on more than one occasion these strikers were legislated back to work. Nevertheless, during the PQ's first term, it treated its public servants very generously.

On the economic front, the PQ made two controversial left-wing moves. Lise Payette, Minister of Consumers, Cooperatives and Financial Institutions, brought in an automobile insurance plan which set up a public scheme for personal injuries but, after much pressure, she left the property damage portion in the hands of private insurance companies. Meanwhile, in late 1977 the government announced that it would nationalize the Asbestos Corporation Ltd. (and Bell Asbestos) by means of a Crown corporation, Société Nationale de l'Amiante. The American owners, General Dynamics Corp., fought the takeover, and details were still before the courts in the 1990s.[135] By then, the global decline in the mining industry, as well as increasing health problems linked to asbestos, prevented much of the anticipated benefit, such as increased processing within the province. The PQ also established new economic development agencies, convened frequent intraprovincial economic summit meetings, modernized the pulp and paper industry with federal assistance, and moved to protect agricultural land. Apart from the Asbestos Corporation takeover, the government made it clear that it planned to rely on the private sector as the main engine of economic development.

The PQ also brought in a redistribution act, and took considerable initiative in municipal reorganization which included new structures, changes in finances, and enhanced emphasis on planning and sewage treatment.[136] Balancing these innovations were rather conservative budgets which, among other things, allowed the province to maintain its credit rating on Wall Street.[137] The Finance minister sought to redistribute the tax burden to some extent to those earning over $30,000, introduced a number of creative touches, retained succession duties after other provinces had abolished them, and gradually increased the provincial deficit.

With regard to federal-provincial relations, harsh words were often exchanged and ministers occasionally left federal-provincial conferences abruptly, but several joint programs were developed. In 1978, for example, Quebec gained control of the entry of immigrants to its territory. Meanwhile, on the fundamental question of separation, further backtracking occurred. Instead of immediately negotiating sovereignty with Ottawa, Lévesque and Morin decided to strive for maximum decentralization until the referendum, then begin serious negotiation only if it carried. Further refinements followed, such as in 1978 when the government stated that sovereignty-association was a hyphenated word and that sovereignty would not be declared unless an economic association with the other provinces could be achieved. A later addition included a second referendum which would be held after negotiations were completed.

On the other side of the fence sat the federal government and the provincial Liberal party. The latter was in shreds after the 1976 election debacle. Bourassa immediately resigned as leader, sought exile in Belgium, and later taught at Harvard, while Gérard-D. Lévesque became interim leader. Since almost everyone connected with the Bourassa regime was somewhat discredited, pressure mounted on *Le Devoir* publisher Claude Ryan to assume the Liberal leadership. Ryan had a well-developed position for a special status for Quebec within Confederation; moreover, he had a reputation for integrity that the party sorely lacked. On the other hand, this tough, hard-working intellectual had a poor public image, that of a schoolmaster who gave long, ponderous lectures. Another possible disadvantage was that his prescribed solution to the Quebec question was quite different from that of Pierre Trudeau, the national Liberal leader. Opposed by the more attractive, conservative, and federalist Raymond Garneau, who had been Finance minister in the Bourassa cabinet, Ryan won at the April 1978 convention. Meanwhile, the federal government was developing its own referendum strategy. Trudeau appointed the Pépin-Robarts Task Force on Canadian Unity in July 1977. But the cabinet ignored its report when it recommended general decentralization, provincial discretion in language legislation, and a kind of distinct status for Quebec, all of which were at odds with the prime minister's approach. The Conservative Clark government, elected soon after, planned to take little part in the referendum campaign.

The 1980s

The 1980s, which began with the defeat of the Parti Québécois referendum, generally witnessed a different and weaker PQ for the rest of the decade. The Liberal party returned to power, but the economic ambience of the province had changed.

At the end of 1979 the PQ had finally issued its white paper on sovereignty-association, "The New Quebec-Canada Agreement," along with the specific question for the referendum.[138] The paper proposed a number of joint Canada-Quebec regulatory authorities in various fields on which Quebec would have parity representation, but other premiers dismissed this as absurd. Because the polls had indicated that the PQ could not win public approval for the principle of sovereignty-association as such, the question was diluted to ask for a mandate to negotiate such an arrangement. A month later Claude Ryan responded with his beige paper entitled "A New Canadian Federation," which was more moderate than many of his previous editorials. The next stage in the referendum battle came in March 1980 with a three-week televised National Assembly debate. This was followed by the public campaign which raged through April and up to May 20.

Although the entire operation was rigidly regulated, both camps naturally tried to maximize their advantages. The PQ brought in a popular budget and awarded a generous public service wage settlement during this period, for example, while the federal government did considerable advertising of its own. To a large extent Claude Ryan was eclipsed by federal Justice Minister Jean Chrétien and four carefully calculated and forceful interventions by Prime Minister Trudeau, re-elected in February 1980 after nine months of Clark Conservatism. Trudeau and several premiers who entered the campaign promised a renewed federalism if the referendum were defeated, but did not specify what form this would take. Two other incidents which may have influenced the result were the "Yvette" and Caisse affairs. Consumers Minister Lise Payette made disparaging remarks about the Liberals trying to attract the support of mere Quebec housewives ("Yvettes"). The Liberals used the hostile reaction to this statement to good advantage, quickly organizing large rallies of women who were proud to be Yvettes and who were also voting "non." Meanwhile, the respected economist Eric Kierans resigned from the board of the Caisse de Dépôt, claiming that the PQ government was exploiting it for political purposes. The result of the referendum was 59.6 percent non and 40.4 percent oui with a turnout rate of 87 percent. This was a great shock to the PQ, given the dilution of the final question; it tried to argue that at least 50 percent of the francophone population had supported its approach, even though this was probably not the case.

However dispiriting the referendum defeat may have been for the PQ, it was not a measure of the legitimacy of the government. Lévesque carried on and did not call an election until April 1981. In the meantime, much constitutional discussion took place, but, after a first ministers' conference failed in September 1980, Trudeau announced he would proceed unilaterally to change the Constitution by getting British approval without provincial consent. The PQ passed a motion in the Assembly opposing such a move.

With 11 straight by-election victories since 1976 and the defeat of the referendum, the Liberal party expected to win the 1981 election. It put forward a program emphasizing the private sector and a slight relaxation of Bill 101, while the PQ set aside the sovereignty issue and promised no referendum during its second term. The PQ still had a reputation as a good government and René Lévesque had much more popular appeal than Claude Ryan. Thus it was not surprising that the PQ was again victorious with 49 percent of the vote to 46 percent for the Liberals, giving them 80 and 42 seats respectively.

Federal-provincial, interprovincial, and judicial consideration of the Constitution continued throughout 1981 and, in October, Ryan supported the PQ government's resolution denouncing Ottawa's unilateral approach. Nine MNAs refused to go along, however, and the provincial Liberal party was badly split. In November, the famous federal-provincial first ministers' conference worked out a constitutional accord which Lévesque refused to sign, partly because the agreement had been reached while he was asleep.[139] He went home humiliated, accused the other participants of betrayal, and attempted to arouse public opinion against the deal. In response, the PQ convention in December opted for sovereignty without association and decided the next election should be fought on that basis. Lévesque had not intended to go so far, however, and threatened to resign unless a referendum among the party's 300,000 members supported his leadership and economic association concept, which it did.[140]

Quebec promptly opted out of all sections of the new national Charter of Rights and Freedoms where it was permitted to do so, although it could not escape the minority language education clause. It also decided to boycott all federal-provincial and interprovincial conferences unless its economic interests were at stake. When the province appealed to the courts to restore its right of veto of constitutional amendments, the Quebec Court of Appeal and the Supreme Court of Canada ruled that Quebec never possessed such a right. Many other federal-provincial disputes occurred in this "state of war," including the fiscal arrangements for 1982-87—which Lévesque called a "bloody rape" and which Parizeau said were designed to destabilize the Quebec government's finances.

The Lévesque government's second term in direct contrast to its first. Among other things, it was plagued with labour problems. In April 1982, at a provincial economic summit, the government revealed it needed $700 million quickly and, because the public sector had been well provided for by the PQ since 1976, it urged the public service unions to reopen their contracts and cancel July and December increases for that year. When the unions would not accept this arrangement, the government legislated a 20-percent pay cut in the first months of 1983 after the current contracts expired, supported by a no-strike clause. This prompted illegal strikes and huge demonstrations by public sector workers, and back-to-work legislation was passed in February. In April, a three-year contract signed with the province's teachers ended the immediate crisis, but the government's actions were sometimes compared to the federal invocation of the War Measures Act and the PQ alienated its largest supporter.

More generally, in the early 1980s Quebec suffered the poor economic situation shared by all provinces, and it did not embark on many innovative courses. Second-term priorities included housing, affirmative action for women and minorities, and the establishment of an external trade ministry to promote Quebec exports. In fields such as environmental protection, the labour code, and language legislation, the government became more conservative. In 1985, for example, it introduced legislation which broke the unity of the labour movement, creating a more decentralized bargaining environment which discouraged the creation of a common front. In other areas, Social Affairs Minister Pierre Marc Johnson drastically cut hospital funding. After holding hearings on language legislation, in 1983 the new minister responsible, Gérald Godin, eased some of the regulations for English-language hospitals and social service agencies by means of Bill 57, and allowed a five-year temporary permit for immigrants from other provinces to attend English-language schools. But the courts struck down any restrictions against Canadian citizens attending English-language schools in Quebec as well as compuslory French-language proficiency tests for professionals.

Poor economic conditions were responsible for the closing of oil refineries and the Iron Ore Company operations at Schefferville, among others. However, Bombardier Inc. received a $1-billion contract to build New York City subway cars and Hydro-Québec signed two long-term multi-million-dollar contracts with American power purchasers. The government unveiled an economic recovery program in November 1983, and devoted considerable effort to creating employment for young people, laid-off miners, and residential construction workers. The tripartite approach of seeking the agreement of labour, business, and government in various sectors ("la concertation") seemed to be reasonably successful in this period.

After the 1981 defeat, Claude Ryan found his Liberal leadership under increasing attack and resigned in August 1982. At the October 1983 Liberal leadership convention, a resurrected Robert Bourassa defeated Pierre Paradis and Daniel Johnson, having "out-worked, out-hustled, out-campaigned and out-toughed" all comers.[141] Bourassa had become a much more self-confident leader but, given that he was once called "the most hated man in Quebec," his was an amazing come-back. The Liberal leader was still preoccupied with hydroelectric power, and his main promise was to sell more power to the United States by means of a second phase of development at James Bay.

On the government side, René Lévesque was under great pressure in this period for having misled the Assembly in connection with a lawsuit involving union sabotage at James Bay. Several of his ministers and MNAs also fell into political or legal difficulty. During 1984-85, the PQ was largely consumed with the sovereignty question. A party convention voted to make sovereignty the issue of the next election, but later in the year Justice Minister Pierre Marc Johnson publicly diverged from this party line. Lévesque indicated that after

Quebecer Brian Mulroney was elected prime minister, there might be a new opportunity to make Canadian federalism work. Calling it a "beau risque," the two leaders sought to establish harmonious relations. The new Conservative federal government, anxious to consolidate its unprecedented support in Quebec, agreed to a $1.8-billion, 10-year regional development program, granted $15 million to save the ailing Petromont petroleum complex, and provided a $150-million interest-free loan to rescue Domtar Inc. operations. Quebec was also awarded the CF-18 fighter plane maintenance contract, a prison in the prime minister's constituency, and many other grants.

When Lévesque announced in November 1984 that he favoured shelving the sovereignty issue for the next campaign, six ministers immediately resigned, including Minister of Finance Jacques Parizeau, Social Affairs Minister Laurin, and Minister of Citizen Relations Denis Lazure. Debate raged within the party for the rest of the year as other ministers left the cabinet, and culminated at the party convention in January 1985 where the Lévesque position carried 65 percent to 35 percent. A public opinion poll conducted at the time indicated that only four percent of the electorate wanted independence and only another 15 percent favoured sovereignty-association. Dissenters walked out of the convention and more ministers resigned. This necessitated an almost complete overhaul of the cabinet, and the new ministers generally had less impressive credentials, were younger, more moderate and pragmatic, more conservative, and more private-sector-oriented than their predecessors. The party's parliamentary majority dwindled, especially after the June 1985 Liberal by-election victories. Lévesque, hospitalized earlier for exhaustion after making a number of bizarre public statements, announced his resignation shortly after the by-elections. This brought forth laudatory commentaries even from those opposed to separatism. He was particularly praised for his role in nationalizing Hydro-Québec and reforming political fund-raising in the province, as well as for giving Quebecers a greater sense of self-confidence. The almost simultaneous resignation of Alberta Premier Lougheed and the previous departures of Pierre Trudeau and Ontario Premier Bill Davis led many to call it the end of an era.

The PQ then embarked on its unique process of selecting a new leader—by a vote of all party members rather than a convention. Justice and Intergovernmental Affairs Minister Pierre Marc Johnson, son of the late Union Nationale premier and brother of the recent candidate for the Liberal party leadership, and was the leading contender from the start. With only one-half of eligible PQ members turning out to vote, Johnson won nearly 60 percent of their support on the first ballot, thereby completing the transformation of the party from its left-wing separatist origins to a somewhat conservative position that virtually abandoned separatism. With a majority of one in the National Assembly and only six months to call the next election, Johnson formed a cabinet and set the crucial election date for December 2.

Although still trailing the Liberals in the polls, the PQ narrowed the gap with its leadership campaign; Johnson's only hope was to maintain this momentum, and he used the strategy of comparing himself personally with Robert Bourassa. The Parti Québécois campaign focused all attention on its leader, as PQ candidates became "Johnson" candidates, using the slogan "Avec Johnson" ("With Johnson"). Despite their generally conservative orientation and emphasis on business issues, both parties made many promises that would entail large expenditures. The role of the federal government became controversial, as Prime Minister Mulroney seemed at first to favour the PQ with the mid-campaign announcement of a $300-million Hyundai car plant to be built in Bromont with $110-million in federal aid, and his decision to allow Quebec to participate in a summit of French-speaking nations (La Francophonie). Criticized by the Liberals, Mulroney withheld other offerings the PQ was expecting. The similarity of the PQ and Liberal parties' positions on almost all issues was such that they were portrayed as Tweedledee and Tweedledum in a cartoon in the *Montreal Gazette*. The Liberals emerged with a massive majority of 99 seats (56 percent of the vote), compared with the PQ's 23 seats (39 percent). However, Bourassa lost his own seat, an indication that Johnson was still the preferred leader and, without him, the PQ would likely have been annihilated.

In the most remarkable political come-back in Canadian history, Robert Bourassa rose from the ashes of his 1976 defeat to assume the premiership for the second time in December 1985.[142] His 28-member cabinet contained four women and four non-francophones, and saw Gérard Lévesque as Finance minister and Claude Ryan in Education and Science. The premier's first priority was the second phase of the James Bay hydroelectric development. In the spring of 1988, Bourassa announced approval of a $7.5-billion plan to build three new dams on La Grande Rivière, shortly after having concluded a $17-billion sale of electricity to New York state. However, Hydro-Québec's reputation suffered under an enormous debt load, repeated blackouts, the loss of an anticipated contract with Maine, and its failure to consult with the Cree inhabitants of the territory in which James Bay II was to be located.

Aluminum production based on abundant hydroelectricity also increased with a new Alcan Aluminum smelter to replace the ancient Arvida plant, a new $1-billion Alouette smelter at Sept-Iles, expansion of the Bécancour and Baie Comeau smelters, and Alumax Inc.'s decision to locate in Quebec rather than Manitoba. Norsk Hydro Canada Inc. planned to add a magnesium plant at Bécancour, Montupet of France began construction of a plant for the casting of aluminum auto engine parts, a Hyundai Auto Canada Inc. assembly plant opened in 1989, and that company announced plans for a body parts plant nearby.

Another major aspect of Bourassa's early economic policy was the privatization of many provincial Crown agencies, the first of which were the Raffinerie de sucre du Québec, Québécair, and most of the assets of SOQUEM, the provincial mining company. He also deregulated and tightened up the regular operations of government. The trend toward privatization reflected the strong francophone entrepreneurial spirit which emerged in the latter half of the decade. Even the general public was involved, primarily through the Quebec Stock Savings Plan (which provided write-offs for investors in Quebec companies), while the assets of the caisse populaire movement and the Caisse de Dépôt reached record levels. Large enterprises no longer had to be publicly owned in order to be Québécois-controlled and many even became multinationals. However, the province suffered from the closing of several oil refineries in eastern Montreal, asbestos fell into disrepute, resulting in the layoff of miners, and the unemployment rate was persistently high.

Although the re-election of Bourassa was thought to symbolize the importance of business in the province and the diminution of linguistic and federal-provincial issues, the latter were never far from the surface. Relations with Ottawa and other provinces remained a prominent aspect of Quebec politics, partly due to the obsession of all three federal parties with currying the favour of the Quebec electorate (and government), given the province's volatility in federal party preferences. Thus Bourassa's five conditions for joining the new Canadian constitutional regime were supported by all three federal parties, and the prime minister persuaded the other nine premiers to concur in the 1987 Meech Lake Accord. The five conditions provided for in the document were the recognition of Quebec as a distinct society within Canada, a requirement of unanimous provincial consent for an expanded range of constitutional amendments (thus meeting Quebec's demand for a veto), granting the provinces the power to nominate candidates for the Senate and the Supreme Court of Canada, allowing them greater freedom to opt out of national programs set up within provincial jurisdiction, and giving Quebec (and any other province which so desired) a greater role in immigration. Eight provinces and the federal parliament ratified the agreement, but new governments in Manitoba and New Brunswick refused to do so, and Newfoundland's Clyde Wells rescinded his province's ratification.

The other major federal-provincial issue of the late 1980s was the Canada-U.S. Free Trade Agreement. Many observers were surprised by Premier Bourassa's strong support of free trade after his initial opposition. To some extent this support appeared to be related to Brian Mulroney's generous response to Quebec's constitutional demands and his equally generous financial treatment of his native province. But the premier also seemed to feel that free trade would encourage even greater hydro-electric sales to the U.S., and he was confident that Quebec's new breed of aggressive, outward-looking, francophone entrepreneurs would take advantage of increased access to the U.S. market. These prospects outweighed the dislocations that the deal could cause in such traditional industries as textiles, furniture, and shoes. Even new PQ leader Jacques Parizeau favoured free trade as a way of reducing Quebec's economic dependence on the rest of Canada.

The federal Tory government directed huge sums of money to Quebec before and after the 1988 federal election, even when, as in the case of the

CF-18 maintenance contract, reason dictated funds should be allocated elsewhere. Federal funding was also directed towards cleaning the St. Lawrence River, and the Canadian Space Agency moved to Montreal.

Bourassa was also faced with the re-emergence of linguistic concerns, the main question being the status of Bill 101, especially with regard to its provision that all store signs must be in French. Bourassa campaigned in 1985 on a platform that the French language had been secured in the province, and that this provision could therefore be relaxed. But, while anglophones and other ethnic groups demanded such reform, hard-core nationalists protested vehemently against change. Rather than keep his promise, Bourassa guaranteed anglophones the right to receive social and health services in English via Bill 142, and then opted to wait for the Supreme Court of Canada's decision on the constitutionality of the sign clause. When the Court ruled in December 1988 that the provision was contrary to the freedom of expression clause in Quebec's Charter of Rights, Bourassa was forced to act. He devised the "outside-inside" compromise in Bill 178: French-only commercial signs would be required externally, but internal bilingual signs were acceptable if French was predominant. Details were spelled out later in reams of regulations. To protect this new legislation from constitutional challenge, Bourassa invoked the "notwithstanding" clause of both the Quebec and Canadian charters. (By invoking the notwithstanding clause, a law can be made to exist even if it violates rights guaranteed in the charter.)

Reaction was swift and heated with protests organized on both sides, and the general social peace of the province was rent asunder. Within Quebec, the Montreal office of Alliance Quebec, the leading anglophone pressure group, was set on fire, non-French groups were appalled at the use of the notwithstanding clause, and Bourassa's three main anglophone ministers resigned. Outside Quebec, there was a profound rejection of Bourassa's approach, especially as most provinces had been expanding French-language services, and many who had been ambivalent about the Meech Lake Accord began to oppose it.

The intolerant stance of many francophones with respect to the signs issue can be traced to their fear for the maintenance of the province's French character, given that Quebec's birthrate was now the lowest in the country. Bourassa attempted to address this problem in the 1988 provincial budget by offering grants of $500 for each of a couple's first two children and $3,000 for each additional child. In subsequent budgets these amounts were raised to $1,000 for the second child and eventually $8,000 for three or more children. At first, such financial incentives seemed to work, but by the mid-1990s the birthrate was falling again. The immigration clause in the Meech Lake Accord was another vehicle for alleviating the low rate of francophone reproduction.

An additional linguistic issue was that of English instruction. The Supreme Court of Canada upheld Quebec's law banning the teaching of English to non-anglophones before Grade 4. Restrictions on the showing of English-language motion pictures in the province were also controversial.

Other social issues to emerge during Bourassa's leadership included a new divorce act providing for the equal distribution of assets; an amended law which eased restrictions on Sunday shopping; a plan for sweeping reform of the health and social service systems; and the progress of the province's Inuit toward self-government with the election of an assembly to draft a constitution.

After 1985, the labour movement seemed to lose much of its militancy, and Bourassa responded with harsh anti-union legislation, such as 1989's Bill 160, which removed seniority as a factor in the employment of health sector employees. Other opposition to the Bourassa government was also exceedingly weak. The official Opposition, the Parti Québécois, was plagued with internal divisions over the sovereignty issue, divisions which persuaded Pierre Marc Johnson to resign as leader shortly after René Lévesque's death in 1987. Former Finance Minister Jacques Parizeau, who made no secret of his commitment to Quebec independence, became leader by acclamation. With the withdrawal or resignation of less independence-minded party members and officials, and the endorsement of the Parizeau approach, party activists seemed more united than they had in many years.

The decade ended with an election in September 1989. Both major parties emphasized environmental protection and demographic decline. The Liberals also focused on their successful economic management, and the PQ proposed a series of mini-referenda designed to wrest various powers from Ottawa pending separation. The Liberals were embarrassed by a whiff of a land-speculation scandal just prior to the campaign, as well as a ridiculous odyssey of toxic PCBs which emerged after a fire at a warehouse in St-Basile-le-Grand. When a deal with Alberta for the destruction of the PCBs fell through, they were transported back and forth across the Atlantic, until the residents of Baie Comeau tried unsuccessfully to prevent their storage near the Manic 2 dam. Public-sector labour problems, especially with regard to the province's nurses, also emerged. Nevertheless, the campaign was a relatively quiet one and, despite these problems, Bourassa was re-elected with 92 seats to the PQ's 29. The Liberals gained 50 percent of the vote while the PQ gained 40 percent, the latter surprising many observers given Parizeau's relatively radical stance on independence. Because of Bourassa's the sign law, the new Equality Party gained much of the urban anglophone vote and won four seats in the Assembly.

The 1990s

The 1990s was a decade of anticipation in the province. Health problems forced Robert Bourassa to resign as premier at the beginning of 1994, and that September the electorate opted for the Parti Québécois in the provincial election. Because Jacques Parizeau had promised a definitive referendum on sovereignty within a year of that election, frenetic referendum activity took place in Quebec, while the rest of the country held its breath.

At the beginning of the decade Quebec was dominated by two main issues: the Meech Lake Accord and the armed standoff at Oka. As the June 1990 deadline for unanimous provincial approval of the Meech Lake constitutional amendment approached, Prime Minister Mulroney convened another week-long first ministers' conference. In its wake, New Brunswick approved the accord, but the deal died when the deadline passed before Newfoundland or Manitoba voted. The demise of Meech Lake led to demands for separation by many Quebec business and labour leaders, to Lucien Bouchard's creation of the federal Bloc Québécois party, and to a separatist victory in a Quebec federal by-election. Bourassa announced that Quebec would henceforth deal with Ottawa only on a bilateral basis. The province later made such an agreement on immigration.

Premier Bourassa appointed a 35-member commission to hold public hearings and recommend a redefined relationship between Quebec and the rest of Canada in the post-Meech Lake era. It was headed by two businessmen, Jean Campeau and Michel Bélanger, and included 18 MNAs representing all parties, three federal MPs, and a variety of municipal, business, labour, and co-operative representatives. In March 1991 the highly nationalistic majority on the commission recommended a referendum on sovereignty in Quebec in the spring or fall of 1992 if Canada had not offered an acceptable deal by then.

At the same time, the Liberal party appointed its own sovereignty committee headed by Jean Allaire. Influenced by a feeling of betrayal with regard to the accord, it recommended a highly decentralized structure, somewhat akin to René Lévesque's sovereignty-association, in which 22 federal powers would be turned over to Quebec. The January 1991 Allaire report became official Liberal policy but, when this angered Claude Ryan, Bourassa made a conciliatory address to the party convention which adopted it. Bourassa passed the bill providing for a referendum as advocated by the Bélanger-Campeau commission, and boycotted the early rounds of constitutional talks in 1991-92. As pressure mounted to return to the table, however, the premier began to sound more like a federalist. In the summer of 1992 he went to Charlottetown to hammer out a deal which gave Quebec everything in Meech plus more explicit new powers. This fell far short of Allaire's recommendations, but Bourassa transformed the October 26, 1992, referendum from one on sovereignty to one on the Charlottetown Accord. Allaire and Liberal youth leader Mario Dumont resigned from the party and later established their own, the Parti Action Démocratique. In the end, 56.7 percent of Quebecers voted against the Charlottetown solution. The Quebec results were not helped when the media released taped telephone conversations of Bourassa's constitutional advisers criticizing his performance at Charlottetown.

The other crisis of 1990 was the armed standoff at Oka between Mohawks and Quebec authorities stemming from a dispute over land claimed by the Natives but scheduled to become an extension to a golf course. One police officer was killed and both sides suffered injuries in repeated scuffles during the 78-day conflict, complicated by the absence of clear-cut leadership on either side.

The Ottawa and Quebec governments tried to co-ordinate their efforts and used the army to supplement the Sûreté du Québec, whom the Mohawks despised. Meanwhile, sympathetic members of the Akwesasne reserve closed the Mercier bridge in Montreal for nine weeks. In the end, the ugly confrontation placed aboriginal concerns firmly and urgently on the national political agenda. It also raised the question of how aboriginal claims might complicate Quebec's bid for separation. By mid-1992, 39 Mohawks were acquitted of charges laid against them and only two received jail sentences, but by 1995 the land dispute had not been resolved. Another leading issue related to Native affairs in the early 1990s was that of the proposed Great Whale hydroelectric project (see Inset 6.1).

Like other provinces in the early 1990s, Quebec made health care reforms a government priority. Among the many controversial aspects of the policy debated in early 1991 was a $5 user fee for people making non-emergency visits to hospital emergency wards. The legislation also gave regional health boards greater authority over the medical profession, and required young doctors to work in under-serviced areas. Angry doctors protested against the reforms with several walkouts but, although some compromises were made, further cutbacks followed.

Language legislation was also high on the Quebec agenda. Because Bill 178 expired in 1993, five years after it was passed, and because a United Nations Human Rights Committee ruled the law infringed freedom of expression, talk of relaxing some provisions began in government circles in 1992. Bill 86, passed in mid-1993, allowed a larger number of children to go to English schools but stopped short of letting immigrant children do so. By this time, the English school system had lost 60 percent of its enrolment and closed 175 schools. Perhaps most significantly, Bill 86 allowed bilingual outdoor signs as long as French was predominant. It also abolished the "language police," the Commission de Protection de la Langue Française.

The deficit did not receive the level of attention it did in other provinces, but it was never far from the Bourassa government's agenda. Public sector workers saw successive wage freezes over the 1991-95 period, and hundreds of jobs were eliminated. All departments suffered from repeated budget cuts, and municipalities were particularly hard hit. The government improved enforcement of child support payments, gave child-care workers a salary boost, but cut back on welfare recipients. It hired 150 new welfare inspectors, whom social assistance recipients found extremely invasive, and penalized able-bodied recipients if they would not take part in make-work projects.

Despite its reductions, the government ran up a series of large deficits as it sporadically announced special spending programs. On the revenue side, to harmonize with the federal Goods and Services Tax, the government extended the provincial sales tax to services at four percent in 1992 (half the rate of the tax on goods). In 1994 it evened out the PST on goods and services at 6.5 percent each. In 1993 the government approved two casinos, one in Montreal and the other in

Charlevoix, but the Kahnawake Mohawks turned down an offer to operate a giant casino of their own. Some of this financial activity can be gleaned from the figures in Table 6.12.

TABLE 6.12   **Government of Quebec Finances, 1990/91–1994/95 (millions)**

	1990/91	1991/92	1992/93	1993/94	1994/95
Total revenues	$36,826	$38,134	$39,111	$40,016	$41,539
Debt charges	5,278	5,532	5,598	6,197	6,457
Total expenditures	40,614	43,365	44,583	45,442	46,548
Deficit	3,788	5,231	5,472	5,426	5,009

Source: Reproduced by authority of the Minister of Industry, 1995, Statistics Canada, *Public Sector Finance, 1994–95*, Financial Management System, cat. no. 68-212 (March 1995). Adapted by author.

With regard to the economy, Quebec had its ups and downs in the first half of the decade. The government adopted a strategy called "Quebec Inc.," which emphasized the development of five industries: aerospace, pharmaceuticals, information technology, electric power generation, and metals and minerals processing. Some companies, including Bombardier, prospered with new markets stretching from Belgium to Turkey, and Desjardins took over the Laurentian Group, becoming the sixth-largest financial conglomerate in the country. Aluminum production expanded with the opening of the heavily subsidized Alouette smelter in Sept Iles. In 1992, the government allowed stores to open on Sunday afternoons as a further boost to the economy. On the other hand, Hyundai closed its car plant in 1993, Lavalin had to be bailed out by the government and then by the SNC Group, and the Norsk magnesium smelter was troubled by duties the U.S. imposed in response to its subsidized hydro rates. The government froze and then reduced the level of immigration, and enacted new pollution standards for the pulp and paper industry.

To regulate its construction industry, Quebec had adopted a policy requiring all construction workers to live in the province. This led to clashes with neighbouring Ontario and New Brunswick, which favoured the free movement of workers across provincial borders. The dispute heated up in 1993 but was resolved by Quebec's decision to deregulate the construction industry. That policy, however, precipitated wildcat strikes and a demonstration by 20,000 outraged construction workers outside the Quebec legislature.

After impressing the public with courage and grace in his fight against melanoma, Robert Bourassa announced his retirement in September 1993. The Liberals unanimously chose Daniel Johnson Jr. as his successor in December.

The son and brother of former premiers, he formed a new government in January 1994. Many government members took advantage of the change in leadership to leave political life. Johnson merged and dismantled departments, reduced the size of the cabinet, signed a major infrastructure deal with Ottawa, reduced taxes and increased funding for job creation in the pre-election budget. He sold Sidbec-Dosco to an Indonesian firm, privatized the Mont-Ste-Anne ski centre, and put the province's liquor stores up for sale. A less equivocal federalist than Bourassa, Johnson took the position that true independence came through jobs, jobs threatened by talk of separation.

One of the most serious problems facing the new regime was that of cigarette smuggling, much of it involving Native reserves. As an alternative to widespread police surveillance of reserves, the provincial and federal governments agreed to lower cigarette taxes to eliminate the profit in smuggling. As Ottawa and other provinces had been deliberately increasing cigarette taxes to curb smoking, this solution did not impress many observers. Neighbouring provinces were extremely annoyed to have to follow suit.

Meanwhile, Jacques Parizeau's stern leadership revived the strength of the PQ, the Equality Party disintegrated, and Mario Dumont took over the Parti Action Démocratique when Jean Allaire developed health problems. Johnson set the election date for September 12, 1994. His campaign centred on the claim that a PQ government, especially if it separated from Canada, would have a serious negative impact on the Quebec economy. Parizeau, on the other hand, pointed out the many faults of the Liberal government, and promised a referendum on sovereignty within a year of the election. The two leaders, both holding doctorates from British universities, squared off in a televised debate. They were generally considered to have come out even. Most polls indicated the Liberals did not have a chance to win the election, and people were surprised when in terms of popular vote the results were nearly a tie, 44.7 percent to 44.3 percent.

Parizeau formed a cabinet with such prominent politicians as Jean Campeau as finance minister, Bernard Landry as vice-premier, and Richard Le Hir as minister in charge of post-referendum planning. Several other ministers had served during the party's earlier term of office. The PQ immediately blamed the Liberals for a $5.7-billion deficit, far beyond pre-election projections, and immediately began to implement a carefully prepared strategy.[143] On December 6, 1994, Parizeau tabled draft legislation declaring Quebec a sovereign country. It established 15 regional committees which would hold public hearings and offer suggestions to fill in gaps in the bill; a central committee would assess these contributions in March, with discussion in the National Assembly in April.

Jacques Parizeau truly believed in an independent Quebec, but even in the first draft of his bill he talked of "sovereignty" rather than "separation" and anticipated the retention of several links with Canada: economic association, joint citizenship, and the use of the Canadian dollar. Opposition leader Daniel Johnson and federal politicians derided and boycotted the public hearings process, calling it a propaganda operation. Repeated polling revealed that even with such links, the original option was not likely to achieve over 50 percent of the vote. Therefore, in order to succeed with the electorate as well as to get Lucien Bouchard and the Bloc Québécois and Parti Action Démocratique onside, Parizeau was forced to make a wrenching *virage* (sharp turn) in his long-held views. He agreed that the sovereignty question would have to incorporate significant ties with Canada, perhaps even a political association. Once he made the change, the three groups managed to work closely together and devised an effective propaganda blitz. Meanwhile, the provincial Liberals recruited Michel Bélanger to head their NO committee and the federal Liberals designated Lucienne Robillard as the minister in charge of fighting separatism.

The 1995 PQ budget projected a deficit of $4 billion in spite of an overall spending freeze, some corporate tax increases, a hike in cigarette taxes, and a further harmonization of the provincial sales tax and federal GST. One of the most controversial implications was the closure of seven hospitals in Montreal and reduction in services at five others, causing one major labour union to withdraw its support for sovereignty. In other developments in its first year in office, the Quebec Nordiques hockey team moved to Denver, and several crown corporation heads left their posts, including Richard Drouin, Jean-Claude Delorme, and Guy Savard. After Parizeau indefinitely postponed the Great Whale power project, the Northern Cree began negotiating with the government again on other matters.

CONCLUSION

Over the past 30 years Quebec has caught up with other provinces in most aspects of its legislative and administrative framework. At the same time, the primacy of the French language has been irrevocably established in the province, and an indigenous francophone economic elite has emerged. Many observers expected these developments would lead to a less idiosyncratic pattern of Quebec politics than in the recent past. Because it was not part of the 1982 constitutional accord, the Quebec government continued to press for entry via the Meech Lake and Charlottetown accords and for further protection for the French language in the province. With the demise of the accords, constitutional, cultural, and linguistic issues remained on the Quebec political agenda. Despite the province's advances, its economy was not very strong, and in 1994 economic problems rather than constitutional issues propelled the PQ back into power. But even if they had voted on economic grounds, Quebec voters had no choice but to address the constitutional question in the 1995 referendum. Whatever the result, the issue would not likely be resolved for many years to come.

TABLE 6.13   Quebec Provincial Election Results Since 1923

Year	Liberals		Conservatives/ Union Nationale		Other	
	Seats	Popular Vote	Seats	Popular Vote	Seats	Popular Vote
1923	64	55%	20	40%	1	5%
1927	75	63%	9	34%	1	3%
1931	79	56%	11	44%	—	—
1935	48	51%	17	19%	25	29%*
1936	14	42%	76	58%	—	—
1939	69	54%	15	40%	2	6%
1944	37	39%	48	39%	6	23%**
1948	8	36%	82	52%	2	12%***
1952	23	46%	68	51%	1	3%
1956	20	45%	72	52%	1	3%
1960	51	52%	43	47%	1	1%
1962	63	57%	31	42%	1	1%
1966	50	47%	56	41%	2	12%****

Year	Liberal		Parti Québécois		Union Nationale		Créditiste		Other	
	Seats	Popular Vote	Seats	Popular Vote	Seats	Popular Vote	Seats	Popular Vote	Seats	Popular Vote
1970	72	45%	7	23%	17	20%	12	11%	—	—
1973	102	55%	6	30%	—	5%	2	10%	—	—
1976	26	34%	71	41%	11	18%	1	5%	1	2%
1981	42	46%	80	49%	—	4%	—	—	—	—
1985	99	56%	23	39%	—	—	—	—	—	5%
1989	92	50%	29	40%	—	—	—	—	4	10%+
1994	47	44.4%	77	44.8%	—	—	—	—	1	11%++

*	Action Libérale Nationale
**	Bloc Populaire 4 (14%); CCF 1 (3%); Nationalist (1%)
***	Independent 2 (2%); Union des Electeurs — (93%)
****	Independent 2 (4%); RN — (5%); RIN — (3%)
+	Equality Party 4 (4%)
++	Action Démocratique 1 (6.5%)

TABLE 6.14   Premiers of Quebec Since 1867

Premier	Party	Year Elected
Pierre Chauveau	Conservative	1867
Gédéon Ouimet	Conservative	1873
Charles Boucher de Boucherville	Conservative	1874
Henri-G. Joly	Liberal	1878
J.-Adolphe Chapleau	Conservative	1879
Alfred Mousseau	Conservative	1882
John Jones Ross	Conservative	1884
L.-Olivier Taillon	Conservative	1887
Honoré Mercier	Liberal	1887
Charles Boucher de Boucherville	Conservative	1891
L.-Olivier Taillon	Conservative	1892
Edmund Flynn	Conservative	1896
F.-Gabriel Marchand	Liberal	1897
S.-Napoléon Parent	Liberal	1900
Lomer Gouin	Liberal	1905
L.-A. Taschereau	Liberal	1920
Adelard Godbout	Liberal	1936
Maurice Duplessis	Union Nationale	1936
Adelard Godbout	Liberal	1939
Maurice Duplessis	Union Nationale	1944
Paul Sauvé	Union Nationale	1959
Antonio Barrette	Union Nationale	1960
Jean Lesage	Liberal	1960
Daniel Johnson	Union Nationale	1966
Jean-Jacques Bertrand	Union Nationale	1968
Robert Bourassa	Liberal	1970
René Lévesque	Parti Québécois	1976
Pierre Marc Johnson	Parti Québécois	1985
Robert Bourassa	Liberal	1985
Daniel Johnson Jr.	Liberal	1994
Jacques Parizeau	Parti Québécois	1994

ENDNOTES

1. Yves Bélanger estimates 60 percent in "Economic Development: From Family Enterprise to Big Business," in Alain-G. Gagnon, ed., *Québec: State and Society* (Scarborough: Nelson Canada, 2nd ed., 1993), p. 391. See also Guy Lachapelle et al., *The Quebec Democracy: Structures, Processes and Policies* (Toronto: McGraw-Hill Ryerson, 1993), ch. 13; and Claude Jean Galipeau, "Le Contre-Courant Québécois," in Keith Brownsey and Michael Howlett, eds., *The Provincial State* (Mississauga: Copp Clark Pitman, 1992).

2. On the English group in Quebec, see S.M. Arnopoulos and Dominique Clift, *The English Fact in Quebec* (Montreal: McGill-Queen's University Press, 1980).

3. Kenneth McRoberts and Dale Posgate, *Quebec: Social Change and Political Crisis* (Toronto: McClelland and Stewart, rev. ed., 1980), p. 15. See also McRoberts' third edition, 1988.

4. Eric Gourdeau, "Québec and the Aboriginal Question," in Gagnon, ed., *Quebec: State and Society.*

5. A.G. Gagnon and Joseph Garcea, "Quebec and the Pursuit of Special Status," in R.D. Olling and M.W. Westmacott, eds., *Perspectives on Canadian Federalism* (Scarborough: Prentice Hall Canada, 1988).

6. Daniel Latouche, "Quebec," in David Bellamy et al., eds., *The Provincial Political Systems* (Toronto: Methuen, 1976); Ralph Heintzman, "The Political Culture of Quebec, 1840-1960," in *Canadian Journal of Political Science* (March 1983); Denis Monière, *Ideologies in Quebec: The Historical Development* (Toronto: University of Toronto Press, 1981); McRoberts and Posgate, *Quebec: Social Change and Political Crisis;* and Léon Dion, "Origin and Character of the Nationalism of Growth," in *Canadian Forum* (January 1964).

7. Herbert F. Quinn, *The Union Nationale* (Toronto: University of Toronto Press, 1963), p. 11.

8. Pierre Elliot Trudeau, "Some Obstacles to Democracy in Quebec," in Trudeau, *Federalism and the French-Canadians* (Toronto: Macmillan, 1968); Quinn, *The Union Nationale*, p. 17.

9. Dale Thomson, *Jean Lesage and the Quiet Revolution* (Toronto: MacMillan, 1984).

10. To some unsympathetic observers, this vital distinction is lost. It is discussed in several sources including David Cameron, "Dualism and the Concept of National Unity," in John Redekop, ed., *Approaches to Canadian Politics* (Scarborough: Prentice Hall Canada, 2nd ed., 1983). One interesting approach is to ask who are the francophone anti-separatists. Daniel Latouche contrasts their disparagement of individual French-Canadians as weak, unstable, and undemocratic, with their intention to take control of the federal government through the strength of their intellect. "Anti-séparatisme et Méssianisme au Québec Depuis 1960," in *Canadian Journal of Political Science* (December 1970).

11. Louis Balthazar, "The Faces of Québec Nationalism," in Alain-G. Gagnon, ed., *Québec: State and Society*, p. 11.

12. David Elkins, "The Sense of Place," in Elkins and Richard Simeon, eds., *Small Worlds* (Toronto: Methuen, 1980).

13. Jeffrey Simpson, *Spoils of Power* (Toronto: Collins, 1988); Hubert Guindon, "The Social Evolution of Quebec Reconsidered," in *Canadian Journal of Economics and Political Science* (November 1960), and "Social Unrest, Social Class and Quebec's Bureaucratic Revolution," in *Queen's Quarterly* (Summer 1964).

14. Simeon and Elkins, "Provincial Political Cultures in Canada," in Elkins and Simeon, eds., *Small Worlds*.

15. Réjean Landry, "Party Competition in Quebec," Marcel Rioux, "The Development of Ideologies in Quebec," and Raymond Hudon, "Ambiguities and Contradictions in Being a Distinct Society," in H.G. Thorburn, ed. *Party Politics in Canada* (Scarborough: Prentice Hall Canada, 6th ed., 1991).

16. On the rise of the Créditistes, see Maurice Pinard, *The Rise of a Third Party* (Montreal: McGill-Queen's University Press, 1975); and Michael B. Stein, *The Dynamics of Right-Wing Protest: A Political Analysis of Social Credit in Quebec* (Toronto: University of Toronto Press, 1973).

17. Reginald Whitaker, *The Government Party* (Toronto: University of Toronto Press, 1977); and Joseph Wearing, *The L-Shaped Party* (Toronto: McGraw-Hill Ryerson, 1981).

18. Don Murray and Vera Murray, "The Parti Québécois: From Opposition to Power," in Hugh Thorburn, ed., *Party Politics in Canada*, (Scarborough: Prentice Hall Canada, 4th. ed., 1979), pp. 248-51.

19. Daniel Latouche, "Universal Democracy and Effective Leadership: Lessons from the Parti Québécois Experience," in Kenneth Carty, ed., *Leaders and Parties in Canadian Politics: Experiences of the Provinces* (Toronto: Harcourt Brace Jovanovich, 1992).

20. Simpson, *Spoils of Power*, p. 197.

21. Duff Spafford found that highway employment increased by over 20,000 employees in the month of the 1952 election, but then declined again since all work had stopped the day afterwards. "Highway Employment and Provincial Elections," in *Canadian Journal of Political Science* (March 1981), p. 142.

22. Heintzman, "The Political Culture of Quebec," p. 45.

23. Rand Dyck, "Relations Between Federal and Provincial Parties," in A.G. Gagnon and A.B. Tanguay, *Canadian Parties in Transition* (Scarborough: Nelson Canada, 1989).

24. Whitaker, *The Government Party*, p. 297.

25. Ibid., p. 288.

26. David Rayside, "Federalism and the Party System: Provincial and Federal Liberals in the Province of Quebec," in *Canadian Journal of Political Science* (September 1978), p. 500.

27. Daniel Latouche, "From Premier to Prime Minister: An Essay on Leadership State and Society in Quebec," in Leslie Pal and David Taras, eds., *Prime Ministers and Premiers* (Scarborough: Prentice Hall Canada, 1988).

28. Mason Wade, *The French-Canadians 1760-1967* (Toronto: Macmillan, 1968), p. 328.

29. Murray and Murray, "The Parti Québécois: from Opposition to Power," p. 244.

30. Graham Fraser, *PQ: René Lévesque and the Parti Québécois in Power* (Toronto: Macmillan, 1984), p. 240.

31. Vincent Lemieux, "Quebec—Heaven is Blue and Hell is Red," in Martin Robin, ed., *Canadian Provincial Politics* (Scarborough: Prentice Hall Canada, 2nd ed., 1978), p. 251.

32. Maurice Pinard and Richard Hamilton, "The Parti Québécois Comes to Power: An Analysis of the 1976 Quebec Election," *Canadian Journal of Political Science* (December 1978), p. 739.

33. Michael Ornstein and Michael Stevenson, "Elite and Public Opinion Before the Quebec Referendum: A Commentary on the State in Canada," in *Canadian Journal of Political Science* (December 1981), p. 774. On different ideologies since 1960 see the articles in the Spring 1983 issue of *Journal of Canadian Studies.*

34. Dale Poel's study of provincial innovations does not analyze any of Lesage's legislation—only earlier historic sites and sales tax legislation—but some of it, such as the election expenses law was clearly more advanced than elsewhere. "The Diffusion of Legislation among the Canadian Provinces: A Statistical Analysis," in *Canadian Journal of Political Science* (December 1976).

35. Marsha Chandler admits Quebec is the only province where more nationalization occurred under non-left than left governments, but this is partly because she defined only the PQ as left, and because of the relative lateness of the election of a left-wing government. Nevertheless, she gives the PQ credit for tightening government control over the state corporations and behaving consistently like other left-wing governments. "State Enterprise and Partisanship in Provincial Politics," in *Canadian Journal of Political Science* (December 1982), and "The Politics of Provincial Resource Policy," in Michael Atkinson and Marsha Chandler, eds., *The Politics of Canadian Public Policy* (Toronto: University of Toronto Press, 1983).

36. A.B. Tanguay, "Recasting Labour Relations in Quebec, 1976-1985: Towards the Disciplinary State?" a paper presented at the Canadian Political Science Association (June 1986).

37. The new emphasis on the francophone private sector is analyzed well in Thomas Courchene, "Market Nationalism," *Policy Options* (October 1986); Alain G. Gagnon and K.Z. Paltiel, "Toward Maîtres chez nous: The Ascendancy of a Balzacian Bourgeoisie in Quebec," *Queen's Quarterly* (Winter 1986); and Alain G. Gagnon and Mary Beth Montcalm, *Quebec: Beyond the Quiet Revolution* (Scarborough: Nelson Canada, 1990).

38. Brian Tanguay, "Quebec's Political System in the 1990s: From Polarization to Convergence," in Gagnon, ed., *Québec: State and Society.*

39. Another motive for this legislation might have been to make the provincial Liberal party financially independent of the federal party, David Rayside, "Federalism and the Party System: Provincial and Federal Liberals in the Province of Quebec," in *Canadian Journal of Political Science* (September 1978), p. 510. On this subject see also H.M. Angell, "The Evolution and Application of Quebec Election Expense Legislation 1960-66," *Report of the Committee on Election Expenses* (Ottawa: Queen's Printer, 1966).

40. A 1982 Quebec court case involving the CEQ decided that the legislation prohibited "third party" advertising during election campaigns.

41. For a comprehensive compilation of such studies see Jean Crête, ed., *Comportement Electoral au Québec* (Chicoutimi: Gaetan Morin editeur, 1984).

42. Richard Hamilton and Maurice Pinard, "The Bases of Parti Québécois Support in Recent Quebec Elections," *Canadian Journal of Political Science* (March 1976).

43. One study indicated that those who split their vote between PQ and Liberal were less in favour of independence than other PQ voting combinations. In a 1976 sample, 45.9 percent voted Liberal-Liberal; 18.7 percent PQ-Liberal; 17.4 percent PQ-non

Liberal; and 17.9 percent PQ-Abstain. David Campbell and Neil Nevitte, "Federal-Provincial Realignments in Quebec," a paper presented at the Canadian Political Science Association (June 1980), p. 14. Some observers think there is a deliberate balancing of different federal and provincial parties, but this author doubts it.

44. Vincent Lemieux, "Quebec," in Robin, ed., *Canadian Provincial Politics,* p. 276.

45. Julien Bauer, "Patrons et patronat au Québec," in *Canadian Journal of Political Science* (September 1976).

46. Lachapelle et al, *The Quebec Democracy,* p. 149.

47. Ibid.; J.I. Gow, *Histoire de l'Administration Publique Québécoise 1867-1970* (Montreal: Presses de l'Université de Montréal, 1986); and E. Cloutier and D. Latouche, *Le Système Politique Québécois* (Ville La Salle: Editions Hurtubise HMH, 1979).

48. Premier Duplessis de-emphasized the lieutenant-governor even earlier, Conrad Black, *Duplessis* (Toronto: McClelland and Stewart, 1977), p. 661.

49. J.R. Mallory, "The Succession of Paul Sauvé and Antonio Barrette," in Paul Fox, ed., *Politics: Canada* (Toronto: McGraw-Hill Ryerson, 3d ed., 1970).

50. Latouche, "From Premier to Prime Minister," p. 151.

51. It has grown from 1867 as follows:

1867-90	65	1931-39	90	1960-66	95
1890-97	73	1939-44	86	1966-73	108
1897-1912	74	1944-48	91	1973-81	110
1912-23	81	1948-56	92	1981-89	122
1923-31	85	1956-60	93	1989-present	125

52. G.W. Kitchin, "The Abolition of Upper Chambers," in D.C. Rowat, ed., *Provincial Government and Politics* (Ottawa: Carleton University, 1973), pp. 74-79.

53. R.J. Fleming, *Canadian Legislatures* (Ottawa: Ampersand Communications, 1988). See also Louis Massicotte, "Quebec: The Successful Combination of French Culture and British Institutions," in Gary Levy and Graham White, eds., *Provincial and Territorial Legislatures in Canada* (Toronto: University of Toronto Press, 1989).

54. Interview with Quebec officials. See also J.I. Gow, "One Hundred Years of Quebec Administrative History, 1867-1970," *Canadian Public Administration* (Summer 1985).

55. Lachapelle et al., *The Quebec Democracy,* p. 79.

56. Stephen Brooks and A. Brian Tanguay, "Quebec's Caisse de Dépôt et Placement: Tool of Nationalism?" *Canadian Public Administration* (Spring 1985). See also Jean-Claude Lebel, "Les Societés d'état au Québec: un outil indispensable," *Canadian Public Administration* (Summer 1984).

57. C.R. Tindal and S.N. Tindal, *Local Government in Canada* (Toronto: McGraw-Hill Ryerson, 2nd. ed., 1984), pp. 85-90.

58. Among the many sources on this period, one of the standards is Wade, *The French Canadians.* There are numerous interpretations in French.

59. I am indebted to Everett Price for many valuable suggestions in this section and others. Some have argued that it is also essential to consider such ideological roots of French-Canadian society as its feudal origins and the influence of the French administration as well as of the Church in providing a basis for the distinctive cultural,

institutional, legal, and social collective identity self-consciously preserved and reinforced by French-Canadian elites up to the 1960s. See, for example, L.E. Hamelin, *Le Canada* (Paris: Presses Universitaires de France, 1964), pp. 73-7; and Marcel Rioux, *Quebec in Question* (Toronto: James Lewis and Samuel, 1971).

60. Among the many sources on this period, one of the most comprehensive is Paul-André Linteau, René Durocher, and Jean-Claude Robert, *Quebec: A History 1867-1929* (Toronto: Lorimer, 1983).

61. Ibid., p. 232.

62. Ibid., pp. 232-3.

63. John Saywell, *The Office of Lieutenant-Governor* (Toronto: University of Toronto Press, 1957), pp. 113-9.

64. Simpson, *Spoils of Power,* p. 199.

65. In spite of the Roman Catholic hierarchy's efforts to persuade its flock to vote Conservative, the Liberals consistently polled over 40 percent of the vote from 1867 to 1896. Skelton quotes one voter of the period: "I cannot vote for M. Laurier for you tell me that if I vote for a Liberal, I shall be damned; I cannot vote for M. Bourbeau, for you tell me that if I do not follow my conscience, I shall be damned; I cannot vote for neither, for you tell me that if I do not vote at all, I shall be damned. Since I must be damned anyway, I'll be damned for doing what I like. I am going to vote for M. Laurier." O.D. Skelton, *Life and Letters of Sir Wilfrid Laurier,* vol. 1 (Toronto: Oxford University Press, 1921), pp. 212-13.

66. Among the many sources on this period are Linteau, *Quebec: A History;* Wade, *The French Canadians;* Quinn, *The Union Nationale;* and B.L. Vigod, *Quebec Before Duplessis: The Political Career of Louis-Alexandre Taschereau* (Montreal: McGill-Queen's University Press, 1986).

67. Laurier wanted to avoid conflict with the Church on this issue because they were already at odds over the Manitoba School Question, Linteau, Quebec: A History, p. 463.

68. Ibid., p. 513; Vigod, *Quebec Before Duplessis.*

69. Linteau., p. 391; Simpson, *Spoils of Power,* p. 203; Vigod, *Quebec Before Duplessis.*

70. Quinn, *The Union Nationale,* p. 63; Vigod, *Quebec Before Duplessis.*

71. Quinn, *The Union Nationale,* ch. 4.

72. Ibid., appendix.

73. Ibid., pp. 49-53.

74. Ibid., p. 64; Vigod, *Quebec before Duplessis.*

75. Quinn, *The Union Nationale;* Black, *Duplessis;* Kenneth McRoberts, *Quebec: Social Change and Political Crisis* (Toronto: McClelland and Stewart, 3rd. ed., 1988); Gérard Boismenu, *Le Duplessisme* (Montréal: Université de Montréal, 1981); Robert Rumilly, *Maurice Duplessis et Son Temps* (Montreal: Fides, 1973); and Cameron Nish, *Quebec in the Duplessis Era, 1935-1959: Dictatorship or Democracy* (Toronto: Copp Clark, 1970).

76. Andre Laurendeau wrote as follows in 1956 as editor of *Le Devoir:* "un fait remarquable, plus de la moitié de nos correspondants refusent de donner publiquement leur nom. Cela traduit exactement l'atmosphère morale du Québec: non point

terreur, car personne ne risque sa vie, mais peur, car des gagne-pain sont en cause. Dans plusieurs cas la crainte parait légitime. En d'autres, la prudence l'emporte nettement sur le courage et le goût du risque ne semble pas notre vice particulier" Gérard Bergeron, *Du Duplessisme au Johnsonisme 1956-1966* (Montreal: Parti Pris, 1967), p. 17.

77. Black, *Duplessis,* p. 218; Wade, *The French Canadians,* p. 930.

78. Even his sympathetic biographer, Conrad Black, calls the early record "very uneven" and admits that "it had certainly not taken too seriously the program on which it was elected." Nevertheless, Black found it more reform-minded than previous Quebec governments, *Duplessis,* p. 217.

79. Wade, *The French Canadians,* p. 944; Black, *Duplessis,* p. 235.

80. The proposal ran into a wall of nationalist opposition in Quebec. The results were as follows: Quebec: 72 percent No, 28 percent Yes; Other provinces: 79 percent Yes, 21 percent No, Total: 64 percent Yes, 35 percent No.

81. To provide capital for the development of these deposits, the Iron Ore Company of Canada was formed from a merger of Hollinger and Hanna and five other American steel companies. In addition to the railway, they built hydroelectric and deep harbour facilities at Sept Iles. Some claimed that the royalty in Quebec was only one cent per ton compared to 33 cents per ton in nearby Newfoundland, but Black denies this, *Duplessis,* pp. 587-8.

82. Quinn, *The Union Nationale,* p. 85.

83. Maurice Pinard, "Working Class Politics: An Interpretation of the Quebec Case," in *Canadian Review of Sociology and Anthropology* (1970); McRoberts and Posgate, *Quebec,* p. 84.

84. David Kwavnick, ed., *The Tremblay Report* (Toronto: McClelland and Stewart, 1973), p. vii.

85. Black, *Duplessis,* p. 687.

86. Quinn, *The Union Nationale,* ch. 7; Simpson, *Spoils of Power,* p. 207.

87. Black, *Duplessis,* pp. 670-5; Pierre Laporte, *The True Face of Duplessis* (Montreal: Harvest House, 1960).

88. Black, *Duplessis,* p. 673.

89. McRoberts and Posgate, *Quebec,* p. 80.

90. Ibid., p. 84; Simpson, *Spoils of Power,* p. 208.

91. Black, *Duplessis,* ch. 20.

92. Ibid., p. 669.

93. For an account of the asbestos strike, as well as an analysis of Quebec society up to that time, see Pierre Trudeau, ed., *The Asbestos Strike* (Toronto: James Lewis and Samuel, 1974).

94. On the role of *Cité Libre* and other opposition in this period see Michael D. Behiels, *Prelude to Quebec's Quiet Revolution* (Montreal: McGill-Queen's University Press, 1985); and Gérard Pelletier, *Years of Impatience 1950-1960* (Toronto: Methuen, 1984).

95. Dale Thomson, *Jean Lesage and the Quiet Revolution;* McRoberts, *Quebec;* and annual accounts in the *Canadian Annual Review.* See also Pierre Vallières, *White Niggers of America* (Toronto: McClelland and Stewart, 1971;) Peter Desbarats, *The State of Quebec* (Toronto: McClelland and Stewart, 1965); David Cameron, *Nationalism, Self-Determination and the Quebec Question* (Toronto: Macmillan, 1974); and Gérard Pelletier, *Years of Choice: 1960-1968* (Toronto: Methuen, 1987).

96. McRoberts and Posgate, *Quebec,* pp. 94-103.

97. André Laurendeau said, for example, that "Not since the days of R.B. Bennett have French-Canadians felt themselves so absent from the affairs of state, as under Mr. Diefenbaker." Peter C. Newman, *Renegade in Power: The Diefenbaker Years* (Toronto: McClelland and Stewart, 1963), pp. 283-4.

98. Thomson, *Jean Lesage,* p. 92.

99. Ibid., pp. 233-48; A.R. Vining, "Provincial Hydro Utilities," in Allan Tupper and Bruce Doern, eds., *Public Corporations and Public Policy in Canada* (Montreal: Institute for Research on Public Policy, 1981).

100. Maurice Pinard, "La Rationalité de l'Electorat: Le Cas de 1962," in Vincent Lemieux, ed., *Quatre Elections Provinciales au Québec 1956-66* (Québec: Presses de l'Université Laval, 1969).

101. Thomson, *Lesage,* pp. 248-288.

102. Ibid., p. 384.

103. McRoberts and Posgate, *Quebec,* p. 109.

104. There is some dispute as to whether the new middle class was the instigator or the product of the Quiet Revolution, but there is little doubt about its overall importance to the movement. William Coleman, *The Independence Movement in Quebec 1945-1980* (Toronto: University of Toronto Press, 1984), p. 8.

105. McRoberts and Posgate, *Quebec,* p. 100.

106. Ibid., p. 121.

107. Some analyses have argued that the Quiet Revolution benefited few beyond the urban middle class, on whom the Liberals depended electorally, and some have emphasized French-Canadians need to enhance their reputation by proving themselves capable of modern accomplishments. Ibid., pp. 101-2. Other interpretations stress the role of the francophone entrepreneurial class or the English-Canadian bourgeoisie. Coleman integrates all three in *The Independence Movement in Quebec.*

108. Lesage had loosened his standards slightly to allow small contracts to be awarded without tender and the road construction budget to be influenced by political considerations. This was not enough for many erstwhile supporters, and many may have stayed home to teach Lesage a lesson. On the other hand, Johnson exploited what little patronage and corruption was left in the system. Thomson, *Lesage,* pp. 151-61; Simpson, *Spoils of Power.*

109. Roberts, *Quebec;* annual accounts in the *Canadian Annual Review;* Dominique Clift, *Quebec Nationalism in Crisis* (Montreal: McGill-Queen's University Press, 1982); Claude Morin, *Quebec Versus Ottawa* (Toronto: University of Toronto Press, 1976); Léon Dion, *Quebec: The Unfinished Revolution* (Montreal: McGill-Queen's University

Press, 1976); Henry Milner, *Politics in the New Quebec* (Toronto: McClelland and Stewart, 1978); and Sheilagh Hodgins Milner and Henry Milner, *The Decolonization of Quebec* (Toronto: McClelland and Stewart, 1973).

110. McRoberts and Posgate, *Quebec*, p. 159; Thomson, *Lesage*, p. 405.

111. Up to this point Pearson responded to Quebec's demands with various pragmatic devices such as opting out. But as the separatist threat increased both he and Trudeau came to the conclusion that there would have to be constitutional changes. At the nationally televised February 1968 conference, federal Justice Minister Trudeau (at that time still relatively unknown) had a dramatic confrontation with Quebec premier Johnson over their divergent views of French-Canadian nationalism. Premier Johnson's views had been articulated in his book, *Egalité ou Indépendance* (Montréal: Editions Renaissance, 1965).

112. Thomson, *Lesage*, p. 362.

113. Ibid., p. 450.

114. John Saywell, *The Rise of the Parti Québécois* (Toronto: University of Toronto Press, 1977), p. 12.

115. The right-wing Regroupement National broke away from the RIN and joined forces with the Ralliement des Créditistes to form the Ralliement National. Gilles Grégoire was the central figure in this.

116. Sources on this period include McRoberts, *Quebec;* Saywell, *The Rise of the Parti Québécois;* Fraser, *PQ;* and annual accounts in the *Canadian Annual Review of Politics and Public Affairs.* See also Réne Lévesque, *My Quebec* (Toronto: Methuen, 1979), *An Option for Quebec* (Toronto: McClelland and Stewart, 1968), and *Memoirs* (Toronto: McClelland and Stewart, 1986); D.C. Rowat, *The Referendum and Separation Elsewhere: Implications for Quebec* (Ottawa: Carleton University, 1978); and W.F. Shaw and Lionel Albert, *Partition: The Price of Quebec's Independence* (Montreal: Thornhill Publishing, 1980).

117. Maurice Pinard and Richard Hamilton, "The Independence Issue and the Polarization of the Electorate: The 1973 Quebec Election," in *Canadian Journal of Political Science* (June 1977).

118. McRoberts and Posgate, *Quebec*, p. 165.

119. There is a large literature on this incident including John Saywell, *Quebec 70* (Toronto: University of Toronto Press, 1971); Gérard Pelletier, *The October Crisis* (Toronto: McClelland and Stewart, 1971); Ron Haggart and Aubrey Golden, *Rumours of War* (Toronto: Lorimer, 1979); and George Radwanski and Kendal Windeyer, *No Mandate but Terror* (Richmond Hill: Pocket Books, 1970).

120. Sandford F. Borins, *Language of the Skies: The Bilingual Air Traffic Control Conflict in Canada* (Montreal: McGill-Queen's University Press, 1983).

121. McRoberts and Posgate, *Quebec*, p. 175.

122. Maurice Pinard and Richard Hamilton, "The Parti Québécois Comes to Power," p. 743.

123. Ibid., p. 748, Alain Albert emphasizes the effect of increased fiscal pressure, union unrest, and high unemployment as reasons to vote against the Liberals. "Conditions

Economiques et Elections: le Cas de l'Election Provinciale de 1976 au Québec," in *Canadian Journal of Political Science* (June 1980).

124. Pinard and Hamilton, "The Parti Québécois Comes to Power," p. 754.

125. Mayor Drapeau had issued assurances that the Olympics could no more have a deficit than he could have a baby.

126. Pierre Dumont, *How Lévesque Won* (Toronto: Lorimer, 1977), p. 27.

127. Pinard and Hamilton, "The Parti Québécois Comes to Power," p. 740.

128. Fraser, *PQ;* L. Ian Macdonald, *From Bourassa to Bourassa* (Montreal: Harvest House, 1984); Coleman, *The Independence Movement in Quebec;* Lévesque, *Memoirs;* and annual accounts in the *Canadian Annual Review of Politics and Public Affairs.*

129. Fraser, *PQ,* pp. 81-2. Except at the francophone Université d'Ottawa.

130. Ibid., p. 98.

131. Some writers, for example Coleman and McRoberts, discount the difference between the two bills—too much in my opinion. Coleman argues that both treated the private sector in much the same way, and that the differences were mostly in local public institutions and access to English-language schools.

132. William Coleman "From Bill 22 to Bill 101: The Politics of Language under the Parti Québécois," *Canadian Journal of Political Science* (September 1981), pp. 482-3.

133. McRoberts argues that the PQ was not a true social democratic party because it did not establish an organic link with organized labour, and prohibited union political contributions. An alternative definition of social democracy is contained in Jean-Louis Bourque, "La Social-Démocratie Québécoise, du Parti Québécois au Gouvernement Péquiste: 1968-1984," a paper presented to Canadian Political Science Association (June 1984), p. 11. On the election expenses issue, see Simpson, *Spoils of Power.*

134. Fraser, *PQ,* p. 123.

135. Stephen Brooks and Brian Tanguay, "Quebec's Asbestos Policy: A Preliminary Assessment," *Canadian Public Administration* (Spring 1985). See also Pierre Fournier, "The National Asbestos Corporation of Quebec," in Allan Tupper and G.B. Doern, eds., *Public Corporations and Public Policy in Canada* (Montreal: Institute for Research on Public Policy, 1981).

136. Vincent Lemieux's study of the laws passed between 1976 and 1981 concluded that the Lévesque government became increasingly interventionist over this period. Farmers, workers, taxpayers, and municipalities were most frequently the beneficiaries of such intervention, while landlords, employers, and professions were most often the victims, "Les Lois du Premier Gouvernement Lévesque," *Recherches Sociographiques* (janvier-avril 1984). A similar study of the 1982-84 period was done by Jean Crête et al., "Changements Electoraux et Politiques," a paper presented to the Canadian Political Science Association (May 1985).

137. But Parizeau was a creative conservative, as he showed in 1978 when federal Finance Minister Jean Chrétien offered to compensate provinces for a general reduction in their sales tax. After being non-committal to Ottawa, Parizeau cut the provincial tax in selective areas rather than across the board and in precisely those

industries where the Quebec economy was the weakest—textiles, clothing, shoes, furniture, and hotel rooms. Chrétien retaliated by cancelling the offer to Quebec and instead sent an $85 income tax rebate to each Quebec taxpayer.

138. "The Government of Quebec has made public its proposal to negotiate a new agreement with the rest of Canada, based on the equality of nations. This agreement would enable Quebec to acquire the exclusive powers to make its laws, administer its taxes and establish relations abroad—in other words, sovereignty—and at the same time, to maintain with Canada an economic association including a common currency. Any change in political status resulting from these negotiations will be submitted to the people through a referendum. On these terms, do you agree to give the government of Quebec the mandate to negotiate the proposed agreement between Quebec and Canada?"

139. Among the books on this subject are Roy Romanow, John Whyte, and Howard Leeson, *Canada...Notwithstanding* (Toronto: Carswell/Methuen, 1984); Keith Banting and Richard Simeon, *And No One Cheered* (Toronto: Methuen, 1983); and David Milne, *The New Canadian Constitution* (Toronto: Lorimer, 1982).

140. There were actually two other conditions: first, that sovereignty had to await a majority of popular vote for the party, not just a majority of seats, and second, that the province continue to be open to minority interests.

141. Fraser, *PQ*, p. 341.

142. On the Bourassa second term, see Jacques Bourgault and Stéphane Dion, "Étude d'une transition gouvernementale: Le cas du Québec en 1985," in Donald Savoie, ed., *Taking Power: Managing Government Transitions* (Toronto: Institute of Public Administration of Canada, 1993); Robert Bourassa, *Power from the North* (Scarborough: Prentice Hall Canada, 1985); and Jean-Francois Lisée, *The Trickster* (Toronto: Lorimer, 1994).

143. On the independence question, see National Executive Council of the Parti Québécois, *Quebec in a New World* (Toronto: Lorimer, 1994); David Bercuson and Barry Cooper, *Deconfederation: Canada Without Quebec* (Toronto: Key Porter Books, 1991); and Paul Boothe, *Closing the Books: Dividing Federal Assets and Debt If Canada Breaks Up* (Vancouver: Fraser Institute, 1991).

READINGS

Books

Canadian Annual Review of Politics and Public Affairs. Toronto: University of Toronto Press. Annual.

Courchene, Thomas. "Market Nationalism." *Policy Options.* October 1968.

Fraser, Graham. *PQ: René Lévesque and the Parti Québécois in Power.* Toronto: MacMillan, 1984.

Gagnon, Alain, ed. *Québec: State and Society.* Toronto: Methuen, 1984; 2nd. ed., Toronto: Nelson, 1993.

Galipeau, Claude Jean. "Le Contre-Courant Québécois." Keith Brownsey and Michael Howlett, eds. *The Provincial State*. Mississauga: Copp Clark Pitman, 1992.

Guindon, Hubert. *Quebec Society: Tradition, Modernity and Nationhood*. Toronto: University of Toronto Press, 1988.

Lachapelle, Guy et al. *The Quebec Democracy: Structures, Processes & Policies*. Toronto: McGraw-Hill Ryerson, 1993.

Landry, Réjean. "Party Competition in Quebec." H.G. Thorburn, ed. *Party Politics in Canada*. 6th ed., Scarborough: Prentice Hall Canada, 1991.

McRoberts, Kenneth. *Quebec: Social Change and Political Crisis*. Toronto: McClelland and Stewart. 3rd ed., 1980.

Parti Québécois. *Quebec in a New World*. Toronto: Lorimer, 1994.

Thomson, Dale. *Jean Lesage and the Quiet Revolution*. Toronto: Macmillan, 1984.

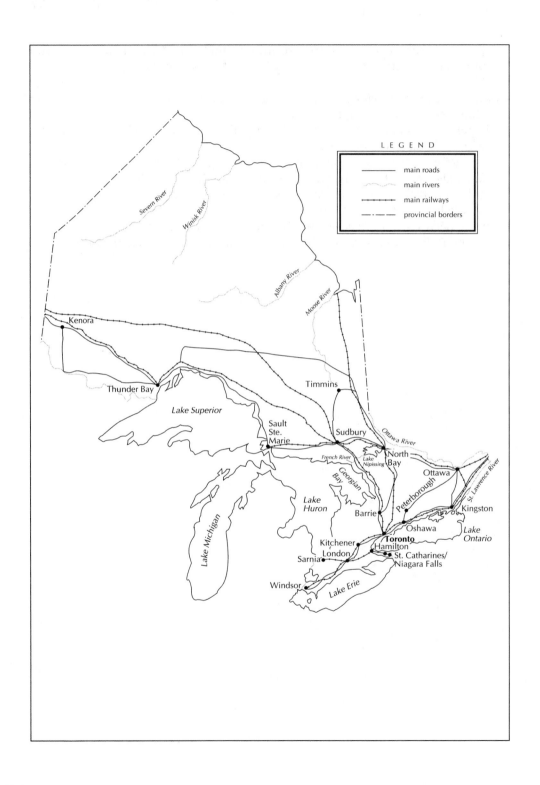

Severn River

Winisk River

Albany River

Moose River

Kenora

Thunder Bay

Lake Superior

Timmins

Sault
Ste.
Marie

Sudbury

Ottawa River

French River

Lake
Nipissing

North
Bay

Georgian
Bay

Ottawa

St. Lawrence River

Peterborough

Lake
Huron

Barrie

Kingston

Lake Michigan

Oshawa

Lake
Ontario

Kitchener

Toronto

London

Hamilton

Sarnia

St. Catharines/
Niagara Falls

Windsor

Lake Erie

ONTARIO

Ontario is sometimes called the keystone province, given that it is prosperous and centrally located, has the largest population, and constitutes Canada's industrial heartland. Blessed with natural resources, Ontario is strategically close to large Canadian and American markets. It has sufficient representation in Ottawa to ensure that national policies usually reflect its interests. It is also the most diversified province in terms of economy and population. Although Ontario remains ahead of the other provinces economic terms, it fell upon hard times in the recession of the early 1990s and its manufacturing sector in particular was savaged. It elected an NDP government during this period, but an economic downturn restrained that party's reformist zeal. More radical change was expected from the right-wing Conservative government elected in 1995.

SETTING

Geography

Ontario is the second-largest province in area; its 1,068,600 square kilometres make it about two-thirds the size of Quebec. Ontario's main physical features consist of the Hudson Bay lowlands and the rocky Precambrian Shield in the north, and the fertile Great Lakes-St. Lawrence lowlands in the south. The Great Lakes and St. Lawrence River divide it from the United States. Given such a geographic expanse, certain regional sentiments naturally developed. Northern Ontario is the most distinctive region, and is demarcated by the French River and Lake Nipissing, but the region itself is so large that further division into northwest and northeast is sometimes appropriate. Metropolitan Toronto is a second clear-cut region, although its labour market area extends well beyond municipal boundaries. Everything east of a vertical line between Toronto and North Bay can be considered eastern Ontario. The rest is sometimes referred to as southwestern Ontario, although that, too, is so large it is sometimes divided further. Different categorizations are used, but include Hamilton-Niagara, Kitchener-London, the Bruce peninsula, and the Windsor area.

Ontario's population in 1991 was 10,084,885, over three million more than Quebec, or 36.9 percent of the Canadian total. By January 1995 it had risen to 11,004,800. Ontario has 11 metropolitan areas with more than 100,000 residents, as seen in Table 7.1.

TABLE 7.1   Metropolitan Areas in Ontario over 100,000 (1991)

Toronto	3,893,046
Ottawa	693,900
Hamilton	599,760
London	381,522
St. Catharines-Niagara	364,552
Kitchener	356,421
Windsor	262,075
Oshawa	240,104
Sudbury	157,613
Kingston	136,401
Thunder Bay	124,427

Source: Reproduced by authority of the Minister of Industry, 1995, Statistics Canada, *1991 Census* cat. no. 93-303, adapted by author.

With nearly 40 percent of the province's population in Toronto's labour market area, that city is Ontario's economic, political, and cultural core, while each of the other 10 centres listed functions as a regional metropolis. These 11 and other large settlements produce the most urbanized province in Canada, with 81.8 percent of the population living in urban areas, mostly in the Windsor to Cornwall corridor. This area is particularly well served by transportation systems—the Macdonald-Cartier Freeway (or Highway 401), railways, airlines, and a matrix of smaller highways. Road, rail, and air links connect the south to the north, and the Ontario Northland Railway extends all the way to Moosonee on James Bay. Toronto's Pearson International Airport is by far the country's busiest in terms of both passengers and cargo, while Ottawa's airport ranks fifth in passengers and ninth in freight. Marine transportation in the province centres on the St. Lawrence Seaway, the world's largest canal system, which includes the Welland Canal around Niagara Falls. The seaway has made Thunder Bay Canada's eighth-largest port, and has increased business to most of the other ports along the way, Hamilton ranking 10th in the country.

Economy

Ontario's gross domestic product is usually about 40 percent of that of the country as a whole. Ontario's economy was originally based on the abundance of

TABLE 7.2   Ontario 1991 Labour Force and Estimated 1995 Gross Domestic Product by Industry

Industry	1991 Labour Force		Est. 1995 GDP ($ millions)	
Agriculture	139,885	2.6%	2,761	1.3%
Fishing	1,965	—	38	—
Logging	13,970	0.3%	614	0.3%
Mining	34,360	0.6%	2,176	1.0%
TOTAL PRIMARY	190,180	3.5%	5,589	2.6%
Manufacturing	942,995	17.4%	54,932	25.8%
Construction	358,895	6.6%	7,908	3.7%
TOTAL SECONDARY	1,301,890	24.0%	62,840	29.5%
Transportation, communications and utilities	376,460	6.9%	21,247	10.0%
Trade	934,830	17.2%	26,013	12.2%
Finance, insurance and real estate	353,225	6.5%	39,294	18.4%
Services	1,867,810	34.3%	46,029	21.6%
Government	411,455	7.6%	12,081	5.7%
TOTAL TERTIARY	3,943,780	72.5%	144,664	67.9%
TOTAL ALL INDUSTRIES	5,435,850		213,094	

Source: Reproduced by authority of the Minister of Industry, 1995, Statistics Canada, *1991 Census,* cat. nos.93-326 and 95-338, and Conference Board of Canada, *Provincial Outlook, Economic Forecast,* Ottawa: Summer 1994, Vol. 9, No 2.

three primary resources—agriculture, mining, forestry—as well as hydroelectricity. Nowadays, however, primary resources provide only 3.5 percent of the province's employment, the lowest proportion in the country. Ontario progressed through a manufacturing phase to the present domination by service industries. Table 7.2 presents figures on employment and GDP by industry.

Ontario usually ranks first among the provinces in terms of the total value of agricultural production. Cattle and dairy products vie for first place within the province, followed by poultry and eggs, hogs, nursery products, soybeans, vegetables, corn, and tobacco. Ontario leads the country in all of the crops mentioned, and competes with British Columbia for first place in fruit; it ranks first in poultry and eggs, second in cattle and hogs, and competes with Quebec for first place in dairy products. Ontario has a maze of marketing boards, one for almost every agricultural product. Most farming takes place in the south, but pockets of agricultural production exist in the north. Ontario had 68,633 census farms in 1991, the largest number in the country, with an average size of just under 200 acres, the second smallest of any province. Agriculture also contributes much of the raw material for the province's processing and manufacturing sectors.

Ontario is second to Alberta in the total value of mineral production—and well ahead if oil and gas are excluded. It has a wide range of minerals, of which nickel and gold have the highest production value and in which Ontario leads the country.[1] These are followed by copper, zinc, and uranium, in all of which it is second among all the provinces. Ontario also has a large supply of salt, silver, and gypsum, of structural materials such as limestone, sand, gravel, stone, and cement, and small amounts of cobalt, iron ore, and petroleum. Inco Ltd. and Falconbridge Inc. in the Sudbury region produce nickel and copper, along with smaller amounts of several other minerals, while Kidd Creek near Timmins produces zinc, copper, and silver. Gold is primarily mined in the Kirkland Lake-Timmins area and at Hemlo near Marathon. Production of uranium has almost ceased in recent years, having been centred in the Denison and Rio Algom mines in Elliot Lake, which cannot compete with Saskatchewan where it is extracted at a lower cost. The last mines in Elliot Lake are scheduled to close in 1996, while the last iron mine is in Wawa. Because the demand for most minerals dropped significantly in recent years, the mining industry has been in decline and employment reduced dramatically.

Ontario ranks third in forestry production, behind B.C. and Quebec. The logging industry, sawmills, plywood mills and other wood processing plants, and pulp and paper production all account for much employment. Logging is usually done by private firms on Crown land under the authority of timber licenses and forest management agreements. The leading companies include Abitibi-Price, Canadian Pacific Forest Products, Domtar Inc., E.B. Eddy, and Mallette Inc., and the leading lumbering, pulp and/or paper producing centres are Cornwall, Dryden, Espanola, Fort Francis, Hearst, Iroquois Falls, Kapuskasing, Kenora, Marathon, Red Rock, Sault Ste. Marie, Smooth Rock Falls, Sturgeon Falls, Terrace Bay, and Thunder Bay. As in other provinces, the record of reforestation and forest management have left much to be desired, but several recent inventories and environmental studies are expected to lead to improvements.

Finally, Ontarians engage in a certain amount of fishing, especially on the Great Lakes. Considerable hunting and trapping activity also takes place, particularly in the north, making Ontario the provincial leader in the value of wild fur pelts.

Ontario has an abundance of hydroelectric power, which has historically been one of the bases of its flourishing manufacturing industry. The Ottawa, Niagara, and St. Lawrence rivers are particularly good sources of electricity, as are a number of smaller installations in the north, especially the Abitibi River. In recent years, however, Ontario has developed several large nuclear power stations, and it now relies on that source for about half of its power requirements. The three nuclear plants in operation are Pickering, Bruce (Kindardine) and Darlington (Bowmanville). Hydraulic and coal-fired generators each presently produce about 25 percent of the total output. Combining all these sources, Ontario is second to Quebec in the total amount of electricity generated. The province is more or less self-sufficient in this respect but, depending on weather and other factors, it may export or import small amounts. With the recession of the 1990s came a fall in demand and the province was in a position to compete with Quebec in exporting electricity to the United States. Ontario Hydro, a Crown corporation, has a virtual monopoly on the providing of electricity and is such an enormous and powerful operation, akin to Hydro-Québec, that many observers over the years feared it was beyond political control.

Manufacturing in Ontario constitutes about 55 percent of the country's total production. The province has had many historical advantages in this respect, some of which have been mentioned: raw materials, cheap and abundant electricity, a pool of skilled labour, good transportation, proximity to markets and to the U.S. automobile production industry, and the protection of the national tariff. These advantages were of limited protection, however, against the global restructuring which began about 1990, augmented by the recession and the Canada-U.S. free trade agreement. Ontario lost over 200,000 manufacturing jobs in the early years of the decade.

Ontario's leading manufactured product by far is automobiles, an industry protected to some extent by the 1965 Canada-U.S. Auto Pact. General Motors, Ford, and Chrysler each have several plants in the province; Suzuki, Toyota, and Honda also make cars in Ontario; and hundreds of smaller firms manufacture auto parts. Other important sectors of manufacturing include food and beverages, chemicals and chemical products, electronics, smelting and refining primary metals, chemicals, primary and fabricated metals, pulp and paper products, machinery, and printing and publishing. Many southern Ontario centres, especially Toronto and environs, produce a variety of manufactured goods, but some locations are more specialized: automobiles in Windsor, Oshawa, Oakville, Brampton, St. Catharines, Ingersoll, and Alliston; food and beverages in Kitchener, London, and Peterborough; wire, heavy machinery, and electrical products in Hamilton; smelting and refining of metals in Sudbury and Port Colborne; petroleum refining, plastics, chemicals and chemical products in Sarnia; steel in Hamilton and Sault Ste. Marie; printing and publishing in Toronto and Ottawa; furniture, rubber, and leather in Kitchener; computers in Ottawa; and transportation equipment in Thunder Bay. Table 7.3 gives an indication of the leading manufacturing sectors in 1990, before the ravages of the recession.

Turning to services, Toronto is the financial capital of Canada. Most of the large chartered banks have headquarters in Toronto, many insurance companies are located there or nearby, and it is the site of the Toronto Stock Exchange. Toronto is home to the main production facilities of the national English-language radio and television networks; and every imaginable business and personal service is also available. Toronto is a key wholesale and retail distribution centre for a wide variety of domestic and imported goods, and it is central to the province's vibrant tourist industry, although Ottawa, Kingston, Niagara,

Stratford, and a host of other cities, towns and wilderness areas are also important in this respect.

TABLE 7.3   Manufacturing in Ontario, 1990

Sector	Workers	Salaries and Wages (millions of dollars)	Value of Shipments (millions of dollars)
Transportation equipment	158,227	$5,850.1	$58,367.1
Fabricated metals	97,317	2,931.5	11,164.3
Electronics and electrical products	89,837	2,916.7	13,932.6
Food and beverages	85,996	2,807.8	21,905.3
Printing and publishing	73,563	2,545.5	7,696.2
Chemicals and chemical products	55,291	2,153.5	15,351.9
Primary metals	54,055	2,317.5	10,389.0
Machinery	47,280	1,555.9	6,771.0
Paper and paper products	39,708	1,486.4	7,921.8
Furniture	32,179	781.9	2,665.6
Plastic	29,693	797.5	3,883.3
Clothing	29,555	602.4	2,070.1
Other sectors	153,229	4,598.9	26,465.0
Total	945,930	31,345.6	$188,583.2

Source: Reproduced by authority of the Ministry of Industry, 1995, Statistics Canada, *Manufacturing Industries of Canada*, cat. no. 31-203, adapted by author.

Given the disproportionate number of federal public servants in the Ottawa area, in addition to the large provincial and municipal government workforces, the public administration sector is another significant factor in the Ontario economy. The provincial public service employs about 90,000; provincial government agencies, boards, commissions and Crown corporations add another 50,000; municipalities and school boards, an additional 300,000; colleges and universities, about 80,000, and health and community services, about 370,000. Thus, the wider provincial public sector employs some 900,000 people,[2] in addition to over 200,000 federal public servants.

Class

Based on this diverse economy, Ontario has traditionally been the most prosperous province; in 1992 it had the highest per capita income at $23,593. In 1991, 12.3 percent of family incomes were under $20,000, while 27 percent were over $70,000, for a median family income of $50,046. This impressive figure is partially due to the fact that the province has one of the highest educational levels in Canada. Ontario is accustomed to having a low unemployment rate (5.1 percent in 1989), but this increased dramatically during the following years, reaching 11 to 12 percent in the mid-1990s primarily due to the closure or downsizing of manufacturing operations.

Organized labour is strong, numbering about 1,325,000 members, although Ontario has the third-lowest rate of unionization in percentage terms in the country, with only 31.6 percent of all paid workers belonging to unions. The Ontario Federation of Labour has a membership of about 800,000. The three largest unions in Ontario are in the public sector—the Ontario Public Service Employees' Union (OPSEU), the Canadian Union of Public Employees (CUPE), and the Public Service Alliance of Canada (PSAC). The largest private sector union is the Canadian Auto Workers (CAW), while Ontario also has the largest number and proportion of workers belonging to international unions, including the United Food and Commercial Workers and the United Steelworkers of America. The success of such unions at the bargaining table has produced relatively high wages, and their size is one reason the NDP is stronger in Ontario than in the five provinces to the east. Although the Bob Rae government enacted many measures designed to benefit the working class, these were largely eclipsed by its 1993 Social Contract legislation which broke existing collective agreements, causing many unions to reconsider their links to that party.

Since Ontario houses more corporate head offices than any other province —45 of the top 100 on the *Financial Post*'s 1994 list—Ontario has a large number of economic titans. Most conspicuous are Ken Thomson, the Reichmann family, Galen Weston, Peter and Edward Bronfman, and the Eaton family. The Thomson interests include newspapers (the *Globe and Mail* and a score of smaller papers), retail stores (The Bay and Zellers), and many other firms in the energy, travel, real estate, and publishing fields. The Reichmanns fell on hard times after building an empire including Abitibi-Price, Olympia and York, Gulf Canada, and Hiram Walker Resources, while Weston controls E.B. Eddy, Holt Renfrew, Westons, Loblaws, and several other firms in the food business. The Toronto branch of the Bronfman family controls such firms as Noranda, Brascan, Trizec, London Life, Royal LePage and the Great Lakes Group. In addition to the chain of department stores which bears their name, the Eaton family owns CFTO-TV, the keystone of the CTV network. Thus, the Ontario economic elite tends to be of national or international stature, and most of the country's major economic decisions are made here. Nearly three-quarters of Peter Newman's "Canadian national business establishment" live in the Toronto area.[3] These include bank presidents (Richard Thomson of the Toronto-Dominion Bank; Al Flood of the Bank of Commerce; P.C. Godsoe of the Bank of Nova Scotia; and Matthew Barrett of the Bank of Montreal); investment dealers and other financial leaders such as Hal Jackman, at least before he became lieutenant-governor; directors of a variety of firms; and some high-profile lawyers. Media lords include John

Bassett (working for Eatons), Conrad Black, Beland and John Honderich, Ted Rogers, and Ken Thomson. Key executives with some of the largest firms in the country also live here: M.W. Hutchins (Ford), Maureen Kempston Darkes (General Motors), Yves Landry (Chrysler), Robert Peterson (Imperial Oil), Michael Sopko (Inco), Frank Stronach (Magna), Frederick Telmer (Stelco), D.W. Kerr (Noranda), R.Y. Oberlander (Abitibi-Price), Trevor Eyton (Brascan), M.A. Cohen (Molson Co.), the Wolfe family (Oshawa Group), and Angelo and Elvio Del Zotto (Tridel), to name just a few.

The most sophisticated class analysis of Ontario politics identifies seven significant classes whose shifting alliances can explain the province's varied electoral outcomes.[4] These are farmers, small capital, large capital, the traditional (private sector) middle class, the new (public sector) middle class, and the private and public sector working classes. During the long period of Conservative dominance after 1943, that party managed to secure the support of almost all of these groups, much of it based on its "progressive" encouragement of the public sector. Frank Miller's change of direction in this respect precipitated the disintegration of this grand, all-class coalition. Since 1985, the public-sector oriented classes in particular have migrated to, and between, the Liberals and the NDP, but in 1995, the Conservatives re-established a broader alliance.

Demography

Ontario's population was once predominantly of British descent, but this group now constitutes only about half of the population. The French are second, followed by Italians, Germans, and Dutch. There are also significant numbers of many other ethnic groups, the largest being Ukrainians, Jews, Portuguese, Poles, and Chinese. Many of these have been assimilated into the "English" culture, as have some of the French, so that 76.6 percent of the total population have English as their mother tongue, and 85 percent as a home language. Only five percent (representing 500,000 people) list French as mother tongue, and 3.2 percent as the language spoken at home.

The French-English cleavage has been a prominent generator of political activity, at first in relation to schools and, more recently, to the question of "official bilingualism." The Conservative government in the early 1980s expanded the range of French-language provincial services but steadfastly refused to recognize the availability of these services as a constitutional right. The Liberals' Bill 8 guaranteed French-language provincial government services in 22 designated regions—wherever French speakers made up at least 10 percent of the local population or total at least 5,000 people. Municipalities within designated areas have the option of providing services in French if they choose. Nevertheless, the French language in the province is not secure: about 37 percent of those with French mother tongue no longer speak it at home.

Ontario has the largest number of residents of aboriginal origin, nearly 250,000 and over 90 percent Indian, but they constitute only 2.4 percent of the population. Little progress has been made on Native land claims in the province, or indeed on other aboriginal demands, although both Liberal and NDP governments addressed these issues and some expansion of reserve lands has taken place. The NDP and aboriginal leaders signed a statement of political relationship in 1991 which recognized the first nations' inherent right to self-government within the Canadian constitutional framework.

Over 18.4 percent of the population have languages other than English and French as mother tongues (chiefly Italian, Chinese, German, Portuguese and Polish), and 11.6 percent of the population's home language is other than English or French. This is a striking reminder of the scale of recent immigration into the province and its marked ethnic diversity. In recent years, immigrants to Ontario have come primarily from Hong Kong, Poland, India, Philippines, Jamaica, and Iran. In fact, almost 25 percent of Ontario residents were born outside Canada. Such "other ethnic groups" have been of political significance in such fields as heritage language programs, government appointments, and bloc voting patterns. The Bob Rae government enacted the most comprehensive employment equity legislation in the country, providing preference for women, francophones, aboriginals, visible minorities, and the disabled, but it created a backlash in the 1995 election campaign. In the name of multiculturalism, it also removed the Queen from the oath taken by police officers in the province. The most overt racism problems in the province are related to the black community and, after an outbreak of rampage and looting in downtown Toronto in 1992, Rae turned to Stephen Lewis to make recommendations on this matter.

TABLE 7.4   Ontario Mother Tongue and Home Language, 1991

	Mother Tongue	Home Language
English	76.6%	85.2%
French	5.0%	3.2%
Other	18.4%	11.6%

Source: Reproduced by authority of the Minister of Industry, 1995. Statistics Canada, *1991 Census*, cat. no. 93-317, adapted by author.

Just as Anglo-Saxon domination has declined, so has the predominance of the Protestant religion. In 1991, only 44.4 percent belonged to such denominations, while the Roman Catholic category numbered 35.5 percent. This left 7.6 percent belonging to other religions, in which Ontario took the lead, and 12.5 percent who had none. Religion has been of considerable political significance in the province, especially in relation to the question of separate schools. The Constitution Act, 1867 guaranteed a Roman Catholic separate school system in

Ontario up to grade 8, which was later extended to Grade 10. After Grade 10, Roman Catholics could attend public or private high schools, but were required to pay taxes to the public system. This was a source of controversy for many years, especially in the 1971 provincial election, and generally led Roman Catholics to vote against the long-dominant Conservatives. Then, Bill Davis promised full public support to the separate school system, to be developed in stages starting in 1985. The implications of the change in policy proved to be far more complicated than anyone had imagined, and were a major factor in the Conservatives' defeat. Other issues with religious overtones, such as abortion and public school prayers, have occasionally surfaced, and other religious groups —especially Jews and fundamentalist Christians—have tried (so far unsuccessfully) to get public funding for their denominational schools.

TABLE 7.5   Religion in Ontario, 1991

Protestant			4,428,305	(44.4%)
United Church	1,410,535	(14.1%)		
Anglican	1,059,910	(10.6%)		
Presbyterian	422,160	(4.2%)		
Baptist	264,625	(2.7%)		
Lutheran	227,915	(2.3%)		
Other Protestant	1,043,160	(10.5%)		
Roman Catholic			3,544,515	(35.5%)
No Religious Affiliation			1,247,640	(12.5%)
Eastern Non-Christian			379,625	(3.8%)
Eastern Orthodox			187,910	(1.9%)
Jewish			175,640	(1.8%)
Other			13,415	(0.1%)

Source: Reproduced by authority of the Minister of Industry, 1995. Statistics Canada, *1991 Census*, cat. no. 93-319, calculations by author.

Thus Ontario has been marked by periodic patterns of ethnic and religious politics, class politics, and regional politics, as well as certain urban-rural conflicts, but none of these have been profoundly divisive. The overriding concern has been economic development, with a lively competition over the location of new industry. Elections have often been fought on such issues as general government performance, leadership, scandal, and, until recently, liquor.

Federal-Provincial Relations

Relations with the federal government have always been an important aspect of Ontario politics but have ranged from hostile to friendly.[5] Generally speaking, basic federal economic policy in such areas as tariffs, transportation, or banking favoured Ontario's interests, largely because a high proportion of policy-makers in Ottawa were Ontarians. In addition, the province's central location meant that it did not develop the sense of distance and alienation characteristic of provinces farther from the national capital. However, many heated battles were waged between Ontario and Ottawa, especially in the Mowat, Hepburn, Drew, and Roberts eras. Oliver Mowat sought to establish and expand the province's constitutional status in a series of court cases and, in co-operation with Mercier of Quebec, to increase provincial revenues. Mitch Hepburn's conflicts with Mackenzie King were more personal and political, often concerning party affairs and the war effort, although some, such as Hepburn's opposition to the central-ist recommendations of the Rowell-Sirois Report, related to the respective roles of government. Drew fought against a centralization in taxation arrangements and shared-cost programs in the post-war period, while Roberts opposed the Pearson government's proposals for national pension and medical insurance plans. In these cases and others, Ontario has also sought maximum fiscal resources and, like other provincial governments, was ready to blame the federal government for any difficulties. This practice was facilitated in that the Ontario government was usually Conservative and the federal government, Liberal. Even so, Ontario had fewer disagreements with Ottawa than most other provinces but, perhaps due to its size, its disputes attained greater national prominence. Over the Trudeau-Davis period, federal-Ontario relations were bet-ter than ever, partly because Ontario was on the defensive as political and eco-nomic power shifted to the West, which began to challenge the central Canadian point of view. Ontario generally supported federal initiatives on keeping energy costs low, combating inflation, and maintaining the Canadian common market free of provincial barriers. In these cases Ontario was not only defending its own economic interests, but supporting a federal position under increasing attack. Davis was able to be a peacemaker between fellow Conservative provincial gov-ernments and the federal Liberal government on many issues, especially on the constitutional issues of the early 1980s. David Peterson was forced to defend the province against federal advocates of free trade and, while he supported the Meech Lake Accord, he had to deal with a federal Conservative government that was primarily concerned with the needs of other provinces.

As a result of the Mulroney government's base in Quebec and the West, and all recent federal governments' obsession with Quebec, Ontario can no longer assume that the national interest as pursued by Ottawa will coincide with its own interests. Ontario opposed the North American Free Trade Agreement with no success, had no more clout in criticizing cutbacks to health and post-secondary education grants, and felt particularly discriminated against by the federal ceiling on Canada Assistance Plan contributions. It joined Alberta and B.C. in challenging this ceiling in court. Not surprisingly, Premier Bob Rae began to chart an "Ontario first" policy. Due to the severity of the 1990s recession,

Ontario received stabilization payments from Ottawa but not to the extent requested by the province. In 1992, Ottawa contributed only 15.6 percent of the Ontario government's revenues, or $6,812 million. The federal government also transferred $357 million to municipalities, $17,134 million to individuals, and $2,055 million to businesses. In recent years, the provincial government has often accused federal cabinet ministers from Ontario of not defending the province's interests well at the national level. Rae criticized the Chrétien government's discriminatory treatment of Ontario, especially in terms of its $3.6 billion cut in health and social program transfers in 1996–98.

POLITICAL CULTURE[6]

Although those in other provinces may view Ontarians as rich, arrogant, and domineering, Ontarians themselves have next to no provincial consciousness. Largely due to the province's central location, and perhaps because the province houses the national capital, Ontarians see themselves primarily as Canadians. Ontarians are the most federally oriented of all Canadians—90 percent, according to *Maclean's* magazine and, at least until recently, lacked a distinctive regional identity and were rather apathetic about provincial affairs. As long as the federal government was pursuing policies favourable to Ontario, and Ontario equated its interests with those of the country as a whole, there was little reason to develop a provincial point of view.[7] Other factors were the high immigration rate and the migration of other Canadians to Ontario. These newcomers identified more with Canada or with their ethnic sub-culture than with Ontario. Lacking a regional economic elite and knowing that the population was so federally oriented, governments in Ontario have generally not pressed for the same degree of provincial power as elsewhere. Now that national policy seems to favour Quebec and/or the West, however, Ontarians are increasingly aware of a distinctive regional interest.

Certain predominant Ontario values and attitudes can be identified: elitism, ascription, hierarchy, continuity, stability, and social order, although these are often associated with the whole country. These values can generally be classified as "conservatism." One source of such values was the United Empire Loyalists; indeed, the province possessed a British-Protestant orientation for generations. On the other hand, Ontario is not as monolithically conservative as the Atlantic region. John Wilson discovered a complementary "progressive" or collectivist side to the Ontario political culture,[8] and felt that the best general label for Ontario would therefore be "progressive conservative." Not only is the Co-operative Commonwealth Federation/New Democratic Party tradition stronger in Ontario but, perhaps partly as a result, even Conservative governments (at least prior to 1995) have been fairly progressive. Wilson maintains that to be successful in the province a party must demonstrate two features—caution and reform. Somewhat similarly, because of some political consciousness on the part of the working class, Ontario is sometimes categorized as a "transitional" political culture, in contrast to the pre-industrial Atlantic provinces. There is also a dynamic, acquisitive aspect to Ontario life not always found elsewhere in the country and, as a result of immigration, it is a very pluralistic, particularistic, multicultural society.

Ontarians generally trust government and feel efficacious about influencing it;[9] on the other hand, the voter turnout rate is not that high. Predictably, interest in federal elections exceeds that of provincial elections, with the voting turnout averaging about 74 percent and 63 percent respectively. This latter figure demonstrates considerable passivity and is the second lowest in the country.

TABLE 7.6   Ontario Voter Turnout in Recent Federal and Provincial Elections

Federal Elections		Provincial Elections	
1974	74%	1977	66%
1979	78%	1981	58%
1980	72%	1985	62%
1984	76%	1987	63%
1988	75%	1990	64%
1993	68%	1995	65%
Average	73.8%	Average	63.0%

Source: *Reports of the Chief Election Officer,* calculations by author.

Thus far, Ontario has been portrayed as having a single political culture, but a northern regional sub-culture is also evident.[10] This is a culture of alienation, dependence, handouts, and frustration, based on isolated settlements, distance from Toronto, poor communications, and inadequate services. The north is ethnically diverse, with Native Peoples, French, Finns, and many other groups. Its economy is based on extraction of natural resources, which means single-industry towns, vulnerability to external markets, processing outside the region, limited employment opportunities, emigration, and pollution. Even when the southern Ontario economy is booming, much discontent is evident in the North. Some observers have drawn parallels between Northern Ontario and Atlantic Canada.

Finally, it can be mentioned that while Ontario does not appear to be as patronage-oriented as the old Quebec or even the modern Atlantic provinces, it is hardly beyond reproach in this respect.[11] A vast patronage system pervaded the province during the 1943–85 period, basically involving the appointment of faithful Conservative supporters to hundreds of semi-independent agencies, boards, and commissions. However, the public service has been based on the merit principle longer than in most provinces, though not so rigidly as in Ottawa.

POLITICAL PARTIES

Party System

Until 1985, the most obvious aspect of the Ontario party system was the dominance of the Progressive Conservative party, which established a modern-day record for political longevity in Canada. While the margin of dominance was not great—there were three minority governments, and the party never won more than 50 percent of the popular vote—the PCs enjoyed 12 consecutive election victories. Among the leading explanations of this phenomenon are the following:[12] given its economic prosperity, Ontario was relatively easy to govern; the federal government was used as a scapegoat for the province's problems; party leaders established favourable personal images; the selection of a new leader every 10 years or so provided an impression of change; the opposition was divided, and therefore no obvious alternative emerged; the party developed a superb electoral organization; the party was flooded with campaign funds as a result of its close ties to business; it maintained a low profile on the assumption that an electorate which barely recognized the provincial government's existence would also be unaware of its faults; the party moulded its policies to the province's progressive conservative political culture; the politicians established and then relied heavily upon a strong provincial public service; and the party governed in accordance with public opinion polls.

The quality of leadership and the alternating of leaders should be particularly emphasized. Ontario was the only province, for example, that did not change governments in the 1970 period, probably because Ontario Tories made such a point about changing from one leader, John Robarts, to another, Bill Davis.

The Conservatives were finally defeated in 1985, and it would seem that five of the factors mentioned earlier were lacking in that campaign. With a Conservative federal government in office, problems could not be blamed so easily on Ottawa; Frank Miller did not establish a favourable image and, given that he was older than the retiring Davis, his selection did not provide an impression of change; Miller chose to establish his own error-prone campaign organization in place of the Big Blue Machine; and his policies were perceived as being too right-wing. This last point was no disadvantage to Mike Harris in 1995.

The Tory defeat emphasizes another respect in which the Ontario party system is unique—it is a more persistent three-party system than elsewhere. Between 1943 and 1951 and since 1967, all three parties have attracted at least 20 percent of the popular vote; the CCF/NDP has formed the official Opposition on four occasions; and, between 1981 and 1995, all three parties elected majority governments. It is often thought that a three-party system is transitional, and that eventually one of the parties will disappear. Some have predicted, for example, that the NDP would displace the Liberals, given the high degree of industrialization and urbanization in the province.[13] But, Ontario has had a relatively stable balance among three parties now for almost 50 years, (see Table 7.7), and especially since the NDP became competitive again in 1967.[14]

TABLE 7.7   Party Support in Ontario, 1970–1995

	Years in Office	Average Percentage of Vote	Percentage of Seats
Conservatives	15 (60%)	37.0	42.4
Liberals	5 (20%)	34.5	33.1
NDP	5 (20%)	26.8	24.4

Source: *Reports of the Chief Election Officer,* calculations by author.

FIGURE 7.1   Percentage of Vote by Party in Ontario Elections, 1970-1995

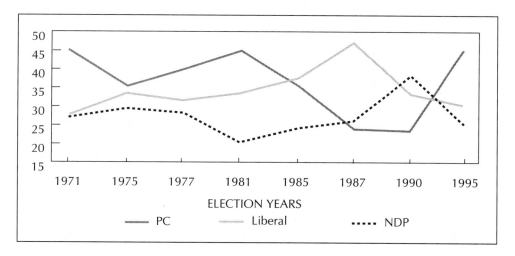

Party Organization

The three parties provide an interesting contrast in terms of their organization.[15] The orientation of the Conservative party in its heyday was almost exclusively electoral, and until 1985 the "Big Blue Machine" repeatedly proved itself to be the most professional, innovative, and successful organization in the election business. It excelled in campaign schools for candidates and organizers, advertising techniques, sophisticated polling, staging of the leader's tour, and in producing glossy brochures and other election paraphernalia. It was not entirely a cadre party, for it sought a large membership and chiefly kept its members involved by providing the excitement of participation or the hope of reward, as opposed to permitting them to contribute to party policy in any meaningful way. The Liberal party, in Opposition, was notoriously weak in organization, run primarily out of the publicly funded leader's office at Queen's Park. By 1988, however, it had developed an impressive extra-parliamentary organization and moved midway between a mass and a cadre party. Its rules on reviewing the leader's performance and voting at nomination meetings are stricter than the Tories, its conventions more frequent, and it recently adopted a new process for making party policy which theoretically combined input from both membership and caucus. The New Democratic Party sees itself as a mass party and, at least in Opposition, generally lived up to the claim in democratic procedures, leadership accountability, and emphasis on membership-generated party policy. In practice, the NDP was not an ideal mass party and a party establishment, which usually got its way, could always be identified. Nonetheless, at least until 1990, there continued to be a significant difference between the operations of the NDP and its competitors. In government, these differences were reduced. Perhaps because of the poor economy, the Rae government repudiated several longstanding party policies, including the nationalization of the car insurance industry. The party then amended its rules, and began to solicit corporate contributions.

Federal-Provincial Party Links[16]

Of the three Ontario parties, the NDP has the closest relationship between its federal and provincial wings. In fact, the NDP is really a single party, while the other two have separate federal and provincial organizations. The NDP has a common federal-provincial membership with a predominantly provincial orientation, although it now establishes separate federal and provincial constituency executives. Leading up to the 1993 federal election, relations between the federal and Ontario parties became strained, especially over the Rae government's decision to break collective agreements with public sector workers.

The Conservatives have long had separate federal and provincial organizations in Ontario with distinctive memberships, constituency executives, and head offices. The extent to which the provincial Tory electoral organization has been at the disposal of the federal party in the latter's election campaigns has depended almost entirely on the relationship between the provincial and federal leaders. Because the Liberals were usually in power in Ottawa after 1943, there was little reason for the provincial Tories to be at odds with the federal Conservative party, although Premier Leslie Frost was not very supportive of George Drew. Problems arose mainly when the party assumed office in Ottawa as well, as in the John Diefenbaker and Joe Clark periods. Bill Davis did all he could to help Brian Mulroney get elected in 1984, through personal appearances and by lending personnel, but he did not aid Joe Clark in 1980. Similarly, Frost was exceedingly active on behalf of John Diefenbaker in 1957-58, but Robarts was not so enthusiastic in the 1960s. The provincial Conservative leader may have sometimes felt a cross-party identity which constrained his support of his federal party leader, such as with Bill Davis and Joe Clark on constitutional and energy questions.

The Liberal situation is even more interesting, primarily because of the war between Mitch Hepburn and Mackenzie King from 1936 to 1942. The battles arose from King's lack of recognition of Hepburn's support for the federal Liberal cause in 1935. This omission was compounded by other slights, imagined or real, and culminated in Hepburn's dissatisfaction with King's approach to the Second World War. This feud not only poisoned intra-party relations at the time, but had lasting effects on the party's federal-provincial relationship. Although relations were sometimes more cordial after 1943, disputes arose over the division of party funds, as did occasional policy differences, especially during the Trudeau era after 1968. In 1976 the Liberal party separated into two organizations, the provincial Ontario Liberal Party and the federal Liberal Party of Canada (Ontario). Henceforth, the party was characterized by separate memberships, constituency associations, finances, provincial executives, and provincial annual meetings, and little co-operation between the respective leaders in election campaigns. When Pierre Trudeau left the picture in 1984, however, relations improved considerably.

The discrepancy in federal and provincial Liberal success in the province after 1900 often led to more able Liberals seeking federal careers, leaving the provincial party with less impressive personnel. Among the provincial Conservative leaders, however, only George Drew went on to lead the federal party. Most federal cabinet ministers from Ontario (with the exception of Oliver Mowat, Newton Rowell, and Sheila Copps), did not have backgrounds in provincial politics. Prime Ministers King and Pearson, for example, showed no previous interest in provincial affairs.

Party Leadership[17]

In the pre-1943 period, three leaders gained prominence: Oliver Mowat, James Whitney, and Howard Ferguson. Each led his party to at least three election victories, and each possessed the two qualities which Wilson has identified as necessary to political success in Ontario—a capacity to manage the affairs of the province in a businesslike way, and the ability to maintain an equitable balance among the principal interests of the province.[18] They also shared a keen sense of the public mood, and an antenna-like sensitivity to what was on the electorate's mind.[19]

In the long Conservative period after 1943, George Drew, Leslie Frost, John Robarts, and Bill Davis also met Wilson's criteria.[20] Managerial capacity was probably most evident in the case of Frost and Robarts, who often spoke of their role in terms of being "chairman of the board," but all four regularly convinced the electorate that they were most capable of "running the store." All came from impeccable Tory (Anglo-Saxon, Protestant, southern Ontario lawyer-business) backgrounds. Yet, they were capable of responding to the demands of other groups in the province, balanced major interests, and demonstrated an amazing flexibility of action when occasion demanded. Drew's social and labour legislation, Robarts' promotion of francophone interests, and Davis' eventual recognition of Roman Catholic educational rights stand out in this respect. Some felt that Davis' approach to official bilingualism was lacking in sensitivity, although he avoided a violent confrontation on the subject through the "politics of stealth." Davis also showed that he was the master of conciliation and compromise on many other issues. He demonstrated courage in splitting from his federal party on the constitutional issue, but he will perhaps be most favourably remembered for his innovative record as Minister of Education. Davis is also living proof that a leader in Ontario need not be charismatic in order to be successful; in fact, it was his image of a decent, cautious, and trustworthy leader that most found so attractive.

Frank Miller, in addition to inheriting the unfortunate Davis legacy of financing separate schools, had too much of a rural-small town orientation for an increasingly urban electorate, was too right-wing, and was thought to be lacking in managerial capacity. But coming from North Bay and being right-wing did not disadvantage Mike Harris in 1995.

While the Conservative party is in power, it grants its leader a good deal of authority and deference, but a defeated leader, as Miller discovered, is not so respected. The striking Ontario Tory practice of "regeneration" has already been mentioned. In order to wash away the stains of the past and to present an image of freshness and vigour, the leader resigned while the party was still in power and still strong, although this practice did not work in 1985.

The Liberal party experienced many leadership problems between the Mowat and Peterson eras, perhaps because the most capable Ontario Liberals entered federal politics. Hepburn's performance as the only Liberal leader to become provincial premier between 1905 and 1985 made life difficult for his successors. A difficult man to deal with on a personal level, he also caused a rift with the federal branch of the party. Then, with luck and skill, David Peterson, who preferred to take more personal initiative in the policy-making process, moved into the leadership vacuum created by the selection of Frank Miller on the Conservative side.[21]

The CCF/NDP has not been so concerned with party leadership, being leaderless for 10 years (1932-42), and then keeping Ted Jolliffe and Donald MacDonald on regardless of election results. However, many would have preferred Stephen Lewis to stay on after 1977, and in 1981 the choice of Bob Rae, then an attractive, articulate, and prominent federal MP, may have been a reflection of an increased concern with leadership image. His leadership was no small contributor to the 1990 NDP victory, after which Rae appeared to run a tight ship. Widely praised for his mastery of the issues, Rae was sometimes criticized for intellectual arrogance and short-circuiting the institutional system. Moreover, once in power, Rae declared that he was not just the leader of the party, but of the government. Party policy resolutions were no longer so sacrosanct; while they were "an important guide" for the government, action had to be determined within the limits "of what we can afford." Much grumbling occurred at party council meetings and conventions after 1990, but party activists were persuaded to criticize with restraint.

The NDP elects its leader at a traditional party convention, but the incumbent must be re-elected every second year. When they chose Mike Harris in 1990 the Conservatives moved to a new system allowing all card-carrying members to vote in their own constituency but weighted the process so that every constituency would have equal clout.[22] The Liberals chose Lyn McLeod in 1992 by another innovation in which delegates to the leadership convention were chosen on the basis of support for the various leadership candidates among all party members voting in each constituency. Leadership candidates in all parties must file a report of their contributions and expenses with the Commission on Election Finance.

Party Ideology

Successful political leaders and parties in Ontario have had both a progressive and a conservative side to their policies. On the one hand they have been businesslike and concerned with the economic development of the province while on the other responding to demands for change from the less privileged elements of society The Conservatives, for example, had close ties to the business community which were reflected in many of their policies: low corporate taxes and tax concessions, minimal regulation in such areas as pollution control or reforestation, exemptions to laws requiring domestic processing, and social program cutbacks in order to maintain the province's Triple-A credit rating.[23] In the natural resource sector, Conservative governments intervened in the economy solely to promote private sector development.[24] Similarly, they had to be dragged into the Canada Pension Plan and medicare, and maintained high health care premiums. However, it is also true that Ontario politics has generally not been as conservative as that of other provinces with Conservative parties in power. Ontario Conservatives were often genuinely progressive, as evidenced by the early creation of Ontario Hydro and the Workmen's Compensation Board, as well as George Drew's 1943 radical post-war election platform, the innovative structure of Metro Toronto, regional government, compulsory seat belts, and rent control. Other Ontario innovations have included a provincial law reform commission and snowmobile legislation.[25] Thus, the two ideological strands were usually kept in balance.

This presented a problem for the Liberal party in Ontario. It often found difficulty adopting an alternative stance when the Conservatives seemed to be all over the ideological map. Hepburn's radicalism was largely empty rhetoric and partly a reaction to the Depression; after his departure, the party was sometimes to the left and sometimes to the right of the Conservatives. When Tory Premier John Robarts opposed medicare, the Liberals supported it and were clearly to the left. But, when the Davis regime sponsored regional government, educational experimentation, and teachers' right to strike, the Liberals were to the right. When Miller assumed the Tory leadership, the Liberals again seized the opportunity to move to the left, this time with greater success. After obtaining their majority, however, they became much more conservative.

In opposition, the CCF/NDP was clearly on the left in its emphasis on social issues such as medicare, rent control, occupational health and safety, workers' compensation, child care, nursing homes, and equal pay for work of equal value, as well as on such economic issues as pollution, disappearing farmland, job security, tax reform, and the decline in the mining and forestry industries.[26] The party also claimed credit for forcing the Conservatives to maintain their moderately progressive stance, as is evidenced by cases such as the 22 points, medicare, rent control, and occupational health and safety, and for popularizing many of the Liberal policies of 1985. On the other hand, the NDP aims for a "pragmatic radicalism," as the fate of the Waffle movement attests.[27] The NDP experienced a period of enormous strain in 1970-72 when the far-left, ultra-nationalistic group known as the Waffle, which had formed within the party in 1969, engaged in public criticism of the NDP leadership and policy. When this internecine dispute began to paralyze party efforts to fight external enemies, Stephen Lewis took aim at the Waffle. The party decided that, while groups could caucus and work for change within the party, they could not hold press briefings, issue public statements, or organize conferences. Lewis also disavowed the nationalization issue and, while a more left-leaning group could usually be identified within the party even after 1972, Bob Rae governed with unanticipated moderation. Debate continues over how much of this ideological restraint reflected Rae's views, and how much resulted from the economic circumstances in which he found himself. Thus it could be said that all three Ontario parties have a progressive and a conservative element, or that all three try to operate within a fairly narrow progressive conservative ideological range. Until the 1995 election, some found it hard to tell the NDP and Liberals apart, but Mike Harris developed a much more right-wing image for the Conservative party.

ELECTIONS

Electoral System

The Ontario electoral system has been a traditional one, never deviating from the basic single-member, plurality system, except for a handful of two- and three-member ridings abolished by 1926. The legislature has been characterized by a certain degree of rural over-representation which benefited the Liberals before 1900, and usually aided the Conservatives afterwards. While the redistribution process was unimpressive, the gerrymandering of constituency boundaries was not as extensive as in many other provinces. Redistributions take place at the whim of the government, on average almost every 10 years. The first ostensibly impartial one was in 1962, followed by others in the mid-1970s and the mid-1980s, the latter being the most effective. The north was guaranteed 15 out of 130 seats, but the commission was otherwise supposed to stay within plus or minus 25 percent. Table 7.8 indicates that while the system was generally satisfactory in the 1990 election, a number of constituencies were far above or below the provincial mean, largely reflecting post-redistribution population changes. The Rae government postponed a redistribution based on the 1991 census until after the 1995 election, and Mike Harris promised to reduce the number of seats.

TABLE 7.8 Representational Disparities in the 1990 Election

Mean no. of voters per constituency	48,584
Largest constituency (York Centre)	101,558 (+109.0%)
Smallest constituency (Algoma)	21,437 (-55.9%)
Average variation from mean	16.5%
Constituencies within ± 10%	45%
Constituencies within ± 25%	80%

Source: *Reports of the Chief Election Officer,* calculations by author.

Following election contribution scandals of the early 1970s, Ontario became one of the pioneers in the area of election finance reform. Passed in time to regulate the 1975 election, its act made provisions for rigid controls on the amounts of contributions, along with disclosure, tax credits, and public subsidies. The Tory party became so successful at using the tax credit system by sending direct mail appeals to individuals that it almost halved its reliance on corporate contributions.[28] The NDP was moderately successful in its efforts to raise funds from individuals after the 1975 act severely limited its union donations, but the Liberal party found it difficult to attract sufficient individual or corporate contributions. The 1981 election, however, revealed that serious problems of equity continued because the act placed no limit on expenditures. Consequently, the 1985 Liberal-NDP pact called for spending limits at both the central and local levels, and other modifications were put in place by 1987. By then the Liberals were awash in corporate contributions; their fund-raising techniques included selling access to the premier or other ministers for $1,000 contributions to the party. In 1989, the Patricia Starr scandal over illegal contributions to the Liberal party revealed loopholes in the legislation, as well as the close relationship between the government and the development industry. Parties now face a spending ceiling of 40 cents per voter, candidates have a spending ceiling averaging about $45,000, the maximum annual contribution is $7,000 (doubled in an election year), and the 75 percent tax credit applies to the first $200 contributed. In addition to the public subsidy for candidates who get at least 15 percent of the vote, parties receive a subsidy of five cents per voter in ridings where their candidate achieved 15 percent of the vote.

Voting Behaviour

Support for the three Ontario parties can be differentiated in a variety of ways. Certain historic regional variations persisted, with eastern Ontario preferring the Conservatives, and the rural southwest the bedrock of Liberal strength. In the urban southwest, all three parties had their strengths, while in the north, the competition was usually between the Conservatives and the NDP, just as in Metro Toronto. In 1987 the Liberals gained province-wide support, as did the NDP in 1990. Thus, although a generally increasing three-party system is evident throughout the province, there are regional differences in party strength, and varied patterns of two- or three-party competition.[29] Rural incumbents have had the advantage of such ridings being safer than urban ones.[30] Traditionally, most of the Anglo-Saxon-Protestant vote has gone to the Conservatives, and the French and Roman Catholic vote to the Liberals. All three parties have made serious efforts to attract the "other ethnic" vote, especially in Toronto, which seems to be genuinely split as a result. The German vote in the Kitchener area has always been Liberal.

Of great interest to academics is whether class voting has displaced the emphasis on ethnicity, religion, and region. Traditional NDP seats tended to be in working-class ridings and the Ontario Federation of Labour tries to convince its members to vote NDP; but many of the party's activists and candidates are middle-class professionals.[31] One reason the NDP has enjoyed greater success in Ontario than in the five more eastern provinces is the strength of organized labour, but the other parties continue to attract much working-class support. Surveys rarely indicate as much class-conscious voting as might be expected in a highly industrialized province.

Two other aspects of Ontario voting behaviour also demand attention: voter apathy, and the federal-provincial relationship. As mentioned, Ontario has a high rate of voter abstention, with only about 63 percent of eligible persons voting in recent years. This is usually related to the lack of provincial orientation among Ontario residents, who have a 10 percent higher turnout in federal elections. It was often said that, before 1985, the governing Conservatives deliberately maintained a low profile between elections so the electorate would ignore provincial politics entirely, making it easier for the incumbents to get re-elected.

On the other hand, Ontario is often the main battleground of federal election campaigns, and a fierce Liberal-Conservative competition normally takes place. Moreover, the Liberals have generally fared better than the Conservatives in federal elections in this province, and have been particularly strong in Northern Ontario and Toronto, where they had been weakest provincially. Survey research bore out the fact that, at least until 1984, many residents voted Conservative provincially and Liberal federally. Evidence also suggests occasional co-operation between the parties, allowing the Conservatives to run strongly in provincial elections in return for limited opposition to federal Liberal candidates. There may be more logic to this phenomenon than meets the eye. The federal Liberal and provincial Conservative parties were both "government" parties, reflecting similar establishment interests. They were both leader-oriented, broker, middle-of-the-road parties, pursuing essentially similar policies.[32] In addition, there was undoubtedly a substantial degree of abstention in provincial elections among those who voted Liberal federally.[33] In 1984-5, however, Ontarians gave the nod to federal Conservatives and provincial Liberals, reversing the usual pattern, and raising the possibility of a deliberate attempt on the part of the electorate to balance their vote. More likely, they were voting against the two incumbent governments. The election of the NDP in 1990 revealed an almost total lack of federal-provincial voter consistency, as did the election of the Conservatives in 1995.

PRESSURE GROUPS AND THE MEDIA

Pressure Groups[34]

Ontario has hundreds of pressure groups, reflecting the diversity of its economy and society as well as the openness on the part of the government to receive input from such sources. Business and professional groups undoubtedly received a warm reception from the many Conservative governments, as well as from the Liberals. Among the many business groups are the Ontario Chamber of Commerce, the Canadian Federation of Independent Business, the Ontario Mining Association, the Ontario division of the Canadian Manufacturers' Association, and various subsidiary manufacturing groups. The insurance industry used its close ties to the Ontario government to challenge federal pension and medicare proposals in the 1960s, as did the Ontario Mining Association in opposing federal tax changes. Another group active at the provincial level is the property industry, including the Housing and Urban Development Association of Canada, the Urban Development Institute, and such individual firms as Tridel, especially as revealed in the Patti Starr scandal. The national head offices of most banks, finance, resource, and manufacturing companies are located a stone's throw from Queen's Park, which gives such companies easier access to government than in other provinces or even Ottawa.

TABLE 7.9   Leading Ontario Pressure Groups

Peak Business	Ontario Chamber of Commerce
	Canadian Federation of Independent Business
	Canadian Manufacturers' Association
	Association of Major Power Consumers of Ontario
Industrial	Ontario Mining Association
	Automotive Parts Manufacturing Association of Canada
	Ontario Forest Industries Association
	Ontario Forestry Association
	Housing and Urban Development Association of Canada
	Ontario Trucking Association
	Ontario Home Builders' Association
	Ontario Road Builders' Association
Agriculture	Ontario Federation of Agriculture
Labour	Ontario Federation of Labour
Professional	Ontario Medical Association
	Law Society of Upper Canada
	Ontario Dental Association
	Ontario Nurses' Association
	Ontario Teachers' Federation
	Ontario Secondary School Teachers' Federation
	Canadian Federation of Students-Ontario
Ethnic	Association canadienne-française d'Ontario
	Ontario Métis Aboriginal Association
	Ontario Multicultural Association
Religious	Ontario Conference of Catholic Bishops
Institutional	Association of Municipalities of Ontario
	Ontario Hospital Association
	Ontario School Trustees' Council
	Ontario Association of Children's Aid Societies
Environmental	Temagami Wilderness Society
	Federation of Ontario Naturalists
	Conservation Council of Ontario
Public Interest	Ontario Social Development Council
	Ontario Coalition Against Poverty
	Ontario Coalition for Better Child Care
	Ontario Coalition for Social Justice

On the professional side, an obvious intimacy once existed between the Conservatives and the Ontario Medical Association (as evidenced in the establishment of a doctors' fee schedule and in allowing doctors to extra-bill), as well as with the Ontario Bar Association. Other professional associations such as the Ontario Teachers' Federation, the Ontario Secondary School Teachers' Federation (OSSTF), and the Ontario Dental Association have experienced more difficulty with the government. Many such professional groups have a special role in the province in that they have been granted powers of self-regulation. Thus, the OMA functions as a pressure group for doctors, while the College of Physicians and Surgeons of Ontario regulates the profession. The same distinction can be made between the Ontario Nurses' Association and the College of Nurses of Ontario, and the Ontario Bar Association and the Law Society of Upper Canada.

Many other pressure groups exist in Ontario: the Ontario Federation of Agriculture, and many specialized agricultural groups; the Ontario Federation of Labour, affiliated with the Canadian Labour Congress and NDP; the Association canadienne-française d'Ontario (ACFO), and an assortment of other ethnic organizations; religious groups including the militantly Protestant Orange Order, still able to voice some opposition to separate schools in 1984, and the Roman Catholic Church; women's groups; the gay community; the Ontario Social Development Council; the Ontario Hospital Association; and various groupings of municipalities. Most of those mentioned are "institutionalized" in the sense that they are permanent organizations and have fairly close relations with the government, especially the bureaucracy. Other groups have chosen to operate through premiers' confidants. Two important issue-oriented groups were the Stop Spadina and People or Planes groups which, temporarily at least, halted construction of the Spadina Expressway and the proposed Pickering airport. Other issue-oriented groups come and go, more recent examples being the Temagami Wilderness Society, the Save the Rouge Valley System, and the Coalition against Sunday Shopping.

The Media

Toronto's *Globe and Mail* aspires to be Canada's national daily newspaper and has influence across the country. Its proprietor is Ken Thomson, who also owns over 20 other less distinguished dailies in Ontario. In 1994 Thomson closed the *Oshawa Times* after its employees went on strike. The Southam Newspaper Group has nine daily papers in the province, while the *Toronto Sun* division of Maclean Hunter Ltd., bought by Ted Rogers, also owns the *Ottawa Sun*. The largest independently owned daily is the the *Toronto Star* which is widely distributed within the province. As can be seen in Table 7.10, the Southam and Thomson chains each have a daily circulation of about 600,000 in Ontario, while the *Toronto Star* alone sits at 500,000.

Toronto is the headquarters of the English division of the Canadian Broadcasting Corporation, as well as the CTV network. CBC television has wholly owned stations in Toronto and Ottawa, as well as eight affiliated stations in other centres. Eaton-owned CFTO in Toronto is the flagship station of CTV, while the other Eaton-owned Baton stations within Ontario are located in Ottawa, Sudbury, Timmins, North Bay, Sault Ste. Marie, Pembroke, London, Wingham, and Kitchener. The Global TV network serves most of the province as does the provincially owned channel, TVOntario. CBC English radio has five wholly owned and four affiliated stations in Ontario, while Radio Canada has one French television station in Ottawa and four French radio stations in the province. A handful of unaffiliated private television stations also exist, as do hundreds of private radio stations.

The press gallery at Queen's Park has about 50 active members, mostly representing the various media outlets mentioned. The *Toronto Star* is probably the most biased newspaper in terms of its coverage of provincial politics, rarely wavering from its Liberal stance. Sometimes the best investigative journalism is done by reporters who are not even members of the press gallery.[35]

TABLE 7.10   Daily Newspapers in Ontario, 1994

Newspaper	Circulation	Chain
Barrie Examiner	12,570	Thomson
Belleville Intelligencer	18,348	Thomson
Brantford Expositor	28,288	Southam
Brockville Recorder and Times	15,903	Independent
Cambridge Reporter	11,376	Thomson
Chatham Daily News	17,017	Thomson
Cobourg Daily Star	5,153	Independent
Cornwall Standard-Freeholder	18,927	Thomson
Fort Francis Daily Bulletin	2,776	Independent
Guelph Mercury	18,253	Thomson
Hamilton Spectator	128,841	Southam
Kenora Daily Miner and News	4,836	Maclean Hunter (Bowes)
Kingston Whig Standard	29,414	Southam
Kirkland Lake Northern Daily News	5,626	Thomson
Kitchener-Waterloo Record	72,288	Southam
Lindsay Daily Post	9,321	Thomson
London Free Press	110,308	Independent
Niagara Falls Review	21,727	Thomson
North Bay Nugget	22,546	Southam
Orillia Packet and Times	10,481	Thomson
Ottawa Le Droit	35,666	UniMédia
Ottawa Citizen	166,639	Southam
Ottawa Sun	51,648	Maclean Hunter (TO Sun)
Owen Sound Sun Times	22,511	Southam
Pembroke Daily News	1,500*	Independent
Pembroke Observer	7,975	Thomson
Peterborough Examiner	26,282	Thomson
Port Hope Guide	3,174	Independent
St. Catharines Standard	39,836	Independent
St. Thomas Times Journal	8,892	Thomson

TABLE 7.10 continued

Newspaper	Circulation	Chain
Sarnia Observer	24,000	Thomson
Sault Ste. Marie Star	24,508	Southam
Simcoe Reformer	9,618	Thomson
Stratford Beacon-Herald	13,180	Independent
Sudbury Star	26,913	Thomson
Thunder Bay Times-News	7,645	Thomson
Thunder Bay Chronicle-Journal	28,902	Thomson
Timmins Daily Press	12,280	Thomson
Financial Post (Toronto)	82,122	Maclean Hunter (TO Sun)
Toronto Globe and Mail	206,920*	Thomson
Toronto Star	502,846	Independent
Toronto Sun	253,837	Maclean Hunter (TO Sun)
Welland-Port Colborne Tribune	17,693	Thomson
Windsor Star	86,236	Southam
Woodstock-Ingersoll Sentinel Review	10,748	Thomson

Source: *Canadian Advertising and Rates Data* (August 1994).

* *Globe and Mail* figures are for Ontario; national circulation is 317,972; *Pembroke Daily News* figures are author's estimate).

GOVERNMENT INSTITUTIONS

Ontario's governmental institutions are distinctive because they operate in the largest province. Moreover, because of their innovative tendency, they have often served as models for other provinces.

Executive

The lieutenant-governor's position has been an orthodox ceremonial one. Some speculation about the lieutenant-governor's role ensued when the 1985 election returned 52 Conservatives, 48 Liberals, and 25 New Democrats. In this case, John Black Aird first asked incumbent premier Frank Miller to form a government and, by the time it was defeated in the legislature on the basis of its throne speech, the NDP and Liberals had signed a two-year pact which guaranteed the security of a Liberal minority government. Miller resigned, and Aird called on Liberal leader David Peterson to form a government, without further controversy.

The cabinet increased from five members to about 26 or 27 over the years, but is not much larger than that of other provinces, with smaller populations.[36] Frank Miller's first cabinet had 33 ministers, largely because of promises made during the leadership convention, while David Peterson's minority government cabinet had only 23, partly because some members had to be free for legislative committee assignments. Ontario premiers have primarily sought an equitable regional balance in forming their cabinets; Peterson's cabinet contained the first black and Oriental ministers in the province; and Bob Rae's 26-member cabinet featured 11 women, including one black female. When Rae revamped his cabinet in 1993, he set up a two-tier structure with 20 ministers invited to cabinet meetings, and seven other ministers without portfolio, attached to senior ministers, who did not attend meetings. This innovation allowed Rae to demote certain ministers without removing them entirely.

The informal cabinet operations became increasingly inefficient over time, leading Premier John Robarts to appoint a committee on government productivity in 1969, headed by the president of Labatt's brewery. In response to its recommendations, in the early 1970s, the entire executive structure was transformed by Robarts' successor, Bill Davis. He established new cabinet committees, including the Policy and Priorities Board, chaired by the premier and perhaps modeled on the priorities and planning committee in Ottawa; the Management Board, which was a revamped Treasury Board; and three policy committees: social development, resources development, and justice, designed to improve the areas of priority-setting, financial management, and policy co-ordination. Another innovation was the "policy minister," a provincial secretary for each of the three main policy fields who had no departmental responsibilities. These policy ministers did not become as powerful as many had feared or expected, and the position was eventually abolished by David Peterson. Indeed, even in the latter Davis period, there seemed to be a general lack of enthusiasm about the way the whole new system operated. Some saw it as delaying rather than improving policy making, and it did not prevent Davis from embarking on sudden personal initiatives, such as having the government buy 25 percent of the Suncor Corporation and reversing government policy on separate schools. That premier's independence from his ministers was also evidenced by his weekly breakfast meetings with his "kitchen cabinet"—party strategists and backroom advisers—which may have been more important than meetings of the cabinet. Finally, it should be added that Davis also reformed the cabinet support system. Somewhat akin to the prime minister's office and privy council office in Ottawa, he established an office of the premier and a cabinet office to provide secretariats to cabinet committees. Under Davis, however, the same person served as head of both offices,[37] unlike the federal model's separation of partisan and bureaucratic functions, adopted by Peterson and Rae. Peterson also set up a premier's council on technology and on health strategy.

Rae's cabinet committees in 1994 consisted of a Policy and Priorities Board, Management Board, and Treasury Board, and committees on social policy, economic development, environment policy, justice, and legislation/regulations. He included the party whip in the cabinet and appointed a number of NDP backbenchers to cabinet committees. A partisan principal secretary headed the premier's office, which included sections responsible for media, scheduling, policy, communications, and liaison with ministers and caucus. Rae's cabinet office was headed by the cabinet secretary, originally a career bureaucrat, but later replaced with the premier's principal secretary, David Agnew. Since the person employed in this position was regarded as the province's top public servant, such a partisan appointment raised much furor, but Rae countered that it was necessary to ensure the government's mandate was implemented. Rae altered Peterson's other agencies somewhat, having a premier's council on economic renewal and another on health, well-being, and social justice, and then combining them.

Legislature

Ontario was the only one of the four original partners in Confederation to establish a unicameral legislature.[38] Ontario institutions were created anew (unlike the situation in Nova Scotia and New Brunswick), and one chamber was deemed sufficient for the minor responsibilities which provinces were expected to assume. In 1938, Ontario officially adopted the name "Provincial Parliament," with members called MPPs, reflecting the fact that the province had become quite important after all.[39] The size of the legislature gradually increased from 82 in 1867 to 130 in 1987.[40]

Until recently, the Ontario legislature operated in a typically "irresponsible" manner, that is, under the complete control of the cabinet. Sessions were short, allowances low, facilities few, and private members had little influence. The cabinet usually governed by regulation and order-in-council, and no proper oral question period existed until about 1970. Since the mid-1970s, however, the Ontario legislature has become the most advanced of any province, with the possible exception of Quebec.

This dramatic transformation resulted mostly from the recommendations of the Camp Commission (1972-75), appointed as an afterthought once the provincial executive branch had been reformed. Another major factor was the minority government situation which existed from 1975 to 1981. The legislature is now characterized by longer sessions (an average of about 90 days per year), a proper question period, the enhanced status of a Speaker elected by all members, and an effective committee system, including busy standing committees, often productive select committee investigations, and an opposition-chaired Public Accounts Committee. House business is better organized, the estimates are more adequately examined, and there is some scope for private members' bills. Most significant, though, are improvements to members' services: offices at Queen's Park and in the constituency, an assistant at each level, caucus research staffs, mailings, telephone lines, accommodation and travel allowances, better pensions, and much higher pay ($42,217 in indemnity and $14,159 in tax-free allowance after a 5.5 percent cut in 1993). A large proportion of members, such as ministers, parliamentary assistants, and party whips, receive supplementary payments for occupying leadership positions. Ontario's members have the highest level of resources among provincial legislators.[41] Most members spend a great deal of time on their "case load," but with the assistance of staff and research support.

The Liberal-NDP pact of mid-1985 significantly upgraded the position of private and opposition members, at least for a two-year period, by allowing them to vote against individual pieces of government legislation without the threat of precipitating an election. The NDP agreed that it would not vote against the government on a non-confidence motion during that time and the Liberals promised not to call an election. The deal also called for a more important role for legislative committees and the introduction of televised coverage of the proceedings. After majority Liberal and NDP governments were elected, certain legislative reforms were retained. Estimates are now examined by a standing committee chaired by an opposition member, and chairs of the other 10 standing committees are distributed in proportion to party standings in the house. Bills can go to standing committees or committee of the whole, or both, after second reading. Both the Liberals and NDP also made rule changes which facilitated the passage of government legislation, by such means as limiting the length of speeches, the time spent on petitions, and the duration of bell ringing.

Bureaucracy[42]

According to Statistics Canada, Ontario employs about 88,000 people in ministries and agencies, another 43,000 in government business enterprises, and a further 200,000 in the wider public sector. Ontario's Civil Service Commission was established in 1918, but this did not prevent patronage appointments to the bureaucracy inevitably coinciding with changes in government. The Conservatives were in office for 42 years after 1943, so the problem of wholesale staff turnovers did not arise; instead, the service grew in partisan association with the Conservative party, with little concern about expertise.[43] The Treasury Board was strengthened in 1954, and the Civil Service Commission experienced many changes in the next 10 years. During the early 1960s, as the complexity of public issues began to place higher demands on the cabinet and legislature, the government recognized the need for a more modern, expert, permanent public service. Since then, the province has developed an increasingly impressive bureaucracy, often capable of challenging federal administrative proposals. The structure of the Ontario public service as well as the cabinet was reformed as a result of the activities of a committee on government productivity in 1970-71. Departments were reorganized, and the Management Board was given greater control over financial and personnel administration. The appointment of an ombudsman in 1975 and the expansion of the office of provincial auditor enhanced control over the bureaucracy; so did the Freedom of Information Act introduced by the Peterson government. Table 7.11 indicates the departmental structure under Bob Rae in 1994.

TABLE 7.11   Ontario Government Ministries, 1994

Agriculture and Food
Attorney General
Citizenship
Community and Social Services
Consumer and Commercial Relations
Culture, Tourism and Recreation
Economic Development and Trade
Education and Training
Environment and Energy
Finance
Health
Housing
Labour
Management Board
Municipal Affairs
Natural Resources
Northern Development and Mines
Solicitor General and Correctional Services
Transportation

Most deputy ministers are career public servants and remain on the job when the government changes. The Rae government criticized the senior bureaucracy for being less than loyal to the new regime, but some observers felt that the fault was more with the NDP, which was overly suspicious of the bureaucracy's loyalty. Most deputy ministers were gradually replaced during the NDP period, but not primarily for partisan reasons. The merit system is otherwise modified by employment equity programs which give preference to women, natives, visible minorities, and the disabled. The public service operates in English, except for the provision of French-language services in designated local areas. Until the NDP regime, the bureaucracy engaged in collective bargaining without the right to strike, but most public servants now have that right as well as broader political rights.

On the other hand, like many other provincial governments, the Rae government broke collective bargaining agreements in both the public service and wider public sectors. Its social contract legislation in 1993 imposed a three-year salary freeze and a number of unpaid days of leave, regardless of what was contained in contracts previously signed. In taking this step, the NDP attracted more criticism than governments of other provinces because of the party's links to organized labour.

Ontario possesses some 700 semi-independent Crown corporations, agencies, boards, and commissions.[44] These were often established to take decisions out of the hands of politicians, such as issuing liquor licenses or censoring films, and to perform commercial or quasi-judicial functions. Most were created during the Conservative regime, and one reason they are so numerous is that they present a façade of limited government appropriate to a conservative party.[45] The largest is Ontario Hydro, pioneer of provincial public power utilities; others include the Ontario Northland Transportation System, the Ontario Municipal Board, the Ontario human rights, water resources, and housing Commissions, the Workers' Compensation Board, and the Ontario Arts Council. While the initial reasons for guaranteeing the semi-independence of such bodies may have been valid, there is growing concern they have become too independent and unaccountable. Each has its own staff, but the governing boards are appointed by the cabinet, and have proven to be a convenient way of rewarding service to the Ontario Progressive Conservative Party and later to the Liberals and NDP.[46] The NDP put a number of sympathetic people on the board of Ontario Hydro, for example, and appointed successive presidents who shared its views, placing the Crown corporation under political control and in a position to begin downsizing operations. The NDP also established new Crown corporations in the fields of transportation, water, and realty, and allowed the former to enter into arrangements with the private sector to build a toll highway. Ontario has also used the royal commission device on many occasions, especially since 1960, to investigate alleged scandals and to study such important policy questions as civil rights and electric power.

TABLE 7.12   Leading Ontario Agencies, Boards, Commissions and Crown Corporations, 1994

Crown Corporations	Ontario Housing Corporation
	Ontario Lottery Corporation
	Ontario Hydro
	Ontario Northland Transportation Commission
	Ontario Place Corporation
	GO Transit
	TVOntario
Agencies, boards, and commissions	Criminal Injuries Compensation Board
	Ontario Municipal Board
	Police Complaints Commissioner
	Employment Equity Commissioner
	Ontario Council on University Affairs
	Environmental Appeal Board
	Rent Review Hearings Board
	Northern Ontario Heritage Fund Corporation
	Ontario Advisory Council on Women's Issues
	Workers' Compensation Board
	Ontario Human Rights Commission

Judiciary

The court structure in Ontario originally consisted of provincial courts, with civil, criminal, and family divisions; intermediate county and district courts; and the Supreme Court of Ontario, divided into the High Court of Justice and the Court of Appeal. In 1990, Attorney General Ian Scott restructured the court system, eliminating the county and district courts by combining them with the high court. He added small claims to this level, which was collectively renamed the Ontario Court of Justice, general division. This left the Ontario Court of Justice, provincial division (criminal and family), as well as justices of the peace who perform marriages and handle minor offenses, at the bottom, and the Court of Appeal at the top. As in the other provinces, judges of the higher courts are appointed by the federal government, while the provincial cabinet names lower level judges. This restructuring was related to a serious backlog of cases in the courts and, after the Supreme Court's 1990 *Askov* decision that a delay of almost two years between a preliminary hearing and trial was excessive, the government abandoned thousands of relatively minor charges. In 1989, the Peterson government began to appoint provincial court judges on the recommendation of a non-partisan committee.

Municipal Government

Given the province's size and largely urban population, municipal government has become a significant operation. In fact, Ontario has one of most decentralized provincial-municipal structures in the country. The municipal units traditionally consisted of cities, towns, villages, and townships.[47] Southern Ontario also possessed counties, upper-tier municipalities on whose council sat representatives of lower-tier units within its boundaries, except for cities and some towns. This pre-Confederation system remained in place for about 100 years, until the creation of the Municipality of Metropolitan Toronto in 1954. That became a two-tier municipal government of a special type, an urban-municipal federation. Each of the 13 local municipalities retained its identity, and all were represented on the Metro council. The smaller units were amalgamated in 1967, and Metro Toronto now incorporates five cities, Toronto, North York, Scarborough, Etobicoke, and York, and one borough, East York. This development was judged so successful that a similar structure called regional government was designed for 11 other large urban centres in the province. These were established in the 1969-74 period and usually included urban areas not entirely contiguous, as well as some surrounding rural territory. The powers of the Metro council have gradually increased at the expense of the lower-tier councils, and suburban representation currently far exceeds that of the central city. This prompted a 1994 referendum in which City residents voted to leave Metro. On the other hand, many see the need for an even larger authority to handle problems extending well beyond Metro's boundaries to the Greater Toronto Area.

Regional government has been much more controversial than metropolitan government in Toronto but, with minor modifications, it seems destined to remain in place. Some of the old county councils have been more or less transformed into regional councils, and others which remain intact have the option of assuming additional powers from the lower-tier municipalities within them, as the restructured county of Oxford has done. In 1970, in a related development, Fort William and Port Arthur were consolidated into the single-tier city of Thunder Bay. That municipalities in Ontario have wide responsibilities, admittedly exercised under strict provincial supervision, means that municipal finance has become a serious problem. Municipal governments feel that they have increased local property taxes to their limits, and are dependent on provincial grants, which have been severely cut back in recent years.

POLITICAL EVOLUTION

1867-1970

Ontario began to assume its modern form with the arrival of thousands of United Empire Loyalists in the 1780s. These immigrants demanded the kind of political institutions to which they had been accustomed and, in response, the British government adopted the Constitutional Act of 1791. This act divided Ontario and Quebec into separate colonies—Upper and Lower Canada—each with a governor, executive and legislative councils, and an assembly, a development which gave rise to two main political groups, the Tories and the Reformers. The Tories were associated with the "Family Compact," the political and economic elite of the day, which monopolized the legislative council, while the Reformers were primarily concerned that the elected assembly be made supreme. As a result of the 1837 rebellion by William Lyon Mackenzie and others, Britain joined Ontario to Quebec in the Act of Union, and the principle of responsible government was soon established.

At that point, the reform movement split into two parts: the Clear Grits advocated other radical republican and democratic causes, while the moderate Reformers were more conservative. George Brown became the guiding spirit of the Clear Grits, John A. Macdonald, the inspiration of the Tories, and John Sandfield Macdonald led a moderate reform government between 1862 and 1864. One striking inheritance from the pre-Confederation period was certain conservative and reform voting patterns—Tories in the eastern towns and counties, much of it Loyalist country, and Clear Grits in the rural southwest. Another was the example of progressive or pragmatic conservatism. This was evidenced in the building of the Welland Canal, which marked the "acceptance of the positive role that government must play in order to counteract the vulnerabilities of the Canadian economy and policy."[48] With Confederation in 1867, Ontario became a separate province once again.

Ontario's first post-Confederation government was a coalition of Moderate Reformers and Conservatives, headed by John Sandfield Macdonald. This government's foremost accomplishment was its education bill, developed with the advice of Egerton Ryerson. Sandfield Macdonald's defeat in 1871 set the stage for 34 years of Liberal rule, during which Oliver Mowat served as premier for 24 years, an Ontario record, although Edward Blake held the position briefly before moving to the federal scene in 1872.

Mowat's long tenure was principally due to his ability to maintain a balance among the various interests in the province: Protestants and Catholics, pro- and anti-liquor groups, businessmen and trade unionists, farmers and urbanities, all regions, and liberals and conservatives. His watchwords were pragmatism and moderation, and he was a model of "conservative reform."[49] Mowat's was an activist government that pursued a policy of developing all sectors of the province—agriculture, mining, forestry, railways, and hydroelectricity—but not neglecting such social services as education, health, prisons, courts, and labour legislation.

Two of the most controversial issues during Mowat's term were alcohol and religion, but he handled both in a competent way. He restricted the sale of liquor to some extent, and held the first of five provincial plebiscites on the question of prohibition in 1894. As for religion, he had inherited a separate school system, and maintained a close alliance with the Roman Catholic hierarchy. Mowat is probably remembered even more for his successful challenge to Prime Minister John A. Macdonald on several matters of provincial rights. Mowat sometimes argued the province's case personally before the judicial committee of the Privy Council, and achieved favourable resolutions of the Manitoba boundary dispute, the question of the status of the lieutenant-governor, and the issue of control of navigable waters.[50] He and Macdonald also fought over the regulation of liquor sales in the province, and Mowat's victory gave subsequent premiers in all provinces considerable patronage opportunities.[51] In the 1894 election, two new groups from the United States entered the fray, the anti-Catholic Protestant Protective Association, and the pro-farmer Patrons of Industry.[52] Mowat remained as premier until 1896, when he accepted Wilfrid Laurier's invitation to join the new federal Liberal cabinet (as did his fellow premiers in Nova Scotia and New Brunswick), and became Minister of Justice in Ottawa.

After Mowat left the scene, the Ontario Liberals began their descent, although they managed to hold on to office for nine more years. Mowat's successor, Arthur Hardy, was chiefly responsible for the "manufacturing condition," the requirement that all pine timber cut on crown land be sawn into lumber in Canada before being exported.[53] His successor, George Ross, introduced a policy of "building up Ontario." Having previously extended the manufacturing condition to exports of pulpwood, Ross wished to survey the newer parts of the province, and to develop and exploit its resources. But the 1902-5 period was dominated by charges of patronage and electoral corruption, as well as by the liquor question. Rewarding party workers with government jobs continued with a vengeance, and false, lost, spoiled, and burned ballots were common.

The second outstanding Ontario premier was the Conservative James Whitney, elected in 1905. Whitney is often regarded as the "father of progressive conservatism" in Ontario, and is praised for two pioneering efforts, the creation of Ontario Hydro as a public corporation in the 1906-10 period, and the Workmen's Compensation Board of 1914.[54] On the hydro question, however, it was Adam Beck who spearheaded the crusade for public control of power as opposed to having companies supply electricity and it was more a businessmen's movement than a radical left-wing measure.[55] Among other things, these measures reflected the fact that Ontario was becoming an urban, industrial province.

Other initiatives in the Whitney era included a reorganization of the University of Toronto, legislation to reduce electoral corruption, lowering of school textbook prices, establishment of the Ontario Railway and Municipal Board (later the Ontario Municipal Board), and hospital and prison reform. These were accompanied by many actions designed to foster economic development, such as building roads and railways, especially the extension of the Temiskaming and Northern Ontario Railroad, assisting agriculture, and furthering northern expansion.

Whitney left several problems unsolved, however, and his record is marred by Regulation 17. Passed in 1912, the regulation restricted the use of French as a language of instruction to the first two years of schooling, and only to districts with sufficient demand. In some ways this was an honest response to public opinion and obvious inadequacies in bilingual schools, and was later slightly relaxed to allow students to receive French instruction beyond Grade 2 if they could not understand English. Whitney believed he was doing francophone Ontarians a favour by preparing them for life in an English-speaking province.[56] The language question became hopelessly complicated by religion, with the Orange Order fighting against the Association canadienne-française d'education d'Ontario, and Irish-Catholics battling with French-Catholics for supremacy on separate school boards.[57] The issue attained its greatest emotional height in the context of the conscription debate at the federal level five years later. Between 1905 and his death in 1914, Whitney had four lopsided electoral victories.

Whitney's successor was William Hearst, who served as premier during the First World War.[58] The two main legacies of the Hearst regime were Prohibition and the enfranchisement of women, although both issues were popularized by the Liberal leader, Newton Rowell. In response to a growing temperance movement,[59] Hearst brought in the far-reaching Ontario Temperance Act in 1916 which, when combined with action taken at the federal level, placed Ontario in an official state of total prohibition for the duration of the war. As suffragette efforts intensified, Hearst began to see the need to recognize women's contribution to the war. By 1919, women were permitted to vote and stand for election.

The Hearst government served a full five-year term before facing the electorate in October 1919. That election coincided with the third referendum on liquor, which further divided the Conservative party, already split on other issues. Moreover, the war, the conscription issue, and the federal wartime coalition government served to upset political loyalties and turned the farming community against both traditional parties. Liberal disunity over conscription and temperance also became evident when Rowell left to join the Union Government in Ottawa. These circumstances led the United Farmers of Ontario to contest the election with its own candidates, co-operating to some extent with the first concerted electoral action by the labour movement in urban areas.

The United Farmers of Ontario was formed in 1914, and its membership grew rapidly between 1917 and 1919. The agricultural community felt insecure because of the reduction in rural population and the perceived threat to the moral standing of the entire Ontario way of life. The withdrawal of promises to exempt farmers' sons from conscription inflamed these sentiments.

The Independent Labour Party was established in 1917, when urban workers began to feel their needs were not being met by the traditional parties. Some of their grievances were related to the war, such as "the conscription of men but not of wealth," but they also sought better legislation with respect to labour standards and collective bargaining. The ILP generally advocated a democratic socialist program that would include a substantial measure of nationalization.

Although they differed on the issues of the tariff and the eight-hour day, the two parties saw that their objectives were compatible and co-operated in the election campaign, forming a coalition government afterwards.[60] It took some time to form a government, however, because the farm party had no recognized leader and not enough members of cabinet calibre had run in the election. E.C. Drury was eventually selected as premier, and a series of by-elections put him and several cabinet colleagues into the House.

The Drury government had a number of accomplishments: a mother's allowances act, a minimum wage for women, extensive highway construction, farm credit legislation, and re-establishment of some degree of government control over the timber and hydro industries. A measure for which the party is less well regarded was its strict enforcement of the Ontario Temperance Act.[61]

The government might have achieved more, but it was plagued by a deep internal division. Radicals within the farmers' movement wanted to eschew any resemblance of "party" activity, believing in the concept of "group government." They argued that each occupational group should establish its own political organization in place of political parties. Drury, on the other hand, wanted to broaden the movement to create a general reform party which would include farmers, labour, and progressive liberals. Serious dissension also broke out within the ILP ranks, which helped cripple the government far more than any disputes between the two partners in the coalition. Thus, it came as no surprise that the government was defeated when Drury called a snap election in 1923, and the Conservatives came to power under Howard Ferguson.

It was the first of three landslide victories in the 1920s for the vigorous new premier.[62] Ferguson had built a strong party organization while in opposition, and had been an effective critic of the Drury government's performance. His approach was to emphasize growth and development, and he allowed the forces of the marketplace to operate with little interference. As a result, much economic development occurred, especially in the mining, lumbering, and pulp and paper industries, with the government providing such infrastructure as power, highways, and railways. Ontario Hydro made rapid expansion of rural and northern electrification its priority. In addition, while Ferguson maintained close ties with the federal party, he separated the federal and provincial organizations in 1920 so that the provincial level would be less affected by federal party fortunes.

On the social side, Ferguson was "slow to recognize the growing deficiencies of existing structures,"[63] but he did make two significant decisions. There was a fifth plebiscite in 1924, and in 1927 Prohibition was replaced with a liquor control act which involved "government control" with a local option. In the same year, Regulation 17 was repealed. Although he authored a gerrymander so offensive it was called a "Fergymander," Ferguson acquired an image of statesmanship and enjoyed a good deal of national popularity.

Ferguson's successor was George Henry, who assumed power in the wake of the Great Depression. Three other issues dominated the 1931-34 period in Ontario: liquor, religion, and electricity, none of which Henry handled very well. On the first question, he timidly put amendments to the Liquor Control Act to a popular vote coinciding with the 1934 election. He then skirted the issue of Roman Catholic demands for a share of corporate and public utility taxes to help finance separate schools by referring the matter to the courts. Finally, he had difficulty refuting Liberal charges of government corruption in connection with hydro contracts, especially when the allegations touched him personally.

Besides these problems and the Depression, Henry faced a dynamic new Liberal leader, Mitch Hepburn. As the Liberal party was regaining strength, the farmer and labour parties almost disappeared. A major factor in the 1934 election results was Hepburn's charisma, described as follows: "his was the radicalism of the demagogue, a red-necked populism that seemed plausible and appealing to a people who longed during the Depression for strong and positive leadership."[64]

With the province beginning to recover from its economic difficulties, the Hepburn government gave some early signs of promise. The cabinet was a solid, progressive one, it passed several pieces of advanced labour legislation, and provided additional assistance to separate schools. Hepburn regarded the compulsory pasteurization of milk as his greatest personal achievement, and enacted other reform measures.

Mitch Hepburn is not generally remembered fondly, however, due to his erratic, immature, and often autocratic behaviour.[65] One example was his intervention in the 1937 strike at the General Motors plant in Oshawa, based on his belief that the advance of unionism under the auspices of the American Congress of Industrial Organizers (CIO) was a Communist-inspired threat to law and order. Hepburn sent in hordes of police officers, and made the strike the central issue of the 1937 election campaign. Although Hepburn's action was generally popular across the province and won him resounding re-election, the experience cost him his two most able ministers, Arthur Roebuck and David Croll. Other unfavourable judgments are based on his slashing of the public service, and his personal weaknesses for liquor and sex, which led to frequent absences from the premier's office.

Hepburn also waged a constant battle with the federal Liberal leader, Mackenzie King. This stemmed from Hepburn's considerable efforts on behalf of the federal party in the 1935 election, and King's refusal to reward him with any kind of influence, especially with respect to political appointments. Hepburn was also profoundly concerned that the King government was not putting forth a maximum war effort, and supported the famous 1940 motion of censure in the Ontario legislature against the King government's war record, an issue which split the provincial caucus right down the middle. This feud had two main adverse consequences—heavy strains on Canada's federal-provincial relations, and long-term damage to the Ontario Liberal party.

While Hepburn was destroying his government and his party, other political parties slowly gained strength. After much turmoil, George Drew eventually emerged as Conservative leader and, at the other end of the ideological spectrum, organizational efforts were undertaken in Ontario on behalf of the Cooperative Commonwealth Federation (CCF) party. Agnes Macphail, an Ontario farmer MP, persuaded that movement to join assorted labour groups and CCF clubs in November 1932 in a kind of triple alliance. The rhetoric of the Cooperative Commonwealth proved to be too radical for the farmer element and the focus too urban-oriented, however, and in March 1934 they withdrew. The CCF's early success was limited to a single seat in the 1934 election, which it lost in 1937.

As these opposition party developments were taking place, Hepburn continued to behave erratically. He resigned as premier (but not as provincial treasurer) in October 1942, and had Attorney General Gordon Conant sworn in as his successor, a move which prompted other cabinet ministers to resign. He left the cabinet in March 1943, a month before a leadership convention at which Harry Nixon was selected as the new leader. Since an election was already overdue, Nixon set the date for August 4, 1943, a day of destiny for Ontario.

The defeat of the Liberals in 1943 was predictable enough, but the rise of the CCF to second place, resulting in a minority Conservative government, was an unexpected development. It paralleled a much improved CCF showing at both the federal level and in many other provinces, and was the result of certain common factors: the party's additional electoral experience, the prospect of a better post-war economy, including such increased social security as the party was promoting, and the rapid urbanization and growth of trade unionism, both of which were byproducts of the war economy.[66] In Ontario, the party had only selected a leader, E.B. "Ted" Jolliffe, in 1942, and he managed to fill a vacuum created by Hepburn and Drew's overriding concern with the war effort and their loss of interest in provincial affairs.[67]

The Conservative leader, George Drew, had previously demonstrated many arch-conservative views; he was anti-labour, anti-French, anti-Catholic, and possessed a hawkish military attitude regarding the Second World War. In 1943, however, he followed the lead of the federal party by changing the name of the provincial Conservatives to the Progressive Conservative party, and then surprised Ontario by announcing a radical 22-point program.[68] Among other things, it promised "economic and social security from the cradle to the grave," increased housing, "the fairest and most advanced labour laws," mother's allowances, old-age pensions, a great array of measures to help returning armed forces personnel, and encouragement for every sector of the economy.

Drew proceeded to form a minority government which lasted until 1945. In this early period, the government created the Labour Relations Board and the Ministry of Planning and Development. When the government was defeated in the legislature, Drew called another election for June 1945. The Liberals were not in good shape, having again selected the discredited Mitch Hepburn as party leader after Harry Nixon's unsuccessful 1943 campaign. The CCF was better organized than it had been, but faced an intense extra-parliamentary right-wing attack. The CCF was fanatically equated with communism, totalitarianism, and dictatorship, in what has been called "the most massive propaganda drive in Canadian political history."[69]

The CCF leader counter-attacked with the contention that the premier maintained a special political police force "to link as many non-Conservatives as possible with the Communist party." Jolliffe claimed that these "Gestapo" reports, however inaccurate, were passed on to right-wing propagandists. Jolliffe's charges were so serious and sensational that they dominated the rest of the campaign, and Drew was forced to appoint a royal commission to investigate.

The election resulted in a strong Tory victory, while the Liberals slipped back into second place almost by default. The period between 1945 and 1948 was one of solid governmental achievement;[70] it was a time of flourishing resource industries and conversion of wartime manufacturing to peace-time production. Among Drew's most heralded decisions were the importation of 10,000 skilled British immigrants, a significant expansion of highways and hydro operations, and advances in day care, homes for the aged, prisoner rehabilitation, hospital grants, and public housing.

Drew called another election for May 1948. Because the government had recently permitted the introduction of cocktail lounges into the province, the once-dormant pro- and anti-liquor forces emerged again, and Drew himself lost his seat to a teetotaling CCFer. The Tories were returned with a reduced majority, and shortly afterwards Drew left to take up the federal Conservative leadership. He was succeeded as premier on an interim basis by Minister of Agriculture Thomas Kennedy, and Leslie Frost became premier in May 1949.

A major factor in the Conservatives' continued success in the 1950s was the province's general prosperity. As Jonathan Manthorpe says, "it was on a sea of billions of dollars of U.S. investment that Frost floated the post-war boom in Ontario."[71] The strength of the party organization was also evident in this period, as was the weak, divided opposition. The most significant aspect of Tory success in the 1950s, however, was the ability and image of the premier himself. Leslie Frost was a strong, forceful leader who maintained strict control of the government. The image he cultivated, however, was one of a simple small-town lawyer, "a gentle, kindly, friendly man,"[72] who took a sincere interest in the welfare of every citizen. Not surprisingly, the 1951 election gave the Conservatives a near monopoly of seats.

The Frost government was highly regarded for its "concrete" initiatives. Highway construction was a top priority, including the Trans-Canada Highway, and three other large, imaginative projects were the establishment of the Ontario Water Resources Commission, a new political structure for Metropolitan Toronto, and the St. Lawrence Seaway, the latter resulting in a great expansion of Ontario Hydro. Frost also undertook a school and hospital construction program of similar dimensions, and was always on hand to officially open all such projects. He remained provincial treasurer until the mid-1950s and, while lavishing money on such projects, kept spending under control and avoided tax increases. By 1959, the Conservatives had agreed to join the comprehensive hospital insurance plan which would be half financed by Ottawa and, around 1960, established several new universities.

But the Conservative performance was frequently marred by scandal. The first involved highways, and became public in January 1955. The Highways minister resigned, three construction companies were fined, and six department officials were fined or jailed for conspiracy to defraud the government. The second, in 1958, involved natural gas, and three ministers resigned after it was revealed that they had bought stock in the Northern Ontario Natural Gas Co. Ltd. (NONG), before sales were made available to the general public.

Frost introduced a three-percent provincial retail sales tax after the 1959 election, but his thoughts were primarily centred on his retirement. He sensed that to maintain the public's confidence, the party needed at least a semblance of rejuvenation.[73] Thus, in deliberately departing when he felt it was in the best interest of the party, Frost engaged in what has come to be called the Tory "regeneration" technique, changing leaders about every 10 years so that the party would be seen "to be vibrant and on the threshold of change."[74] A party convention in October 1961 selected Minister of Education John Robarts as Frost's successor.

Robarts hailed from London, Ontario, and his background included degrees in business administration and law, and a distinguished wartime naval service. He had a "chunky, formal handsomeness" and was seen as safe, "sincere, earnest, diligent, personable, orthodox, careful [and] conservative."[75] After some experience in office, his image became that of the tough executive, the manager in full control of provincial affairs.

This period was also significant for the CCF. After experiencing declining support in both federal and provincial elections, discussions began in the late 1950s with the goal of creating a new party. In 1961 the CCF was transformed into the New Democratic Party (NDP), with support from the Canadian Labour Congress. Within Ontario, CCF leader Donald MacDonald automatically became leader of the new party.

On the legislative front, the early 1960s were dominated by a host of new Conservative initiatives. These included such measures as a redistribution of constituency boundaries with the addition of 10 new seats, new minimum wage legislation, substantially increased university grants, funding for subway construction in Toronto, and a new foundation tax plan, sponsored by Education Minister Bill Davis, to provide additional financial assistance to separate schools.

In response to charges that organized crime was spreading throughout the province, Robarts created the Ontario Police Commission and then a royal commission on the subject. The latter concluded that a serious increase in organized crime had occurred, but found no corruption in the attorney general's department. The controversy over crime spilled over into the 1963 election campaign, however, where the Liberal leader insisted on revealing "a scandal a day." The NDP campaign was an improvement over those of the CCF, and an attempt was made to portray a completely new image.[76] Robarts, however, was easily re-elected.

The legislative record of the 1963-67 period included a pioneering legal aid plan, a new Department of University Affairs, the start of the community college system, consumer and mental health legislation, amendments to the liquor licence laws, a consolidated structure for Metro Toronto, and a reform of legislative operations. On the negative side, Ontarians witnessed much intergovernmental conflict on the pensions and medicare issues. In this connection, Premier Robarts and the federal Liberal Health and Welfare Minister Judy LaMarsh engaged in a protracted and colourful debate. Later in the 1960s, Robarts was forced to join both federal pensions and medicare schemes.

The only major problem for the Conservatives in the mid-1960s was again crime-related—legislation introduced in 1964 to give the Ontario Police Commission extraordinary powers in its fight against organized crime. Among other things, it permitted the imprisonment without the laying of charges of those who refused to answer questions on the subject. The resignation of the attorney general, the deletion of the most offensive clauses, and the appointment of the McRuer Royal Commission on Civil Liberties permitted the government to avoid any long-term consequences.

Compensating for any flaws in the government's record was the stature of the premier himself. Robarts' impressive reputation within the province was increasingly strengthened by his emergence as a national figure in the Canadian unity issue. Thus, in the euphoria of Canada's centennial year, Robarts called an election for October 1967. The Liberals entered the campaign with a new and relatively unknown leader, Robert Nixon, who inherited a party with no policy, exhausted by two leadership conventions and frequent disputes between its federal and provincial wings.

The election returned the Conservatives to office but with reduced support, while the Liberals held their own. Most significant was the NDP rise to 26 percent of the popular vote, marking the start of the sustained Liberal-NDP competition for official Opposition status, and the beginnings of a true three-party system in the province.

Robarts' last three years in office were full of action. Immediately after the election, he convened the Confederation for Tomorrow Conference, a meeting of provincial premiers to discuss the future of Confederation, mainly in an attempt to fathom the position of Quebec. Robarts followed this with an increased recognition of Franco-Ontarian rights. The government provided language training for a limited number of civil servants, allowed MPPs to use French in the legislature and, most importantly, introduced French-language high schools. The latter naturally caused some difficulty at the local school board level, but the principle raised little controversy in the legislature. The government also established a maze of community colleges and implemented a massive consolidation of local school boards. Hard on the heels of this latter development, it raised the equally controversial issue of regional government. There was much evidence that these issues and others were becoming more complicated and controversial: longer legislative sessions; the host of studies and reports which preceded any government decision; and an increased incidence of protests and demonstrations. In spite of aiming for a pragmatic, middle-of-the-road approach, the government often angered factions on the extremes.

At the end of the decade, two changes in party leadership took place. Donald MacDonald of the NDP resigned in 1970 after warding off a challenge to his leadership in 1968. He was succeeded by Stephen Lewis, who had a reputation as a skilful organizer and was a commanding presence in the House. In December 1970, having come to the same conclusion Frost had reached about 10 years earlier, Robarts announced his resignation.[77] The party thus engaged in another round of "regeneration," as the first three decades of modern Tory rule in the province drew to a close.

The 1970s[78]

In the 1971 Tory leadership race, Bill Davis, a Brampton lawyer who had served impressively as Robarts' Education Minister, was the "establishment" candidate. Despite his "monotonous delivery and convoluted grammar,"[79] he won a narrow victory and immediately set out to change things. His cabinet contained seven new faces, replacing several older ones, giving the public appearance of a new team. Davis also engaged his opponent's skilled organizational team, which became his party and election "Big Blue Machine." This new party organization undertook a major public opinion survey to determine attitudes toward parties, leaders, and issues. Davis then turned his attention to policy, making several major executive decisions and proposing a plethora of new legislation. Among these, nationalist, environmentalist, and youth-oriented concerns predominated: he awarded $1 million to the publishing firm of McClelland and Stewart to prevent an American takeover, gave Canadians preferred access to Crown land, created a new environment ministry, halted logging in Quetico Park, initiated a multi-million dollar pollution-related lawsuit against Dow Chemical Canada Ltd., and reduced the voting and drinking ages to 18 years. Perhaps most significantly, the cabinet stopped construction of the Spadina Expressway in Toronto, and confirmed its policy of no additional funding for Roman Catholic separate schools. These two decisions seemed to serve political purposes—demonstrating change and decisiveness in the first case, and avoiding the alienation of the Conservatives' basic Protestant constituency in the second. In any event, by this "legislative whirlwind"[80] the government completed the regeneration process, distinguished itself from the Robarts' regime, and transformed "Bland Bill" into "Decisive Davis."[81] It also set the stage for the October 1971 election.

The most striking aspect of that campaign was the Conservatives' saturation of the media and their selling of Bill Davis "like a can of tomatoes."[82] The opposition parties had less money and therefore put more emphasis on policies; in fact, the Liberals issued a detailed "Blueprint for Government" which contained an array of policies, including one on separate schools, which was sometimes called the silent issue of the campaign. In the end, the results were not substantially different from those of 1967.

Davis immediately restructured the entire executive branch, implementing recommendations of the committee on government productivity. In addition to changes mentioned earlier, the treasurer's position became an extremely powerful one when held by Darcy McKeough, who was given responsibility for Treasury, Economics and Intergovernmental Affairs. Otherwise, however, the next four years were not happy ones for Ontario politics.

First, the government plunged into a series of questionable ministerial activities which acquired the loose label of "scandals." Most damaging were charges in connection with the construction of new head office buildings for Ontario Hydro and the Workmen's Compensation Board. It was revealed that Fidinam (Ontario) Ltd., the firm which won the contract to build the WCB office, had made a $50,000 contribution to the Conservative party shortly before the contract was awarded. In the Hydro case, the contract had gone to Gerhard Moog, who promoted himself as a close friend of the premier. In response, the government introduced an election finances reform act. This legislation, which was implemented before the 1975 election campaign, limited annual political contributions, set a limit on advertising expenditures, required the disclosure of the names of contributors of over $100, and partially reimbursed the expenses of candidates receiving over 15 percent of the vote.

The government also faced many policy problems, the first of which was labour unrest in the public service. The issue climaxed in late 1973 with teachers' rallies, protests, and a one-day province-wide walkout, which resulted in legislation granting teachers the right to strike. Another problem was the escalating cost of education and health in the province, which the government tried to control, and partly financed with a two-percent increase in the retail sales tax. Transportation was also an issue, especially in the absence of an alternative to the Spadina Expressway. The government found it necessary to partially reverse the Spadina decision and allowed an "arterial road" to be built.[83] It later created the Urban Transportation Development Corporation, which was supposed to find a substitute mode of transportation. In a related matter, the province decided not to provide the infrastructure for the proposed Pickering airport, forcing the federal government to abandon the idea. Davis passed new planning legislation and created a new Housing ministry, but these did little to assuage the serious housing shortage. Finally, the initial implementation of regional government in larger urban centres proved controversial.

Other government initiatives were more popular. The legislature was reformed in accordance with the recommendations of the Camp commission, and the appointment of the province's first ombudsman brought much congratulation. The government established more French-language high schools, abolished medicare premiums for seniors, introduced a new Guaranteed Annual Income System (GAINS) for the elderly, blind, and disabled, and implemented a free prescription drug program for needy pensioners and social assistance recipients.

The government also fought back with an election-oriented 1975 budget and a well-publicized attack on federal petroleum pricing policies, coupled with the imposition of a provincial 90-day freeze on such prices. The Liberal election strategy was to attack the government's integrity, and the party tried to transform Robert Nixon from a "nice guy" into a fighter. The NDP chose to deal exclusively with four "bread and butter" issues, conveniently covered by the acronym HELP—Housing, Energy, Land, and People. As the campaign progressed, Stephen Lewis spent more and more time detailing abusive rent increases and advocating rent controls. With his litany of stories of rent gouging, couched in concrete, human terms, the issue caught the public's attention, and the other parties were forced to propose measures in this area. From this electoral cauldron emerged a minority Conservative government, and the NDP, with a significantly smaller share of the popular vote than the Liberals, obtained its greatest number of seats to that date and became the official Opposition.

The most pressing legislative business of the next session was the implementation of rent controls, a commitment made in one form or another by all three parties. The bill introduced by the Tories was strengthened by opposition amendments, the first concrete sign the Conservatives were no longer in complete control. Another major event of the fall of 1975 was the federal announcement of wage and price controls. Finding itself harassed by public service salary demands at the very time it was trying to exercise restraint, the Davis government put provincial and municipal employees' salaries under federal control with indecent haste. The government's financial difficulties also led Health Minister Frank Miller to close several hospitals and increase health care premiums.

Health and environmental concerns featured prominently in this period. The Ham royal commission on the health and safety of mine workers, appointed largely as a result of NDP pressure, reported in August 1976. Stephen Lewis was also successful in getting the Workmen's Compensation Board to recognize asbestos as a cause of cancer. The government appointed a royal commission to study its previous decision to give the Reed Paper Co. timber rights to 49,210 square kilometres of northwestern Ontario. This gift was especially controversial because that firm had polluted the English-Wabigoon river system near Dryden, severely affecting resident Native settlements. Reed later withdrew its proposal, by which time the government had extended the mandate of the royal commission to the question of development north of the 60th parallel.

As for the opposition parties, Robert Nixon resigned the Liberal leadership. A newly elected 37-year-old psychiatrist from Hamilton, Stuart Smith, emerged as his successor, winning narrowly over David Peterson, another new MPP from London. A few months later, the Liberals separated their federal and provincial organizations. The 1976 session was particularly difficult for Smith, new to the legislature and the party leadership, and placed in the crucial balance-of-power position in the minority government. Stephen Lewis' New Democrats, on the other hand, luxuriated in the role of official opposition, and delighted in referring to the Liberals as "the third party."

The 1977 session opened with Davis under considerable pressure from his party to call an election, the polls looking favourable for the government. He introduced a rent control bill covering the period after August 1, 1977, granting the cabinet the power to set a ceiling no higher than eight percent on rent increases. The Liberals then introduced an amendment with a six-percent ceiling, which the NDP supported. This two-percent difference was all the excuse Davis needed to call an election.

The Tories unveiled a "Charter for Ontario" reminiscent of Drew's 22 points in 1943, but it became something of a joke. The NDP were continually forced to defend such policies as nationalization of resource companies and the $4 minimum wage. Smith's hastily prepared platform concentrated on job creation and limiting the increase in provincial taxes. Later, he spoke more philosophically about a range of conservative values—the work ethic, thrift, restraint, and educational fundamentals.[84] The electorate again denied the Conservatives a majority government, the Liberals finished ahead of the NDP to regain the official Opposition, and the NDP ended up a depressing third, prompting Lewis to resign the party leadership.

Before going to the polls again, Davis served a full four years, the term characterized by high unemployment and inflation. For the first time since the 1930s, Ontario experienced substantial layoffs and plant closures, both in manufacturing, especially automobiles, and in primary industries, mostly mining. One government response was the establishment of an employment development fund to provide grants to companies as incentives to expand or modernize existing operations. The pulp and paper and automobile industries were the main beneficiaries. The economic downturn also forced the government to introduce legislation in response to closings and layoffs, providing better severance pay for discontinued employees. This period was also marred by many strikes and several instances of back-to-work legislation. More appealing to the union movement was a new law which had the employer automatically deduct union membership dues from each employee's pay cheque.

Pollution was also becoming a serious problem. It included acid rain, the leading Canadian source of which was Inco Ltd.'s smelter in Sudbury; mercury pollution from pulp and paper mills; and lead emissions, radioactive mine tailings, dioxins, and liquid industrial wastes. Pollution also thrust Ontario Hydro into the spotlight. Its coal-fired generators were the second-largest source of acid rain in the province, but an even greater danger came from its increasing reliance on nuclear energy and involved leaks in its operations and waste disposal. Many other aspects of Hydro's nuclear program also came under attack, including large rate increases in 1976-77, and the multi-billion deal to buy uranium from Denison Mines Ltd. and Rio Algom Ltd., which many observers saw as excessively generous to the mining companies. Another problem was the cost (especially with regard to interest on necessary loans) of developing such nuclear capacity, the Darlington plant being particularly controversial. These questions were only partially answered by the long-awaited Porter royal commission report on electric power planning, and the Crown corporation was sometimes called "a juggernaut out of control."[85]

The government's efforts to limit spending on health, education, and welfare also created problems. Continuing controversy arose over health insurance premiums and doctors opting out of the province's health insurance plan. Opposition leader Stuart Smith probably had his finest hour in 1978 when he forced the government to reduce by half a proposed 37.5 percent increase in OHIP premiums. It was a rare case of Treasurer Darcy McKeough being forced to back down and not long afterwards he resigned.

Bilingualism was another continuing concern. The government cautiously but progressively increased French-language services, especially in the courts, and began to translate statutes into French. For obvious political motives, it also offered limited encouragement to heritage language programs and multiculturalism.

Among other developments, the government passed a comprehensive occupational health and safety act, a family law reform act, and bills providing for compulsory automobile insurance and for a citizens' complaint board against the Toronto police. It extended rent control, and raised the legal drinking age to 19. Operation of the legislature was altered substantially in the minority government situation, such as in the appointment of an NDP member as Speaker, and in greatly increased resources for private members. Judicial inquiries routinely cleared the government of charges of election bribery and corruption.

The 1980s

The early 1980s saw intense federal-provincial interaction, especially with regard to energy policy and constitutional reform. To protect Ontario's manufacturing sector, Davis tried to make a case for lower oil and gas prices in Ottawa's negotiations with the producing provinces, a move which naturally brought him into conflict with the West. Somewhat similarly, Ontario sided with the federal government on its constitutional proposals, and in the end both Davis and Attorney General Roy McMurtry played key roles in engineering a federal-provincial consensus on the Charter of Rights and Freedoms.

By early 1981, however, it was time for another election. The BILD program (Board of Industrial Leadership and Development), a five-year multi-million dollar economic development plan, was the focus of the Conservative campaign, in addition to its usual emphasis on the appeal of "Bill" Davis. The public's lack of interest in the campaign was confirmed when only 57 percent of the electorate bothered to vote. They gave the Conservatives their long-awaited majority, with the NDP the biggest loser, returning with only 21 seats. These results led to the resignation of both opposition party leaders and almost simultaneous leadership conventions in February 1982. David Peterson, the London lawyer-businessman who had run second to Stuart Smith six years before, captured the Liberal crown. The NDP prevailed upon the young Toronto labour lawyer and federal finance critic, Bob Rae, to assume the provincial party leadership.

Economic problems, especially high unemployment, continued over the next four years. Inco Ltd., Chrysler, Massey-Ferguson, General Motors, American Motors, and McDonnell-Douglas, as well as the pulp and paper industry and various mining operations, all suffered significant layoffs. Many industries experienced serious strikes, including the 1981 walkout of non-medical hospital workers, a controversial and illegal action for which union leaders were fired, suspended, and/or jailed for contempt of court. BILD projects provided some relief from the unemployment situation, but were of little overall significance. Inflationary pressures eased after 1982, but the government deficit

CHAPTER 7: Ontario **347**

continued to grow despite what many considered intolerable cutbacks in social programs. Foremost among the government's efforts to restrain its expenditures was a wage control program introduced in 1982 which applied to all workers in the public sector, including teachers, hospital workers, and university personnel, as well as provincial and municipal public employees.

Another controversial initiative was the government's 1981 purchase of 25 percent of the shares of Suncor, the Sun Oil Co. This was done at the whim of the premier; his rationalization was that, as a consuming province, Ontario required a "window" on the petroleum industry. Many, even members of the cabinet, felt the $650 million could have been better spent, especially because it appeared that the shares had been overpriced.

The next issue to arise involved trust companies and an incredibly complicated transaction in which more than 10,000 apartment units in Toronto were sold, or "flipped," several times in quick succession at increasing prices. Initially attention focused on the sales' impact on rent controls, to which the government responded with a temporary five percent ceiling. But greater concern developed over the province's regulation of financial institutions. Other developments in this period included the introduction of new human rights code provisions relating to the handicapped and sexual harassment, a new planning act, a new child and family services act, reform of the Workers' Compensation Board, and a new emphasis on "special education." The repeated opening and closing of the Morgentaler abortion clinic in Toronto, with accompanying arrests, charges, acquittals, and appeals, was a new experience for Ontario, as was the protracted investigation into the mysterious deaths at Toronto's Hospital for Sick Children. Increasing conflict between the government and the medical profession centred on medical fees and the continuing problem of doctors opting out of OHIP. Doctors resorted to various kinds of strike action before settling for a fee increase of two or three times the ceiling imposed on others whose incomes were derived from public sources. The government granted French the status of an official language in the Ontario courts in 1983, and introduced legislation guaranteeing an education in French for any student in the province. Finally, the majority government substantially changed the legislature's operations. The old Tory arrogance returned and, among other things, Davis appointed a Conservative MPP as Speaker without consulting the Opposition.

The most controversial event of this period was Davis' sudden announcement in June 1984 that the government would fund the Roman Catholic secondary school system to the same extent as the public system, starting with Grade 11 in 1985. Davis' change of heart on the issue apparently reflected the province's increasing proportion of Roman Catholic residents, as well as the new intimacy between Davis and Cardinal Emmett Carter, whose frequent presence at Conservative party events had been noted.[86] No one anticipated the impact that this move would have on the teaching profession (with regard to questions of seniority, layoffs, and religious affiliation), or on the administration of local school boards (as a substantial switch in enrolment occurred from the public to the separate system). Shortly thereafter, Davis resigned.

Bill Davis was warmly feted, especially for his decency, at the January 1985 leadership convention called to choose his successor.[87] In the end, Industry Minister Frank Miller, 57, emerged victorious. He was a former treasurer and health minister, and a well-educated resort operator from Muskoka. But many observers wondered about such a succession—could Miller, two years older than Davis, be considered a rejuvenation, and was he too right-wing and too rustic for the electorate?

Miller was torn between calling an immediate election to take advantage of the party's high position in the polls or convening a short session of the legislature to establish his own record of achievement. He soon opted for the former course, probably due to indications that the separate school issue was heating up and that provincial and federal budgets would not be popular. In preparation for the election, Miller unveiled a $1.5-billion, three-year economic development program, Enterprise Ontario, focusing on retraining young people and women. It was reminiscent of Davis' BILD program, but was narrower in scope, emphasizing tax cuts for small business and technological adaptation.

At the start of the race, the Gallup poll reported 51 percent voter support for the Conservatives, 29 percent for the Liberals, and 20 percent for the NDP. All three leaders were new, and David Peterson and Bob Rae were recognized as party leaders by only about one-quarter of the public. Peterson in particular had made little impact at Queen's Park. Both opposition parties also felt vulnerable in the wake of the Conservative sweep in the 1984 federal election. Moreover, several of the brightest Ontario Liberals had resigned, some to become federal candidates, an indication of their view of the prospects of a provincial party regularly described as "disorganized and demoralized."

Miller decided to shun the Big Blue Machine. His new advisers persuaded him to avoid a televised leaders' debate and remain inaccessible to the media and the public except for carefully staged events.

The Liberal party was well prepared and fast off the mark. David Peterson stuck to a limited number of issues throughout the campaign: job creation, an end to extra-billing, the abolition of medicare premiums, the introduction of a denticare program, sales tax breaks, rent controls, equal pay for work of equal value, day care, increased job skills training in high schools, and selling beer and wine in small variety stores. He had once been seen as a rather conservative Liberal, but most of his new positions were somewhat left-wing; indeed, the NDP accused him of stealing several of its policies. In contrast to his performance in the legislature and to that of the new Conservative leader, Peterson proved to be a dynamic presence—a modern, progressive, urban, likeable, young, attractive professional—and his boundless energy was an inspiration for local candidates.

The NDP mounted a curiously low-key campaign, protecting its incumbents and promoting another 20 or so candidates with the best chances of winning.

Bob Rae stressed five themes: job creation and security, pollution control, tax reform, equal pay for work of equal value, and social programs, including an end to extra-billing.

The results were a startling upset: 52 Conservatives, 48 Liberals, and 25 New Democrats. The Liberals actually gained the largest share of popular vote, 38 percent compared to 37 percent for the Tories, and 24 percent for the NDP. According to post-election polls, Miller had been a liability to the Tory party[88] and much of the responsiblity for the defeat was attributed to his advisers. As far as issues were concerned, no less than 31 percent of the electorate was concerned with separate school funding, even though all parties had studiously avoided it. The question was legitimized when, a week before the election, a Toronto Anglican archbishop compared Davis' actions on the extension of funding to methods used by Adolf Hitler. This issue worked against the Conservatives, presumably because they could be held responsible. Peterson's "yuppie" image also helped the Liberals take a number of urban and suburban seats away from the Conservatives in Toronto.

Amid great speculation, Lieutenant-Governor John Black Aird asked Miller to carry on as premier for the time being. The NDP, with the balance of power, announced that it was open to accepting offers for its support. Both Liberals and Conservatives agreed to appoint negotiating teams to meet with the NDP committee to see what could be arranged. From the start, the NDP had a more encouraging response from the Liberals, although both Liberals and Conservatives were willing to agree to most of its policy demands. The key differences were that the Liberals were more amenable to a written pact guaranteeing a period of political stability, while the Tories preferred ad hoc support. The NDP also raised but did not pursue the question of a formal coalition government. Finally, on May 24, Rae announced that the NDP would support the Liberals, and four days later the precedent-setting pact was made public.[89] The most innovative aspect of the agreement was that the NDP would support the Liberals on non-confidence votes for a two-year period during which the government promised not to call an election. This left the NDP free, as an opposition party, to defeat individual Liberal initiatives. The two parties went on to establish a detailed list of legislative priorities.

Despite their impending defeat, the Tories introduced a full-scale speech from the throne. After the eight-day "throne speech debate," the 42-year-old Ontario Conservative government fell on June 18, 1985, as the Liberals and the NDP joined forces to vote against it. Miller submitted his resignation without requesting an election, and the lieutenant-governor called on David Peterson to form a government. Peterson's cabinet included three "super-ministers", Robert Nixon as treasurer, Sean Conway as education minister, and Ian Scott as attorney general. With unprecedented haste, the new premier recalled the legislature for July 2, primarily to address the separate school funding issue. Rather than start a new session with his own speech from the throne, Peterson read a statement outlining the government's plans.

The government introduced legislation on the separate school question and promised implementation by the fall. At the same time, it sent a reference case to the Ontario Court of Appeal on the bill's constitutionality. Many groups such as the Ontario Secondary School Teachers' Federation opposed the measure, and the costs of the program were estimated to be much higher than Davis originally indicated.

The next two years witnessed a bewildering barrage of government actions and a rapid implementation of most of the items in the Liberal-NDP Accord. These included a freedom of information act, an audit of forest resources, an extension to all private rental dwellings of the four-percent limit on rent increases; the proclamation of the "spills bill" which would compel polluters to pay for the clean-up of chemical spills; an increase in Workers' Compensation benefits; the promise of tougher enforcement of occupational health and safety legislation; and an end to favouritism in the awarding of government advertising contracts. Other legislation would ban extra-billing by doctors, provide OHIP financing for medically necessary travel for northern residents, and allow first-contract arbitration for labour disputes. The government introduced television into the legislature; compensated the Natives of the English and Wabigoon River region; and decided to locate a toxic waste disposal site near St. Catharines (although this project did not materialize over the next 10 years). In addition, as provided for in the accord, the government passed an election finances reform bill to limit both contributions and expenditures, and brought in legislation dealing with nursing homes, job security, farm financing, and equal-pay-for-work-of-equal-value, which would eventually cover large firms in the private sector as well as the public service. Robert Nixon's budget emphasized job creation and training for young people, and an expansion of non-profit housing, but his increase in the gasoline tax was withdrawn after NDP opposition. Not surprisingly, Wall Street lowered the province's credit rating.

Measures adopted between 1985 and 1987 which were not provided for in the accord included Bill 8 on French-language services, which passed unanimously but raised much controversy later; the go-ahead to complete the Darlington nuclear plant, contrary to David Peterson's earlier views; northern development initiatives, such as the relocation of government offices to the north; improved university and hospital funding; and amendments to the human rights code including one making it illegal to discriminate against a person based on his or her sexual orientation.

The provincial economy remained strong throughout this period, as Ontario welcomed the construction of a $300-million Toyota Canada Inc. plant in Cambridge, the expansion of the Honda Canada Inc. plant in Alliston, and a new General Motors-Suzuki plant for Ingersoll. Privatization in Ontario was limited to selling Minaki Lodge in Kenora to Four Seasons Hotels, and the Urban Transit Development Corporation to Lavalin Industries of Montreal. It was later rescued from bankruptcy by Bombardier.

The two years of minority government thus reflected well on the Peterson administration, and witnessed the defection of two New Democrats to the Liberal fold. The accord had provided the government with a legislative agenda and a timetable, while Peterson himself was surprisingly sure-footed in the premier's chair. Some attributed the latter to the talents of his chief adviser Hershell Ezrin but, whatever the reason, Peterson continued to develop a positive public image. Treasurer Robert Nixon supplied prudent financial management, and only two apparent ministerial conflict-of-interest situations marred the government's record. Meanwhile, Frank Miller wearied of the internal wrangling of the Tory party and announced his resignation as leader. The second Tory leadership convention of 1985, held in November, chose Larry Grossman, who had finished second earlier in the year.

By mid-1987 the premier was ready to go to the people in the hope of achieving a majority government. The polls foretold the September landslide Liberal victory, as Peterson toured the province in its carefree summertime slumber, and the Tories and NDP battled for second place. The NDP tried desperately to inspire interest in the automobile insurance issue, while the even more desperate Conservative leader turned to the right to consolidate his party's rock-bottom support. With a turnout rate of 63 percent, the Liberals captured 95 seats compared with 19 for the NDP and 16 for the Tories. The Liberals were finally able to extricate themselves from their southwestern Ontario base, and won the largest share of the vote in every region of the province, including Toronto, the north, and the east. In this context, Bob Rae was happy to finish second, while the once dominant Conservative party was shattered, with leader Larry Grossman losing his seat. Grossman soon announced his intention to retire, and the Tory caucus selected Andy Brandt as interim leader.

With the overwhelming majority, the pace of Liberal reform slackened noticeably. However, Peterson appointed a record number of women and members of ethnic groups to his cabinet, moved quickly to bring in conflict-of-interest legislation, and established a northern Ontario heritage fund to assist that sector's economy.

Automobile insurance continued to be a major issue after the election. Premiums rose so rapidly that the government instituted a freeze. After two increases in 1988 and a recommended increase of 17 percent for 1989 from the new Ontario Automobile Insurance Board, the government stepped in and set a ceiling of 7.6 percent. The board later recommended a no-fault insurance system and, in early 1990, the government introduced a new no-fault automobile insurance plan. While the legislation promised relief from escalating insurance premiums, more than 90 percent of accident victims would lose the right to sue. The legislation was opposed by lawyers, consumer groups, and trade unions, and supported primarily by the insurance companies.

Housing and health were two other problem areas. The housing situation was characterized by serious shortages of affordable accommodation, in particular in the Toronto area, and by horrendous delays in the rent review process. The government introduced a new provincial home ownership savings plan and other piecemeal programs such as a requirement that 25 percent of new housing developments in any community be allocated for affordable housing. In the health field, a major confrontation over doctors' fees occurred in 1988, while nurses gained more clout on hospital committees. Robert Nixon eliminated health care premiums as of 1 January 1990, replacing them with a payroll tax on employers.

One of the province's most controversial decisions was leaving the thorny question of Sunday shopping to the discretion of individual municipalities. The public was deeply divided on the issue, and most municipalities did not want this added responsibility, fearing that they would be forced into Sunday shopping by competing communities nearby.

In the north, the controversy over extending logging in a provincial wilderness park in the Temagami region stood out. A long battle brewed with logging companies and their workers on the one hand, and environmentalists, Native peoples, and cottage owners on the other. Attempts at compromise were unsuccessful, and demonstrations, arrests, and numerous court appearances continued for years. Also, the mining industry saw severe layoffs in the uranium mines at Elliot Lake, and the closing of most of the remaining iron mines. The government ordered the worst air polluters in the province to reduce their emissions by 50 percent by 1994, while kraft pulp and paper mills were also told to clean up.

Bill Davis' decision to provide full public funding of the Roman Catholic separate school system continued to raise difficulties. Transferring public high school properties to separate boards became controversial in many parts of the province, while the 1989 budget gave separate schools a greater share of local commercial and industrial taxes. Further complications were caused by francophone demands for French-language school trustees and complete French-language school boards. Meanwhile, the Ontario Court of Appeal struck down the compulsory recitation of the Lord's Prayer in public schools.

In other legal matters, the province accredited the Morgentaler abortion clinic in the wake of the Supreme Court decision on this matter, but Dr. Henry Morgentaler still had to get a court injunction to keep picketers from harassing his clients. The government set up an investigation into allegations of racism after several black suspects were injured or killed by Toronto-area police. It also established a new impartial system of appointing provincial court judges, and began a reform of the court structure. Even so, thousands of backlogged court cases existed in certain regions, and the Supreme Court of Canada ruled that the resulting delays in bringing cases to trial were excessive.

The 1989 budget promised some $400 million to reform of the welfare system, increase social assistance rates and provide more incentives to work. These actions constituted the beginning of the implementation of the 1988 government study known as the Thomson Report. Under employer pressure, the government diluted changes to the occupational health and safety act which allowed workers to shut down dangerous workplaces. The NDP saw reforms to the workers' compensation program in 1988-89 as a backward step, and mounted a bitter filibuster. General Motors announced it would close its van assembly plant in Scarborough, and Peterson signed a contract with Manitoba to purchase $5 billion worth of electricity, giving Ontario more time to consider its energy options.

On the major federal-provincial issues of the period, the legislature overwhelmingly endorsed the Meech Lake Accord and opposed free trade. Peterson demonstrated his dislike of the Canada-U.S. trade deal with legislation asserting provincial jurisdiction over the water, energy, and health facilities in the province and including the right to set prices for water exports to the U.S., the right to charge a higher export than domestic price for electricity, and the right to give funding preference to Canadian-owned non-profit health facilities over American-owned ones. Federal-provincial agreement was reached on the gradual phase-out of subsidies to the wine industry, however, consistent with GATT and free trade restrictions.

In 1989, Solicitor General Joan Smith resigned after the Opposition criticized her personal intervention in two Ontario Provincial Police investigations, and the Patricia Starr scandal erupted. Starr was chairman of the Toronto branch of the National Council of Jewish Women (NCJW), and a hard-working provincial Liberal volunteer rewarded for her party services with the chair of Ontario Place. She had used part of a provincial sales tax credit on an NCJW housing project constructed by the development firm Tridel to make large, illegal political donations, mostly to provincial Liberals. The situation was further complicated in that Tridel's president, Elvio Del Zotto, served as president of the federal wing of the Liberal Party in Ontario, and his company was involved in many other projects receiving public funds. When it was revealed that Peterson's new right-hand man Gordon Ashworth had benefited personally from the Starr-Tridel relationship, Ashworth resigned and the premier called a judicial inquiry into the scandal. Starr's lawyers challenged the constitutionality of the inquiry and, after the revelation of more evidence, it was disbanded. Starr was charged with several electoral law violations and served a jail sentence, but the Liberal party officials and politicians on the receiving end were not charged with any offences.[90] In a major cabinet shuffle, Peterson purged most of the ministers with links to Starr, as well as several others who had outlived their usefulness.

The 1990s

In 1990 Ontario began to be consumed by recession and, by the middle of the year, widespread layoffs and shutdowns occurred. Meanwhile, the Conservatives decided to hold their leadership convention on the "progressive" basis of giving every party member a vote. Mike Harris eventually triumphed over Dianne

Cunningham in a lacklustre contest. In these circumstances, Peterson called an election for September 6, only three years after he had gained his majority, no doubt hoping to take advantage of the distracted summertime atmosphere in the province as he had in 1987. He also wanted to go to the polls before the recession became severe, before he might be mistakenly blamed for the federal GST scheduled to take effect in January 1991, and before Patti Starr's date in court. Although Peterson claimed to need a mandate to protect Ontario's interests in Confederation and negotiate Canada's constitutional future, he never convinced the electorate he was anything but opportunistic. This was clearly a case where the voters resented a premature election.

When Peterson called the election, an Environics poll showed his party held 50 percent of the public's support compared to the NDP's 26 percent and 22 percent for the Conservatives. Until the campaign forced them to focus on the Liberal record, the electorate was generally content. The arrogance and opportunism of the early call, plus Opposition revelation and reiteration of Liberal faults, apparently changed many voters' minds. The Toronto garbage crisis and a backlog of thousands of rent review and court cases were frequently mentioned. Several observers argued that Peterson was a victim of a general antipathy towards all governments and politicians at the time, largely caused by public resentment against Ottawa, and he probably suffered from his association with Mulroney, Bourassa, and Meech Lake. Other voters felt the Starr affair was symptomatic of more widespread provincial Liberal corruption. The Liberal campaign was poorly organized, zigzagged between attacking the Conservatives and the NDP, and Peterson ran into unexpected protests at almost every campaign stop.[91]

The NDP began the campaign by welcoming voters turned off by the Liberals, but eventually issued a platform, "An Agenda for People." The platform promised tax reform—a minimum corporate tax, succession duties on estates over $1 million, a tax on real estate speculation, provincial assumption of 60 percent of the local education budget, and elimination of income taxes on the poor. Bob Rae also emphasized pay equity, child care, indexed private pensions, public automobile insurance, an increased minimum wage, greater environmental protection, rent control, and, to cope with layoffs, longer notice, better severance pay, and more retraining programs.

The new Tory leader was saddled with a lack of voter recognition and a $4-million party debt, but Mike Harris called himself "the taxfighter" and ran a one-note campaign accusing the government of having raised 33 taxes. Perhaps in response, Peterson promised in mid-campaign to reduce the sales tax from eight to seven percent (having raised it two years earlier), but this issue backfired and added to the electorate's sense of Liberal opportunism. Harris surprised many observers by holding his own in a lively but inconclusive televised leaders' debate.

At the last minute, the Tories managed to run a full slate of candidates, and the three major parties were joined by 68 Family Coalition candidates, 39 Greens, 46 Libertarians, and an assortment of others. Seventy-four New Democrats, 36 Liberals (not including David Peterson), and 20 Conservatives were elected. Due to the abundance of fringe candidates, the NDP won a majority of seats with only 37.6 percent of the vote. It secured more seats than either of the other parties in all regions of the province, winning in places where it had always been weak. A total of 28 women were elected, 20 of them on the government side, and the new NDP MPPs also included many social activists and union organizers.

As surprised as anyone at his victory, Bob Rae chose a cabinet which included 11 women, 12 newly elected MPPs, and Floyd Laughren as deputy premier and treasurer.[92] Immediately after the election, officials revealed that the NDP would inherit a government deficit in the $2-billion range. The worsening recession provided the context for Rae's cancellation of a $55-million grant which Peterson had committed to a new Toronto ballet-opera house, for withdrawal of NDP opposition to a British takeover of Consumers Gas and for the province's exit from Varity Corporation. The first Ontario NDP throne speech was a reiteration of campaign promises, less specific, less immediate, and less inspiring than many supporters had hoped, but more moderate than others expected. Most of its commitments were to be implemented gradually over a four-year term, and many promises required additional study before being enacted. After five years of savage recession, many of its promises and commitments remained unfulfilled.[93]

As in other provinces in the first half of the 1990s, Ontario politics were dominated by the issue of public finance. By the time of the NDP government's first budget in April 1991, the 1990-91 deficit had risen to $3 billion. The budget boldly declared war on the recession, but at the cost of an unprecedented $9.7 billion deficit, which reached $10.8 billion by the end of the fiscal year. The 1992-93 deficit was supposed to be $9.9 billion but rose to $12.4 billion, a fate repeated in subsequent years, as seen in Table 7.13. Thus, the NDP added almost $50 billion to the accumulated provincial debt over its five years in power. It fought with the Provincial Auditor over the size of the deficit, but was lauded for the introduction of Ontario Savings Bonds to help repatriate the debt.

Soon after the 1991 budget and, partly as a result of pressure from bond rating agencies and lending institutions, the premier and the minister of Finance began to express concern about the province's finances and initiated serious efforts to contain the growth of the debt. Every year Laughren would announce new cost-cutting measures with the hope of not going above a symbolic $10-billion figure. It is not surprising that the NDP had to swallow its principles in many areas, especially those involving increased expenditure of public funds. Even so, the provincial credit rating was regularly downgraded.

TABLE 7.13   Government of Ontario Finances, 1990/91–1994/95 (millions)

	1990/91	1991/92	1992/93	1993/94	1994/95
Total revenues	$47,917	$45,744	$46,106	$48,174	$49,388
Debt charges	5,226	5,652	6,831	8,117	8,959
Total expenditures	50,261	56,555	58,525	60,902	60,377
Deficit	2,344	10,812	12,419	12,728	10,989

Source: Reproduced by authority of the Minister of Industry, 1995, Statistics Canada, *Public Sector Finance, 1994–95*, Financial Management System, cat. no. 68-212 (March 1995). Adapted by author.

Apart from its deficit budgets, the NDP's most controversial move was its Social Contract legislation of 1993. The government claimed the 1993-94 budget would reach a deficit of $17 billion unless drastic measures were taken, so to achieve a more manageable $9 billion, $8 billion had to be found in a combination of additional revenues and expenditure cuts. The government chopped $4 billion out of program spending and brought in $2 billion worth of tax increases. The remaining $2 billion had to be cut via the Social Contract, spreading that amount among eight sectors of the wider public sector. In essence, it was a three-year salary freeze, combined with up to 12 days per year of unpaid leave for about 900,000 people earning over $30,000 annually. Rather than impose uniform cuts across the board, as many other provincial governments were doing, the NDP tried to establish framework agreements within the sectors, allowing negotiation within individual workplaces, primarily over the number of days of unpaid leave. These could be reduced if other savings could be found, so that incentive existed for employees to negotiate an agreement rather than be subdued by general legislation. In the government's eyes, such negotiations had a semblance of a "contract." But this was not how unionists saw the issue: they felt the government, an NDP government at that, had opened and altered sacred collective agreements. The government argued that the alternative was a massive layoff of public sector workers. Although the public sector had done well in salary increases in previous years and had been spared the layoffs prevalent in the private sector, union leaders condemned the Social Contract in vehement terms and many, especially the Canadian Union of Public Employees, pledged to oppose the NDP in the next election.

The second striking break with NDP tradition was the decision not to nationalize the automobile insurance industry, a move largely motivated by the recession and one which upset many longtime party activists. The government argued that it would have cost an estimated $1.4 billion to provide compensation to the companies in question, and the operation of a single, more efficient Crown corporation in the field would have resulted in the loss of about 5,600 jobs. Instead, the NDP amended the Liberals' legislation to allow accident victims wider scope in suing for damages for pain and suffering, and to increase the benefits, but it also removed the right to sue for economic loss. Most Ontario residents soon saw increases in their car insurance premiums. Other initiatives included the introduction of photo radar to deter speeding, a graduated system for drivers' licenses, and approval of longer trucks on the province's highways.

The government did try to follow up on its promise to regulate Sunday shopping, but public opinion forced it to repeal its legislation. Then, even though the NDP had an antipathy to lotteries, gambling, and casinos, the prospect of revenue from these sources led the government to set up a casino in Windsor and to plan for a second, run by aboriginals, on Rama reserve near Orillia. In this case, the government faced the certainty that casinos would spring up just outside the province's borders if it failed to act. However, the about-face on these two issues caused one NDP MPP to quit and sit as an Independent. Also, rather than reducing university and college tuition fees as it had promised, the NDP repeatedly increased them although, as in many other cases, it blamed cutbacks in federal grants to the province as a contributing factor.

The government also decided its promise of heavier corporate taxation needed further study and appointed the Fair Taxation Commission. In its 1993 report, the commission agreed with the party's position on inequities in the Ontario taxation system, while noting some could only be rectified at the national level. The government introduced a diluted minimum corporate income tax and, instead of establishing inheritance and wealth taxes as the commission recommended, Finance Minister Floyd Laughren raised income taxes for more affluent individuals, as well as taxes on alcohol and tobacco, and extended the retail sales tax in what was called the largest tax grab in provincial history. The 1994 budget, however, contained no new taxes and even allowed companies a one-year holiday from paying the payroll health tax for new employees.

The government's cutbacks in health spending were both lauded and condemned. Clamping down on out-of-province billings was one means of getting the health budget under control but, when the province imposed a maximum daily limit of $100 a day for health care outside the country, the Canadian Snowbirds Association filed a lawsuit and Ottawa suggested that this limit violated the Canada Health Act. The government also tightened up the drug benefit plan for seniors and those on social assistance, as well as medical lab fees and pharmacists' dispensing fees. It removed several medical procedures from OHIP coverage, including in-vitro fertilization, but continued to cover annual physical checkups as a preventive measures. On the other hand, the government expanded cancer treatment facilities, anonymous HIV testing, and, in 1992, abortion clinics—the same time the Morgentaler abortion clinic in Toronto was bombed. The NDP gave midwives and nurse practitioners more prominence in the health-care system, established binding arbitration to settle fee disputes with doctors, and clamped down severely on sexual misconduct of health professionals. To reduce fraud, it introduced a new digitized photo health card, and brought in a drug plan to subsidize the costs of prescription drugs for the working poor. It also stiffened anti-smoking laws, making 19 the minimum age to buy tobacco and prohibiting cigarette sales in drug stores. But it was reluctantly forced to reduce taxes on cigarettes to counter the smuggling of contraband tobacco from Quebec and the United States.

If the Bob Rae government broke faith with organized labour in its Social Contract, it did its best to live up to its promises of labour legislation. It was pounded by the business community over Bill 40, which made it easier both to form a union (requiring a secret vote on whether to establish a union after 40 percent of workers had been signed up), and to get a first contract (automatic access to arbitration 30 days after a strike or lockout). It also extended union membership to previously excluded groups. Most significantly, the bill prohibited the use of replacement workers in a strike or lockout, although companies were allowed to transfer work to other plants and use supervisors to do the work of strikers. Although the NDP did not succeed in setting the minimum wage at 60 percent of the average industrial wage in the province, it repeatedly increased it until it reached the highest level in the country. It also enacted legislation which gave public servants the right to strike, a right they received much later than their counterparts in most other provinces. As promised, the government enacted a wage protection plan for workers whose employers closed down owing them wages and vacation, severance, or termination pay. Rae conducted a major overhaul of the Workers' Compensation Board, removing its top officials, scrapping the indexing of benefits, and discovering widespread fraud in its operations.

The NDP also showed its concern for jobs by intervening when several major plants threatened closure. In Kapuskasing and Sault Ste. Marie respectively, the government helped keep Spruce Falls Pulp and Paper and Algoma Steel plants alive under majority employee ownership with a combination of cash and pressure on the former owners. When Boeing threatened to close de Havilland aircraft in Toronto, the NDP joined forces with Ottawa and Bombardier to keep it viable. In the case of Elliot Lake, there was no reason to subsidize the uranium mines, but the government did everything it could to try to minimize the shattering effects of the closings. It bought Ontario Bus Industries for $1, but hoped to find a private sector buyer; it sold the province's remaining Suncor shares, as well as the Toronto SkyDome and the Algoma Central Railway, and allowed the National Basketball Association to enter the province in the form of the Toronto Raptors. Rae helped fund an expansion of the Toronto subway system and the Toronto convention centre, and build a new trade centre at the Canadian National Exhibition. The premier was proud of the "partnerships" he established with industries in the private sector in pursuit of jobs. He also made a number of foreign trips in search of investors, although the province's trade offices around the world were casualties in the battle to confine the deficit.

The NDP's main job-creation program, called jobsOntario, had several ingredients. Under the jobsOntario training fund, the government provided up to

$10,000 to employers for every unemployed person hired. The jobsOntario capital fund provided an estimated 10,000 jobs in infrastructure projects, and the jobsOntario homes fund stimulated the slumping construction industry. Although the government put considerable money and publicity into it, the program had trouble gaining credibility. For every job created, however, more than one was lost, due to a serious cyclical downturn in the economy and long-lasting restructuring. Such statistics not only exceeded those of the recession of the early 1980s but, to a much greater extent, represented firms closing their doors for good.

In the housing sector, the NDP promoted non-profit and co-operative housing, and legalized the use of basement apartments to help ease the housing shortage. It passed its own rent control act and, in response to a royal commission report, introduced a new planning system which sought to protect farmland, be friendly to pedestrians and public transit, and speed up the development process. Unfortunately financial bungling, if not fraud, forced the government to fire the entire board of the Metro Toronto Housing Authority.

On the social policy side, the NDP enacted the most comprehensive employment equity legislation in the country, in all but smaller businesses giving preference in hiring to women, aboriginals, the disabled, and visible minorities. It also made progress addressing other aboriginal concerns. It extended spousal employment benefits within the public service to same-sex partners, but failed to pass a general law on the issue in a free vote after Liberal leader Lyn McLeod changed her mind on the issue and even some New Democrats opposed it. The NDP cracked down on welfare by decreasing or freezing social assistance benefits and hiring inspectors to eliminate fraud and overpayments, but it also absorbed responsibility from municipalities for sole support parents on general welfare. It sought to get welfare recipients employed via a program called jobLink, but the strategy suffered from lack of funds. The government had all new court orders for father's child support payments deducted automatically from the employee's paycheque, promoted the conversion of for-profit child-care operations to non-profit, and streamlined services for the elderly. It also compensated victims of sexual abuse at Grandview Training School for Girls. On the other hand, it raised nursing home rates and delayed implementing pay equity legislation. In addition to introducing curriculum changes in the school system, the government appointed a royal commission on learning and began to implement its recommendations. The Ontario Court of Appeal upheld provincial policy which refused to fund Jewish or private Christian schools, citing historic constitutional rights for the public funding of the Roman Catholic system.

The NDP secured political control of Ontario Hydro and redirected its operations. Rae's appointment of high-profile environmentalist-businessman Maurice Strong as Hydro president meant the Crown corporation abandoned its expansion plans, downsized its workforce (with much labour unrest), and eventually turned a profit. With regard to the environment, the government told municipal politicians in the Greater Toronto area to dispose of their garbage within the region to encourage citizens to produce less trash. While the NDP produced an environmental bill of rights and strengthened environmental standards with respect to mining companies, it exempted the private sector from environmental assessment rules.

In intergovernmental affairs, Bob Rae was a passionate advocate of the Charlottetown Accord, especially after persuading his fellow premiers to include a social charter in the document. Possibly due to Rae's efforts, the Ontario electorate voted narrowly in favour of the accord. Also, Ontario and Quebec continued a long-standing dispute over the latter province's restrictions on non-resident construction workers. This dispute reached heated proportions in 1994, when the restrictions were removed and a mutual agreement on government procurement was signed.

Such achievements were largely overshadowed by the unprecedented number of cabinet resignations from 1990 to 1995. Unlike most previous governments, however, none of the resignations involved personal benefit at public expense. Instead, most were relatively minor violations of excessively rigid guidelines for the conduct of cabinet ministers, and some were semi-humorous, at least to outside observers. Peter Kormos was allegedly fired for posing as a fully clothed pin-up boy in the *Toronto Sun*, but the real reasons were his poor judgment and inability to function as a team player. Zanata Akande resigned over accusations she had exceeded the rent review guidelines in apartment buildings she owned, although she was later cleared. Evelyn Gigantes resigned twice, once for inadvertently disclosing the name of an out-of-province OHIP claimant, and once for her attempts to settle an internal dispute at a co-operative housing project. Peter North resigned over a job he offered in exchange for sexual favours, and Will Ferguson over an alleged sexual incident which happened 20 years before. Like Akande, he was later acquitted. Rae's communications director resigned for leaking the criminal record of the woman who brought the accusations against Ferguson. But Shelley Martel did not resign after she said she had seen the file of a Sudbury dermatologist fighting the government's cap on OHIP billings and that he would be charged with overbilling. She later confessed to having fabricated these statements in the heat of an argument. She did resign, however, after writing a letter, approved by her legal advisers, found to violate the Privacy Act.

The government had a persistently tense relationship with police officers, especially those in Metro Toronto, primarily over budgets, accusations of racism, and the investigation of complaints. In 1992, the government enraged the police community by requiring reports be submitted whenever an officer drew a gun in public. For about seven weeks, officers protested by refusing to issue tickets for minor offences or wear full uniforms (opting for baseball caps), culminating in a protest at Queen's Park. With an eye to the safety of officers, the government restricted the sale of ammunition, authorized the police use of pepper spray, and replaced their .38 calibre revolvers with semi-automatic pistols. Possibly to make peace with the police, it fired the head of the Special Investigations Unit and the provincial parole board.

Unfortunately for Bob Rae, the NDP's public image was made up of budgetary deficits, cabinet resignations, and policy reversals. Although this was only one side of the picture, it was the prevailing view as the party entered the 1995 election. Meanwhile, in 1992 the Liberals chose Lyn McLeod as their new leader. McLeod won by nine votes over Murray Elston, who had entered the convention with more support from committed delegates. Over the following three years, however, she failed to establish her identity with the electorate.

Having fallen below 20 percent in the polls (with the Liberals at over 50 percent), Rae was in no rush to call an election. He and his ministers criss-crossed the province in the early months of 1995 distributing over $1 billion in handouts, but rather than call the legislature into session with a full-fledged budget, the Finance Minister issued a financial statement. In the meantime, Conservative leader Mike Harris produced his call for a "Common Sense Revolution" (CSR), which advocated the elimination of the deficit over five years along with 13,000 government jobs; a cut of 20 percent in all government expenditures except health, law enforcement, and classroom funding; a reduction in the personal income tax rate of 30 percent; a reduction in welfare benefits to 10 percent above the national average, with mandatory "workfare" and "learnfare" for all except lone parents with young children; and repeal of the Employment Equity Act and the NDP labour legislation, Bill 40.

Trying to clone the Chrétien "red book" strategy of the 1993 federal election, and deliberately carving out a position slightly to the left of the Common Sense Revolution, Lyn McLeod's Liberals unveiled a provincial red book which promised to balance the budget over four years, eliminate 12,000 government jobs, reduce taxes by 5 percent, increase health funding, save $1 billion through welfare reform, including a reduction in benefits for those who refused training or work, and amendments to employment equity and Bill 40. Once he called the election, Rae had much less of a detailed program to offer than his opponents, generally emphasizing job creation, saving health care, standing up to Ottawa, and living within Ontario's means.

Whether it was because of attacks from both left and right, their lack of principle, their indistinct leader image, the gender of their leader, or other causes, the Liberals' campaign lead quickly evaporated. By election day, most of this floating vote had moved into the PC camp. It seemed that even if many voters did not believe the Tory figures of a tax cut, they did support the general thrust of the CSR: concentrate on the deficit, reduce taxes, eliminate employment equity, get rid of Bill 40, and make those on welfare go to work. Such a thrust was out of character for Ontario, and even for the Ontario Progressive Conservative Party—indeed, it was borrowed from the Reform Party and Ralph Klein's adaptation of Reform policy in Alberta. But times had changed, the debt had more than doubled, and the Ontario Liberals' imitation of the CSR had helped to give it legitimacy. Mike Harris garnered 82 seats (45 percent of the vote), the Liberals were returned with only 30 (31 percent of the vote), and the NDP, with 21 percent of the vote, fell to 17 seats.

CONCLUSION

Until 1985 modern Ontario politics was distinguished by a Tory dynasty and a three-party system. After a unique two-year period of Liberal-NDP minority government, the province gave the Liberals a landslide victory but retained its three-party character. The shift from Conservative to Liberal dominance was dramatic, but the new government continued in a manner similar to that of its Tory predecessor. Then, to everyone's surprise, the restless electorate returned a majority NDP government in 1990. The NDP provided a pragmatically progressive government, but deficits, cutbacks, tax increases, and cabinet resignations forced it into a low position in the polls. In 1995, the electorate returned the Conservatives to power, but on the basis of a right-wing platform that challenged prior understanding of the moderate ideological character of Ontario politics.

TABLE 7.14   Ontario Provincial Election Results Since 1919

Year	Conservatives		Liberals		CCF/NDP		Other	
	Seats	Popular Vote	Seats	Popular Vote	Seats	Popular Vote	Seats	Popular Vote
1919	25	33%	28	23%	11	10%*	47	31%
1923	75	50%	14	21%	4	5%*	18	24%
1926	74	56%	21	22%	1	1%*	16	21%
1929	92	57%	13	32%	1	1%*	6	10%
1934	17	40%	70	50%	1	7%	2	3%
1937	23	40%	66	51%	–	5%	1	4%
1943	38	36%	16	31%	34	32%	2	1%
1945	66	44%	14	30%	8	22%	2	4%
1948	53	41%	14	30%	21	27%	2	2%
1951	79	48%	8	32%	2	19%	1	1%
1955	84	49%	11	33%	3	17%	–	–
1959	71	46%	22	37%	5	17%	–	–
1963	77	48%	24	35%	7	16%	–	–
1967	69	42%	28	32%	20	26%	–	–
1971	78	45%	20	28%	19	27%	–	–
1975	51	36%	36	34%	38	29%	–	–
1977	58	40%	34	32%	33	28%	–	–
1981	70	44%	34	34%	21	21%	–	–

TABLE 7.14 continued

Year	Conservatives		Liberals		CCF/NDP		Other	
	Seats	**Popular Vote**	**Seats**	**Popular Vote**	**Seats**	**Popular Vote**	**Seats**	**Popular Vote**
1985	52	37%	48	38%	25	24%	–	–
1987	16	25%	95	47%	19	26%	–	–
1990	20	24%	36	32%	74	38%	–	6%
1995	82	45%	30	31%	17	21%	1	3%

*United Farmers or Progressives won all "other" seats from 1919 to 1937, except for two in 1919 and one in 1923; their percentage of the popular vote was 24, 22, 11, 5, 1, and 1 respectively from 1919 to 1937; the "others" from 1943 to 1951 were Communists.

TABLE 7.15 Premiers of Ontario Since 1867

Premier	Party	Year Elected
John Sandfield Macdonald	Coalition	1867
Edward Blake	Liberal	1871
Oliver Mowat	Liberal	1872
A.S. Hardy	Liberal	1896
George Ross	Liberal	1899
James Whitney	Conservative	1905
William Hearst	Conservative	1914
E.C. Drury	United Farmers	1919
Howard Ferguson	Conservative	1923
George Henry	Conservative	1930
Mitch Hepburn	Liberal	1934
Gordon Conant	Liberal	1942
Harry Nixon	Liberal	1943
George Drew	Progressive Conservative	1943
Tom Kennedy	Progressive Conservative	1948
Leslie Frost	Progressive Conservative	1949
John Robarts	Progressive Conservative	1961
Bill Davis	Progressive Conservative	1971
Frank Miller	Progressive Conservative	1985
David Peterson	Liberal	1985
Bob Rae	NDP	1990
Mike Harris	Progressive Conservative	1995

ENDNOTES

1. Ministry of Northern Development and Mines, *Ontario Mineral Score 1992* (Toronto, 1994).

2. These figures are based on Social Contract documents rather than the Statistics Canada figures used in other chapters. According to the latter, there are about 330,000 provincial employees and 425,000 municipal employees.

3. Peter C. Newman, *The Canadian Establishment* (Toronto: Seal Books, Rev. ed., 1979), pp. 251-258. See also Newman's *Debrett's Illustrated Guide to the Canadian Establishment* (Toronto: Methuen, 1983). Corporate takeovers and changes of personnel are so frequent it is more difficult to keep up with them than with political developments.

4. Keith Brownsey and Michael Howlett, "Ontario: Class Structure and Political Alliances in an Industrialized Society," in Brownsey and Howlett, *The Provincial State* (Mississauga: Copp Clark Pitman, 1992).

5. Rand Dyck, "The Position of Ontario in the Canadian Federation," in R.D. Olling and M.W. Westmacott, eds., *Perspectives on Canada Federalism* (Scarborough: Prentice Hall Canada, 1988); Robert Vipond, "Constitutional Politics and the Rise of the Provincial Rights Movement in Ontario," an address to the Canadian Political Science Association (June 1984); Richard Simeon, "Ontario in Confederation," in Donald C. MacDonald, ed., *The Government and Politics of Ontario,* 3rd ed., (Scarborough: Nelson, 1985); and Christopher Armstrong, *The Politics of Federalism: Ontario's Relations with the Federal Government, 1896-1942* (Toronto: University of Toronto Press, 1981).

6. Robert Drummond, "Is There an Ontario Identity?" in Eli Mandel and David Taras, *A Passion for Identity* (Toronto: Methuen, 1987); Royce MacGillivray, *The Mind of Ontario* (Belleville: Mika Publishing, 1985); Canadian Broadcasting Corporation, *Ontario at 200,* transcript of Ideas programs, April 30-May 3, 1984; F.-P. Gingras, "Ontario," in David Bellamy, et al., eds., *The Provincial Political Systems,* (Toronto: Methuen, 1976); Peter Oliver, "On Being Ontarian," in Oliver, *Public and Private Persons* (Toronto: Clarke Irwin, 1975); three articles in MacDonald, ed., *The Government and Politics of Ontario,* 3rd ed.: Desmond Morton, "Sic Permanet: Ontario People and Their Politics," S.F. Wise, "Ontario's Political Culture," and Tom Miller, "Cabin Fever: The Province of Ontario and its Norths"; the Morton and Wise articles in White, ed., *The Government and Politics of Ontario,* 4th ed. (Scarborough: Nelson, 1990); and John Wilson, "The Red Tory Province: Reflections on the Character of the Ontario Political Culture," in MacDonald, ed., *The Government and Politics of Ontario,* 2nd ed., (Toronto: Van Nostrand Reinhold, 1980).

7. Dyck, "The Position of Ontario."

8. Wilson, "The Red Tory Province."

9. Richard Simeon and David Elkins, "Provincial Political Cultures in Canada," in Elkins and Simeon, eds., *Small Worlds* (Toronto: Methuen, 1980); and Marsha A. Chandler and William M. Chandler, *Public Policy and Provincial Politics* (Toronto: McGraw-Hill Ryerson, 1979), pp. 74-83.

10. Gingras, "Ontario"; Miller, "Cabin Fever"; G.R. Weller, "Hinterland Politics: The Case of Northwestern Ontario," in *Canadian Journal of Political Science* (December 1977); Matt Bray and Ernie Epp, eds., *A Vast and Magnificent Land* (Toronto: Ontario Ministry of Northern Affairs, 1984); and Weller's article in White's fourth edition.

11. Jeffrey Simpson, *Spoils of Power* (Toronto: Collins, 1988), ch. 11.

12. These are gleaned from various sources including Morton's introduction to MacDonald's *Government and Politics of Ontario;* Norman Penner, "Ontario, The

Dominant Province" in Robin, *Canadian Provincial Politics;* John Wilson, "The Red-Tory Province," and newspaper accounts of the party's 40th anniversary in office, for example, *Toronto Star,* 31 July 1983, and of Davis' retirement in mid-October 1984.

13. See, for example, John Wilson and David Hoffman, "Ontario, a Three-Party System in Transition," in Robin, *Canadian Provincial Politics.*

14. Robert Williams, "Ontario's Party Systems: Under New Management," in H.G. Thorburn, ed., *Party Politics in Canada* (Scarborough: Prentice Hall Canada, 6th ed., 1991).

15. Joseph Wearing, "Political Parties: Fish or Fowl?" in MacDonald, *The Government and Politics of Ontario,* and Wearing's article in White's fourth edition.

16. On this subject, see Dyck, "Relations Between Federal and Provincial Parties," in A.G. Gagnon and A.B. Tanguay, eds., *Canadian Parties in Transition* (Scarborough: Nelson, 1989); Joseph Wearing, *The L-Shaped Party* (Toronto: McGraw-Hill Ryerson, 1981); Robert Williams, "Ontario's Party System"; and especially Reginald Whitaker, *The Government Party: Organizing and Financing the Liberal Party of Canada, 1930-58* (Toronto: University of Toronto Press, 1977).

17. White, "Governing From Queen's Park: The Ontario Premiership," in Pal and Taras, eds., *Prime Ministers and Premiers* (Scarborough, Prentice Hall Canada, 1988).

18. Wilson, "The Red-Tory Province," pp. 226-230.

19. All their biographers make this point in one way or another. Humphries also points out that the early premiers had no public opinion polls; thus Bill Davis' skill at reading public opinion seems less impressive, because it was based on extensive polling.

20. See also the *Toronto Star,* July 31, 1983; various newspapers in mid-October 1984, including Tom Axworthy's column in the *Toronto Star,* 14 October 1984; Graham White, "Governing From Queen's Park: The Ontario Premiership"; and Donald C. MacDonald, *The Happy Warrior* (Toronto: Fitzhenry and Whiteside, 1988), ch. 20.

21. White, "Governing From Queen's Park," p. 170.

22. Peter Woolstencroft, "Tories Kick Machine to Bits: Leadership Selection and the Ontario Progressive Conservative Party," in Kenneth Carty, ed., *Leaders and Parties in Canadian Politics: Experiences of the Provinces* (Toronto: Harcourt Brace Jovanovich, 1992).

23. Norman Penner, "Ontario, The Dominant Province" in Robin, *Canadian Provincial Politics,* emphasizes government assistance to business, hydro, roads, tax concessions, and the camaraderie of government and business leaders. This obviously suggests a form of elite accommodation was at work.

24. Marsha Chandler, "The Politics of Provincial Resource Policy," in Michael Atkinson and Marsha Chandler, eds., *The Politics of Canadian Public Policy,* (Toronto: University of Toronto Press, 1983), p. 61. See also the *Journal of Canadian Studies* (Spring 1983).

25. Dale Poel also lists a human tissue act, senior citizen housing, and cost of credit legislation as Ontario innovations, giving it the highest innovation score apart from Saskatchewan, "The Diffusion of Legislation among the Canadian Provinces: a Statistical Analysis," in *Canadian Journal of Political Science* (December 1976). It might also be considered the pioneer in legal aid. See also K.J. Rea, *The Prosperous Years: The Economic History of Ontario 1939-75* (Toronto: University of Toronto Press, 1985), ch. 10.

26. Gerald Caplan, *The Dilemma of Canadian Socialism: The CCF in Ontario* (Toronto: McClelland and Stewart, 1973); J.T. Morley, *Secular Socialists* (Montreal: McGill-Queen's University Press, 1984); and MacDonald, *The Happy Warrior.*

27. Penner points out that NDP candidates identified as Wafflers fared as well as others in this period; maybe so, but the larger question is to what degree did the Waffle Movement paralyze the party.

28. Dyck, "Electoral Reform," in MacDonald, *The Government and Politics of Ontario,* 2nd ed.

29. Robert Williams, "Ontario's Party Systems: Federal and Provincial," in Thorburn, *Party Politics in Canada,* 5th ed., Robert Drummond, "Voting Behaviour: Dancing in the Dark on a Moving Floor," in Donald C. MacDonald, *The Government and Politics of Ontario,* 3rd ed.

30. Grossman, "'Safe' Seats: The Rural-Urban Pattern in Ontario," in *Canadian Journal of Economics and Political Science* (August 1963); Dennis Wrong, "Ontario Provincial Elections, 1934-55: a Preliminary Survey of Voting," in *Canadian Journal of Economics and Political Science* (August 1957). On socio-economic variables and voting behaviour, see Drummond, "Voting Behaviour: Casting the Play"; Drummond in White's fourth edition; and Wilson and Hoffman, "Ontario, a Three-Party System in Transition."

31. Dyck, "A Profile of the Candidates in the 1977 and 1981 Ontario Provincial Elections," an address to the Canadian Political Science Association (June 1983).

32. Williams, "Ontario's Party Systems," in Thorburn, *Party Politics;* Robert Cunningham, Janet Rubas, and Graham White, "Differential Loyalties: Split Identification and Voting at the Federal and Provincial Levels," an address to the Canadian Political Science Association (June 1972).

33. John Wilson and David Hoffman, "The Liberal Party in Contemporary Ontario Politics," in *Canadian Journal of Political Science* (June 1970), argue that abstention is the main cause of the federal-provincial discrepancy, but others disagree.

34. James MacKenzie, "Interacting with Government," in MacDonald, *The Government and Politics of Ontario;* T.G. Myhal, "Interest Groups: The Property Development Industry," in D.C. Rowat, *Provincial Policy-Making;* M.W. Bucovetsky, "The Mining Industry and the Great Tax Reform Debate," in Paul Pross, ed., *Pressure Group Behaviour in Canadian Politics* (Toronto: McGraw-Hill Ryerson, 1975); and the Jacek article in White's fourth edition.

35. Frederick Fletcher, "The Crucial and the Trivial: News Coverage of Provincial Politics," in White, *The Government and Politics of Ontario.*

36. On the subject of the cabinet, see Graham White, "Governing From Queen's Park: The Ontario Premiership," in Pal and Taras, eds., *Prime Ministers and Premiers;* Fred Schindeler, *Responsible Government in Ontario* (Toronto: University of Toronto Press, 1969); Hugh Segal, "The Evolving Ontario Cabinet: Shaping the Structure to Suit the Times," in MacDonald, *The Government and Politics of Ontario,* 3rd ed.; The Reports of the Committee on Government Productivity; J.D. Fleck, "Reorganization of the Ontario Government," in *Canadian Public Administration* (Summer 1972) and "Restructuring the Ontario Government," in *Canadian Public Administration* (Spring 1973); Kenneth Bryden, "Executive and Legislature in Ontario: A Case Study on

Governmental Reform," in *Canadian Public Administration* (Summer 1975); and the Loreto and White article in White's fourth edition.

37. Edward Stewart, *Cabinet Government in Ontario: A View from Inside* (Halifax: Institute for Research on Public Policy, 1989).

38. Graham White, *The Ontario Legislature: A Political Analysis* (Toronto: University of Toronto Press, 1989); Graham White, "Ontario: A legislature in adolescence," in Gary Levy and Graham White, eds., *Provincial and Territorial Legislatures in Canada* (Toronto: University of Toronto Press, 1989); MacDonald, "Modernizing the Legislature"; MacDonald, *The Government and Politics of Ontario,* 3rd ed.; the Camp Commission Report; and Graham White, "The Life and Times of the Camp Commission," in *Canadian Journal of Political Science* (June 1980).

39. Schindeler, *Responsible Government,* pp. 85-7

40.

1867-74	82	1902-08	98	1955-63	98
1874-85	88	1908-14	106	1963-67	108
1885-89	90	1914-26	111	1967-75	117
1889-94	91	1926-34	112	1975-87	125
1894-1902	94	1934-55*	90	1987-present	130

*The reduction in the number of seats was an economic move prompted by the Depression.

41. Vaughan Lyon argues that opposition members were so moved by perks and by their new importance in a minority situation, and so wedded to the British parliamentary model, that they did not press for significant reforms which would have survived a return to majority government, "Minority Government and Majority Rule: Ontario 1975-1981," *Canadian Journal of Political Science* (December 1984).

42. Schindeler, *Responsible Government;* C.R. Tindal, "The Public Service," in MacDonald, *The Government and Politics of Ontario,* 2nd. ed.; the Loreto article in White's fourth edition; George G. Bell and Andrew D. Pascoe, *The Ontario Government: Structure and Functions* (Toronto: Wall and Thompson, 1988); and E.A. Lindquist and Graham White, "Streams, springs, and stones: Ontario public service reform in the 1980s and the 1990s," *Canadian Public Administration* (Summer 1994).

43. Hodgetts and O.P. Dwivedi, "Administration and Personnel," in Bellamy et al., *The Provincial Political Systems.*

44. John Eichmanis and Graham White, "Government by Other Means: Agencies, Boards and Commissions," in MacDonald, *The Government and Politics of Ontario,* 3rd ed.; Eichmanis' article in White's fourth edition; Publications Ontario, *Guide to Agencies, Boards and Commissions of the Government of Ontario* (Toronto, 1994); and D.C. MacDonald, "Ontario's Agencies, Boards and Commissions Come of Age," *Canadian Public Administration* (Fall 1993).

45. Schindeler, *Responsible Government,* p. 80.

46. Simpson, *Spoils of Power,* p. 219. The Liberals reformed the system to the extent that appointees usually had qualifications beyond service to the party.

47. On municipal government, see C.R. Tindal and S.N. Tindal, *Local Government in Canada* (Toronto: McGraw-Hill Ryerson, 2nd. ed., 1984); two articles in MacDonald, *The Government and Politics of Ontario,* 3rd ed., Henry Jacek, "Regional Government and Development: Initiation, Implementation and Impact," and Allan O'Brien,

"Holding Pattern: A Look at the Provincial-Municipal Relationship"; and the Siegel article in White's fourth edition.

48. Wise, "Upper Canada and the Conservative Tradition," in *Profiles of a Province: Studies in the History of Ontario* (Toronto: Ontario Historical Society, 1967), p. 30. The standard history of Ontario is Joseph Schull, *Ontario Since 1867* (Toronto: McClelland and Stewart, 1978); H.V. Nelles, *The Politics of Development* (Toronto: Macmillan, 1974), is also excellent.

49. Wallace, "Political History: 1867-1912," in A. Shortt and A.C. Doughty, eds., *Canada and Its Provinces* (Toronto, 1914), p. 177. Other material on Mowat includes Donald Swainson, ed., *Oliver Mowat's Ontario* (Toronto: Macmillan, 1972); Margaret Evans, "The Mowat Era 1872-1896: Stability and Progress," in *Profiles of a Province,* and "Oliver Mowat, the Pre-Premier and Post-Premier Years," in *Ontario History* LXII (1970); and Sir John Willison, *Reminiscences: Political and Personal* (Toronto: McClelland and Stewart, 1919).

50. Morrison, "Oliver Mowat and the Development of Provincial Rights in Ontario: A Study in Dominion-Provincial Relations, 1867-1896," in *Three History Theses* (Toronto: Ontario Department of Public Records and Archives, 1961).

51. Simpson, *Spoils of Power.*

52. James Watt, "Anti-Catholicism in Ontario Politics: The Role of the Protestant Protective Association in the 1894 Election," in *Ontario History* LIX (1967); Janet Kerr, "Sir Oliver Mowat and the Campaign of 1894," *Ontario History* LV (1963); and S.E.D. Shortt, "The Patrons of Industry," in Swainson, ed., *Oliver Mowat's Ontario.*

53. Nelles, *The Politics of Development,* p. 73.

54. Charles Humphries, *Honest Enough to Be Bold: The Life and Times of Sir James Pliny Whitney* (Toronto: University of Toronto Press, 1985); and "The Sources of Ontario 'Progressive' Conservatism, 1900-1914," historical papers presented at the annual meeting of the Canadian Historical Association, 1967.

55. Nelles, *The Politics of Development,* p. 248. See also A.R. Vining, "Provincial Hydro Utilities," in Allan Tupper and G.B. Doern, eds., *Public Corporations and Public Policy in Canada* (Montreal: Institute for Research on Public Policy, 1981).

56. Humphries, *Honest Enough to Be Bold,* p. 204.

57. Peter Oliver, "Regulation 17: The Resolution of the Ontario Bilingual Schools Crisis 1916-1929," in Peter Oliver, *Public and Private Persons* (Toronto: Clarke Irwin, 1975); Marilyn Barber, "The Ontario Bilingual Schools Issue: Sources of Conflict," in *Canadian Historical Review* XLVII (1966); and Margaret Prang, "Clerics, Politicians, and the Bilingual Schools Issue in Ontario, 1910-1917," in *Canadian Historical Review* XLI (1960).

58. Brian Tennyson, "The Succession of William H. Hearst to the Ontario Premiership—September 1914," in *Ontario History* LVI (1964).

59. Margaret Prang, *N.W. Rowell, Ontario Nationalist* (Toronto: University of Toronto Press, 1975) and "The Evolution of a Victorian Liberal: N.W. Rowell," in Evans, *Profiles of a Province.*

60. On the United Farmers of Ontario period, see E.C. Drury, *Farmer Premier: Memoirs of the Hon. E.C. Drury* (Toronto: McClelland and Stewart, 1966); Tennyson, "The Ontario

General Election of 1919: The Beginnings of Agrarian Revolt," in *Journal of Canadian Studies IV* (1969); David Hoffman, "Intra-Party Democracy: a Case Study," in *Canadian Journal of Economics and Political Science* XXVII (1961); and Charles Johnston, *E.C. Drury: Agararian Idealist* (Toronto: University of Toronto Press, 1986).

61. Oliver, "The New Order: W.E. Raney and the Politics of Uplift," in Oliver, ed., *Public and Private Persons.*

62. Peter Oliver, *G. Howard Ferguson: Ontario Tory* (Toronto: University of Toronto Press, 1977).

63. Ibid., p. 308

64. Gerald Caplan, *The Dilemma of Canadian Socialism: the CCF in Ontario* (Toronto: McClelland and Stewart, 1973), p. 67. McKenty was slightly more charitable: "Hepburn had astonishing ability to take a complicated issue, translate it into easily grasped bread-and-butter language, dramatize it, and wrap it in emotional overtones. He had as well the priceless gift of establishing almost immediate rapport with the 'little man' and the 'have nots,' a power unmatched by any other Ontario politician in the hungry thirties," McKenty, *Mitch Hepburn* (Toronto: McClelland and Stewart, 1967), p. 54. See also John Saywell, *Just Call Me "Mitch": the Life and Times of Mitchell F. Hepburn* (Toronto: University of Toronto Press, 1991).

65. McKenty, *Hepburn,* p. 254; Jonathan Manthorpe, *The Power and the Tories* (Toronto: Macmillan, 1974), ch. 2; Saywell, *Just Call Me "Mitch".*

66. Caplan, *The Dilemma of Canadian Socialistm,* p. 88.

67. Interview with E.B. Jolliffe.

68. Toronto *Globe and Mail,* 9 July 1943 and 17 July 1943; and the pamphlet, *The Constructive Platform of the Progressive Conservative Party in the Province of Ontario,* approved at the general meeting in Toronto, 3 July 1943. Manthorpe is obviously in error in suggesting the platform was pencilled by Drew on the back of an envelope; in fact, it was drawn from the 1942 Port Hope conference.

69. Caplan, *The Dilemma,* p. 126.

70. Manthorpe, *The Power and the Tories,* p. 37, and Schull, *Ontario Since 1867,* ch. 15.

71. Manthorpe, *The Power and the Tories,* p. 44. See the Frost biography Roger Graham, *Old Man Ontario: Leslie M. Frost* (Toronto: University of Toronto Press, 1990).

72. Ontario Progressive Conservative Association, *1957 Annual Meeting Souvenir Program,* p. 3.

73. "I am firmly of the opinion that in the interest of our party ... a change of leadership [should take place] at a time when the party is in power, when it is strong and its prospects are bright....," quoted in J. Saywell, *Canadian Annual Review of Politics and Public Affairs, 1961* (Toronto: University of Toronto Press, 1963), p. 56. See also MacDonald, *The Happy Warrior.*

74. Manthorpe, *The Power and the Tories,* p. 45.

75. Ibid., p. 63; *Canadian Annual Review* (Toronto: University of Toronto Press, 1961), p. 57; A.K. McDougall, *John P. Robarts: His Life and Government* (Toronto: University of Toronto Press, 1986).

76. *Canadian Annual Review,* 1963, p. 101; D.M. Cameron, "The New Democratic Party and the Ontario General Election of 1963," M.A. thesis, University of Toronto, 1964, p. 69; and MacDonald, *The Happy Warrior.*

77. "My own personal philosophy leads me to believe that in the very fast-moving times in which we live, government policies and actions need to be continuously reviewed, revised and rethought. I have never believed that any one man or one group had a monopoly of ideas, and I firmly believe it is necessary to provide opportunity for new approaches to be made available," quoted in the *Canadian Annual Review of Politics and Public Affairs 1970,* (Toronto: University of Toronto Press, 1971), p. 199; McDougall, *John P. Robarts.*

78. On this period see the annual accounts of Ontario in the *Canadian Annual Review of Politics and Public Affairs,* and Claire Hoy, *Bill Davis* (Toronto: Methuen, 1985).

79. Manthorpe, *The Power and the Tories,* p. 87.

80. Oliver, "Ontario," *Canadian Annual Review* (1971), p. 116.

81. Manthorpe, *The Power and the Tories,* p. 161.

82. Ibid., calls this "the most spectacular political sales job the country had ever seen," p. 189.

83. That is, two lanes each way instead of three, but extending no farther downtown than Eglinton Avenue. This was after Davis had been given the "Transportation Man of the Year" award for halting Spadina.

84. Robert J. Drummond and F.J. Fletcher, "Party and Leader Images and Media Use in the 1977 Ontario Election," a paper presented to Canadian Political Science Association (June 1979); and "Preliminary Results of the 1977 Ontario Election Study," a paper presented to the Canadian Political Science Association, (May 1978); Oliver, "Ontario," in *Canadian Annual Review of Politics and Public Affairs, 1977* (Toronto: University of Toronto Press).

85. Paul McKay, *Electric Empire* (Toronto: Between the Lines, 1983).

86. Hoy, *Bill Davis,* ch. 19; Rosemary Speirs, *Out of the Blue: the Fall of the Tory Dynasty in Ontario* (Toronto: Macmillan, 1986).

87. Davis echoed his predecessors in his retirement statement: "It has always been my wish to leave the party and the Government in as strong and dynamic a circumstance as possible," saying it was "time for new leadership with the kind of new ideas and new perspectives such a change will bring," Toronto *Globe and Mail,* 9 October, 1984, p. 2; Speirs, *Out of the Blue.*

88. *Toronto Star,* 2 June 1985, and 3 June 1985; Speirs, *Out of the Blue.* 81.

89. The full document was included in the first edition of this book; Speirs, *Out of the Blue.*

90. Patti Starr, *Tempting Fate* (Toronto: Stoddart, 1993).

91. Georgette Gagnon and Dan Rath, *Not Without Cause: David Peterson's Fall from Grace* (Toronto: HarperCollins, 1991).

92. Graham White, "Traffic Pile-ups at Queen's Park: Recent Ontario Transitions," in Donald Savoie, ed., *Taking Power: Managing Government Transitions* (Toronto: Institute of Public Administration of Canada, 1993).

93. Early works on the NDP period were quite critical: George Ehring and Wayne Roberts, *Giving Away a Miracle* (Oakville: Mosaic Press, 1993); Thomas Walkom, *Rae Days: the Rise and Follies of the NDP* (Toronto: Key Porter Books, 1994).

READINGS

Brownsey, Keith, and Michael Howlett. "Class Structure and Political Alliances in an Industrial Society." Keith Brownsey and Michael Howlett, eds. *The Provincial State*. Mississauga: Copp Clark Pitman, 1992.

Canadian Annual Review of Politics and Public Affairs. Toronto: University of Toronto Press, annual.

Ehring, George, and Wayne Roberts. *Giving Away a Miracle*. Oakville: Mosaic Press, 1993.

Gagnon, Georgette, and Dan Rath. *Not Without Cause: David Peterson's Fall from Grace*. Toronto: Harper Collins, 1991.

Monahan, Patrick. *Storming the Pink Palace: Bob Rae, the NDP and the Crisis of the Canadian Left*. Toronto: Lester, 1995.

Speirs, Rosemary. *Out of the Blue: The Fall of the Tory Dynasty in Ontario*. Toronto: Macmillan, 1986.

Walkom, Thomas. *Rae Days: The Rise and Follies of the NDP*. Toronto: Key Porter Books, 1994.

White, Graham, ed. *The Government and Politics of Ontario*. 4th ed., Scarborough: Nelson Canada, 1990.

White, Graham. "Traffic Pile-ups at Queen's Park: Recent Ontario Transitions." Donald Savoie, ed. *Taking Power: Managing Government Transitions*. Toronto: Institute of Public Administration of Canada, 1993.

Williams, Robert. "Under New Management." H.G. Thorburn, ed. *Party Politics in Canada*. 6th ed., Scarborough: Prentice Hall Canada, 1991.

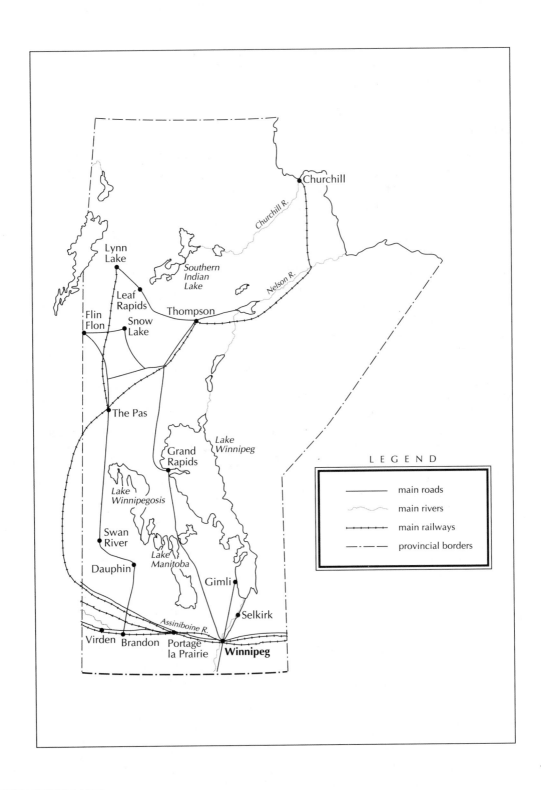

Churchill

Churchill R.

Nelson R.

Lynn
Lake

Southern
Indian
Lake

Leaf
Rapids

Flin
Flon

Snow
Lake

Thompson

The Pas

Grand
Rapids

Lake
Winnipeg

Lake
Winnipegosis

Swan
River

Lake
Manitoba

Dauphin

Gimli

Selkirk

Virden   Brandon   Portage
la Prairie

Assiniboine R.

Winnipeg

LEGEND

——————— main roads

~~~~~~~~~ main rivers

+++++++++ main railways

—·—·—·—· provincial borders

CHAPTER 8

MANITOBA

Manitoba has in many ways become Canada's median or average province. The "gateway to the West," it is centrally located and traditionally served as the location where eastern manufactured goods were exchanged for western raw materials. In modern times, the decline of railways, the advent of air travel and telecommunications, and the emergence of substantial manufacturing capacity in the West have reduced Manitoba's role in interprovincial trade. It is still the median province in terms of size, and is more advanced economically than the Atlantic region but behind the three richest provinces. It has a relatively balanced economy, not being identified with any particular industry, and is somewhat "average" in terms of its ethnic distribution, with a medium-sized francophone community.

SETTING

Geography

Manitoba's area is 649,947 square kilometres, about the same size as the other Prairie provinces, although with lakes Winnipeg, Winnipegosis, and Manitoba, it has significantly less land area and more water surface. It also differs from Alberta and Saskatchewan in having access to ocean shipping at the Port of Churchill on Hudson Bay. Although the province's topography is level, it contains three main geographical formations: a triangular section of agricultural land in the south, the Precambrian shield in the north and, farther north still, the Arctic tundra. For political purposes, the province could be divided into three main regions, the Winnipeg area, the rich agricultural southwest, and the marginal north, through which run powerful rivers, especially the Nelson.

Manitoba's population rose to just over the one-million mark in 1976, reaching 1,091,942 in 1991, and 1,132,800 in January 1995, slightly larger than that of Saskatchewan.[1] A total of 652,354 or about 60 percent of Manitobans live in the Winnipeg metropolitan area. The only other urban concentrations are Brandon (38,567), Thompson (15,046), and Portage la Prairie (13,186). Statistics Canada calculates that 72.1 percent of the population live in urban centres, statistically placing the province between Alberta and British Columbia on the one hand, and Saskatchewan on the other.

Winnipeg has always been a central service and distribution centre for Western Canada.[2] Although its importance has declined somewhat in comparison with other Western cities, it is still the home of the Canadian Wheat Board and Winnipeg Commodity Exchange. Transportation and communication, especially railways, have also been important in this respect. Even though larger urban concentrations have developed in the West, and air services have encroached on the primacy of trains, Winnipeg continues to be a major node in the national transportation system with both Canadian National Railway Company and Canadian Pacific Ltd. lines traversing the city and maintaining extensive marshalling yards, as well as repair, training, and distribution facilities. Winnipeg also has rail connections to the United States, while another railway line stretches from The Pas to Churchill, with branches to Flin Flon, Lynn Lake, and Thompson, permitting that northern port to export wheat and nickel. Winnipeg International is the eighth busiest airport in Canada in terms of passengers and fifth in cargo, and seven of the country's largest trucking firms have their headquarters in the province. A highway links Winnipeg to Thompson and, at Portage La Prairie, the northern Yellowhead route of the Trans-Canada Highway branches off from the southern route which crosses the province.

Economy

Manitoba's economy is balanced among various primary industries and among primary, secondary, and tertiary sectors. Although this economy is not outstanding in any particular respect, the province manages to remain relatively stable and prosperous. The provincial gross domestic product averages about 3.5 percent of the national total.

Agriculture was once the predominant industry in the province, and it is still the most valuable primary industry both in gross provincial product and in numbers employed, ranking fifth in the country. Manitoba's farming is more diversified than that of Saskatchewan, if not Alberta, for, while wheat is the largest single product, canola, barley, and flaxseed are also grown in large amounts. The value of crops exceeds that of livestock, which includes cattle, hogs, dairy products, and poultry and eggs. Other agricultural activities include horticulture, hay, and specialty crops such as sunflower seeds, lentils, and field peas. In 1991, Manitoba had 25,706 farms with an average size of 740 acres.

Mining is the second-largest primary industry. Nickel and copper are the leading minerals, the province ranking second and fourth respectively on a national basis in these two fields. Oil, lead, zinc, tantalum, gold, cobalt, and silver round out the Manitoba mining picture. The main mining centres are the Inco Ltd. company town of Thompson, which primarily produces nickel, and Flin Flon, Leaf Rapids, and Snow Lake, where Hudson Bay Mining and Smelting produces copper and zinc. Both of these companies operate smelters or refineries in the province. In addition, led by Chevron Resources Ltd., Manitoba produces a limited amount of crude oil from the Virden and Waskada areas in the southwest corner of the province.

The Precambrian shield also supports a forestry industry. This includes logging, lumber, lumber products, pulpwood and the manufacture of kraft paper, newsprint, and paper products. Large sawmills operate in The Pas, Swan River, and Dauphin regions of the north and the Pineland region in the southeast, and processing facilities tend to be located in the same areas. The Manfor kraft plant at The Pas, now owned by Repap Enterprises Inc., and the Abitibi-Price Inc. newsprint plant recently purchased by Pine Falls Paper are the two largest manufacturing operations based on forestry. The government adopted a 20-year forest management plan in 1981, with an emphasis on sustainable development.

TABLE 8.1   Manitoba 1991 Labour Force and Estimated 1995 Gross Domestic Product by Industry

	1991 Labour Force		Est. 1995 GDP ($ millions)	
Agriculture	44,570	8.0%	997	5.1%
Fishing	1,215	0.2%	26	0.1%
Forestry	1,815	0.3%	45	0.2%
Mining	6,140	1.1%	390	2.0%
TOTAL PRIMARY	53,735	9.6%	1,458	7.4%
Manufacturing	61,660	11.0%	2,389	12.1%
Construction	29,605	5.3%	929	4.7%
TOTAL SECONDARY	91,265	16.3%	3,318	16.9%
Transportation, communications and utilities	51,890	9.3%	3,185	16.2%
Trade	91,330	16.4%	2,791	14,2%
Finance, insurance & real estate	29,360	5.3%	2,876	14.6%
Services	191,690	34.2%	4,566	23.2%
Government	50,040	9.0%	1,482	7.5%
TOTAL TERTIARY	414,310	74.1%	14,900	75.7%
TOTAL ALL INDUSTRIES	559,305		19,676	

Source: Reproduced by authority of the Minister of Industry, 1995, Statistics Canada, *1991 Census* (cat. nos. 93-326 and 95-359); and Conference Board of Canada, *Provincial Outlook, Economic Forecast*, Ottawa: Summer 1994, Vol. 9, No. 2.

The largest bodies of water, especially Lake Winnipeg, are home to a commercial fishing industry of which the leading species are whitefish, pike, and walleye. The province also hosts a substantial trapping industry.

Like Newfoundland and Quebec, Manitoba has an abundance of hydroelectric power, and claims to have the lowest electricity rates in North America. The Crown corporation Manitoba Hydro, along with the city-owned Winnipeg Hydro, furnish all of the province's electricity, more than 95 percent of which comes from water power. The largest source of hydroelectricity is the Nelson River in the north, which has five major generating stations, including the Limestone dam completed in 1992. The Winnipeg River in the south services six smaller, older stations, while another hydro generating station is located at Grand Rapids, and thermal (coal) stations at Brandon and Selkirk. Manitoba exports electricity to Saskatchewan, Ontario, and especially the United States. A $13.5-billion deal with Ontario signed in 1989 was supposed to ensure the construction of the $5.5 billion Conawapa dam as well, but Ontario later cancelled the deal, and the proposed dam has yet to be built.

Manufacturing has always been important in Manitoba and continues to employ more people than the primary industries collectively. Much manufacturing activity is still related to the farming community, either in the form of processing agricultural products or in supplying manufactured goods for the farmers of Western Canada. The leading manufacturing sectors are food and beverages, transportation equipment, primary and fabricated metals, and electrical products. Next, related to the province's forests, are paper and allied products, printing and publishing, wood products, furniture, and fixtures. Other manufacturing includes machinery, clothing and textiles, chemicals, and pharmaceuticals. Most of the manufacturing, except for primary resource processing, is located in Winnipeg, which also specializes in aeronautics, even after the National Defence Department's CF-18 fighter plane maintenance contract went to Montreal. Wheat, cattle, aircraft parts, motor vehicles and parts, canola, electricity, and nickel constitute the province's largest exports.

Manitoba has a relatively heavy reliance on the services sector, including such transportation industries as railways, air, trucking, and courier services; finance, such as the historic Great-West Life and Investors' Group; colleges, universities, and medical research; and engineering and data processing services. Like New Brunswick, Manitoba is trying to attract telemarketing and other communications services, and early successes included Canada Post, Canadian Pacific, and Unitel. In tourism, Manitoba combines the big-city cultural attractions of Winnipeg with historic sites, festivals, beaches, and great wilderness areas. Public administration is also a significant part of the economy, with large government establishments: nearly 50,000, 45,000, and 30,000 people are employed by the provincial, municipal, and federal governments respectively.

Class

Manitoba was once the most prosperous Western province, but has been surpassed by Alberta and B.C., largely because of their abundance of petroleum. Manitoba had a per capita income of $19,862 in 1992, fifth after Quebec. In 1991, the median family income was $40,671, with 18.3 percent making under $20,000 and 16 percent over $70,000. In recent years Manitoba's diversified economy, coupled with deliberate government policy, have resulted in one of the lowest unemployment rates of any province, but that rate still exceeded nine percent in the early 1990s.

The labour movement is not particularly strong in the province, the Manitoba Federation of Labour having a membership of about 100,000. The largest unions are in the public sector—Manitoba Government Employees Union (MGEU) and the Canadian Union of Public Employees (CUPE), followed by the private sector unions, the United Food and Commercial Workers, the Steelworkers, and the Canadian Auto Workers. In 1986 the province had a total of 157,600 union members or 37.1 percent of its paid workers, the fourth highest rate of unionization in the country.

Manitoba's economic elite is headed by the Richardson family, whose interests are almost as diverse as those of the Irving family in New Brunswick. They include Richardson Securities, Pioneer Grain Company Ltd., insurance, feed and fertilizer factories, pipeline construction, real estate, farming, oil exploration, and many others. A second Manitoba dynasty was the Riley family, involved for generations in the insurance business, especially Great-West Life Inc. and the Investors' Group Inc. both now owned by Paul Desmarais of Montreal. More recent successes include Izzy Asper (CanWest Global Communications Group), Jack Fraser (Federal Industries Ltd.), Randy Moffat (communications), and the Cohen family (Gendis Inc., Saan Stores Ltd., Sony of Canada Ltd., and oil and gas).[3] The large American agricultural firm Cargill Ltd. has its Canadian headquarters in Winnipeg; United Grain Growers Ltd. has recently transformed itself from a co-operative to a shareholder-owned company; while Manitoba Pool Elevators and the Canadian Wheat Board are also important institutions in the province. An imaginary line which dissects Winnipeg can be drawn across the province and, generally speaking, both the urban dwellers and the farmers south of this line are well off, while north Winnipeggers and northern rural residents are economically underprivileged.

A class analysis of Manitoba politics can start with the basic economic forces in society—originally farmers, business and labour—and how they translated their interests into political action. The long Liberal-Progressive period was basically dominated by an alliance of business and farmers. Starting in 1958, Duff Roblin, a Progressive Conservative, instituted a Keynesian modernization, incorporating a much more active provincial state. Since then, the province has experienced major ideological shifts between social democratic and neo-conservative governments. They have essentially differed on the size and role of the state, and in whose interests government activity should be taken.[4]

Demography

With the exception of Quebec, Manitoba has the country's smallest percentage of inhabitants of British descent. This is partly because it has the largest francophone minority west of Ontario, but mostly because of the diversity of other ethnic groups in the province. As in the other prairie provinces, francophones are outnumbered by those of German and Ukrainian background. After about 116,000 residents (10.8 percent) with aboriginal origins come Dutch, Polish, and Scandinavians.

The high rate of francophone and other assimilation is evident from mother tongue and home language statistics. Three-quarters of Manitobans have English as their mother tongue and 87.7 percent speak it at home, compared to 4.7 percent and 2.3 percent French, and 20.3 percent and 9.9 percent other languages. The same imaginary line drawn through the centre of Winnipeg which separates rich from poor tends to divide the Manitoba population in ethnic terms: most people south of it are Anglo-Saxon (or Mennonite) and most to the north are of other ethnic origins, while the French are concentrated in the St. Boniface district of Winnipeg and the southeast corner of the province.

TABLE 8.2   Manitoba Mother Tongue and Home Language, 1991

	Mother Tongue	Home Language
English	75.0%	87.7%
French	4.7%	2.3%
Other	20.3%	9.9%

Source: Reproduced by authority of the Minister of Industry, 1995, Statistics Canada, *1991 Census,* cat. no. 93-317, adapted by author.

At its creation in 1870, Manitoba had an approximately equal number of French and English inhabitants, and was designated an officially bilingual province. Confederation and the railway brought an influx of Ontarian and overseas immigrants into Manitoba, and the English population quickly outnumbered the French. In 1890, this new majority dismantled the original bilingual framework and revoked the official status of French in the province. This action caused some controversy at the time, but the issue did not arise again until the Quiet Revolution in Quebec in the 1960s awakened the consciousness of the ever-diminishing francophone minority in Manitoba, and the Roblin and

Schreyer governments made some attempt to protect the rights of French-speaking Manitobans. The real pressure for change came when the Supreme Court of Canada ruled in 1979 that the Manitoba legislature had acted unconstitutionally in 1890. By 1979, however, Franco-Manitobans were numerically inferior to many other ethnic groups, and the judicial restoration of French as an official language was a matter of great controversy. Howard Pawley's NDP government tried to establish a minimum level of French-language services, but the provincial Conservatives under Sterling Lyon fuelled the flames of ethnic discord by opposing this initiative.

Since 1979, new laws have been passed in both official languages, old unilingual English laws have been translated into French, provincial services are increasingly offered in both languages, and francophone educational and judicial rights have been secured. From its St. Boniface headquarters, "la Société franco-manitobaine, de concert avec le Manitoba français, protège les intérêts de la francophonie, facilite l'épanouissement de la vie française, et fait la promotion du français au Manitoba.[5]

As in other provinces, Manitoba Natives have been discriminated against or overlooked. The Aboriginal Justice Inquiry of 1988-91 revealed the extent of the discrimination, however, and new megaproject proposals inspired Natives to object to disruption of their lives. Reflecting the fact that it has the highest proportion of residents of aboriginal origin, Manitoba has seen several Natives elected to the legislature, and Elijah Harper's veto of the Meech Lake Accord in that chamber was the first dramatic indication that aboriginal Canadians would no longer be ignored.

The large proportion of Manitoba residents of neither British nor French origin is a reflection of immigration that took place decades ago. Germans, Ukrainians, Dutch, Poles and Scandinavians are largely assimilated, or at least integrated, into provincial life. One group of newcomers peculiar to Winnipeg is the Filipino community.

At least at first, ethnic and linguistic issues were closely tied to religion. Since the French population was Roman Catholic and the English were Protestants, there was an even split in religious affiliation. The early immigrants were largely Protestants, however, and the Catholic minority soon found itself on the defensive. The separate school system, established in 1870 along the lines of that in Ontario, was abolished in 1890, but a resolution of this issue occurred when Prime Minister Laurier drew up a compromise agreement with the provincial premier in 1897. Today the population is 51 percent Protestant and 30.3 percent Catholic. Prominent among the Protestant sects are the United and Anglican churches, but the Mennonites and Lutherans are also strong, reflecting the large German population. Religion was not a serious political problem between 1897 and 1960, when the issue of separate schools emerged once again.

TABLE 8.3   Religion in Manitoba, 1991

Protestant	550,120	(51.0%)
United Church	200,375	(18.6%)
Anglican	94,190	(8.7%)
Mennonite	66,000	(6.1%)
Lutheran	55,130	(5.1%)
Other Protestant	134,425	(12.4%)
Roman Catholic	327,785	(30.3%)
No Religious Affiliation	148,170	(13.7%)
Eastern Orthodox	20,655	(1.9%)
Eastern Non-Christian	16,590	(1.5%)
Jewish	13,670	(1.3%)
Other	2,400	(0.2%)

Source: Reproduced by authority of the Minister of Industry, Statistics Canada, *1991 Census,* cat. no. 93-319, adapted by author.

Overall, Manitoba had a stormy 30 years of ethnic and religious conflict, followed by about 80 years of relative peace before ethnic politics became predominant again. After 1920, the provincial political scene was incredibly peaceful, permitting successive coalition governments, although a certain amount of urban-rural tension persisted and a lively class-conscious minority in north Winnipeg provided a consistent level of support for the CCF/NDP and occasionally for the Communist party. A little more political excitement developed after 1955, but it was only in the late 1960s that the province's less affluent population, largely composed of minority ethnic groups, put the NDP into power.[6] Nevertheless, the significance of class and ethnicity in Manitoba politics is not constant.

Federal-Provincial Relations

The 30 years following 1870 also saw much conflict between Manitoba and the federal government.[7] One issue was the location of the eastern boundary of the province, although this dispute was actually a fight with Ontario in which Ottawa took Manitoba's side to no avail. A second disagreement arose over repeated federal disallowance of provincial attempts to thwart the monopoly clause in the Canadian Pacific Railway charter by establishing independent railway links to the United States. The federal government was also involved in the separate schools question because the 1867 Constitution Act allowed a religious minority whose separate school system was abolished by a province to appeal to Ottawa for remedial legislation. Finally, Ottawa's withholding of control over provincial natural resources created a serious conflict that was not resolved until 1930, when control was transferred to all three prairie provinces.

In addition to issues of provincial rights, intense opposition to many federal policies emerged, particularly in the 1920s. Indeed, Manitoba resorted to a provincial farmers' government in part as a means of fighting such policies, especially the tariff on imported manufactured goods which raised the prices Westerners had to pay. The transportation issue, which largely centred on the question of freight rates, was also prominent in this period. However, since 1930 or so, relations with Ottawa have been more friendly, reflecting Manitoba's increased economic diversity and a "national" approach to many issues. Of course, like other provinces, Manitoba has tried to obtain as much federal funding as possible, and such efforts were particularly desperate during the Great Depression. More recently, however, antagonism has centred on the Constitution, when Conservative Premier Sterling Lyon was fundamentally opposed to the Trudeau approach and led the provincial attack against it. Manitoba was outraged when the CF-18 maintenance contract was awarded to Quebec in 1986. With a change of government in 1988, Manitoba supported free trade, but the minority Filmon government backed away from Meech Lake under Opposition pressure.

With its medium provincial income, the province obtains about 30 percent of its revenues from Ottawa, less than the Atlantic provinces, but more than the other five. In addition to the $1,899 million which Ottawa transferred to the provincial government in 1992, it gave $51 million to municipalities, $2,298 to individuals and $477 to businesses.

POLITICAL CULTURE

Manitoba is a province without a distinctive political culture. If Manitobans have a self-image, it is probably one of a moderate, medium, diversified, and fairly prosperous but unspectacular province. Many value its ethnic heterogeneity; others, its intermediary position in federal-provincial affairs, interpreting west to east and vice versa. It is now one of the more federally oriented provinces, despite what has been said about Western alienation. With Saskatchewan, it occupies a position just below Ontario in the proportion of residents who think of themselves as Canadians first—about 80 percent. This is undoubtedly the result of its central geographic position and its economic reliance on Ottawa, a relatively high dependence when compared with other Western provinces.

Manitoba was initially populated largely by ex-Ontarians, and this dominant group laid the foundations for a basic value structure just slightly more progressive and politically experimental than central Canadian liberalism.[8] Even in the period of agrarian revolt in the 1920s, the province's leading political figures, T.A. Crerar and John Bracken, did not stray far from Ontario rural liberalism. In fact, Manitoba experienced a long period of non-partisan "businesslike" government with an emphasis on "sound administration." All it demanded was a change in such federal policies as the tariff, and the basic assumptions of eastern

Canadian liberalism went unchallenged. Manitoba has certainly been more conservative than the radical, populist provinces to its west.

The more radical element in Manitoba was not the farming community but the British working-class immigrant population, largely Methodists influenced by the social gospel. They, along with a minority of continental European immigrants, formed the basis of labour, socialist, and communist parties. Once the majority of working-class continental Europeans shrugged off their deferential Liberal loyalties, the province witnessed a more balanced division of classes. With this class-based politics, authorities such as John Wilson and Jane Jenson would undoubtedly claim Manitoba has become a modern, developed political culture. Unfortunately, this hypothesis is contradicted somewhat by the recent outbreak of anti-French ethnic conflict and the resurrection of the provincial Liberal party.

Manitoba is also difficult to classify in terms of such measures as efficacy and trust. For Richard Simeon and David Elkins, it ranked high in these respects; more recent research, however, suggests a lower ranking.[9] Manitoba's voter turnout rate has been in the medium-to-low range, 72 to 73 percent, in both federal and provincial elections in recent years.

TABLE 8.4   Manitoba Voter Turnout Rate in Recent Federal and Provincial Elections

Federal Elections		Provincial Elections	
1974	70%	1977	76%
1979	77%	1981	72%
1980	69%	1986	68%
1984	77%	1988	74%
1988	75%	1990	69%
1993	69%	1995	69%
Average	72.8%	Average	71.3%

Source: *Reports of the Chief Electoral Officer,* calculations by author.

POLITICAL PARTIES

Party System

The Manitoba party system has experienced several transformations and the province has see-sawed between a period of harmony among all parties in 1940, to the highly partisan and bitter competition of the early 1980s, and since to greater inter-party consensus. For the first 30 years after Confederation, parties were not well organized and, after a brief two-party system composed of the

TABLE 8.5   Party Support in Manitoba, 1970-95

	Years in Office	Average Percentage of Vote	Percentage of Seats
NDP	14	36.4	43.4
Conservatives	11	41.9	47.4
Liberals	–	19.9	9.3

Source: *Reports of the Chief Electoral Officer,* calculations by author.

FIGURE 8.1   Percentage of Vote by Party in Manitoba Elections, 1970–90

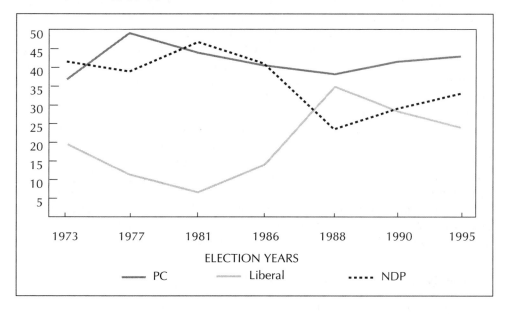

Liberals and the Conservatives, farmer and labour groups introduced two long-standing new political organizations around 1920. The farmers formed the government after 1922 under the United Farmers and Progressive labels, but later merged with the Liberals in a Liberal-Progressive coalition, while the Labour party maintained a distinct identity and became the Co-operative Commonwealth Federation (CCF). A handful of Social Credit members complicated the situation in the legislature after 1936. From this conglomeration emerged a lengthy and ever-broadening multi-party, no-name coalition, which at one point incorporated all parties. The CCF eventually broke away from the coalition, followed by the Conservatives, while Social Credit disappeared, leaving the old Liberal-Progressive alliance intact. Between 1958 and 1986 all parties declined in popularity, except the Conservatives and the NDP, who constituted a clear-cut two-party system in the province for a time. Just when it appeared Manitoba had become an ideologically polarized party system in an industrialized society in which a class cleavage displaced ethnic and religious concerns, ethnic conflict emerged again. In addition, the Liberal party revived to take second place in 1988, but finished third in 1990 and 1995. Thus, as Table 8.5 illustrates, Manitoba has changed from a two- to a three- to a two-and-a-half-party system over the past 25 years.

Party Organization

Whatever their ideological differences, the parties are not far apart in terms of organization. While the NDP naturally has some marks of a mass party, such as regular policy conventions and an annual leadership review, one observer has gone so far as to label it a cadre party not much different in operation from the Conservatives.[10] Until the 1980s, the CCF/NDP in Manitoba never developed the obsession with internal democracy which characterized its counterparts in some other provinces. Much reliance was placed on the leader, especially in the Schreyer period, and the premier, cabinet, and caucus had little difficulty with the party rank and file. In fact, one of the reasons for its 1977 defeat was probably that the party organization had been largely ignored both as a source of policy and as an organizational force with which to fight elections. A legislative liaison committee was set up to maintain a close link between the government and the party organization, but Premier Schreyer regarded party policies as "guidelines" rather than as edicts, and he used the annual party convention to endorse and promote government policy.[11] As for mass party characteristics, both the Conservatives and the NDP featured successful challenges to the incumbent leader, in 1975 and 1968 respectively.

Federal-Provincial Party Links[12]

As befits a province on the margin of the Western revolt against central Canada, Manitoba parties have often had an ambivalent relationship with their national counterparts. Close ties between the federal and provincial branches of both main parties existed in the 1900-20 period, but Premier John Bracken's non-partisan coalition complicated party lines in the province for the next 35 years. He had generally close relations with the national Liberal party, especially as Mackenzie King sought to woo the Progressives back into his fold but, once the provincial Conservatives joined the Liberal-Progressive coalition in 1940, Bracken personally moved closer to the federal wing of that party. This alliance was consumated in 1942-43 when he became federal Tory leader and the national party changed its name to Progressive Conservative to make him feel more comfortable. It was awkward for the two parties to compete with each other in federal elections in Manitoba when they were allies provincially throughout this post-1940 period. The situation became even more bizarre when Bracken's successor, Stuart Garson, later went to Ottawa as a Liberal. After the Conservatives left the coalition, Progressive leader Douglas Campbell was seen as Liberal but found federal Prime Minister Louis St. Laurent too "socialistic" for his taste. Thus, for some time after 1958, relations were not close between the two Liberal organizations. They were not helped by the later personal animosity between federal cabinet minister Lloyd Axworthy and provincial leader Sharon Carstairs.

Premier Duff Roblin established such warm ties with the Diefenbaker party that he ran for the federal Tory leadership in 1967. Harmonious relations continued until the 1980s when bilingualism and Meech Lake badly split the federal and provincial wings. In the case of the NDP, federal-provincial party relations have generally been good, but were severely strained when Ed Schreyer temporarily endorsed Liberal Prime Minister Pierre Trudeau's wage-and-price control program even though the federal NDP condemned the plan. In addition, Schreyer was perceived as having a mind of his own, and a slightly different version of social democracy.[13] This frequently led to speculation that he would join the Trudeau cabinet, but the closest he got was becoming governor general. Before 1958, therefore, federal-provincial party relations in Manitoba were somewhat confused; since then the pattern has been clearer, but serious conflicts have arisen on occasion.

Party Leadership

Manitoba had one of the longest-serving premiers in Canadian history, John Bracken, who held office from 1922 to 1943. This term was, in one respect, even longer than 21 years in that he also set the leadership style for years after his departure. A political neophyte when he assumed the premiership, he practised non-partisan, administrative politics, and was the antithesis of charisma. In fact, until the end of his career, he remained self-conscious about his ability to deliver a good speech. Bracken had firmly held convictions about hard work, thrift, and economy, and was essentially a 19th-century liberal who believed in capitalism. As a Westerner, he also saw a role for government in some situations and for co-operative effort in others, but he was not a radical, progressive, agrarian populist. He is remembered for little but his style, since his initiatives were deliberately few, and his immediate successors left even less of a mark on the province.[14]

In comparison, Duff Roblin, Sterling Lyon, Ed Schreyer, and Howard Pawley did not serve long, but each had more impact on the province. Roblin came from a business background but had a progressive point of view and was distinctly left of his predecessors, the Liberal-Progressives. He built up the Progressive Conservative organization almost from scratch and governed confidently despite his youth. He also had a national perspective and might have had more success as federal Conservative leader than did Robert Stanfield. His successor, Walter Weir, was more rural and conservative in outlook. All accounts of the 1969-77 period emphasize the image and dominance of Ed Schreyer.[15] He was young, attractive, thoughtful, and easily bridged the rural-urban gap. As both premier and Opposition leader, Sterling Lyon was usually described as a spellbinding speaker, cocky and abrasive. He was at his best scorning the NDP or the federal Trudeau government, relishing the role of a fighter. Howard Pawley was not seen as such a strong leader, being described instead as bland, quiet-spoken, and having a collegial style. However, he was regarded as honest and sincere and perhaps the province had had enough of a strongman such as Lyon by 1981 when Pawley's gentle competence triumphed.[16] Filmon is businesslike, but no more charismatic; he is conciliatory, congenial, and low-key, but his insistence on changes to the Meech Lake Accord enhanced his stature within the province sufficiently to secure a bare majority in 1990. The PC party was reelected on his coattails in 1995.

Party Ideology

For many decades after 1900, and certainly after 1919, two ideological streams were evident in the province: a general conservatism, and a radical, labour, working-class element in north Winnipeg. Even the Rodmond Roblin government of 1900-1915 introduced some progressive measures, and the Norris regime of 1915-1920 was particularly innovative. After 1920, however, "Brackenism" took hold, and a basic conservative ideology held sway under the guise of non-partisanship. Reductions were made in social services before the Great Depression, and the knife cut even more deeply in those miserable years. Right up to the 1958 defeat of the Liberal-Progressives, a long-term alliance of farmers and business interests, the only sign of an ideological alternative to such profound conservatism was the small opposition force in the legislature.

The progressive and conservative elements have been more evenly balanced since 1958 and, while the CCF/NDP has been consistently progressive, the other two parties have alternated from one ideological pole to the other.[17] Under Duff Roblin, for example, the Progressive Conservatives were genuinely progressive, instituting enormous increases in public spending between 1958 and 1967, vast improvements in social services, and a broad process of economic planning. Under Walter Weir, the party made a distinct move to the right, so much so that the electorate apparently looked for a more progressive alternative in 1969.

The Schreyer government represented a left-of-centre option to Weir's and Lyon's Conservatives, but some wondered how left-wing it genuinely was.[18] While the premier himself was careful to use the expression "social democratic" rather than "democratic socialist," Schreyer and his colleagues took actions of a collectivist or equalizing nature. The nationalization of automobile insurance, the taking over of faltering firms to preserve the jobs involved, the myriad health and social service initiatives, the protection of rights likely to be violated, and income redistribution through changes in the tax system were all within the bounds of his stated ideological position. Three distinctive social democratic features were income equalization, economic planning, and government involvement in natural resource industries.[19] On the other hand, Schreyer supported wage-and-price controls and rejected Eric Kierans' recommendation to nationalize the mining companies. Schreyer was consistently left of centre, but not too far left; he had a carefully considered ideological position, based on a combination of the Swedish social democratic experience and the Roosevelt New Deal.[20] He also realized how fundamentally conservative his province remained.

The Conservatives opted for a progressive leader in Sidney Spivak in 1971, as Schreyer drew both opposition parties leftward. However, as taxes rose and ill-fated public enterprises continued to lose money, Sterling Lyon saw the opportunity to appeal for restraint and successfully challenged Spivak for the party leadership in 1975. He won the premiership in 1977 but, after only three years of consistent neo-conservativism, voters returned the NDP to power under Howard Pawley, who essentially continued the Schreyer social democratic approach. Premier Gary Filmon exercised a much more middle-of-the-road conservatism, concerned about the government deficit, for example, but not as obsessed as premiers in other provinces.

The Liberals' move to the right with Robert Bend gave the NDP an opportunity to make gains in the centre, especially because Weir was also on the right at the time. Just as Lyon was pulling things to the right in 1977, the Liberals chose a left-wing leader in Charles Huband, and the party again "found itself in the wrong place at the wrong time."[21] The electorate was becoming understandably confused about where the Liberals fit and increasingly ignored the party. Sharon Carstairs finally revived it with new enthusiasm, new leadership, and a centre-right ideological position indistinguishable from that of Filmon.

ELECTIONS

Electoral System

Manitoba possesses an orthodox single-member, first-past-the-post electoral system, but it experimented earlier and with more alternatives than did other provinces. The original French-English equality in the legislature was soon discarded and, from 1920 to 1945, Winnipeg was one 10-member constituency employing proportional representation. From 1945 to 1953 it had three four-member ridings, using a preferential ballot. Somewhat similarly, the rural areas used a single-member transferable or preferential system between 1927 and 1936. These experiments were in the Progressive tradition, and may have been to the advantage of the Liberal-Progressive party. For example, the CCF would probably have done better with single-member constituencies in Winnipeg; on the other hand, that would have made it more difficult for a Communist or Independent to get elected.

For a long period, Winnipeg accounted for about 33 percent of the population but was allotted only 18 percent of the seats—a totally unjustifiable disparity. To its credit, however, Manitoba pioneered an independent redistribution process. Since 1950, the principle of impartiality has prevailed in regular decennial redistributions and, in recent years, the province has reduced the urban-rural imbalance. From 1958 to 1968, the electoral map was drawn on the principle of seven urban voters for every four rural voters, which was at least an improvement on the previous four-to-one ratio. In 1968, the rural-urban distinction was dropped for a new rule stating that no constituency could vary from the size of the average provincial constituency by more than 25 percent. Under this scheme, Winnipeg and Brandon obtained a combined 29 seats between them compared with 28 rural ridings. By 1990, Winnipeg alone had 31 of 57 seats in the legislature. Except in the four northern ridings, which can vary from the mean by up to 25 percent, Manitoba constituencies must now be within a range of plus or minus 10 percent. At the time of its adoption in 1988, the new electoral map had only one constituency exceeding 10 percent and, as seen in Table 8.6, by the time of the 1990 election, the map was still one of the most equitable in the country: only two constituencies exceeded plus or minus 25 percent of the mean.

TABLE 8.6   Representational Disparities in the 1990 Election

Mean no. of voters per constituency	12,504
Largest constituency (Tuxedo)	16,009 (+28.0%)
Smallest constituency (Point Douglas)	8,450 (-32.4%)
Average variation from mean	7.7%
Constituencies within ± 10% (42 of 57)	73.7%
Constituencies within ± 25% (55 of 57)	96.5%

Source: *Report of the Chief Electoral Officer,* calculations by author.

Election-day treating and other forms of corruption were common in the early years, especially 1914, but have since become infrequent. Manitoba has also been relatively free from scandal in the area of party finance. The last real scandal of this sort was the Legislative Buildings affair which brought down the Rodmond Roblin government in 1915. A bill on election financing was passed in 1970 and later amended, and is now among the country's most satisfactory laws on this subject. The measure limits party, candidate, and advertising expenditures; provides public subsidies for candidates and tax credits; requires disclosure of contributions over $250; and, unlike most other provinces, makes a public subsidy available for party expenditures.

Voting Behaviour

From 1920 to 1958, Manitoba voters divided into four main groups. The working class of British background in north Winnipeg voted labour or CCF. The southern English and Mennonite farmers and prosperous residents of south Winnipeg supported the Liberals, Progressives, or Conservatives. The northern rural residents of non-English background also supported the coalition, while other ethnic groups in north Winnipeg were split, some voting for the government and others for the Communist party, depending on their ideological background. The French exhibited bitterness when T.C. Norris abolished French-language schools, but later reverted to their traditional Liberal allegiance. In the Duff Roblin period, the Conservatives gained the upper hand among Anglo-Saxons in south Winnipeg and the rural southwest, the Liberals were limited to the French and deferential "other ethnics" in the rural north and north Winnipeg, while the NDP inherited the British working class in the northern half of the capital.

This pattern changed suddenly in 1969 when the ethnic vote in northern rural areas and in north Winnipeg shifted from the Liberals to the NDP. This was partly because Ed Schreyer's rural, ethnic, Catholic background contrasted sharply with that of Liberal leader Robert Bend, but this pattern intensified, outlasting Schreyer's departure from the scene. At first sight, 1969 represented an "ethnic revolt" as residents of non-English origin defied the advice of their ethnic leaders and moved en masse to the NDP. A simultaneous change in religious voting patterns occurred, as the CCF/NDP had previously relied primarily on Protestants, and now made significant inroads among Roman Catholic, Ukrainian Catholic, and Greek Orthodox adherents.[22] Since ethnicity, class, and location all basically coincide, however, it is possible that class factors were part of the explanation for the change in voting patterns. Some observers emphasize the class factor, arguing that, as voters of non-Anglo-Saxon background became semi-assimilated, they were less susceptible to appeals directed at their ethnic distinctiveness.[23] Given the clear ideological difference between the Conservatives and the NDP, class position took priority. Others emphasize Schreyer's ethnic as well as class appeal, and point out that even more prosperous ethnic groups voted NDP.[24] In any case, the NDP has basically been supported by workers, poorer farmers, "ethnics," and northerners, while the Tories have been backed by the middle class, the richer farmers, "Anglos," Mennonites, and southerners. In 1988, however, the Liberals suddenly reclaimed the ideological and geographic centre of the Manitoba political spectrum, especially in Winnipeg.

A reasonably close correspondence exists between federal and provincial voting behaviour in Manitoba. North Winnipeg regularly chose CCF/NDP candidates after 1921, especially J.S. Woodsworth and Stanley Knowles, and until 1957-58, most of the rest of the province returned Liberals and Liberal-Progressives. Diefenbaker and Roblin put an end to that, and since 1957 the

Liberals have been almost as unpopular in federal elections in Manitoba as elsewhere in the West. During the Trudeau era, the Conservatives and NDP captured the bulk of the vote in Manitoba federally as well as provincially, but the Liberal party hung on to some support in central Winnipeg, and has now resurfaced at both levels.

PRESSURE GROUPS AND THE MEDIA

Pressure Groups

In the early years, the leading pressure group was the United Farmers of Manitoba, which was so prominent that it became the government in 1922. In 1928 it reverted to pressure group status, but remained influential, especially while the Liberal-Progressives held power. It later became the Manitoba Farm Bureau and was perceived as representing the more prosperous farmers. The National Farmers Union speaks for their poorer brethren in Manitoba, as elsewhere. In the wake of the dispute over federally subsidized freight rates (the Crow Rate), the MFB disintegrated, later reappearing in the form of Keystone Agricultural Producers.[25] Labour has also been active since 1920, both as a party and as a pressure group, primarily in the form of the Manitoba Federation of Labour, and has predictably been most influential when the NDP is in office. As in other provinces, however, business groups have had most influence. The Winnipeg and Manitoba Chambers of Commerce are always prominent, the Canadian Federation of Independent Business is particularly active in the province, and the Canadian Manufacturers' Association has a division in Manitoba. At the height of the Autopac controversy over the nationalization of the province's automobile insurance industry, much pressure was applied by insurance groups in opposition to the plan.

Other leading groups in recent years have been the Manitoba Medical Association, with which the NDP regularly battled, the Manitoba Teachers' Society, and the Société franco-manitobaine, which attained such status that the government negotiated with it over a proposed constitutional amendment.

TABLE 8.7   Leading Manitoba Pressure Groups

Peak Business	Manitoba Chamber of Commerce
	Canadian Federation of Independent Business
Industrial	Manitoba Forestry Association
	Manitoba Home Builders Association
	Mining Association of Manitoba
	Tourism Industry of Manitoba

TABLE 8.7 continued

Labour	Manitoba Federation of Labour
Agriculture	Keystone Agricultural Producers
	National Farmers Union
Professional	Manitoba Association of Registered Nurses
	Manitoba Teachers' Society
	Manitoba Bar Association
	Manitoba Medical Association
	College of Physicians and Surgeons
Ethnic	Société franco-manitobaine
	Assembly of Manitoba Chiefs
	Manitoba Métis Federation
Institutional	Manitoba Association of School Trustees
	Manitoba Association of Urban Municipalities
	Union of Manitoba Municipalities
	Manitoba Health Organizations
Environmental	Manitoba Eco-Network Inc.
Public Interest	Manitoba Association for Rights and Liberties

The Media

Throughout the province's history, the *Winnipeg Free Press* has been a very important influence. It was closely associated with the federal Liberal party, especially in the John Dafoe-Mackenzie King era; it generally supported the provincial coalition government up to 1958, and was particularly critical of the NDP after 1969. Table 8.8 lists all the daily newspapers in the province. The Canadian Broadcasting Corporation operates English and French radio and television stations out of Winnipeg, with an English television affiliate in Brandon, while Randy Moffat owns the CTV affiliate in Winnipeg and other radio and television stations in the province.

TABLE 8.8   Daily Newspapers in Manitoba, 1994

	Circulation	Chain Affiliation
Winnipeg Free Press	142,841	Thomson
Winnipeg Sun	45,883	Quebecor
Brandon Sun	20,456	Thomson
Portage La Prairie Daily Graphic	4,158	Maclean Hunter (Bowes)
Flin Flon Reminder	3,600	Independent

Source: *Canadian Advertising Rates and Data* (August 1994).

GOVERNMENT INSTITUTIONS

Manitoba has essentially the same governmental institutions as other provinces. Many of these institutions, however, have functioned somewhat differently. Until about 1900, the province was not really prepared to operate autonomously and, from 1920 to 1955, it possessed a strange succession of coalition and non-partisan governments which resulted in deviations from normal partisan cabinet and legislative procedures.

Executive

Due to Manitoba's initial lack of well-developed governmental structures, the first two lieutenant-governors after 1870 actually ran the province.[26] In addition to their general administrative functions, the lieutenant-governors regularly reserved provincial legislation for the consideration of the federal cabinet, secured amendments to provincial bills to meet federal objections, and acted as confidential advisers to Prime Minister John A. Macdonald. Since 1900 and the development of party government, however, the lieutenant-governors have assumed the more conventional social and ceremonial position.

Apart from the first 30 years, when both the lieutenant-governor and the legislature were unusually active, Manitoba has been governed essentially by the premier and cabinet. As mentioned earlier, the province was chiefly distinctive for the succession of coalition and non-partisan governments. While these governments were marked by compromise and inaction, the lack of activity was more the result of their conservative, administrative mentality than of dissension within the ranks. In 1994, the Manitoba cabinet had 18 members, a marked increase over the nine ministers who made up that body as recently as 1963. French-Catholic representation in the cabinet has declined, and for three periods (1890-1913, 1914-1922, and 1958-1969) no French representation was included.[27] The Schreyer government in 1969 was the first to diverge from this Anglo-Saxon-Protestant predominance. It included members from a variety of ethnic and religious backgrounds, many of whom were carried over into the Pawley cabinet. Just as ethnic and religious representation did not greatly concern premiers until recently, so too has regional representation in the cabinet been largely ignored.

The cabinet operated very informally until 1958, when Duff Roblin appointed a cabinet secretary and upgraded the Treasury Board. Then, in 1968, the otherwise conservative Walter Weir pioneered the use of planning and priorities and management committees of cabinet at the provincial level. The Schreyer government added a health, education and social policy committee in 1971, and abolished the planning and priorities committee in 1973 in the belief that the whole cabinet should be present for crucial decisions. Under Howard Pawley, however, the committee reappeared in the form of a strategy committee. Gary Filmon had no such inner cabinet, but employed a wide range of cabinet committees, including Treasury Board, which he chaired, and economic development, human services, sustainable development, native affairs, management and reform, urban affairs, land use, multicultural affairs, and assessment reform. Roblin and Schreyer also strengthened the cabinet support systems with an executive council Office. Filmon had a premier's office and a cabinet office, both headed by the clerk of the executive council, but also including a more partisan principal secretary.

Legislature

Just as the province discarded its official bilingualism and separate school system shortly after its founding, so it abolished its bicameral legislature. A two-chamber legislature for a population of 12,000 people was even more ridiculous than in Prince Edward Island, and in 1876 the Legislative Council was eliminated on instructions from Ottawa, which was still providing most of the province's funds. Twice the seven-member council vetoed its closure but on a third attempt the bill was passed on the understanding that members would be given equivalent positions elsewhere.

This left the Legislative Assembly, which originally had 24 members and whose constituency boundaries were designed to produce equal representation of French and English and Protestants and Catholics. By 1879 this principle of equality was dropped, and by 1881 no attempt was made to relate electoral boundaries to ethnic or religious settlements. Manitoba has a semi-circular chamber unique in Canada, which has grown to 57 seats.[28] Although its first 50 years were lively ones, the coalition and non-partisan governments which ruled from 1920 to 1955 produced a desultory legislature. The Bracken, Garson, and Campbell governments (1922-1958) were marked by a virtual absence of legislative activity, simply because these cabinets did not see the need for additional legislation. The farming community also felt that the cabinet should listen directly to pressure groups rather than to the legislature and, as a result, cabinet domination was even more complete.[29] To some extent legislative action was also superseded by plebiscites. Although the 1916 Initiative and Referendum Act was thrown out by the courts on the grounds that it interfered with the discretion of the lieutenant-governor, seven plebiscites occurred on the subject of liquor.

Since the return of party government in 1958, the Manitoba legislature has operated more conventionally with a daily oral question period, a full set of standing committees, and an Opposition member chairing the public accounts committee. Bills presumed to be of interest to all members are usually referred to the committee of the whole, while others go to a standing or special committee. Such committees may include ministers, but are chaired by non-ministerial members from the government side. The estimates are scrutinized by the committee of supply. Legislative committees have held numerous public hearings across the province in recent years, especially on constitutional matters.

Manitoba ranks among the lowest provinces in terms of MLA remuneration ($28,780 with a non-taxable expense allowance of $14,390 in 1994) and in other services for legislators, although those with special responsibilities receive more. After the 1995 election, Manitoba was the first province to scrap the tax-free allowance and pay ordinary MLAs a straight taxable indemnity of $56,500. The existing MLA pension plan was also eliminated, but more funds were provided for the operation of constituency offices. In the early 1990s, the Manitoba legislature sat more days per annum than almost any other. It then adjourned for eight months in July 1993 and sat only briefly in 1994, partly because of the government's precarious position.

Bureaucracy

Manitoba employs about 12,700 people in regular departments and agencies, another 12,000 in government business enterprises, and 23,000 more in the wider public sector. It was among the first provinces to adopt a civil service commission in 1918, prior to which appointments had been made on a patronage basis. This action was prompted in large part by the "notorious corruption of the [Rodmond] Roblin regime" and by a recognition of the need for more competent personnel.[30] Still, its public service was small and unprofessional as long as the cabinet and legislature sought to minimize governmental activity. The public service remained relatively stagnant until a new act was passed in 1947, but it remained fairly inactive until the Duff Roblin government was elected in 1958. Since that time, the Manitoba public service has expanded enormously with a corresponding increase in expertise, although it is still relatively small on a per capita basis. Table 8.9 shows the government department structure in 1994.

In addition to its regular departments, Manitoba has many semi-independent bodies, including a variety of agricultural marketing boards, several Crown corporations—especially Manitoba Telephone System, Manitoba Hydro, and Manitoba Public Insurance Corporation—as well as the usual municipal board, public utilities board, arts council, and liquor commission, to name but a few. The Lyon and Filmon governments both privatized a number of NDP creations and acquisitions, and Filmon created a Crown corporations council in 1989 to ensure that these institutions stayed within their mandates and remained accountable to the public. Given the long period of coalition and non-partisan government, patronage was for many years a less prominent part of politics in Manitoba than in any other province.[31] Since 1958, however, a change in government has usually meant a turnover in the personnel heading agencies, boards, commissions, and Crown corporations, a change which is perhaps justifiable because of the difference in party ideology. Similarly, several deputy ministers usually depart voluntarily (or as in the case of Sterling Lyon, involuntarily) when a new government takes office.

TABLE 8.9   Manitoba Government Departments, 1994

Agriculture
Consumer and Corporate Affairs
Culture, Heritage and Citizenship
Education and Training
Energy and Mines
Environment
Family Services
Finance
Government Services
Health
Highways and Transportation
Housing
Industry, Trade and Tourism
Justice
Labour
Natural Resources
Northern Affairs
Rural Development
Urban Affairs

TABLE 8.10   Leading Manitoba Agencies, Boards, Commissions and Crown Corporations

Crown Corporations	Liquor Control Commission of Manitoba
	Manitoba Public Insurance Corporation
	Manitoba Housing and Renewal Corporation
	Manitoba Development Corporation
	Manitoba Mineral Resources Ltd.
	Leaf Rapids Town Properties Ltd.
	A.E. McKenzie Company Ltd.
	Manitoba Hydro-Electric Board
	Manitoba Telephone System
	Manitoba Water Services Board
Agencies, Boards, and Commissions	Communities Economic Development Fund
	Crown Corporations Council
	Manitoba Hazardous Waste Management Corporation
	Manitoba Labour Board
	Manitoba Lotteries Corporation
	Workers' Compensation Board

Judiciary

The Manitoba judiciary consists of provincial courts and the Court of Queen's Bench, both of which sit in the larger centres throughout the province, and the seven-member Court of Appeal located in Winnipeg. Manitoba is one of the few provinces that has established a Family Division of the Court of Queen's Bench.

Municipal Government

Few municipal governments operated in the province until 1902.[32] Now, with almost 60 percent of the population resident in the Winnipeg metropolitan area, that city is the focus of any discussion of municipal government and has a whole provincial department (Urban Affairs) at its disposal. A large number of independent suburbs such as St. Boniface and St. James sprang up around the city of Winnipeg and, from 1950 onward, authorities were concerned with co-ordinating local services in this region. In 1960, a central second-tier based on the Metropolitan Toronto model was added to the 15 or so municipalities in the area. Although the new structure represented an improvement in many ways, it was very controversial at first, and the Schreyer government considerably altered it in 1972. The lower tiers were more or less abolished with the creation of one great "unicity" governed by a 50-member council. Thirteen community committees in the old municipal units were also provided for to perform limited administrative and communication functions. This bold step, an alternative to the two-tier Toronto model, did not work as well in practice as in theory, and in 1977 some changes were made, such as reducing the size of the council to 29 and the number of community committees to six. Recent boundary adjustments to the city of Winnipeg involved the secession of the Headingley municipality. Meanwhile, the government has begun to pay more attention to the other 200 municipalities in the province—other cities, towns, villages and rural municipalities, to say nothing of a plethora of school boards and other local authorities—and has recognized that their reform is overdue.

POLITICAL EVOLUTION

1870-1970

Manitoba was small and primitive when it became a province in 1870, lacking the other six provinces' pre-Confederation experience with representative and responsible government. It was not until the turn of the century that Manitoba functioned in a manner more becoming a province, after having relied to that point on federal funding and the administrative skill of the lieutenant-governor. About 12,000 people inhabited the area in 1870, including 1,560 whites who were descendants of Lord Selkirk's Red River settlement of 1812, 560 Indians,

5,750 Métis, and 4,080 of English-Native origin.[33] Given this population mix, the province had a slight French/Catholic majority at the time.

Manitoba had the most violent entry into Confederation of any province. The area involved was owned and governed by the Hudson's Bay Company but, as the territory passed from company to Canadian jurisdiction, authority broke down and the colony began to descend into anarchy. In this vacuum, Métis leader Louis Riel and others formed a provisional government, seized Fort Garry, and organized the election of 12 English and 12 French delegates who drafted terms for union with Canada. A team was sent to negotiate with the Macdonald government in Ottawa, which had been notoriously insensitive throughout. The provisional government was not recognized unanimously within the territory and at least three deaths occurred in the confused situation, including the execution of Thomas Scott, an Ontario member of the Orange Order, a militant Protestant group.

The province was established in 1870 at Riel's insistence. It was to be officially bilingual and have a guaranteed separate school system, a bicameral legislature (partly so that the Hudson's Bay Company could have representation in the Legislative Council), and a federally appointed lieutenant-governor. Moreover, the Assembly was based on equal French and English representation. On the other hand, the federal government retained control of Crown lands and natural resources, arguing that this was necessary to pursue its policies of populating the West and building a transcontinental railway.[34]

An election was held in 1870, but for several years the lieutenant-governor really ran the province; he even attended meetings of the cabinet, a body carefully constructed with two French and two English members and one English-Native representative. The election of 1874 gave Manitoba its first real premier, R.A. Davis, and in 1876 this government abolished the Legislative Council. Considerable immigration occurred in the 1870s, mostly English-speaking Ontarians, Mennonites, Icelanders, and some French Canadians.

After the election of 1878, John Norquay became premier. He was returned in 1879 and again in 1883, when the party designations Liberal and Conservative were used for the first time, together with a wide array of other party labels. Nominally a Conservative, Norquay was involved in two main issues—the battle with Ontario over the eastern boundary of the province, and the fight for adequate railway service, in which he had to fight the federal government and the Canadian Pacific Railway.

Both Manitoba and Ontario claimed the territory between the tip of Lake Superior and Lake of the Woods, and both gave it representation in their provincial legislature and established local governments in the area. John A. Macdonald disallowed the Ontario statute which purported to take over the territory, but the British Privy Council ruled in Ontario's favour in 1884. Nevertheless, Manitoba's boundaries were enlarged in 1881, mainly to the north and west, so that it no longer resembled a postage stamp.

On the railway issue, Manitoba objected to Canada Pacific's monopoly, which allowed it to charge unlimited rates while refusing to construct badly needed branch lines. But Norquay's provincially approved railway charters for links to American lines were disallowed by the federal cabinet as a violation of the monopoly clause.

Party labels were hardly evident in the 1888 election—indeed, that election and two others which followed were scarcely contested—although the victor, Thomas Greenway, was considered a Liberal. The railway issue continued to preoccupy the early days of his administration. He successfully persuaded the federal government to buy out Canadian Pacific's monopoly clause and build a rail line to the United States. Disappointed by the railways' decision not to build a proposed line to Hudson Bay, Greenway turned his attention to matters of language and religion.

By this time, a clear-cut English/Protestant majority had developed, largely due to immigrants from Ontario who began to make "the old dual community over in the image of their natal province."[35] The issues of bilingualism and separate schools were distinct but related, and the fate of French and Catholic rights was much the same. Even before 1890, in fact, the French lost their parity position in the cabinet and in the legislature. In 1890, the legislature abolished the use of French in its proceedings and in the courts, even though it was guaranteed in the Manitoba Act of 1870.

The same legislature dismantled the separate school system in 1890. Those affected took this initiative to the courts, in the case of *Barrett v. the City of Winnipeg.* The Manitoba courts upheld the abolition, the Supreme Court of Canada overturned it and, the British Privy Council ultimately agreed to it on the grounds that the legislation did not deny Catholics the right to operate their own schools—it only required them to pay taxes to the public school system as well. The other course of action open to the Catholic minority was to use section 93 of the 1867 Constitution Act which provided for an appeal to the federal cabinet and the passage of remedial legislation on the issue by the Parliament of Canada. The federal Conservative government, led by Mackenzie Bowell, a former Grand Master of the Ontario Orange Order, surprised some observers by ordering the Greenway government to provide support for separate schools. Greenway refused, and won the 1896 provincial election on the issue. Ottawa then introduced the remedial legislation, but the government's five-year term expired before it passed. Ironically, in the subsequent 1896 federal election, the largely English/Protestant Conservatives favoured such federal action, while the French/Catholic Liberal leader, Wilfrid Laurier, opposed it. He argued that education was a matter of provincial rights and, after being sworn in as prime minister, negotiated a compromise with Greenway under which minimal educational rights were returned to the Catholic minority in 1897.[36]

By 1899, the province felt it was time for a change, and elected the Conservatives in a contest in which party lines were clearly drawn. The new government assumed office in early 1900 under Hugh John Macdonald, the son of Sir John; a few months later, the premiership passed to Rodmond Roblin, the real architect of the party's success.

The Roblin government was in office for 15 years, presiding over a rapid expansion of the provincial population, and leaving behind both positive and negative monuments. The provincial population more than doubled between 1901 and 1916 in response to the wheat boom, world-wide prosperity, and the federal government's aggressive immigration policy led by Clifford Sifton, former attorney general of Manitoba. Ukrainians were a major component of the new immigrant population. During this period, Winnipeg became the great metropolis of the West and, appropriately enough, provincial boundaries were more than doubled to their present location.[37]

The prosperous times and the growth of the province's population and territory generated much government revenue, which Roblin used to improve the still inadequate railway system. Then, when Bell Telephone applied for a charter in the province, the government decided to establish a public telephone system with the objective of ensuring that remote rural areas would be serviced even if it were unprofitable. In this way Manitoba created the first publicly owned telephone system in North America. The government also built the St. Boniface stockyards and meat packing plant, and Winnipeg began to supply its own hydroelectricity.

With this innovative record (coinciding with the equally activist Whitney Conservative government in Ontario), Roblin was re-elected in 1903, 1907, 1910, and 1914. Over that time Roblin faced only one major setback—the public purchase of a line of grain elevators, a scheme which ran serious deficits and had to be abandoned—and problems in the grain handling area therefore continued. A more general problem for the Roblin government was that in spite of its record of innovation, certain groups began demanding even more reform. Charges of bribery, corruption, and election-day treating and intimidation also grew over the years, although the Opposition may have been equally at fault. There was also a major scandal involving the construction of the new Legislative Building in 1914-15 which caused the departure of the Roblin government. The lieutenant-governor felt compelled to intervene and appointed a royal commission to investigate. Its report not only exposed serious contract violations in which the public purse had been defrauded of nearly $1 million, but also revealed that much of this money was kicked back into party coffers. The Roblin government resigned before the full extent of the scandal was known, but the investigation continued, uncovering corruption in many other parts of the government.[38]

The Liberal party had become a threat to Roblin even before 1914, largely because a variety of reform groups associated themselves with the party. These included the Manitoba Grain Growers, the Temperance and Social Gospel movements, Tax Reform and Direct Legislation leagues, feminists, trade unions, and various Protestant churches. The Liberals, under T.C. Norris, took over upon Roblin's resignation in 1915 and won a commanding election victory later that year. The next five years witnessed the implementation of a far-reaching reform program, including new electoral laws which reduced corruption, while a civil service commission was established to remove patronage in the bureaucracy. Norris made primary education compulsory, and adopted Prohibition in 1916. Manitoba was the first province to grant women the right to vote, also in 1916, and the first to provide mothers' allowances. Some of this relatively advanced treatment of women could be attributed to the presence of Nellie McClung, one of the pioneers of the Canadian women's movement. As in other provinces, the Prohibition and women's suffrage initiatives were linked to the Canadian war effort. Norris also introduced legislation in the areas of workers' compensation, factory safety, labour standards, and agricultural credit and research, and created the Manitoba Hydro-Electric Board. He established a public health nursing system, and road development continued. On the other hand, the Norris government's abolition of the bilingual schools provision of the 1897 Laurier-Greenway compromise has become a source of controversy in recent years, although it appeared as a necessary measure to the Anglo-Saxon majority of the time. Prohibition did not work any better in Manitoba than elsewhere, and another measure that proved unworkable was the Initiative and Referendum Act of 1916. This Act provided that the legislature had to response to a popular petition for action, but it was declared unconstitutional by the Privy Council in 1919. All in all, it was a very innovative period, with Manitoba often leading the country.

Although they had been backed by labour and farmer groups in 1914-15, the Liberals were unable to maintain this support in spite of legislation designed to appeal to these sectors. The major labour dispute of the period, of course, was the 1919 Winnipeg General Strike. The First World War had greatly increased the ranks of organized labour, but had not improved their overall economic situation. After the war, a serious recession was made worse by the increased supply of labour as soldiers returned home. Thus, in May 1919, questions of wages and hours and the principle of collective bargaining forced Winnipeg workers, especially in the building and metal trades, to call for a general strike. Although the city was divided into two hostile camps, the Citizens' Committee of 1,000 and the Strike Committee, the strike would probably have been settled peaceably except for the interference of the federal government, which had the strike leaders arrested. This precipitated an illegal mass meeting during which the police attacked, killing two men. Several labour leaders were imprisoned on the charge of seditious conspiracy, and others were deported. Many of the leaders involved later became active in provincial or federal politics, and north Winnipeg has had a radical reputation ever since. The 1920 election was contested by the newly formed Independent Labour Party, as were elections in other provinces at the same time, and several of the strike leaders were elected while still in prison.

The Liberals' loss of farmer support proved to be an even more serious problem. The political consciousness of the agricultural community had grown gradually as farmers contended with disagreeable federal tariff and transportation policies, exploitative middlemen and suppliers—the banks, railways, elevator operators and implement companies—and a hazardous climate. One organization, the Patrons of Industry, entered Manitoba in the early 1890s, but was replaced by the Manitoba Grain Growers in 1903. The latter became an increasingly active farmers' pressure group, and changed its name to the United Farmers of Manitoba in 1919. After the Roblin government's grain elevator scheme collapsed, the Grain Growers took up the cause, and amalgamated with groups in other provinces to form the giant United Grain Growers co-operative. Although less radical than some of their counterparts farther west, and indeed quite conservative in most respects, the Manitoba farmers rejected the party system, at least as it then existed, with both parties dominated by eastern Canadian interests. The farmers' impatience with federal Liberal and Conservative party policies and practices was exacerbated by the formation of a coalition government in Ottawa and the adoption of conscription in 1917. This discontent was compounded by the post-war recession, which reduced the price of wheat but not of farm supplies, and the federal government's abandonment of the orderly wartime grain marketing system (an earlier version of the Canadian Wheat Board). Manitoba farmers, unlike those in Ontario, felt little in common with labour groups in the province, especially after the Winnipeg General Strike, except perhaps that both were fighting eastern domination and the "big interests."[39] The farmers felt that, in addition to its connection with national parties, the Norris government was too urban-oriented, too progressive, contained too many lawyers, and was spending too much money.[40] With a successful electoral effort in Ontario the year before, it is therefore not surprising that a number of farmer candidates contested the 1920 Manitoba election.

Thus, in spite of its innovative record (and partly because of it), the Norris Liberal government faced labour and farmer opposition candidates in the election of 1920. The results were 21 seats for the Liberals, 12 Farmers, 11 Labour, seven Conservatives (still discredited from 1915), and four Independents, reducing Norris to a minority government. As in the House of Commons from 1921 to 1925, the farmer group was the second-largest party, but it declined to function as the official Opposition. Norris struggled on, but was defeated in the legislature in 1922. In the subsequent election, aided by rural over-representation in the electoral system and a more organized campaign, the United Farmers of Manitoba won 28 seats, while the Liberals elected only nine, the Conservatives seven, and Labour six, in a culmination of the effort to get rid of "politics" in the province.[41] The farmers thereupon assumed the mantle of government.

The party took office without a leader, but eventually persuaded the president of the Manitoba Agricultural College, John Bracken, to become premier. Bracken held this position from 1922 to 1943 without interruption, longer than any Manitoba premier before or since. His leadership reflected the conservative values of the dominant rural and urban, farmer and business, Anglo-Saxon interests in the province. He headed a succession of farmer and coalition governments, and was determined to be honest, economical, efficient, businesslike, and non-partisan, treating Manitoba as one large municipality. His governments were so economy-minded that he hardly undertook any new initiatives during his 21 years in office; in fact, one of Bracken's first moves was to reduce the level of mothers' allowances.[42] Moreover, his successors, Garson and Campbell, continued this style of administration for an additional 15 years, so that, in many ways, Manitoba was 35 years behind the times when a new government finally took over in 1958.

By 1927, the Bracken government ran under the generic and inappropriate label of the Progressive party, and the results of that election were substantially the same as in 1922. Then, in 1928, the United Farmers organization decided to withdraw from electoral politics, leaving its legislative members in mid-air.[43] Under strong Conservative attack, Bracken arranged an informal entente with the Liberals. He successfully made an issue of the Conservatives' refusal to join in the coalition in 1931, when a united front might have been useful in demanding more money from Ottawa to help Manitoba cope with the Great Depression. Bracken formalized his alliance in 1932, as three Liberals entered the cabinet, and the new Liberal-Progressive party won an easy victory at the polls.[44]

Bracken has been described as a modest, colourless, able administrator, a non-drinking moralist, and a man who paid great attention to detail.[45] In 1923 and again in 1928, he relaxed the Prohibition laws but countered this by banning smoking in the legislature and introducing film censorship. In an effort to balance the budget, Bracken introduced a personal income tax, but also reduced expenditure on welfare, schools, and hospitals. Acting as his own provincial treasurer until 1932, he also decreased the size of the public service and cut public sector salaries. On the other hand, like most conservative administrations, his government promoted economic development by providing infrastructure such as roads, railways, and hydroelectricity. In spite of the awkward situation whereby the federal government owned the province's natural resources until 1930, mining flourished at Flin Flon under the Hudson Bay Mining and Smelting company, while the lumbering and pulp and paper industries also expanded. In addition, the Hudson Bay Railway was completed in 1931 with federal assistance.

Given the availability of even less tax revenue, the Depression offered an excuse for greater economic restraint in government, and that is precisely what Bracken practised. The world-wide economic collapse meant that farmers often could not sell their wheat, and when they did, it was at rock-bottom prices. The farmers' misery was made worse by the simultaneous occurrence of drought and, when grain did grow, it was promptly consumed by grasshoppers. Thus, there was rarely much wheat to sell. Many people were reduced to near starvation, municipalities defaulted, and the province came close to bankruptcy, a predicament that was not substantially eased by minimal federal relief grants.

Out of this desperate situation emerged one promising policy innovation that is sometimes identified with Bracken—the federal government's assumption of responsibility for unemployment insurance in 1940. The Manitoba government presented an eloquent brief to the Rowell-Sirois Commission in the late 1930s in this regard, and federal responsibility became one of the commission's main recommendations.

By 1936, the Co-operative Commonwealth Federation had absorbed the Independent Labour Party in the province, and had chosen J.S. Woodsworth as its first national leader. He was a Methodist-Social Gospel minister who had been active in the Winnipeg General Strike, and who was elected to represent north Winnipeg in the House of Commons from 1921 onward. The Social Credit party had come to power in Alberta in 1935, and made an appearance in Manitoba a year later. When the 1936 election at first appeared to leave him in a minority position, the non-partisan Bracken repeated his offer of coalition, and the five new Social Credit members responded with a promise of general support, just as a deferred election gave the Liberal-Progressives a narrow majority.[46] Finally in 1940, using the pretext of the war and the need for provincial unity in pressing for the implementation of the recommendations of the Rowell-Sirois Report on reforming federal-provincial financial relations, Bracken again invited all parties to join him in a coalition government. In this case, the Conservatives, CCF, and Social Credit did so. In the 1941 election the incumbents of this new nameless coalition did not run against each other, and there were more acclamations and fewer opposition members elected than usual. The CCF was not entirely comfortable with this arrangement, and withdrew from the coalition when Bracken left the premiership in 1943.[47] Strangely enough, he was persuaded to become leader of the federal Conservative party, even though he had usually been antagonistic toward Tories both in Manitoba and in Ottawa. He was also entering a highly partisan federal political environment after a provincial career based on non-partisanship. On the other hand, Bracken was attractive to the Conservatives as the leading Western spokesman on agriculture, and he had become increasingly impatient with federal Liberal policies. The Conservatives had recently modified their policy somewhat, bringing it into line with his own, and Bracken insisted on the addition of the adjective "Progressive" to the party name, reflecting his origins.[48] His political longevity in Manitoba was not repeated at the federal level, however, and he was replaced in 1948 after a lacklustre performance.

In Manitoba, Bracken was succeeded by his chief lieutenant, Stuart Garson. The new premier led the coalition to re-election in 1945 against strong opposition from the CCF, which actually received more popular vote than any other party. By this time, post-war reconstruction and tax-rental agreements served as incentives to continue the Liberal-Progressive Conservative-Social Credit coalition. Garson was a lawyer, but otherwise much like his able, hardworking, and very serious predecessor. In 1948 he followed Bracken to Ottawa, but to the federal Liberal rather than the Conservative party. Another long-time minister, farmer Douglas Campbell, then became premier. The coalition continued to cope with debt reduction and was re-elected in 1949, but no Social Credit members were successful and four dissident Tories, including Duff Roblin, were elected as Independent Conservatives. One of the most significant events of the Campbell period was the Winnipeg flood of 1950, a disaster for which the provincial government was totally unprepared.[49] In the same year, the Conservatives officially withdrew from the coalition, displacing the CCF as official Opposition, although some Tories converted to Liberal-Progressive, causing much confusion in their ranks. The Conservatives placed second to Campbell's party in the 1953 election and, in 1954, Duff Roblin, the grandson of Rodmond Roblin, successfully challenged the incumbent Tory leader, Errick Willis, to become Opposition leader. Campbell loosened the provincial purse-strings slightly to finance a road-building program in the early 1950s, but the government did nothing in response to studies which proposed changes in the health and education systems. Over this period the province also drifted into public ownership of the hydro system, the expansion of rural electrification being one of the coalition's most significant accomplishments.[50] One long overdue reform, which completely sealed the aging government's fate, was a redistribution of seats in the legislature prior to the 1958 election. The rural over-representation which had served the Liberal-Progressives so well for so long ended, and Winnipeg was finally given a fairer share of seats.

Among the other factors contributing to the defeat of the 36-year-old Liberal-Progressive regime were Duff Roblin's personal popularity and the appeal of his reform policies. Roblin reconstructed the provincial Conservative party[51] and, perhaps most significant, the federal Tory party had swept the nation—and especially the West—in the 1958 federal election, a victory which centred on John Diefenbaker. The new prime minister had governed well since 1957, completely transforming federal voting patterns on the prairies by his understanding of Western concerns and his government's impressive export sales of wheat.

Whatever he owed to Diefenbaker at the start, and however much increased federal funding assisted him over the next decade, Roblin soon established a popular reputation of his own, and a fresh spirit engulfed the province. He and his ministers prepared a program of expansion in almost every field and probably engaged in more innovation in the 1960s than any other province except Quebec and New Brunswick.[52] Roblin was initially elected to a minority position, but easily obtained CCF support by introducing hospital insurance, and adopted a CCF resolution on old-age pensions. Defeat on a procedural motion in 1959 provided an excuse to call another election, in which the Tories were returned with a solid majority.

One of Roblin's most significant reforms was undoubtedly in education, which had been starved for funds for more than 30 years. He increased grants for new school construction and raised teachers' salaries. The 1960 MacFarlane royal commission on education recommended consolidation of small school districts, full funding for separate schools, and increased use of French as a language of instruction, but Roblin moved cautiously in all three respects. The province eventually assumed two-thirds of all education costs, established new vocational schools, consolidated local school districts, established a university grants commission, and expanded the Manitoba Institute of Technology. Roblin also introduced a tepid proposal for shared services between public and separate schools, and allowed increased instruction (up to half a day) in French for francophone students. In 1967, he raised Brandon College to autonomous university status, as he did with United College, which became the University of Winnipeg.

Roblin also spent significant sums to improve health and welfare services, such as new hospitals and senior citizen housing, and reduced hospital insurance premiums. To pay for these services, the government raised existing taxes and introduced new ones and, because he acted as his own provincial treasurer, Roblin bore the brunt of the criticism for doing so.

Other reforms included creating the Metropolitan Corporation of Greater Winnipeg in 1960 to provide badly needed co-ordination and equalization of municipal services in the city and its autonomous sprawling suburbs. Similarly, the government improved the provincial highways network, including a perimeter road around Winnipeg, and started work on the construction of a huge floodway—later dubbed "Duff's Ditch"—designed to divert surplus water around Winnipeg and to protect the city from a recurrence of sometimes disastrous floods.

On the economic front, Roblin initiated an economic development strategy in which the government played a major role. He established a planning process, including an industrial development board to encourage new private initiatives with industrial parks and other infrastructure, and created the Manitoba Development Fund, which provided companies with tax concessions, grants, and low-interest loans. Manitoba Hydro constructed a large power development at Grand Rapids, 250 miles north of Winnipeg, where operations began in 1965.

On the Opposition side, the Co-operative Commonwealth Federation became the New Democratic Party, the Liberal-Progressives became the Liberals, and both parties changed leaders during this period. But, when Roblin called a snap election in 1962, the Conservatives were easily returned.

The mid-1960s was a relatively prosperous period, and Roblin established several provincial economic planning agencies. Inco Ltd. expanded its operations in Thompson, and in 1966 the town was incorporated and elected a mayor and council. With federal assistance, a transmission line to Winnipeg was constructed from the hydro development at Kettle Rapids on the Nelson River. There was, however, some question as to whether the Manitoba Development Fund was being operated in a responsible and efficient manner.

In 1966, in these mixed but still generally favourable circumstances, Roblin called another election. The various parties proposed different versions of medicare but, in general, the issues were not clearly defined. In the end, the government was returned, having lost some ground, and the NDP came a close third behind the Liberals. Increased government expenditures subsequently caused Manitoba to adopt a five-percent retail sales tax, leaving Alberta the only province without such a levy. This prompted Joe Borowski, professional protester, ex-miner, and merchant from Thompson, to camp on the grounds of the legislature to demonstrate against Roblin's implementation of the tax. Other government reforms included new liquor legislation, a redevelopment program in Winnipeg, and a 10-year $85-million federal-provincial ARDA plan for the interlake district.

Then, at the last minute, Duff Roblin entered the 1967 race for the federal Conservative party leadership, announcing he would quit as premier regardless of the outcome of that campaign. As a successful premier of a central province, an unusual bilingual Westerner sympathetic to the French cause, Roblin might have bridged the gulf between the Diefenbaker and Dalton Camp factions in the party. Nevertheless, he was narrowly defeated on the final ballot by his fellow premier, Nova Scotian Robert Stanfield. Roblin was also defeated as a candidate in Winnipeg in the 1968 federal election but many years later, after another stint in business, he was appointed to the Senate and for a time served there as government leader in the Mulroney cabinet.

In the contest to succeed Roblin, Highways Minister Walter Weir, a young and somewhat rustic undertaker, defeated the urbane Attorney General Sterling Lyon. The party apparently wanted a respite from Progressive Conservatism, for Weir was seen as the more conservative of the two at the time.[53] The Weir interlude, from November 1967 to June 1969, was conservative indeed, and the new premier suspended several proposals which Roblin had undertaken. Weir also regularly fought with the federal government. He threatened to stay out of the national medicare scheme and, when he finally agreed to enter the program, the province set high premiums and over half of Manitoba's doctors opted out.[54] Both within the province and at the federal-provincial constitutional conference of February 1969, Weir demonstrated his lack of sympathy for any extension of bilingualism, while his government ignored requests for the teaching of other languages or for separate school support. He halted the rapid increase in public expenditures which marked the Roblin period, but still had to raise property taxes, hydro rates, and hospital insurance premiums to help finance them. On a more innovative note, Weir reorganized the government apparatus, became the first premier to introduce cabinet committees on planning and management, and established a new securities commission.

One of the most difficult issues on the government's agenda in 1969 was a proposed hydro development at Southern Indian Lake, 60 miles northwest of Thompson. Manitoba Hydro planned to dam the lake, divert most of the Churchill River into the Kettle Rapids generating plant on the Nelson River, and flood the surrounding land. This would displace a band of about 600 Natives and

Métis, to whom Hydro offered to pay a total of $60,000 for relocation. At the height of the controversy, Premier Weir unexpectedly called an election for June 25. This decision was made so quickly that the Conservative party did not even have time to reorganize along the new constituency boundaries after the recent redistribution. The Liberals were severely hampered by the words and actions of their federal counterparts—especially Prime Minister Pierre Trudeau's apparent preference for selling bilingualism rather than wheat, and his confirmation that the Air Canada maintenance base in Winnipeg would be transferred to Montreal. The new provincial leader, old-time Liberal-Progressive Robert Bend, seemed to share most of Weir's basic conservative values. Weir's election call caught the NDP in the middle of a leadership race with a convention scheduled for the end of June, but the party brought it forward to June 7.

The 1970s[55]

With the exception of north Winnipeg, Manitoba had never shown much receptiveness toward democratic socialism; yet in 1969 the province suddenly opted for an NDP government, and the New Democrats were as surprised as anyone. The NDP cause was helped by the recent redistribution of legislative seats, which gave Winnipeg a much greater proportion, by Weir's move to the right, and by the apparent similarity of the other two parties. Of striking significance was the cross-province debating tour of NDP leadership contenders, coupled with the lengthy free television coverage of the leadership convention itself, which occurred in the middle of the election campaign. Weir's attempt to catch the NDP with its pants down backfired as "the media generated an unprecedented level of public awareness of the provincial NDP."[56] All analyses of the NDP's victory, as well as of its re-election in 1973, centre on the leadership of Ed Schreyer.

People liked what they saw—a fresh, moderate new leader, a farm boy who was first elected to the legislature in 1958 at the age of 22, then served in the House of Commons, and had also taught political science at the University of Manitoba. Moreover, he was a Roman Catholic of non-Anglo-Saxon background, another departure for party leaders in the province. The Manitoba electorate was transformed, with the NDP extending its support beyond the working class of north Winnipeg to the entire non-Anglo-Saxon northern part of the province. An "ethnic revolt" took place in which the NDP was seen as more receptive than the Liberals or Conservatives. To a large extent, the non-Anglo-Saxon population was also the have-not group in the province, so that 1969 can also be seen as a sudden realization of class-consciousness among this group. Schreyer preached a moderate social democratic message, but there was no mistaking his appeal to the less prosperous element of the population. Schreyer was sworn in as premier with a cabinet of varied ethnic and religious backgrounds.

The legislative record of the first four years of the Schreyer government was chock full of progressive reforms. In the health field, for example, the government reduced medicare premiums in 1969 and abolished them entirely in 1973; it included nursing homes in hospital insurance coverage, expanded hospitals, and introduced a drug benefit program for the elderly. Schreyer raised welfare allowances, cut bus fares for pensioners, expanded the supply of public housing, and established new neighbourhood health clinics. The NDP also passed a new consumer protection act and set up a consumer complaints bureau. Other related new agencies included an ombudsman, a human rights commission, a law reform commission, and a new landlord and tenant act, while a rentalsman was appointed to help negotiate disputes over rent.

In the economic sphere, Schreyer created a department of cooperative development, provided farmers with increased credit and other assistance, and aided fishermen with a freshwater fish marketing agency. A radical new labour code simplified the union certification process, and the minimum wage was raised. The government encouraged job creation under the Winter Employment Act, and increased grants to municipalities. It resolved the Southern Indian Lake hydro project dispute with the Native community remaining in place, and developed an assortment of social and economic programs and grants of benefit to Native peoples. The government formed the Department of Northern Affairs and the Communities Economic Development Fund, and designed the planned town of Leaf Rapids in connection with new mining developments.[57]

Other miscellaneous initiatives included reform of election expenses legislation and the extension of legal aid. The government also authorized restoring French as a language of instruction, and erected a statue of Louis Riel on the grounds of the legislature. On the question of public support of separate schools, Schreyer took the unusual step of allowing a free vote because both the cabinet and NDP caucus were split on the issue. Schreyer himself urged the extension but, when a combination of Opposition members and New Democrats defeated it, the premier responded by saying that he had done all that he could.

Two innovations bearing an unmistakable democratic socialist mark were the new municipal structure for metropolitan Winnipeg and the nationalization of automobile insurance. Unicity Winnipeg was to cover the entire metropolitan area with a strong centralized administration, but it also involved a decentralized community committee mechanism to encourage popular political participation. The automobile insurance industry in Saskatchewan had been taken over by the CCF government of T.C. Douglas, and the Schreyer government pursued the same path by establishing an insurance plan called Autopac. This move provoked predictable opposition from private insurance companies and chambers of commerce, and the *Winnipeg Free Press* became hysterical in editorials about the advance of socialism in the province. The principal motivations for this takeover were the high litigation costs and duplication of administrative expenses involved in private insurance schemes. Schreyer restored peace to the situation by assisting individual insurance agents damaged by the public plan, and insurance premiums dropped as anticipated.

Other initiatives of an ideological nature included increases in personal and corporate taxes and in the mining royalties tax, while a grant scheme was introduced to reduce the education tax levy of homeowners on fixed incomes. This property tax rebate was accompanied by an increase in the provincial share of local education costs to 80 percent. The government also conducted a limited federal-provincial guaranteed annual income experiment. While automobile insurance was the only deliberate extension of government ownership, Schreyer stepped in to save many firms from going bankrupt and to preserve the jobs of their employees. Consequently, the government ended up owning all or part of the following firms: the Lord Selkirk cruise ship, Morden Fine Foods (a vegetable canning factory), McKenzie Seeds, Venture Tours, Saunders Aircraft, Flyer Industries (bus manufacturing), and Tantalum Mining. Other governments might have bailed such companies out with grants, but Schreyer had the Manitoba Development Corporation take an equity share in them. On the other hand, when McGill economist and former federal Liberal cabinet minister Eric Kierans submitted a 1973 report recommending a gradual government takeover of the large northern mining companies, Schreyer responded that such action was too drastic. His version of social democracy did not extend government ownership that far.

The biggest headache in the area of economic development was Churchill Forest Industries, a project which Schreyer inherited from the Roblin and Weir regimes.[58] In 1966, the Manitoba Development Fund agreed to lend money to a Swiss-American syndicate to construct a sawmill and pulp and paper complex at The Pas. The project would give that economically deprived region a boost, as well as provide employment for a large number of Natives and Métis. The project quickly aroused suspicions concerning the extent of public funding, but neither Roblin nor Weir took much action. By 1969, the general alarm about the project contributed to Weir's election defeat, and Schreyer established an inquiry into the venture even as his government extended more public funds. Then, in 1971, the government abruptly took possession of the project and appointed a special commission of inquiry to unravel the maze of companies involved.

Responsibility for mismanagement of the project was divided among many participants, as the province ended up paying about $100 million, the entire cost of the complex, for assets worth only $70 million. Although the paper and lumber complex continues to operate today as Manitoba Forest Resources Ltd. (Manfor), and has been privatized and bought by Repap, it was once called "the most disturbing of any provincial government's attempting industrial development in the history of Canada."[59] It was yet another example of politicians being so obsessed with economic development that they gave away huge sums to mysterious international promoters, and of public servants being incapable of assessing the merits of such proposals.

Among other political developments over the 1969-73 period, both Liberal and Conservative parties chose new leaders—extending the non-Anglo-Saxon precedent in that both new leaders were Jewish. I.H. (Izzy) Asper, a prominent tax lawyer, became Liberal leader in October 1970 and, when Weir was finally persuaded to resign as Tory leader in February 1971, the party reverted to the progressive days of Duff Roblin by replacing him with Sidney Spivak. Joe Borowski was named to the NDP cabinet, but did not remain long. After repeated conflicts with other ministers, he was finally forced to resign for opposing government policy on abortion. He later left the party because he felt that its new film classification system was not sufficiently opposed to pornography.[60]

It had been a period of prodigious legislative output, and Schreyer was happy to campaign on his record in the 1973 election. The Liberals and Conservatives both called for tax reductions, cuts in government spending, and more incentives for economic growth in the private sector. They were assisted by the Group for Good Government, essentially the same collection of people who opposed the NDP in Winnipeg municipal politics by backing the Independent Citizens Election Committee. This group sought to identify the opposition candidate in each riding, whether Liberal or Conservative, with the best chance of defeating the NDP. In several constituencies it also arranged for a single candidate to oppose the New Democrat nominee.[61]

In spite of the new opposition party leaders and the protest group (eight of whose candidates were elected), the NDP was returned with an increased margin. After such an active first four years and, in the face of Opposition demands for less government activity, Schreyer's second term involved much less innovation. However, perhaps the most significant development was a 1977 package of family law reforms which provided for equal division of all property and financial holdings in the case of divorce. He extended the drug benefit program to every citizen and allotted more funds to ambulance services and day care. The government also invested in housing lots and provided mortgage loans to low-income earners. In an effort to reduce the gap between high and low incomes, Schreyer increased the property tax rebate again, and introduced a new income tax credit system. The government also fought with the medical profession over fees, and imposed a new metallic minerals royalty on mining companies in response to the Kierans report. It provided greater political rights for public servants, and expanded provisions of its human rights act. At the same time, the government introduced new conflict of interest legislation which governed the activities of MLAs, municipal councillors, and senior civil servants. It expanded language rights, established a French-language teachers' college, and permitted school boards to provide instruction in languages other than English or French.

In measures that might be regarded more socialistic, Schreyer extended Autopac to all forms of insurance other than life insurance, and introduced rent controls. Another innovation was the "stay option," which sought to keep farmers on their land by protecting them from bankruptcy and stabilizing their incomes. The government also established a new Crown corporation in the mining field, Manitoba Mineral Resources Ltd., and the Criminal Injuries

Compensation Board. However, many thought Schreyer was betraying party ideology when he supported federal wage and price controls, and applied the program to all provincial and municipal employees. Shortly afterward, the premier said the federal approach was unjust, and announced his intention to withdraw from the program and set up his own form of controls.[62] In 1977, in what could be seen as another compromise, the structure of Unicity was altered in a tacit admission that many of its intended benefits had not materialized.

Both opposition parties changed leaders again in 1975. Asper was succeeded as Liberal leader by Charles Huband, a prominent Winnipeg lawyer, and Spivak was challenged by Sterling Lyon, former attorney general in the Roblin government. This caused a bitter fight within the Conservative party, but the right-wing Lyon was ultimately successful.

The 1977 election campaign saw the NDP place even greater emphasis on Schreyer's leadership. This was probably because of certain weaknesses in the cabinet and the party organization, and also because the party had either run out of ideas or was afraid to publicize new proposals when it was under attack for raising taxes and taking over companies that continued to lose money. Its most important new promise was a comprehensive social insurance plan. Lyon, on the other hand, advocated severe retrenchment in government operations, and promised to eradicate unprofitable government takeovers and cut taxes. He appealed for the votes of all those unhappy with the NDP, won the election, and assumed office in October 1977.

Sterling Lyon's term in Manitoba represented Canada's first experience with neo-conservatism, as he practised "acute, protracted restraint." He predictably charged the NDP with socialist irresponsibility and overspending, especially in the case of Manitoba Hydro and, among all of his right-wing moves, his reductions in social and health services were likely the most controversial. These cutbacks included raising fees for day care, freezing university grants, limiting hospital grants, and reducing cultural and other social programs.

Several deputy ministers were dismissed on ideological grounds, the civil service was reduced, and a task force was immediately established to recommend ways of limiting government spending. Lyon explicitly overturned several NDP measures, including an overtime pay provision in the minimum wage law and the most progressive features of the family law bill; he froze $50 million of public works spending and abolished rent control in two stages over 1978-80, although an appeal board was left in place. He set up commissions to investigate the operations of Manitoba Hydro and the Public Insurance Corporation. These naturally resulted in scathing reports of mismanagement, but the Tory government did not dismantle Autopac. It did divest itself of the Lord Selkirk cruise ship, Morden Fine Foods, Tantalum Mining, and many smaller enterprises, but failed to find buyers for other candidates for privatization. Several NDP appointments were replaced, such as the Hydro chairman and the entire Film Classification Board.

Lyon quickly abolished succession duties and lowered personal and corporate income taxes. He later removed Schreyer's super-royalties on mining companies, raised university tuition fees, no longer used gasoline tax revenues to help finance Autopac, and froze hydro rates for five years. The electorate appeared to resent restraint and cutbacks in government spending and the removal of rent controls more than it appreciated the tax reductions, for the government faced a succession of demonstrations and labour unrest, especially in 1978. But generally speaking, at least for the first three years, Lyon kept to his course: smaller government, restraint, fiscal responsibility, lower taxes, and reliance on the private sector.

Other initiatives were less ideological or even somewhat contrary to what was expected. Lyon altered the NDP's property tax rebate and cost of living tax credit scheme, but to the benefit of those most in need. He added a tax credit provision for political contributions, and altered electoral boundaries on a non-partisan basis. More surprisingly, Lyon gradually started making direct grants to separate schools, a change of policy that aroused little controversy. After accusing the NDP of over-expanding Hydro, he permitted the utility to grow again following a two-year freeze.[63]

Lyon spent much of his term as premier fighting Prime Minister Pierre Trudeau's proposals for constitutional change. In addition to opposing some of the specific provisions such as language rights, he was philosophically opposed to a charter of rights and an increased role for the courts, preferring to rely on the age-old British principle of parliamentary sovereignty. He was even more upset with Trudeau's unilateral approach, and gladly referred the matter to the Manitoba courts. Due to the 1981 provincial election campaign, Lyon was forced to leave that year's constitutional conference before the final agreement was reached. On the subject of language rights, the Supreme Court of Canada decided in the 1979 *Forest* case that the 1890 statute abolishing official bilingualism in the province was unconstitutional, and Manitoba was therefore still officially bilingual. Lyon complied with the ruling, albeit unenthusiastically, by starting to institute bilingualism in the legislature, courts, and laws.

In other political developments, Ed Schreyer was named Canada's governor general in December 1978. This necessitated a 1979 NDP leadership convention, which was won by Howard Pawley, Schreyer's attorney general. Although seen as uninspiring and unassuming, Pawley immediately began developing stronger constituency associations. More excitement was provided by Conservative back-bencher, Robert Wilson, who was convicted of conspiracy to import marijuana and sentenced to seven years in jail. He was expelled from the Tory caucus, but refused to resign his seat until a special act declared it to be vacant.

The 1980s

As the province moved towards another election, Manitobans had mixed feelings about the performance of the Lyon government. Some were still upset about the cutbacks, and many were disappointed that the economic boom promised by proponents of free enterprise conservatism had not materialized.[64] In particular, the pattern of emigration continued because the economy had left a high rate of unemployment. The government did increase the civil service and government spending as the election approached, but at the expense of a large deficit which contradicted its neo-conservative philosophy. In these circumstances, Lyon tried to soften his image as a bully and a scrapper, and began to speak almost exclusively of three megaprojects under consideration which dominated the election campaign called for October 1981.

The first megaproject was a $600-million aluminum smelter to be built by the Aluminum Company of Canada just north of Winnipeg. The second was a Western power grid, which involved shipping electricity to Saskatchewan and Alberta from new generating facilities to be constructed in Manitoba. The third was a $400-$600 million potash development by the International Mineral Co. (Canada). For its part, the NDP promised to restore rent control and introduce interest rate relief. It criticized Lyon's cutbacks, the lack of economic growth, and his "giveaway" of resources, promising instead to establish a government-owned oil company. The party benefited from the strong organization which Pawley had laboured to build, but suffered from the defection of Sid Green and two other dissidents who had formed a new political party, the Progressives. The results showed Manitoba had become even more polarized between the Conservatives and the NDP. The NDP gained 47 percent of the vote and 34 seats to the Tories' 44 percent and 23 seats, as Lyon made way for another NDP regime. No other party won a seat and all other parties combined collected less than 10 percent of the vote.[65]

Like other provinces, Manitoba suffered through a difficult economic period between 1981 and 1984. In spite of a series of layoffs, bankruptcies, and company closings, however, the provincial unemployment rate remained one of the lowest in the country.[66] Driven by recessionary revenue losses, the new government put a hiring and wage freeze on the public service and cut government spending in some areas, despite its fight against such actions while in Opposition. Somewhat similarly, it raised taxes, introducing a payroll tax in 1982, and then increasing the sales tax to six percent in 1983. It also allowed hydro rates to rise by 9.5 percent, even though Lyon's five-year freeze on these rates had not expired.

In spite of a shortage of funds, the Pawley government was able to implement some of its priority measures. Most importantly, it reintroduced rent controls, established a Crown petroleum corporation, ManOil, and gave interest rate relief to small businessmen, farmers, and lower income homeowners. Pawley improved health care benefits for the elderly, introduced a denticare plan for children, expanded day care facilities, and froze tuition fees. The government reformed labour legislation which, among other things, further eased the process of union certification. It also brought forward several measures of agricultural support, and amended Conservative legislation to tighten restrictions on non-resident and corporate ownership of farmland. The government's main economic initiative, the Manitoba Jobs Fund, was initiated in 1983 with $200 million and was extended with an additional $200 million in 1984 and in 1985, emphasizing the creation of long-term employment.

The Pawley government also struggled with another problem not of its own making, the court-imposed restoration of official bilingualism. Pawley soon realized it would take years to translate nearly a century of provincial legislation into French, although the pressure to do so mounted with a second court challenge by Roger Bilodeau regarding the constitutionality of the province's English-only laws. In May 1983, Pawley negotiated a deal with the federal government and the Société franco-manitobaine. The province would be given until 1995 to translate all its laws, the court case would be postponed and, in return, a constitutional amendment would guarantee bilingual services in all central offices of the provincial government and in regional offices where a demand existed. The Manitoba Conservatives, still led by Sterling Lyon, adamantly opposed this compromise, and brought the legislature to a virtual halt in the latter part of 1983 and early 1984.

Meanwhile, the federal parliament debated a resolution supporting the Pawley-Ottawa agreement in September 1983, shortly after Brian Mulroney became national Tory leader and leader of the official Opposition. It was a difficult situation for Mulroney, who knew the provincial Conservative party's stand (shared by some of his Manitoba MPs), and some saw an element of political opportunism in the proposal on the part of Prime Minister Trudeau. By allowing only each party leader to speak, however, the resolution was adopted unanimously in the House of Commons. A plebiscite held by 20 Manitoba municipalities during the local elections in October complicated the issue. In total, some 76 percent of those who voted were opposed to extending bilingualism.

In any case, the provincial Conservatives filibustered the bilingual services deal until February 1984 when the legislative session ended and the compromise died. The Bilodeau court case went forward, and in June 1985 the Supreme Court of Canada rendered its decision. It ruled that all 4,500 English-language laws in the province were constitutionally invalid, but could remain temporarily in effect to prevent legal anarchy. In November the Supreme Court endorsed an agreement made among the federal, Manitoba, and Quebec governments as well as the Société franco-manitobaine and Monsieur Bilodeau which gave the province until December 1988 to translate current laws, rules, and regulations, and another two years to translate all other laws. No one was happy with this result, least of all the francophones who preferred the extension of services to the translation of laws.

The government faced several other problems during this period. A protracted conflict with the province's doctors over fees and the means of settling fee disputes was resolved in January 1985 with legislation to outlaw extra-billing; in return, the doctors received a fee increase and a system of binding arbitration for fee disputes. The NDP's claim to radicalism was severely tested by Dr. Henry Morgentaler's decision to open an abortion clinic in Winnipeg in May 1983. The clinic met with predictable opposition from Joe Borowski, now proprietor of a Winnipeg health food store. After repeated police raids on the clinic, charges against the doctor were stayed by the attorney general until an analogous court case was resolved in Ontario. The only bright spot on the provincial horizon was the NDP's plan to increase Manitoba Hydro's generating capacity. Construction of the Limestone generating station on the Nelson River began in 1985 after a contract was signed with Northern States Power Co. to sell $3.2 billion of electricity over a 12-year period beginning in 1993. This was expected to generate $1.7-billion profit, half of which would be placed in a heritage trust fund to support the economic and social development of the province. Hydro sales and dam construction became the NDP's greatest hope for re-election, although with substantial private investment and redevelopment of the North Portage area of Winnipeg, the economy generally improved from 1984 onward.

Sterling Lyon resigned as Tory leader in December 1983 to be succeeded by Gary Filmon, a 41-year-old Winnipeg businessman of mixed ethnic background who had been Minister of Consumer Affairs. A few months later, the Liberals chose Sharon Carstairs, a teacher of about the same age as Filmon, as their new leader. She was the daughter of Harold Connolly, who had served briefly as premier of Nova Scotia and later in the Senate. In the 1984 federal election a new anti-bilingualism party, the Confederation of Regions, was quickly established and had its greatest success in Manitoba, gaining 9.8 percent of the vote.

Given the difficulties he had encountered, especially over bilingualism, and the consequent low party standings in the polls (less than 20 percent at its nadir),[67] Howard Pawley waited until almost the end of his five-year term to call a provincial election for March 1986. His hopes that the Limestone project would outweigh language concerns in the public mind were fulfilled; his New Democrats were re-elected by the narrowest of margins: 30 seats with 41.4 percent of the vote compared with 26 seats and 40.4 percent of the vote for Gary Filmon's Conservatives. Meanwhile, the Liberals regained representation in the legislature when Sharon Carstairs won her seat.

After the election, Pawley faced new problems, most notably a scandal involving MTX Telecom Services, a subsidiary of the Crown corporation Manitoba Telephones, in its dealings with Saudi Arabia. On the positive side, the annual deficits of both being an embarrassment, he found a Dutch buyer for Flyer Industries, and began negotiations to sell ManFor, the Crown corporation created when the government was forced to take over Churchill Forest Industries at The Pas. For the most part, 1986 was a year of housekeeping, but the government became bolder in 1987, making discrimination on the basis of sexual orientation illegal under the Human Rights Code and planning the takeover of Inter-City Gas to reduce natural gas rates. This reversal of the privatization plans of other provinces was ultimately abandoned, however, as was anticipated legislation to implement pay equity in the private sector. Although federal transfer payments continued to decrease, Pawley decided to preserve social and health services by increasing income and corporate taxes and implementing a one-percent increase in the sales tax. Such taxes allowed the NDP to cut substantially the provincial deficit. The economy remained generally strong and the unemployment rate low and, by making additional hydro sales, the government appeared to be in no danger, either in terms of finances or popularity.

Another reason the government felt reasonably secure was that, despite the Tories' near win in 1986, that party lacked momentum afterwards. Gary Filmon was under attack from within his own ranks, and federal Health and Welfare Minister Jake Epp came close to challenging him for the provincial leadership. The federal Conservatives did not help their provincial colleagues by awarding the CF-18 fighter plane maintenance contract to Canadair of Montreal, even though Bristol Aerospace of Winnipeg had submitted a technically superior and cheaper bid. Even the normally placid Howard Pawley hit the roof at this point. He also teamed up with David Peterson against free trade, and was a reluctant signatory to the Meech Lake Accord.

At the beginning of 1988, the NDP suddenly plummeted in the polls after raising public automobile insurance premiums by some 24 percent to cover an accumulated Autopac deficit. Protests abounded, the Opposition smelled blood, and all eyes turned towards unhappy NDP backbencher, Jim Walding. He had been Speaker of the legislature during the 1983-84 period and his party had never forgiven him for allowing the Tory filibuster against bilingualism. After trying unsuccessfully to deny him a nomination in 1986, Pawley left Walding to harbour his hostility on the backbenches rather than appoint him to the cabinet. Walding's vote on the budget was crucial because, after the appointment of a Speaker from the NDP ranks and the resignation from the legislature of one NDP member, the government had 28 votes to a combined opposition of 27. Thus, when Walding decided to support the Opposition motion of non-confidence in the budget, the government fell by a count of 27 to 28, the first time in Canadian history that a majority government had been defeated by the vote of one of its own members.[68]

Pawley obviously had to call an election, but he startled the Manitoba electorate by announcing his resignation as party leader, and by setting the date of an NDP leadership convention for less than one month before the election, just as in 1969. Pawley may have been planning to run in the 1988 federal election and hoped that his resignation would absolve the new NDP leader of responsibility for the insurance rate increase, which the government later reduced to about 18 percent. Urban Affairs Minister Gary Doer ultimately triumphed at the convention, while Pawley agreed to stay on as premier until the election was over.

Doer could not prevent the NDP's inevitable defeat and, although the Tories began the campaign with an enormous lead in the polls, Filmon's lacklustre performance caused his party to steadily lose steam. An opening was thus created for the provincial Liberal party, and in strode an aggressive, dynamic Sharon Carstairs. Polls indicated that she was the favourite of the three leaders and, with the federal Liberals no longer in office and Trudeau removed from the scene, it was respectable once again to be a Liberal in Manitoba. Both Carstairs and Filmon criticized tax increases, the deficit, and Crown corporation losses. On election night, the Tories finished with 25 seats and 38 percent of the vote, the Liberals with 20 seats and 35 percent, and the NDP with 12 seats and 24 percent. In an amazing Liberal comeback, Carstairs swept most of Winnipeg, while the Tories held on to the prosperous rural south, and the NDP was reduced to the marginal rural north.

Gary Filmon formed a minority government and moved cautiously in office so as not to offend the Opposition. Prolonged droughts reduced hydro production, the Morgentaler clinic in Winnipeg reopened, but Filmon's biggest headache was the Meech Lake Accord. Prime Minister Mulroney pressured him to seek legislative approval for Meech Lake, but Carstairs (a Chrétien Liberal) was adamantly opposed, and the provincial NDP was divided on the issue. Filmon finally found the courage to introduce the Meech Lake resolution into the legislature in December 1988, but withdrew it three days later, after Quebec Premier Bourassa used the notwithstanding clause to override the Supreme Court ruling on bilingual signs. In the spring of 1989, however, the premier established an all-party legislative committee to hold public hearings on the Accord; its unanimous report, issued in October, called for major changes to the document.

Among Filmon's policy initiatives were the sale of four Crown corporations: ManFor, to Repap Enterprises Inc. of Montreal; ManOil, to Tundra Oil and Gas controlled by the Cohen and Richardson families in the province; the data processing company Manitoba Data Services; and the general insurance arm of Manitoba Public Insurance Corporation. Repap's $1-billion plans for expansion and conversion to chlorine bleached softwood kraft pulp were immediately opposed by environmentalists. The Conservatives proclaimed the NDP's freedom of information act, and Filmon attended a meeting of the Société franco-manitobaine to announce a continuation of the NDP language policy of gradually expanding French-language services, a policy the Conservatives had adamantly opposed in the past. They toughened laws for impaired driving and introduced conflict of interest legislation. Manitoba welcomed increased equalization payments and the rise in mining revenues which allowed an income tax cut in the 1989 budget, as well as federal promises of health and agricultural labs for Winnipeg, but the closing of the Canadian Forces Base Portage La Prairie raised almost as much furor as that of Summerside, P.E.I. More positively, Filmon signed a major hydro contract with Ontario that would permit construction of the proposed $5.5-billion Conawapa dam, although it also raised objections from Native groups and environmentalists. He also announced the decentralization of 700 government jobs out of Winnipeg, while Inco Ltd. planned a $300-million expansion in Thompson.

The most prominent issue in Manitoba in 1989 was aboriginal injustice; a two-man inquiry of the subject began after a public outcry over two cases involving Native victims. Helen Betty Osborne, a teenager in The Pas, was picked up by four white men, raped, and brutally murdered. The case was covered up for 16 years and only one man was eventually convicted. J.J. Harper was a Native leader who bled to death after being shot in a scuffle with Winnipeg police. The inquiry investigated these two cases specifically, as well as the subject of aboriginal justice generally, by travelling to every corner of the province and holding informal hearings in Native villages and on reserves. The Winnipeg Police Association was unsuccessful in trying to block the inquiry, and one officer committed suicide during the course of its proceedings.

The 1990s

Filmon took Carstairs and Doer with him to the June 1990 first ministers' meeting regarding the Meech Lake Accord. Although he secured their approval to amendments, the agreement evaporated on its June 23rd deadline when the Manitoba legislature was still debating it, largely due to the delaying tactics of Native NDP MLA, Elijah Harper. He felt the Accord offered nothing for aboriginal peoples and that it was time for them to stand up and be counted.

Then, although the 1988-90 period had been one of moderate, consensual, and businesslike minority government, Gary Filmon decided to take advantage of his post-Meech Lake popularity (over 50 percent in the polls) to call an election for September 1990, a week after the Ontario vote. The Conservative campaign focused on its leader to the extent of downplaying the party's name, issues, and federal connection. At the same time, the federal Conservative party helped with direct mail and computerized soliciting that gave voters the impression they were receiving a personalized letter from Filmon. The Tories also emphasized their record of fiscal responsibility, clinched a deal with the medical profession in the middle of the campaign, and found extra money for hospitals and highways. Liberal Sharon Carstairs emphasized economic issues such as research and development, but the fact that she had joined her Tory and NDP counterparts in accepting the Meech Lake Accord, with minor modifications, was held against her because of her earlier fierce opposition. She may also have suffered from the unexpected defeat of the Ontario Liberal government. The NDP, which focused its campaign on environmental, health, housing, taxation, labour, and farmer issues, probably benefited from the party's success in neighbouring Ontario. Leader Gary Doer took an aggressive approach in the televised leaders' debate, and tried to saddle Filmon with the unpopularity of the federal

GST. Several other non-televised leader debates were also held, including one on Native issues, while at least eight aboriginal candidates sought office.

The results confirmed Winnipeg was the main battleground, as both the Conservatives and NDP won back seats the Liberals had taken there in 1988. The Conservatives lost popularity during the campaign, receiving a bare majority of 30 seats (42 percent of the vote), compared to the NDP's 20 seats (29 percent), and the Liberals' seven seats (28 percent). Once again, at least in terms of seats, southern Manitoba and south Winnipeg were solidly Tory, northern Manitoba and north Winnipeg were securely NDP, and seven Liberal seats were squeezed between them in the middle of the capital.

With this slim majority, and with by-elections making his position even more precarious, Gary Filmon carried on for a full five-year term. No longer dependent on Opposition support, he turned to the right, as did all provincial governments during the 1990-95 period. For example, he lost no time repealing what he regarded as pro-labour legislation, passed by the NDP, which allowed an independent arbitrator to impose on both parties a final contract offer of either side. In 1991, Filmon's government also tightened the Workers' Compensation Act. At the same time, Filmon designed several initiatives to help existing businesses or attract new industry to the province, such as a new oil and gas act, tax breaks and tax credits to encourage research, development, manu-facturing, and processing, and a reduction of payroll taxes paid by business. The province trumpeted its skill in attracting several firms in the telecommunications field. On the other hand, the recession took its toll, with layoffs at Great-West Life, and the closing of the Campbell Soup plant.

One of the principal issues of the period was the August 1991 publication of the report of the Aboriginal Justice Inquiry, after it spent $3 million, travelled 18,000 kilometres, and took 21,000 pages of testimony. The report detailed sys-tematic discrimination against Natives by the legal system and police forces. It recommended aboriginal self-government and a separate, parallel aboriginal jus-tice system. Filmon's government rejected this latter recommendation, but promised to address other faults in the system. In 1994, the federal and provin-cial governments and the Assembly of Manitoba Chiefs announced Manitoba would be a test case for Native self-government and the first province in which the Indian Act would be dismantled.

Manitoba witnessed several constitutional developments during this period. First, the province's post-Meech Lake legislative committee on the Constitution held more public hearings and reported in October 1991. Manitobans later voted 62 percent to 38 percent against the Charlottetown Accord. On francophone questions, the Supreme Court of Canada continued to fine-tune Manitoba's defi-nition of official bilingualism. In January 1992, the Court decided the province did not have to translate all orders-in-council, only those of a legislative nature, with the force of law, and affecting a large number of people. In March 1993 the same Court determined that, like other provinces, Manitoba must establish independent French-language school boards, placing French schools under the exclusive management and control of the French-language minority.

With regard to economic issues, in 1992 Ontario cancelled the deal to purchase Manitoba electricity, eliminating the need to build the Conawapa dam, which would have been the largest construction project in the province's history. Unfortunately, Saskatchewan showed little interest in a proposal to swap its natural gas for Manitoba's electricity. In 1992, the speech from the throne announced Sunday shopping would be allowed in the province. In 1993, a no-fault automobile insurance scheme was introduced. To reduce costs in the publicly owned system, the bill prohibited injured parties from suing for compensation. The government also set up an Economic Innovation and Technology Council in 1992, and unveiled a Framework for Economic Growth in 1993. This 10-point strategy included fiscal management, skills training, innovation, infrastructure investment, and new industries such as health care products, aerospace, information and telecommunications, and agri-food processing.

The program of fiscal conservatism became most apparent in the series of Filmon government budgets. In 1990, the government imposed a three-percent ceiling on public sector wage increases (except for nurses). In 1991, it froze the wages of 48,000 public service employees and eliminated about 1,000 jobs, only half of them by attrition. Moreover, by cutting $12 million in grants to non-profit groups, the government indirectly caused a larger number of layoffs. In 1992, it cut another 300 government positions, and about 500 and 400 more in the following two years respectively. The terms of the 1993 budget were particularly harsh: a wage rollback and work week reduction plan (10 days off without pay called "Filmon Fridays") for 100,000 public sector workers, including teachers; elimination of the children's dental plan; and reduction of tax credits for pensioners, tenants, property taxpayers, and those receiving social assistance and workers' compensation benefits. The 1994 budget contained 10 more Filmon Fridays, with provincial judges challenging their inclusion in that plan. Victims of government retrenchment in 1994 included foster parents, home care, students on bursaries, and schools and universities. The government also continued its privatization initiatives, and provided a variety of corporate tax breaks.

Despite such measures and the exhaustion of the provincial fiscal stabilization fund over the 1991-93 period—and partly because it refused to raise major taxes—the government continued to run large annual deficits, as seen in Table 8.11. This resulted in a downgrading of Manitoba's credit rating. In 1993, however, the government declared its intention to balance its books over the following four years. Not surprisingly, many of the resulting cutbacks led to protest rallies. In fact, the "progressive" measures which Filmon adopted over this period are relatively few: strengthening of tenants' rights, tax freezes, a federal-provincial welfare scheme for single mothers, more assistance for the mentally retarded, and incentives for first-time home buyers.

PRENTICE HALL
GINN PUBLISHING
ALLYN & BACON
C A N A D A

539 Collier Macmillan Drive,
Cambridge, Ontario N1R 5W9
1-800-567-3800

1

| DATE | PAGE |

P.O. NUMBER SUN420000019601161 10/23/95   1

SHIP TO: INVOICE NO.   2737040

PROF. A SALOOJEE
RYERSON POLYTECH UNIVERSITY
POLITICS & SCH OF PUB ADMIN
350 VICTORIA ST
TORONTO   ON M5B 2K3

SHIP BY: BOOKMAIL   **OCT 26 1995**

INV.	OPT 1	OPT 2	CM/BO REF.	DEL. BILL	SOURCE KEY
IN	SMP	WH4			

SALESMAN BILL	SHIP	TERRITORY BILL	SHIP	O/C	ROY	COMM	PAY	REG #
116	116	100	100	ZE	NO			678

STOCK NO.	QUANTITY	BIN	BULK	CRTN QTY	RET TO STK
0134433912	1	06-074-9			
PROV POLITICS CDA 3/E					
0134392175	1	06-096-9			
PARTY POLITICS IN CANADA 7/E					

# CTN.	CORR. WGT.	PACKER SIGNATURE	CARRIER SIGNATURE

TOTAL UNITS	TOTAL WEIGHT	GROSS ORDER VALUE	BILLED WT. %	V	C	B.C.
2	1.88			0	N	

IN# 2737040 VIA:BKM CO#10- ID#6784

OCT 26 1995

"Received, subject to the Rules for the Carriage of Express and
Non-Carload Freight Traffic and tariffs in effect on the date of
issue of this original shipping contract (bill of lading), goods
described below, in apparent good order, except as noted
(contents and conditions of contents of packages unknown),
marked, consigned and destined as indicated below, which said
company agrees to carry to its usual place of delivery at said
destination, if on its road, otherwise to deliver to another carrier
on the route to said destination. It is mutually agreed, as to each
carrier of all or any of said goods over all or any portion of said
route to destination, and as to each party at any time interested
in all or any of said goods, that every service to be performed
hereunder shall be subject to all the terms and conditions
(which are hereby incorporated by reference and have the
same force and effect as if the same where severally, fully
and specifically set forth herein), approved by the Express
and Non-Carload Freight Traffic Terms and Conditions Approval
Order and also available at all express and railway agency
stations and express and freight offices upon request, when said
goods are carried by a rail carrier and which are agreed to by the
shipper and accepted for himself and his assigns."

1. approved by the National Transportation Agency by General Order No. T-5, dated February 1, 1965 set forth in the Canadian Freight Classification and also available at all Railway agency stations and freight offices upon request when said goods are carried by a rail carrier; and which are agreed to by the shipper and accepted for himself and his assigns; or

2. approved by the National Transportation Agency by General Order No. T-43, set forth in the Rules for the Carriage of Express and Non-Carload Freight Traffic and also available at all express and railway agency stations and express and freight offices upon request when said goods are carried by a rail carrier and which are agreed to by the shipper and accepted for himself and his assigns; or

3. of the bill of lading set forth in or prescribed by the relevant tariffs, classification, statutes and regulations pertaining to motor carrier's services when said goods are carried by a motor carrier; or

4. of the bill of lading form as described in the Trucking Regulations (1988) 120 G.O. II 791 as approved by the Quebec Transport Commission when said goods originating in Quebec are to be carried by a motor carrier; or

5. of the bill of lading of the water carrier as approved in its tariffs of Rules and Regulations when said goods are carried by a water carrier.

TABLE 8.11   **Government of Manitoba Finances, 1990/91–1994/95 ($ millions)**

	1990/91	1991/92	1992/93	1993/94	1994/95
Total revenues	$6,125.9	$6,467.5	$6,214.0	$6,458.8	$6,484.3
Debt charges	1,328.4	1,384.4	1,475.3	1,485.5	1,519.8
Total expenditures	6,395.9	6,902.1	7,029.5	6,825.4	6,889.0
Deficit	270.0	434.6	815.5	366.6	404.7

Source: Reproduced by authority of the Minister of Industry, 1995, Statistics Canada, *Public Sector Finance, 1994–95*, Financial Management System, cat. no. 68-212 (March 1995). Adapted by author.

The principal controversies of the period included the lease of $7 million worth of government office space without public tender to a company with Tory connections, an immigrant investor scandal, and partisan appointments. Other problems facing the Filmon government included the 1991 nurses' strike, the longest in the province, a court decision ordering the province to pay for abortions performed in the Morgentaler clinic, and criticism from the auditor that the government had not included pension benefits in its books. While Natives pressed for approval for casinos on reserves, the government established two new casinos in Winnipeg, bringing the province considerable revenue. The fate of the Winnipeg Jets National Hockey League team was up in the air after it threatened to move to the U.S., but a combination of private, community, and government support kept it in town.

The biggest political change occurred when Sharon Carstairs stepped down as Liberal leader, and MLA Paul Edwards, a Winnipeg lawyer, won the party leadership in a June 1993 contest in which all party members could mail in their ballot or vote at four regional polling centres. Later, after the publication of her autobiography, Carstairs was appointed to the Senate by Prime Minister Jean Chrétien. Several MLAs resigned to run in the 1993 federal election, Elijah Harper switching from the NDP to the Liberals in the process. In September 1993 this necessitated five by-elections in which, even after a major cabinet shuffle, the Conservatives lost one seat, leaving them only one ahead of the combined opposition. The 1994 speech from the throne and budget passed only with the Speaker voting in their favour and, after these close calls, Filmon adjourned the legislature without transacting much other business.

After a somewhat artificial 1995 balanced budget, Filmon called an election for April 25 and won an increased majority (31 seats). The NDP took second place (23 seats) with a campaign focused entirely on preserving medicare. Independent Aboriginal candidates in three northern ridings, possibly encouraged by the PCs to split the NDP vote, had no impact on the outcome. Liberal Party support declined to 24 percent during the course of the campaign, and Paul Edwards was not among the three Liberals to win a seat.

CONCLUSION

In 1979, just as Manitoba began to move to a two-party system based on ideological and class differences, the ethnic issue of bilingualism became prominent again. In the process, the Liberal party was revived to create a three-party system, and once Gary Filmon became leader of the Conservatives, the bitter ideological divisions among the parties largely evaporated. In 1988 the province found itself confused politically and ended up electing a minority Conservative government with a Liberal Opposition. In 1990 and 1995, the NDP regained second place, and Filmon gained a majority. Based on a more moderate platform than its Ontario and Alberta counterparts, the Filmon team looked forward to a more secure existence as it approached the turn of the century.

TABLE 8.12   Manitoba Provincial Elections Results Since 1920

Year	Liberal		Conservative		CCF/NDP		Other	
	Seats	Popular Vote	Seats	Popular Vote	Seats	Popular Vote	Seats	Popular Vote
1920	21	36%	7	17%	11	21%*	16	27%**
1922	5	24%	7	17%	6	16%*	33	43%**
1927	7	21%	15	27%	3	10%*	30	42%**
1932	38	40%***	10	36%	5	17%*	2	6%
1936	23	36%***	16	29%	7	12%	9	23%
1941	21	35%***	15	22%	3	17%	10	26%
1945	25	32%***	15	16%	10	34%	5	18%
1949	31	40%***	10	13%	7	26%	9	21%
1953	35	41%***	12	21%	5	17%	5	21%
1958	19	35%***	26	41%	11	20%	1	4%
1959	11	30%***	36	47%	10	22%	–	2%
1962	13	36%***	36	45%	7	15%	1	4%
1966	14	33%	31	40%	11	23%	1	4%
1969	5	24%	22	36%	28	38%	2	2%
1973	5	19%	21	37%	31	42%	–	3%
1977	1	12%	33	49%	23	39%		
1981	–	7%	23	44%	34	47%	–	2%
1986	1	14%	26	40%	30	41%	–	5%
1988	20	35%	25	38%	12	24%	–	3%
1990	7	28%	30	42%	20	29%	–	1%
1995	3	24%	31	43%	23	33%	–	1%

* Labour
** 1920: Farmer 12 (16%); 1922: United Farmers of Manitoba 28 (33%); 1927: Progressive party 29 (33%)
*** Liberal-Progressive party

TABLE 8.13   Premiers of Manitoba Since 1870

Premier	Party	Year Elected
A. Boyd*		1870
N.A. Girard*		1871
H.J.H. Clarke*		1872
N.A. Girard*		1874
R.A. Davis		1874
John Norquay	Conservative	1878
D.H. Harrison	Conservative	1887
T. Greenway	Liberal	1888
H.J. Macdonald	Conservative	1900
Rodmond Roblin	Conservative	1900
T.C. Norris	Liberal	1915
John Bracken	United Farmers of Manitoba	1922
Stuart Garson	Liberal-Progressive	1943
Douglas Campbell	Liberal-Progressive	1948
Duff Roblin	Progressive Conservative	1958
Walter Weir	Progressive Conservative	1967
Ed Schreyer	New Democratic Party	1969
Sterling Lyon	Progressive Conservative	1977
Howard Pawley	New Democratic Party	1981
Gary Filmon	Progressive Conservative	1988

* These men were not really premiers but were in charge of the administration of the province.

ENDNOTES

1. Up to the 1911 census, Manitoba was the largest Western province in terms of population. After that, it was second until 1931, when it was third largest. It was fourth from 1941 to 1971, and third again since 1971.

2. Winnipeg was the largest city in terms of population in Western Canada until the 1931 census when it was overtaken by Vancouver. Now Edmonton and Calgary are also larger.

3. Peter C. Newman, *The Canadian Establishment* (Toronto: Seal Books, rev. ed. 1979), pp. 241-248; *Debrett's Illustrated Guide to the Canadian Establishment* (Toronto: Methuen, 1983), p. 116. Newman also mentions Alan Sweatman, Marty Freedman, and G.H. Sellers, among others.

4. Alex Netherton, "Manitoba: The Shifting Points of Politics, a Neo-Institutional Analysis," in Keith Brownsey and Michael Howlett, eds., *The Provincial State: Politics in Canada's Provinces and Territories* (Mississauga: Copp Clark Pitman, 1992).

5. From the telephone book of government services in French published by the Société franco-manitobaine. See also Nelson Wiseman, "The Questionable Relevance of the Constitution in Advancing Minority Cultural Rights in Manitoba," *Canadian Journal of Political Science* (December 1992).

6. Thomas Peterson, "Manitoba, Ethnic and Class Politics," in Martin Robin, ed., *Canadian Provincial Politics* (Scarborough: Prentice Hall Canada, 1978); Donald Swainson, "Ethnic Revolt: Manitoba's Election," in *Canadian Forum* (August 1969); G.A. Rawlyk, "The Manitoba Miracle, June 25, 1969," in *Queen's Quarterly* (August 1969).

7. On this subject, see M.A. Donnelly, *The Government of Manitoba* (Toronto: University of Toronto Press, 1963), ch. 3.

8. Nelson Wiseman, "The Pattern of Prairie Politics," in H.G. Thorburn, ed., *Party Politics in Canada* (Scarborough: Prentice Hall Canada, 5th. ed. 1985); David Laycock, *Populism and Democratic Thought in the Prairies, 1910-1945* (Toronto: University of Toronto Press, 1989); and Zenon Kulchyckyj, "Subfragmentation and the Political Culture of the Canadian West," Canadian Political Science Association (May 1981). Wiseman writes in his book *Social Democracy in Manitoba* (Winnipeg: University of Manitoba Press, 1983) as follows: "Manitoba had enough of Ontario in it to have sustained the only provincial Conservative party west of Ontario that has never collapsed. But it also had enough of modern Britain and continental Europe to provide CCFer J.S. Woodsworth and provincial Communist leader W.A. Kardash with parliamentary seats. Manitoba also had enough of the prairies in it to produce national and provincial Progressive parties," p. 149.

9. Richard Simeon and David Elkins, "Provincial Political Cultures in Canada," in Elkins and Simeon, eds., *Small Worlds: Provinces and Parties in Canadian Political Life* (Toronto: Methuen, 1980); William M. and Marsha A. Chandler, *Public Policy and Provincial Politics* (Toronto: McGraw-Hill Ryerson, 1979).

10. James McAllister, *The Government of Edward Schreyer* (Montreal: McGill-Queen's University Press, 1984), p. 140.

11. Ibid., ch. 10.

12. Rand Dyck, "Relations Between Federal and Provincial Parties," in A.G. Gagnon and A.B. Tanguay, eds., *Canadian Parties in Transition* (Scarborough: Nelson Canada, 1989).

13. Even as a backbencher, Schreyer had often broken rank; McAllister, *The Government of Edward Schreyer,* p. 18.

14. Nelson Wiseman, "The Pattern of Prairie Leadership," in Leslie Pal and David Taras, eds., *Prime Ministers and Premiers* (Scarborough: Prentice Hall Canada, 1988).

15. For example, Russell Doern, *Wednesdays Are Cabinet Days* (Winnipeg: Queenston House, 1981), ch. 8; McAllister, *The Government of Edward Schreyer,* pp. 3, 125, and ch. 2; Wiseman, *Social Democracy in Manitoba,* pp. 120-132.

16. Nelson Wiseman, "From Jail Cell to the Crown: Social Democratic Leadership in Manitoba," in R.K. Carty, ed., *Leaders and Parties in Canadian Politics: Experiences of the Provinces* (Toronto: Harcourt Brace Jovanovich, 1992).

17. Netherton talks of "major paradigmatic shifts" in his chapter in Brownsey and Howlett, eds., *The Provincial State.*

18. Norman Wiseman, *Social Democracy in Manitoba,* pp. 125-6 and 139-40; James McAllister, *The Government of Edward Schreyer;* and Harold Chorney and Phillip Hansen, "Neo-Conservatism, Social Democracy and 'Province-Building': the Experience of Manitoba," *Canadian Review of Sociology and Anthropology* (1985).

19. Schreyer's concept of equalizing incomes was sometimes stated as specifically as this: that no one should make more than two-and-one-half or three times what anyone else received, or that no one should make more than two-and-one-half times the average industrial wage; McAllister, *The Government of Edward Schreyer*, p. 54; Doern, *Wednesdays Are Cabinet Days*, p. 116. "We are committed and determined to work toward greater equality of the human condition," in Paul Beaulieu, ed., *Ed Schreyer, A Social Democrat in Power* (Winnipeg: Queenston House, 1977), p. 195. As for planning, he set up a planning secretariat, headed by J.C. Weldon and then by Marc Eliesen, which prepared a comprehensive planning document, *Guidelines for the Seventies*. Schreyer involved the whole cabinet in the planning process and H.G. Thorburn writes that this "generated the political will to act, a unique experience in Canada." See H.G. Thorburn, *Planning and the Economy* (Toronto: Canadian Institute for Economic Policy, 1984), p. 133. With respect to the role of government in natural resource development, Marsha A. Chandler emphasizes the managerial role of Manitoba Mining Resources Ltd. and points to the super-royalties which Schreyer levied on the mining companies, "The Politics of Provincial Resource Policy," in Michael M. Atkinson and Marsha A. Chandler, eds., *The Politics of Canadian Public Policy* (Toronto: University of Toronto Press, 1983), p. 57. See also John N. McDougall, "Responses to the Kierans Report on National Resources Policy in Manitoba," Canadian Political Science Association (June 1987).

20. Wiseman, *Social Democracy in Manitoba*, p. 119; Beaulieu, *Ed Schreyer*, p. 190. He also admired John Kenneth Galbraith.

21. Joseph Wearing, *The L-Shaped Party* (Toronto: McGraw-Hill Ryerson, 1981), p. 129.

22. McAllister, *The Government of Edward Schreyer*, p. 121.

23. Peterson, "Manitoba, Ethnic and Class Politics" in Robin, *Canadian Provincial Politics.*

24. McAllister, *The Government of Edward Schreyer*, p. 123.

25. Bob Stirling and John Conway, "Fractions Among Prairie Farmers," Canadian Political Science Association (June 1985).

26. Donnelly, *The Government of Manitoba*, ch. 7.

27. Roblin briefly had a franco-Manitoban in his cabinet in 1959, but he died.

28. 1870-1883:   24
    1883-1886:   30
    1886-1888:   35
    1888-1907:   40
    1907-1914:   41
    1914-1920:   49
    1920-1949:   55
    1949-present: 57
    On this subject, see Andy Anstett and Paul Thomas, "Manitoba: The Role of the Legislature in a Polarized Political System," in Gary Levy and Graham White, eds., *Provincial and Territorial Legislatures in Canada* (Toronto: University of Toronto Press, 1989).

29. Donnelly, *The Government of Manitoba*, pp. 67 and 105; Donnelly and others decry the effect the coalition had on the province's political institutions.

30. Ibid., p. 121; Jeffrey Simpson, *Spoils of Power* (Toronto: Collins, 1988), ch. 12.

31. Simpson, *Spoils of Power*, p. 253.

32. On municipal government, see C.R. Tindal and S.N. Tindal, *Local Government in Canada* (Toronto: McGraw-Hill Ryerson, 2nd. ed., 1984); and Donald Higgins, *Local and Urban Politics in Canada* (Toronto: Gage, 1986). Much has been written about the Unicity experiment.

33. W.L. Morton, *Manitoba: A History* (Toronto: University of Toronto Press, 1957), p. 145.

34. Morton argues that this initial discrimination against Manitoba, repeated in 1905 against Alberta and Saskatchewan, was the spark which ignited the whole syndrome of Western discontent in "The Bias of Prairie Politics," in Donald Swainson, ed., *Historical Essays on the Prairie Provinces* (Toronto: McClelland and Stewart, 1970).

35. W.L. Morton, *Manitoba: A History,* p. 250.

36. It permitted religious exercises in the school if authorized by the school board; it required the hiring of a Roman Catholic teacher if there were a specific number of Catholic students; and, on the related language question, bilingual schools were provided where 10 pupils spoke French or any language other than English.

37. Laurier established the northern boundary of Alberta and Saskatchewan at 60° North in 1905, but refused to extend Manitoba's to the same latitude. This became an issue in Manitoba in the 1911 federal election, and the new Conservative Borden government took appropriate action in 1912, extending Manitoba's northern border.

38. Ed Whitcomb, *A Short History of Manitoba* (Stittsville: Canada's Wings, 1982), p. 33. The record was also blemished by reducing the minimum wage for child labour and increasing the maximum hours of work for women and children in 1914; Wiseman, *Social Democracy in Manitoba,* p. 6. See also Simpson, *Spoils of Power.*

39. Donnelly, *The Government of Manitoba,* p. 59.

40. Whitcomb, *A Short History of Manitoba,* p. 40.

41. Morton, *Manitoba: A History,* p. 379. The categorization of some members was unclear and some accounts therefore have slightly different results.

42. Wiseman, *Social Democracy in Manitoba,* p. 12.

43. Morton, *Manitoba: A History,* p. 405.

44. John Kendle, *John Bracken: A Political Biography* (Toronto: University of Toronto Press, 1979), pp. 121-6.

45. Ibid., p. 49. Another description was "an earnest young man ... quite without frills." Peterson, "Manitoba, Ethnic and Class Politics," in Robin, *Canadian Provincial Politics,* p. 77.

46. Donnelly, *The Government of Manitoba,* p. 64. At this point, Bracken invited the Conservatives to join the coalition, indicating a willingness to divide the cabinet positions and even to alternate the premiership; Kendle, *John Bracken,* p. 145.

47. It was the only time the party entered such a formal coalition anywhere and, although there was opposition to the move from the start, the majority felt Bracken was so popular and the CCF so weak it would be wiped out if it rejected the invitation. The CCF leader was added to the cabinet as minister of Labour, but he was not

supported by Bracken on most of his legislative initiatives, Wiseman, *Social Democracy in Manitoba*, ch. 2.

48. Although Bracken was not literally "progressive," he was more so than the Conservatives had been to that point. By altering their stance slightly, the Tories became progressive enough for him, even though the insistence on the name change had more to do with his origins than his current ideology.

49. Among other things, the Bracken personal papers and the CCF party files were lost in the flood. In total, 1,800 square kilometres were under water, causing property damage of $26 million and forcing the evacuation of over 100,000 people.

50. Peterson, "Manitoba, Ethnic and Class Politics," p. 88; James Jackson, *The Centennial History of Manitoba* (Toronto: McClelland and Stewart, 1970), p. 245.

51. Donnelly, *The Government of Manitoba*, p. 67.

52. Jackson, *The Centennial History of Manitoba*, p. 249.

53. *Canadian Annual Review*, 1967, p. 152.

54. Ibid., 1969, p. 126.

55. McAllister, *The Government of Edward Schreyer*; Wiseman, *Social Democracy in Manitoba*; Doern, *Wednesdays are Cabinet Days*; Beaulieu, ed., *Ed Schreyer, A Social Democrat in Power*; as well as the *Canadian Annual Review of Politics and Public Affairs*.

56. Wiseman, *Social Democracy in Manitoba*, p. 120.

57. McAllister calls the Department of Northern Affairs the Schreyer government's most significant bureaucratic creation, *The Government of Edward Schreyer*, p. 24. See also Geoffrey Weller, "Managing Canada's North: The Case of the Provincial North," *Canadian Public Administration* (Summer 1984).

58. Philip Mathias, *Forced Growth* (Toronto: James Lewis and Samuel, 1971), ch. 6; Nick Hills, "The Churchill Forest Industries Scandal," in Kenneth M. Gibbons and Donald C. Rowat, eds., *Political Corruption in Canada* (Toronto: McClelland and Stewart, 1976); and "The Real Story Behind CFI," in *Canadian Dimension*, 1971.

59. Mathias, *Forced Growth*, p. 178.

60. Borowski had tried the patience of Schreyer and his cabinet colleagues on many other occasions. For an account of this colourful character, see Doern, *Wednesdays are Cabinet Days*.

61. Debicki, "Why the Voters Didn't Play the Game," an address to the Canadian Political Science Association (June 1975).

62. Schreyer had a well-developed concept of "rational restraints" which he defended in spite of the federal party position; Beaulieu, ed., *Ed Schreyer, A Social Democrat in Power*, pp. 241-2.

63. Alex Netherton, "The Opportunities and Limitations of a Hydro Development Strategy: the Case of Manitoba 1960-1980," Canadian Political Science Association (June 1983).

64. *Canadian Annual Review*, 1980, p. 290; 1981, p. 400.

65. Howard Pawley and C. Lloyd Brown-John, "Transitions: The New Democrats in Manitoba," in Donald Savoie, ed., *Taking Power: Managing Government Transitions* (Toronto: Institute of Public Administration of Canada, 1993).

66. One of the casualties was Assiniboia Downs racetrack, just as Princess Anne was about to be honoured by a race in her name; *Canadian Annual Review 1982*, p. 262.

67. Surveys showed that the NDP trailed the Conservatives by about 35 percent at one point and by 15 percent in March 1985. In April 1984, 33 percent said bilingualism was of most concern to them. In October 1983, 56 percent opposed the government proposal; Institute for Social and Economic Research, University of Manitoba, "Attitudes of the Manitoba Population toward Bilingualism Policies Proposed by the Provincial Government"; "Political Preferences of Manitobans"; and "Political Attitudes of Western Canadians."

68. Bosiask, "By One Vote: The Defeat of the Manitoba Government," *Canadian Parliamentary Review* (Spring 1989).

READINGS

Canadian Annual Review of Politics and Public Affairs. Toronto: University of Toronto Press, annual.

Canadian Dimension. Winnipeg, monthly.

Carstairs, Sharon. *Not One of the Boys*. Toronto: Macmillan, 1993.

McAllister, James. *The Government of Edward Schreyer*. Montreal: McGill-Queen's University Press, 1984.

Netherton, Alex. "The Shifting Points of Politics: A Neo-Institutional Analysis." Keith Brownsey and Michael Howlett, eds. *The Provincial State*. Mississauga: Copp Clark Pitman, 1992.

Pawley, Howard and C. Lloyd Brown-John. "Transitions: The New Democrats in Manitoba." Donald Savoie, ed. *Taking Power: Managing Government Transitions*. Toronto: Institute of Public Administration of Canada, 1993.

Wiseman, Nelson. *Social Democracy in Manitoba: A History of the CCF/NDP*. Winnipeg: University Press, 1984.

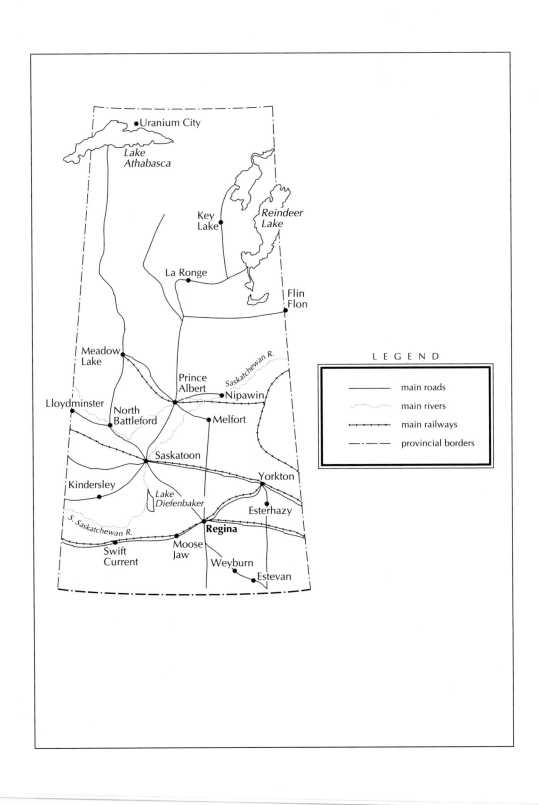

Uranium City

Lake
Athabasca

Key
Lake

Reindeer
Lake

La Ronge

Flin
Flon

Meadow
Lake

Saskatchewan R.

Prince
Albert
Nipawin

Lloydminster
North
Battleford
Melfort

Saskatoon

Kindersley

Yorkton

Lake
Diefenbaker
Esterhazy

S. Saskatchewan R.
Regina

Swift
Current
Moose
Jaw
Weyburn

Estevan

CHAPTER 9

SASKATCHEWAN

The Saskatchewan landscape of vast stretches of wheat fields highlighted by stately grain elevators is a stark reminder of the province's heavy dependence on a single industry. Saskatchewan's reliance on wheat entailed growth and prosperity in its first 25 years, but this was followed by economic disaster in the Great Depression, and slow improvement afterwards. The boom and bust cycle and the spirit of co-operation it engendered contributed to Saskatchewan's second unique characteristic, the election of a Co-operative Commonwealth Federation government in 1944 and the subsequent experience with "agrarian socialism." During the 1970s, the province was subject to a third striking development—rapid growth and prosperity based on its mining industry. Saskatchewan consequently became a middle-ranking province economically, no longer synonymous with wheat. The problems of that industry in the 1980s and early 1990s, compounded by a global recession, resulted in general economic decline, but the province has brighter prospects as it approaches the turn of the century.

SETTING

Geography

Saskatchewan is 651,900 square kilometres in area and contains two basic geographic regions: the rich level plains in the south, and the Precambrian shield of the north. The dividing line is a little more than halfway up from the American border. In addition to this natural division, the cities of Regina and Saskatoon constitute individual regions, and it is often convenient to speak of two kinds of settlement, rural and urban.

Saskatchewan celebrated surpassing the one million mark in population in 1983-84, but it subsequently lost population. In the 1991 census it stood at 988,928, but the population stabilized afterwards at just over one million, rising

431

to 1,017,200 in January 1995. Saskatoon, with a population of 210,023, and Regina, with 191,692, are the two main and almost equally sized urban poles. The other large urban centres are Prince Albert (41,257), Moose Jaw (35,552), North Battleford, Yorkton, and Swift Current. Lloydminster sits astride Saskatchewan's western border, with 7,241 of the town's residents in that province and 10,042 in Alberta. Saskatchewan is the least urbanized Western province (63 percent), exceeding the 50 percent urban mark in 1971, but less rural than the Atlantic region.

Saskatchewan is crossed by the southern and northern (Yellowhead) routes of the Trans-Canada Highway, as well as by Canadian Pacific and Canadian National rail lines. In addition, it has an amazing network of local roads and railway branch lines, although many of the latter have closed in recent years. Roads extend to the three main uranium mining areas in the north, but that region depends primarily on air travel.

Economy

Saskatchewan is very much a resource-based economy. It has the highest proportion of residents of any province engaged in primary employment, the lowest proportion in manufacturing, and the second-lowest in service industries. Overall, its gross domestic product is about three percent of the national total.

Saskatchewan has 42 percent of the arable land in Canada and, for decades, wheat provided the basis of Saskatchewan's economy. In a good crop year it is still the province's most important industry, constituting about 60 percent of the national total. Wheat overshadows other crops, although barley, oats, and canola are also grown in sizeable amounts, such that the value of Saskatchewan crops exceeds that of any other province. Throughout the 1980s, however, the wheat crop was plagued by bad weather and problems such as grasshoppers, significantly reducing production and the province's overall prosperity. At the same time as Saskatchewan's production fell, the rest of the world produced a greater supply of wheat, resulting in a decline in demand and price. Even in good years, western Canadian grain farmers were heavily subsidized, but Europe and the U.S. could afford to subsidize their farmers even more. Given these combined difficulties, the future of the industry is uncertain, and many governments have sought ways of keeping farmers in operation when creditors were threatening to foreclose on them. Most farm families must now derive supplementary income from off-farm employment, while diversification into new specialty crops, forages and feed grains, as well as into a greater reliance on livestock is also part of the solution. Even the appearance of the grain industry is changing, as concrete elevators replace the classic wooden ones. Saskatchewan currently ranks fourth in the country in livestock, with emphasis on cattle, hogs, and sheep. Saskatchewan used to rank second to Ontario in total value of agricultural production, but in recent years it has also been surpassed by Alberta. In 1991, the province's 60,840 farms had an average size of 1,090 acres, the largest in the country.

The mining industry sometimes exceeds the value of agriculture in economic terms, with the province now usually ranking fourth in the country in value of annual production. The three main mineral products are petroleum, potash, and uranium.

Saskatchewan is second to Alberta as a producer of crude oil, about one third of which is categorized as "heavy oil," and another third each as medium and light. The heavy oil, dark, thick and sticky, is located mainly in the Lloydminster and Kindersley-Kerrobert region in the west, and must be converted into a lighter, higher-quality product. For this purpose, Saskatchewan has two heavy oil upgraders, the NewGrade Upgrader operating in Regina since 1988, and the Bi-Provincial Upgrader which opened in Lloydminster in 1992. The southeastern Weyburn-Estevan area has light and medium varieties of oil, and a smaller, medium field is found near Swift Current. Production began in the late 1940s with the value of production growing to $100 million by 1960, $200 million by 1970, and over $1,400 million in 1992. After a slump in the early 1980s, petroleum activity has revived somewhat, and Saskatchewan has become the leader in horizontal drilling. Much of the crude oil goes to the oil upgrader in Regina or asphalt plants in Moose Jaw and Lloydminster. Natural gas is also found along the western border, the province ranking third in the country in this resource. Saskatchewan exports more than half of the oil and natural gas it produces, the former to the United States in large part, and the latter to eastern Canada.

The potash industry began production in 1962 with the real boom starting about 1970. Potash is found in a south-central band across the province with most of the 10 mines located near Saskatoon or Esterhazy in the southeast, and one near Moose Jaw. Four of the mines are owned by the Potash Corporation of Saskatchewan, which the NDP transformed into a Crown corporation in the 1970s and which the Conservatives privatized about 15 years later. Two are owned by International Minerals and Chemical Corp., and one by each of Rio Algom Ltd., Kalium Canada Ltd., Noranda Inc., and Cominco Ltd. Although potash sales fell after 1980, the future of the Saskatchewan industry looks reasonably optimistic; the province contains about 50 percent of the world's known potash reserves and there is a continuing need for potash-based fertilizer. Most of the product is exported to the United States, but the Pacific rim is another promising market. Saskatchewan has its own large fertilizer plant, Saskferco Products Inc., just outside Regina.

A large reserve of rich uranium ore has been found in the Athabasca basin of northern Saskatchewan. Although the original mine at Uranium City was abandoned by Eldorado Nuclear, and despite a sharp decline in sales in the 1960s, uranium exploration flourished in the 1970s. Saskatchewan has three production areas—Rabbit Lake, Key Lake, and Cluff Lake. The first two are owned by Cameco Corp. (two-thirds) and the German company Uranerz Exploration and Mining Ltd. (one-third), while Cluff Lake is owned by the French firm Cogema Resources Inc. Key Lake is the largest uranium mine in the world, and Cameco and other companies are developing other projects at McClean Lake, Cigar Lake, Midwest Lake, and other sites. After 1983, Saskatchewan surpassed Ontario as the country's leading uranium producer, but the ore is so rich that great precautions must be taken and strict environmental assessments made.

The province also contains a limited amount of coal, in which it is the third largest producer in the country. Mined at six sites along the U.S. border, the coal is of the lignite variety, particularly suitable for thermal electric generation. Most of it is therefore used in four thermal-electric generating stations within the province. Saskatchewan also has an assortment of minerals including gold, copper, zinc, and nickel near Flin Flon, on the Saskatchewan-Manitoba border; a number of sodium sulphate and salt plants; a variety of clays and other construction materials; and the prospect of producing diamonds.

Compared with agriculture and mining, the province's forestry industry is relatively small, and in most respects exceeds only that of Prince Edward Island. Nevertheless, a large portion of Saskatchewan is covered by forest, and production from the central part of the province includes lumber, posts and poles, plywood, particle board, pulp wood, and kraft pulp. The largest pulp mill is owned by Weyerhaeuser Canada Ltd. at Prince Albert; a new Millar Western Pulp Ltd. mill has opened in Meadow Lake and its state-of-the-art technology means zero effluent is being released into the environment. Lastly, there are small commercial fishing and trapping industries.

Lacking the mighty rivers of Manitoba and some other provinces, Saskatchewan depends on its own lignite coal to produce about 70 percent of its electricity needs. The remaining 30 percent is derived from five main hydro generating stations. In 1928 a Crown corporation, Saskatchewan Power Corporation, was established to oversee the development of the province's power resources, and in 1949 it purchased the remaining private companies. The corporation was also responsible for distributing natural gas until that division was severed into a separate company in 1989.

Saskatchewan has a limited manufacturing sector, smaller than that of Nova Scotia or New Brunswick. Food and beverages are naturally most important, including meat packers, bakeries, and breweries, but the spinoffs of the oil and potash industries include chemicals, fertilizers, paints, and plastics. Regina has a steel mill and pipe plant (Interprovincial Pipe and Steel Co. or IPSCO), and other manufacturing takes the form of foundries, agricultural implements, sheet metal products, and printing and publishing. Recent developments include electronics and telecommunications, making Saskatchewan a pioneer in the field of fibre optics. Innovation Place in Saskatoon was the first research park in Western Canada.

TABLE 9.1   **Saskatchewan 1991 Labour Force and Estimated 1995 Gross Domestic Product by Industry**

Industry	1991 Labour Force		Est. 1995 GDP ($ millions)	
Agriculture	91,140	18.2%	2,292	11.8%
Fishing	245	–	11	–
Forestry	1,795	0.4%	61	0.3%
Mining	12,000	2.4%	2,294	11.8%
TOTAL PRIMARY	105,180	21.0%	4,658	24.0%
Manufacturing	26,995	5.4%	1,201	6.2%
Construction	25,770	5.2%	890	4.6%
TOTAL SECONDARY	52,765	10.6%	2,091	10.8%
Transportation, communications and utilities	37,365	7.5%	2,342	12.1%
Trade	79,670	15.9%	2,434	12.5%
Finance, insurance & real estate	22,750	4.6%	2,973	15.3%
Services	164,865	33.0%	3,683	19.0%
Government	37,265	7.5%	1,242	6.4%
TOTAL TERTIARY	341,915	68.5%	12,674	65.3%
TOTAL ALL INDUSTRIES	499,870		19,425	

Source: Reproduced by permission of the Minister of Industry, 1995, Statistics Canada, *1991 Census,* cat. nos. 93-326 and 95-366, and Conference Board of Canada, *Provincial Outlook, Economic Forecast,* (Ottawa: Summer 1994), Vol. 9, No. 2.

As mentioned, the services sector is small compared to that of other provinces. However, recent additions include Sears' western Canadian call centre in Regina, Crown Life's move to Regina from Toronto, and the relocation of Atomic Energy of Canada's research facilities to Saskatoon. As for government, Saskatchewan has about 40,000 provincial employees, 45,000 municipal employees, and 15,000 federal employees.

Class

After a long period as a have-not province, Saskatchewan enjoyed an above-average per capita personal income in the 1970s, in the same ranking as Manitoba and Quebec. In the early 1990s, however, its per capita income fell below that of Nova Scotia. In 1992 Saskatchewan had a per capita personal income of $18,448, while in 1991 the median family income was $38,531. Just over 20 percent of families made under $20,000 and 15 percent over $70,000. Saskatchewan often has the lowest unemployment rate of any province, between seven and eight percent, but this is partly due to the tendency of the unemployed to leave the province.

The Saskatchewan Federation of Labour has about 100,000 members. In total, 114,000 workers are unionized, which represents 32.9 percent of the province's paid workers, the fourth-lowest rate in the country. These figures reveal that the strength of the CCF/NDP has rested with the farming community as well as organized labour. The largest unions are found in the public service—the Saskatchewan Government Employees' Union (SGEU), and the Canadian Union of Public Employees (CUPE). The Communications, Energy and Paperworkers (CEP), the United Food and Commercial Workers, and the Steelworkers are the largest unions in the private sector.

Saskatchewan's long domination by a party which relied heavily on public activity has meant that the province has not developed much of a private-sector power structure. In addition, many of the large private corporations there have come from outside the province. Nevertheless, a handful of successful and influential resident entrepreneurs can be identified, especially the Fred Hill family of Regina, now worth some $1 billion and headed by Fred's son Paul. The Hills are heavily involved in insurance, resources, energy, the media, Crown Life, and real estate development—Hillsdale subdivision. Other prominent business figures are the Mitchell family (Intercontinental Packers), the Knight family (development), and the Pinder family (pharmacies).[1]

If the corporate sector is abnormally small, co-operative organizations in the province are unusually strong. This tradition originated with the early settlers who had to deal with the challenges of climate and distance. Co-operatives were also organized as counterweights to federal government policies and central Canadian corporations. The largest single co-operative is the Saskatchewan Wheat Pool, while Federated Cooperatives Ltd. is a collection of co-operatives, both of them among the largest employers in the province. Similar to the United Grain Growers, the Wheat Pool decided to change its co-operative status to some extent in 1994 by selling shares to the public. Hundreds of other co-operatives flourish, and their variety is startling: more than 200 retail stores, over 220 credit unions, more than 600 service co-ops (child care centres, laundromats, local bus lines, recreation facilities, and health clinics), and over 200 producer and marketing co-ops.

Demography

Saskatchewan has a diverse ethnic distribution. Less than 40 percent of the population is of British descent, followed by those of German and Ukrainian origin and Native Peoples, while the French are fifth. The next largest groups are Scandinavians, Poles, and Dutch. On the other hand, 84.2 percent have English as mother tongue, and 94.4 percent speak it at home.

Saskatchewan has a smaller francophone minority than Manitoba or Alberta, and its assimilation rate is the second highest in the country. Thus, in 1991, only 2.2 percent of the population had French as its mother tongue, and only 0.7 percent used it in the home. As Saskatchewan and Alberta were settled, schools were established in either English or French, according to local needs, and the territorial government began on a bilingual basis. When an English-speaking majority emerged, however, the territorial assembly passed an Ordinance in 1888 which removed French as an official language of the assembly, and instruction in French was restricted to the first two or three years of school. After 1901, French could also be used for one hour per day in any grade but, with lax supervision, was probably more common than the laws and regulations permitted.[2] Then, in 1931, the government eliminated French language instruction and the issue diminished in importance.

The French factor was revived by the federal government from the mid-1960s onward, and since then Saskatchewan has relaxed the restrictions on the use of French in its schools. After the 1988 Supreme Court decision in the *Mercure* case, Saskatchewan passed a language act which set out how far it would go in the area of official bilingualism. It began to translate some of its laws, allowed French to be spoken in the legislature and in the courts, established French schools, and made a few provincial services available in French. Further legislation in 1993 anticipated the establishment of eight "fransaskois" school boards, managed by Saskatchewan residents of French origin.

Saskatchewan has nearly 100,000 residents of aboriginal origin, comprising 10 percent of the population. Regina and Saskatoon both contain relatively large proportions of urban aboriginals, and native concerns are an increasingly important item on the province's political agenda. In 1992, the premier, prime minister, and chiefs of 22 Saskatchewan bands signed the Treaty Land Entitlement Framework Agreement, which provided bands with about $450 million over 12 years to buy land to settle outstanding treaty land entitlements. It was the largest treaty-based land deal in Canadian history.

TABLE 9.2   Saskatchewan Mother Tongue and Home Language, 1991

	Mother Tongue	Home Language
English	84.2%	94.4%
French	2.2%	0.7%
Other	13.5%	4.9%

Source: Reproduced by permission of the Minister of Industry, 1995, Statistics Canada, *1991 Census,* cat. no. 93-317, adapted by author.

The fact that over 60 percent of its population is of non-British origin but most speak English means that Saskatchewan's immigration largely occurred decades ago. In 1991, 81 percent of its population was born in the province and

94 percent in Canada so, apart from those who leave, Saskatchewan now has a relatively stable population. The use of other languages was permitted in Saskatchewan schools for one hour per day between 1901 and 1918, but was discontinued at that point.

Ethnicity in Saskatchewan has often been linked to religion. The province is currently made up of 53.4 percent Protestants, 32.5 percent Catholics, 11 percent of no religious persuasion, and two percent Eastern Orthodox. The United Church is the largest Protestant sect but, a reflection of the high proportion of Germans, Lutherans outnumber Anglicans, while Mennonites are in fourth place. Religious controversy also predated the creation of the province and continued to be an issue until about 1930. The territorial board of education originally had separate Catholic and Protestant sections, and grants were made equally to both types of schools. The policy of parity and separate administration was abandoned in 1892, perhaps due to the Manitoba precedent. In original autonomy bills creating Saskatchewan and Alberta, Prime Minister Wilfrid Laurier re-established dual religious administration and increased the financial obligations of the provinces toward separate schools. Laurier eventually reversed this decision, and the two provinces were created much like Ontario, with public and separate schools under direct government administration, and government grants guaranteed to separate schools only at the elementary level. The question died down until a 1913 dispute erupted over the allocation of corporate taxes. Then, in the late 1920s, the Ku Klux Klan began protesting the operation of separate schools, and the issue became prominent in the 1929 election. It was not until 1964 that full funding and tax support were extended by right to separate high schools in the province, some 20 years before Ontario. Since then, the province has also contributed to certain other private high schools that follow the authorized curriculum.

TABLE 9.3   Religion in Saskatchewan, 1991

Protestant		521,680 (53.4%)
United Church	222,120 (22.8%)	
Lutheran	82,160 (8.4%)	
Anglican	69,930 (7.2%)	
Mennonite	25,240 (2.6%)	
Other Protestant	122,230 (12.5%)	
Roman Catholic		316,935 (32.5%)
No Religious Affiliation		107,225 (11.0%)
Eastern Orthodox		19,505 (2.0%)
Other		10,690 (1.1%)

Source: Reproduced by permission of the Minister of Industry, 1995, Statistics Canada, *1991 Census*, cat. no. 93-319, adapted by author.

In summary, ethnicity and religion were sources of much political conflict in Saskatchewan for the first 25 years. This was accompanied by a certain rural-urban tension, as well as some regional antagonisms. Since 1930, however, the province has increasingly adopted a more ideological character, and ethnicity and religion have been less prominent. The class-based, ideological pattern of politics finds wealthier farmers, business and self-employed professionals on one side, and poorer farmers, labour, and salaried professionals on the other. It usually reflects a rural-urban split as well.

Federal-Provincial Relations

Saskatchewan's relations with Ottawa have been dominated by the question of control of the province's natural resources, and by the issue of federal tariff and freight rates. Saskatchewan and the other prairie provinces pressured Ottawa for 25 years in an attempt to gain jurisdiction over their natural resources. Farmers were anxious for changes in the tariff and freight rates, and felt exploited by the railways, the banks, the farm machinery companies, the grain elevators, and the Winnipeg Grain Exchange. From 1935 to 1957, ex-premier Jimmy Gardiner was the province's representative in the federal cabinet and his solicitude toward the farming community largely pre-empted serious issues from arising. The concern shown by John Diefenbaker and Alvin Hamilton in the 1957-63 period also eased farmer discontent. It was mainly after 1963 that the province felt ignored by the federal government, often because it did not elect a single federal Liberal and was therefore unrepresented in the federal cabinet. Issues in this period included freight rates, grain movement, rail line abandonment, agricultural stabilization, and opposition to the federal bilingualism policy.[3] Later, in the 1970s, the second phase of Ottawa-Saskatchewan discord over natural resources erupted. In two key constitutional challenges to Saskatchewan resource legislation, the federal government intervened to help overturn the provincial laws. Saskatchewan took an ambivalent but constructive stance on the constitutional reform package in the early 1980s, supporting the amendments which would reverse these two court decisions, but unenthusiastic about other provisions and about the manner in which the question of patriation was approached.[4] In the Mulroney-Devine era, relations were for the most part harmonious, and Chrétien and Romanow were old allies from the 1980-82 constitutional wars.

In 1992, the Saskatchewan government received 28.3 percent of its revenues from Ottawa, or $1,663 million. The federal government also transferred $7 million to municipalities, $2,082 to individuals, and $944 to businesses.

POLITICAL CULTURE

Saskatchewan's one-crop economy has to a large extent defined its self-image and influenced its political culture. Saskatchewan views itself as a politically sophisticated but relatively rural, ethnic, grain-growing province which has had to battle a "stark frontier environment." This required individual co-operation in the first instance, and then co-operation of a more formal nature. The horror of the Depression experience persuaded residents to erect certain safeguards to protect themselves—largely in the form of collective government programs—and since that time they have possessed an experimental, utilitarian perspective on the role of the state.[5] Much has changed in this respect over the past 20 years and, at least in the 1970s, Saskatchewan bristled with self-confidence in its more prosperous and diversified economy. This self-confidence may return as it approaches the turn of the century.

Prior to 1960, however, almost everything in Saskatchewan centred on wheat. Despite this dependence on agriculture, a farmers' party did not take office in the early 1920s. The Liberal government of Saskatchewan was able to resist most of the radical democratic populist demands of the Progressives, and functioned in a "crypto-liberal" populist manner until the Co-operative Commonwealth Federation period ushered in a somewhat different kind of reform—social democratic populism. Radical democratic populism and social democratic populism had much in common, such as an emphasis on co-operation as the true moral principle of social interaction, co-operation as the means of establishing a "countervailing power" to that of the foes of the people, and co-operation as a system of economic relations which prevented exploitation while allowing for the individual ownership of agricultural land.[6] The social democrats and the more radical populists also shared a vigorous mass organizational opposition to central Canadian domination and a belief in participatory democracy. Where they differed was in radical democracy's penchant for methods of direct democracy, compared to social democracy's acceptance of party discipline and executive paramountcy, and its unbounded faith in planning and in the provincial state bureaucracy.

These differences between the Progressives in Manitoba or Alberta and the Co-operative Commonwealth Federation in Saskatchewan were partly the result of different settlement patterns. Unlike Manitoba, rural Saskatchewan was populated by many members of the British working class but fewer Ontario liberals. There were also fewer Americans than in Alberta, and those U.S. citizens who were attracted to Saskatchewan were more likely to be of Scandinavian than English background, and socialists rather than those only interested in monetary reform.[7]

The most extensive account of the rise of the CCF in Saskatchewan is Seymour Martin Lipset's *Agrarian Socialism*, published in 1950.[8] In his analysis, Saskatchewan was receptive to the social democratic message primarily because of the province's co-operative traditions. Saskatchewan's farmers faced long cold winters, dry hot summers, hail, snow, and early frost, as well as other natural problems such as pests and plant diseases. These environmental hazards were compounded by a feeling of exploitation by central Canada and the loneliness and social isolation of pioneer life. To cope with these problems, farmers were forced into co-operative action of many kinds. They co-operated in establishing grain elevators, retail stores, telephone service, roads, medical and hospital facilities, marketing pools, social events, and even churches. When co-operative efforts failed or were insufficient, the farm leaders advocated a collectivist political approach. As the co-operative movement transformed itself into a political party, activists of the former became the leaders of the latter. There were many devout socialists among the farm leadership and as conditions became increasingly desperate in the Great Depression, they were able to convince their followers to opt for a radical left-wing political solution. Some observers feel that the CCF merely provided the most effective response to the farmers' concerns in Saskatchewan and that, whatever the government's ideological orientation, the electorate was essentially pragmatic and conservative.[9] While no one would claim that all who voted for the CCF saw themselves as socialists, it would seem that an ethic of co-operation and collective public action was ingrained in the province and permitted a socialist party to take root. The CCF was more than a party based on pragmatism—its aim was to take the co-operative principle a step further in establishing a co-operative commonwealth within Saskatchewan.

Saskatchewan residents also felt at the mercy of, and hostile towards, the federal government and the central Canadian corporate elite.[10] On the other hand, to establish national standards and equalize wealth across the country, the CCF government of T.C. Douglas was invariably in favour of a stronger federal government, a sentiment not shared by the New Democratic Party under Allan Blakeney or the Liberal or Conservative administrations since 1964. This may have been partly a reaction to the policies and practices of the Trudeau government, however, and not entirely a matter of constitutional principle.

Perhaps because the farmers never came to power as a movement, the province lacked the strong moralistic streak which earlier reduced the incidence of patronage and corruption in Manitoba and Alberta. The Liberal party of Jimmy Gardiner, circa 1930, is usually regarded as a classic electoral machine which engaged in every manner of dubious political activity to secure its election.[11] In Noel's terms, this could be seen as the second stage of clientelism in which the electorate must establish a patron-client relationship with the governing party to fulfil its needs.[12] On the other hand, the election of the CCF in 1944 brought this phase to an abrupt end with the development of modern bureaucratic government. Thus, the third stage of clientelism arrived earlier in Saskatchewan than in any other province. The CCF government's only concern about relying on an expert bureaucracy was that it might blunt the party's purpose; the party therefore tried to combine merit with a general sympathy for the government's overall objectives in its hiring practices.

Embedded in the preceding discussion are the four main features of the Saskatchewan political culture identified by Christopher Dunn and David Laycock: populism, alienation, bipolarity, and modernization.[13] Alienation is a general characteristic of western Canada, but the Saskatchewan variant includes an element of vulnerability. They note that populism takes the form of "a widespread popular desire to wrest power from established elites and to democratize important social, political, and economic institutions." Modernity refers to the willingness to experiment with different political parties, policies, and institutions, and bipolarity, to the ideologically polarized party system.

Wilson placed Saskatchewan at the top of the "developed" provincial political cultures because of its class-based two-party system.[14] Saskatchewan was a peculiar place for a democratic socialist party to become successful, given the weakness of its urban working class; nonetheless, economic position essentially replaced ethnicity and religion as a determining factor in party preference. Like modern British Columbia, the province has two ideological streams reflected in the party system, one to the left and the other to the right of centre, respectively emphasizing individualism and co-operation.[15] Unlike B.C., however, the left-wing point of view has been the predominant one in Saskatchewan since 1944.

Saskatchewan residents rank high in political participation, especially in provincial voter turnout, which is typically about 82 percent, and also above average in federal turnout, at about 75 percent. This is consistent with active participation in community organizations; Lipset, for example, studied farmers' organizations and found one elective position for every two or three farmers.[16] Saskatchewan residents are also among those most likely to work in a political campaign, to contact public officials and to work with others in the community to solve a local problem. They could thus be said to possess a participant political culture.

TABLE 9.4   Saskatchewan Voter Turnout in Recent Federal and Provincial Elections

Federal Elections		Provincial Elections	
1974	72%	1971	83%
1979	79%	1975	80%
1980	71%	1978	79%
1984	78%	1982	84%
1988	78%	1986	82%
1993	69%	1991	83%
Average	74.5%	Average	81.8%

Source: *Reports of the Chief Electoral Officer*, calculations by author.

POLITICAL PARTIES

Party System

At first glance, Saskatchewan appears to have been characterized by two periods of one-party dominance—the Liberals from 1905 to 1944 and the CCF/NDP for the past 50 years. On the other hand, power changed hands regularly, and the province could also be seen as having a competitive two-party system. Since 1960, as seen in Table 9.5, Saskatchewan has had the highest two-party predominance of any Western province in popular vote, and a very high two-party preponderance of seats. The ingredients of the party system have changed since 1905, from Liberals and Conservatives to Liberals and the CCF/NDP, and now to the NDP and Conservatives, but some form of two-party system has persisted. Furthermore, at least since 1934, the party system has been ideologically polarized.

Of course, third parties have existed alongside the main two. The Progressives actually outpolled the Conservatives in 1921 and 1925, but did not function as a unified party. There was small Social Credit representation in the legislature in 1938 and 1956, and the Conservatives often won substantial popular vote without translating it into seats in the 1934-1971 period. The transitional 1975 election, however, was the only one in which three parties did well in terms of both seats and votes but, in 1991, the Liberals rebounded somewhat in popular vote, and then came in second in 1995.

Saskatchewan is distinguished from Manitoba and Alberta not only by its long history of two-party dominance but, ironically, by the fact that this most agricultural of provinces was the only one of the three not to elect a farmers' government. The Liberal party was able to withstand the Progressive challenge in the early 1920s primarily because it was a farmer's party in everything but name: it co-opted Saskatchewan Grain Growers Association leaders, implemented their policies, and disowned the federal Liberal party. Having survived the Progressive threat, and having been fortunate to lose the 1929 election, the Liberals continued to thrive in the post-1934 period. In another example of the Pinard theory, the Depression caused voters to turn to a new third party, the Co-operative Commonwealth Federation, when they were ready to abandon the discredited Conservatives. The Depression, a cataclysmic experience for Saskatchewan, allowed an agrarian socialist party to emerge, built on the extensive network of co-operative organizations and the co-operative spirit of the province.

On the other hand, the Liberal party decline after 1970 and its replacement by the Conservatives was not unique to Saskatchewan.[17] The decline at the federal level was primarily the work of John Diefenbaker more than 10 years earlier, and Saskatchewan residents were merely aligning their federal and provincial voting patterns by eliminating the Liberals from consideration. If Diefenbaker seriously wounded the Liberal party in the west, however, it was the policies and attitudes of the Trudeau government which killed it, both federally and provincially. The result was a polarized NDP-Conservative two-party system, at least until 1991.

TABLE 9.5   Party Support in Saskatchewan, 1970-95

	Years in Office		Average Percentage of Vote	Percentage of Seats
NDP	15	(60%)	46.2	57.7
Conservatives	9	(36%)	32.2	33.8
Liberals	1	(4%)	21.2	8.5
Total	25	(100%)	96.6	100.0

Source: *Reports of the Chief Electoral Officer*, calculations by author.

FIGURE 9.1   Percent of Vote by Party in Saskatchewan Elections, 1970-91

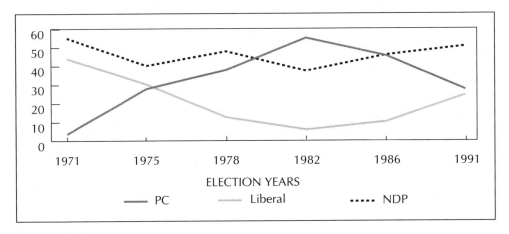

Party Organization

In terms of party organization, the CCF/NDP claimed to be a distinctive mass party in such respects as finance, leadership review, policy making, and general democratic operations. Research generally indicates that it was, even during the periods it held office. The CCF was financed primarily from individual contributions, while the NDP also relied on union support; the leadership was open for re-election at the annual party convention in both cases; and there was active year-round local membership activity, especially in the CCF period. Devices which ensured the legislative branch of the party responded to its grassroots included the initiation of policy resolutions in constituency associations; the pre-dominance of policy discussions at the annual party convention; the legislative advisory committee, a liaison body between the two wings of the party; and the prohibition of MLAs from holding top party positions. The CCF managed to reconcile such democratic party procedure with strong centralized cabinet control, and instances of the cabinet departing from party policy were rare. This represented a remarkable similarity of views between the party leadership and rank and file, a respect by the leader for the democratic traditions of the party and, on occasion, a willingness by the membership to be persuaded to follow the leader's recommended course.[18] However, on at least three occasions, serious discord erupted between the party and the government: in the late 1940s, Douglas persuaded CCF delegates that the oil industry should be developed by the private sector; in the 1970s, Blakeney convinced the party that the province should embrace uranium development; and, after the party changed its uranium policy in the interim Opposition period, Romanow repeated this act in the 1990s. On the other hand, today's NDP is less preoccupied with policy making and more with winning elections, and is thus less distinct in its organization from other parties in the province.

Federal-Provincial Party Links[19]

Because federal policies have almost always been seen to discriminate against the province, all three parties have at one time or another dissociated themselves from their federal counterparts. The Conservatives did this at the very start by using the name "Provincial Rights" party until 1911. The Liberals used this device to their advantage in the 1919-22 period when the federal party was not as receptive to lowering tariffs as the provincial government expected. This dissociation had a major part to play in Saskatchewan's continued support of the Liberal party. Federal-provincial Liberal party relations improved under Dunning and especially Gardiner, and as long as Saskatchewan was the third-largest province, it was a pillar of the federal party's strength. All this changed with the advent of John Diefenbaker followed by Pierre Trudeau, during which time the federal Liberal party in the province rapidly declined.

During the tenure of Liberal Premier Ross Thatcher, relations with the federal party reached an all time low.[20] This was partly because of significant ideological differences between Thatcher and Lester B. Pearson and Pierre Trudeau, and partly because of provincial opposition to many federal policies of a non-ideological nature, such as bilingualism, grain transportation, and the Constitution. Relations continued to be strained in the period that Otto Lang was the federal spokesman in the province, and are only more harmonious now that the Trudeau years are a distant memory.

Even the provincial CCF maintained its distance from the federal party to some extent. Until 1967, long after the federal party had changed its name to the NDP, the provincial party carried on under the CCF label for fear of appearing to shed its agricultural image for a labour-oriented one. Later, while Ed Broadbent sought to defend the Saskatchewan position in constitutional talks and helped achieve the section 92A amendment on provincial control over natural resources, the provincial party showed little gratitude, dissatisfied with Broadbent's quick support of the Trudeau constitutional position.

Party Leadership

Saskatchewan provincial politics have more often than not been dominated by the factor of party leadership.[21] Even in the early period, Walter Scott, W.M. Martin, and C.A. Dunning each contributed much to the success of the Liberal party, especially to its ability to withstand the attraction of a Progressive alternative. More recently, Jimmy Gardiner, T.C. "Tommy" Douglas, Ross Thatcher, Allan Blakeney, Grant Devine, and Roy Romanow stood out as strong men with well-developed views and a solid grasp of their respective governments. Each of these dominant leaders had a distinctive style.[22] Gardiner was the aggressive machine politician, primarily concerned with promoting the Liberal party and controlling every aspect of party affairs, even after moving on to the federal cabinet. Douglas, the longest-serving premier, was a genial, folksy stump orator who was the best salesman for socialism. His geniality masked a determined ideological orientation and a pioneering spirit. Thatcher, on the other hand, was the autocratic, tough free-enterpriser who personally reconstructed the Liberal party. Both Douglas and Thatcher had a kind of charisma, however different in its appeal. Blakeney had a shrewd, sharp, analytical mind, and a more bureaucratic style,[23] and was willing to share the spotlight with Attorney General and Deputy Premier Roy Romanow. Grant Devine had some of Douglas' folksiness and geniality but became as determinedly right-wing as Douglas was left. Romanow, the first premier of Ukrainian descent, is usually described as politically cautious, competitive, gregarious, eloquent, and urbane.

Party leaders in Saskatchewan have been chosen at traditional delegate conventions. The first break with this tradition was the Conservative leadership race in November 1994 in which all party members were entitled to vote. After paying a $20 fee, they could either attend the convention in Regina or vote by telephone from their residences. The party took advantage of the "tele-democracy" technology previously used by the Liberals in Nova Scotia and British Columbia.

Party Ideology

In the 1905-1922 period Saskatchewan was characterized by the same reformism as Ontario and Manitoba, that is, labour and welfare legislation and a certain amount of nationalization. Some of these measures, many relating specifically to the farming community, were enacted by the Liberal government to forestall Progressive political involvement in the province. In the 1930s, the Co-operative and Liberal governments were preoccupied with the Great Depression and did not follow any distinct ideological line, although opposition forces increasingly polarized on the left.

The CCF began in the mid-1930s as a clear-cut socialist party, using that term without reservation and advocating widespread government ownership. When it discovered that many people were frightened by the socialist label and the prospect of such comprehensive nationalization, it began to moderate its stance. The party assured voters that land would remain in private hands and the main objects of government ownership would be natural resources and public utilities. Once in office, it pursued the nationalization of most utilities, so that electricity, natural gas distribution, and telephones were all effectively owned by the public. However, it did not nationalize the emerging oil industry, as party policy originally demanded, the government position being that it did not have the funds or expertise to embark on such a risky business. The CCF thus left itself open for great debate, then and since, about how socialistic it really was.[24]

There is no doubt that the Douglas government was more willing to use the tool of public ownership than any contemporary administration in Canada. Indeed, some of its actions such as public automobile insurance have since been duplicated only by NDP or Parti Québécois governments. There is also no question that his government resorted to other kinds of public intervention (for example, taxation, regulation, and provision of services) to a much greater extent than any other government of the time. The CCF introduced myriad innovations on the social side, especially hospital and medical insurance and other health services, all of which served as models for later programs in other provinces and at the federal level. In these respects and many others, the Douglas CCF was a unique phenomenon in Canadian political life.[25] On the other hand, the party's program was regularly toned down as it tried first to obtain and then to retain office, for its leadership was aware that the electorate was more conservative than the government. Like any new government, especially one of this nature, the CCF also had to contend with bureaucratic conservatism.[26] It could therefore be said that the Douglas government was as radical as it could have been in the circumstances, given the constraints of a federal system, a capitalist economy, a shortage of provincial resources, a conservative bureaucracy, and a desire for re-election. It did not upset the framework of existing economic and social order, but could still be said to have practised "moderate democratic socialism."[27]

Eventually, of course, the government was defeated by the Liberals and Ross Thatcher, who claimed, "There's nothing wrong with socialism except it doesn't work." Once in office, his performance became more conservative, although it never quite matched his fulminating rhetoric. Although he left the CCF governmental apparatus more or less intact, he did little to extend it, and encouraged private enterprise to develop the province's resources.

The Blakeney NDP government, riding a wave of greater provincial prosperity and renewed radicalism from having been in Opposition, came to office with a surge of reform, but its most distinctive feature was to pick up on the old CCF idea of nationalizing natural resources. In taking over about half of the potash industry and establishing a strong government presence in oil and uranium, it proved the NDP's distinctiveness, and also created a contrast with the more moderate approach of the Schreyer government in Manitoba. Opposition forces throughout the 1970s promised a less interventionist government, and on this platform Grant Devine was elected in 1982. He modified some programs like the Land Bank, and encouraged the private sector to expand its operations in resource development. Later, Devine embarked on a massive privatization program of dismantling CCF/NDP Crown corporations, only slowing down in late 1989 after public opinion polls indicated that the electorate felt he had gone too far. On the other hand, Devine used various incentives to attract business to the province including joint ventures and loan guarantees. Roy Romanow claimed he was less ideological than his CCF/NDP predecessors and, inheriting a massive debt from Devine, governed in a less interventionist and more fiscally conservative manner than the Conservatives. He raised taxes, cut expenditures, closed or converted 52 rural hospitals, made partnerships with the private sector, and produced a balanced budget four years later.

ELECTIONS

Electoral System

Since 1967 all constituencies in Saskatchewan have been represented by a single member; however, between 1921 and 1964, the three cities had two, three, four, or five representatives. Between 1964 and 1967, Regina was divided into two two-member ridings and two single-member constituencies.[28] Until 1975, there was a wide discrepancy in the size of constituencies, due in part to gerrymandering and in part to rural and northern over-representation.[29] Gerrymandering was especially prevalent in the early history of the province and in 1970 was revived with a vengeance by Ross Thatcher. This action became an issue a year later and, rather than guarantee re-election, it probably contributed to the government's defeat. The Blakeney government introduced legislation to redistribute seats by means of an independent commission, a process which was carried out twice in the 1970s and which allowed only a plus or minus 15 percent variance from the mean. After 1981, Regina and Saskatoon had 31 percent of the seats, while their populations constituted 33 percent of the province. Even this independent redistribution does not guarantee that a party's popular vote will correspond to its proportion of seats, as the 1986 election showed. The Devine government brought in its own redistribution legislation in

1987 which specified that there be 35 rural, 29 urban, and two northern con-stituencies. It also increased the permissible variation from the mean to plus or minus 25 percent, and increased the size of the legislature to 66 members. The new map drawn up on this basis, enacted via the Representation Act 1989, obvi-ously over-represented the rural parts of the province where the governing Conservatives were strong. When a group of citizens threatened litigation, the government referred the constitutionality of the legislation to the Saskatchewan Court of Appeal who appointed Roger Carter to represent the opposing side, and the case became known as the "Carter case." The court ruled the legislation unconstitutional and, with little time before the next election, the government appointed a new redistribution commission that quickly designed fairer bound-aries. However, when the Carter case was appealed to the Supreme Court of Canada, that Court upheld the challenged electoral map, calling for effective, not necessarily equitable, representation.[30] Most experts could not believe the lati-tude which the majority of the Court was willing to leave to the politicians, and the deviations from equal representation which it found acceptable. The election was therefore fought on the first set of boundaries but, in spite of the fact that urban constituencies had an average of 1,000 more voters than rural ones, the Conservatives lost. Upon its victory, the NDP introduced new legislation to reduce the size of the legislature to 58 for the 1995 election. That includes two northern ridings, and 56 southern ridings whose population cannot vary from the southern population quota by more than plus or minus five percent. In other words, after the 1991 controversy, Saskatchewan adopted the most strin-gent rules in the country. A new electoral map reflecting these rules was designed by an impartial constituency boundaries commission in 1993.

TABLE 9.6   Representational Disparities in 1991 Election

Mean no. of voters per constituency	9,882
Largest constituency (Saskatoon River Heights)	13,224 (+33.8% of the mean)
Smallest constituency (Athabasca)	5,635 (−43.0% of the mean)
Average variation from mean	12.7%
Constituencies within ± 10% (29 of 66)	44%
Constituencies within ± 25% (60 of 66)	91%

Source: *Reports of the Chief Electoral Officer,* calculations by author.

An anomaly of the Saskatchewan system until 1952 was that elections in the two northern ridings were held a few weeks later than the rest of the province. The two main parties were almost tied in 1929, making the northern battle particularly intense.

Election-day treating and party financial scandals have been relatively rare in Saskatchewan, especially in recent times. In 1916-17, however, four assembly members were found guilty of bribery and corruption in connection with liquor administration and road work, and one was sent to prison. In 1974, the government passed legislation in the area of election expenses, providing for spending ceilings for parties and candidates, disclosure of contributions of over $100, and public reimbursement for candidates and parties that gained at least 15 percent of the vote.[31] An unusual aspect of Saskatchewan law is that government advertising is prohibited during an election campaign.

Voting Behaviour

The pattern of voting behaviour in terms of such variables as geography, ethnicity, religion, and class is not as clear-cut as might be expected in the province which has most frequently elected a "socialist" government.[32] Prior to 1944, for example, the more prosperous farmers—those most active in various co-operative organizations—were the backbone of CCF support and the party had very limited urban appeal.[33] The CCF came to power the year it extended its base of support to less prosperous farmers in rural districts and blue collar workers in urban areas, making its first serious pitch for the labour vote. During the 1944-64 period, many of the richer farmers drifted toward the Liberal party, as might be expected, and the CCF base was increasingly made up of less prosperous farmers and the urban working class. In fact, the latter became its most reliable source of support. The groups most opposed to the CCF were urban and small-town professionals, as well as businesspeople and their employees who competed with the co-operatives to service the rural community. Economic position was also complicated by ethnic and religious factors: a strong connection existed between the Liberal party and Catholics and non-English voters. In modern times, the NDP has done relatively better in urban than rural areas, taking most of the urban seats in recent elections and improved its standing with less prosperous farmers and the working class. In the 1990s, the NDP is not so much a farmer/labour alliance as a coalition of "progressive" farmers, urban unions, middle-class professionals, and public sector workers.[34] The Liberals and Conservatives are stronger in more prosperous farming districts and among urban and small-town business people and professionals.

Perhaps more remarkable was the lack of consistency between federal and provincial electoral results, especially between 1958 and 1975. During that period, Saskatchewan returned Conservative members to the House of Commons almost exclusively, but the party received next to no support provincially. This federal Tory vote appeared to come from both Liberal and NDP provincial supporters, each group preferring the Conservatives to the alternative.[35] Diefenbaker himself had once been an unsuccessful provincial Conservative leader, but at the federal level his Saskatchewan compatriots supported him fully. As the provincial Liberals declined (and even fell below the level of federal Liberal party support), voters were more consistently divided between Conservatives and NDP at both levels of government.

PRESSURE GROUPS AND THE MEDIA

Pressure Groups

In the early years, only one pressure group was prominent: the Saskatchewan Grain Growers' Association. Its strategic decision not to become a political party, unlike its counterparts in other provinces, has been mentioned earlier in this chapter. Later, another more radical farm group, the United Farmers of Canada (Saskatchewan Section), developed and absorbed the Grain Growers. However, after the United Farmers helped create the Farmer-Labour Party, it returned to pressure group status, this time under the name Saskatchewan Farmers' Union. It then became the Saskatchewan Federation of Agriculture which later dissolved as a result of divisions over the Crow rate issue. The Western Canadian Wheat Growers' Association has arisen to fill its place, although it is not affiliated with the Canadian Federation of Agriculture. The Saskatchewan Wheat Pool has always been influential in its own right, as have other agricultural groups including the National Farmers Union.[36] Labour became more significant with time, now taking the form of the Saskatchewan Federation of Labour, which is linked to the NDP. CCF/NDP initiatives in the health field gave rise to early active roles for the Saskatchewan College of Physicians and Surgeons and the Saskatchewan Hospital Association. In recent years there has been much conflict with the Saskatchewan Medical Association over doctors' fees. The health programs and public automobile insurance plan greatly upset the private insurance industry and generated much pressure on its part. The Blakeney government was challenged by large individual oil and potash companies and the pressure groups which represented them collectively, such as the Saskatchewan Mining Association and the Saskatchewan Potash Producers Association. Of course, as in other provinces, the Saskatchewan Teachers' Federation is active, as are urban and rural municipal associations and women's groups.

TABLE 9.7   Leading Saskatchewan Pressure Groups

Peak Business	Saskatchewan Chamber of Commerce
Industrial	Saskatchewan Mining Association
	Saskatchewan Potash Producers Association
	Saskatchewan Construction Association
	Saskatchewan Home Builders Association
Labour	Saskatchewan Federation of Labour

TABLE 9.7 continued

Agriculture	Western Canadian Wheat Growers Association
	National Farmers Union
	Saskatchewan Livestock Association
Professional	Saskatchewan Medical Association
	Saskatchewan Teachers' Federation
Ethnic	Ukrainian National Federation
	Federation of Saskatchewan Indian Nations
	Association culturelle franco-canadienne de la Saskatchewan
	Métis Society of Saskatchewan
Institutional	Saskatchewan Association of Health Organizations
	Saskatchewan Association of Rural Municipalities
	Saskatchewan Association of Urban Municipalities
	Saskatchewan School Trustees' Association
Environmental	Saskatchewan Eco-Network
	Saskatchewan Environmental Society
Public Interest	Saskatchewan Association on Human Rights

The Media

Saskatchewan's leading newspapers are the *Saskatoon Star-Phoenix* and the *Regina Leader-Post*, both owned by the Armadale chain. Moose Jaw and Prince Albert have daily newspapers owned by Thomson Newspapers Ltd., and one weekly French newspaper exists. The Canadian Broadcasting Corporation operates both English and French radio and television from Regina, and English radio out of Saskatoon, while CTV also has television stations in the two large cities.

TABLE 9.8   Daily Newspapers in Saskatchewan, 1994

	Circulation	Chain affiliation
Regina Leader-Post	66,457	Armadale
Saskatoon Star-Phoenix	60,129	Armadale
Prince Albert Daily Herald	10,915	Thomson
Moose Jaw Times-Herald	9,689	Thomson

Source: *Canadian Advertising Rates and Data* (August 1994).

GOVERNMENT INSTITUTIONS[37]

Saskatchewan's government institutions are generally similar to those of other provinces. Where they differ, it is primarily due to innovations adopted by the CCF and NDP during their long periods in power.

Executive

The lieutenant-governor has generally performed routine functions, except for incidents in 1905 and 1961.[38] In the first instance, to secure partisan control of the province, the Liberal Laurier federal government made it known to the lieutenant-governor (also a Liberal), that the Liberal leader Walter Scott should be chosen as premier instead of the pre-1905 leader, F.W.G. Haultain, a Conservative. Scott was selected, as directed, and Haultain became a vigorous Opposition leader. In 1961, the lieutenant-governor reserved a bill for the consideration of the federal cabinet, 24 years after the power had last been exercised in any other province and long after it was considered obsolete. It was a somewhat controversial CCF government bill which dealt with the alteration of certain mineral contracts. Prime Minister John Diefenbaker, himself from Saskatchewan, made it clear that whatever their views, lieutenant-governors were expected to approve all legislation and federal assent was readily forthcoming.[39] Governors were originally expected to do a lot of entertaining but, especially after the CCF closed Government House, the social and ceremonial aspects of the office have declined. Several recent occupants of the office did not even take up residence in Regina.

The premier and cabinet are the focal points of government in Saskatchewan as elsewhere. Although the cabinet has to some extent been kept more accountable to the legislature than in other provinces, it has been even more powerful because of the scope of government activity. In constructing their cabinets, premiers are generally concerned with maintaining a geographic balance between rural and urban areas, between the two major cities, and among the other regions of the province. Some emphasis is also placed on religious balance, but Roman Catholics have usually been under-represented. In the 1940s the CCF emphasis on planning and the authority of the cabinet in this process led to the establishment of four central agencies unique for their time: an economic advisory and planning board, a cabinet secretariat, a budget bureau, and a government finance office. The CCF administration also experimented with program budgeting techniques. In 1961, the new premier Woodrow Lloyd strengthened the cabinet secretariat, tightened cabinet procedures, and made more use of cabinet committees. Ross Thatcher exerted more personal control over cabinet operations, but Allan Blakeney reverted to the earlier CCF attitude toward "orderly cabinet procedure."[40] Grant Devine's cabinet once reached 25 members, but was gradually reduced to 17, with the premier himself serving as Agriculture minister after 1985. Roy Romanow had an 18-member cabinet in 1994, and retained a cabinet committee system similar to that of his precedessor, with a planning and priorities committee, a Treasury Board, a legislative review committee, a regulations review committee, and an order-in-council review committee. Under Romanow, the Department of the Executive Council had two sides, one political and the other non-partisan. The political side was headed by the premier's chief of staff and looked after correspondence, speeches, and media relations, while the deputy minister and cabinet secretary headed the non-partisan side which included the policy and planning and cabinet secretariats.

Legislature

Politics in Saskatchewan has avoided both the overwhelming legislative majorities of successive governments found in Alberta, and the coalition style governments of Manitoba; as a result, the Saskatchewan legislature has always been a more balanced and competitive debating chamber. Provision for direct legislation was once suggested in Saskatchewan but never adopted, although six plebiscites were held, mostly on the liquor question.

The legislature was created as a single house with 25 members and, with rapid increases in population, it soon rose to 63, only to decrease as a result of the Depression and emigration. After the Second World War, however, the size of the legislature once again began to grow, reaching a high point of 66 members.[41] Legislative sessions were planned according to the weather and the seasonal schedule of the farmers and were usually held between February and seeding time, although since 1973 a post-harvest fall session has usually been held as well. The increasing pressure of legislative business and the decreasing proportion of farmer representatives have meant that it is now common to have committees sit between sessions; and these bodies often conduct public hearings around the province. Legislative debates have been recorded since 1947 and an oral question period, informally permitted previously, has been officially sanctioned since 1975. A sophisticated television system was installed in 1982.

Just as Saskatchewan has been a pioneer of many public policies, so its legislative operations established a number of precedents. Ministers do not sit on regular legislative committees, and it has had an effective public accounts committee with an Opposition chairperson since 1967. The standing committee on Crown corporations, which resulted from the number of government enterprises created by the CCF, has always been a lively forum. Another innovation, perhaps also a result of greater CCF government activity, was the committee on regulations which, like the public accounts committee, has a government majority but an Opposition chair. The committee on non-controversial bills is also unusual in having an Opposition chair and majority. By joint agreement of the government and the Opposition, bills are sent to it even before second reading, but it cannot amend them—only approve them or return them to the House. Most other public bills are considered in committee of the whole, as are the estimates in committee of finance. The Speaker is now elected by secret ballot by all MLAs.

The role of an MLA in Saskatchewan is increasingly a full-time job. While some of its legislative procedures are more advanced than those of other provinces, MLAs do not have the same level of services and remuneration as in

Ontario and Quebec. In 1994, members earned $38,546, with a tax-free expense allowance of $7,622, as well as per diem allowances for attendance in the legislature and at caucus meetings which typically total about $15,000 annually. The Saskatchewan legislature meets for an average of 72 days per year, and ranks in the middle of the provinces in this respect. In 1977-78, when defections from the Liberals gave both opposition parties the same number of seats, the Speaker recognized no official Opposition, but the Conservatives accused him of collusion with the Liberals. Three Conservative members were suspended from the legislature for five days for being disrespectful of the Speaker. In recent years, both the NDP and Conservatives have engaged in long walkouts as an Opposition tactic.

Bureaucracy

Saskatchewan employs about 9,800 people in regular government departments and agencies, over 11,000 in government business enterprises, and another 16,600 in the wider public sector. The public service in Saskatchewan has also been distinctive, although before 1944 it operated much as in other provinces with rampant patronage in spite of the appointment of a civil service commissioner in 1913 and the development of a short-lived public service act in 1930. The CCF inherited a partisan Liberal public service in 1944, but within three years had established a public service commission with all the trappings of a non-partisan administration: competitive examinations, grading and classification, merit, efficiency, security of tenure, and a ban on discrimination. It extended collective bargaining rights to civil servants in 1945, 20 years before any other province, and in 1947 passed legislation allowing public servants to engage in political activity as long as it did not impair their usefulness on the job. Provincial cabinets have reserved the right to make order-in-council appointments at senior levels on the grounds that these employees must share the overall perspective of the government, an assertion which may be justifiable in an ideologically polarized province. Some 100 top civil servants resigned when the Liberals took office in 1964, some of them going to New Brunswick or Ottawa; another 31 departed when the NDP returned to power in 1971.[42] There was an even larger purge, considered excessive by most observers, when Grant Devine formed his Conservative government in 1982, and Roy Romanow cut many partisan heads of Crown corporations and deputy ministers when he took over in 1991.[43] Among the administrative innovations of the Allan Blakeney period was a program budgeting system and the full service Department of Northern Saskatchewan, which looked after everything in that region to the exclusion of other government departments.[44] Devine planned to decentralize about 10 percent of the public service from Regina to small towns throughout the province, but the NDP was elected just in time to cancel this project.

TABLE 9.9   Saskatchewan Government Departments, 1994

Agriculture and Food
Economic Development
Education, Training and Employment
Energy and Mines
Environment and Resource Management
Finance
Health
Highways and Transportation
Justice
Labour
Municipal Government
Provincial Secretary
Social Services

TABLE 9.10   Leading Saskatchewan Agencies, Boards, Commissions and Crown Corporations, 1994

Crown Corporations	Saskatchewan Liquor Board
	Saskatchewan Power Corporation
	Saskatchewan Telecommunications
	Saskatchewan Transportation Company
	Saskatchewan Forest Products Corporation
	Saskatchewan Government Insurance
	Saskatchewan Housing Corporation
	Saskatchewan Opportunities Corporation
	Saskatchewan Water Corporation
	SaskEnergy Incorporated
	Saskatchewan Property Management Corporation
	Saskatchewan Crop Insurance Corporation
Agencies, Boards, and Commissions	Crown Investments Corporation of Saskatchewan
	Public Service Commission
	Saskatchewan Municipal Board
	Saskatchewan Gaming Commission
	Saskatchewan Arts Board
	Saskatchewan Energy Conservation and Development Authority
	Saskatchewan Municipal Board
	Saskatchewan Workers' Compensation Board

Saskatchewan has been identified since 1944 with its unique collection of Crown corporations. Two main ones predated the CCF: a 1908 provincial telephone system (now Saskatchewan Telecommunications), and in 1928 public electricity (now Saskatchewan Power Corporation). In the 1944-64 period the CCF consolidated these and created a number of other public enterprises: a bus service (Saskatchewan Transportation Company), a sodium sulfate mine (Saskatchewan Minerals), Saskatchewan Forest Products Corporation, Saskatchewan Government Insurance, and the Saskatchewan Economic Development Corporation. The Thatcher government essentially left these in place but, after 1971 the NDP government added substantially to the province's family of Crown corporations with the Saskatchewan Oil and Gas Corporation (SaskOil) and Saskatchewan Housing Corporation, the Saskatchewan Development Fund Corporation, Potash Corporation of Saskatchewan, and the Saskatchewan Mining Development Corporation, which had a share of the Cluff Lake and Key Lake uranium developments, and the Agricultural Development Corporation (Agdevco).

In addition to the number and scope of its Crown corporations, Saskatchewan established a unique relationship between these agencies and the government. Rather than operate semi-independently as is usually the case, Saskatchewan's Crown corporations were under the direct control of a minister and the cabinet. A board of directors was appointed in most cases, but the relevant minister was made chair of the board. To integrate Crown corporations into the overall government planning process, the cabinet also exercised ultimate control over corporation policy. In addition, the financial aspects of their operations were supervised by the government finance office, through a type of holding company later renamed the Crown Investment Corporation (CIC). While in other jurisdictions complaints were made of Crown corporations being too remote from cabinet direction, in Saskatchewan the opposite charge was sometimes made. Consequently, when Grant Devine became premier in 1982 he replaced the CIC with the Crown Management Board, giving Crown corporations a clearer mandate and reducing political interference in their operations. A full-time outside appointment was made chair of each corporation, ministers became vice-chairs, and MLAs were eligible to sit on the boards. Then, in 1988-89, Devine engaged in a privatization rampage in which the government sold or obtained legislative authorization to sell many of these "Crowns," most notably SaskOil (which became Wascana Energy Inc.), the Prince Albert Pulp company, the Potash Corporation of Saskatchewan, Agdevco, Saskatchewan Minerals Corporation, and the Saskatchewan Computer Utility Corportion. Devine also sold the oil and gas assets of Saskatchewan Power Corporation, and the Saskatchewan Mining Development Corporation was jointly privatized with the federal Crown corporation Eldorado Nuclear, becoming Cameco Corporation. The Saskatchewan government retained about 25 percent of the Cameco shares, and a lesser proportion of Wascana Energy. When the NDP came back to power in 1991, it made changes somewhere between the hands-on approach of Blakeney and the hands-off directive of Devine with respect to the direction of Crown corporations. The Crown Investments Corporation of Saskatchewan was resurrected as a holding company for most of the "commercial Crowns" and given more political authority over their operations with a particular emphasis on debt reduction. The CIC board of directors is essentially a cabinet committee, while the CIC staff provides corporate, human resources, and financial analysis and accounting services for all the Crown corporations within its jurisdiction.

Judiciary

The upper level of the Saskatchewan judiciary consists of the Supreme Court, with its two divisions, Court of Appeal and Court of Queen's Bench. Amendments in 1994 created a family law division of the court and required a mediation session in the early stages of civil and family law disputes. The lower level is made up of provincial courts distributed throughout the province. Provincial court judges went to court in 1994 to demand a 20-percent pay increase when the government gave them only five percent.

Municipal Government

Local government in Saskatchewan has not changed dramatically in structure since 1905. The province currently has 12 cities, along with towns and villages, while the rural municipalities form a grid of 18-mile squares throughout the southern part of the province. The northern half of the province is not organized for municipal purposes. Overall, Saskatchewan has a centralized local government system, with most of the health and welfare functions being carried out by the province.

POLITICAL EVOLUTION

1870–1970

After Manitoba and British Columbia became provinces in 1870 and 1871 respectively, the territory in between remained the Northwest Territories under the jurisdiction of Ottawa. Between 1870 and 1876, the lieutenant-governor of Manitoba doubled as the governor of the Territories, but after 1875 the North-West Territories Act provided for a separate lieutenant-governor and an appointed council supplemented by elected members, with the territorial capital established in Regina.

The most significant development of the next few years was the coming of the transcontinental railway and, partly as a result, the destruction of the Native and Métis way of life. In 1884 Louis Riel was invited by Métis leaders to return from exile in the United States to take up the Métis cause. With little federal response to moderately worded demands for the relief of the starvation of aboriginal peoples and the displacement of Métis by homesteaders, the situation became violent. A series of clashes ensued between Métis and the Canadian forces, rushed to the site on the still unfinished Canadian Pacific Railway, and about 100 people were killed. Riel surrendered in May 1885 and, despite a jury recommendation of mercy,[45] was hanged for high treason in November.

Shortly after the violence ended, the CPR was completed, immigration increased, and the territories were granted an elected assembly of 22 members and representation in the House of Commons. The governor was then allowed to select four members of the assembly as an advisory council, later called an executive committee, but they had a limited role in policy matters and in deciding how money provided by the federal government would be spent. After considerable pressure, the principle of responsible government was recognized in 1897 when F.W.G. Haultain assumed a position analogous to premier and a fledgling territorial government took form. Demands for provincial autonomy, especially for more local control over public finance, soon followed. Much of the federal reluctance to grant autonomy was based on the fear of a separate schools dispute similar to the one in Manitoba in 1890. The politics of the Territorial government was essentially non-partisan for, while Haultain was a Conservative, he led a coalition cabinet. The other leading politician of the time was Walter Scott, a Regina newspaper publisher and Liberal member of the House of Commons, who actively pursued the autonomy question in Ottawa. Both parties advocated provincial autonomy in the 1904 federal election.

Negotiations proceeded between the two governments and in February 1905 the autonomy bills creating the provinces of Saskatchewan and Alberta were introduced. Prime Minister Wilfrid Laurier decided to create two provinces rather than one, largely to keep them the approximate size of Manitoba, which was sensitive about its eastern and western borders, and to prevent the development of a large counterweight to Ottawa. A second key decision was to leave the federal government in charge of the new provinces' public lands, just as it still controlled those of Manitoba. This was done at the insistence of Clifford Sifton, the Minister of the Interior, who argued that giving the provinces such management rights might jeopardize the success of the massive immigration program then in operation. In return, Ottawa gave the new provinces financial concessions. The most controversial issue in the whole autonomy package concerned separate schools. Laurier's original act seemed to guarantee a return to religious control of education. This prompted Sifton to resign, and he did not rejoin the cabinet even after Laurier backed down under pressure from Protestant Ontario. (Laurier then had to deal with a backlash from Quebec's Henri Bourassa and other French-Canadian Roman Catholics.) Liberal Walter Scott had submitted his resignation as an MP on another issue—CPR exemption from property taxation—but was called upon by the lieutenant-governor to become the first premier of Saskatchewan.

Scott was selected as provincial Liberal party leader in August 1905 and was sworn in as premier in September. After his government was securely in place, he called the first provincial election for December. F.W.G. Haultain became leader of the Opposition, discarding the Conservative label for that of the Provincial Rights Party. This was to take advantage of the previous non-partisan atmosphere in the territory, and to protest certain aspects of the autonomy bill such as the natural resources provisions which he felt were unjustly imposed on an unwilling province. The parties were chiefly divided on the issue of separate schools, and Haultain was dissatisfied even with Laurier's compromise of a separate school system operating under the supervision of the Department of Education. The Liberals took full advantage of patronage, election timing, and the support of the federal government, and made special efforts to appeal to the new immigrant vote and to farmers by naming to the cabinet the president of the Territorial Grain Growers' Association (TGGA), W.R. Motherwell. Not surprisingly, the Liberals won the election, and began an uninterrupted 24-year rule.

The first few years were occupied with establishing the administrative machinery of the province, which included government departments, judicial institutions, schools, railways, and roads. This task was complicated by the province's increasing population, largely composed of homesteaders. As a result, Saskatchewan was the third-largest province in Canada between 1911 and 1951. Scott established the University of Saskatchewan, with its college of agriculture and effective extension department which served the educational needs of the farming community. He created a system of local government and a provincially owned telephone system, constructed the impressive legislative building, and sponsored such labour legislation as factory acts and workers' compensation.

The main focus of government attention, however, was the agricultural community. When the Saskatchewan Grain Growers' Association (SGGA, the successor to the TGGA in 1906) demanded a publicly owned grain elevator system, Scott responded by giving government support to a farmers' co-operative in this field, the Saskatchewan Co-operative Elevator Co., which had C.A. Dunning as its General Manager. It also passed a hail insurance act.

Under provincial Treasurer J.A. Calder, the Liberals also established an efficient party machine. Patronage was pervasive, especially in the form of low-level civil service jobs for party supporters. Those receiving government contracts were expected to demonstrate their gratitude, and manipulation of the voters' lists was routine.[46]

By 1913 the wheat boom was over and the outbreak of the First World War had many implications for the province. Saskatchewan contributed to the war effort with flour, manpower, and funds; it also had to face the wartime-related questions of temperance and women's suffrage. The government gave women the vote in 1916, and moved gradually toward Prohibition over the 1915-17 period, Saskatchewan being among the leaders in both respects.[47] Meanwhile, W.M. Martin took over as Liberal premier. Wartime also brought linguistic and religious aspects of education to the fore, while 1917 saw the initiation of conscription as well as the formation of a coalition government in Ottawa. The resulting split in the federal Liberal party also divided Saskatchewan Liberals, some supporting the Union Government and others the Laurier wing in Opposition.

Until this point, the Liberal party in Saskatchewan had continued to recruit farm leaders to the cabinet, and the government almost automatically implemented the resolutions passed at annual SGGA conventions. The Non-Partisan League made a brief appearance in the province in 1916-17 but did not prevent Martin from leading the Liberals to their fourth consecutive election victory. The next five years, however, would be a test of whether the Liberal strategy of co-opting farmer leaders could succeed against the increased political militancy of the farmer organizations.

In 1917, the SGGA endorsed the Farmers' Platform of the Canadian Council of Agriculture, but the organization was undecided about whether to enter electoral politics given that it already had a sympathetic government in the province. A post-war recession and the abandonment of an orderly wheat marketing system heightened the farmers' traditional complaints against federal policy, but Premier Martin strategically drew an increasing distinction between the federal and provincial Liberal parties, and brought more farmer representatives into the cabinet.

Even more shrewdly, Martin called the 1921 election before the SGGA had decided whether to become involved directly, and dropped the Liberal party label in favour of "Government" candidates. The Conservative party was leaderless and in disarray, and the isolated local farmer involvement had no overall direction. Forty-six Progressive or Independent candidates opposed the government, but 46 Martin "Government" supporters were returned, compared with six Progressives, seven Independents, and a smattering of others; the best the Progressives could do was to form the official Opposition. The Liberal party thus continued in office in Saskatchewan just as it was being defeated in neighbouring provinces by an organized farmers' movement.

The Saskatchewan farmers' organization had no hesitation in contesting the federal election in 1921, and 15 Progressives were elected out of 16 seats, despite Martin's uncharacteristic endorsement of the federal Liberals. He was replaced as premier shortly afterwards by C.A. Dunning, a long-time farm leader, and it was only in 1922 that the SGGA finally opted to enter provincial politics. Even then, the decision was subject to local discretion and—faced with such an ideal Liberal party leader, a declining membership, and competition from the new Farmers' Union of Canada (a more radical group established in 1921)—the SGGA reversed its stance in 1924. In the 1925 election many fewer Progressive and Independent candidates came forward, while the Conservatives had regrouped somewhat under their new leader, J.T.M. Anderson. With Dunning as leader, and Highways Minister James Gardiner as party organizer, the Liberals won another easy victory; and with the Progressive threat behind them, they could work more closely with the federal Liberal party.

Apart from the question of the political involvement of the farmers, several prominent issues dominated the 1917-29 period. One was the difficulty of enforcing Prohibition, a task entrusted to the provincial police force which existed between 1917 and 1928. After the war, the rationale for Prohibition disappeared and, after a plebiscite in 1924 approved its repeal, government liquor stores began to operate again. The increasing number of automobiles in this era had widespread consequences including demands for more and better roads, new regulatory legislation, and a reversal of much of the province's social isolation. Always sensitive to farmers' needs, the government sponsored the Saskatchewan Farm Loans Act in 1917, and set up a debt adjustment bureau in 1922 to help those who faced the loss of their farms. Co-operatives of many kinds abounded, some with government support and some without. The greatest accomplishment in this respect was the creation of the Saskatchewan Wheat Pool in 1923, simultaneous with parallel developments in Alberta and Manitoba. A joint product of the Farmers' Union and the SGGA, the new organization purchased the Saskatchewan Co-operative Elevator Co. in 1926 to give it a string of elevators and grain terminals. The two farmers' organizations merged as the United Farmers of Canada (Saskatchewan Section) in 1926, and the association took a leftward turn under the influence of new leaders who came mainly from the Farmers' Union.[48]

The government made many advances in health and welfare in this period including mothers' allowances, a child welfare bureau, hospitals, a Department of Public Health, better treatment of the deaf, blind, and mentally ill, an increase in old age pensions, and the establishment of vocational schools.[49] When C.A. Dunning was named to the federal cabinet in 1926, Jimmy Gardiner succeeded him as premier. Retaining the highways portfolio and responsibility for party organization, he proceeded to construct an even more impressive provincial Liberal party machine.[50] One of his chief initiatives was the Power Commission Act which set the stage for the provincial control of electricity.

Besides farmer support, the Liberal Party's strength lay in the "other ethnic" community, but after 1917 controversy emerged in this area. In response to increasing pressure to promote the assimilation of non-anglophones, in 1918 the Martin government tried to eliminate the use of languages other than English in the province's schools. This prompted W.R. Motherwell's resignation from the cabinet, which forced the government to backtrack slightly on French but not on other languages. The public concern continued, however, and took the form of opposition to separate schools as well as demands for more selective immigration. Organizations such as the Protestant Orange Order and the Independent Order of the Daughters of the Empire and even farmers' groups took part in such protests. By 1927 the province had become ripe for an invasion of the U.S.-based white supremacist group the Ku Klux Klan. The Klan did not create anti-Catholic or anti-ethnic feelings, but coalesced the formerly diffuse opposition.[51] It appealed to submerged prejudices but its message could be presented in a positive light, such as preserving the virtues of a British, Protestant, and

"Canadian" way of life. It had no official alliance with the Conservative party, but its campaign against Liberal government policies helped to bolster the Conservative cause.

The Liberal defeat in 1929, after 24 years in office, can be explained by a variety of factors: the emotional, religious and ethnic upheaval aroused by the Klan; the fact that residents wanted a change from a stagnant government which had managed to alienate individuals and communities; and the desire to break the Gardiner machine, to extricate corruption, and to institute a non-partisan civil service. J.T.M. Anderson invited all those opposed to the Liberal government to join him; the Progressives did so and, in many ridings, the Progressives, Independents, and Conservatives did not run against each other. The results were 28 Liberals, 24 Conservatives, six Independents, and five Progressives. The electoral alliance remained firm on the promise of civil service reform, and the Progressives and Independents decided to support the Conservatives rather than Gardiner. Anderson took office in September 1929, forming what he called a "Co-operative" government.

In three main respects the new government was true to its word. Its public service act removed patronage from the provincial bureaucracy, leaving only deputy ministerial, board, and commission appointments to the discretion of the cabinet. The display of religious symbols and the wearing of religious dress were prohibited in public schools, while French was eliminated as a language of instruction and could be taught as a subject no more than one hour per day. Mostly as a result of previous negotiation, the province finally obtained control of its natural resources in 1930. The onset of the Great Depression two months after the Anderson government took office, however, effectively neutralized any other ambitious plans.

During the Depression, Saskatchewan was the hardest hit province. This was partly because of the province's one-crop economy and the collapse in the price of wheat, but it was exacerbated by the dramatic decline in wheat production as a result of nine straight years of drought compounded by grasshoppers, rust disease, and wind erosion. The southwest part of the province, the Palliser Triangle, was worst off, and the average per-capita income in the province fell by 72 percent between 1929 and 1933.[52] Premier Anderson responded with debt adjustment legislation and by setting up the Saskatchewan Relief Commission in 1931. In addition, many voluntary agencies provided aid, much of it in the form of food, clothing, and shelter. As individuals and municipalities went bankrupt, the province became increasingly dependent on the federal government, and Anderson worked closely with the Bennett Conservative government in Ottawa. They established relief camps, but a riot in a Saskatoon camp led to the death of a Royal Canadian Mounted Police officer in 1933, while a coal miners' strike in Estevan involving a clash with police resulted in three deaths in 1931.

In 1931 the United Farmers of Canada (Saskatchewan Section), under the control of the more radical farm leaders, decided to enter politics directly. An Independent Labour Party had also been founded in 1925 with Regina school principal and alderman, M.J. Coldwell, as its leader. These two groups coalesced in 1932 to form the Farmer-Labour Party, and chose Coldwell as the leader of the new group. Since the UFC was by this time espousing such left-wing concepts as "social ownership and co-operative production for use" and a "use-lease" system of land tenure in place of private ownership, the two groups experienced little difficulty effecting such an alliance. The Farmer-Labour Party participated in the founding of the CCF in Calgary in 1932 and in Regina a year later, and began an intensive organizational drive in the province. With the Liberal party now challenged from the left, it began to see itself less as a reform party and more as a defender of the status quo.[53]

Anderson called an election for June 1934 and, like his fellow Conservatives in Nova Scotia, New Brunswick, P.E.I., Ontario, B.C., and Ottawa, he suffered a resounding defeat. As elsewhere, this could be blamed primarily on the Depression, an event which only the coalition government in Manitoba survived. In addition, the different elements within the Saskatchewan coalition often quarrelled, and considerable dissension existed within Anderson's own Conservative party. Then, too, the removal of patronage as well as the curtailed and non-partisan pattern of highway construction upset many erstwhile supporters. The Farmer-Labour party platform called for the nationalization of farmland, with a leaseback system for existing occupants, and made no effort to disguise its socialist message, rendering it a particularly vulnerable target.[54] Besides fighting the Liberal attack, the Farmer-Labour party found itself the object of a Roman Catholic Church statement which repudiated socialism.[55] In the end, the Liberals returned to power under Gardiner, the Farmer-Labour Party became the Opposition, and the Conservatives failed to win a single seat.

The Liberals immediately abolished the public service commission and returned to the spoils system, dismissing most civil servants and replacing them with partisan friends. They also introduced legislation to cope with the Depression in various ways, such as seed grain, relief, tax arrears, and debt adjustment, and made provision for municipal and other group-sponsored hospital and medical services, which provided a base for later public plans. When the trek of the unemployed to Ottawa in July 1935 was halted in Regina by Prime Minister Bennett, the RCMP interruption of a public meeting caused a riot in which a city policeman was killed. Later that year, a federal election was held in which the Liberals were victorious (M.J. Coldwell and T.C. Douglas being the two Co-operative Commonwealth Federation candidates elected in Saskatchewan), and Gardiner left to become Canadian Minister of Agriculture. He was replaced as premier by W.J. Patterson, but Gardiner became the source of federal patronage in Saskatchewan and continued to take an interest in provincial affairs. At the federal level, the Prairie Farm Rehabilitation Administration, established in 1935, provided funds for a variety of agricultural purposes such as conservation, irrigation, and reclamation.

By the time of the 1938 Saskatchewan election, the provincial Conservatives had a new leader in John Diefenbaker and the Farmer-Labour Party had become the Co-operative Commonwealth Federation (CCF). In addition, the Social Credit party had been elected in Alberta and was making inroads in Saskatchewan, taking protest votes away from the CCF. For its part, the CCF dropped the term "socialism" from its platform, as well as the provision for nationalization of land, and instead emphasized government planning. This less radical direction prompted the Catholic Church to withdraw its censure of the party, but the Liberals were re-elected. The Saskatchewan party system had clearly been realigned into a two-party system composed of the Liberals and CCF, as the latter drove out the vestigial second party. The readjustment in political allegiances and the realignment of partisan appeals that this required were complex and gradual. This was especially so because the new party embraced a socialist doctrine which had roots in Saskatchewan's agrarian progressive tradition but which went far beyond anything formally advocated by a political party or farmers' organization.[56]

The Second World War dominated the scene between this election and the next, and most of the legislation passed at the provincial level was of a housekeeping nature. Some of the more interesting measures were credit union legislation, an extension of Gardiner's health legislation, an act providing for school district consolidation, a cancer control act, and a 1943 decision to postpone the next provincial election for one year. Meanwhile, CCF leader George Williams enlisted in the army and was posted overseas, opening the way for T.C. Douglas to return from Ottawa to take over the party leadership.

CCF support was rapidly increasing in almost every part of the country in the early 1940s. This was due to an increase in trade union membership and in the political consciousness of the union movement, and to the attractiveness of the CCF's post-war program—a vision of a better world to follow the sacrifices endured during wartime. Farm security, better labour legislation, and a complete system of socialized health services were among the party's priorities. Voters felt resentment at many aspects of federal Liberal policy, and the Conservatives did not offer much of an alternative. While the CCF did well in many provincial elections in this period and in the federal election of 1945, how can its even greater success in Saskatchewan be explained?

A significant factor in this success was the co-operative, agrarian, populist, radical base established by the Saskatchewan Grain Growers' Association, the United Farmers of Canada, and the Farmer-Labour Party. Central to gaining such support was the CCF's abandonment of its program for the socialization of land. In addition, the provincial Liberal government was unpopular for many policies, such as its insistence that farmers repay debts incurred in the 1930s for seed grain, and the party's organization was in disrepair. Furthermore, the Liberal party was forced to become more oriented towards private enterprise and was discredited by its extreme anti-socialist campaign. The postponement of the election from 1943 to 1944 gave the impression that the Liberals were running scared and allowed the CCF another year of intensive organization. Perhaps the most important factor of all, however, was the choice of T.C. (Tommy) Douglas as the new party leader. The enthusiastic, populist oratory of this former Baptist minister, who combined humour with parable, gave the party the spark it needed to take advantage of these favourable circumstances.

The first few years of the CCF administration are usually seen as a hotbed of experimentation and innovation.[57] Many of its programs were the inspiration of Joe Phelps, Minister of Natural Resources and Industrial Development, and could be categorized as "import-substitution" manufacturing endeavours: a brick manufacturing plant, a shoe factory, a tannery, a woollen mill, and a box factory.[58] Phelps' initiatives in the resource field included a timber board and a sodium sulfate mine. These efforts were justified as a means of diversifying the economy, creating jobs, and generating revenue for expanded social services. Other ministers created provincial utilities, such as a printing company, a bus company, a northern airline, and the government automobile insurance corporation. The initial rationale of the public insurance scheme was to provide minimal compensation for those injured by drivers who were not insured; only later was it extended to a full-scale insurance plan.[59] While the CCF inherited public telephone and power systems, it expanded these by taking over municipal telephone operations and private power companies, creating integrated, efficient public monopolies. The government also took action to aid the farm community in 1944 in the form of the controversial Farm Security Act, which allowed farmers to keep their land and still pay off previously accumulated debts. It also introduced a community pastures program and a new Department of Co-operatives and Co-operative Development.

On the social side, Douglas personally assumed the Public Health portfolio and immediately set up the Health Services Planning Commission, which provided a detailed agenda for health policy that guided the government in this high-priority field for 20 years. The public hospital insurance scheme, which went into operation in 1947 and which necessitated much hospital construction and expansion, was probably the government's greatest achievement in this early period. In addition, it made improvements in preventive services; the province became a leader in mental health care, as well as in the treatment of cancer and tuberculosis; it provided free medical, dental, and hospital services and prescription drugs to pensioners; it established a college of medicine; and inaugurated an air ambulance service. The government passed advanced labour legislation, including a labour relations board, and improved and equalized education in a number of ways. It brought in an innovative bill of rights in 1947 and established a Saskatchewan arts board in 1948.

With this impressive conglomeration of new government activity, an obvious need developed for more central co-ordination, and the 1946-48 period was primarily concerned with such administrative innovation. In 1945 the government replaced the initial small and academic economic advisory committee with a powerful planning board, which played an especially influential role for many years in recommending an appropriate division between public and private activity. The other key central agencies were the budget bureau and the government finance office. To staff these agencies and other new and expanding departments, the government recruited an expert professional public service. These were mostly "Fabians" who believed in "socialist planning," and the result was a combination of progressive cabinet ministers and ideologically compatible and innovative bureaucrats who designed and implemented change from the centre.[60] Other bureaucratic reforms included the introduction of collective bargaining for public servants.

When Douglas called an election for June 1948, the government was returned but with slightly reduced support. The CCF then consolidated programs and engaged in considerable debate about the role of government in the development of natural resources. With the expertise assembled in the Saskatchewan Power Commission, it decided that that agency, already actively involved in extending rural electrification throughout the province, would be given responsibility for distributing natural gas as well. Witnessing the prosperity in Alberta, especially after the Leduc oil field discovery in 1947, the Saskatchewan CCF was impatient to see its oil industry expand, and a majority in the cabinet eventually became more moderate in their view of the role of the government in the economy. Although party policy advocated social ownership of natural resources, the government was increasingly conscious of its limited finances and expertise in this area, and began to believe that regulation and taxation might be sufficient means of public control. Douglas frequently emphasized that government ownership, co-operative development, and private enterprise all had a role to play in the province. Thus, the CCF eventually left the development of natural resources to the private sector but, to attract companies to do the work, the government had to promise not to expropriate the industry.[61] A similar decision was made in 1945 with respect to potash, although this industry was slower to get started, and uranium production began in 1952 under federal auspices.

Moderation in government policy was also encouraged by extensive opposition "free enterprise" publicity campaigns, and the government was not immune to criticism of the largely unsuccessful fate of its early manufacturing enterprises.[62] The realization that it had underestimated the difficulties of creating secondary industry in the province sparked another debate within the government which centred on the relative emphasis to be given to resource development as opposed to manufacturing. The public apparently preferred the more moderate approach which reduced the role of government ownership in general and placed less emphasis on nurturing the manufacturing industry, and the party substantially increased its support in the 1952 election. A comprehensive Royal Commission on Agriculture and Rural Life reported in 1955 and inspired much government activity afterwards, including the 1958 Agricultural Machinery Act and the 1960 Family Farm Improvement Act and Crop Insurance Act. Farmers also benefited from improvements in rural roads and extensions of rural electrification and telephone service.

In 1957, the federal Progressive Conservatives led by Saskatchewan's own John Diefenbaker took power in Ottawa. New federal Tory policies were of great benefit to the province, especially massive export sales of wheat, and the South Saskatchewan River Dam project was started after years of discussion. The completed dam was named after Jimmy Gardiner and provided both electricity and irrigation. Meanwhile, the government began a province-wide grid road building program, and Saskatchewan became the first province to complete its section of the Trans-Canada Highway. When the federal government began to pay half the cost of a national hospital insurance scheme in 1957, the CCF felt that the savings involved in financing its own program would finally allow it to embark on a public medical insurance program (that is, to cover doctor's bills as opposed to hospital bills). Douglas announced the proposal in 1959, but the medical profession immediately expressed its opposition. In the same year, the Liberals chose a new leader. Ross Thatcher, a vigorous and forceful personality, had been a CCF MP from 1945 to 1955 but left the party to sit as an Independent, and then became a Liberal. Possessing all the fire of a new convert, he immediately shook up the party, working on memberships, finance, organization, policy, and candidate recruitment, and made the 1960 election much more lively than usual. Nevertheless, the CCF was returned with only a slight loss of support, and considered the victory an endorsement of its medical care plan.

The 1961-64 period in Saskatchewan was particularly exciting. First, the lieutenant-governor refused to sign a piece of government legislation, reserving it for the federal cabinet's consideration, an action that had not occurred in Canada since 1937. Second, in November 1961 T.C. Douglas was persuaded to become leader of the national alliance of the CCF and Canadian Labour Congress, to be called the New Democratic Party. Long-time Education Minister Woodrow Lloyd became the new Saskatchewan premier. Third, in October 1961 the government introduced its medicare plan. To finance the scheme, it increased a variety of taxes and established small premiums, but excluded deterrent fees except for specialist services. The Liberals supported the bill on second reading, but opposed it on third.[63]

Prior to the start of the scheme on April 1, 1962 (later postponed to July 1 of that year), the opposition of the medical profession continued with threats of a mass exodus to the United States. "Keep our doctors" committees formed throughout the province and other hysterical activity took place, culminating on July 1 with a doctors' strike. The government recruited British doctors to alleviate the situation, a British Labour peer and doctor, Lord Taylor, was invited to mediate the situation, and on July 23 a settlement was reached. Allan Blakeney was moved to the Health portfolio and given the delicate task of implementing the program. The government was hindered somewhat by the defection to the Liberals of former Health Minister Walter Erb and former national CCF leader Hazen Argue, and lost several by-elections in the wake of the conflict.

In 1963-64, however, with the medicare dispute settled, the CCF appeared to bounce back. Wheat, oil, and the beginning of potash production led to an economic boom, and new industry diversified the Saskatchewan economy. Interprovincial Steel Corporation opened in Regina and the government established the Saskatchewan Economic Development Corporation (SEDCO), which provided funds to stimulate private industry. Lloyd extended full tax and grant support to Roman Catholic high schools in 1964, constructed regional vocational schools, improved teacher training, established a new Regina campus of the University of Saskatchewan, and built new auditoriums in the two largest cities. The government expanded hydro and road systems, and even introduced devices to improve legislative scrutiny of the executive. All signs pointed to another CCF/NDP victory.

Yet the CCF was defeated in the 1964 election after 20 years in office, proving that, at least in Saskatchewan, a buoyant economy and a progressive government record are no guarantee of re-election. The parties presented different perspectives on the province's prosperity, the CCF comparing it to the situation 20 years earlier, and the Liberals, to the current affluence of neighbouring Alberta. The levelling off of CCF support was likely due to the departure of Tommy Douglas and other stalwarts, memories of the medicare crisis which had exhausted the participants and rallied the government's diverse opponents, and the electorate's fear that the creation of the NDP had changed the nature of the party.[64] Thatcher blamed the CCF for high taxation, slow economic growth, and Saskatchewan's declining population.

Ross Thatcher's first term was one of continued economic prosperity and optimism.[65] He combined tax reductions with increased spending on highways and education, including free textbooks for Grade 9. The government raised the minimum wage, as well as pensions for teachers and civil servants, made an effort to deal with the problems of aboriginal peoples and the Métis, established a Youth Department, and took over the administration of social aid from municipalities under the new Saskatchewan Assistance Plan. Innovations occurred in legal aid and criminal injuries compensation, Thatcher extended consumer protection with respect to interest rate disclosure, and expanded the use of French as a language of instruction in the school system. Most of these initiatives were at odds with the premier's blunt anti-socialist rhetoric.

On the other hand, the government clearly moved to the right in some areas, such as making an immediate budget cut of $20 million and increasing health care premiums. Thatcher concentrated on the exploitation of the province's natural resources through private and often foreign investment, announcing two large potash developments, a new sawmill, a base-metal mine, and incentives for petroleum exploration. The Liberals' showpiece was a new pulp mill near Prince Albert, established in 1966 by the U.S. firm Parsons and Whittemore. In return for a 30 percent share of equity, the government guaranteed the company's loan of $50 million, gave it access to nearly one-third of the province's commercial forest, provided subsidized pulpwood, and saw that it received a large federal Department of Regional Economic Expansion grant.[66] The Liberals dismissed the recommendations of a CCF-appointed royal commission on taxation; made somewhat restrictive amendments to the Trade Union Act; and halted the Saskatchewan Power Commission strike in 1966. While leaving most Crown corporations intact, the Liberals removed their monopoly position in a number of cases. Several leading public servants felt distressed at the new atmosphere in Regina and left the government service, just as Thatcher appointed a royal commission to study government administration. His subsequent appointments of an independent auditor and a comptroller of the Treasury, however, were widely applauded.

Prior to the 1967 election the government redistributed legislative seats in its own interest. That contest centred on the government's claim of bringing prosperity to the province via private enterprise, and the Opposition's charge that the Liberals had given the province's resources away to outside interests. The party finally dropped the CCF label and ran unashamedly under the NDP banner. Conservative support dropped by nine percent, allowing the Liberals to secure narrow re-election.

The Liberals' second term did not match the progress of their first years in office. This was largely due to an economic downturn which reduced provincial revenues. Immediately after the election, Thatcher announced an austerity program in provincial spending which particularly affected school teachers, and began a long dispute over direct financial control of the university. The 1968 budget increased the sales tax, as well as most other provincial taxes and fees, and imposed deterrent (or utilization) fees on medical and hospital services. This raised much animosity in the province, as did 1969 amendments to the Trade Union Act. A series of strikes by hospital workers occurred; more ceilings were imposed on public sector wage increases in 1970; and the Essential Services Emergency Act was applied to end the strike of construction workers.

The government was not helped by problems in the wheat industry. Even in those years which produced a good crop, international sales and prices fell dramatically. The federal government responded with programs which encouraged farmers to leave their fields fallow or switch to another crop, precipitating many protests including long lines of farmers driving tractors slowly along the highway. Even the potash industry was troubled by oversupply, which led Thatcher to negotiate an agreement with authorities in New Mexico, the source of U.S. potash, on prices and production. Each mine was assigned a proration quota, meaning each was allowed to produce only a certain percentage of its capacity.

The one consistently progressive concern of the Thatcher Liberals was the fate of the province's aboriginal peoples. In 1969, it established a separate government department for Métis and Indians and designed a variety of programs to assist them. The government also extended French language rights and erected a statue of Louis Riel.

During this period, the Waffle movement developed within the NDP, with Saskatchewan becoming a secondary base of its operations. Woodrow Lloyd, who had revived discussion of public ownership after 1964, supported this left-wing movement over the objections of the party establishment, and this act led to pressure which hastened his departure from the provincial leadership.[67] Lloyd was replaced by Allan Blakeney, a lawyer by training, a Saskatchewan public servant from 1950 to 1958, and a prominent member of the pre-1964 CCF cabinet. In the same year, the government resorted to even more blatant gerrymandering.

The 1970s

The 1970s was a decade of unprecedented economic prosperity in Saskatchewan, coinciding with the election of the NDP under Allan Blakeney.[68] In the 1971 election, the Liberals tried to make the two-party contest one of socialism versus free enterprise. They emphasized their record, proposed labour courts to replace existing legislation including the right to strike, and unveiled a proposal for a second pulp mill to be built by Parsons and Whittemore.[69] The NDP faulted the government for its future plans as well as its past sins of deterrent fees, neglect of pollution and reforestation, and its poor record in labour relations, and presented a full basket of alternative proposals. In explaining the NDP victory, most observers emphasized the heavy-handed approach of Thatcher and his government compared with the dynamic, fresh image of Allan Blakeney. Thatcher accepted full responsibility for the defeat, and died of a heart attack a month later.

The NDP initially emphasized reversing several actions of the preceding government. It cancelled the second pulp mill, removed deterrent fees for hospital and medical services, and repealed offensive labour legislation. The Blakeney government then introduced its own program, with almost as many innovations as the Douglas government had undertaken in 1944-48. In this respect, the Land Bank Commission of 1972 stood out in terms of both inventiveness and controversy. In an effort to preserve the family farm, the commission would buy land from retiring farmers and lease it, with an option to buy, to those who wanted to get started in the industry. The Opposition, however, saw dark parallels to the concept of land nationalization in the early 1930s. In 1973 the FarmStart program was designed to encourage young farmers in the livestock industry, while other legislation in this area limited the foreign and corporate ownership of agricultural land. In addition, the government amended the Forest Act to allow the alteration of contracts between private lumber companies and the former Liberal government, giving the province more power to promote reforestation. The government also purchased shares in the Interprovincial Steel and Pipe Corporation of Regina and Intercontinental Packers of Saskatoon.

Other early NDP initiatives included the appointment of an ombudsman and the establishment of a human rights commission, a new Department of Consumer Affairs, and a Human Resources Agency to replace the Indian and Métis Department. Responsibility for Native peoples was also assumed by a second administrative innovation, the Department of Northern Saskatchewan. The government also introduced occupational health and safety legislation, a province-wide salary bargaining plan for teachers, a new Saskatchewan Housing Corporation to give lower-income families increased accessibility to affordable housing, and cash supplements to the working poor under the Family Income Plan. In the realm of health, the government brought chiropractic services under medicare, and unveiled a free preventive dental care plan for children and a universal pharmacare plan to subsidize the cost of prescription drugs. Two milestones in higher education were the establishment of community colleges and the transformation of the University of Regina into an autonomous institution under the Saskatchewan Universities Commission.

Beginning in 1973, the government's attention turned increasingly to the question of resource development, an area which would involve much conflict between the government and industry, and between Regina and Ottawa. Under the Oil and Gas Conservation, Stabilization and Development Act of 1973, the government bought 90 percent of the province's oil and gas reserves, for which companies were compensated, and gave itself the power to control wholesale petroleum prices and production. In an even more controversial move, it imposed a surcharge of 100 percent of the difference between the market price of oil and the pre-1973 base price. This provision was designed to allow the province to recover the windfall profits created by the sharp rise in the world price of oil established by the Organization of Petroleum Exporting Countries (OPEC) cartel. The government created a Crown corporation, Saskatchewan Oil and Gas Corporation (SaskOil), to enter all phases of the petroleum industry and it began to drill wells in 1974. These initiatives were in part devised to protect provincial control of the industry in the face of federal efforts to increase tax revenues in this field. Canadian Industrial Gas and Oil Ltd. (CIGOL) challenged the province's legislation in the courts and, in 1977, the Supreme Court of Canada ruled the act involved both indirect taxation and interprovincial regulation of trade, and therefore could not be enacted by the province. The court also ordered that the $500 million collected under the act be repaid but, because the money had already been spent to acquire potash companies, the government introduced the Oil Well Income Tax Act to accomplish the same end directly and retroactively. In fact, negotiations with individual firms ultimately produced a harmonious settlement. Ottawa's decision to support the private company in its legal fight strained federal-provincial relations, especially when Alberta, Manitoba, and Quebec joined the Saskatchewan side. The two levels of government also fought over a new federal feed grains policy and over the Saskatchewan scheme for prorationing the output of potash mines.

Potash became the other main focus of resource policy.[70] After the Thatcher government's introduction of the prorationing plan, world demand increased and, by 1974, all mines were allowed to produce to capacity. In December 1972, however, Central Canada Potash began a court challenge of the provincial prorationing legislation. The government launched a thorough review of potash policy in 1973, and was determined to increase its tax revenues from this industry. The party convention in that year decided that "in every possible instance, priority be given to developing our natural resources by or through Crown corporations and co-operatives."[71] When the private potash companies refused to allow the government to see their financial statements, the NDP announced in October 1974 that a new reserve tax would be imposed on potash companies. The government would participate as either a majority partner in joint ventures or as full owner in the development of all new potash mines in the province. Later, the government suggested that the reserve tax might be reduced in cases where the desired corporate data were supplied. In February 1975, it created the Potash Corporation of Saskatchewan, while most potash companies refused to pay the reserve tax and challenged it in the courts. Meanwhile, a great debate brewed within the NDP cabinet and caucus over how far the government should go to control the industry—regulation, taxation, or nationalization of some or all of the existing mines. The Kierans report on mining in Manitoba, virtually ignored in that province by Ed Schreyer, became the inspiration for NDP action in the Saskatchewan potash industry.[72] The cabinet was worried about public acceptance of what might appear to be radical action, however, and eventually decided on nationalization as a last resort:

> It was therefore less a sense of commitment to public ownership than a sense of outrage at corporate ploys intended to vitiate government endeavours to influence the pace of potash development and to maximize its revenues that convinced the Cabinet to proceed with the take-overs.[73]

The government announced that it intended to take control of the Saskatchewan potash industry by purchasing some or all of the province's producing potash mines and negotiated with individual companies over the 1976-77 period. In the end, it offered sufficient compensation to acquire a 40 percent share without having to resort to expropriation. The necessary funding came from a combination of oil revenues and borrowing, so that no new taxation was required. The Liberals filibustered the legislation, but the three main adversaries—the companies involved, Ottawa, and the U.S. government—were essentially reconciled to the decision.[74] When the Supreme Court of Canada rendered its decision in the Central Canada Potash case in the middle of the 1978 election campaign, ruling that the prorationing scheme encroached on federal powers over interprovincial trade, Blakeney was quick to lash out at Ottawa for trying to gain control of provincial resources.

Prior to the 1975 election, both the Liberals and Conservatives chose new leaders. Dave Steuart succeeded Ross Thatcher, and the Conservatives appeared to gain a new lease on life with the colourful wheeler-dealer, Dick Collver. The NDP, influenced by the Waffle faction, adopted several radical-sounding resolutions, but the party establishment denied Waffle members election to key posts, and the group left the party in 1973.[75] After this turmoil subsided, an independent redistribution of electoral boundaries was carried out for the first time, and the government adopted a bill on election finance.

In the June 1975 election, the NDP was returned with 39 seats, but lost 15 percent of its 1971 vote, while the Liberals maintained their 15 seats, but lost 10 percent of their earlier support, partly due to the unpopularity of the federal party. Collver's Conservatives came out of nowhere to capture seven seats and 18 percent of the popular vote.

Between the 1975 and 1978 elections, the government agreed to the proposed uranium development at Cluff Lake after receiving assurances from the companies involved with regard to proper environmental safeguards and a commitment to give northern residents first chance at the new jobs. Another main thrust of public policy in this period was related to the federal wage-and-price control program. Blakeney gave the program qualified support, but insisted on setting up his own provincial body to administer it. This naturally enraged the Saskatchewan Federation of Labour, which regarded such regulation as heretical for the NDP, but Blakeney argued he was concerned about inflation and believed in economic planning. Meanwhile, the province also instituted rent control, which was equally unpopular among landlords. In 1977, Colin Thatcher, son of the late Liberal premier, defected to the Conservatives. This, together with other converts and by-election victories, gave the Conservatives the same number of MLAs as the Liberals, resulting in an unpleasant battle for official Opposition status.

With the economic situation appearing favourable, Blakeney called an election for October 1978. He campaigned on his government's record in promoting local ownership and/or control of the potash, oil, and uranium industries, which had diversified the economy and provided revenue to expand social services. The NDP emphasized the need for strong leadership and also touted Blakeney's anti-federal stand on accumulated grievances, in particular over Ottawa's treatment of the province on oil and potash issues. Tory leader Dick Collver combined considerable organizational talent with an evangelical platform style, but was plagued by a highly publicized lawsuit against his former business partners and the Saskatchewan Government Insurance Office. Meanwhile, the Liberals changed leaders, choosing Ted Malone, a Regina lawyer. Malone offered a peculiar platform promising three referenda on various right-wing issues. The result was another solid NDP victory and, for the first time since 1905, the Liberals failed to win a seat. They also ended up heavily in debt because they did not even qualify for the subsidy given to parties which garnered 15 percent of the popular vote.

Federal-provincial relations dominated the Saskatchewan political scene in the 1979-82 period. One of the main issues was grain handling and transportation, including controversy over the Crow rate, branch line abandonment, and insufficient and antiquated grain cars. In 1979 Saskatchewan purchased 1,000 hopper cars, railway cars that carry grain, with $50 million from its Heritage

Fund and persuaded Alberta to follow suit; even Ottawa agreed to lease 2,000 more cars. Then, in 1980 the National Energy Program adversely affected the province's oil industry but, after a revised energy agreement was signed in 1981, the industry expanded. The third intergovernmental issue in this period was the Constitution. Saskatchewan Attorney General Roy Romanow was joint chairman with Jean Chrétien of a federal-provincial group which tried to arrive at a consensus on the subject in the summer of 1980. About the same time, national NDP leader Ed Broadbent arranged a deal with Prime Minister Pierre Trudeau whereby the reform package would include a constitutional amendment to clarify and enlarge provincial jurisdiction over natural resources to overcome the effects of the 1977 and 1978 Supreme Court decisions. Given this federal NDP support, Trudeau felt confident taking unilateral action on the patriation issue when the 1980 federal-provincial constitutional conference collapsed. Saskatchewan opposed unilateral action and was dissatisfied with other provisions in the package, but Blakeney and Romanow were instrumental in the ultimate settlement reached in November 1991.

On the provincial front, the government adopted a new human rights code, amended the Workmen's Compensation Act, reformed pension legislation, and took action on day care and urban transit, activated another redistribution of ridings, and set up a new beef stabilization scheme. A home owner's protection act was introduced to assuage the effects of high interest rates, but large utility rate increases occurred at the same time. Despite concern about the nuclear option raised at NDP conventions, the government assumed a larger role in the uranium industry, with controlled development, expansion, and partial ownership of the Cluff Lake and Key Lake projects. This growth was offset, however, when Eldorado Nuclear closed operations at Uranium City.

Dick Collver left the Tory leadership with a flourish in 1979.[76] He was succeeded by Grant Devine, a 35-year-old agricultural economist at the University of Saskatchewan, a farm boy who had gone on to acquire a PhD. The Liberals abandoned the architect of their right-wing approach, Ted Malone, and in 1981 chose defeated Liberal MP Ralph Goodale as their new leader. Thus, although the NDP government's third term had not been as exciting as the first two, Blakeney seemed "solidly entrenched" as the decade ended.[77]

The 1980s

The 1980s was a difficult decade for Saskatchewan. It involved economic problems, a change of government, and a major shift in government policy. As a result of the recession at the start of the decade, the oil, potash and uranium industries both suffered, but all three mineral industries remained strong and accounted for large amounts of provincial revenue. Then, in early 1982, the federal government announced an end to the Crow rate, arguing that freight rates would have to be increased to reflect the actual cost of shipping grain if the railways were to be able to finance improvements in the system. Since the Crow rate was of greater concern to Saskatchewan wheat producers than to any other agricultural group in the West, the Blakeney government organized an intense publicity campaign against the change. At the same time, it brought down a budget which expanded the rural natural gas network, froze natural gas prices, and promised interest relief for homeowners whose mortgage rates exceeded 15 percent. With these initiatives, Blakeney called an election for April 1982.

Although divisions over the Crow rate destroyed the Saskatchewan Federation of Agriculture, it did not catch on as an election issue. A strike of hospital personnel had to be ended by legislation, alienating much of the NDP's labour support. The focus of the campaign became the different NDP and Conservative plans to make use of the province's natural resource revenues. Based on a public opinion survey, the Tories promised to eliminate the 20-percent provincial tax on gasoline and to subsidize all mortgages above 13.25 percent. Devine also pledged to end the Land Bank purchases, and to freeze and control utility rates. The NDP countered with the elimination of the school property tax for homeowners, universal dental care, and other medicare extensions. To everyone's astonishment, the Conservatives won a landslide victory, capturing 55 seats to nine for the NDP. However prosperous the province, the electorate preferred the populist Tory approach to the technocratic, bureaucratic tenor of the Blakeney New Democrats.

Grant Devine's government moved quickly to implement its election promises.[78] It abolished the gasoline tax, guaranteed mortgages at 13.25 percent, froze utility rates, and created the Public Utilities Review Commission. The Farm Purchase Program replaced the Land Bank scheme so that prospective farmers could borrow money from the Farm Credit Corporation to purchase, rather than lease, farmland. Another dimension of the changeover was a purge of the civil service. The NDP had terminated 69 order-in-council appointments before it left office, but the Tories rid the government of well over 200 other senior public servants and Crown corporation officials.[79]

During 1982-83, the new Conservative government reorganized departments, imposed wage restraint in the public sector, introduced a new $3,000 provincial grant for first-time home buyers, and turned its attention to Crown corporations and the resource industry. It established a Crown Corporation Review Commission to examine the province's collection of Crown agencies, which reported that financial returns were poor, political influence was excessive, and objectives were ill-defined. This led Devine to transform the Crown Investments Corporation into the Crown Management Board, with the intention of accomplishing the review commission's recommended objectives.

In the area of natural resources, the new government pledged to halt further public intervention and welcomed the private sector into resource industries with the slogan "Saskatchewan is open for business." Mineral Resources Minister Colin Thatcher introduced a number of incentives for private investment in the oil industry, including a one-year royalty holiday, and reduced the budget of SaskOil. These actions rejuvenated the private oil industry, and in mid-1983 the federal and provincial governments signed an agreement regarding the construction of a $600-million heavy-oil upgrading plant in Regina. This was followed in 1984 with Husky Oil's announcement of a massive $3.2-billion heavy-oil project with more wells, a second upgrading plant at Lloydminster, and pipeline networks to the two adjacent provinces. The industry boomed as the royalty holiday, which was later extended, encouraged light oil development. Then, in a further boost to the industry, the new federal Mulroney government signed the "Western Accord." Even the Crown-owned SaskOil prospered in these circumstances in spite of Devine's preference for private sector expansion. Later, though, the government decided to sell a one-third interest in SaskOil to individual shareholders.

In contrast to this promising picture, agriculture began a decade-long decline. The Crow rate controversy was ultimately resolved against the wishes of a majority of Saskatchewan farmers, but that was the least of the industry's problems. Devine introduced a farm land security act in 1984 in response to numerous farm foreclosures. The act was designed to give farmers financial breathing space, and allowed them to postpone payments on mortgage debts until the end of 1985. Droughts exacerbated the situation, as did a grasshopper invasion, and in these circumstances irrigation became the main concern of an extended federal-provincial Economic and Regional Development Agreement grant. In another attempt to counter the problems, Devine became his own Minister of Agriculture, and the government spent massive sums to assist farmers, resulting in a $2-billion deficit. The deficits contained in provincial budgets of this period were also related to spending on job creation, although Saskatchewan's consistently low unemployment rate was also due in part to emigration.

As Saskatchewan edged closer to the 1986 election, the economic decline among its major industries worsened. In all four sectors—wheat, oil, potash, and uranium—prices were low and markets poor. Devine's position was not helped by the actions of his Minerals Minister Colin Thatcher. After a controversial trial, Thatcher was convicted of murdering his ex-wife and then expelled from the legislature.

The opposition parties roundly criticized the deficit in the October election campaign, but it did not stop Devine or NDP leader Blakeney from making further expensive promises, primarily in the areas of agriculture, housing, and pensions. The Conservative leader outshone Blakeney on the public platform, pursuing a "rural strategy" by perfecting his farm-boy image complete with slang expressions. Devine was also significantly helped by the federal government's mid-campaign announcement of a $1-billion farm aid package (announced after Devine's pleading phone call to the prime minister was overheard by the press), as well as by its delaying until after the election the announcement that the

CF-18 fighter plane maintenance contract would go to Quebec instead of Western Canada. The election results indicated a discrepancy between popular vote and seats; the NDP actually outpolled the Conservatives 45.2 percent to 44.6 percent, but the Tories won 38 seats to the New Democrats' 25. The Liberals doubled their vote to 10 percent, and by winning his riding leader Ralph Goodale returned the party to the legislature for the first time since 1975. The Conservatives captured almost all of the rural seats but only four urban ones, while the NDP won all remaining urban seats but only three in rural areas, plus the two in the north. Blakeney resigned the NDP leadership in 1987 and was succeeded by the more charismatic Roy Romanow. Goodale resigned his position and seat to contest the 1988 federal election, and later became Prime Minister Jean Chrétien's Agriculture minister; the provincial Liberals chose a telegenic clinical psychologist, Lynda Haverstock, to replace him.

After the election the government shifted dramatically to the right.[80] This neo-conservative focus was attributed to the decline in government revenue, which had caused the deficit to rise to $3.3 billion, but many viewed it as the party's hidden agenda. In the 1987 budget, the government made substantial cuts in social, health, and education spending. In particular, it fired 300 dental therapists who operated the children's dental plan, part of a total layoff of 700 government employees and an elimination of 2,000 positions. The government instituted a $125 deductible per family in the province's prescription drug plan, tried to force welfare recipients to work, and eliminated provincial grants to many social agencies. Not surprisingly, this fundamental change in social policy led to numerous protests and demonstrations and a sharp decline in Conservative support in public opinion polls.

The economic side of this neo-conservative philosophy included a two-percent increase in the retail sales tax along with other tax increases, the hiring of a British privatization consultant, Oliver Letwin, and the privatization of many Crown corporations and government services. The prospect of cash from such sales to offset the provincial deficit coincided with the government's ideological preference for the private sector. Thus, the government sold the oil and natural gas reserves of the Saskatchewan Power Corporation to SaskOil, which itself was almost fully privatized; it sold Saskatchewan Minerals Corporation to two Ontario firms; and sold the Prince Albert Pulp Mill to Weyerhauser Ltd., a branch plant of an American firm. The privatization philosophy of both the Mulroney and Devine governments inspired the merger of the federal Crown corporation Eldorado Nuclear with the provincially owned Saskatchewan Mining Development Corporation. The two governments agreed that both would later sell off their shares in the new company, Cameco (Canadian Mining and Energy) Corp., the world's largest uranium producer. Other Crown corporations sold by Devine included Saskatchewan Government Printing, Saskatchewan Forest Products Corporation, and Saskatchewan Computer Utility Corp, while SaskTel privatized its telephone book's "yellow pages" to an employee group. The privatization process was overseen by the new Department of Public Participation which was given the power to make further sales without specific legislative authorization.

The prospects for the potash industry were dim in the latter part of the decade. In addition to the problems of poor demand and low prices, a dispute erupted with the United States during which that country temporarily imposed prohibitive duties on Canadian exports. The province retaliated with legislation which gave the government the power to control production to reduce output and force prices upward. The government also wrote off the $800-million debt of its own Potash Corporation of Saskatchewan, perhaps to make it a more attractive candidate for privatization.

The issue of privatization became even more controversial in 1989. Although Devine had promised never to privatize a provincial utility, he first detached the natural gas distribution system of SaskPower to form a separate Crown corporation, SaskEnergy, and then announced its sale in early 1989. The NDP Opposition boycotted the legislature and let the division bells ring for 17 days, giving in only after the government agreed to public hearings on the matter. Immediately afterwards, the NDP filibustered the bill to privatize the Potash Corporation of Saskatchewan, only to have the government invoke closure for the first time in Saskatchewan history. In both cases, certain safeguards were written into the legislation, but not enough to satisfy the Opposition. In the end, SaskEnergy remained a Crown corporation, but a majority of the potash corporation's shares were eventually sold to individual members of the public. Later, Devine severed the general insurance division of Saskatchewan General Insurance from the auto insurance wing of the company, but the former's privatization was successfully challenged by the union involved, the courts ruling that such action required legislation, not just a cabinet decision. By this time, Devine was running out of government assets he could sell to help cope with his financial problems.

Somewhat later in the decade the petroleum industry revived due to a new royalty holiday and natural gas sales to Ontario. Then, in September 1988, just before the anticipated federal election, the federal, Alberta, and Saskatchewan governments re-announced their commitment to help Husky Oil Ltd. build the Bi-Provincial heavy oil upgrader in Lloydminster. Even though studies indicated it was the least economically viable of Canada's potential energy megaprojects, the three governments and Husky agreed to make contributions of $400 million, $305 million, $222 million, and $340 million respectively. By this time, the NewGrade heavy oil upgrader, a joint project of the province and Federated Co-operatives, was operating in Regina, but with many technical problems. Uranium markets also improved marginally over this period.

In the midst of the controversy surrounding the government's social and economic policies, the issue of bilingualism erupted in early 1988. The Supreme Court of Canada ruled in the *Mercure* case that a provision of the 1886 Northwest Territories Act (similar to Section 133 of the British North America Act), requiring all laws to be passed in English and French and granting the right to speak French in the courts, was still valid. The Court also noted, however, that the Saskatchewan legislature could amend this provision with a bilingual law validating all English-only laws passed since 1905. Devine took this route but also decided to permit French to be spoken in the legislature and in the courts. He began translating laws, starting with those related to the courts and judicial system. Prime Minister Brian Mulroney requested that Devine expand and speed up the process, contributing $60 million over 10 years in support of this initiative. Unfortunately, a scandal developed in the translation of provincial statutes into French. At the behest of such Tory friends as Senator Michel Cogger and pollster Ken Waschuk, Devine granted $4 million to Montreal businessman Guy Montpetit and his GigaText Translation Systems to complete the work using computers. The system did not work, and the translation was later carried out using more conventional means.

From time to time, the Opposition and media charged that Devine had rewarded many other friends. They uncovered scores of untendered government contracts in such fields as law, advertising, and property business; a variety of other financial irregularities; and criticized many questionable government appointments. Another controversial social issue—Sunday shopping—also emerged, but the government followed Ontario's lead in handing the problem over to municipalities. Greater controversy surrounded government investment of $64 million, as well as loan guarantees of $305 million in a large fertilizer plant, Saskferco, built just west of Regina in partnership with the U.S.-based Cargill Grain. The agreement upset environmentalists, other fertilizer producers, and the NDP, which called it a "sweetheart deal" between the government and a company gradually extending its ownership of all aspects of the prairie agricultural industry. Meanwhile, the wheat industry continued to decline.

Another major difficulty for the government was the $154-million Rafferty-Alameda Dam project on the Souris River near the American border. It was designed to create a large water reservoir to cool a coal-fired power plant, conserve water for irrigation and recreational purposes, and control flooding in North Dakota, prompting the U.S. government to contribute $50 million. However, environmentalists persuaded the Federal Court to quash the project's licence in the middle of construction because of an inadequate federal environmental assessment. The issue dragged on for several years, involved several federal environment ministers, a series of court decisions, endless federal-provincial meetings and recriminations, and the appointment and resignation of environmental assessment panels. Construction, however, continued relentlessly.

The 1990s

The 1990s in Saskatchewan saw the usual decennial change of government and a gradual improvement in the economy. Even though it was another NDP decade, it was generally a period of government contraction rather than expansion.

Given his many political and economic problems, and the fact that he would have to face the electorate again before November 1991, Grant Devine devoted 1990-91 to improving his prospects for re-election. One unusual initiative was the establishment of "Consensus Saskatchewan," an advisory group of some 100 people who held public meetings across the province. Its recommendations focused mainly on the deficit. As for federal-provincial relations, Devine was generally the federal prime minister's most loyal supporter, as he demonstrated by agreeing to make Saskatchewan the second province to harmonize its retail sales tax with the federal goods and services tax. Among other things, this involved extending the provincial tax to children's clothing, restaurant meals, books, natural gas, and electricity. Neither this nor his support of the Meech Lake Accord won Devine much support within the province. On the other hand, considering the unpopularity of the Mulroney government, the federal-Saskatchewan tussle over the Rafferty Dam and a simultaneous conflict with the Canadian Radio-television and Telecommunications Commission over the province's new educational television network probably did the premier no harm.

Knowing he had little residual support in the cities, Devine did his best to shore up his rural support. First, he introduced the Fair Share Saskatchewan program which involved moving nearly 1,400 or 10 percent of government jobs from Regina to small towns. The initiative was naturally opposed by the public service unions, and cost Devine a leading cabinet minister. Second, because federal grain subsidies had helped his re-election in 1988, Devine was pleased to participate in a new joint subsidy program introduced in early 1991. The Gross Revenue Insurance Program (GRIP), provided a safety net guaranteeing farmers a minimum income against both crop losses and low prices. Its costs were shared by Ottawa, the provinces, and farmers. Just before the election, Devine distributed early crop insurance payments of $6,000 each for a total of $800 million. Unfortunately, this was about $500 million short of the farmers' expectations. Third, Devine brought in a new electoral map which considerably over-represented rural areas. Nine university professors challenged the boundaries and the Saskatchewan Court of Appeal ruled the map offended the democratic rights provided in the Charter of Rights and Freedoms. While appealing the decision to the Supreme Court of Canada, the government established a new boundaries commission which soon issued a revised map with 31 urban, 33 rural, and two northern seats. But, when the Supreme Court allowed the original boundaries to stand, Devine happily scrapped the more recent and more equitable proposal.

To compensate for moving government jobs out of Regina, and to bolster the economy in general, Devine sought to attract new companies to the province. Because Crownx Inc. wanted to sell its troubled Toronto-based Crown Life, the Saskatchewan government provided a loan guarantee to Haro Financial Corp., headed by the Hill family, to purchase 42 percent of the company shares and move it to Regina. New Brunswick had earlier declined a similar deal. The premier was also successful in persuading Ottawa to move the Farm Credit

Corporation to Regina, and signed a memorandum of understanding with Atomic Energy of Canada Ltd. to move 120 research jobs to Saskatoon. Among other government initiatives in this period was a bill to provide for plebiscites and referenda, and budgets which contained severe spending cuts to finance the provincial share of GRIP. Devine cut 600 government jobs over two years, streamlined government organization, and reduced the size of the cabinet.

None of these tactics made much impression, given the depressed state of the province's agricultural industry. Low grain prices, high interest rates, severe droughts, voracious grasshoppers, and a global glut of wheat meant farm fore-closures, a decline in population, and an increase in the use of food banks. On the political front, Devine faced an exodus of cabinet ministers, the provincial auditor's revelations of misdeeds in Crown corporations, an 11-day nurses' strike, a two-week NDP filibuster over the provincial sales tax-goods and services tax merger, a libel case with the Canadian Broadcasting Corporation over cover-age of his land dealings, his record of 10 straight budget deficits, failure to pass the 1991 budget and his reliance on questionable special warrants, and a court decision suspending the decentralization of government jobs.

In these circumstances, no one was surprised the NDP won the long-delayed October 1991 election, with 55 seats to Devine's 10 and Liberal Lynda Haverstock's one. The Tory victories were all in the rural south, but the NDP won a larger number of rural constituencies, plus all the urban ones except for the Liberal seat in Saskatoon. Roy Romanow had won in spite of not spelling out a clear-cut NDP program, promising only to create wealth by co-operating with the private sector, slash government spending, and hold taxes. While it opted for the NDP, the electorate proved to be conservative on three simultane-ous plebiscite votes: No to government-funded abortions, Yes to balanced bud-gets, and Yes to plebiscites on constitutional amendments.

Roy Romanow formed a government in November 1991 with an 11-mem-ber cabinet, including six newcomers and four women. A brief session of the legislature in December cleared up urgent business, including the passage of the Conservative budget and cancellation of both Fair Share Saskatchewan and the harmonized provincial sales tax. The new government revealed that the 1991-92 deficit would be over a billion dollars more than Devine had anticipated, and the most significant influence on the NDP government's actions throughout the fol-lowing four years was the $5.2-billion debt accumulated over the Devine era, one of the highest per capita provincial debts in the period. Not surprisingly, bond rating agencies reduced the province's credit rating.

Other influences also pushed Romanow in a conservative direction, includ-ing the recession of the early 1990s, the prevailing public attitude against gov-ernment deficits, and the tradition of fiscal responsibility of the Saskatchewan CCF/NDP. The Saskatchewan government no longer owned Crown corporations with which to intervene in the economy, and had no money to buy them back; federal free trade agreements imposed restrictions on government intervention;

and section 92A of the Constitution allowed Saskatchewan to tax natural resource companies without having to own them.[81]

Romanow appointed the Gass Financial Management Review Commission to discover the full extent of government debt and recommend ways of making government more economical and effective.[82] The government transformed the Saskatchewan Economic Development Corporation into the Saskatchewan Opportunities Corp. and, by way of the Crown Investments Corporation, emphasized debt reduction among remaining Crown corporations.

The annual budgets of the Romanow years were exercises in raising taxes and slashing expenditures. The retail sales tax rose to eight percent in 1992 and to nine percent in 1993, when the government extended it to cover such items as adult clothing. Among its other tax increases was a 10-percent income surtax in 1992, while it regularly cut grants to hospitals, schools, municipalities, and universities. As a result of such financial decisions, the government halved the 1992-93 deficit (eliminating 500 government jobs), and reduced the 1993-94 deficit by the same proportion (with a loss of 390 more positions). After further cuts to municipalities, school boards, and hospitals, the 1994-95 deficit was halved again. One additional source of revenue would be new casinos in Regina and Saskatoon, run by a new Crown corporation, Saskatchewan Gaming Corp. But the government was forced to make a deal with the Federation of Saskatchewan Indian Nations on this subject, shutting down unauthorized casinos on reserves in return for the federation obtaining one-quarter of casino profits and one-half of casino employment.

TABLE 9.11   Government of Saskatchewan Finances, 1990/91–1994/95 ($ millions)

	1990/91	1991/92	1992/93	1993/94	1994/95
Total revenues	$6,137.0	$5,672.7	$5,598.3	$6,120.5	$6,265.9
Debt charges	1,214.9	1,309.9	1,421.0	1,211.5	1,211.3
Total expenditures	6,458.5	7,318.2	6,489.5	6,524.9	6,510.8
Deficit	321.5	1,645.5	891.2	404.4	244.9

Source: Reproduced by authority of the Minister of Industry, 1995, Statistics Canada, *Public Sector Finance, 1994–95*, Financial Management System, cat. no. 68-212 (March 1995). Adapted by author.

Given the fact that so much of Canada's health system was pioneered in Saskatchewan, one of the most striking aspects of the first term of the Romanow government was its reduction in health sector spending. The cuts included reducing health-care coverage for eye examinations and chiropractic services; restricting the universal drug plan to low-income families and seniors; and limiting the children's dental plan to the needy. Then, in August 1992, the government unveiled a comprehensive plan to restructure health care, with 30 new regional community-based health boards and health centres to preside over every aspect of medical care. The government eliminated funding to 52 small-town hospitals, arguing that Saskatchewan had Canada's highest per capita number of hospital beds, but many were converted to health centres.[83]

One of the few areas in which spending rose was welfare and social services, partly because of the recession and partly because the government placed a priority on reducing child poverty. Indeed, the government introduced a variety of youth- and family-oriented measures: raising the legal age for buying cigarettes to 19; providing a telephone hotline and other support for victims of spousal abuse; establishing a special investigative team to handle cases of sexual abuse of children, as well as a safe home for such victims; and setting up a unified family court.

Another priority was reform of labour legislation. A new law made it easier for a union to gain certification and a first contract, improved maternity and family leave benefits, and increased the time of notice required in layoffs or dismissal. Most controversial was the path-breaking requirement for larger companies to extend dental, medical and life insurance benefits to part-time workers on a pro-rated basis. On the other hand, the government rejected a ban on replacement workers during strikes as well as a ban on strikes in essential services.

The Romanow government was initially uncertain how to handle the deal Devine had made with Atomic Energy of Canada Ltd., partly because the NDP party was divided on the nuclear energy issue. But, at the 1992 party convention, cabinet members successfully persuaded a majority of delegates to support the expansion of the uranium industry, after which the government reaffirmed the AECL deal and began feasibility studies and design work in Saskatoon on the Candu 3 reactor. This change in party policy, along with a new contract with Ontario Hydro, allowed the cabinet to approve new uranium mining projects.

With regard to the economy as a whole, the government issued an economic plan in November 1992 called *Partnership for Renewal: A Strategy for the Saskatchewan Economy,* which many found to be uninspired or pro-business in tone. It identified six sectors for future emphasis: mining, forestry, tourism, energy, agriculture, and information and communications technology. The government set up a provincial action committee on the economy to advise on the links between the government and business, as well as regional economic development authorities to try to salvage rural Saskatchewan.

The government took a number of more specific economic initiatives. Being strapped for funds and independent of the rural vote, the NDP repeatedly reduced support payments to grain farmers. Its changes to the Gross Revenue Insurance Program precipitated an 18-day Tory walkout from the legislature in 1992. More amenable to farmers was the Farm Land Leaseback Program which allowed farmers whose mortgages were being foreclosed to lease their land back from lending institutions for six years of secure tenure. Then, in mid-1994, a major binational fight erupted over exports of Canadian wheat to the United States, and many Canadians were dissatisfied at the outcome, whereby Canada agreed to voluntarily cut back wheat exports to the U.S. for at least a year to avoid trade sanctions. Another dispute developed between the provincial government and Federated Co-operatives, joint owners of the NewGrade heavy oil upgrader in Regina. After a flurry of charges and countercharges, they compromised on restructuring the operation's finances, helped by $125 million from Ottawa. As for the Bi-Provincial Upgrader at Lloydminster, when the federal and Alberta governments pulled out in 1994, Saskatchewan invested an additional $43 million to keep the project alive. Romanow also restructured the Crown Life deal to reduce the province's financial responsibility.

Among measures of a non-economic nature, Romanow went ahead with Devine's Treaty Land Entitlement Framework Agreement with Saskatchewan's native peoples. He also brought in a conflict of interest law and code of ethics for MLAs, established a new impartially designed electoral map which would result in only 58 seats after the following election, and added discrimination on the basis of sexual orientation to the Human Rights Code. The government reformed automobile insurance to a no-fault system. Accident victims received a maximum of $125,000 in place of the right to sue for pain and suffering, but retained the right to go to court for loss of income.

When Romanow returned to an 18-member cabinet in 1983, he appointed Janice MacKinnon as the province's first female Finance minister. Then, with the budget in balance, he called an election for June 1995 and was easily returned. More interesting was the change of position of opposition forces. The new Progressive Conservative leader Bill Boyd was plagued with a dozen former Conservative MLAs facing fraud charges, leaving Lynda Haverstock to lead her Liberals to second place.

CONCLUSION

The 1980s were a difficult decade for farming, and the long-term prospects of the industry are mixed. In some years one or another of Saskatchewan's mineral resources is able to offset downturns in the fortunes of agriculture, but the oil, potash, and uranium industries have also experienced difficulties. Saskatchewan is the home of Canada's most successful social democratic party and, along with British Columbia, its longest-standing polarized two-party system. At least until Devine's privatization campaign of the late 1980s, the ideological alternative to the CCF/NDP, whether Liberal or Conservative, was never as extreme as in Manitoba or B.C., and most of the left-wing innovations had remained intact despite fairly frequent government turnovers. The provincial Liberal party was a casualty of such ideological polarization, as well as the unpopularity of its federal counterpart, and did not rebound as quickly as in Manitoba or Alberta. Given the many economic and political problems of the Devine government, it is no surprise the NDP came back to power in 1991, but the next four years revealed a major shift in policy from the party's left-wing traditions. Such a shift kept it in power in 1995, unlike its Ontario counterpart.

TABLE 9.12   Saskatchewan Provincial Election Results Since 1921

Year	Liberal		CCF/NDP		Conservatives		Other	
	Seats	Popular Vote	Seats	Popular Vote	Seats	Popular Vote	Seats	Popular Vote
1921	46	51%	6	8%*	3	7%	8	34%**
1925	50	52%	6	23%*	3	18%	4	6%**
1929	28	46%	5	7%*	24	36%	6	9%**
1934	50	48%	5	24%***	—	27%		
1938	38	45%	10	19%	—	12%	4	24%****
1944	5	35%	47	53%	—	11%		
1948	19	31%	31	48%	—	8%	2	14%****
1952	11	39%	42	54%	—	2%	—	4%****
1956	14	30%	36	45%	—	2%	3	21%****
1960	17	33%	37	41%	—	14%	—	12%****
1964	32	40%	25	40%	1	19%		
1967	35	46%	24	44%	—	10%		
1971	15	43%	45	55%	—	2%		
1975	15	32%	39	40%	7	28%		
1978	—	14%	44	48%	17	38%		
1982	—	5%	9	38%	55	54%	—	4%****
1986	1	10%	25	45%	38	45%		
1991	1	23%	55	51%	10	26%		
1995	11	35%	42	47%	5	18%		

* Progressives
** Mostly Independents
*** Farmer-Labour Party
**** Social Credit (in 1948 Social Credit got two seats and six percent of the vote)

TABLE 9.13   Premiers of Saskatchewan Since 1905

Premier	Party	Year Elected
Walter Scott	Liberal	1905
W.M. Martin	Liberal	1916
C.A. Dunning	Liberal	1922
James Gardiner	Liberal	1926
J.T.M. Anderson	Co-operative	1929
James Gardiner	Liberal	1934

TABLE 9.13 continued

Premier	Party	Year Elected
W.J. Patterson	Liberal	1935
T.C. Douglas	Co-operative Commonwealth Federation	1944
W.S. Lloyd	Co-operative Commonwealth Federation	1961
Ross Thatcher	Liberal	1964
Allan Blakeney	New Democratic Party	1971
Grant Devine	Progressive Conservative	1982
Roy Romanow	New Democratic Party	1991

ENDNOTES

1. Peter C. Newman, ed., *Debrett's Illustrated Guide to the Canadian Establishment* (Toronto: Methuen, 1983), p. 117. Newman also lists such names as Graham Walker, W.E. Bergen, Sidney Buchwold, and Lloyd Barber. See also Christopher Dunn and David Laycock, "Innovation and Competiton in the Agricultural Heartland," in Keith Brownsey and Michael Howlett, eds., *The Provincial State (*Mississauga: Copp Clark Pitman, 1992).

2. Keith McLeod, "Politics, Schools and the French Language, 1881-1931," in Norman Ward and Duff Spafford, eds., *Politics in Saskatchewan* (Don Mills: Longmans, 1968), p. 131.

3. Evelyn Eager, *Saskatchewan Government* (Saskatoon: Western Producer Prairie Books, 1980), p. 184.

4. For the central role played by Allan Blakeney, Roy Romanow, and officials, see Roy Romanow, John Whyte, and Howard Leeson, *Canada...Notwithstanding* (Toronto: Carswell-Methuen, 1984).

5. John Archer, *Saskatchewan, a History* (Saskatoon: Western Producer Prairie Books, 1979), pp. 347-50.

6. These distinguishing terms come from David Laycock, *Populism and Democratic Thought in the Prairies, 1910-1945* (Toronto: University of Toronto Press, 1989).

7. Norman Wiseman, "The Pattern of Prairie Politics," in H.G. Thorburn, ed., *Party Politics in Canada* (Scarborough: Prentice Hall Canada, 5th ed., 1985).

8. S.M. Lipset, *Agrarian Socialism, The Co-operative Commonwealth Federation in Saskatchewan* (Berkeley: University of California Press, 1950); also the Anchor Books edition of the same title (New York: Doubleday, 1968). A paper by John Archer, "The Political Development of Saskatchewan," quoted in J.C. Courtney and David E. Smith, "Saskatchewan, Parties in a Politically Competitive Province," in Martin Robin, ed., *Canadian Provincial Politics* (Scarborough: Prentice Hall Canada, 1978) is also helpful here.

9. In her otherwise excellent book, Eager puts too much emphasis on this point, just as she does in her article, "The Conservatism of the Saskatchewan Electorate," in Ward and Spafford, *Politics in Saskatchewan*. She makes a good point when she states that

the CCF government after 1944 was more radical than the electorate, but she underestimates the distinctiveness of that electorate. For example, Lipset in *Agrarian Socialism* says that the average farmer belonged to four or five co-operatives (p. 54) and adds that the "collectivist ideas, which were to mature in the CCF in the 1930s, were based on the farmers' day-to-day experiences" (p. 69). The campaign for the Wheat Pool had also organized farmers into a "self-conscious class" (p. 86), and "a large proportion of the farming population supported an agrarian socialistic program designed to eliminate private profits by governmental or co-operative action before an explicitly socialist party appeared upon the scene" (p. 94). Even in 1934, when it was advocating socialism and state ownership of land, the Farmer-Labour party received almost 30 percent of the rural vote (p. 138). This is not conservative.

10. Courtney and Smith, "Saskatchewan," in Robin, *Canadian Provincial Politics,* consider the federal system to be one of the prime influences in Saskatchewan politics, p. 283.

11. Escott Reid, "The Saskatchewan Liberal Machine Before 1929," in *Canadian Journal of Economics and Political Science* (No. 1, 1936), reprinted in Thorburn, *Party Politics in Canada;* and in Ward and Spafford, *Politics in Saskatchewan;* see also Jeffrey Simpson, *Spoils of Power* (Toronto: Collins, 1988).

12. S.J.R. Noel, "Leadership and Clientelism," in David Bellamy, et al., *The Provincial Political Systems* (Toronto: Methuen, 1976).

13. Dunn and Laycock, "Saskatchewan: Innovation and Competition in the Agricultural Heartland," in Brownsey et al., eds., *The Provincial State.*

14. John Wilson, "The Canadian Political Cultures," in *Canadian Journal of Political Science* (September 1974).

15. Eager, *Saskatchewan Government,* p. 2.

16. Lipset, *Agrarian Socialism,* p. 245.

17. Barry Wilson, *Politics of Defeat: the Decline of the Liberal Party in Saskatchewan* (Saskatoon: Western Producer Prairie Books, 1980), and David E. Smith, *The Regional Decline of a National Party: Liberals on the Prairies* (Toronto: University of Toronto Press, 1981).

18. F.C. Engelmann, "Membership Participation in Policy-Making in the CCF," in *Canadian Journal of Economics and Political Science* (May 1956); Lipset, *Agrarian Socialism,* pp. 257-8; and Eager, *Saskatchewan Government,* chs. 5 and 11. Eager writes of the remarkable degree of concurrence in the direction of party and of government as follows: "Throughout the twenty years of CCF rule, the cabinet carried out its executive and legislative duties with the leadership and decisiveness necessary in parliamentary government while paradoxically upholding consistently the principle of party supremacy. This reconciliation ... was accomplished through seemingly perpetual consultation between the two groups, including careful consideration by the cabinet of all CCF convention resolutions and equally careful explanation to the party for those it felt could not be implemented ... Mr. Douglas ... managed by consummate skill to avoid collision through keeping party and government running along parallel courses" (p. 175).

19. Rand Dyck, "Relations Between Federal and Provincial Parties," in A.C. Gagnon and A.B. Tanguay, eds., *Canadian Parties in Transition* (Scarborough: Nelson Canada, 1989).

20. Joseph Wearing, *The L-Shaped Party* (Toronto: McGraw-Hill Ryerson, 1981), pp. 119-139.

21. "Politics has been as much a politics of personalities as of parties," Courtney and Smith, "Saskatchewan," in Robin, *Canadian Provincial Politics*, p. 303.

22. See Nelson Wiseman, "The Pattern of Prairie Leadership," in Leslie Pal and David Taras, eds., *Prime Ministers and Premiers* (Scarborough: Prentice Hall Canada, 1988).

23. See his book, *Political Management in Canada* (Whitby: McGraw-Hill Ryerson, 1992).

24. Lipset, for example, wavers on this point. He says it changed gradually from an agrarian socialist party to a liberal agrarian protest movement (p. 188), but then argues there is little doubt the government's socialization program established a qualitative difference between the CCF and other agrarian reform parties (p. 299). For Eager it was not radical enough to call "socialist," see Eager, *Saskatchewan Government*, pp. 55-61.

25. In his study of policy innovations in the Canadian provinces, Dale Poel found that Saskatchewan accounted for 10 out of a national total of 25, and seven stemmed from the CCF period, "The Diffusion of Legislation among the Canadian Provinces," in *Canadian Journal of Political Science* (December 1976), p. 619. See also Jean Larmour, "The Douglas Government's Changing Emphasis on Public, Private and Co-operative Development in Saskatchewan, 1944-1961" and Jim Pitsula, "The CCF Government in Saskatchewan and Social Aid, 1944-1964," both in William Brennan, *Building the Co-operative Commonwealth* (Regina: Canadian Plains Research Centre, 1984).

26. Lipset has an excellent discussion of this problem in *Agrarian Socialism*, ch. 12.

27. Courtney and Smith, "Saskatchewan," in Robin, *Canadian Provincial Politics*, p. 303. Marsha A. Chandler also found the NDP resource polices to be distinctive, "The Politics of Provincial Resource Policy," in Michael M. Atkinson and Marsha A. Chandler, eds., *The Politics of Canadian Public Policy* (Toronto: University of Toronto Press, 1983).

28. Moose Jaw had two members between 1921 and 1967; Saskatoon had two between 1921 and 1960, three from 1960 to 1964, and five from 1964 to 1967; Regina had two from 1921 to 1952, three from 1952 to 1960, and four from 1960 to 1964.

29. Peter McCormick, "'One Man, One Vote' in Provincial Politics: The Case of Saskatchewan, 1929-1982," Canadian Political Science Association (June 1984).

30. *Reference Re Prov. Electoral Boundaries (Sask.)* [1991] 2 SCR 158.

31. The Liberals objected to this provision in 1978, but the other parties would not bend the rule and left them seriously in debt.

32. Lipset, *Agrarian Socialism*, ch. 8; Sanford Silverstein, "Occupational Class and Voting Behaviour: Electoral Support of a Left-Wing Protest Movement in a Period of Prosperity," in the Anchor edition of *Agrarian Socialism*.

33. Lipset explains this paradox in these terms: "within an exploited economic group, those who possess economic and social status within the class are most resentful of a threat to their security. The poorer, social outcast groups ... are likely to be politically apathetic rather than rebellious ... An upswing in the business cycle may prove to be

the stimulus that gives the depressed members of society enough personal security to engage in politics" (pp. 204-5).

34. Ken Rasmussen, "Economic Policy In Saskatchewan, 1991-1994: the Politics of Declining Expectations," Canadian Political Science Association, June 1994.

35. John Courtney and David E. Smith, "A Constituency Study of Saskatoon City," in Ward and Spafford, *Politics in Saskatchewan.*

36. Bob Stirling and John Conway, "Fractions Among Prairie Farmers," Canadian Political Science Association (June 1985).

37. Eager's book, *Saskatchewan Government,* is an excellent account of the province's political institutions, at least up to 1980.

38. Eager, *Saskatchewan Government,* ch. 8.

39. Mallory, "The Lieutenant-Governor's Discretionary Powers: The Reservation of Bill 56 in Saskatchewan," in *Canadian Journal of Economics and Political Science* (November 1961). The bill forced oil companies to renegotiate contracts with farmers who had given away their mineral rights long before there was any prospect of discovering oil in the province.

40. Eager, *Saskatchewan Government,* p. 138.

41. The size of the legislature has varied as follows:

1905-1908: 25	1952-1960: 53	1991: 66
1908-1912: 41	1960-1964: 55	1995: 58
1912-1917: 54	1964-1971: 59	
1917-1934: 63	1971-1975: 60	
1934-1938 55	1975-1982: 61	
1938-1952: 52	1982-1991: 64	

On this subject, see David E. Smith, "Saskatchewan: Approximating the Ideal," in Gary Levy and Graham White, eds., *Provincial and Territorial Legislatures in Canada* (Toronto: University of Toronto Press, 1989).

42. E.G. Jamieson, "Provincial Employees," in Donald C. Rowat, ed., *Provincial Government and Politics* (Ottawa: Carleton University, 1972), p. 206.

43. H.J. Michelmann and J.S. Steeves, "The 1982 Transition in Power in Saskatchewan: the PCs and the Public Service," *Canadian Public Administration* (Spring 1985).

44. Geoffrey Weller, "Provincial Ministries of Northern Affairs: a Comparative Analysis," in R.W. Weir et al., eds., *Resources and Dynamics of the Boreal Zone,* (Ottawa: Association of Canadian Universities for Northern Studies); and D.M. Wallace, "Budget Reform in Saskatchewan: A New Approach to Program-based Management," in *Canadian Public Administration* (Winter 1974).

45. Archer, *Saskatchewan, A History,* ch. 6.

46. David E. Smith, *Prairie Liberalism: The Liberal Party in Saskatchewan, 1905-71* (Toronto: University of Toronto Press, 1975), pp. 28-31; see also Simpson, *Spoils of Power.*

47. June Menzies, "Votes for Saskatchewan Women," in Ward and Spafford, *Politics in Saskatchewan.*

48. Duff Spafford, "The 'Left Wing' 1921-1931," in Ward and Spafford, *Politics in Saskatchewan.*

49. Smith, *Prairie Liberalism,* p. 150.

50. Reid, "The Saskatchewan Liberal Machine Before 1929," in Ward and Spafford, *Politics in Saskatchewan;* and Smith, *Prairie Liberalism.*

51. Patrick Kyba, "Ballots and Burning Crosses," Ward and Spafford, *Politics in Saskatchewan;* and Smith, *Prairie Liberalism,* pp. 143-8. The creed of the Klan read as follows: "The Klan believes in Protestantism, racial purity, Gentile economic freedom, just laws and liberty, separation of Church and state, pure patriotism, restrictive and selective immigration, freedom of speech and press, law and order, higher moral standards, freedom from mob violence, and one public school." Thus not all of its planks were blatantly offensive (Kyba, p. 109). One of its particular concerns was that a few public schools in Catholic areas were governed by Catholic boards who hired nuns as teachers and permitted crucifixes and other emblems to be placed in the schools. If there were not enough Protestants in the area to justify a school of their own, Protestant children might be exposed to such "alien" influence (Kyba, pp. 114-5).

52. Smith, *Prairie Liberalism,* p. 204.

53. Ibid., p. 216.

54. The land policy was designed to keep the farmer on his land and stop foreclosures, rather than to move towards collectivized farming.

55. Lipset, *Agrarian Socialism,* p. 137.

56. Ibid., p. 242.

57. Ibid; Smith, *Prairie Liberalism;* Archer, *Saskatchewan, A History;* Eager, *Saskatchewan Government;* C.H. Higgenbotham, *Off the Record: The CCF in Saskatchewan* (Toronto: McClelland and Stewart, 1968); Diane Lloyd, *Woodrow* (Regina: Woodrow Lloyd Memorial Fund, 1979); Doris French Shackleton, *Tommy Douglas* (Toronto: McClelland and Stewart, 1975); L.R. Lovick, *Tommy Douglas Speaks* (Lantzville, B.C.: Oolichan Books, 1979); Lewis H. Thomas, *The Making of a Socialist, The Recollections of T.C. Douglas* (Edmonton: University of Alberta Press, 1982); Robert Tyre, *Douglas in Saskatchewan: The Story of a Socialist Experiment* (Vancouver: Mitchell Press, 1962); and William Brennan, ed., *Building the Co-operative Commonwealth* (Regina: Canadian Plains Research Centre, 1984).

58. John Richards and Larry Pratt, *Prairie Capitalism: Power and Influence in the New West* (Toronto: McClelland and Stewart, 1979), pp. 116-7.

59. Thomas, *The Making of a Socialist,* pp. 221-2.

60. Richards and Pratt, *Prairie Capitalism,* pp. 139-41.

61. Ibid., p. 136.

62. The shoe factory was closed in 1949 with a deficit of $156,000, the woollen mill in 1954 with a deficit of $830,000, and the box factory in 1957 with a deficit of $500,000. The fish board was turned into a co-operative in 1959, while the Liberal government sold the airline and the brick plant in the 1960s. This experience should have been an early warning about the provincial government's lack of expertise in assessing the viability of proposed economic development projects. Unfortunately, most other provinces had to make the same mistake themselves.

63. The Liberal position on medicare actually wavered through more variations than this, at one point including the promise of a plebiscite. On the doctors' strike, see R.F. Badgley and S. Wolfe, _Doctors' Strike_ (Toronto: Macmillan, 1967); E.A. Tollefson, _Bitter Medicine: The Saskatchewan Medicare Feud_ (Saskatoon: Western Producer Prairie Books, 1963); Tollefson's article in Ward and Spafford, _Politics in Saskatchewan;_ and two articles in the Anchor edition of Lipset's _Agrarian Socialism,_ J.W. Gouldner, "The Doctors' Strike: Change and Resistance to Change in Saskatchewan," and C. Krueger, "Prairie Protest: The Medicare Conflict in Saskatchewan."

64. Ibid., Smith, _Prairie Liberalism,_ p. 298.

65. Dale Eisler, _Rumours of Glory: Saskatchewan and the Thatcher Years_ (Edmonton: Hurtig, 1987).

66. Richards and Pratt, _Prairie Capitalism,_ pp. 119-120; Philip Mathias, _Forced Growth_ (Toronto: James Lewis and Samuel, 1971), ch. 4.

67. Lloyd, _Woodrow,_ ch. 11.

68. On this period see Dennis Gruending, _Promises to Keep: A Political Biography of Allan Blakeney_ (Saskatoon: Western Producer Prairie Books, 1990); Richards and Pratt, _Prairie Capitalism;_ and annual accounts in the _Canadian Annual Review of Politics and Public Affairs._

69. Archer, _Saskatchewan, A History,_ p. 334; Mathias, _Forced Growth._

70. J.K. Laux and M.A. Molot, "The Potash Corporation of Saskatchewan," in Allan Tupper and G.B. Doern, eds., _Public Corporations and Public Policy in Canada_ (Montreal: Institute for Research on Public Policy, 1981); M.A. Molot and J.K. Laux, "The Politics of Nationalization," in _Canadian Journal of Political Science_ (June 1979); Roy Romanow's speech on the second reading of _An Act respecting the Development of Potash Resources in Saskatchewan, 1976;_ as well as Richards and Pratt, Archer, and Smith.

71. _Canadian Annual Review, 1973,_ p. 194. In the 1971 election campaign, party literature said that an NDP government "will consider the feasibility of bringing the potash industry under public ownership."

72. Richards and Pratt, _Prairie Capitalism,_ p. 260.

73. Laux and Molot, "The Potash Corporation of Saskatchewan," in Tupper and Doern, _Public Corporations and Public Policy,_ p. 194.

74. Molot and Laux, "The Politics of Nationalization," in _Canadian Journal of Political Science._

75. The one Waffler elected as an NDP MLA, John Richards, decided at this point to sit as an Independent in the legislature.

76. In the middle of the night he resigned and, in an apparently intoxicated state, fired off a .357 magnum revolver from the window of his Regina apartment and was charged with illegal possession and improper use of a firearm. _Canadian Annual Review,_ 1979, p. 366.

77. _Canadian Annual Review,_ 1982, p. 282.

78. Three contrasting accounts of the Devine period can be found in J.M. Pitsula and Ken Rasmussen, _Privatizing a Province_ (Vancouver: New Star Books, 1990), Lesley Biggs and Mark Stobbe, eds., _Devine Rule in Saskatchewan: a Decade of Hope and_

Hardship (Saskatoon: Fifth House Publishers, 1991), and Don Baron and Paul Jackson, *Battleground: The Socialist Assault on Grant Devine's Canadian Dream* (Toronto: Bedford House Publishing, 1991).

79. According to the *Toronto Star,* more than 400 people with NDP ties were rooted out, May 6, 1984; H.J. Michelmann and J.S. Steeves, "The 1982 transition in power in Saskatchewan." For his view of the new government, see Colin Thatcher, *Backrooms* (Saskatoon: Western Producer Prairie Books, 1985).

80. Murray Dobbin, "Tory blitzkrieg in Saskatchewan: PC program and budget cuts," *Canadian Dimension* (September 1987); Dobbin, "Laying Waste to Saskatchewan Democracy," *Canadian Forum* (April 1990).

81. Ken Rasmussen, "Economic Policy In Saskatchewan, 1991-1994."

82. *Report of the Saskatchewan Financial Management Review Commission* (Regina), February, 1992.

83. Phillip Hansen, "Saskatchewan: The Failure of Political Imagination," in *Studies in Political Economy* (Spring 1994).

READINGS

Biggs, Lesley and Mark Stobbe, eds. *Devine Rule in Saskatchewan: a Decade of Hope and Hardship.* Saskatoon: Fifth House Publishers, 1991.

The Canadian Annual Review of Politics and Public Affairs. Toronto: University of Toronto Press, annual.

Dunn, Christopher, and David Laycock. "Innovation and Competition in the Agricultural Heartland." Keith Brownsey and Michael Howlett, eds. *The Provincial State.* Mississauga: Copp Clark Pitman, 1992.

Lipset, S.M. *Agrarian Socialism, The Co-operative Commonwealth Federation.* Garden City, New York: Anchor Books, Rev. ed., 1968.

Rasmussen, Ken. "Economic Policy in Saskatchewan, 1991-1994: the Politics of Declining Expectations." An address to the Canadian Political Science Association, June 1994.

Richards, John, and Larry Pratt. *Prairie Capitalism: Power and Influence in the New West.* Toronto: McClelland and Stewart, 1979.

Saskatchewan Bureau of Statistics. *Economic Review,* annual.

Saskatchewan Bureau of Statistics. *Saskatchewan Economic Statistics,* annual.

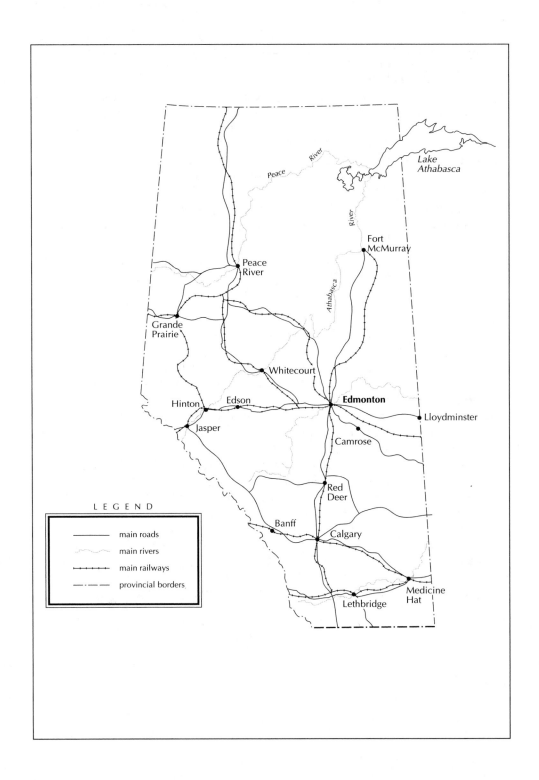

LEGEND

——————	main roads
∿∿∿∿	main rivers
+++++	main railways
—·—·—	provincial borders

Peace River

Lake Athabasca

River

River

Athabasca

Fort McMurray

Peace River

Grande Prairie

Whitecourt

Hinton

Edson

Jasper

Edmonton

Lloydminster

Camrose

Red Deer

Banff

Calgary

Medicine Hat

Lethbridge

CHAPTER 10

ALBERTA

Alberta is the home of fabulous petroleum wealth, gorgeous mountain scenery, and smouldering Western alienation. The first of these characteristics was not truly significant until after 1947, while the others have been constant. Alberta was a poor agricultural province for its first 40 years and, in spite of the prosperity of the next 45 years, a distinctive political pattern has remained. Alberta has experienced four long periods of often overwhelming one-party dominance. In the 1990s, however, Alberta was less prosperous and had a more balanced legislature, and it seemed likely its political behaviour would become less unusual. As it approached the turn of the century, it stood out in having the country's most radical right-wing government.

SETTING

Geography

Alberta is 661,000 square kilometres in area, and is separated from Saskatchewan by an arbitrary straight line and from British Columbia by the Rocky Mountains. The province is mainly composed of the Western Plains, but there is a bit of the Precambrian Shield in the northeast corner and a slice of the Western Cordillera in the southwest foothills and mountains. The south is made up of prairies; the centre, of parkland—a combination of plains and forests; and the north, of forest and muskeg. The two urban poles of Calgary and Edmonton dominate the southern and northern regions of the province respectively. It is therefore common to divide the province into north and south, but smaller regions are also identifiable, such as the Lethbridge-Medicine Hat area in the far south, the Red Deer region halfway between Calgary and Edmonton, the Peace River country northwest of Edmonton, and the Fort McMurray region northeast of the capital.

Alberta's population grew rapidly in the 1970s, mostly as the result of inter-provincial migration, to exceed the two million mark in 1979 and reach 2,545,553 by 1991 and 2,726,900 by January 1995. Since 1951, its population has been second to British Columbia in the West and is fourth largest in the country. Calgary and Edmonton have always been in intense competition over just about everything, not the least of which is the size of their population. In recent years, the population of the city of Calgary (710,677 in 1991) has exceeded that of the city of Edmonton (616,741) but, in terms of metropolitan area, Edmonton came out ahead 839,924 to 754,033. This is because there are several self-contained municipalities just outside the capital. In any case, between them Calgary and Edmonton contain 62.6 percent of the province's population. The other urban centres are Lethbridge (60,974), Red Deer (58,134), Medicine Hat (52,681), Fort McMurray (49,204) and Grande Prairie (28,271). Alberta is now the third most urbanized province in the country at 79.8 percent, and considerable conflict has always existed between rural and urban perspectives.

The province is crossed from east to west by Canadian Pacific and Canadian National railways. CN also maintains a line from Edmonton through the Peace River block to Hay River and Pine Point in the Northwest Territories, as well as a line from Edmonton to Fort McMurray. Alberta possesses an extensive network of roads, including two east-west routes of the Trans-Canada Highway, the busy Calgary-Edmonton corridor, and roads that parallel the railway from Edmonton to Fort McMurray, and to Peace River and the Northwest Territories. Among the many airlines operating in the province is Canadian Airlines International with its headquarters in Calgary. Once called Pacific Western Airlines and owned by the province, it grew to such a point that it took over Canadian Pacific Airlines. The Calgary International Airport is the fourth busiest in the country in terms of both passengers and cargo, while Edmonton International is eighth in cargo and ninth in passengers.

Economy

Petroleum completely dominates the modern Alberta economy and, relative to the national average, Alberta has a higher proportion of people employed in primary industries and fewer in the secondary sector. Its economy constitutes about 10.6 percent of the national gross domestic product.

Earlier development of gas and oil, especially around Turner Valley, had made Calgary the centre of the Canadian petroleum industry, but its true beginnings may be dated from 1947, when oil was discovered at Leduc, just south of Edmonton. Since then, exploration has led to the development of oil fields at many locations including Redwater, Swan Hills, West Pembina, Rainbow Lake, and the central foothills region. The province is also graced with natural gas wells and processing plants, an industry valuable in itself and also the base of the petrochemical industry. Alberta accounts for about 82 percent of the country's national crude oil production and about 83 percent of the natural gas. A network of oil and gas pipelines crosses the province and leads to the east, west, and south. The Interprovincial Oil Pipeline extends from Edmonton to Wisconsin, Sarnia, Toronto, and Montreal. The Trans-Mountain Pipeline supplies oil to the west coast and the northwestern United States. The Westcoast Transmission Pipeline carries natural gas to British Columbia, with more recent connections to California, and the controversial Trans-Canada Pipeline, built in 1958, now supplies gas to Quebec City, Chicago, and New England. Alberta natural gas is also carried directly south into the United States. In 1993 about 22 percent of the province's oil stayed in Alberta, 34 percent was destined for other provinces, and 44 percent was exported to the U.S.; for natural gas, the proportions were 17 percent, 30 percent, and 53 percent respectively. That year saw an expansion of oil pipeline capacity to Chicago and a new gas pipeline to California.

The decline of conventional oil supplies led to the production of synthetic crude oil which can be recovered from the oil or tar sands. These huge reserves are located in the Athabasca, Cold Lake, Peace River, and Wabasca areas, all north of Edmonton. Thus far, two major oil sands plants operate: the Suncor Inc. plant, completed in 1967, and the Syncrude Canada Ltd. plant which started to produce in 1978. Both are located close to Fort McMurray, and are surface-mined. A number of experimental underground schemes also exist, and synthetic crude oil accounts for between 15 and 20 percent of the country's total oil production. Inset 10.1 provides more detail on the petroleum industry and Figures 10.1, 10.2, 10.3, and 10.4 respectively show the location of petroleum in western Canada, the finished products derived from crude oil, petrochemical products, and pipelines.

The industry flourished for 35 years, especially after the 1973 Organization of Petroleum Exporting Countries (OPEC) crisis, until a combination of factors around 1980, including the National Energy Program, caused a significant slowdown. The province reacted with programs to reduce oil company taxes and royalties to keep the industry afloat, and the Mulroney government scrapped the NEP, and by mid-1985 the situation was improved considerably. Unfortunately, the international price for oil plummeted shortly afterwards, causing another major economic downturn in the province, although natural gas was less affected.

Alberta is also the leading source of sulphur and many other by-products of natural gas processing, called petrochemicals. Among the major petrochemical plants are Dow Chemicals Canada Inc. (Fort Saskatchewan), A.T. Plastics Inc. and Celanese Canada Inc. (Edmonton), Union Carbide Canada Ltd. (Prentiss), Shell Canada Ltd. and B.F. Goodrich Canada Ltd. (Scotford), and Novacor Chemicals Canada Ltd. (Joffre and Medicine Hat).

While petroleum makes Alberta the leading province in mining, the industry is not confined to oil and gas. Alberta is also one of Canada's two largest coal producers. This is located in the southern mountains, foothills, and plains. As in Nova Scotia, the industry declined in the 1950s, but was rejuvenated due to the rapid escalation in the cost of petroleum. Coal is used primarily to generate electricity in the province and for export to Japan. Alberta has virtually no metallic mineral production, but it does contain peat and such structural materials as cement, limestone, clay, sand, and gravel. The combined aspects of the mining industry, with a production value in 1992 of almost $17 billion, completely overshadow other sectors of the gross domestic product.

INSET 10.1 The Petroleum Industry in Western Canada

Petroleum is Alberta's greatest asset and most distinctive feature. Between 80 and 85 percent of Canadian production comes from this one province, and the industry constitutes the foundation of Alberta's prosperity.

Petroleum can be divided into two raw products: oil and natural gas. Conventional crude oil comes in three main types: light, medium, and heavy. Light and medium grades are readily refined into usable products, but heavy oil must be upgraded into a lighter state before it is ready to be refined. Most of Alberta's oil is either light or medium, but considerable heavy oil is found along the Saskatchewan border. The Bi-Provincial heavy oil upgrader is therefore conveniently located in Lloydminister, while another is in Regina. The upgraded heavy oil is called synthetic crude.

As known supplies of conventional crude began to diminish in the 1960s, another type of oil was discovered—bitumen, which is found in oil or tar sands. The two large tar sands plants near Fort McMurray—Syncrude Canada Ltd. and Suncor Inc.—recover the bitumen by open-pit techniques and then separate it from the sand, clay and water accompanying it. In other locations, the bitumen is below the surface and must be mined by "in situ" techniques such as steam injection. Imperial Oil's plant at Cold Lake is the largest such project to date. Like heavy oil, bitumen must be upgraded into synthetic crude, and the two upgraders mentioned are capable of doing so. Drilling for conventional crude oil is less expensive than producing oil from tar sands but Canada is running low on the former and has huge reserves of the latter. In the early 1990s, about 15 percent of Canada's oil production was synthetic. Figure 10.1 indicates the location of conventional crude and tar sands in western Canada, as well as of natural gas. Figure 10.2 illustrates many finished products derived from crude oil following the refining process, the most important being gasoline and diesel fuel.

Large reserves of natural gas are spread more uniformly throughout the province. Natural gas is produced by the same drilling techniques as conventional crude oil and, when they are found together, the oil and gas are separated. Natural gas must be refined to remove by-products and impurities, especially sulphur and hydrogen sulphide, so that what is used for heating purposes is largely methane. Distinct from natural gas are natural gas liquids, which are heavier gaseous hydrocarbons such as ethane, propane, and butane. They are used as fuels in their own right, as well as in petrochemical plants and oil refineries.

Petrochemicals use natural gas as their primary feedstock, but oil is also a source. Petrochemical plants convert natural gas into such substances as methanol, ethylene, propylene, butadiene, butylenes, benzene, toluene and xylene. These are further processed by other industries into an array of finished products as illustrated in Figure 10.3. These include plastics, film, anti-freeze, adhesives, paints, textiles, rubber, carpets, cosmetics and pharmaceuticals, insulation, herbicides and pesticides.

Because Alberta uses only about one-quarter of the oil and gas it produces, the rest is transported by pipeline to other provinces and to the United States. Figure 10.4 shows current pipeline routes in Canada and into the United States. In rough terms, about one-quarter is consumed in other provinces and about one-half is exported.

Because of the large amount of revenue involved, both federal and provincial governments tax various aspects of the petroleum industry beyond the normal corporate income taxes. The producing provinces derive revenues from royalties, the sale of Crown leases, rentals and fees. The federal government, which ordinarily leaves natural resources to be taxed by the provinces, has greatly annoyed producing provinces whenever it levied its own taxes on petroleum companies. Both levels of government also levy retail taxes on petroleum products, such as the gasoline tax.

If taxation of the petroleum industry produces intergovernmental conflicts, so does the issue of pricing. The price of most natural resources is determined by the market forces of supply and demand, but for many years governments intervened to set prices in the petroleum industry. The provincial and federal governments were often at odds about the appropriate price as well as the constitutional authority to set it. These questions were at the heart of the conflict over the 1980 National Energy Program, but after the "Western Accord" of 1985 both levels of government backed out of pricing. Oil prices were allowed to rise to international levels, at one time controlled by the OPEC cartel. That organization is now less effective than it once was in establishing international prices. The price of natural gas also depends on market forces determined by North American supply and demand. Unfortunately for producers and producing provinces, the world oil price fell 50 percent in 1986, just after deregulation. It gradually rose in subsequent years, only to fall again in 1993-94, but the resulting reduction in exploration is expected to increase the price by the end of the century. Meanwhile, the natural gas price is strong due to U.S. demand and increased pipeline capacity.

Among the primary industries, agriculture ranks ahead of mining in employment, but a distant second in value of production. Overall, Alberta is normally second to Ontario in the value of agricultural production, and its agricultural scene is diversified. The province has the largest cattle industry in the country, centred on ranches in the southwest foothills and feedlots throughout the province. Cattle farming has recently been the largest source of agricultural income, followed by wheat, in which Alberta is second in the country. Other crops include barley, oats, and canola. Hogs, dairy farming, sugar beets, poultry and eggs, other livestock, potatoes, vegetables, and horticulture complete the picture. Although southern Alberta is dry, the number of acres served by irrigation exceeds that of any other province, and it ranks second in the use of fertilizer. The number of farms in 1991 was 57,245 with an average size of 898 acres.

FIGURE 10.1 Location of Petroleum in Western Canada

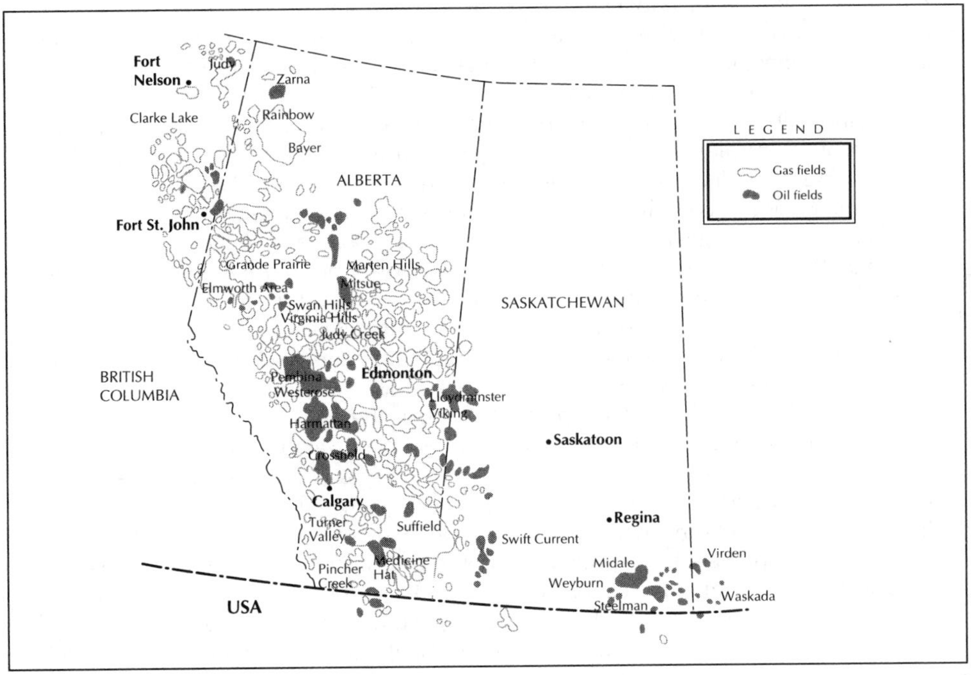

Source: Petroleum Communication Foundation.

With 60 percent of the province covered by trees, forestry is another significant primary industry. This industry was slow to get started in Alberta, allowing the province to put into place a mandatory reforestation policy at the outset, and it maintains a commendable commitment to sustainable forest development. There are 25 major sawmills and over 200 in total, two older pulp mills (Weldwood in Hinton and Weyerhaeuser in Grande Prairie), and assorted plywood, veneer, oriented standboard, panelboard, paper, and furniture operations. Alberta ranks fourth in primary forest and lumber production, but it has experienced a great increase in pulp and paper production in recent years. It how has six pulp mills in operation, the newer ones being Alberta-Pacific (Al-Pac) at Athabasca, Millar Western at Whitecourt, Daishowa Forest Products Ltd. at Peace River, and Alberta Energy Company's plant at Slave Lake. There is one newsprint plant, Alberta Newsprint Co. at Whitecourt, and two paperboard plants, one in each of the two large cities.

Alberta has left its electric power industry in private or municipal hands. There is some hydro production generated by the upper reaches of the Bow and South Saskatchewan rivers, and considerable potential in the rivers of the north, but most electricity is produced by burning coal. The two largest firms are Alberta Power Ltd. in the north and TransAlta Utilities in the south.

FIGURE 10.2   Finished Products from Crude Oil

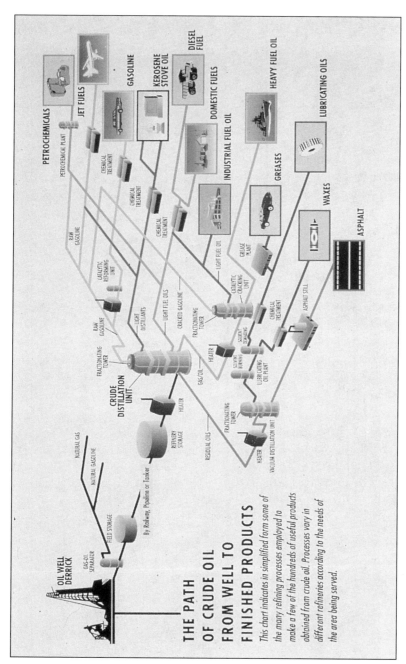

Source: Petroleum Communication Foundation.

FIGURE 10.3 Petrochemical Products

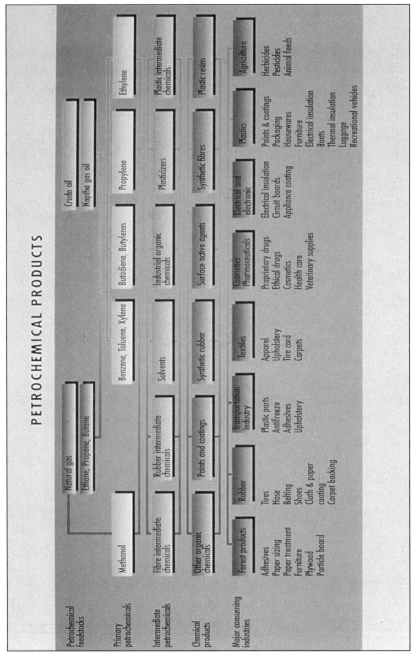

Source: Petroleum Communication Foundation.

FIGURE 10.4   Major Oil and Natural Gas Pipelines

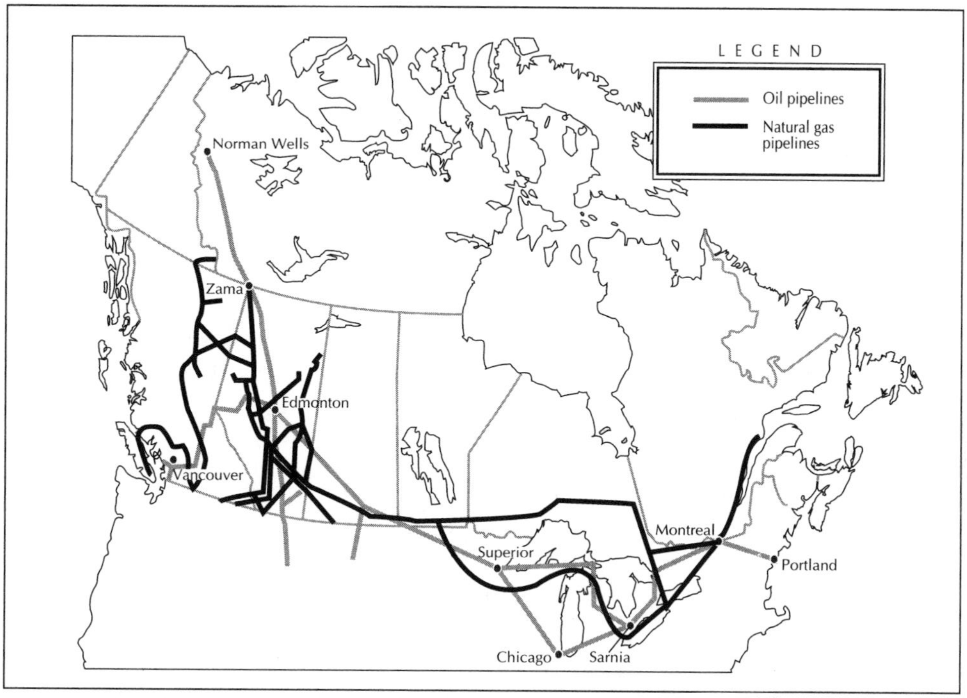

Source: Petroleum Communication Foundation.

Alberta ranks fourth among all provinces in manufacturing, with recent expansion related to the rapid growth of the Western Canadian population, low taxes and energy costs, and availability of skilled labour and local financing. Chemicals and chemical products (including petrochemicals) lead the list, followed by food and beverages. Machinery and transportation equipment rank third, including mobile homes made by the indigenous ATCO Ltd. followed by wood, paper and applied products, and printing and publishing. Alberta's main exports include both primary and manufactured goods, especially crude petroleum, natural gas, petrochemicals, wheat, forest products, coal, and meat and livestock.

The service sector is the largest employer, heavily dependent on the petroleum industry, and largely centred in Calgary and Edmonton. Calgary has become the financial centre of prairie Canada, with regional offices of such national institutions as the chartered banks, and the headquarters of some smaller financial institutions. The West Edmonton Mall is famous as a shopping centre, and tourism constitutes a large part of services and trade, based in large part on the spectacular attraction of national parks in the mountain regions and the cosmopolitan atmosphere of the two largest cities, ranging from the high culture of

TABLE 10.1 **Alberta 1991 Labour Force and Estimated 1995 Gross Domestic Product by Industry**

Industry	1991 Labour Force		Est. 1995 GDP ($ millions)	
Agriculture	94,320	6.7%	2,991	4.4%
Fishing	380	–	11	–
Logging	6,045	0.4%	186	0.3%
Mining	79,695	5.7%	15,056	22.0%
TOTAL PRIMARY	180,440	12.8%	18,223	26.6%
Manufacturing	106,905	7.6%	5,488	8.0%
Construction	102,090	7.3%	3,804	5.5%
TOTAL SECONDARY	208,995	14.9%	9,292	13.5%
Transportation, Communications and Utilities	111,295	7.9%	8,002	11.7%
Trade	237,270	16.9%	7,131	10.4%
Finance, Insurance and Real Estate	70,640	5.0%	11,275	16.4%
Services	493,730	35.1%	11,485	16.7%
Government	102,470	7.3%	3,165	4.6%
TOTAL TERTIARY	1,015,400	72.2%	41,058	59.9%
TOTAL ALL INDUSTRIES	1,404,835		68,573	

Source: Reproduced by permission of the Minister of Industry, 1995, Statistics Canada, *1991 Census*, cat. nos. 93-326 and 95-373, and Conference Board of Canada, *Provincial Outlook, Economic Forecast*, Summer 1994, Vol. 9, No. 2.

theatre and orchestras to the Calgary Stampede. In 1992, the federal government had 43,138 employees in Alberta, the province had 82,157, and the municipalities 134,814, for a total government workforce of 260,109.

Class

Petroleum development in particular has made Alberta a wealthy province and, while things are not as rosy as they were before 1980, Alberta had a per capita income in 1992 of $22,389, slightly lower than Ontario and British Columbia. In 1991, 15.4 percent of its families made under $20,000 and 22.8 percent over $70,000, for a median family income of $46,146. Albertans also rank with Ontarians and British Columbians in having the highest average level of education in the country.

Alberta's unemployment rate reached a high point of 9.6 percent in the recession of the early 1990s, and it often vies with Manitoba as the second-lowest in the country. The Alberta Federation of Labour has about 150,000 members. The unionized work force of 296,100 represents some 26.4 percent of paid workers in the province, the lowest proportion in the country. This reflects a certain conservatism on the part of residents, successive government policies which have discouraged unionization, and a "seduction by high wages and the prospects of continued prosperity."[1] It is also partly the reason for the weakness of the provincial New Democratic Party. The largest unions are the Alberta Union of Provincial Employees, the Communications, Energy and Paperworkers, the Canadian Union of Public Employees, and the United Food and Commercial Workers.

Much has been said in recent years of Alberta's new-found prosperity, but not all of the Alberta corporate elite are newly rich and not all made their money in oil. Peter Newman includes the Cross (ranching and brewing) and Lougheed families of Calgary among the longstanding dynasties, to which he might have added the Mannix family (construction), with whom ex-premier Peter Lougheed was first associated.[2] Prominent Alberta oilmen include Chuck Shultz (Gulf Canada Resources), James Baroffio (Chevron Canada), Ted Newall (Nova Corp.), David O'Brien (PanCanadian Petroleum), James Stanford (Petro-Canada), Charles Wilson (Shell Canada), George Watson (TransCanada Pipelines), Grant Billing (Norcen Energy Resources), Don Stacy (Amoco Canada Petroleum), Philippe Dunoyer (Total Petroleum), Brian MacNeil (Interprovincial Pipelines Co.), Stan Milner (Chieftain International), Bill McGregor (Numac Oil and Gas), Donald Harvie (Devonian Foundation), and the Seaman brothers (investment firms). Corporate leaders in other fields include Ron Southern (ATCO), Peter Pocklington (Edmonton Oilers), Charles Allard (broadcasting), John Jope (Canada Safeway), Kevin Jenkins (PWA Corp.), J.R. Shaw (Shaw Communications), Jeffrey McCaig (Trimac), Ken McCready (TransAlta Corp.), Art Child (Burns Foods), and the four Ghermezian brothers, famous for their West Edmonton Mall. Many corporate leaders have close ties to the Conservative government.

One of the earliest class analyses of Alberta was conducted in 1953 by C.B. Macpherson in an attempt to explain the peculiar provincial party system. He concluded that the province was overwhelmingly made up of small commodity producers and that everyone essentially belonged to the same class.[3] His was a kind of Marxist interpretation that looked for class cleavages, but found the conflict of class interests not so much within the society as between that society and the forces of outside capital. However homogeneous then, it has obviously become a more mature industrial society with attendant class divisions, and yet, the province still often behaves like a classless society.

More recent analyses, however, discovered the existence of several classes in Alberta society and attributed many government policies to their presence.[4] Albertans have seen countless examples of government assistance to big capital (especially petroleum and forestry companies) and to the rural petite bourgeoisie. The urban middle classes, at first a backbone of Conservative support, moved to support opposition parties when restraint programs of the 1990s limited their incomes. The working classes have rarely had much influence, as can be seen in the province's labour legislation, and the Ralph Klein revolution could be expected to mobilize large portions of the middle and lower classes to protest against government cutbacks.

Demography

Alberta has a slightly larger proportion of residents of British descent than Manitoba or Saskatchewan, although this group accounts for just over 40 percent of the population. German background is the second most common, Ukrainian third, and French fourth. These are followed by Scandinavian, Dutch, Native, Polish, and Chinese. The most significant geographic concentration of any ethnic group is the Ukrainian community in the Edmonton region. Only 57.6 percent of Alberta's residents were born in the province, while 27.2 percent migrated from other parts of the country, and 15.2 percent came from abroad.

As in the other prairie provinces, the French have largely been assimilated: only 2.3 percent have French as their mother tongue compared with 82.5 percent English, and only 0.8 percent use French at home, while 91.5 percent use English. The language transfer rate from French mother tongue to non-French home language is 64.5 percent. As discussed in the previous chapter, the removal of French as an official language occurred in the days when Alberta and Saskatchewan had a common territorial government, and little conflict of a linguistic nature surfaced in Alberta afterwards. The 1988 Language Act allows French to be used in the legislature and certain courts and, in the wake of the Charter of Rights and Freedoms, the courts decided that in several localities, the number of francophone students warrants a French-language school, and that francophones have the right to manage and control them.[5] After legislation was passed in 1993, the first three francophone school boards were established in the Peace River, Lakeland, and Edmonton regions.

TABLE 10.2   Alberta Mother Tongue and Home Language, 1991

	Mother Tongue	Home Language
English	82.5%	91.5%
French	2.3%	0.8%
Other	15.2%	7.7%

Source: Reproduced by permission of the Minister of Industry, 1995, Statistics Canada, *1991 Census*, cat. no. 93-317, adapted by author.

Alberta has the third-highest number of residents of aboriginal origin (nearly 150,000) and the third-highest proportion among all provinces (5.9 percent).

As elsewhere, Native issues command increasing political attention. Alberta set up an investigation into Native justice after incidents somewhat parallel to those in Manitoba, but in recent years has probably treated its Métis population better than other provinces have done. The same cannot be said of other Aboriginals.

In terms of religion, 48.4 percent of Albertans are Protestant, 26.5 percent Catholic, and 19.7 percent have no religious preference. Among the Protestant groups, the United Church is most popular, followed by the Anglicans and the Lutherans. Alberta is distinctive in that Baptists are the fourth-largest Protestant sect, Pentecostals are fifth, Presbyterians are sixth, and the Mormons are seventh. The issue of separate Roman Catholic schools was settled in 1905 and since then has not been much of an issue, although in the 1990s a major change in school board structures and funding produced opposition from the Roman Catholic community. The main political significance of religion in Alberta was the relatively high proportion of fundamentalist groups—Baptists, Mormons, and Pentecostals—who tend to be located in the southern part of the province and who had a particular attraction to Social Credit and the fundamentalist religious leaders of that party, William Aberhart and Ernest Manning. Accredited private schools (often with a religious orientation) that follow the authorized curriculum and hire certified teachers are funded at a rate of 75 percent.

TABLE 10.3   Religion in Alberta, 1991

Protestant			1,219,240 (48.4%)
United Church	419,600	(16.7%)	
Anglican	173,160	(6.9%)	
Lutheran	137,145	(5.4%)	
Baptist	63,735	(2.5%)	
Pentecostal	52,990	(2.1%)	
Presbyterian	48,385	(1.9%)	
Mormon	46,830	(1.9%)	
Other Protestant	277,395	(11.0%)	
Roman Catholic			666,785 (26.5%)
No Religious Affiliation			496,150 (19.7%)
Eastern Non-Christian			78,460 (3.1%)
Eastern Orthodox			42,720 (1.7%)
Other			15,825 (0.6%)

Source: Reproduced by permission of the Minister of Industry, 1995, Statistics Canada, *1991 Census*, cat. no. 93-319, adapted by author.

Alberta thus appears to have been remarkably free of internal ethnic and religious cleavages over its history and, while income disparities exist, the general prosperity and the small extent of organized labour are such that they have not produced a significant class cleavage. Certain regional tensions are evident —between rural and urban, between Calgary and Edmonton, and between north and south—as is some conflict between the agricultural and petroleum industries, but none has caused great difficulty.

Federal-Provincial Relations[6]

Alberta's relative internal political calm stands in sharp contrast to the habitual antagonism which exists between the province and the federal government.[7] The sources of conflict have been discussed in the chapters on Manitoba and Saskatchewan, but these issues often generated stronger feelings in Alberta, which was further removed geographically from Ottawa. In addition, the province was sometimes more seriously affected by contentious federal policies and was more unorthodox in its response than were its prairie neighbours. Thus, the question of tariffs, freight rates, and natural resources jurisdiction led to the election of a provincial farmers' government in 1921; the problems of credit and the centralized banking system produced the Social Credit movement of the 1930s; and the unorthodox legislation introduced by Social Credit resulted in severely strained relations with Ottawa.

Bilingualism, the Constitution, and federal resource policy, especially the National Energy Program (NEP), temporarily raised the threat of a separatist government in the province in the early 1980s. The NEP generated the most heated conflict between the province and the federal government in more than 40 years, and even led the Lougheed administration to reduce the flow of oil to eastern Canada. "Let the eastern bastards freeze in the dark" was a fairly popular slogan in the province at the time. In addition, federal policies on medicare and cutbacks in shared-cost programs were received with considerable hostility, partly because Alberta does not qualify for equalization payments and the federal government's contribution to provincial revenues in 1992 was only 15.1 percent, second-lowest in the country. In addition to the $2.4 billion it transferred to the provincial government, Ottawa sent $58 million to municipalities, $4,027 million to individuals and $824 million to businesses. With a diversified agricultural community and some hope of additional local manufacturing, Alberta was generally happy with the changes to the Crow rate, except for the method of payment, ecstatic over free trade, and excited over the prospects of Senate reform.

More recent federal-Alberta issues included reforming fiscal arrangements, Alberta desiring greater flexibility in designing its own personal income tax; reducing overlap and duplication, especially in such areas as energy, agriculture, economic development, labour market policy, and the environment; and eliminating interprovincial trade barriers. Also on the provincial agenda is the funding of such programs as the Trans-Canada Highway, agricultural support, immigration, the grain transportation system, minority language education, and various projects in the petroleum industry.

POLITICAL CULTURE

Albertans have a very positive self-image. They reside in a rich, beautiful, confident, and increasingly sophisticated province, and their only problem seems to be that they are restrained by federal government policies and the corporate practices of central Canada. Albertans have been so close to a consensus on internal objectives that they felt particularly affronted when others stood in their way. To some extent this is simply the response of a wealthy, Western conservative sub-culture, but it also constitutes a continuity of a tradition encompassing more unusual political movements in the province, such as the United Farmers and Social Credit. In particular, it incorporates populism, without much participation, conservatism, and alienation.

The United Farmers of Alberta (UFA) came to power in 1921 based on a "radical democratic populism" similar to that in Manitoba or the co-operative movement in Saskatchewan.[8] The UFA abhorred common party practices such as patronage and corruption, as well as the lack of independence of the legislature's private members, who were subjected to rigid party discipline after policies had been determined by majority vote in secret caucus meetings. The UFA sought more democracy, particularly in such forms of direct legislation as the referendum (in which a law does not take effect until approved in a vote by the electorate), the initiative (in which a specific number of names on a petition would require the legislature to pass a law), and the recall (in which a specific proportion of electors could require an MLA to resign). While the UFA government in practice accepted most of the conventions of parliamentary-cabinet government, there was a lingering minority group which never lost the radical spirit of what was really "social democratic populism."

In 1935, with the Depression as a catalyst, and with Saskatchewan becoming socialist, the populist movement in Alberta was transformed into the Social Credit League. That Saskatchewan should embrace left-wing populism in the 1930s while Alberta opted for what became right-wing populism can be partly explained by the difference in the composition of their populations. The British working-class element was smaller and the proportion of American immigrants much larger than in Saskatchewan. Furthermore, the Americans who flocked to Alberta, many coming from the American Bible Belt, tended not to be socialists, as in Saskatchewan, but rather radical, populist, individualistic liberals who were preoccupied with monetary theories.

At first sight, Social Credit carried forward many of the UFA traditions, such as opposition to federal policies and an increasing farmer interest in monetary reform.[9] It soon became apparent, however, that the new movement was in some ways the antithesis of the UFA, in that Social Credit was essentially authoritarian and anti-participatory and advocated "plebiscitarian populism."[10] It urged people to vote for results, but not to be concerned about establishing the means to achieve them, for such matters were best left to the experts. Social Credit presented a vision of a benevolent, technocratic regime in which the technical experts would be given free rein, but the party lacked the commitment to participation, co-operation, or equality that marked other strains of populism in the Canadian West.

The Social Credit government soon abandoned its attempts at monetary reform and found a new bogeyman in socialism. Because no more than a minority of UFA supporters had ever been social democratic populists, this was a popular stance and its appeal grew as the development of oil made the province increasingly prosperous and conservative. Thus, just as the UFA had sown the seeds of Social Credit with its opposition to federal policies and its later interest in monetary reform, Social Credit laid the groundwork for the Conservative party by promoting conservatism and provincial rights. When the UFA was replaced by Social Credit in 1935, popular participation was jettisoned from the provincial political culture; when Social Credit gave way to the Conservatives, nothing changed except the names and faces.

The lack of a participatory spirit in Alberta can still be seen in the election turnout rate. The average voter turnout in the most recent six provincial elections is 57.6 percent, the lowest in the country, and 67.5 percent in federal elections, the second-lowest behind Newfoundland. Of course, this phenomenon can also be accounted for by a lack of opposition to the Conservative party at both the federal and provincial levels. A Conservative landslide has often been a foregone conclusion, and many voters do not bother to take part in the exercise. But the low turnout is also a reflection of a basic tenet of the provincial political culture which accepts the existence of an authoritarian or one-party government.

TABLE 10.4   Alberta Voter Turnout in Recent Federal and Provincial Elections

Federal Elections		Provincial Elections	
1974	67%	1975	60%
1979	68%	1979	59%
1980	61%	1982	66%
1984	69%	1986	47%
1988	75%	1989	54%
1993	65%	1993	60%
Average	67.5%	Average	57.6%

Source: *Reports of the Chief Electoral Officer*, calculations by author.

If populism combined with limited popular participation and a fundamental conservatism are the first two strains of the province's political culture, the third, "Western alienation,"[11] also merits considerable attention. While this feeling is shared by the other three Western provinces, it is most deeply ingrained in

Alberta. Originally the province's discontent centred on high tariffs, high freight rates, and the difficulty of obtaining credit at the centralized banks. It seemed that Ottawa was acting in the interests of central Canadian corporations, specifically the manufacturers, the railways, and the banks, and this generated a feeling of economic exploitation among Albertans. Over the years the national banks have decentralized and expanded their Western operations, and even the Trudeau government permitted regional banks. Most dramatically, Prime Minister Brian Mulroney gave Alberta free trade with the United States, partly at the urging of ex-premier Lougheed. Of the three main original complaints, freight rates continue to be the greatest source of contention, but here the Alberta case is weakest, because the high rates are mainly a reflection of the province's distance from the concentrated markets and manufacturing bases of central Canada and the United States.[12]

A new set of economic grievances arose in the 1973-84 period, primarily in connection with the petroleum industry. The Alberta government wanted to receive the bulk of the revenue, as well as to control the selling price and the rate of production. It also hoped to establish a petrochemical industry in the province, rather than see its resources used to expand petrochemical operations in Sarnia, Ontario. This attitude was based on the non-renewable character of the resources and the need to plan for the future when the oil and gas reserves would be depleted. With the downturn in the industry around 1980, for which the National Energy Program was only partly responsible, Western alienation temporarily became Western separatism for many Albertans. Most calmed down in 1981, when Premier Lougheed was finally able to negotiate changes in the energy program, and modifications were made in the Trudeau constitutional package.

These separatist sentiments were also a reaction to Albertans' antipathy toward Quebec and French-Canadian influence within the federal government. The French minority in the Western provinces was so small that it was difficult for most Albertans to accept the notion of English-French duality in the country, especially in the West. The appearance of French signs and labelling was galling to many, but of more significance was the problem unilingual Albertans had in obtaining employment with the federal government. Even worse, Ottawa was so preoccupied with the language question as a means of fighting Quebec separatism that it ignored the economic aspirations of the West.

Another factor in the feeling of alienation was the weak, if not non-existent, Western representation in the federal Liberal cabinet and caucus, while the French and Quebec contingent was so strong. The result was that Alberta often felt excluded from the national decision-making process. It had always been sensitive about its minority status in the councils of the federal parties, being outnumbered by members from Ontario and Quebec, but the total lack of representation in the federal government party for such a lengthy period made the situation critical. The solution, as many Albertans saw it, was to enlarge provincial jurisdiction in various areas so that the Western provinces could pursue their own policies. Alberta's main concern was more control over resource matters. Lougheed always saw the solution primarily in expanding the number of government decisions made in Edmonton, and reducing those made in Ottawa and Toronto, although Alberta also supported the alternative of greater inclusion in the national society, such as with a reformed Senate, in which the provinces would have increased representation at the federal level. While the election of the Mulroney Conservative government in 1984 assuaged the alienation of Western Canada to some extent, the Tories also proved to be obsessed with Quebec. The Reform Party was therefore able to press the traditional western complaints with great electoral success in the early 1990s.

The Reform party's original slogan was "The West wants in"—that is, it wanted westerners to play a larger part in federal decisions rather than address issues at the provincial level. In fact, for all the criticism of Ottawa, all probes of the Alberta psyche have found an underlying attachment to Canada.[13] Asked if they think of themselves as a Canadian or an Albertan first, nearly three-quarters of the province's residents opt for the former—above the national average.

Due in part to the province's progressive and "Bible Belt" traditions, its politics have been largely free of scandal, patronage, and corruption, both at the electoral level and in the operation of the government.[14] Scandal did arise on two main occasions, but was considered such a serious matter that it helped defeat the government. Just as the socialist cause was sufficient to overcome the inducements of the Liberal party machine in Saskatchewan, so the succession of evangelical-style causes—agricultural, religious, and anti-socialist — obviated the need for more material political rewards in Alberta.

By most accounts, Alberta falls into the medium category of provinces, along with Saskatchewan, in terms of political trust and efficacy,[15] but with a lower voter turnout rate consistent with the level of other forms of political participation. On the other hand, in Wilson's categorization of provinces based on level of development according to the importance of social class, Alberta ranks high. Religious and ethnic voting patterns have largely been replaced by an ideological one, although this has by no means produced a balance between left and right. The province's political culture is a very conservative one, and the free enterprise spirit is strong. The Conservative party, just as Social Credit before it, receives an overwhelming proportion of the popular vote. Thus a strong but (formerly) pragmatic conservatism coexists with a weak social democratic alternative.

POLITICAL PARTIES

Party System

Alberta has had a unique succession of four periods of one-party dominance: the Liberals, 1905-1921; the United Farmers of Alberta, 1921-1935; Social Credit, 1935-1971; and the Conservatives, since 1971. What is also remarkable is that each time the change in government was dramatic—the spectacular rise of one party coupled with the spectacular demise of another.[16] Even more interesting is that in 1921 and 1935, the new government was formed by a non-traditional party in its first outing, although the new party always seemed to have at least something in common with the discredited government it replaced. Since 1935, the province has been ruled by three principal men, William Aberhart, Ernest Manning, and Peter Lougheed, and the government party has controlled all but a handful of seats. In his book, *Democracy in Alberta*, C.B. Macpherson called the Alberta situation a "quasi-party system," that is, a special kind of one-party dominance characterized by a homogeneous class structure in the province. Macpherson believed that Albertans were almost uniformly petit-bourgeois independent commodity producers who considered themselves held in a quasi-colonial relationship with eastern Canada and exploited by the interests of eastern capitalism. Hence, they elected a strong provincial government to fight against this colonial treatment.[17] Macpherson's interpretation is related to the non-party tradition in the West, which was further enhanced by the anti-party sentiment resulting from the early Liberal party scandal in Alberta. The petit-bourgeois nature of the protest movements allowed an oscillation between radicalism and conservatism, evident in both the UFA and Social Credit periods. This insightful theory includes some important distinctions between the UFA and Social Credit regimes, but has produced many detractors.[18] Macpherson has been faulted for overestimating the dominance of the rural, agricultural population, ignoring provincial class divisions among urban labour, the professional middle class, and the small urban businessmen, and underestimating the degree to which Social Credit was originally supported by the working classes. He may also have over-emphasized the degree of one-party dominance by considering the proportion of seats held by the government party, rather than its percentage of popular vote. Even Macpherson recognized that industrial workers outnumbered farmers after 1941, and the proportion of independent commodity producers has certainly declined since then. Furthermore, the electorate has now opted for the provincial branch of one of the national parties rather than a regional protest party[19] and, admittedly, the degree of one-party dominance declined in recent years.

In spite of these developments, much of what Macpherson observed is still valid—a one-party dominant situation persists and is based to a considerable extent on rejection of perceived colonial treatment by eastern Canada.[20] Thus, even if the class structure of the province is more complicated than Macpherson suggested, the population continues to behave as an almost homogeneous unit. Indeed, it has been argued that, while Alberta at present is not really exploited by the east, residents "still talk as though it were," and the "obsession with real estate" shows a persistence of the petit-bourgeois mentality.[21]

The Maurice Pinard theory postulates that in such a one-party dominant situation, voters dissatisfied with the government will opt for a new force rather than the traditional weak opposition party. This theory seems appropriate to 1921 and 1935. In the context of scandal, internal division, and federal party disruption, the switch from Liberal to UFA in 1921 is not surprising. Similarly, with the Farmer government unable to take effective action in the Depression, the about-face to the magnetic William Aberhart is also understandable. In 1971, Harry Strom had replaced Ernest Manning, and Peter Lougheed presented a much more appealing image without any substantive change; thus the electorate's action on that occasion also appears to be a logical shift. It is said that the overthrow of Social Credit was due to the forces of urbanization, secularization, geographic mobility, and affluence,[22] and that Lougheed added to Social Credit's free-enterprise conservatism by giving it an "urban middle-class respectability, a comfortably vague social conscience and a little political excitement."[23] The three shifts of power in Alberta—1921, 1935, and 1971—coincided with similar changes in most other provinces; what is more striking, then, is that the changes in Alberta were so few.

TABLE 10.5   Party Support in Alberta, 1970-95

	Years in Office	Average Percentage of Vote	Percentage of Seats
Conservatives	24	52.6	78.6
Liberal	–	13.6	7.9
NDP	–	17.9	6.6
Social Credit	1	11.7	5.9

Source: Reports of the *Chief Electoral Officer,* calculations by author.

FIGURE 10.5   Percentage of Vote by Party in Alberta Elections, 1970-1993

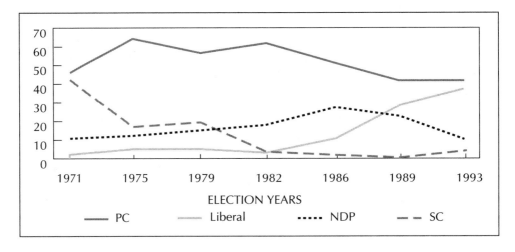

In the mid-1990s, the Conservatives continued to maintain impressive popular support as well as a preponderance of seats. "No party openly calling itself conservative has ever achieved such success under conditions of universal suffrage in the entire history of the world."[24] Social Credit and the Liberals, the leading parties between 1935 and 1967, virtually disappeared in the 1980s, the former for purely provincial reasons, the latter partially because of the policies of its federal counterpart. Until 1989, this left only two sources of opposition to the government: the NDP, which presented a left-wing alternative; and an assortment of separatists, quasi-separatists, and remnants of Social Credit, whose orientation was to the right of the Conservatives. After 1989, the province seemed to be moving towards a three-party system as the Liberals revived, and in 1993 to more of a two-party system as the NDP collapsed.[25]

Party Organization

The distinctive United Farmers of Alberta and Social Credit approaches to party organization and gauging popular will—delegate democracy and plebiscitarian democracy respectively—have already been mentioned. Peter Lougheed constructed the Conservative party almost single-handedly in the 1960s, and it was thus very much under his personal control.[26] Of greater significance, however, is the theory on which his government operated—that in the face of a federal threat and in the absence of internal conflict, there was no need for an official Opposition; democratic nominating conventions and caucus procedures could accommodate all demands.[27] Those who wished to have influence would work through the Conservative party; opposition parties were not part of the policy-making process; and those voters who chose not to join the government party were permitted only to assess the performance every four years or so. It was a kind of plebiscitarian democracy somewhat similar to that of Social Credit.[28] Lougheed even allowed votes to be taken in caucus, since those in the formal legislature were perfunctory.

Federal-Provincial Party Links[29]

Given the tradition of regional protest in Alberta, relations have often been strained between the provincial and federal wings of various parties. The failure to dissociate itself from the federal Liberal party was certainly a factor in the provincial Liberal defeat in 1921, and even the UFA contingent was a distinctive bloc within the national Progressive Party in the 1920s. Since the federal Social Credit party was to a large extent a creation of the Alberta party, relations were generally quite close until the group of Quebec Social Credit MPs suddenly arrived on the scene in 1962.

Alberta has traditionally been the weakest link in the federal Liberal party and it is said that federal patronage was often the main focus of Liberal attention to the province. In the 1950s, the two branches of the Liberal party did not relate well, and provincial Liberal leader Harper Prowse fought with the Alberta federal cabinet minister, George Prudham, who seemed loath to offend the provincial Social Credit regime. In 1966, the provincial Liberal leader resigned over appointments to the federal campaign committee in Alberta,[30] and in 1977 the provincial Liberals officially separated from the federal party. The Co-operative Commonwealth Federation and early NDP were sometimes seen as too federally oriented to have much appeal in the province, but this was less true after a split of some consequence occurred between provincial NDP leader Grant Notley and federal leader Ed Broadbent over the issue of constitutional reform. Finally, Peter Lougheed was perceived as somewhat contemptuous of Joe Clark as federal party leader because Clark had been one of his assistants. However, the premier welcomed the accession of Brian Mulroney to the party leadership (in preference to Clark or Bill Davis), and relations between the two leaders began on a favourable note. Lougheed served notice that he expected the federal government to take action on three fronts: dismantle much of the NEP, pay more attention to agriculture, and pursue free trade with the United States, all of which Mulroney proceeded to do. Later, Don Getty would have occasion to complain about federal Tory policies and attitudes, but free trade and the prospect of an elected Senate generally appeased him. By the time Ralph Klein took over, the federal party had almost ceased to exist and the Reform party had swept the province in the 1993 federal election. Indeed, Getty and Klein did their best to pre-empt entry of the Reform Party into the provincial scene by appropriating its policies, while many Conservative party members and even MLAs belonged to that federal party rather than their own.

Party Leadership

Especially since 1935, leadership has probably been the single most important factor in Alberta politics, with three dominant leaders in 50 years. Indeed, this emphasis on leadership has sometimes bordered on hero worship. William Aberhart served eight years as premier, Ernest Manning, 25, and Peter Lougheed, 14. Aberhart's and Manning's styles were both founded in religion, morality, sincerity, and strength, but while Aberhart has been called a demagogue for his emotional flamboyance and a genius for his organizational skills, Manning would more properly be labelled cautious and rational with a cooler kind of charisma.[31]

Lougheed, on the other hand, acquired the image of a modern manager. Although less spontaneous and somewhat impersonal, he could also be considered charismatic and took to the TV studio whenever the going got tough. Lougheed was often described as ambitious, intense, competitive, and very sensitive to criticism. That his own family lost its fortune during the Great Depression probably explained his obsession with economic diversification in the province. He ran Alberta with an almost iron hand, and this somewhat autocratic style was sometimes held responsible for the large turnover of Tory MLAs and ministers before every election. The praise was lavish when he retired—describing him as the Western strongman who had built his party from scratch, who had implanted his definition of Canada in the new Constitution, and who had made Alberta central to all national issues.[32] Getty, his successor, demonstrated a more affable and easy-going manner which was rare in Alberta politics.[33] His ineffectiveness guaranteed a short term in office, but the party continued in power under the populist Ralph Klein. An overwhelming proportion of the population mystically identified with this chubby, frank, down-to-earth, unsophisticated, and often uninformed ex-broadcaster and ex-mayor of Calgary. Even after he initiated massive cuts in government services to balance the provincial budget almost overnight, his popularity held up remarkably; the public liked his folksy charm and common touch and intuitively trusted him.

Until the election of Ralph Klein as Conservative leader in 1992, parties held traditional leadership conventions in the province. In the 1992 Tory race, each member of the party was allowed to cast a vote, and a second ballot took the form of a preferential vote among the top three contenders. One analysis of the process suggested that the average socio-economic status of such a large group of voters would be lower than that of a delegate convention. When the Liberals replaced Laurence Decore in 1994, they used the televote system previously pioneered by that party in Nova Scotia and British Columbia.

Party Ideology

Since the mid-1940s, Alberta has possessed a predominantly conservative political culture, but before that the UFA was the most radical of any of the farmer movements. Alberta was the first province to establish a wheat pool, for example, although neither the early Liberals nor the UFA nationalized the electric power industry. Aberhart's Social Credit was a unique ideological phenomenon appealing to the dispossessed, promising them debt relief and new purchasing power, but otherwise firmly committed to the capitalist system. It was not surprising, therefore, that Manning should make the Co-operative Commonwealth Federation and socialism the object of his attack after the Socreds had been unsuccessful in their attempt to reform the banks. The "right-wing populism" of Social Credit differed dramatically from the "left-wing populism" of the CCF, and after 1944 Social Credit acquired a more orthodox conservative ideology.[34] Manning came to rely on multinational oil companies to develop the province's petroleum resources, many of his policies were very conservative (for example, no Department of Labour until 1959, rather repressive labour legislation, and opposition to universal medicare), and he used a great deal of right-wing rhetoric. On the other hand, his government generally provided good social services, such as in the areas of education and welfare and an early version of non-universal, privately administered hospital insurance. Then, as he was in the process of retiring as premier, Manning called for political realignment and "social conservatism," but this concept did not really represent any change in ideology—it was simply an appeal to Conservatives to merge with Social Credit. In a study of provincial policy innovations in the 1950-1974 period, Alberta was cited for the first Canadian ombudsman and the first condominium legislation.[35]

Little ideological shift occurred when Lougheed came to power with his slogan "free enterprise which cares." It was merely a switch from the rural right to the urban right and, while Social Credit formed the official Opposition until 1982, it was hard to tell the two parties apart because both were staunchly anti-federal. Lougheed, like Manning, found it difficult to be too conservative with so much revenue at his disposal, and many of the services he introduced were exceptional, especially those relating to senior citizens. About the only difference between Manning and Lougheed was that the former was reluctant to interfere at all with market forces, while the latter's approach to economic development sought to establish an indigenous entrepreneurial class, provided some overall governmental direction, and utilized a number of at least quasi-public agencies. In short, Lougheed engaged in "province-building."[36] On the other hand, Lougheed's reliance on the private sector, his use of health-care premiums, and his insistence on the right of doctors to extra-bill can all be distinguished from the left-wing NDP strategy in Saskatchewan. While the Alberta super-royalties and occasional move to public ownership reflect a superficial similarity to its eastern neighbour, there was a difference in form and function. Rather than supplant private enterprise, as sometimes occurred in Saskatchewan, the Alberta government acted to promote the private sector, "to strengthen the province's hand vis-à-vis outsiders, and to benefit the province's business community and urban middle-class."[37] Alberta was the last province to require the use of seat-belts, the last to outlaw extra-billing by doctors, and one of the few to leave the provision of electricity in private hands. After an indistinct record under Don Getty, the Conservative party turned sharply to the right under Ralph Klein. In an era when even NDP provincial governments were cutting public services, Klein went far beyond all other provinces in his effort to balance the budget in four years. This involved slashing the budgets of all departments.

The Alberta Liberal party has always faced a dilemma: should it espouse its traditional centre or slightly left-of-centre policies or abandon this position in the face of a conservative provincial political culture. In the early 1960s, for example, it was split on the issue of nationalizing private power companies. In more recent years, it has not offered much of an ideological alternative to the Conservatives. The NDP, with its limited audience in the province, strives to represent an ideological alternative—greater public ownership and control of power and other utilities, selective nationalization of resource industries, a pro-union stance on labour legislation, more concern with unemployment, and defence of social programs.

ELECTIONS

Electoral System

Since 1959 Alberta has had only orthodox single-member constituencies; earlier, however, it tried two major electoral variations. From 1921 to 1959, Edmonton and Calgary were multiple-member ridings using proportional representation from 1926 onward.[38] This probably resulted in a greater degree of minority party representation than would otherwise have been the case, especially because opposition to the government came more from the cities than from the countryside. In rural areas, a preferential single-member system was used between 1926 and 1959, but the combined anti-government vote in any constituency was rarely enough to elect an Opposition member. Until 1968, the two large cities were notoriously under-represented and, while they have been treated somewhat more fairly since, Alberta continues to be one of the most extreme examples of rural over-representation.[39] This rural-urban discrepancy can be seen as a deliberate act of the governing parties to enhance their electoral prospects, since the UFA, Social Credit, and now the Tories all fared better in rural than in urban ridings.

The 1990 redistribution of seats in Alberta was even more of a fiasco than in Saskatchewan, and far too complicated to detail here. Suffice it to say that a new act passed in 1990 was widely referred to as a "Gettymander" because its over-representation of rural areas benefited the Conservative party. At the same time that the government appointed an electoral boundaries commission in 1991, it referred the new legislation to the Alberta Court of Appeal. In the wake of the Supreme Court of Canada's decision in Saskatchewan's Carter case, the Alberta Court upheld the Alberta act. But the members of the redistribution commission found the legislation unworkable, the original chairman resigned, and the five commissioners issued five individual reports. In this confused situation, the government reverted to having the electoral map drawn by a committee of the legislature. But when several Opposition members, knowing they would be out-voted in the end, boycotted the committee, the four Conservative members drew the lines themselves.

General rural over-representation thus remains part of the problem with the Alberta system. Constituencies must be within plus or minus 25 percent of the provincial mean, but up to four can be up to 50 percent below the mean. There is also a particular problem with the designation of 43 urban constituencies, five "rurban" seats, and 35 rural seats. If the courts uphold the defective Alberta act, the electoral map drawn in 1992 and used in the 1993 election—which even then had 14 constituencies beyond the 25-percent range—will remain in effect until after the census of 2001.[40]

Alberta is one of three provinces with a semi-permanent voters' list, usually updated 21 months after an election and then annually until the next election. With modern computer technology, further changes in the enumeration process can be expected at both federal and provincial levels.

TABLE 10.6   Representational Disparities in the 1993 Election

Mean number of voters per constituency	19,840
Largest constituency (Calgary-Egmont)	28,498 (+43.5% of the mean)
Smallest constituency (Cardston-Chief Mountain)	9,043 (-54.4% of the mean)
Average variation from mean	15.7%
Constituencies within ± 10% (30 out of 83)	36%
Constituencies within ± 25% (69 out of 83)	83%

Source: *Reports of the Chief Electoral Officer,* calculations by author.

Given the moralistic nature of the UFA and Social Credit, and presence of the province's Bible Belt, evidence of election-day treating was rare after the early Liberal days; indeed, an offer of alcohol could have been counter-productive. There have been few scandals within political parties, although many individual cabinet ministers or ex-ministers sought to enhance their personal financial situations by exploiting their positions within the government.[41] Election expenses legislation was passed in 1977, with disclosure of the source of contributions exceeding $100, limits on the amount of contributions, and a tax credit system. This legislation has not prevented the Conservative party from attracting enormous amounts of corporate contributions. After some controversy about the relationship between such donations and government contracts, the Conservatives amended the legislation in 1984 so that companies controlled by the government, such as those partly owned by the Alberta Energy Company (itself partly owned by the government), were not permitted to make political contributions. Minor changes were also made in 1993.

Voting Behaviour

With the overwhelming majorities that successive governments have achieved in Alberta, even in terms of popular vote, a discussion of provincial voting behaviour becomes to a large extent a question of identifying those who opposed the government. A difference in voting behaviour between the north and south has been evident, with the south voting more heavily first for the UFA, then for Social Credit, and now the Conservatives than the north. The southern part of the province was mainly composed of those of English, German, or Scandinavian extraction, while the north had more Ukrainian and French residents; thus this ethnic cleavage coincided to some extent with the regional one but, in general, the salience of ethnic distinctions has been low.[42] As for religion, it is usually thought that religious fundamentalists were the backbone of Social Credit strength, considering the concentration of Mormons, Baptists, and other related sects in the southern part of the province. These groups were certainly the most intense Socred enthusiasts, while the Roman

Catholic-Liberal link, the Protestant-Conservative connection, and the tendency of NDP supporters to have no affiliation to any church are all found in Alberta as elsewhere.

A variation between urban and rural voters was also evident, urban voters being relatively more likely to oppose a UFA, Social Credit, or Tory government, and residents of small towns and the countryside more likely to support them. Without going as far as Macpherson does in categorizing Alberta as a society made up of one homogeneous class, it is evident that class cleavages "are not as sharply defined" in Alberta as they are in many other provinces.[43] Nevertheless, it would appear that the UFA attracted the less affluent, while more prosperous urban professionals continued to vote Liberal or Conservative in that period, and the same pattern prevailed at least during the Aberhart period of Social Credit. As Ernest Manning became increasingly anti-socialistic in his rhetoric and pro-business in his legislation, the nature of Social Credit support shifted to some extent, although he managed to retain most of his early supporters. The CCF and especially the NDP activists have essentially been a combination of workers and intellectuals, while specific issues brought the party some middle-class votes as well.

In 1967 Peter Lougheed began his assault on the Social Credit bastion, gaining most of his support among the new urban middle class. However, since 1971 it has become difficult to differentiate Tory support—it comes from all regional, ethnic, religious, and economic groups, in almost equal proportions. Opposition strength in this period, whether Liberal or NDP, has been strongest in Edmonton, the northern part of the province, and Calgary.

Alberta has usually shown a strong consistency between federal and provincial voting behaviour. The provincial Liberal period saw mostly Liberal MPs elected, the UFA period had mainly farmer representatives in Ottawa, and for most of the Social Credit era the province largely sent members of that party to the federal parliament. Between the 1958 Diefenbaker revolution and 1971, however, a certain inconsistency developed with the electorate voting Social Credit provincially and Conservative federally, although there was no ideological inconsistency even then. Between 1971 and 1993, the federal and provincial patterns were almost identically Tory blue. In 1993, Albertans re-elected the provincial Conservatives and then sent a large delegation of ideologically similar Reformers to Ottawa.

PRESSURE GROUPS AND THE MEDIA

Pressure Groups

The main interest group in early Alberta was the United Farmers organization which became both a party and the government in 1921. It briefly affiliated with the Co-operative Commonwealth Federation after 1933 and a regrouping in 1948 produced the Farmers Union of Alberta, which established a friendly relationship with Social Credit.[44] In 1969 Unifarm emerged to represent more prosperous farmers; in the same year the National Farmers Union was formed and began to set up locals in the province. Unifarm enjoyed good relations with the provincial government, although relations between the NFU and the government were not so close. In the post-1947 period two more influential groups were established, the Canadian Petroleum Association and the Independent Petroleum Association of Canada. The former represents the major multinationals, while the latter speaks for the smaller Canadian firms. Of course, both the Manning and Lougheed governments dealt closely with individual petroleum companies. The Alberta Federation of Labour has become more vocal in recent years and its leadership at least is more supportive of the NDP. Nevertheless, its membership is relatively small and it has rarely had much influence with the Tory government.[45] The Alberta Teachers' Association and the Alberta Chamber of Commerce are influential, as are the municipal associations—the Association of Municipal Districts and Counties and the Urban Municipalities Association. The Alberta Healthcare Association, the Association canadienne-française de l'Alberta, the Métis Association of Alberta, and the United Nurses of Alberta are among many others that could be mentioned.[46]

TABLE 10.7   Leading Alberta Pressure Groups

Peak Business	Alberta Chamber of Commerce
Industrial	Canadian Petroleum Association
	Independent Petroleum Association of Canada
	Alberta Chamber of Resources
	Alberta Construction Association
	Alberta Forest Products Association
	Alberta Home Builders' Association
	Canadian Gas Association
	Tourism Industry Association of Alberta
Labour	Alberta Federation of Labour
	United Nurses of Alberta
Agriculture	Unifarm
	National Farmers Union
	Western Cattlemen's Association
Professional	Alberta Medical Association
	Law Society of Alberta
	Association of Professional Engineers, Geologists, and Geophysicists of Alberta
	Alberta Teachers' Association
Ethnic	Association canadienne-française de l'Alberta
	Indian Association of Alberta
	Métis Association of Alberta

TABLE 10.7 continued

Institutional	Alberta Urban Municipalities Association
	Alberta School Boards Association
	Alberta Association of Municipal Districts and Counties
	Alberta Healthcare Association
Environmental	Friends of the Oldman River
Public Interest	Alberta Human Rights and Civil Liberties Association

The Media[47]

The Southam-owned *Calgary Herald* and *Edmonton Journal* are the province's leading newspapers, but both cities also publish a *Sun* affiliated with the Toronto paper of the same name. These and other dailies are listed in Table 10.8. The Canadian Broadcasting Corporation has an English television station in Edmonton and three affiliated stations in the province, English radio stations in the two major cities, and French radio and television stations in Edmonton. The CTV Network has stations in both Calgary and Edmonton, and the province hosts a number of private television stations, many private radio stations, and one weekly French newspaper.

TABLE 10.8   Daily Newspapers in Alberta, 1994

	Circulation	Chain
Calgary Herald	117,190	Southam
Calgary Sun	71,059	*Toronto Sun*
Edmonton Journal	161,376	Southam
Edmonton Sun	80,203	*Toronto Sun*
Fort McMurray Today	5,413	Bowes
Grande Prairie Herald-Tribune	8,331	Bowes
Lethbridge Herald	24,350	Thomson
Medicine Hat News	14,484	Southam
Red Deer Advocate	21,003	Independent

Source: *Canadian Advertising Rates and Data* (August, 1994).

GOVERNMENT INSTITUTIONS

The distinctiveness of government institutions in Alberta is largely related to the lop-sided legislative majorities characteristic of the province. It also reflects the province's very conservative political culture.

Executive

The role of the lieutenant-governor has been rather controversial in Alberta on several occasions, especially in the first few years of the Social Credit regime.[48] Prime Minister Wilfrid Laurier was determined to establish Alberta on a good Liberal foundation, just as with Saskatchewan, so he directed the new lieutenant-governor to select Alexander Rutherford, the provincial Liberal leader, as the first premier. In 1937 lieutenant-governor J.C. Bowen reserved three pieces of Social Credit legislation for the consideration of the federal King cabinet. Alberta challenged the constitutionality of the powers of reservation and disallowance, and the Supreme Court of Canada ruled that (at least in law) these powers still existed. The province reacted by closing the lieutenant-governor's residence and curtailing services available to him.

Prior to the election of the Conservatives in 1971, the cabinet functioned mainly as a collective decision-making body, but Lougheed introduced cabinet committees about the same time as most other provinces. Two regimes later, the key cabinet committee in Ralph Klein's Alberta is the agenda and priorities committee, chaired by the premier. The provincial treasurer chairs the Treasury Board, but the four cabinet policy committees are rather inexplicably chaired by Conservative backbenchers, with ministers functioning as vice-chairs: financial planning, community services, agriculture and rural development, and natural resources and sustainable development. Getty's cabinet once reached the size of 27, but Klein's contained only 17 members in 1994. The cabinet is assisted by the executive council office, headed by the deputy minister, and the premier's office, presided over by the executive director.

Legislature

The Alberta legislature was created with 25 seats and has grown gradually with the province's population to its current complement of 83.[49] Alberta has been characterized by massive government majorities in the legislature, especially in the Social Credit (1935-1971) and Conservative (1971-present) periods. This has meant the cabinet had little difficulty effecting whatever changes it wished, and opposition influence was virtually nil. Occasionally there would emerge an impressive opposition party leader—Harper Prowse (Liberal, 1948-58), Peter Lougheed (Conservative, 1967-71), or Grant Notley (NDP, 1971-84)—who by sheer eloquence and persistence would have some impact on government policy. There were never enough bodies on the opposition side, however, to alter government initiatives by voting power alone, nor even enough members to make effective use of the normal opposition devices such as question period, committee work, filibusters, or examination of the estimates. With so many members on the government side, those without ministerial appointments had little to do and few regarded their legislative duties as a full-time job. Consequently, Alberta had a medium level of remuneration until a controversial

30-percent raise in 1989, which presumably reflected an increasing workload. Over the 1990-93 period, the Alberta legislature sat more days per annum than that of any other province. In 1994, members received a taxable indemnity of $36,420 and a non-taxable allowance of $18,210, along with many other benefits and allowances. Given their sparse numbers in the past, it was crucial that the Opposition be given adequate resources, a point that led to disputes over who would be designated official Opposition after the 1982 election of two NDP members, and two Independents, who had formerly been Social Credit MLAs. After much suspense, the Speaker recognized the NDP as official Opposition and it received the leader's indemnity and additional support funds. In short, it has been easy to overlook the Alberta legislature because, to an even greater extent than in other provinces, almost all of the action takes place in the executive branch.

To denigrate the position of the legislature even further, Alberta flirted with the concept of direct democracy even before the UFA came to power.[50] The Sifton Liberal government adopted the Direct Legislation Act in 1913 which permitted the government to hold a plebiscite on a law of its choosing, and required it to respond to a petition from the electorate requesting a vote on a legislative proposal. Unlike in Manitoba, the law was not challenged in the courts, presumably because it did not make the electorate's decision binding. A 1931 UFA amendment allowed the government to refer a question to the public before taking legislative action. Under this law, seven plebiscites were held, four on liquor (1915, 1920, 1923, and 1957), two on daylight saving time (1967 and 1971), and one in 1948 which concerned public ownership of power companies. The statute was amended in 1958 and the new legislation conformed to that of other provinces by providing for popular consultation primarily on the question of whether liquor should be sold in the community. In 1993, a law made a provincial referendum compulsory on changes to the Constitution.

Over the last 25 years, some attempt has been made to improve legislative operations. A hansard was finally instituted in 1972; there is a daily question period; an active public accounts committee has an Opposition chair and is supported by an independent auditor general; bills are scrutinized in committee of the whole; and the estimates are examined for 25 days in committee of supply. Most work is done in the government caucus or legislative chamber, with the only standing committees in 1994 as follows: Heritage Savings Trust Fund Act; law and regulations; legislative offices; members' services; private bills; privileges and elections, standing orders and printing; and public accounts.

At least on the surface, the Alberta legislature made revolutionary changes in its operations over the 1992-93 period.[51] These included electing the Speaker by secret ballot, allowing private members' bills and motions to come to a vote, allowing the Opposition leader to designate five departments' estimates for examination in supply subcommittees, a change in the timetable of sittings, and a daily slot for members' statements. These sweeping reforms sprang from an all-party agreement, and the government and Opposition house leaders also expressed a willingness to allow free votes. Whether such changes actually increased the significance of private members or reduced the control of the cabinet remained to be seen; at least they gave the Opposition more warning of what the government wants the legislature to approve. Of perhaps greater immediate impact was the fact the legislature discontinued pensions for MLAs who retired or were defeated after 1989.

Bureaucracy

Alberta employs about 35,000 people in departments and agencies, another 5,000 in government business enterprises, and a further 40,000 in the wider public sector. As in most provinces, Alberta's bureaucracy was not particularly impressive until the post-1971 period. It had a civil service commission as early as 1918, and the UFA abolished the patronage system. The Aberhart regime brought in certain Social Credit experts and, under Manning's leadership, a better bureaucracy slowly emerged. However, the civil service act itself was never strong, and was weakened by amendments passed in 1947, 1954, 1957, and 1959.[52] Alberta has a relatively large public service as well as an enormous number of regulatory agencies, and in 1967 was the first province to appoint an ombudsman. The prohibition of strikes in the public service has become a controversial issue in recent years, and the province was one of the last to pass a freedom of information act. Alberta maintains offices in such key financial and business centres as Hong Kong, London, New York, Seoul, and Tokyo.

TABLE 10.9   Alberta Government Departments, 1994

Advanced Education and Career Development
Agriculture, Food and Rural Development
Community Development
Economic Development and Tourism
Education
Energy
Environmental Protection
Family and Social Services
Health
Justice
Labour
Municipal Affairs
Public Works, Supply and Services
Transportation and Utilities
Treasury

TABLE 10.10 Leading Alberta Agencies, Boards, Commissions and Crown Corporations, 1994

Crown Corporations	Alberta Agricultural Development Corporation
	Alberta Heritage Savings Trust Fund
	Alberta Mortgage and Housing Corporation
	Alberta Municipal Finance Corporation
	Alberta Opportunity Company
	Alberta Resources Railway
	Alberta Treasury Branches
Agencies, Boards, and Commissions	Alberta Advisory Council on Women's Issues
	Alberta Energy and Utilities Board
	Alberta Human Rights Commission
	Alberta Liquor Control Board
	Environmental Appeal Board
	Labour Relations Board
	Municipal Government Board
	Workers' Compensation Board

Alberta's large number of agencies, boards, and commissions has continued since Manning's day and may reflect a conservative approach to government which preferred those forms of organization to a proliferation of regular departments. Some of the more distinctive agencies include the Alberta Hail and Crop Insurance Corporation, the Alberta Mortgage and Housing Corporation, the Alberta Opportunity Company, the Alberta Research Council, and the Oil Sands Technology and Research Authority. An inheritance from the Social Credit years is the network of Treasury Branches, a kind of provincial bank. While the early Liberal period established Alberta Government Telephones as a Crown corporation, it was privatized by Getty in 1990. The Lougheed government nationalized Pacific Western Airlines in 1974 (although it was privatized in 1983-84), but electric power has been left in private hands. Among the significant semi-independent agencies is the powerful Alberta Energy and Utilities Board, a recent combination of the Energy Resources Conservation Board and the Public Utilities Board. Another is the Petroleum Marketing Commission, which has broad powers relating to the sale of oil and gas produced from the province's Crown leaseholds, and a third is the Alberta Oil Sands Equity. Mention should also be made of the well-known Alberta Heritage Savings Trust Fund, established in 1976 from a portion of the province's revenues from oil and natural gas royalties. The heritage fund officially stood at about $11.5 billion in 1994, with 53 percent of its funds invested in corporate securities (such as TransCanada Pipelines, Nova Corp., Alberta Energy Company Ltd., and Canadian Western Bank), loans to other provinces (the four Atlantic provinces and Hydro-Québec), and project investments (Bi-Provincial Upgrader, Al-Pac, the Prince Rupert grain terminal, Millar Western pulp, and Syncrude). The other 47 percent is invested in the securities of the Alberta government and Crown corporations (Alberta Opportunity Company, Alberta Agricultural Development Corp, Alberta Municipal Finance Corp., and Alberta Mortgage and Housing Corp.). The heritage fund also contributes to capital projects within the province but which are not considered part of its assets—medical research, hospitals, irrigation, parks, and rail hopper cars, to name a few. The fund lacks independence, however, because the cabinet makes investment decisions after receiving advice from the Treasury and private sector consultants.

Judiciary

The Alberta judiciary consists of the Court of Appeal and the Court of Queen's Bench which resulted from a 1978 amalgamation of district courts and the trial division of the Supreme Court. There are also a large number of provincial courts, plus small claims courts in Calgary and Edmonton, and family and juvenile courts in all the cities. As in several other provinces, Alberta judges went to court to challenge a five-percent cut in their salaries.

Municipal Government[53]

Municipal government in Alberta began with cities, towns, and villages, but by 1912 a new municipal system was established which included rural municipalities and local improvement districts. After 1942 the government encouraged amalgamation as a means of reducing the number of rural units, now called municipal districts, and in 1950 it created the Alberta county, a unique rural municipal structure. The county is a one-tier rural government combining educational responsibilities with usual municipal functions, and the majority of the populated rural areas are organized into 30 such units. The province currently has a total of 16 cities, and Calgary and Edmonton have become very large one-tier metropolitan centres. Edmonton still has large suburbs that remain independent entities: Fort Saskatchewan, Spruce Grove, and St. Albert are cities in their own right. A major new municipal government act in 1995 deregulated much of the provincial supervision of municipal operations. At the same time, the provincial government reduced the number of school boards to 60 from 140, assumed the financing responsibility, and even appointed the superintendents.

POLITICAL EVOLUTION

1870-1970[54]

Between 1869 and 1905, Alberta and Saskatchewan formed a single territory and, as outlined in the previous chapter, Ottawa appointed a territorial lieutenant-governor and a council in 1875. It created a legislative assembly in 1888;

recognized F.W.G. Haultain, representative of an Alberta constituency, as premier in 1891; and granted responsible government in 1897. The territorial capital was Regina because that part of the region had a larger population. Alberta was not involved in the Riel Rebellion of 1885; instead, its principal interaction with aboriginal peoples consisted of Treaties 6 and 7 in 1876-77 under which the natives surrendered central and southern Alberta in return for reserves and other "benefits." These "benefits" were such that the Natives endured long periods of destitution in following years. After 1885, the population of the territories grew substantially as the the Canadian Pacific Railway and federal Homestead policy attracted increasing numbers of settlers, particularly Germans, Ukrainians, French, Scandinavians, and among other Americans, Mormons.

As discussed in the preceding chapter, the controversies surrounding the establishment of the two new provinces included separate schools, federal retention of natural resources, and the creation of two provinces rather than one. The lieutenant-governor chose as the new Liberal Alberta premier Alexander Rutherford, a Strathcona lawyer who had been a member of the Northwest Territories Legislative Assembly since 1902. Edmonton was selected as provincial capital over its more Conservative southern rival, Calgary. Rutherford took office, named a Liberal cabinet, and won an overwhelming victory in the first Alberta provincial election in November 1905. The provincial Tories were led by R.B. Bennett, a Calgary lawyer who was solicitor for the highly unpopular CPR as well as other companies such as Bell Telephone. Bennett did not even win his own seat.

The 1905-09 period was one of establishing the institutional foundations of the province such as government departments, public buildings, the legal system, and schools. Calgary expected to be named the location of the provincial university, but in 1908 Edmonton was also the victor in this competition. Rutherford built the usual public works, such as roads and bridges, and in the labour field brought in workmen's compensation and an eight-hour day for coal mines. As in other prairie provinces, the government took over the telephone service from the Bell company because of dissatisfaction with the company's monopoly position and its lack of interest in rural expansion. The Rutherford government's chief concern, however, was railway construction. A second transcontinental line, later to be incorporated into the Canadian National system, was built through Edmonton. The Rutherford government guaranteed bonds for various railway companies to establish a network of branch lines throughout the province. This included the Alberta and Great Waterways (AGW) Railway, a 350-mile line from Edmonton to Fort McMurray, built on terms that were even more generous than usual.

Almost immediately after the 1909 election, controversy emerged regarding the awarding of the Alberta and Great Waterways Railway contract.[55] The government appointed a royal commission to investigate the deal but, even before it reported, the staunchly Liberal lieutenant-governor persuaded Rutherford to step down to minimize the damage to the party, writing to Laurier as follows: "I am afraid that I had to do a few things that a Lieutenant-Governor is not supposed to do, but I think I was justified by the results."[56] He selected Arthur Sifton, chief justice of the province, to be premier. The AGW issue remained prominent for years, especially as it lost money, and the province assumed control after prolonged and unsuccessful litigation. That experience did not prevent Sifton from guaranteeing the finances of even more rail lines. In 1911 several provincial members moved to the federal scene, including R.B. Bennett; in 1912 the majestic new legislative building opened; and in 1913, the Sifton government implemented several resolutions of the United Farmers of Alberta convention, including a direct legislation act, agricultural schools, and the incorporation of the Alberta Farmers Cooperative Elevator Co.

The First World War broke out after Sifton was re-elected in 1913, and provincial politics generally took a backseat to national and international issues. As in other provinces, the war effort aided the temperance and suffragette movements. Sifton enacted prohibition in Alberta in 1916 as a result of the direct legislation act, and granted women the right to vote. He also established a provincial police force which found itself saddled with the difficult task of enforcing Prohibition. The government introduced other initiatives such as farm credit legislation largely at the behest of the United Farmers, and in 1917 the Alberta Farmers Cooperative Elevator Co. joined the United Grain Growers chain. Oil and natural gas were found at Turner Valley in 1914, and other natural resources such as minerals, forests, and electric power were also developed.

Because Sifton provided strong leadership and satisfied farmer demands, and because the electoral map continued to favour the government, the Liberal party machine was almost as effective as its legendary counterpart in Saskatchewan.[57] Thus, the 1917 election returned a majority of Liberals, two representatives of the Non-Partisan League, and, for the first time in Canada, two women. Sifton then left to join the federal Union Government and, deprived of his commanding presence, the provincial Liberal party soon began to disintegrate. His successor, Charles Stewart, was a popular farmer but lacked the skill required to keep the various factions united. This was especially difficult after a split occurred in the federal Liberal party between conscriptionists and Laurier supporters. Stewart was also unable to deflect criticism of the national Liberal policy regarding tariffs, freight rates, and retention of natural resources, and the post-war recession was a blot on all incumbent governments, federal or provincial. Within the province, the Stewart government set up the Alberta Research Council but was plagued by continuing railway difficulties and the taint of patronage and corruption. The leaderless provincial Conservatives were even more divided, and were condemned for the federal party's cancellation of the conscription exemptions for farmers' sons. With both parties discredited, the time was ripe for the entry of a new, agrarian party.

The United Farmers of Alberta organization was formed in 1909. Given that farmers represented the largest single interest in the province and that a substantial proportion belonged to the UFA, successive Liberal governments were only too ready to respond to the organization's demands. The relationship between the government and the farmers' group during the Sifton and Stewart periods had been almost as close as in Saskatchewan, but, like their brethren in Manitoba and Ontario, Alberta farmers also opted for direct electoral activity. One reason for the difference in strategy was the leadership of Henry Wise Wood, president of the UFA from 1916 to 1930,[58] a transplanted American wheat farmer who believed that farmers should co-operate and present a united front in their economic and political environments. Suspicious of political parties that claimed to be all-inclusive, he persuaded the UFA to take political action as an occupational group rather than an orthodox party. The organization's other theorist was William Irvine, who sat in parliament at various times as a Labour, UFA, and CCF MP.[59] The new political organization ran candidates in the 1921 provincial election and, even though it had no leader, was successful in winning 38 seats to the Liberals' 15. Wood chose to remain head of the extra-parliamentary organization, so the premiership fell to Herbert Greenfield, a British-born farmer. In the federal election held shortly afterwards, the UFA won 11 of 12 Alberta seats.

The first UFA cabinet contained J.E. Brownlee as attorney general, and one Labour member, even though the UFA had an overwhelming majority in the legislature. In the early years it had some difficulty reconciling the constraints of cabinet government with the principle of delegate democracy at the heart of the UFA organization. In 1925, the caucus informed Premier Greenfield that it preferred Brownlee as leader and, without much resistance, the transition was made. Described as a "man of rare firmness, intelligence and integrity," Brownlee was a much stronger premier than Greenfield, and remained in the position until 1934.[60]

The outstanding achievement of the UFA era was probably the establishment of the Alberta Wheat Pool in 1923. The wheat pool also demonstrated that although the UFA "may have seemed political novices, they were not organizational novices."[61] Wood, Greenfield, and Brownlee were central to the idea, and invited an eloquent American expert, Aaron Sapiro, to solicit support for the plan. In a few months' time, 27,000 farmers representing 45 percent of the total wheat acreage in Alberta had signed a contract with the pool. This co-operative organization offered farmers several benefits: a fairer price, an advance payment, and a better marketing system. Sapiro later helped establish the Saskatchewan and Manitoba wheat pools. All three provincial pools then incorporated the Canadian Cooperative Wheat Pool Ltd. which would handle and market all grain received at terminal elevators, and which some observers described as "the greatest agricultural cooperative organization in the world."[62]

Other legislative achievements relating to agriculture in this period were successful dairy, egg and poultry, and livestock pools. The UFA also claimed that its pressure on the federal government resulted in lower freight rates and improved grain handling facilities in Vancouver. In non-agricultural areas, the government ended the unenforceable Prohibition in 1923 and abandoned the provincial police force in the early 1930s. The UFA government joined with the other prairie provincial governments to gain control over its natural resources in 1930, and managed to sell the AGW and other northern railways to the CN and CP systems and remove that albatross from the province's neck. The UFA also benefited from Brownlee's administrative competence and, by rewarding merit rather than using patronage in government appointments, it increased the efficiency of government departments, railways, and the telephone system. Neither the Liberal nor Conservative parties mounted a sustained effort during this period, and the UFA was easily re-elected in 1926 and 1930.[63]

After the Great Depression began in 1929, the province was almost exclusively concerned with the issue of debt. The provincial government had to bail out the Alberta Wheat Pool as well as municipalities, and placed much reliance on federal relief funds. Although Alberta was marginally less affected than Saskatchewan, it was still badly hit and the problem was felt most deeply by farmers already in debt. On the assumption that prices would remain strong, farmers had borrowed heavily for years to expand their operations and buy machinery. While they had long demanded a moratorium on their debts, and a debt adjustment act permitted a one-year delay before foreclosure, the urgency increased after 1929 when grain prices fell precipitously. In 1931, the government established the Alberta Rural Credit Corporation and temporarily suspended the Tax Recovery Act. In 1933, it passed a new debt adjustment act similar to legislation enacted in Saskatchewan and Manitoba. The government also established a new provincial income tax and increased other taxes to help cover interest payments on the provincial debt.

Two other developments characterized this period. The first was a bewildering array of fundamentalist evangelical organizations which established Bible schools and colleges and began to broadcast radio programs in the mid-1920s. The most successful was the Calgary Prophetic Bible Institute's William Aberhart, who had a weekly Sunday program. The second development, related to the debt moratorium issue, was the emergence of theories on monetary reform. Of all the schemes proposed over the years, mostly by former Americans, the one that attracted most attention was Social Credit as espoused by a Scottish engineer, Major C.H. Douglas. Aberhart accidentally came across Douglas' writings in 1932 and began to incorporate them into his weekly religious program. Although Premier Brownlee frowned on Douglas' theories and felt that, in any case, monetary reform was beyond provincial jurisdiction, more and more UFA members became interested in Social Credit. In 1934 the premier was forced to invite Aberhart and Douglas to present their views to a legislative committee.

Meanwhile, Brownlee faced another problem—he was the defendant in a civil court action, accused of seducing a girl whom his family had befriended and whom he had helped to obtain a government job. Brownlee denied the allegations, and judges and juries over-ruled each other all the way to the Supreme Court of Canada. Whether or not there was any truth to the charges, given the evangelical atmosphere of the province Brownlee could not continue as premier. In July 1934 he resigned and was succeeded by a farmer, R.G. Reid.[64]

To understand the strange and dramatic rise of Social Credit in 1935, one must first imagine the impact of the Depression on Alberta.[65] The economy was devastated; farmers were hopelessly in debt; foreclosures were common; wheat prices were ridiculously low; and very few people had cash. The UFA was discredited by its inaction in the circumstances and by the allegations of scandal. Into this chaotic economic situation marched William Aberhart, high school principal during the week and radio evangelist on Sunday. As the Depression wore on, he gradually increased the proportion of Social Credit content in his weekly broadcast, a program which eventually reached an estimated audience of half a million people. He developed his own simplified version of Douglas' work which he skilfully fitted to the realities of Alberta society at the time. Aberhart was an organization man, with tremendous energy, drive, and self-confidence, and he encouraged his religious followers to set up Social Credit study groups around the province. He and disciple, Ernest Manning, would travel around to address these gatherings on weekends and school holidays. Aberhart was a powerful performer, both on radio and on the public platform, a master of crowd psychology, and charismatic in the true sense of the term. He was a "born showman," and "the great spellbinder never failed to lift his audiences to a state of hysterical enthusiasm."[66] Graced with a sonorous voice, he employed charts, diagrams, political skits, and all sorts of popular analogies and slogans to catch people's attention. He aroused such great passion that many of his followers regarded him as a deity and would brook no criticism of their new saviour. Others saw him as a hypocrite who deliberately set out to win power through the use religion,[67] and called him "Bible Bill" with derision. There seems little doubt that he was sensitive to the human misery around him, but that he also had an authoritarian personality in which emotion and fundamentalism were prominent.

In addition to Aberhart's charisma, Social Credit offered an explanation of the economic conditions, a remedy, and an invitation to participate in a program of social action. His explanation of the Depression relieved people of any feeling of personal guilt by identifying as the villains the banks, the "50 Bigshots," the East, the old-line parties, the federal government (and in its wilder moments, an international Communist-Jewish conspiracy). Social Credit offered a simple, partial remedy which involved tinkering with the banking system, and a reform of credit and interest policies. It did not advocate a wholesale transformation of capitalism or disruption of the basic tenet of private ownership—just the promise of a monthly $25 dividend for each Albertan, an electrifying amount given the economic circumstances. At the height of the movement's popularity, over 1,600 study groups in the province examined Aberhart's proposals, giving the participants a feeling of political efficacy.

When the 1935 election came, Aberhart transformed his religious-economic reform following into a political party. He chose all the Social Credit candidates, but declined to stand for election himself. His mammoth picnics opened and closed with a hymn, and he often told his admirers that they did not have to understand the theory of Social Credit to vote for the party—all could be safely left in the hands of the experts. The appeal of Social Credit spread quickly as people linked the economic theory with divine inspiration, viewing Aberhart as a man of God, the prophet above politics. With the Liberals and Conservatives not considered viable alternatives, and with the UFA in disrepute, the Alberta electorate opted en masse for a party less than one year old, just as it had done in 1921. Alberta became another province where an election at the depth of the Depression wiped out the incumbent government, as Social Credit won 56 seats, the Liberals, five, and the Conservatives, two.

Aberhart's governmental performance over the next eight years varied considerably from what he had promised. Manning was made provincial secretary and minister of Trade and Industry, while the premier kept the Education portfolio for himself and won a seat in a by-election. He was bailed out of some immediate financial commitments with $2 million in credit from Ottawa, but in 1936 the provincial government defaulted on nearly $3-million worth of debt. It introduced an austerity budget and halved the interest payable on all funded debt. The latter was a blow to low-income Albertans living off the interest from such bonds as well as to the province's credit rating for years to come. In the same year, the government introduced a system of provincial currency called "prosperity certificates" or "scrip." Each certificate was supposed to be worth $1, but acquired value only if holders affixed a one-cent stamp on the back of it every Thursday so that after two years (104 weeks), the scrip could be redeemed for real money. Aberhart decreed that the certificates would be used in lieu of money in certain government transactions, but most people regarded them as "funny money," and he had to abandon the whole scheme within a year. Another Social Credit measure released farmers from liability for debt and mortgage payments but this, as well as three bills which attempted to cut interest rates, was thrown out by the courts. Aberhart repealed the Recall Act in 1937 just as a petition was circulating in his own constituency to recall him because of lack of interest in local affairs. Among the few early initiatives that remained on the books was an hours of work act.

In 1937 Aberhart also faced a serious backbenchers' revolt; about half the caucus was upset that after 18 months in office there was still no monthly dividend, nor had other Social Credit promises been carried out.[68] Aberhart survived by creating a Social Credit Board ("the experts"), a five-man body with full power to establish Social Credit in the province, but the government encountered great difficulty with the legislation designed to achieve this objective.[69] The Bank Taxation Act was clearly intended to drive the chartered banks out of the province and was declared unconstitutional by the courts. The Bank Employees

Civil Rights Act and the Judicature Act, which forbade any constitutional challenge to provincial legislation without the cabinet's consent, were both disallowed by the federal cabinet, as were three related Social Credit measures. When Aberhart introduced two banking bills a second time, along with the Accurate News and Information Act or "press bill," the lieutenant-governor reserved all three for the consideration of the federal cabinet. The press bill was a reaction to the hostile reception given the new government by most of the province's newspapers. It would have required newspapers to print corrections at the direction of the government and to supply the source of any information published, a clear violation of the principle of freedom of the press. When the attorney general refused to vouch for the validity of the laws before the lieutenant-governor, Aberhart dismissed him and assumed the position (normally held by a lawyer) himself. The invalidating actions of the federal cabinet and Supreme Court did not necessarily embarrass Aberhart in the eyes of the public; to some extent they only confirmed the power which outside institutions held over the province. One Social Credit measure allowed to stand provided for a kind of provincial bank, the Treasury Branches, soon established throughout the province. Little more was heard of Social Credit after 1937 although many people still anticipated their monthly dividend.

On a more positive note, the government overhauled the education system, passed more labour legislation, and provided free hospital treatment for maternity, tuberculosis, cancer, and polio cases. Also significant was the creation of the Oil and Gas Conservation Board which supervised and regulated all exploration and production of oil and natural gas in the province.

On the question of the decision-making process in the Aberhart period, Macpherson termed this era one of "plebiscitarian democracy," in that "people gave up their right of decision, criticism and proposal, in return for the promise that everything will be done to implement the general will."[70] Aberhart rarely spoke in the legislature himself, partly because he preferred forums where no one could talk back, and partly because he was implementing the general will which needed no discussion. He ran the cabinet, caucus, and party in the same autocratic manner he had operated his high school. This plebiscitarianism extended to the electorate who were told to vote for results, not methods, for the means would be left to the experts. Some people saw traces of fascism in this invitation to so blindly follow a leader.

The economic situation reached its nadir in 1937, but recovered somewhat after the outbreak of the Second World War, and the government's record was acceptable in many respects. Liberal and Conservative opponents of the Aberhart regime collected under the "Unity Party" umbrella to fight the 1940 election, but had no leader or positive policy alternative. By this time the CCF had also entered the scene, although it suffered somewhat from its affiliation with the discredited UFA.[71] The Unity forces received almost as much popular support as the government, but Aberhart won a majority of seats.

The next three years were relatively uneventful except for more federal-provincial conflict. Ottawa exercised its power of disallowance again in 1942 and 1943 to invalidate several more Alberta bills relating to debts, while Aberhart was unco-operative about the Rowell-Sirois commission, set up by Ottawa to study federal-provincial finance, and the constitutional amendment regarding unemployment insurance. Aberhart died in 1943, and his political and religious disciple Ernest Manning became leader of both the political and religious organizations.

Manning faced an early election and, with Social Credit theory effectively laid to rest, he needed to find a new platform for the party. Because CCF support was at its height across the country, he found a ready target: Social Credit would lead the fight against socialism. Although the two doctrines took organizational form in Canada at about the same time, and although both were in large part a response to the Depression and designed to help the dispossessed, they soon parted company and became vehemently antagonistic toward each other. In essence, the CCF was against all the abuses of capitalism, if not capitalism itself, while Social Credit has profoundly committed to the capitalist system, except for the role of the banks. A certain contradiction always existed between Manning's anti-socialist rhetoric and the actions of his government, which generally speaking provided a high level of public services, but the two groups differed fundamentally in their attitude towards internal democracy. Even though the religious credentials of the CCF were as solid as Manning's (although the social gospel origins of the CCF were quite a different brand of religion), he saw the CCF as godless and materialistic. The 1944 CCF victory in Saskatchewan occurred during the Alberta election campaign, and this made Manning's case concerning the socialist threat more persuasive. Manning's constant repetition of the anti-socialist message over the years likely contributed to the subsequent conservatism of Alberta's political culture, his populist origins and religious connections giving the charge credibility.[72] He captured 51 seats and 52 percent of the vote, but the CCF had its best showing in the history of the province, gaining 25 percent of the vote and electing two members.

Manning's first priority after the election was to restore the province to financial respectability. He gave up trying to establish social credit at the provincial level, and proceeded to undo the damage that the theory had already caused. This involved reimbursing bondholders for debts upon which the province had defaulted and for the interest payments which had been reduced or left unpaid. Backed by a combination of new government revenues from the petroleum industry, federal contributions, and a new issue of provincial bonds, the Provincial Securities Exchange Act of 1944 essentially rectified the situation. This was followed, however, by one last attempt to establish Social Credit in the form of the Alberta Bill of Rights of 1946 which provided for credit certificates and a board of credit commissioners. The scheme was quickly deemed unconstitutional by the courts. Finally, after an embarrassing anti-Semitic report in 1947, Manning abolished the social credit board, and all that remained of Douglas' and

Aberhart's theories were periodic outbursts from party fundamentalists about the evils of the banks.

Having rid himself of the last vestiges of Social Credit, and having established the defence of private enterprise against the threat of socialism as the new raison d'être for his party, Manning's next course of action became clear when oil was discovered at Leduc in 1947, and later at other locations across the province. The rest of his tenure focused on the developing of the petroleum industry. The basic strategy was to open the province's doors to private and mostly foreign investors, reflecting Manning's own ideological orientation which equated the interests of the multi-national oil companies with those of the province. He based the Alberta regulatory system on American private ownership precedents, especially those of Texas, and his strategy of rapid development favoured the largest U.S. companies.[73] Such companies had to obtain approval from an oil and gas conservation board to test drill, while the government received rent for such drilling rights and collected production royalties once the oil began to flow.

The province became wealthy almost overnight, and most residents were satisfied with the resulting low level of individual taxation and high level of services. On the other hand, some raised questions about the rate of taxation on the oil companies, the possibility of public ownership, the lack of encouragement for private Canadian firms in the industry, and the absence of requirements to use Alberta manpower, management, or supplies.[74] Calgary continued to house the Canadian headquarters of the oil companies, but Edmonton was now more central to the actual production and refining of petroleum, and this gave rise to a rivalry between the two cities for the title of "Canada's Oil Capital."

On the basis of the new oil wealth, Manning had no trouble in the 1948 election, although it coincided with a public power ownership plebiscite that was narrowly defeated with government opposition. By then the province could afford to provide free medical and hospital care for those receiving old age assistance, mothers' allowances, and some disability pensions.

Liberal leader Harper Prowse was the only opposition politician to give Manning much trouble during his 25 years as premier. To most observers, Manning seemed more sincere about religion than Aberhart, and received less criticism for using his "Back to the Bible Hour" broadcasts to further his political aims. Prowse, however, felt that Manning's religiosity was a sham and, given their personality differences and Prowse's oratorical talent, an intense bitterness developed between the two. They differed, for example, on the question of exporting natural gas, an issue in the 1952 election. With another victory, Manning had the green light to export, and incorporated the Alberta Gas Trunk Line Co. in 1954 as the agency that would collect all the natural gas in the province and deliver it to export pipelines. Although he rejected the idea of a Crown corporation on ideological grounds, Manning ensured that Albertans would own the company through a province-wide distribution of shares.[75]

Meanwhile, pipelines were also under construction to export Alberta oil to the east and west. Prowse fared best in the 1955 election after he had raised several charges of scandal, especially over the government's lease of an Edmonton office building which was owned by two Social Credit MLAs. This was a violation of the Legislative Assembly Act, and the two were told to resign. In a campaign full of "allegation and denials, of innuendoes, hints and dark suspicions,"[76] Prowse managed to gain 31 percent of the vote and elect 15 members. But Manning carried on in office, while Prowse resigned as Liberal leader in 1958 and was appointed to the Senate in 1966.

With the tremendous petroleum revenues generated in the 1950s and 1960s, the Manning government established a first-class system of roads, schools, universities, hospitals, and social services. In fact, despite the premier's declared opposition to bureaucracy and big government, Alberta spent more money per capita in the 1950s than any other province.[77] In 1957 and 1958, the government paid each citizen over 21 a small cash dividend which was somewhat reminiscent of its promises in 1935. In the early 1960s, the government developed a subsidized medicare program for those who could not afford private medical insurance, but a few years later it was adamantly opposed to any federal comprehensive public scheme. It made several improvements in the welfare field in 1966 in connection with the new federal Canada Assistance Plan: day care, preventive and counselling services, and a new child welfare act. In other developments, Manning granted Natives the right to vote in provincial elections in 1965, created a Department of Youth in 1966 to attract younger voters to the aging party, and passed a bill of rights which prohibited various forms of discrimination. An independent University of Calgary emerged, with the University of Lethbridge following shortly after. Because the extent and power of administrative agencies had been the subject of criticism for some time, the government appointed an ombudsman, the first in North America.

In addition to the expansion of the conventional oil and gas industry, especially the new find at Rainbow Lake in 1966, two large economic projects took form in this period. In 1964 the government gave approval to Great Canadian Oil Sands, or Sunoco, to establish a plant in the Athabasca tar sands and construct a pipeline to Edmonton. The government insisted, however, that 125,000 $100 debentures be made available to Albertans. In 1965 construction started on the Alberta Resources Railway which was designed to serve the Peace River district, and especially to assist in the extraction of coal which was to be shipped to Japan.

On the party front in the mid-1960s, Manning wrote a small book called *Political Realignment* in which he called for a new ideological grouping of "social conservatism" and invited the Conservative party to join Social Credit. The CCF was slow to transform itself into the NDP, but the new party won its first seat in a by-election in 1966. The most important political occurrence, however, was the selection of the young, able, and attractive Peter Lougheed as the new Conservative leader in 1965.

In the 1967 campaign, Lougheed stressed procedural issues such as excessive government by order-in-council and the power of administrative tribunals. In the end, Manning retained 55 seats, the Conservatives doubled their share of the popular vote to 26 percent and won six seats, while the Liberals suffered the greatest losses. A simultaneous plebiscite on the introduction of daylight saving time was narrowly defeated.

The new enlarged Conservative Opposition gave government measures and spending proposals much more serious scrutiny than before, and was successful in persuading the government to appoint an Opposition chair of the public accounts committee, the first province to do so. The report of the commission under Mr. Justice W.J.C. Kirby, set up to investigate conflict of interest charges, chided ministers and ex-ministers for lacking discretion in some of their business dealings. Several substantial new laws were passed in 1968 including the Municipal Government Act, the Alberta Housing Act, and the Irrigation Act. The government authorized an increase in the amount of French-language instruction in the schools, and provided more funding for the Alberta Resources Railway. Meanwhile, the provincial revenue picture was not as bright as in the past, and generous expenditures left the government with a deficit in 1967-68. Then, having served 25 years, the second-longest tenure of any premier in any province, Manning retired at the end of 1968. After a heated battle, Harry Strom, one of Manning's veteran ministers, was elected as his successor. Manning continued to preach on the weekly "Back to the Bible Hour," set up a consulting company with his son, Preston, and was appointed to the Senate in 1970. However, in a move considered by some to be heresy, given the traditional Social Credit antipathy to the banks, he soon joined the board of directors of the Canadian Imperial Bank of Commerce.

Manning's longevity was based on several factors, the most important being the great prosperity of the province. A second aspect was his personal stature. He possessed a strong administrative ability, often holding several portfolios including attorney general. His stern moral reputation and his religious radio program reinforced his image of honesty, while an enticing air of mystery resulted from his intense personal privacy.[78] He was also assisted by the feedback mechanisms of his caucus and the Social Credit League. The league was a good channel of public opinion as well as a highly efficient election-day machine. Despite his rigid opinions on moral issues and his strong private enterprise stance, Manning could bend with the public mood. For example, when a plebiscite in 1957 favoured relaxation of the liquor laws, the government complied despite Manning's own views on the matter. He also created and depended on an increasingly competent civil service.

Harry Strom was premier for 33 months, a period of considerable government activity but one marked by a lack of strong leadership and the increasing growth of Conservative opposition. Strom was subject to conflicting streams of advice which he was unable to reconcile, generally preferring to opt for the ways of the past. Those innovations that were adopted were not explained to the electorate in a way that would create a new progressive image for the party, as had been done by the Ontario Conservatives, for example, in 1971.

Strom created a new Environment department, and after first announcing that the province would not join the federal medicare program, he later reversed his stand. Reports critical of provincial penal and mental health systems led to substantial changes in these two fields in 1970, and new criminal injury compensation was introduced. Housing was another priority, with the Alberta Housing Corporation created to encourage urban renewal, public housing, and low-income home ownership. Just before the 1971 election, the government raised the homeowners' tax discount to $75 and doubled that for the elderly in need. Other developments included expanding the college system, a new hail and crop insurance corporation, creating the Alberta Police Commission, and amalgamating the Oil and Gas Conservation Board and Alberta Power Commission into the Energy Resources Conservation Board. Strom relaxed Sunday-closing laws, and set 18 as the minimum age to vote and drink in a new age of majority act, while the labour movement forced alterations to proposed amendments to the labour act dealing with compulsory arbitration.

The 1970s[79]

Peter Lougheed was descended from one of Alberta's pioneering families. He played football for the Edmonton Eskimos, received a law degree, and added a master of business administration degree from the Harvard Business School before joining the Mannix Corp. construction firm in Calgary. Lougheed's initial strategy as Conservative leader involved building a viable organization, and impressing everyone with his hard work, dedication, and dynamism. Trips to other provinces demonstrated to him that strong leadership was the key to success, and that a solid central organization and active constituency associations should all owe their primary allegiance to the leader. In the legislature the Tory performance was also impressive, especially in the unusual practice of introducing bills from the Opposition side.[80] His six members became 10 by 1971 as the party captured two by-elections, and two other opposition members joined the Tory ranks. Besides organization, Lougheed was concerned with developing a political philosophy and image. Because Social Credit was ideologically in tune with the province's political culture and because he had no quarrel with its moderate brand of conservatism, Lougheed concentrated on image, emphasizing momentum and the need for change. The key words were "enthusiasm, enterprise, fresh, drive, new, vigorous and young," and the campaign slogan was "NOW!"

Thus the 1971 election was a competitive two-party race. It was essentially a campaign of images, personalities, and styles—the youthful, urban, dynamic, modern Lougheed against the tired, rural, wooden, but decent Harry Strom.

There was little difference between them in terms of actual policy or ideology. In fact, the substantive similarity between the two leaders made Lougheed even more appealing; he represented a safe change, a continuity in policy coupled with a new, better educated, younger, more energetic team.[81] Most Albertans were already voting Conservative in federal elections. The NDP also ran a strong campaign, but the Liberals put up very little effort, the leader being ousted when it was revealed he had been conducting secret negotiations with Social Credit regarding a possible alliance of the two parties. Thus, Lougheed scored a stunning upset of almost the same magnitude of those of 1921 or 1935: 49 seats and 46 percent of the popular vote to 25 seats and 42 percent for Social Credit, while the NDP elected its leader, Grant Notley. The Conservatives did relatively better in the north than in the south and were helped by the redistribution which eliminated three rural seats and created 13 new urban ones. Overall, it seems that between newcomers to the province and new voters between the ages of 18 and 21, some 30 percent of the electorate were newly enfranchised in 1971, and the Conservatives did especially well among this group.[82] Paralleling Aberhart's mastery of radio, Lougheed was particularly effective on television.[83] The poor state of both the national and provincial economies was another contributing factor in Alberta's change of government; the province was one of nine that changed governments around the same time.

Under Lougheed the government came to be even more preoccupied with petroleum resources, as the fate of the industry rose and fell and then began to rise again. In the first instance, however, the new government's priorities were civil rights, senior citizens, and mental health. Lougheed's bill of rights included the usual civil liberties plus the right to own property, and was to be paramount over other provincial legislation. The government absolved senior citizens of having to pay medicare premiums and exempted them from the education tax on their homes. Lougheed rewrote the Mental Health Act and substantially increased funding in this area. Other innovations in 1972 included the Agricultural Development Fund, the Alberta Opportunity Fund, and the Alberta Arts Foundation. The Conservatives devoted more money to the provincial grid road program, workers' compensation payments, and the handicapped. While a plebiscite in 1967 defeated the adoption of daylight saving time, another in 1971 had approved it, and Lougheed followed through with appropriate legislative action.

More initiatives followed in 1973 and 1974: the province assumed the cost of all basic education funding and 90 percent of the local cost of social services, and made more funds available for kindergartens and urban transportation systems. When the government unexpectedly purchased Pacific Western Airlines, Lougheed explained that this rather socialistic move was necessary to ensure that the company expand and service Alberta's growing needs.

Oil prices rose again over the 1971-73 period and substantially increased the government's revenues, but in 1972 Lougheed raised the rent on oil leases and the royalty rate with his natural resources revenue plan, an action taken with no advance discussion with the industry. In 1973 the Organization of Petroleum Exporting Countries (OPEC) suddenly increased the international price of oil, and in 1974 the government was almost exclusively concerned with related issues. As an immediate response to OPEC, the federal government imposed a freeze on domestic oil prices and an export tax on oil of which the producing provinces originally received 50 percent of the revenue. Then, at a federal-provincial conference in January 1974, Ottawa announced a single domestic price, necessitating the subsidization of oil prices in the east which was dependent on imported oil. The producing provinces benefited from an increased domestic price, but lost their share of the export tax. Alberta agreed to these arrangements, but was upset that the federal budget of 1974 no longer permitted oil companies to deduct provincial royalty payments from the calculation of their federal income tax. In response to both federal and provincial legislation, companies cut back their activity in 1974, and in December of that year Lougheed reacted by reducing various provincial charges on the industry and providing more drilling incentives. He created the Alberta Energy Company in 1973, with 50 percent government ownership, as the province's agent in the Syncrude Canada Ltd. project, other unconventional developments such as Suffield natural gas, and joint ventures with private companies. Lougheed granted new powers over petrochemical feedstocks to the Energy Resources Conservation Board and established an oil sands technology authority, while Alberta Gas Trunk Lines led a consortium which planned to construct a large $300-million petrochemical plant. The Alberta government was distressed to hear of Ottawa's plans to have the federal Crown corporation, Petrosar, build a similar plant in Sarnia, and fought unsuccessfully against it.

The end of 1974 and beginning of 1975 were dominated by the crisis of the Syncrude project, the second tar sands development at Fort McMurray. With costs escalating, Atlantic Richfield decided to withdraw from the consortium, threatening the continuation of the project. In February 1975, after a great deal of difficult negotiation, an agreement was reached whereby the remaining partners would invest $1.4 billion and retain 70 percent equity, the federal government would provide $300 million for 15 percent equity, Ontario would invest $100 million for five percent, and Alberta would supply $200 million in return for a convertible debenture, and would also finance a $200 million power plant and a $100-million pipeline. Many were relieved at this solution, but others found reasons to criticize the agreement.[84]

Armed with the Syncrude settlement, Lougheed called an election for March 1975. The NDP was the only opposition party to field a full slate of candidates and was particularly critical of the Syncrude deal. The result was another landslide for the Tories who won 69 of 75 seats and 63 percent of the popular vote, compared with four seats and 18 percent for Social Credit, and Notley's single seat and 13 percent for the NDP. Thus the rout of the Social Credit party was complete, and the transformation in Alberta politics in the early 1970s as overwhelming as in 1921 and 1935.

After the election, Lougheed raised provincial royalties again, permitting increased government expenditure. In response to the federal wage-and-price control program in the fall of 1975, Alberta introduced temporary rent controls and legislation compatible with the federal intervention. In 1976, the government announced a new coal policy and began to limit provincial spending increases which had been rising at about 33 percent a year. The latter was difficult to impose, however, with thousands of interprovincial migrants arriving each year and demanding provincial and municipal services. The federal government resisted Alberta's purchase of the PWA Corporation, and did its best to stop the transfer of the airline's headquarters from Vancouver to Calgary. Alberta responded by taking a strong provincial rights stance in constitutional discussions initiated by Ottawa, and enunciated its position in full in a 1978 document called "Harmony in Diversity." The biggest event of the period, however, was the creation of the Alberta Heritage Savings Trust Fund. About 30 percent of non-renewable resource revenue was to be contributed to the fund, which would be used to finance capital projects in the province such as irrigation, the Southern Alberta Cancer Centre and other medical facilities, oil sands research, reforestation, and recreation facilities, in an effort to strengthen and diversify the province's economy. Loans to other provinces would also be made. The main criticism of the fund was directed at the discretion it permitted the cabinet in investing such large sums without prior legislative approval. Under the terms of the enabling legislation a legislative committee could only examine the reports after the investments had been made.

In 1977-78, oil companies announced two new megaprojects. Shell Canada Ltd. planned a third tar sands project on behalf of the Alsands group, while Imperial Oil Ltd. unveiled plans for a $4-billion heavy oil plant at Cold Lake. In 1978, the export of natural gas became a prominent issue as both provincial and federal governments wished to increase domestic markets first, against the companies which wanted to export.

In other developments, the government introduced major changes to the Planning Act, the Environmental Conservation Act, the Landlord and Tenant Act, and the Matrimonial Property Act, the latter providing for the equal division of property upon divorce. In financial matters, it removed retail gasoline and diesel fuel excise taxes while raising medicare premiums. Lougheed provided increased funding for highways, hospitals, home mortgages and public housing, welfare and the handicapped, and property tax refunds for senior citizens.

Early 1979 saw another election in the province. To render their situation even more secure, the Tories made $2 billion worth of electoral promises in such areas as municipal grants (virtually eliminating municipal debts), transportation, medical resources, urban parks, and low-interest mortgages.[85] The Conservatives won the predicted landslide victory, with 74 of 79 seats representing 57 percent of the popular vote; Social Credit retained its four seats, and the NDP elected only its leader.

The 1970s are often depicted as a period in which a New West took form, especially in Alberta. Viewed by the federal government as a dangerous degree of decentralization and provincial power at the expense of the nation, and by central Canada as a cause of its economic decline, this phenomenon had a much more positive image within Alberta—one of "province-building."[86] Those most intimately involved in the development were sometimes referred to as a new bourgeoisie, a new middle or capitalist class. They included Alberta businesspeople from such firms as ATCO Ltd., Nova Corp., and Mannix Corp.; petroleum professionals such as lawyers, geologists, engineers, and consultants; the state administrative elite in the various provincial departments and regulatory agencies; and others involved in such fields as real estate, construction, ranching, agribusiness, sports, and tourism. Their general objective was to transfer wealth, power, careers, decision making, and industry to the West. These Albertans wanted to create an industrial core in the province rather than be an extractive periphery; they wished to free themselves from the influence of the old Montreal-Toronto establishment, eastern financial interests, and the federal government; and they hoped to make arrangements for their own future following the eventual decline of the oil industry. More specifically, the new middle class sought to develop backward and forward linkages from the petroleum industry to manufacture the equipment necessary for the industry and then to upgrade energy resources at the source, thus reducing the export of raw materials and jobs. One way to accomplish this was to create a petrochemical industry in the province. They also extended provincial constitutional control over natural resources as far as possible, and maximized resource revenues for the province. Rather than following the nationalization technique of neighbouring Saskatchewan (except for the temporary takeover of PWA), Alberta opted for quasi-state enterprises and joint ventures, such as Syncrude Canada Ltd., the Alberta Energy Company, and Nova Corp. While it may not have believed in nationalization, Alberta did prescribe an activist government to steer development and devise a relatively coherent planning strategy, including a strong provincial public service. This Lougheed strategy of "economic provincialism" differed from the Social Credit approach in several ways: it was less deferential to the multi-national oil companies; it was determined to extract a greater proportion of the revenues involved; and it sought to give local entrepreneurs a larger share of the action in contrast to their earlier "frustrated marginal role." In short, the provincial government was involved with indigenous capitalists "in a close alliance for the purpose of regional empire-building."[87]

The 1980s

All sectors of the Alberta economy enjoyed exceptional prosperity at the beginning of the 1980s; real estate values skyrocketed and new construction abounded, especially in Calgary.[88] In addition to the high level of private sector development, government revenues continued to increase, and highways, hospitals, educational institutions, housing, social services, and agriculture all benefitted from large increases in public funding. The government matched Saskatchewan in purchasing 1,000 hopper cars and then provided most of the funding for a new grain export terminal in Prince Rupert, B.C., while Edmonton and Calgary both gained new light rail transit systems. It was not until the end of 1981 that the effects of the recession began to be felt seriously in the province: unemployment climbed, office space went unoccupied, and thousands of home foreclosures occurred. The province reduced the proportion of resource revenue to the heritage fund from 30 percent to 15 percent, began to use all interest generated from the fund for current expenditures, and projected a budget deficit in 1982-83.

The re-election of the Trudeau Liberal government in 1980, after a brief stint of Conservative rule under the province's own Joe Clark, inaugurated a very troubled period in federal-Alberta relations. The conflict centred on the energy and constitutional issues and spawned the strongest separatist movement the province had ever seen. In the matter of energy, the most important battle involved the price of oil. Alberta wanted substantially higher prices for a variety of reasons—as an incentive for expensive and non-conventional exploration and development, to set aside more money from this non-renewable resource for the day when it would be largely depleted, and to encourage conservation. On the other hand, the federal Liberal government had been re-elected on a promise to keep oil price increases below those proposed by Joe Clark to tame inflation, spur manufacturing, and reduce Ottawa's subsidy to eastern Canadian consumers. Alberta unilaterally increased the price in August 1980, but the federal government responded with the National Energy Program in October.[89] The NEP raised oil prices, but not as much as Alberta wanted; it imposed a variety of new federal taxes on the industry, including an export tax on natural gas; it provided for a new division of revenues which gave Ottawa a larger share; it included incentives for Canadianization of the industry and for conversion from oil to natural gas; and it aimed for national self-sufficiency. Lougheed reacted with a province-wide television broadcast in which he firmly stated the Alberta case: Ottawa was invading provincial territory and, unless a mutual agreement was reached, the province would challenge the natural gas export tax in the courts; it would halt the construction of new tar sands plants; and it would phase in a reduction in oil production of 60,000 barrels per day at three-month intervals, beginning March 1st, 1981.

The premier then took his message to central Canada and to a series of federal-provincial meetings. In September 1981, after the damage was done to the industry and to the popularity of Trudeau, the Liberal Party and the federal government, a compromise modified many aspects of the NEP. The settlement included federal withdrawal of the export tax on natural gas and a complicated agreement on oil and gas price increases and the division of revenues. Despite the agreement, the NEP had helped fan the coals of separatism, led to a decline in oil exploration, and contributed to the suspension or abandonment of several major heavy oil and oil sands projects. In 1981 Esso Resources Enterprises Ltd. pulled out of the Cold Lake development (later revived) and the Alsands megaproject was abandoned in 1982. Although many Albertans blamed the NEP for these problems and more, it happened to coincide with an international recession, high interest rates, and a levelling off of world oil price increases. The NEP has thus to some extent been unfairly blamed for the decline of the petroleum industry and the Alberta economy as a whole.

The Lougheed government opposed several features of the Trudeau constitutional package, especially the proposed amending formula and the unilateral approach Trudeau had adopted, and joined several other provinces in challenging the constitutionality of the legislation in the courts. After the Supreme Court forced the two sides back to the bargaining table, Alberta was relatively pleased with the resolution of the constitutional question: the package included its own amending formula and enhanced provincial jurisdiction over natural resources.

The federal NEP and unilateral constitutional announcements in the fall of 1980 gave western separatist movements a big boost, and for a few weeks huge rallies were held. Lougheed kept a wary eye on the separatist groups in the province, rejecting their approach but understanding many of the causes of their discontent, and by the end of the year the movement seemed to have been reduced to a handful of right-wing radicals. In early 1982, however, the separatist Western Canada Concept (WCC) won a by-election, attracting the support of a variety of discontented groups, including religious fundamentalists and those concerned with freight rates, oil pricing, bilingualism, metrification, and gun control.

As the next provincial election approached, the Lougheed government faced charges of patronage, extravagance, secrecy, and mismanagement of the heritage fund. One Tory MLA, Tom Singlinger, was expelled from the party for his dissidence, and formed the Alberta Reform Movement. The NDP began a campaign for lower interest rates, arguing that Alberta residents should reap more benefit from the heritage fund, which had a value of about $13 billion, and Lougheed announced that home mortgages, small businesses, and farmers would be eligible for reduced interest rates. He also put PWA up for sale in order to counter accusations that he was too socialistic. The November 1982 election featured an amazing array of candidates, all with their own idea of how to spend the heritage fund. Both the Tories and NDP ran full slates, the WCC had 78 candidates, and they were joined by 29 Liberals, 13 Social Credit candidates, 14 from the Alberta Reform Movement, eight Communists, and 34 Independents. In spite of this wide selection, the downturn in the economy, the limited success of the Lougheed government in diversifying and strengthening the province's economic base, and the lack of a specific anti-federal issue, the Conservatives attracted 63 percent of the vote, compared to 19 percent for the NDP, 12 percent for the WCC, and six percent for all the rest. The Conservatives won 75 seats, the NDP won two, and two incumbent Social Credit members running as Independents were also returned. In 1983 the Speaker decided to recognize the NDP as the official Opposition, and Grant Notley took over as Opposition leader.[90] Shortly afterwards, the Social Credit party effectively passed into history.

The next few years constituted a painful readjustment for Alberta. Even though it drew on the heritage fund for expenditures, the government ran a deficit and had to cut back some services and reduce the number of civil service jobs. It limited the increase in grants to public institutions to five percent, raised medicare premiums, and increased the personal income tax by 13 percent. Over the 1983-84 period, Alberta was the only province to lose population, and it scrapped planned oil and gas price increases. Controversial labour legislation removed the hospital workers' right to strike, and unionized construction firms were allowed to establish non-union subsidiaries. The government sought to encourage job creation with increases in its capital budget and tax reductions for the corporate sector. A protracted dispute simmered with the federal government over its plan to penalize the province for allowing doctors to extra-bill their patients and hospitals to charge user fees.[91] One positive development was the construction near Swan Hills of the Alberta Special Waste Treatment Centre, a $20-million hazardous waste disposal system unique in the country.

On the opposition front, ex-Socred leader Ray Speaker, sitting as an Independent, formed the Representative Party with a moderate conservative and federalist stand. In October 1984, NDP leader Grant Notley died in an airplane crash, but the party regrouped under his successor, Ray Martin, and continued to form the official Opposition after winning the resulting by-election. Nick Taylor continued to lead the Liberals, but in 1985 the party added a leadership review mechanism to its constitution.[92]

The Alberta economy began to recover in 1984. Drilling and production increased, and several new projects were unveiled including expansions at the two original tar sands plants. By 1985 the Heritage Fund contained over $14 billion and investment income provided $1.6 billion or 16 percent of provincial budgetary revenues. Alberta celebrated the election of the Mulroney government in 1984, and the "Western Accord" signed by federal and provincial energy ministers in March 1985. This deal essentially deregulated oil prices, allowing them to float to world levels, and removed a number of federal taxes. The oil export and Canadian ownership charges were abandoned and the petroleum and gas revenue tax, which claimed 12 percent of well-head revenues, was phased out, as were the Petroleum Incentive Program grants which encouraged frontier exploration at the expense of conventional sites. The resulting increased revenue for oil companies was expected to be reinvested to create jobs and increase future supplies. The accord virtually eliminated the National Energy Program, but its critics stressed that it amounted to a loss to the federal treasury of several billion dollars over the next four years, as well as an end to efforts to

Canadianize the industry. There was also no guarantee that increased profits would be reinvested in Canada, and many feared that consumers and taxpayers would ultimately bear the burden. Lougheed followed the accord with further incentives for exploration and development: a combination of provincial royalty reductions and tax breaks for oil and natural gas producers which would benefit the industry by an additional $420 million per year.

With the strength of the petroleum industry renewed, Lougheed made educational reform a priority in 1984. He devoted some $250 million to employment training initiatives, primarily to cope with the unemployment problem, significantly increased financial assistance to post-secondary students, and proposed changes in the school curriculum to prepare graduates for the marketplace. On the other hand, three outstanding problems included disputes with the Alberta Medical Association over fee increases for doctors, with the Alberta Teachers' Association on the creation of a new body to advise on teacher standards and discipline, and with the public sector unions. The unions challenged the prohibition on strikes by provincial government employees, hospital workers, and municipal police and firefighters under the "freedom of association" provisions in the Charter of Rights and Freedoms. With these exceptions, Premier Lougheed had put his house in order, and announced his resignation in June 1985.

The race to succeed Lougheed was dominated by Don Getty, a 51-year-old former Edmonton Eskimos' quarterback who had been elected to the legislature in 1967. He had served as Energy minister and then minister of Intergovernmental Affairs between 1971 and 1979, when he returned to the private sector as an energy consultant and corporation director. In spite of his early advantage, Getty's aggressive organization tended to tarnish his reputation for integrity, and his second ballot victory was surprisingly narrow.[93] Getty assumed the premiership in November 1985, and won an Edmonton by-election a month later. While he had to deal with party unity strained from fierce infighting during the leadership campaign and difficult problems in the agricultural sector, a popular new natural gas policy was announced after much federal-provincial negotiation.

Getty called an election for May 1986. It was a foregone conclusion that the Conservatives would be re-elected, but their support was much lower than expected. Only 47 percent of the voters bothered to cast their ballots, most of the abstainers presumably being former Tory supporters who had lost their enthusiasm. Of those who did vote, 51 percent voted Conservative, compared with a record high of 29 percent for the NDP, 12 percent for the Liberals, and five percent for the Representative Party. Only the Tories and NDP ran a full slate of 83 candidates, while the Liberals fielded 63, and 104 others represented a variety of right-wing fringe groups. Getty lost six cabinet ministers, but his forces won 61 seats compared with Ray Martin's 16 New Democrats. Long-time Liberal leader Nick Taylor was finally elected, along with three colleagues, and two former Social Crediters running for the Representative Party were also successful. The major gap in the Tory blue that covered the province was caused by 12 NDP and two Liberal seats in Edmonton.[94]

Later in 1986 a severe drop in the world price for oil wiped out the economic advances that had flowed from the 1985 Western Accord, and the oil industry remained in the doldrums for the rest of the decade. In this situation, the provincial government provided $1 billion worth of tax cuts and incentives for oil companies, and eventually persuaded Ottawa to provide over $400 million in compensation for loss of revenue. After the demise of the National Energy Program and its incentives for Canadianization, several takeovers occurred in the "oil patch." Most controversial was the American-owned Amoco Canadian Petroleum Company Ltd. takeover of Dome Petroleum, but British Gas (Canada) Ltd. bought Bow Valley Industries, and the Li Ka-shing family of Hong Kong took majority control of Husky, leaving Nova Corp. with 43 percent. Nova had the sweet revenge of acquiring control of the Ontario-based petrochemical and energy firm, Polysar Ltd., to become one of the largest such firms in the country. Megaprojects such as the Lloydminster heavy oil upgrader and various proposed tar sands plants were postponed and only mini-projects proceeded.

The government also had to offer expensive assistance to farmers due to successive droughts. By early 1987, a $3.3-billion deficit forced Getty to cut grants to municipalities, schools, and hospitals even prior to the budget, which then stunned taxpayers with a combination of further spending cuts and $1-billion worth of tax increases. Getty froze all new capital projects, and further cuts to hospital budgets led to reductions in staff and the closing of beds. The province also dropped medicare coverage for "non-essential" services such as birth control counselling, sterilization, vasectomies, intrauterine devices, circumcisions, and eye examinations for those aged 18 to 65. He increased personal income and business taxes, raised health-care premiums 28 percent, imposed a new gasoline tax, and suspended the transfer of 15 percent of resource revenue to the heritage fund. Henceforth all resource revenue would be used for current purposes.

The decline in the energy industry, depressed real estate values, internal mismanagement, and lax government supervision combined to precipitate the collapse or near-collapse of several Alberta-based financial institutions. Among the largest bankruptcies in the province were the Canadian Commercial Bank and the Northland Bank in 1985, and the Principal Group Ltd., a huge financial services conglomerate, in 1987. Meanwhile on the labour front, a bitter strike at Peter Pocklington's Gainers Inc. meat packing plant continued for over six months in 1986. Because the law permitted hiring replacement workers during a legal strike, many demonstrations and arrests took place. Pocklington later gained an even more unsavoury reputation when he "sold" star hockey player Wayne Gretzky to the Los Angeles Kings. A major nurses' strike lasted for 19 days in early 1988. Because provincial law prohibited nurses from taking such action, the walkout was illegal, but the nurses felt that government cutbacks had left them no choice.[95]

At this point, the forest industry suddenly became a bright spot in the provincial economy. Because Alberta had a larger unallocated harvest than traditional forestry provinces, it attracted a dizzying number of investors. The projects included Alberta Newsprint Co. and Millar Western Pulp plants in Whitecourt; two plants based on Japanese investment, Daishowa Canada (pulp) in Peace River, and Alberta-Pacific Forest Industries (pulp and paper) in Athabasca; Alberta Energy Co.'s pulp mill near Slave Lake; and expansion of the older pulp mills at Hinton and Grande Prairie. Needless to say, the provincial government provided assistance of one kind or another for these projects—usually highways and railways—which annoyed British Columbia Premier Bill Vander Zalm who felt the firms would otherwise have located in his province.

Several aspects of the French question also surfaced in Alberta during the late 1980s. First, when a newly elected Franco-Albertan New Democrat, Leo Piquette, asked a question in French in the legislature in 1986, it was disallowed by the Speaker. A rule change in 1987 allowed French to be spoken, but only with advance notice, the Speaker's approval, and if accompanied by an English translation. Then, in the wake of the 1988 Supreme Court of Canada *Mercure* decision on bilingualism in Saskatchewan (a decision which presumably applied to Alberta as well), the government introduced a bill to validate its English-only laws but without the corresponding Saskatchewan initiative of translating any laws into French. The bill merely provided that members could speak French in the legislature without the permission of the Speaker and that French could be used in court proceedings. Finally, while the province's French-language schools were guaranteed by the Charter of Rights of 1982, where numbers warranted them, the parents involved sought to manage and control such schools. When their demands were denied, they brought the matter before the courts, and won their case in the 1990 *Mahe* decision.

Throughout the ups and downs of the economy, the strikes and the ethnic conflicts, Premier Getty demonstrated little political leadership. Several crises found him on the golf course, whether in the province or in Palm Springs. But despite his lacklustre performance, neither opposition party was able to make much headway. The Liberals held a leadership convention in October 1988 where Nick Taylor was defeated by Edmonton mayor, Laurence Decore, a 48-year-old lawyer and businessman who was a stiff and uninspiring speaker. Being in favour of free trade he was at odds with his four caucus members and his national leader on the main question of the day. About the same time, Preston Manning's new Reform Party won an impressive 15 percent of the Alberta vote in the federal election and a by-election victory shortly afterwards. Several ministers chose the moment to retire, but Getty recruited new blood: Calgary mayor Ralph Klein, a former Liberal; Edmonton TV anchorman Douglas Main, a former Reform Party candidate; and leader of the Representative Party Ray Speaker. At this point the other Representative MLA retired, and their two-man party disappeared.

Three days after a speech from the throne which emphasized family values, Getty called an election for 20 March, 1989. Getty chose three issues on which to conduct the usual battle with Ottawa: high interest rates, the proposed federal sales tax, and the idea of electing Alberta's next Senator. Later, he promised to spend billions of dollars for such purposes as seniors' programs and services, drug control programs, mortgage assistance, and roads, but was vague about the amounts and details involved. Such promises provided Decore with an issue, because his main claim to fame was his reduction of the Edmonton municipal debt while he had been mayor. With a turnout rate of 53.6 percent, the Conservatives dropped to 59 seats and 44 percent of the popular vote, the NDP maintained its 16 seats but dropped to 26 percent of the vote, and the Liberals dramatically revived to take eight seats and 29 percent of the vote. Almost all the opposition seats were in Calgary and Edmonton, while the Tories continued their near-monopoly of rural Alberta. Getty was personally defeated, but decided to continue as premier, and soon won a by-election in Stettler. Shortly thereafter, the government raised medicare premiums again and postponed the balancing of the budget, both contrary to its election promises.

The Report of the Code Inquiry on the collapse of the Principal Group was issued in July 1989. It accused president Donald Cormier and the Principal officers of fraud, deemed Alberta's regulation of financial institutions inadequate, and concluded that Connie Osterman, Minister of Consumer and Corporate Affairs, had been negligent in failing to enforce the regulations. Getty fired her when she refused to assume the political responsibility and resign. In the end, the government compensated most investors to a level of 85-90 percent, almost 50 percent being retrieved from the sale of company assets. The Royal Canadian Mounted Police chose not to press criminal charges, and a new financial consumers act was designed to prevent a repeat occurrence.

Another prominent issue in the province was the Senatorial election held at the time of municipal elections in October 1989, as Getty tried to pursue the Triple-E Senate proposal on an informal basis. This was a proposal to reform the federal senate so that senators would be Elected, with an Equal number per province and Effective powers. It would protect the west from the central Canadian majority in the House of Commons. The election was won by the Reform Party candidate Stan Waters and, after considerable delay and provincial government pressure, Prime Minister Brian Mulroney appointed Waters to the upper chamber.

The 1990s

Generally speaking, Alberta did not experience the increase in prosperity of other provinces in the second half of the 1980s, but neither did it share their traumatic recession in the first half of the 1990s. On the other hand, beginning in 1993, it lived through the most radical neo-conservative budget-cutting any province has ever seen.

Alberta was largely cushioned from the recession by the health of its petroleum industry. For example, after exhaustive environmental hearings Shell started construction of a $825-million gas-sulphur project at Caroline from the largest Alberta gas find in 20 years. Nova Corp. expanded its gas transmission system as several proposals were made for new pipelines to export natural gas to the United States. A 1990 National Energy Board ruling was all that Albertans could have asked for, giving TransCanada Pipelines the green light for a $2.6-billion pipeline expansion, most of which would increase natural gas exports to the American market. These advances resulted in improved real estate values in Calgary and encouraged downtown development, while Nova Corp., Dow Chemical Canada Inc., and Union Carbide Canada Ltd., also enlarged their petrochemical operations. The most negative aspect of the industry was the abandonment of another major tar sands project, the OSLO project, when the federal government withdrew its support.

Getty's largest privatization scheme involved Alberta Government Telephones (AGT, now called Telus Corporation), but the whole project became something of a nightmare. In 1983 AGT and Nova Corp. established Novatel, which produced cellular telephones. Nova abandoned the scheme in 1989, leaving Novatel an AGT subsidiary. At first it was privatized along with AGT but, when its financial losses tarnished the value of the larger corporation's shares, the government bought Novatel back for $160 million and laid off 220 personnel. In 1992 the government sold Novatel to Northern Telecom at a $560-million loss to Alberta taxpayers. To make matters worse, Telus laid off 1,500 employees. Another financial mess occurred when Peter Pocklington defaulted on repayment of loans to his Gainers meat packing plant, and the government of Alberta ended up owning it. A third problem was the computer firm Myrias Research Corp., which carried a $20-million government loss. A fourth, also involving loan guarantees, was a $100-million magnesium smelter at High River. In 1992 the provincial auditor general wrote a scathing report about these and other cases of government financial mismanagement.

Two main environmental problems occurred in the early 1990s. Natives joined with other environmentalists and the Friends of the Old Man River, but failed to stop the construction of a $350-million irrigation dam near Pincher Creek. In addition to the efforts of Peigan Indians to divert the course of the river (claiming it would otherwise destroy a sacred burial ground), the dam was the subject of an almost comedic series of federal and provincial environmental assessments and court cases, with many parallels to the Rafferty-Alameda saga in Saskatchewan. About the time the dam was completed, the Supreme Court of Canada upheld federal power to hold an environmental review. On the other hand, an agreement between the government and Alberta Métis gave the latter a land base with partial self-government in eight Alberta settlements, and included resource revenues and $310 million for social services and economic development.

Environmentalists were otherwise concerned with the many proposed pulp and paper projects in the province. The provincial government allowed the Daishowa Forest Products Ltd. bleached kraft pulp mill in Peace River to proceed in spite of environmental and other concerns, but delayed the Alberta-Pacific Forest Industries (Al-Pac) mill at Athabasca a number of times. At a cost of $1.6 billion, the Al-Pac project would be the largest pulp mill in the world. It received government approval after it changed the bleaching agent it planned to use.[96]

On the constitutional front, Getty tried to attract Reform-minded voters with public speeches denouncing official bilingualism and multiculturalism. About the same time an Alberta legislative committee reported on the subject, the government passed a bill requiring a binding referendum in the province on any change to the Constitution. It was partly because of this law (as well as similar legislation in Quebec and British Columbia), that the first ministers decided to have a national referendum on the Charlottetown Accord later in 1992. Getty lost a senior minister, Ray Speaker, to the federal Reform party and, in the by-election to succeed him, both Liberal and Conservative provincial candidates belonged to the federal Reform party. Fortunately for existing provincial parties in Alberta, Reform Party leader Preston Manning decreed that his party would only operate at the federal level. Alberta also lost its court challenge of the federal Goods and Services Tax.

During the seven years he was premier, Getty accumulated a provincial debt of some $15 billion. This was a striking amount for a province that had experienced such prosperity for the preceding 40 years. In the 1990-92 period alone, the government cut public service jobs, raised medicare premiums, limited transfer payments, and promised to balance the budget without success. Every year the final budget deficit was larger than anticipated. To make the government's balance sheet even worse, Getty introduced a new oil and natural gas royalty structure which further reduced government revenues.

Given these problems, the unpopularity of the federal Conservatives, and Canadians' apparent disillusionment with all governments, Getty's government fell in the polls. The premier's health problems and uninspiring leadership led to talk of inserting a leadership review clause into the provincial party constitution. After staring down dissidents, Getty immediately fell into controversy over private oil investments he had made while holding public office. This led him to institute new conflict of interest rules for ministers and MLAs, with provisions including the appointment of an ethics commissioner and prohibiting cabinet ministers from assuming another public position within six months of leaving office. Getty was also faulted for making patronage appointments, for bringing an excessive number of public works into his own constituency, and for controversial travels at public expense. Then, just after he initialled the Charlottetown Accord in the fall of 1992, he yielded to increasing pressure to resign.

The Conservative party decided on a leadership-selection process based on the principle of one member-one vote. Memberships cost $5 and were often bought in blocks and given away by leadership candidates. When the first results were tabulated, Health Minister Nancy Betkowski led Environment Minister Ralph Klein by one vote. After the campaign's frenetic final week, in which memberships could be taken out until the last minute and in which five of the less successful candidates threw their support to Betkowski, the ultimate result gave Klein a surprising 60 percent of the 78,000 votes cast.[97]

In many similar federal and provincial cases where an unpopular party switched leaders just before an election, the new leader did not manage to save the day. However, in 1993 Ralph Klein went on to win another Tory victory in Alberta. His cabinet was unorthodox, excluding the five Getty ministers who ran against him as well as representatives from Edmonton. His populism also led him to set up four standing cabinet super-committees headed by backbenchers. Among pre-election developments was the adoption of a new electoral map, a process involving a badly split boundaries commission, a court decision, and a partisan legislative committee. Adopted under closure in the legislature, the new map continued to under-represent Calgary and Edmonton, the main sources of opposition support. The government also eliminated pensions for MLAs elected in 1989 or later, and reduced the pension of those elected earlier. Meanwhile, the government and Opposition agreed on substantial changes to legislative procedures.

With regard to the economy, in early 1993 Klein delivered an economic strategy paper which promised to balance the budget by 1997 and to do so without raising taxes. The Deficit Elimination Act was passed to this effect. His 1993 budget entailed eliminating 2,500 government jobs, increasing health-care premiums and other fees, and amalgamating or eliminating many government agencies. Another priority was reducing the welfare budget by getting social assistance recipients into jobs or training programs. In an attempt to reduce the welfare caseload by 10,000 people a year for three years, the government introduced a variety of programs involving make-work projects and/or training, and slashed welfare allowances and related services. Another 1,800 government jobs would be eliminated by privatizing 200 liquor stores, as well as motor vehicle and property registration services. The sale of the last block of Alberta Energy Co. shares would also help the financial situation, but a government-appointed financial review commission's claim that the heritage fund was worth only $7.6 billion was not good news. A year later it was officially determined to be $11.4 billion.[98] A unique federal-Alberta economic summit produced funding for the Trans-Canada Highway, oil sands and heavy oil projects, and agreement on future joint environmental assessments. Ministers sometimes made disparaging remarks about homosexuals, welfare recipients, and other ethnic groups, and Alberta remained one of the few provinces that did not include discrimination on the basis of sexual orientation in its Individual Rights Protection Act. A later court decision, however, read such a clause into the act.

The unprecedented Tory election victory in June 1993 was based on Klein's personal appeal, as well as his ability to distance himself from the Getty record and portray himself as an agent of change determined to balance the books. The election was billed as the "battle of the mayors"—Klein formerly mayor of Calgary and Decore formerly mayor of Edmonton—now leading the two major parties. The Liberals ran a close second in popular vote, while the NDP was wiped out in terms of seats. Ray Martin quit as NDP leader shortly afterwards, to be replaced by Ross Harvey. Despite leading the largest Opposition in Alberta history, Laurence Decore faced considerable dissent within his party. He resigned in July 1994, and the Liberals used a televote system (with several hitches) to choose Grant Mitchell to replace him. Mitchell did not endear himself to certain party members and Liberal MLAs by insisting on a more liberal ideological stance for the party to distinguish it from the Klein Conservatives, and later backtracked on health care cuts.

The period after June 1993 was almost completely consumed by cutting government services to eliminate the operating deficit by 1997. Such was the thrust of the August speech from the throne and the September mini-budget. The 1994 budget sought to cut the operating deficit by 37 percent—by over $900 million—to $1.5 billion for 1994-95. It included eliminating nearly 1,800 public service jobs and raising $81 million in 80 new or increased fees. It was accompanied by a massive "business plan" which outlined a three-year plan, including spending targets and savings,[99] for each government department. Table 10.11 shows the province's financial picture in Statistics Canada terms.

TABLE 10.11   Government of Alberta Finances, 1990/91–1994/95 ($ millions)

	1990/91	1991/92	1992/93	1993/94	1994/95
Total revenues	$14,907	$14,186	$13,973	$14,919	$14,397
Debt charges	1,888	1,899	1,916	2,231	2,152
Total expenditures	16,050	16,316	16,875	16,414	15,369
Deficit	1,143	2,130	2,902	1,495	972

Source: Reproduced by authority of the Minister of Industry, 1995, Statistics Canada, *Public Sector Finance, 1994–95,* Financial Management System, cat. no. 68-212 (March 1995). Adapted by author.

All government departments had to cut 20 percent from operating budgets, all public servants had to absorb a five-percent pay cut in 1994 (partly in the form of seven unpaid days of leave) and had salaries frozen for the next two years. Ministers made daily announcements of other spending reductions. The government continued to privatize Crown corporations, including ACCESS, the educational television system and, along with Ottawa, bought its way out of the Bi-Provincial heavy oil upgrader at Lloydminster. After a year of operation, however, few customers found the sale of the government's liquor outlets to be satisfactory, let alone an improvement. Bill 57 permitted the cabinet to delegate by means of a contract the operation of almost any government program to the private sector, so that it could be administered on a fee-for-service basis with little legislative scrutiny.

As in other provinces, one of the the main cost-cutting objectives was a leaner health delivery system. The government amalgamated 204 hospital boards into 17 regional authorities, and gave them the power to decide which hospitals would be closed. Unlike Saskatchewan, where these tended to be rural hospitals, in Alberta mainly urban hospitals were affected: two in Calgary and one in Edmonton, with others reduced to the status of community clinics. The number of acute care beds was to be halved over three years, and many other medical services were reduced or eliminated. Several individual cases of medical tragedy were reported and, in spite of the cuts, the government raised medicare premiums. Alberta also fought with the federal Health minister over the funding of private clinics serving the affluent.

Welfare funding continued to be slashed and recipients removed from welfare rolls. The government's ultimate objective was to provide welfare only for the unemployable, not the unemployed. Many recipients hoped to find a more hospitable environment by moving to British Columbia, and the government provided some 6,000 with a one-way bus ticket. Fifteen support programs for seniors were eliminated or reduced, and included a 40-percent cut on seniors' eyeglasses and dental care. Seniors making over $18,000 now had to pay their own medicare premiums and lost the government subsidy of their property taxes, while those between $10,000 and $18,000 had such benefits partially reduced. Klein also increased nursing home fees.

In education, the government reduced the number of school boards to 60 from 142 and made them virtually impotent. Klein reduced grants to kindergartens by 50 percent, which often resulted in user fees being charged. Class sizes increased as the government cut education budgets by 12 percent and post-secondary grants by 14 percent. The government raised tuition fees and ordered universities to weaken the system of tenure for professors. There was also a $113-million cut in operating grants to municipalities, forcing them to make up the difference with increased property taxes.

Not surprisingly, these unprecedented government cutbacks precipitated numerous hostile demonstrations, and many opponents spoke of the meanness of the exercise and the two-class society it was creating, including a large increase in the use of food banks. What surprised many observers, however, was the docility of the majority of the population in accepting such reforms. Had Preston Manning been successful in convincing his fellow Albertans of the horrors of government deficits, or was Ralph Klein so popular that people would accept whatever he did? Once the self-imposed budgetary suffering had been achieved, what would he do for an encore? And was his personality enough to keep the majority of the public onside?

The government hoped the private sector would compensate for job losses in the public sector by creating 110,000 jobs by the end of 1997. It offered to help exporters in particular and, as luck would have it, government resource revenues for 1994-95 were $800 million more than expected. Soaring revenues from video lottery terminals and a generally buoyant economy also helped to produce a balanced budget by mid-1995 instead of mid-1997, as the $972 million deficit predicted in Table 10.11 evaporated. Nevertheless, treasurer James Dinning, who was often seen as the brains behind the whole operation, carried on with further cuts in his 1995 budget.

In action not directly related to finances, the Klein government doubled stumpage fees for softwood lumber production after complaints from outside the province that they were too low. It also simplified the petroleum royalty system, and was pleased to announce the establishment of two new panel board plants at Grande Prairie. However, it was not praised for its protection of the environment.

From the outset of the Klein regime, Ken Kowalski had served as deputy premier. In charge of several departments and agencies, he was often seen as the person who ran the day-to-day operations of the government while Klein handled public relations. But Kowalski frequently made controversial statements, engaged in blatant patronage, and interfered in processes better left alone. This led to Kowalski's resignation in mid-1994, when Klein aroused angry public reaction by appointing his ex-deputy head of the Alberta Energy and Utilities Board. Klein was forced to withdraw the appointment, which in any case would have violated conflict of interest rules requiring a six-month cooling-off period for ex-ministers. Once again, Klein defused a potentially troublesome situation.

CONCLUSION

Peter Lougheed dominated Alberta politics for 15 years, and even those who did not always agree with him found him to be an impressive leader. No new leader ever inherited a party so deeply entrenched in power as did Don Getty when he took over the Tory reins in Alberta in 1985. While no one expected the new leader to be a match for the old, almost everyone was disappointed with the drift which ensued during the Getty period. The prospects for opposition parties in Alberta substantially improved, although they could not dislodge the Conservatives from power. It was the widespread expectation that he could not win again which forced Getty from office in 1992 but, even as the Liberal party overtook the NDP as the alternative, the electorate latched on to the populist new Conservative leader, Ralph Klein. However much they identified with this "very ordinary guy," many began to regret their decision when he became obsessed with the budget deficit and slashed everything in sight to balance the budget. Thus, just as Alberta politics began to look more competitive and orthodox than ever before, Klein managed to demonstrate another facet of its uniqueness.

TABLE 10.12   Alberta Provincial Election Results Since 1921

Year	Liberal		Conservative		CCF/NDP		Other	
	Seats	Popular Vote	Seats	Popular Vote	Seats	Popular Vote	Seats	Popular Vote
1921	38	(44%)	15	(35%)	1	(5%)	7	(15%)
1926	43	(41%)	7	(26%)	4	(23%)	6	(10%)
1930	39	(39%)	11	(25%)	6	(14%)	7	(22%)

Year	Social Credit		Liberal		CCF/NDP		Conservative		Other	
	Seats	Popular Vote	Seats	Popular Vote	Seats	Popular Vote	Seats	Popular Vote	Seats	Popular Vote
1935	56	(54%)	5	(23%)	–	–	2	(6%)	–	(16%)
1940	36	(43%)	1	(1%)	–	(11%)	–	–	20	(45%)*
1944	51	(52%)	–	–	2	(25%)	–	–	4	(23%)
1948	51	(56%)	2	(18%)	2	(19%)	–	–	2	(7%)
1952	52	(56%)	4	(22%)	2	(14%)	2	(4%)	1	(4%)
1955	37	(46%)	15	(31%)	2	(8%)	3	(9%)	4	(5%)
1959	61	(56%)	1	(14%)	–	(4%)	1	(24%)	2	(2%)
1963	60	(55%)	2	(20%)	–	(10%)	–	(13%)	1	(2%)
1967	55	(45%)	3	(11%)	–	(16%)	6	(26%)	1	(3%)

Year	Conservative		Social Credit		NDP		Liberal		Other	
	Seats	Popular Vote	Seats	Popular Vote	Seats	Popular Vote	Seats	Popular Vote	Seats	Popular Vote
1971	49	(46%)	25	(41%)	1	(11%)	–	(1%)	–	–
1975	69	(63%)	4	(18%)	1	(13%)	–	(5%)	1	(1%)
1979	74	(57%)	4	(20%)	1	(16%)	–	(6%)	–	(1%)
1982	75	(63%)	–	(1%)	2	(19%)	–	(2%)	2	(16%)**
1986	61	(51%)	–	–	16	(29%)	4	(12%)	2	(8%)***
1989	59	(44%)	–	–	16	(26%)	8	(29%)	–	(1%)
1993	51	(44%)	–	(2%)	–	(11%)	32	(40%)	–	(3%)

*   The others in 1940 were the Unity Party or Independents.

** In 1982 two former Social Credit members were elected as Independents, while the Western Canada Concept won 12 percent of the vote but no seats.

***In 1986 the Representative Party won two seats and five percent of the vote.

TABLE 10.13   Premiers of Alberta

Premier	Party	Year Elected
Alexander Rutherford	Liberal	1905
Arthur Sifton	Liberal	1910
Charles Stewart	Liberal	1917
Herbert Greenfield	United Farmers of Alberta	1921
J.E. Brownlee	United Farmers of Alberta	1926
R.G. Reid	United Farmers of Alberta	1934
William Aberhart	Social Credit	1936
Ernest Manning	Social Credit	1943
Harry Strom	Social Credit	1968
Peter Lougheed	Progressive Conservative	1971
Don Getty	Progressive Conservative	1985
Ralph Klein	Progressive Conservative	1992

ENDNOTES

1. Jack Masson and Peter Blaikie, "Labour Politics in Alberta," in Carlo Caldarola, ed., *Society and Politics in Alberta* (Toronto: Methuen, 1979), p. 282.

2. Peter C. Newman, *The Canadian Establishment,* (Toronto: Seal Books, rev. ed. 1977), pp. 258-265; and Newman, *Debrett's Illustrated Guide to the Canadian Establishment* (Toronto: Methuen, 1983), pp. 118-132. Many of the original oil barons are also mentioned in Peter Foster, *The Blue-Eyed Sheiks* (Toronto: Collins, 1979).

3. C.B. Macpherson, *Democracy in Alberta: Social Credit and the Party System* (Toronto: University of Toronto Press, 1953).

4. For example, Peter J. Smith, "Alberta: A Province Just Like Any Other?" in Keith Brownsey and Michael Howlett, eds., *The Provincial State* (Mississauga: Copp Clark Pitman, 1992).

5. *Mahe v. Alberta* [1990] 1 SCR 342.

6. For this and most of the following sections, see Allan Tupper and Roger Gibbins, eds., *Government and Politics in Alberta* (Edmonton: University of Alberta Press, 1992).

7. David Elton, "Alberta and the Federal Government in Historical Perspective, 1905-1977," in Caldarola, *Society and Politics.*

8. David Laycock, *Populism and Democratic Thought in the Prairies, 1910-1945* (Toronto: University of Toronto Press, 1989).

9. J.F. Conway, "The UFA and Social Credit Regimes in Alberta: Some Continuities," an address to the Canadian Political Science Association (June 1980).

10. Macpherson, *Democracy in Alberta;* Laycock, *Populism and Democratic Thought in the Prairies;* Zenon Kulchyckyj, "Subfragmentation and the Political Culture of the Canadian West," an address to the Canadian Political Science Association (May 1981); Peter Sinclair, "Class Structure and Populist Protest: The Case of Western

Canada," in Caldarola, *Society and Politics;* Harvey Rich, "Plebiscitarian Democracy in Alberta," an address to the Canadian Political Science Association (June 1980).

11. Roger Gibbins, *Prairie Politics and Society* (Toronto: Butterworths, 1980), ch. 5; Gibbons, "Western Alienation and the Alberta Political Culture," in Caldarola, *Society and Politics;* Larry Pratt and Garth Stevenson, eds., *Western Separatism* (Edmonton: Hurtig, 1981); and John Barr and Owen Anderson, eds., *The Unfinished Revolt* (Toronto: McClelland and Stewart, 1971). Political scientists might find it useful to distinguish among three objects of alienation—the authorities (the Liberal government), the regime (minority status in Ottawa), and the political community (wanting to separate from Canada).

12. Kenneth Norrie, "Some Comments on Prairie Economic Alienation," in Caldarola, *Society and Politics,* makes an interesting case that the problem is not with discriminatory federal policies, but rather the operation of market forces, leaving the West at a disadvantage for a number of reasons including its small population base and its geographic isolation. He says that, apart from federal taxation of resources, the real dissatisfaction is with the market economy and that Western policy proposals in these areas are actually demands for intervention in the market. Ironically, it is usually those most wedded to the private market who are most critical of the lack of federal intervention.

13. Thelma Oliver, "Aspects of Alienation in Alberta," an address to the Canadian Political Science Association (1975); David Elton and Arthur Goddard, "The Conservative Takeover, 1971–" in Caldarola, *Society and Politics,* p. 68.

14. Jeffrey Simpson, *Spoils of Power* (Toronto: Collins, 1988), ch. 14.

15. Marsha A. Chandler and William M. Chandler, *Public Policy and Provincial Politics* (Toronto: McGraw-Hill Ryerson, 1979), pp. 77-83; John Wilson, "The Canadian Political Cultures," in *Canadian Journal of Political Science* (September 1974); Richard Simeon and David Elkins, "Regional Political Cultures in Canada," in Elkins and Simeon, eds., *Small Worlds* (Toronto: Methuen, 1980).

16. Elton and Goddard use the word "spectacular" in "A Return to Consensus Politics in Alberta," a paper presented to the Canadian Political Science Association (June 1976), p. 1; many others have made the same observation, for example, L.G. Thomas, *The Liberal Party in Alberta* (Toronto: University of Toronto Press, 1959), pp. xi-xii, and Harvey Rich, "Plebiscitarian Democracy in Alberta," p. 2.

17. Macpherson, *Democracy in Alberta,* p. 246.

18. Among them Seymour Martin Lipset, "Democracy in Alberta," in *Canadian Forum* (1954); John Richards and Larry Pratt, *Prairie Capitalism: Power and Influence in the New West* (Toronto: McClelland and Stewart, 1979), pp. 149-53; and Edward Bell, "Class Voting and the First Alberta Social Credit Election," *Canadian Journal of Political Science* (September 1990).

19. Terrence J. Levesque and Kenneth H. Norrie, "Overwhelming Majorities in the Legislature of Alberta," in *Canadian Journal of Political Science* (September 1979).

20. J.A. Long and F.Q. Quo find the theory inappropriate for the Tory period, "Alberta, Politics of Consensus," in Martin Robin, ed., *Canadian Provincial Politics* (Scarborough: Prentice Hall Canada, 2nd. ed., 1978), pp. 22-24.

21. Garth Stevenson, "Quasi-democracy in Alberta," in Thorburn, *Party Politics in Canada* (Scarborough: Prentice Hall Canada, 5th ed., 1985), pp. 280-1.

22. Howard Palmer and Tamara Palmer, "The 1971 Election and the Fall of Social Credit in Alberta," in *Prairie Forum* 1 (1976).

23. Richards and Pratt, *Prairie Capitalism*, p. 165.

24. Stevenson, "Quasi-democracy in Alberta," p. 278.

25. Allan Tupper, "Alberta Politics: The Collapse of Consensus," in H.G. Thorburn, ed., *Party Politics in Canada* (Scarborough: Prentice Hall Canada, 6th ed., 1991).

26. Meir Serfaty, "The Rise of the Conservative Party in Alberta under Lougheed, 1965-71," an address to the Canadian Political Science Association (June 1979).

27. Stevenson, "Quasi-democracy in Alberta," p. 282.

28. Harvey Rich, "Plebiscitarian Democracy in Alberta," pp. 27-32.

29. Rand Dyck, "Relations Between Federal and Provincial Parties," in A.G. Gagnon and A.B. Tanguay, eds., *Canadian Parties in Transition* (Scarborough: Nelson Canada, 1989).

30. Joseph Wearing, *The L-Shaped Party* (Toronto: McGraw-Hill Ryerson, 1981), pp. 122-3; Reginald Whitaker, *The Government Party* (Toronto: University of Toronto Press, 1977), pp. 359-368.

31. John J. Barr, *The Dynasty* (Toronto: McClelland and Stewart, 1974), p. 120. See also Nelson Wiseman, "The Pattern of Prairie Leadership," in Leslie Pal and David Taras, eds., *Prime Ministers and Premiers* (Scarborough: Prentice Hall Canada, 1988).

32. On Peter Lougheed, see Allan Hustak, *Peter Lougheed* (Toronto: McClelland and Stewart, 1979), and David Wood, *The Lougheed Legacy* (Toronto: Key Porter Books, 1985).

33. Keith Archer and Margaret Hunziker, "Leadership Selection in Alberta: The 1985 Progressive Conservative Leadership Convention," in R.K. Carty, ed., *Leaders and Parties in Canadian Politics: Experiences of the Provinces* (Toronto: Harcourt Brace Jovanovich, 1992).

34. Long and Quo, "Alberta, Politics of Consensus," p. 7; Peter Sinclair makes the point that there was little in the Social Credit program on co-operatives, state control of monopolies, or state welfare in "Class Structure and Populist Protest: The Case of Western Canada," in Caldarola, *Society and Politics*, pp. 76, 82. See also Masson and Blaikie, "Labour Politics in Alberta," in Caldarola, *Society and Politics*, p. 275.

35. Dale Poel, "The Diffusion of Legislation among the Canadian Provinces: a Statistical Analysis," in *Canadian Journal of Political Science* (December, 1976).

36. M.L. McMillan and Kenneth H. Norrie, "Province-Building versus a Rentier Society," *Canadian Public Policy VI Supplement* (February 1980); Larry Pratt, "The State and Province-Building: Alberta's Development Strategy" in Leo Panitch, ed., *The Canadian State* (Toronto: University of Toronto Press, 1976); Peter Smith, "Alaska and Alberta —The Politics and Management of Plenty: A Comparative Analysis," an address to the Canadian Political Science Association (May 1981). On the takeover of PWA, see Allan Tupper, "Pacific Western Airlines," in Allan Tupper and Bruce Doern, eds., *Public Corporations and Public Policy in Canada* (Montreal: Institute for Research on Public Policy, 1981).

37. Marsha A. Chandler, "The Politics of Provincial Resource Policy," in Michael Atkinson and Marsha Chandler, eds., *The Politics of Canadian Public Policy* (Toronto: University of Toronto Press, 1983).

38. Medicine Hat had two members in 1921 and 1926.

39. John Anthony Long, "Maldistribution in Western Provincial Legislatures: The Case of Alberta," in *Canadian Journal of Political Science* (September 1969); Terrence J. Levesque and K.H. Norrie, "Overwhelming Majorities in the Legislature of Alberta"; H.E. Pasis, "The Inequality of Distribution in the Canadian Provincial Assemblies," an address to the Canadian Journal of Political Science (1972).

40. This sordid story is related in Rainer Knopff and F.L. Morton, "Charter Politics in Alberta: Constituency Apportionment and the Right to Vote" and David Bercuson and Barry Cooper, "Electoral Boundaries: An Obstacle to Democracy in Alberta," in John Courtney, *Drawing Boundaries* (Saskatoon: Fifth House Publishers, 1992).

41. In my opinion, Jeffrey Simpson underestimates the scandals and patronage of the Social Credit period in *Spoils of Power*, ch. 14. See Alvin Finkel, *The Social Credit Phenomenon in Alberta* (Toronto: University of Toronto Press, 1989).

42. Thomas Flanagan, "Ethnic Voting in Alberta Provincial Elections," in Caldarola, *Society and Politics*, p. 320.

43. Roger Rickwood and Bhagwan Dua, "Human Resources Management in a Changing Alberta Environment: Need for Policy Changes," an address to the Canadian Political Science Association (1981), p. 13; Long and Quo, "Alberta, Politics of Consensus," pp. 19-20; Stevenson, "Quasi-democracy in Alberta," p. 279.

44. Grace Skogstad, "Farmers and Farm Unions in Alberta," in Caldarola, *Society and Politics*, p. 227.

45. Masson and Blaikie, "Labour Politics in Alberta," in Caldarola, *Society and Politics*; Rickwood and Dua, "Human Resources Management in a Changing Alberta Environment," Canadian Political Science Association.

46. Richard Baird, "Interest Groups and the Government and the Politics of Alberta," *Political Science 100 Readings* (Edmonton: University of Alberta, 1993).

47. Tupper and Gibbins, *Government and Politics in Alberta*, ch. 8.

48. John Saywell, "Lieutenant-Governors," in David Bellamy et al., eds., *The Provincial Political Systems* (Toronto: Methuen, 1976).

49.

1905-1909	25	1959-1963	65
1909-1913	41	1963-1967	63
1913-1921	56	1967-1971	65
1921-1926	61	1971-1979	75
1926-1940	63	1979-1986	79
1940-1952	57	1986-present	83
1952-1959	61		

On this subject, see F.C. Engelmann, "Alberta: From One Overwhelming Majority to Another," in Gary Levy and Graham White, eds., *Provincial and Territorial Legislatures in Canada* (Toronto: University of Toronto Press, 1989).

50. Agar Adamson, "We Were Here Before: The Referendum in Canadian Experience," *Policy Options* (March 1980).

51. Thomas Bateman and David Thomas, "The Rhetoric and Reality of Parliamentary Reform in Alberta," *Canadian Parliamentary Review* (Winter 1993-94).

52. J.E. Hodgetts and O.P. Dwivedi, *Provincial Governments as Employers* (Montreal: McGill-Queen's University Press, 1974), pp. 18-9; E.G. Jamieson, "Provincial Employees," in Donald C. Rowat, ed., *Provincial Government and Politics* (Ottawa: Carleton University, 1973), pp. 196-7.

53. Jack Masson, *Alberta's Local Governments* (Edmonton: University of Alberta Press, 1994).

54. Useful sources on this period include Ernest Watkins, *The Golden Province* (Calgary: Sandstone Publishing 1980); J.G. MacGregor, *A History of Alberta* (Edmonton: Hurtig, 1981); L.G. Thomas, *The Liberal Party in Alberta* (Toronto: University of Toronto Press, 1959); Macpherson, *Democracy in Alberta;* and two articles in Caldarola's *Society and Politics:* Lewis G. Thomas, "The Liberal Party in Alberta, 1905-1921"; and C.F. Betke, "The United Farmers of Alberta, 1921-1935."

55. See Thomas, *The Liberal Party in Alberta,* pp. 97-106.

56. Saywell, "Lieutenant-Governors," pp. 302-3.

57. See Thomas, *The Liberal Party in Alberta,* pp. 172-4. On the 1913 election, J.G. MacGregor says: "The election was a bitter battle where dubious practices vied with political juggling and assorted shenanigans. Electors were bribed, ballot boxes lost or stuffed, and the candidates, with the hearty approval of most of the electors, dragged out all the tricks known to successful politicians of the day," p. 215.

58. Among other sources on this subject are Macpherson, *Democracy in Alberta,* ch. 2; and W.K. Rolph, *Henry Wise Wood of Alberta* (Toronto: University of Toronto Press, 1950).

59. William Irvine, *The Farmers in Politics* (Toronto: McClelland and Stewart, 1920; reprinted in 1976 in the Carleton Library series); Anthony Mardiros, *William Irvine: The Life of a Prairie Radical* (Toronto: Lorimer, 1979).

60. MacGregor, *A History of Alberta,* p. 256.

61. Betke, "The United Farmers of Alberta," p. 23.

62. Watkins, *The Golden Province,* p. 70.

63. Macpherson, *Democracy in Alberta,* chs. 2 and 3. Macpherson argues that the UFA should be viewed in contrast with other parties, rather than in terms of the difference between its theory and practice, pp. 91-2.

64. Unfortunately for the UFA, the minister of Public Works at the time was embroiled in a scandal involving financial discrepancies, of which he was later exonerated, as well as a contested divorce suit.

65. The leading works on this period include John Irving, *The Social Credit Movement in Alberta* (Toronto: University of Toronto Press, 1959); J.R. Mallory, *Social Credit and the Federal Power in Canada* (Toronto: University of Toronto Press, 1954); Macpherson, *Democracy in Alberta;* Barr, *The Dynasty;* L.H. Thomas, *William Aberhart and Social Credit in Alberta* (Toronto: Copp Clark, 1977); Joseph Boudreau, *Alberta, Aberhart and Social Credit* (Toronto: Holt, Rinehart and Winston, 1975); Watkins, *The Golden Province;* MacGregor, *A History of Alberta;* L.P.V. Johnson and Ola MacNutt, *Aberhart of Alberta* (Edmonton: Institute of Applied Art, 1970); David Elliott and Iris Miller, *Bible Bill*

(Edmonton: Reidmore Books, 1987); Finkel, *The Social Credit Phenomenon in Alberta;* and Harold Schultz, "Portrait of a Premier: William Aberhart," *Canadian Historical Review* (1964).

66. Irving, *The Social Credit Movement,* p. 308; Barr, *The Dynasty,* p. 38. See also Edward Bell, *Social Classes and Social Credit in Alberta* (Montreal: McGill-Queen's University Press, 1994).

67. Watkins, *The Golden Province,* p. 93.

68. Harold Schultz, "The Social Credit Back-benchers' Revolt," *Canadian Historical Review* (March 1960).

69. Mallory, *Social Credit and the Federal Power in Canada;* H.J. Whalen, "Social Credit Measures in Alberta," in *Canadian Journal of Economics and Political Science* (November 1952).

70. Macpherson, *Democracy in Alberta,* p. 233.

71. Myron Johnson, "The Failure of the CCF in Alberta: An Accident of History," in Caldarola, *Society and Politics;* Alvin Finkel, "Obscure Origins: The Confused Early History of the Alberta CCF," in William Brennan, ed., *Building the Co-operative Commonwealth* (Regina: Canadian Plains Research Centre, 1984).

72. Johnson, "The Failure of the CCF," in Caldarola, *Society and Politics,* p. 105.

73. Richards and Pratt, *Prairie Capitalism,* p. 83.

74. Barr, *The Dynasty,* pp. 140-44; Richards and Pratt, *Prairie Capitalism,* pp. 85-91. Richards and Pratt point out that oil brought prosperity, which gave rise to a new middle class, and populism was "swallowed up in the maw of Americanization."

75. Richards and Pratt, *Prairie Capitalism,* p. 67.

76. Watkins, *The Golden Province,* p. 177. Many were concerned, for example, that long-time Minister of Lands and Mines Nathan Tanner had recently resigned to make his own fortune in the petroleum industry. Manning himself made a little money on some land transactions, but was not criticized for doing so, p. 183.

77. Barr, *The Dynasty,* p. 133.

78. Ibid., p. 154.

79. This period is covered in accounts in the *Canadian Annual Review of Politics and Public Affairs;* Richards and Pratt, *Prairie Capitalism;* Hustak, *Peter Lougheed;* and Wood, *The Lougheed Legacy.*

80. Serfaty, "The Rise of the Conservative Party of Alberta under Lougheed, 1966-71."

81. Barr, *The Dynasty,* p. 235.

82. Elton and Goddard, "The Conservative Takeover," and "A Return to Consensus Politics;" Edward Bell, "The Rise of the Lougheed Conservatives and the Demise of Social Credit in Alberta: A Reconsideration," *Canadian Journal of Political Science* (September 1993).

83. Barr, *The Dynasty,* ch. 13, documents the disarray in the Social Credit campaign between various factions and personalities; Richards and Pratt compare Aberhart and Lougheed, *Prairie Capitalism,* p. 165.

84. Larry Pratt, *The Tar Sands* (Edmonton: Hurtig, 1976) is one such criticism.

85. *Canadian Annual Review of Politics and Public Affairs,* 1979, p. 372.

86. This paragraph is a condensation of Richards and Pratt, *Prairie Capitalism,* chs. 7 and 9.

87. Ibid., p. 237.

88. For a negative perspective on the growth, see Chuck Reasons, ed., *Stampede City, Power and Politics in the West* (Toronto: Between the Lines, 1984).

89. For a very critical account of the National Energy Program, see Peter Foster, *The Sorcerer's Apprentices: Canada's Super-bureaucrats and the Energy Mess* (Toronto: Collins, 1982). C.L. Ruthven, "Canadian Federalism and the Regulation of Oil: 1960-1984," an address to the Canadian Political Science Association (May 1985).

90. Howard Leeson, *Grant Notley: The Social Conscience of Alberta* (Edmonton: University of Alberta Press), 1992.

91. Another problem was the solicitor general who resigned after studying the province's prostitution problem personally in the comfort of his car.

92. James Lightbody, "Dancing with Dinosaurs: Alberta Politics in 1986," *Canadian Forum* (January 1986).

93. Keith Archer and Margaret Hunziker, "Leadership Selection in Alberta: The 1985 Progressive Conservative Leadership Convention," in Carty, *Leaders and Parties in Canadian Politics.*

94. Allan Tupper, "New Dimensions of Alberta Politics," *Queen's Quarterly* (Winter 1986).

95. Andrew Nikiforuk, Sheila Pratt, and Don Wanagas, *Running on Empty: Alberta After the Boom* (Edmonton: NeWest Press, 1987).

96. Larry Pratt and Ian Urquhart, *The Last Great Forest: Japanese Multinationals and Alberta's Northern Forests* (Edmonton: NeWest Press, 1995).

97. David Stewart, "Electing the Premier: an Examination of the 1992 Alberta Progressive Conservative Leadership Election," an address to the Canadian Political Science Association, 1994.

98. Glen Mumey and Joseph Ostermann, "Alberta Heritage Fund: Measuring Value and Achievement," *Canadian Public Policy* (March 1990).

99. Alvin Finkel, "The Arsenal of the Right: the Klein Revolution," *Canadian Dimension* (October-November, 1994); Kenneth Whyte, "Klein of the Times," *Saturday Night* (May 1994); Mark Lisac, *The Klein Revolution* (Edmonton: NcWest Press, 1995).

READINGS

Bell, Edward. *Social Classes and Social Credit in Alberta.* Montreal: McGill-Queen's University Press, 1994.

Canadian Annual Review of Politics and Public Affairs. Toronto: University of Toronto Press, annual.

Finkel, Alvin. *The Social Credit Phenomenon in Alberta.* Toronto: University of Toronto Press, 1989.

Lisac, Mark. *The Klein Revolution.* Edmonton: NeWest Press, 1995.

Macpherson, C.B. *Democracy in Alberta: Social Credit and the Party System.* Toronto: University of Toronto Press, 1953.

Richards, John, and Larry Pratt. *Prairie Capitalism: Power and Influence in the New West.* Toronto: McClelland and Stewart, 1979.

Stevenson, Garth. "Quasi-democracy in Alberta." H.G. Thorburn, ed. *Party Politics in Canada.* Scarborough: Prentice Hall Canada, 5th ed., 1985.

Tupper, Allan and Roger Gibbins, eds. *Government and Politics in Alberta.* Edmonton: University of Alberta Press, 1992.

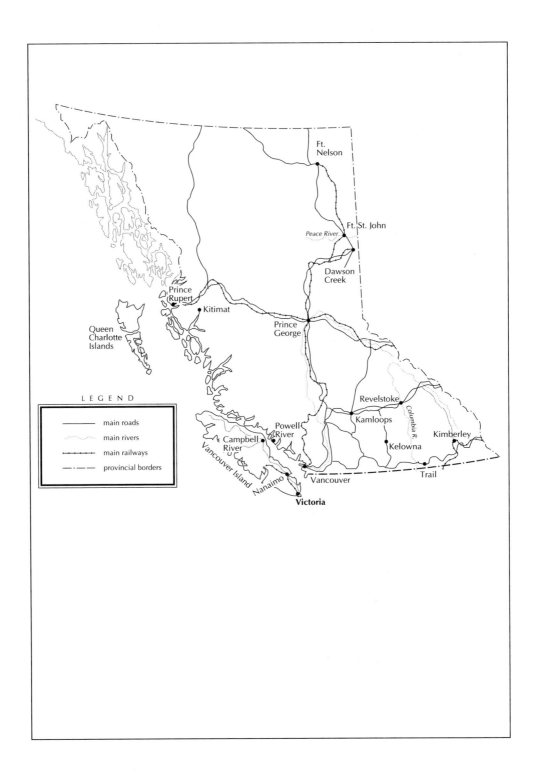

BRITISH COLUMBIA

With its mild climate, lush vegetation, abundant forest and mineral resources, magnificent scenery, and widespread prosperity, British Columbia is the lotus-land of Canada. Isolated from the rest of the country by the Rocky Mountains, B.C. is often unorthodox, being either innovative and avant garde or ultra-conservative and behind the times. It is not always a peaceful paradise, for the pattern of resource exploitation in this rich province has created conflict between labour and management and between left and right. British Columbian society has often been more polarized than that of any other province, but as it approaches the turn of the century, politicians on both sides have tried to maintain a more moderate position.

SETTING[1]

Geography

British Columbia is 948,596 square kilometres in area, the third-largest province in both area and population. It is mainly categorized as being part of the Western Cordillera physiographic region, which consists of four principal parts: the coastal mountains, the interior plateau, the Rocky Mountains in the southeast, and a large triangular continuation of the central plains in the northeast. There are several major rivers—the Fraser and the Columbia flow southwestward, the former ending at Vancouver and the latter in the United States, and the Peace River travels northeastward through Alberta to the Arctic. The province consists of the mainland portion and many islands, the main ones being the Queen Charlottes and Vancouver Island, the latter constituting about three percent of the total area and containing the capital city, Victoria. The mainland is divided between the lower Fraser Valley which is dominated by Vancouver; the interior, which includes various strips of development in the south such as the Kootenays, Okanagan, and Cariboo; and the north. In total, the province officially recognizes eight development regions. Many coastal communities are isolated, and some interior settlements have only recently been linked with roads and railways.

British Columbia's population first exceeded that of Saskatchewan in 1951. It has been rapidly increasing in size ever since, surpassing three million in early 1989, and reaching 3,282,061 in 1991. By January 1995, it had risen to 3,719,400. Vancouver is the dominant urban centre, with 471,844 city residents and 1,602,502 people living in the metropolitan area, which includes such self-contained municipalities as North and West Vancouver, Burnaby, New Westminster, and Coquitlam. Vancouver has been the largest city in Western Canada since 1931, and much of its growth can be attributed to its increased importance as a port. Furthermore, Vancouver is the economic and cultural core of British Columbia and, with exactly half of the provincial population living in the area, it easily overshadows the interior hinterland as well as the political capital, Victoria. That city is second largest in the province, with a population of 287,897. Other cities include Matsqui (113,562), Kelowna (111,846), Nanaimo (73,547) and Prince George (69,653). In 1991 British Columbia became the second most urbanized province, at 80.4 percent.

Given its terrain, British Columbia's economic development depends heavily on its transportation and communications infrastructure. The province's transportation system includes the two national railways terminating in Vancouver, a Canadian National line crossing to Prince Rupert, and the provincially owned BC Rail, which stretches from North Vancouver through Prince George and Fort St. John to Fort Nelson, and connects with the Northern Alberta Railway at Dawson Creek. All railway companies have made major capital improvements in recent years. In addition to the southern roads, including two branches of the Trans-Canada Highway, the Alaska Highway (built during the Second World War) links Dawson Creek-Fort St. John to Fort Nelson and the Yukon, while another highway parallels the railway between Prince George and Prince Rupert and then sweeps north to meet the Alaska Highway at the Yukon border. Major deep-sea bulk cargo facilities are located at North Vancouver, Surrey, Port Moody, and Roberts Bank, making Vancouver by far the largest port in Canada. It has had container capabilities since 1976. Prince Rupert is rapidly becoming an important port as well, now ninth busiest in the country. Both B.C. products and prairie produce are exported from these ports, with the most common destinations being the United States and Japan. Coastal shipping includes the British Columbia Ferry Corporation, which operates the largest ferry fleet in the world, principally between the mainland and Vancouver Island. The province is also served by many airlines, Vancouver's airport being the country's second largest. In 1992, a local airport authority assumed control of the facility from the federal government.

Economy

British Columbia is rich in all four basic primary products—mining, forestry, agriculture, and fishing—and is heavily dependent on the extraction, processing, and export of such raw materials.[2] But it is increasingly dependent on secondary and tertiary sectors, however much these are based on natural resources. In the 1990s, some observers noted a dual economy in the province—a flourishing Vancouver, specializing in services, and a stagnant resource-based interior.

B.C. is the leading Canadian province if all aspects of forest production are combined; it is far ahead in logging and the production of lumber, ranks second in woodpulp and newsprint, and third in other paper and paperboard. Much of the industry is still located in its original locations—the mainland coast, including Powell River, and on Vancouver Island, at Port Alberni—but with improved inland transportation, the interior forest is also being exploited. B.C. is famous for its towering Douglas fir, but its other and often more important species are lodgepole pine, spruce, hemlock, balsam, and cedar. Forestry is the largest export industry in the province and the base of the main segment of manufacturing. The pattern of production is for the province to sell timber rights on public land to private companies, which leads to a close relationship between the government and the principal corporations in the field such as MacMillan Bloedel Ltd., Fletcher Challenge Canada Ltd., Canfor Corp., Crestbrook Forest Industries Ltd., Crown Forest Industries Ltd., Weldwood of Canada Ltd., Western Pulp, Weyerhaeuser Canada Ltd., and Cariboo Pulp and Paper. Although clear-cutting operations caused controversy in the past and the logging of old growth forest continues to foment opposition, the government now regulates the industry more rigidly and puts considerable effort into reforestation through its silviculture program.

Large numbers are employed in all aspects of the forestry industry—logging, sawmilling, and pulp and paper—and it is very sensitive to shifts in the U.S. economy. American recessions always cause a serious drop in demand because of a reduction in residential construction, and in the 1980s U.S. lumber producers also sought to impose a countervailing duty on exports of Canadian softwood lumber and cedar shakes and shingles. As a consequence, enormous layoffs in all aspects of the B.C. forestry industry provided an incentive for "free trade." An increasing proportion of the forest production is being processed into more sophisticated, value-added products, such as paper, windows, and doors. The largest pulp and/or paper mills are located on Vancouver Island, across the strait between Vancouver and Powell River, and at Quesnel, Prince George, Mackenzie, Prince Rupert, and Kitimat.

The province's mining industry, although exceeded by that of Alberta and Ontario, is of great importance. Copper has now become the leading mineral in B.C., one in which it ranks first in the country, and is mainly found in the interior plateau, frequently accompanied by molybdenum deposits. The second-most valuable mineral is coal, of which the province competes with Alberta as the leading Canadian producer. Historically coal was mined in the extreme south-east corner of the province where B.C. shares a seam with southwestern Alberta. In response to expanded export markets, Robert Banks just south of Vancouver has become a coal superport. In 1984 Quintette Coal (half owned by Denison Mines) and Tech Coal undertook a large coal development in the northeast. This project was based on a long-term agreement with Japan and involved building railways, highways, a power plant, and a new town of Tumbler Ridge, as well as new port facilities at Prince Rupert. The next most important mineral is gold, in which British Columbia ranks third, while it leads the country in the production of silver. Both are mined in the northwest part of the province. B.C. remains a significant source of lead and zinc, which are mainly produced at the Sullivan Mine at Kimberley, one of the first major developments in the province. They are processed at the nearby Cominco smelter, one of the largest in the world, at Trail. A small amount of asbestos was found at Cassiar in the north, but this mine closed in 1992, as did a number of others. The province also has an abundance of structural materials such as sand, gravel, gypsum, stone, and cement. The Alcan smelter at Kitimat, with its large supply of hydroelectricity, transforms imported bauxite into aluminum, as in Quebec.

B.C. ranks second in the country in terms of natural gas and natural gas byproducts, and third in oil, although it must also import the latter from Alberta. These petroleum resources are found in the northeast plains, particularly in the Dawson Creek-Fort St. John and Fort Nelson areas. Pipelines deliver the petroleum to southern parts of the province and to Prince Rupert, and a natural gas pipeline between the mainland and Vancouver Island was completed in 1991. On the other hand, several Vancouver-area oil refineries closed in the early 1990s.

British Columbia ranks sixth among all provinces in agriculture, but this industry is also a major source of provincial wealth. The value of livestock exceeds that of crops, as B.C. features cattle ranching in the interior plateau, dairy farming, especially in the lower Fraser Valley, poultry and eggs. As for crops, it specializes in nursery products and fruit and vegetables. It rivals Ontario in the production of fruit, with the Okanagan valley being famous for its apples, grapes, and other tree fruit. There is also grain grown in the Peace River district. In 1991, B.C. had 19,225 farms with an average size of 307 acres, but this figure disguises a wide range from huge cattle and grain farms to tiny greenhouse or poultry businesses. More and more agricultural production is being processed into canned and frozen products, including fruit drinks and wine.

Even though the B.C. fishing industry has been spared the trauma characterizing its Atlantic counterpart in the 1990s, it is still smaller than that of the Atlantic coast, with B.C. second to Nova Scotia among individual provinces. B.C.'s specialty is salmon, which constitutes over 50 percent of the value of the fishing industry. The salmon is located along the entire west coast as well as around Vancouver Island, and can be sold fresh, chilled, frozen, canned, filleted or smoked. In recent years, much has been done by way of aquaculture to support the rather fragile and unpredictable catch, but it has suffered seriously from poaching, excessive quotas, and the failure to enforce such quotas. Roe herring is also becoming important, especially in the Japanese market, and exceeds the value of groundfish, while the other main catches are shellfish and halibut. In addition to salmon farms, the province boasts shellfish and trout farms. As on the Atlantic coast, attempts have been made to rationalize the fishing fleet, and disputes have erupted with the United States over respective fishing zones. The extension of the 200-mile limit in 1976 was a major boost to the industry, and, although it did not end the problems, in 1985 a treaty was finally signed with the U.S. concerning disputed salmon fishing territory off the northwest coast. Most of the fish processing plants are located in the Prince Rupert and Vancouver areas.

TABLE 11.1   British Columbia 1991 Labour Force and Estimated 1995 Gross Domestic Product by Industry

Industry	1991 Labour Force		Est. 1995 GDP ($ millions)	
Agriculture	41,290	2.4%	744	1.0%
Fishing	9,900	0.6%	228	0.3%
Forestry	39,280	2.3%	1,834	2.6%
Mining	19,550	1.1%	1,822	2.5%
TOTAL PRIMARY	110,020	6.4%	4,628	6.5%
Manufacturing	193,520	11.2%	9,546	13.3%
Construction	129,295	7.5%	6,799	9.5%
TOTAL SECONDARY	322,815	18.7%	16,345	22.8%
Transportation, communications and utilities	141,550	8.3%	9,221	12.9%
Trade	303,460	17.6%	9,035	12.6%
Finance, insurance and real estate	100,155	5.9%	13,329	18.6%
Services	630,105	36.6%	15,720	21.9%
Government	113,575	6.6%	3,386	4.7%
TOTAL TERTIARY	1,288,845	74.9%	50,691	70.7%
TOTAL ALL INDUSTRIES	1,721,680		71,664	

Source: Reproduced by authority of the Minister of Industry, 1995, Statistics Canada, *1991 Census,* cat. nos. 93-326 and 95-385, and Conference Board of Canada, *Provincial Outlook, Economic Forecast,* (Ottawa: Summer 1994), Vol. 9, No. 2.

British Columbia has several mighty rivers and generates most of its electric power from hydro sources. It ranks second in the production of electricity from such sources, and third in total supply. Some of the leading dams are on the

Columbia River at the Revelstoke, Mica, and Seven Mile locations, while the Gordon Shrum and Peace Canyon dams are located on the Peace River. Electricity can also be produced from thermal sources, especially natural gas, and private resource companies such as Alcan Ltd. generate their own power and sell the excess to the British Columbia Hydro and Power Authority. The electric power industry was left in private hands until the company was nationalized in 1961. Underwater cables transmit electricity from the mainland to Vancouver Island, and the province exports significant quantities to the United States. B.C. built three storage dams on the Columbia River in the 1960s and leased the downstream rights to the U.S. for 30 years. These rights will revert to the province in 1998.

B.C. ranks third among the provinces in terms of manufacturing, with about eight percent of the national total. Manufacturing is the third-largest employer in the province, and the value of this industry far exceeds all primary industries combined. Most of the manufacturing is based on the primary resources, especially wood—pulp and paper, plywood, newsprint, shingles, shakes, other wood products, and paper and allied products. Food and beverages are second and largely involve the processing of agricultural and fish products. Refined petroleum and coal products are third. The mining industry is also the base for metal fabricating, primary metals, non-metallic mineral products, and chemicals and chemical products. Printing and publishing, transportation equipment, and machinery (especially sawmill, logging, and pulp and paper equipment) round out the leading manufacturing industries. The production of electrical equipment and other higher technology products as well as plastics and clothing is also increasing. The Greater Vancouver area contains most of the manufacturing with smaller, more specialized secondary industry and processing located on Vancouver Island (pulp, wood), in the Prince Rupert-Kitimat area (wood, fish, aluminum), in the Okanagan (food and beverages), and at Trail (smelting and fertilizer).

B.C. has a higher proportion of residents employed in the tertiary sector than any other province. The service and trade sectors are its two major employers, with tourism a particularly important element given B.C.'s mountain, island, and coastal scenery, provincial and national parks, skiing facilities, mild climate, and Okanagan wine tasting, as well as the many attractions of Vancouver and Victoria. British Columbia is increasingly becoming a retirement base, especially in the Vancouver Island, Vancouver, and Okanagan regions. The province also has a large financial sector, including the headquarters of the HongKong Bank of Canada and the Vancouver Stock Exchange. The federal government employs 54,108 people in B.C., the province, 135,837, and municipalities, 95,263.

British Columbia's chief exports are softwood lumber, pulp, coal, newsprint, copper, paper and paperboard, machinery, aluminum, and natural gas. Its leading customers are the United States (about 50 percent) and Japan (about 25 percent). The construction of the Panama Canal in 1914 opened new markets in Europe, and the European Union remains the province's third-largest customer.

Class

During the past 20 years or so, British Columbia has often been ranked as the most wealthy province. In 1992 its per capita income was $22,662, between that of Ontario and Alberta. In 1991, 15.1 percent of families made less than $20,000, fewer than any province except Ontario, while 22 percent of B.C. residents received more than $70,000, for a median family income of $46,151. The province also has one of the country's highest levels of educational attainment. One reason incomes are so high is that it is the second most heavily unionized province in the country, with 38.7 percent of paid workers belonging to unions. The largest unions are the B.C. Government Employees' Union; the International Woodworkers of America (Canada); the Canadian Union of Public Employees (CUPE); the Communications, Energy and Paperworkers; the B.C. Teachers' Federation; and the United Food and Commercial Workers. More than half of the 519,500 unionized workers (350,000) belong to the B.C. Federation of Labour. This strength of organized labour is related to the prominence of the NDP at the political level. On the other hand, the B.C. unemployment rate is often high, sometimes exceeding that of the Maritime provinces. In the early 1990s, however, it paralleled Ontario's, and was only slightly higher than that of the prairie provinces, hovering just below 10 percent.

Among the prominent B.C. corporations and chief executive officers are the following: John Sheehan (B.C. Hydro), Brian Canfield (B.C. Telecom), Peter Bentley (Canfor Corp.), Gary Charlwood (Century 21 and Uniglobe Travel Ltd.), Robert Hallbauer (Cominco Ltd.), Douglas Whitehead (Fletcher Challenge), Conrad Black (Hollinger Inc.), Jimmy Pattison (Jim Pattison Ltd.), Robert Findlay (MacMillan Bloedel), John Willson (Placer Dome Inc.), James Shepard (Finning Ltd.), Michael Phelps (Westcoast Energy Inc.), and Hank Ketcham (West Fraser Timber Co. Ltd.). The key provincial dynasty used to be the Woodward family of department store fame, but it was racked by a bitter family feud in 1985 as well as rival takeover bids, and the Hudson's Bay Co. picked up the remaining pieces.

Many analyses of British Columbia politics emphasize the class dimension, and concentrate on the division between labour and capital. In the forestry and mining company towns found throughout the province a class division was evident—workers versus management—with no intervening middle class.[3] Vancouver itself experienced a long history of class consciousness on the part of workers and of labour political activity, undoubtedly reflecting the early immigration of British trade unionists. Thus both in the metropolitan centre and in towns in the hinterland, a class cleavage was felt and then politicized. More recently, Michael Howlett and Keith Brownsey have restated the significance of class, but argued that the situation is more complex. They say that "at least six classes and class fractions compete and collude with the aim of attaining electoral success."[4] They divide capital into two classes, large and small; the middle class into the traditional petite bourgeoisie and the new middle class; and the working class between public (non-manual) and private sector (manual). They point to shifting coalitions of these six classes in explaining B.C. election results, rather than emphasizing more superficial factors such as party leadership.

Demography

In terms of ethnicity, about one-half of British Columbians are at least partly of British descent, a higher proportion than in the other Western provinces. Of those with single origins, the Chinese segment has recently overtaken the Germans. Those of East Indian, other Asian, French, Scandinavian, Dutch, and Aboriginal heritage follow. The French minority has been effectively assimilated and B.C. has the highest language transfer rate of any province. Only 1.6 percent list French as their mother tongue, and only 0.4 percent of the total population use it at home, compared with 90 percent who use English. Given this situation, the status of the French language has never been an internal political issue in the province, and official recognition is limited to a handful of French-language schools and a number of other mixed schools. On the other hand, the significant number of Asians was once the source of much conflict and, with high recent immigration from Hong Kong, China, Taiwan, India, and the Philippines, it threatens to be so again. B.C. now offers credit courses in Mandarin, Japanese, and Punjabi in some of its high schools. This is the only province in which less than half of its residents were born in the province (49 percent), with 29 percent coming from elsewhere in Canada, primarily lured by the climate, and 22 percent from abroad.

British Columbia has the second-largest number of residents with aboriginal origins, and the fourth-largest proportion, and it is the province in which Native land claims are most prominent and problematic. The Royal Proclamation of 1763 recognized aboriginal title and said that only the Crown could acquire lands from aboriginal inhabitants and only by treaty, but the policy was not pursued west of the Rocky Mountains, and few treaties were signed when European and Asian immigrants began to arrive. The Hudson's Bay Co. purchased aboriginal land and only a limited number of small reserves were created as protection from aggressive settlers. Moreover, in 1916, lands were cut off from 34 reserves without aboriginal consent. The Nishga tribe went to court and in 1973 the Supreme Court of Canada's recognition of aboriginal title prompted Ottawa to start negotiating comprehensive claims. But the province's policy was to deny the validity of aboriginal title, and it refused to participate. Some recent progress has been made on this difficult issue, including the Sechelt band's acquisition of a quasi-municipal form of aboriginal self-government and, after a change of provincial policy, tripartite negotiations began in 1990 with the Nisga'a Tribal Council. The Harcourt government recognized aboriginal title and the inherent right to self-government, transferred certain programs to First

Nations control, and established the British Columbia Treaty Commission to oversee the process of negotiating modern treaties.

TABLE 11.2   British Columbia Mother Tongue and Home Language, 1991

	Mother Tongue	Home Language
English	80.5%	89.6%
French	1.6%	0.4%
Other	17.9%	9.9%

Source: Reproduced by authority of the Minister of Industry, 1995, Statistics Canada, *1991 Census,* cat. no. 93-317, adapted by author.

TABLE 11.3   Religion in British Columbia, 1991

Protestant			1,446,475 (44.5%)
United Church	420,755	(13.0%)	
Anglican	328,580	(10.1%)	
Lutheran	108,190	(3.3%)	
Baptist	84,090	(2.6%)	
Pentecostal	70,620	(2.2%)	
Presbyterian	63,985	(2.0%)	
Mennonite	39,055	(1.2%)	
Jehovah Witness	33,665	(1.0%)	
Other Protestant	297,535	(9.2%)	
No Religious Affiliation			987,985 (30.4%)
Roman Catholic			603,080 (18.6%)
Eastern Non-Christian			159,965 (4.9%)
Other			50,005 (1.5%)

Source: Reproduced by authority of the Minister of Industry, 1995, Statistics Canada, *1991 Census,* cat. no. 93-319, adapted by author.

This ethnic distribution reflects the fact that only 18.6 percent of the province's population is Roman Catholic, while 44.5 percent is Protestant. B.C. leads the country in terms of the proportion of residents who have no organized religion (30 percent), as well as those who belong to the Eastern Non-Christian group. Among the Protestant sects, the United and Anglican churches are the largest, but Baptists and Pentecostals are relatively stronger than in most other provinces including Alberta. As with language, religion has rarely been of much political significance in the province, except to some extent as a base for the Social Credit party. British Columbia does not have a Roman Catholic separate school system, but the government provides partial funding for some independent schools.

As in most provinces, politics in B.C. have been preoccupied with economic development. However, despite this general focus and the lack of ethnic and religious tensions, the province is affected by regional cleavages and class divisions. B.C. has experienced the usual regional rivalry, exacerbated by geographic barriers and generally centred on the distribution of government works; but it has also felt serious conflicts between different regionally based industries as well as a particular resentment in the hinterland against the dominant role of Vancouver. That city is often seen as being parasitic, siphoning the wealth produced in the interior and controlling the fate of those who do the real work in harvesting the resources. Consciousness of class, whether two or six in number, has led to a more polarized ideological party system than in any other province.

Federal-Provincial Relations

British Columbia's attitude towards Ottawa has more often been one of indifference than the hostility so commonly experienced on the Prairies. With the geographic barrier of the Rocky Mountains, British Columbians have gone about their work by developing their resources, selling them to the world, and interacting with the western United States and the Pacific rim in relative isolation from the rest of Canada.

B.C. has made the usual Western demands on the federal government concerning tariff, transportation, monetary and language policies, insufficient representation in national political institutions, and interference in provincial jurisdiction.[5] The specific complaints, however, reveal a distinctive B.C. perspective on such issues—an imbalance between federal expenditures in the province and revenues derived from it; inadequate transportation and communication links to the rest of the country; and insufficient assistance to the provincial transportation infrastructure, ignoring the high costs incurred by projects such as highway construction in mountainous areas. B.C. is ineligible for equalization payments, so in 1992 Ottawa transferred $2.3 billion to the B.C. government, only 13 percent of the province's revenues. The federal government also transferred $107 million to B.C. municipalities, $6.6 billion to individuals, and $405 million to businesses.

During the 1870s, a separatist threat emerged because the Canadian Pacific Railway line was not finished on schedule and other items in the Terms of Union were unfulfilled. A second major confrontation occurred in 1907 in connection with a revision of federal-provincial grants. Discriminatory freight rates became a serious issue in 1920, as did the Rowell-Sirois Report in the 1937-40 period. After 1952, W.A.C. Bennett was usually at odds with Ottawa over one aspect of public finance or another, but the most controversial dispute of that era was the Columbia River Treaty, although the federal government ultimately agreed with Bennett's position. Since 1975 new conflicts have developed, especially over the National Energy Program, the Constitution, finances, and aboriginal issues. A variety of resource issues with a particular B.C. flavour have arisen due to the importance of the forestry and mining sectors in the province and the export orientation of these industries. "The reality is a rather complex triangular interaction among the two jurisdictions and the dominant resource industries."[6] The province works closely with these industries to influence federal policies on transportation facilities and costs, tariffs and other trade restrictions, monetary policy, and the exchange rate of the Canadian dollar. The key questions have been duty-free export of lumber, newsprint, and pulp to the United States, the opening of the Japanese market to B.C. lumber and coal, low tariffs on imported machinery and equipment, and taxation of the mining industry. Thus, the province's recent demands on Ottawa have generally related more to help on the export scene than to changes in domestic policy. It has followed Alberta's lead on petroleum matters, and it has deferred to federal jurisdiction over fisheries, although it supports the concept of concurrent jurisdiction over off-shore fisheries. In the 1990s, the two levels of government first co-operated and then fought over the KAON particle accelerator facility at the University of British Columbia. The province also opposed unilateral reductions in federal transfer payments, especially the cut to its share of Canada Assistance Plan funds. Greater co-operation was forthcoming on the Treaty Commission established to oversee negotiations with the province's First Nations.

POLITICAL CULTURE[7]

Given the province's wealth and isolation, its residents present a distinct image of optimism, self-centredness, and self-satisfaction. With the province's mountains and sea-coast, pleasant climate and varied resources, British Columbians consider themselves the envy of the rest of the country. Their model is the relaxed, "laid-back," and often off-beat style of California. British Columbia is the end of the line, appealing to those who want to make their fortune and those who want to "do their own thing." Indeed, one reason for the lack of a more substantive self-image is the constant immigration to the province. Historically, a large proportion of immigrants went directly to B.C. without any contact with the perspectives of central Canada. The province thus has a "parvenu" or frontier orientation, its society has hardly had time to congeal, and it is unstable and lacks traditions, all of which foster a mentality centred on future growth rather than past accomplishments.[8] Martin Robin discusses the many fortune seekers, buccaneer capitalists, boodle hunters, plunderers, and promoters who were attracted to the province.[9]

The *Maclean's* surveys of 1990 and 1994 consistently showed that only 17 percent of B.C. residents saw themselves first as citizens of their province, compared to an average of about 80 percent who felt themselves first to be Canadians (more than in Alberta). These surprising figures apparently reveal the provincial orientation of British Columbians is based less on hostility than on feelings of "defensive and disinterested detachment."[10] Of course, B.C. has pressed its material claims upon the federal government and provincial politicians have not hesitated to damn Ottawa when it has suited their purposes; but the electorate has never developed a protracted and intense bitterness towards Ottawa, perhaps due to the lack of an agrarian revolt. In some respects the obstacles to communication and the weakness of integrative institutions within the province have retarded the development of provincial sentiment; and, while B.C. constitutes a "small world" unto itself in many respects, it is also proof that people can be in favour of their province without being against the country.[11] For reasons of both geography and mentality, B.C. is often categorized as a fifth separate region in the country.

While both W.A.C. Bennett and Dave Barrett practised a kind of populist politics, B.C. does not have the same agrarian populist tradition as the Prairie provinces. With a small agricultural base, the province had virtually no farmer politics, even in the 1921 period, and adhered to no particular theories which emphasized democratic participation, although eight plebiscites were held between 1900 and 1952.

TABLE 11.4   British Columbia Voter Turn-out Rate in Recent Federal and Provincial Elections

Federal Elections		Provincial Elections	
1974	72%	1972	69%
1979	75%	1975	70%
1980	71%	1979	69%
1984	78%	1983	78%
1988	79%	1986	77%
1993	68%	1991	75%
Average	73.8%	Average	73.0%

Source: *Reports of the Chief Electoral Officer,* calculations by author.

B.C. was also marked by a long entrenchment of clientelism.[12] Parties did not develop for more than 30 years after it had become a province, so much scope was left for individual politicians to grant favours to various clients, including themselves. A long period of second stage clientelism followed, in which patronage was dispensed by the government party.[13] B.C. experienced considerable political corruption well into the Vander Zalm era. A good deal of "public works" and "highway" politics also took place but, because of the limited role accorded to the bureaucracy, such government favours were dispensed by politicians long after this practice had ceased in most other provinces. Third stage clientelism, in which the public service has the major role in distributing patronage, arrived late in B.C. because bureaucrats did not render advice unless it was solicited, which did not occur until 1972.

By the standards of Simeon and Elkins, British Columbia has the most highly developed political culture of any province. It is high in both feelings of trust and efficacy,[14] although the actual level of voter turn-out is not so impressive, 74 percent and 73 percent in federal and provincial elections respectively. Given the sense of partisan difference in the province, it is surprising that the voter turn-out rate, especially in provincial elections, is not higher.

The most significant aspect of the British Columbia political culture has been its bipolarity, its division into two ideological camps with much resulting discord and an intense political hostility between the two major parties. Given that this is largely a class-based cleavage, observers such as Wilson regard the province as having a "developed" political culture.[15] The basis of this bipolarity is the dominance of the resource industry, especially forestry and mining, which fosters a "politics of exploitation."[16] Both industries are characterized by a relatively small number of large, capital-intensive firms, operating in a series of single-industry company towns. Each was divided clearly between workers and management, with a few business people and professionals on the management side. Class consciousness was a natural result, with workers gravitating to a left-wing political party, and the others, to the right. The lumber and mining camps were an excellent incubator of radical union activity, among British and American Marxists as well as continental European immigrants.[17] Meanwhile, in Vancouver a similar class cleavage developed, largely influenced by British trade unionist immigrants. They came to the province at the turn of the century with the experience of union organization, strikes, and the beginnings of the British Labour party. Many others who arrived from Edwardian England, however, intended to make their fortunes in the province and wished to dissociate themselves from manual workers.

The working-class elements across the province found common cause in a variety of often extreme labour and socialist movements, eventually producing the more moderate CCF/NDP. The middle class and entrepreneurs recognized their mutual interests were embodied in the Liberal, Conservative, or Social Credit parties. The province witnessed a prolonged ideological conflict between the forces of acquisitiveness and individualism on the one hand and equality and collectivism on the other, although it was not as all-inclusive as the "extravagant rhetoric" on the part of politicians on each side would suggest. Yet rather than regard the province as possessing two political cultures, they are best seen in combination, because "the existence of each is vital to the maintenance of internal discipline within the other."[18] This rigid division may be breaking down somewhat in the 1990s.

POLITICAL PARTIES

Party System

When parties began to take form in British Columbia after 1903, the province had a non-polarized two-party system consisting of Liberals and Conservatives, although a labour-socialist element always existed. This system remained intact until the mid-1930s when the CCF entered the fray. The "socialist" threat propelled the Liberals and Conservatives into a provincial coalition government in 1941 with the CCF as the official Opposition. Ten years later, as the coalition was breaking up, the partners introduced an electoral system designed to keep the CCF out of government, even as coalition members went their separate ways. The new system achieved that purpose, but instead of benefiting the Liberals or Conservatives, the experiment backfired to the advantage of Social Credit. That party represented a change from the warring coalition parties but also provided ideological continuity. Thereafter the Liberals and Conservatives declined in provincial politics, although the former retained about 20 percent of the vote, and the province might be said to have had a two-and-one-half or three-party system until 1972. W.A.C. Bennett followed the example of previous successful government parties in the province: developing its resources but also showing concern for the welfare of the people. The Social Credit vehicle was appropriately anti-socialist and pro-development, but it produced bountiful revenues with which to improve social services.

The NDP finally came to power in 1972, after having been the official Opposition for almost 40 continuous years, at about the same time that most other provinces also changed governments. The national economic situation, especially inflation, was undoubtedly a factor in the party's success but, as in other locations, the B.C. electorate turfed out a government that had grown stale after many years in office. Dave Barrett and the NDP presented a fresh, moderate alternative. Three-and-one-half years later, the province blamed Barrett for a lack of government competence, for a too-rapid pace of change, and for his treatment of the large resource corporations. A new Opposition coalition united behind Bill Bennett, as he invited remnants of the Liberal and Conservative parties into his renewed Social Credit ranks. By 1979, the NDP had developed a coalition of its own by absorbing other politically homeless elements, so that the province was left throughout the 1980s with a balanced and ideologically polarized two-party system, Social Credit and NDP. Because neither of the national major parties was significant at the provincial level, B.C.'s was sometimes called a "protest party" system.

Thus, while the polarized ideological rhetoric before 1975 was always some-what diluted by the presence of the moderate Liberals, it was unrestrained for the next 15 years. The degree of ideological polarization in the last half of the 1980s was extreme, and the government genuinely neo-conservative. The NDP defeated Social Credit again in 1991, after which the Socred party disintegrated. Some of its support drifted into a provincial Reform party, not officially affiliated with Preston Manning's federal party of the same name, and the rest helped catapult the Liberals into the position of major contender.

TABLE 11.5   Party Support in British Columbia, 1970-95

	Years in Office	Average Percentage of Vote	Percentage of Seats
Social Credit	18	41.8	44.8
NDP	7	42.3	48.1
Combined	25	84.0	92.9
Liberal	—	11.0	6.3

Source: *Reports of the Chief Electoral Officer,* calculations by author.

FIGURE 11.1   Percentage of Vote by Party in British Columbia Elections, 1970-1991

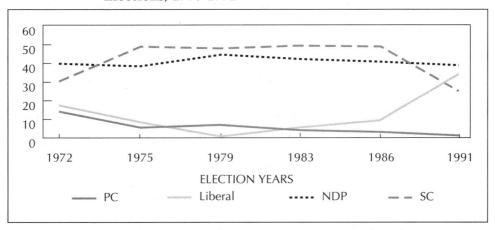

During the almost 40 years in which B.C. residents were electing Social Credit provincial governments, they were sending an almost balanced number of Liberal, Conservative, and CCF/NDP members to Ottawa. With the Socreds essentially out of the federal picture, and with different issues, leaders, candidates, and strategies involved in national campaigns, it is not surprising that the results differed from those of provincial elections. The same electorate produced two quite different party systems in national and provincial politics, a situation which emphasizes the effect which federalism has on the development of political institutions.[19]

Party Organization

The coalition government from 1941 to 1952, one of the rare examples of such in the Canadian experience, presented an interesting case of party organization. At first the two components worked together fairly easily even though they maintained separate organizations, conventions, and caucuses. As the leadership changed and the CCF threat appeared to diminish, however, pressure increased from both federal parties to have their respective provincial wings disengage; and within the coalition itself growing disagreement over policy, spoils, and future prospects forced the partners to go their separate ways.

Although both W.A.C. Bennett and Dave Barrett had populist streaks, neither gave his party organization much influence over the conduct of government. Resolutions contradicting government policy were regularly passed at annual Socred conventions but were largely ignored. The NDP was theoretically a mass party in which the organization determined party policy and then forwarded these policies to the government for implementation. In actuality, Barrett governed in general conformity with party policy but was not bothered by any discrepancies. On occasion the party was angered because of the premier's disregard for its policy work. As Harcourt was besieged with problems, the NDP organization rallied around him in the mid-1990s.

Federal-Provincial Party Links

Given the lack of symmetry between the provincial and federal party systems in British Columbia since 1941, it is not surprising that difficulties in federal-provincial party relations have developed. In the Liberal party these problems pre-dated the coalition, as relations between Premier T.D. (Duff) Pattullo and Prime Minister Mackenzie King worsened after 1935.[20] In this case it was largely a question of policy and ideological differences, and King was happy to see Pattullo ousted from the provincial leadership in 1941. The simultaneous federal and provincial elections in 1949 caused great stress, as the two parties were friends at one level and enemies at the other. Provincial Liberal and Conservative leaders generally saw themselves as head of both wings of the party, but national leaders were reluctant to give them control over federal matters in the province because of the provincial coalition. This situation divided the

Tories into two antagonistic camps and, in the early 1950s, caused a public clash between the federal and provincial wings, especially between the two leaders, George Drew and Deane Finlayson. This rift lasted until Davie Fulton left Ottawa to become provincial conservative leader.[21] Because the split persisted through three different pairs of leaders, it was obviously more than a personality conflict; on the other hand, there were no apparent differences over policy. After the brief Fulton period, the problem re-emerged. Given that the federal Conservatives attracted the bulk of Socred provincial voter support, they were reluctant to offend Social Credit by actively assisting the provincial Conservatives. On many occasions a provincial Tory leader has complained of a lack of federal party help, and Brian Westwood was so upset about the situation that he resigned to join the Western Canada Concept.[22] Over the years there was considerable movement of provincial Liberal leaders to or from the federal scene, but at times the lack of effort on the federal level seemed designed to avoid alienating Social Credit support for federal Liberal candidates. In 1991, the B.C. Liberals opted to separate the federal and provincial branches of the party.

The two wings of the CCF/NDP have rarely been in conflict; indeed a fairly consistent support existed at both levels. Each branch recognized the need for support from the other, and the federal and provincial parties were essentially identical. Even on the 1981-82 constitutional issue, where the Saskatchewan and Alberta wings of the party were opposed to the Broadbent approach, Barrett supported the federal line. The national Social Credit party was rarely significant enough to present any problems in maintaining party unity. W.A.C. Bennett did, however, ally himself with Réal Caouette and the Quebec wing, opposed to Manning and Robert Thompson of the Alberta contingent. In fact, once it had helped him get elected, Bennett had little contact with his fellow Social Credit government next door.

Party Leadership[23]

Although ideology has been a more significant factor than leadership in B.C. politics, the province has produced several colourful, controversial, and dominant political leaders. Among the earlier premiers, Richard McBride and Duff Pattullo stand out, but so, too, do several recent premiers. W.A.C. Bennett was in office for 20 years, the longest-serving premier in the province's history, but at first sight one might wonder why. Several writers have remarked on his lack of articulateness, and his manner of speech has been called "jerky, nervous and tumbled."[24] This was offset, however, by his "beaming personality and windmill style," and by his populist, jaunty, and exuberant optimism. His public joviality and unassuming style aside, Bennett was a rather authoritarian, paternalistic leader who invariably got his own way, as exemplified by the nationalization of B.C. Electric or the terms of the Columbia River Treaty. He was fond of the formal trappings of the office and the symbolic and ceremonial aspects of leadership, but he also ran the province almost single-handedly with virtually no staff support. His public appeal was based on his image of sound, economical, and effective management and his "elaboration of the grandeur and potential of the province."[25] He was a devotee of building, development, and growth, and had the good fortune to govern when economic prosperity was high.

Except for being garrulous and populist in style, Dave Barrett was almost Bennett's opposite. He was casual, informal, collegial, fraternal, self-deprecating but bright, articulate, and entertaining. Some felt that he went too far in "demystifying the office of premier,"[26] and most believed that he did not have a firm enough hand to be in charge of both the finance portfolio and the Treasury Board.[27] His cabinet meetings were marked by "improvisational enthusiasm," and his style was creative but rudderless. On the other hand, no one doubted his sincere concern for the disadvantaged.

Bill Bennett was hardly more articulate than his father W.A.C. and sometimes exhibited a weak grasp of issues, but he was deadly serious in contrast to his always smiling father. The younger Bennett developed a technocratic style, improved the decision-making processes, surrounded himself with a more adequate complement of advisers, and earned a reputation as a dedicated, hardworking leader. No one ever suspected, however, that he had the comprehensive and well-considered ideological position revealed in 1983, although adviser Pat Kinsella had been working on his "tough guy" image for some time.[28]

Bill Vander Zalm was extremely colourful—exuberant, folksy, optimistic, and often painfully frank. Opponents derided his views, policies, and intelligence but, initially at least, he represented a breath of fresh air. He later fell victim to a fatal conflict of interest and much other political controversy, but retained some fervent admirers even afterwards.[29]

In contrast, Mike Harcourt was a bland, awkward public speaker, who tried to develop a middle ground between the previous ideological extremes which had divided the province. Many welcomed Harcourt's consensual approach, but it also contributed to his image as a weak leader not completely in command.

NDP and Socred leaders have been chosen by traditional delegate conventions, but the Liberals used the "televote" system to choose Gordon Campbell in 1993.[30] Fortunately for them, the technology worked better than in Nova Scotia and Alberta.

Party Ideology

Ideology has been the most important factor in British Columbia provincial politics, whether one listened to the party leaders, compared party policies, or even probed the orientations of the electorate. Almost every election since 1933 has been portrayed as an intense ideological conflict between the forces of left and right, democratic socialism and private enterprise. Between 1952 and its demise in 1991, Social Credit claimed to be defending ordinary people against the socialist hordes and labour leaders who would drive away investment, while the NDP portrayed itself as shielding the people from the ravages of unscrupulous capitalists.

Social Credit under W.A.C. Bennett was something of an anomaly in ideological terms. In one rhetorical flourish he claimed that his government was "more conservative than the Conservatives in financial matters, more liberal than the Liberals in terms of providing the nation's highest old-age and social assistance benefits, and even more in favour of public ownership than the CCF because of our ferry system and hydro programs."[31] The essence of his approach, however, was the business of resource exploitation. He did not hesitate to use government to promote economic growth in the private sector. Bennett was an "activist, interventionist, state capitalist" who encouraged development with highways, bridges, access roads, ferries, railways, and hydroelectric power, but then left well enough alone. His labour legislation was backward but, with considerable revenues available, he implemented generally progressive social services in a paternalistic fashion.[32] Between 1972 and 1975, the NDP moved rapidly, perhaps too much so, to have the province catch up with the rest of the country—or occasionally surpass it—in all areas neglected by Bennett. Innovative labour and agricultural legislation was introduced, and the great expansion of social programs reflected the NDP's ideology of redistribution. The NDP rule was marked by much government involvement in the economy, but it was of a different form than under Social Credit, and included increased regulation and taxation and more nationalization. One specific measure of the ideological difference was with respect to the mining industry. In its dealings with that sector, the NDP employed all four revenue instruments (profits tax, royalties, super-royalties, and public ownership), and granted the minister a larger management role.[33] Bill Bennett reversed some but not all of the NDP initiatives. He tried to maintain greater control of provincial finances, abandoned many social innovations, and transferred most of the new Crown holdings to the private sector in the form of British Columbia Resources Investment Corporation (BCRIC). After 1983 he practised restraint with a vengeance and declared war on organized labour, thereby becoming a far more consistent conservative or neo-conservative than his father ever was. Indeed, unlike his father, whose private enterprise rhetoric always exceeded his performance, Bill Bennett went beyond what was promised in the ideological battle of the 1983 election campaign. Vander Zalm was more erratically right wing, and his privatization plans surpassed those of Bill Bennett.[34] Like other provincial NDP governments in the 1990s, especially that of Saskatchewan, the Mike Harcourt regime was in most respects rather conservative, but lacked the reputation for businesslike management.

ELECTIONS

Electoral System

The British Columbia electoral system has probably had more distinctive features than that of any other province. Although the multiple-member constituencies declined over the years and have now disappeared, for example, the number of two-member constituencies increased from seven to 18 in 1986. While Prince Edward Island had historical reasons for adopting a two-member system, partisan advantage was the only real reason for its existence in B.C. This relates to a second aspect of the province's electoral system—the persistent lack of an independent redistribution system and a significant degree of rural over-representation. Although the redistribution process was regularly set in motion by statute every six years or after every two elections, the extent of gerrymandering was greater in B.C. than anywhere else in the country. Because the law required that an electoral district must receive increased representation when its population exceeded its electoral base by more than 60 percent, a favourite technique was to convert single-member Social Credit ridings to two-member ones, while eliminating some held by the NDP. The NDP might have been expected to reform this system as a matter of principle or because it generally worked to its disadvantage, but Barrett called an election in 1975 just before the results of an independent redistribution were to be implemented. It was therefore left to the courts to require an equitable distribution of seats in B.C., the first province where such judicial intervention occurred.[35]

The B.C. Civil Liberties Association went to court in 1986 to challenge the existing set of riding boundaries and, in the 1989 *Dixon* case, Madam Justice Beverly McLachlin ruled them unconstitutional in terms of section 3 of the Charter of Rights. The provincial law prescribed a plus or minus 25 percent margin, but allowed exceptions in very special circumstances. Without actually agreeing that a margin of 25 percent was acceptable, McLachlin decided that when 32 percent of the districts exceeded that figure, the existing electoral boundaries were a "gross violation of the fundamental concept of representation by population which is the foundation of our political system." She wrote that "equality of voting power" was the single most important factor to be taken into account in the redistribution process.[36] Even though the province had to repeat the exercise, by the time of the 1991 provincial election only 73 percent of ridings remained within the 25 percent range, as indicated in Table 11.6.

On the question of election expenses, the 1975 election also occurred before the new act in this area was passed, and, before 1995, only a tax credit provision for political contributions existed in the law. Political scandals in the province have been commonplace, but most incidents have involved individual ministers or premiers exploiting their positions and have not discredited the entire party. Nevertheless, the existing electoral system benefited Social Credit with its ample corporate contributions, and the revelation of W.A.C. Bennett's Free Enterprise

Education Fund exploded the myth that Social Credit was financed by the little people.[37] In fact, the only restrictions he introduced prohibited union check-off contributions to the NDP, but the unions were ingenious enough to find other ways to manifest their support. It could be added that the province's ideological politics are taken too seriously for election-day treating to be much of a factor in influencing votes.

TABLE 11.6   Representational Disparities in the 1991 Election

Mean no. of voters per constituency	26,521
Largest constituency (Okanagan West)	38,523 (+45.3% of the mean)
Smallest constituency (Peace River North)	15,407 (-41.9% of the mean)
Average variation from mean	17.6%
Constituencies within ± 10% (23 of 75)	30.7%
Constituencies within ± 25% (55 of 75)	73.3%

Source: *Reports of the Chief Electoral Officer,* calculations by author.

B.C. has also remained rather backward in determining who is eligible to vote. It first relied on a partisan system of collecting names, followed by one of individual registration, rather than the more common method of pre-election enumeration, although it has now moved to a permanent computerized voters' list. While this pioneering effort may seem out of context, it is in line with B.C.'s long-time peculiarity in this field, and is not necessarily an improvement over the system used in most other provinces. In one respect B.C. was a genuine pioneer: it listed the candidate's party affiliation on the ballot as early as 1939, but it was the last province to reduce the voting age to 18.

The most dramatic aspect of the B.C. electoral system was the experiment with the alternative or preferential system used in 1952 and 1953, for without it the subsequent hegemony of the Social Credit party might never have occurred. Once consolidated in power after 1953, however, Social Credit reverted to the first-past-the-post system.

Voting Behaviour

British Columbia has been characterized by a greater extent of class voting than any other province. A 1979 study showed, for example, that a majority of the working class voted NDP and majorities of the middle and upper-middle classes preferred Social Credit.[38] With an economy dominated by large corporations and big unions, and a geography sprinkled with company towns often divided sharply between workers and management, this voting pattern is not difficult to explain. The B.C. working class has historically been more unionized, more politicized, and more militant than anywhere else in the country. Hence, at least from 1933 onward, the unionized workers have opted for the CCF/NDP, and businesspeople and the middle class for the Liberals, Conservatives, or Social Credit. The latter also attracted most of the farmers and non-unionized clerical vote. Given that both major post-1952 parties had an anti-elitist orientation, however, the professional-managerial elite continued to vote Liberal until about 1975.

Many subtleties must be added to this general picture. One is that B.C. electoral behaviour is quite different in federal politics, raising questions as to the true significance of class divisions. In addition, the labour movement is divided and does not necessarily give unanimous support to the NDP. Just over half of the unionized workers belong to the B.C. Federation of Labour and, while the Bennett actions of 1983-85 brought the labour movement together to some extent, many inter-union divisions persist. The B.C. Federation of Labour has even had its disagreements with the NDP over the years, and recently loggers often sided with forestry companies against the environmentalists in the party. As mentioned, members of the non-unionized working class were quite likely to vote Social Credit rather than NDP; on the other hand, such professionals as teachers, social workers, and public servants were more inclined to support the NDP, especially after 1983, so that the NDP is not devoid of middle-class support. In any case, only a minority of voters are subjectively class conscious, yet many others seem to be unconsciously guided by class in their voting decisions. Thus, while it could be concluded that class is the single most important socio-economic determinant of voting behaviour in B.C. provincial politics, the ideological gulf between Social Credit and the NDP did not correspond perfectly with class divisions, and each party had pockets of support in all classes.[39] By 1991, Social Credit had been discredited, and the Liberals began to assume most of the support of those who could not bring themselves to vote Socred or NDP.

Ethnicity is not that significant in the province, nor is religion, except perhaps for the "non-believers" who largely vote NDP, and the fundamentalists who voted for Social Credit. Geographical or regional divisions, however, have been important. Distinct regional bases of party strength are evident: CCF/NDP was centred in Vancouver, the island, the north coast, and the Kootenays; Social Credit was supported in the Okanagan, Cariboo, Fraser Valley, and Peace River regions; while the Liberals or Conservatives held on to the high status constituencies in Vancouver and Victoria from 1952 to 1979. One study indicated that local issues and local candidates were particularly important before 1952, resulting in wide variations in election results from one constituency to another. For the next 10 years or so, fairly uniform province-wide trends occurred, a development that could be related to the advances of modern communications and transportation, including the electronic media.[40] While still apparent, these regional distinctions declined to some extent in the last 20 years, and changed dramatically in 1991.

How do federal and provincial voting behaviour relate to each other in British Columbia? The general picture, of course, is that NDP voters have been fairly consistent at both levels, and that Social Credit supporters switched to the Conservatives, or to a lesser extent the Liberals, in federal elections. In 1979, for example, when the two elections were almost simultaneous, approximately 65 percent of those who voted provincially switched to another party federally. The Reform party swept most of the B.C. seats in the 1993 federal election.

PRESSURE GROUPS AND THE MEDIA

Pressure Groups

Pressure groups have been a very visible part of British Columbia politics for many years. In the early 1990s, for example, endless disputes erupted between forestry companies and loggers on the one hand and environmentalists and aboriginal groups on the other. Two such groups were Greenpeace and the American Rainforest Action Network. More generally, the Council of Forest Industries of B.C. represents the interests of the major forestry companies. Forestry and mining companies usually have a close relationship with the B.C. government, and the government often acts as the industry's representative in Ottawa. The mining industry is represented by the Mining Association of B.C., consisting of the major multinational companies active in the province, and the B.C. and Yukon Chamber of Mines, a joint venture which includes prospectors and smaller exploration companies. Both exerted a special effort against the mining initiatives of the 1972-75 period.[41]

The insurance industry's protest centred on the B.C. branch of the Insurance Bureau of Canada but it was less successful in its opposition to the Barrett government, partly because the government had other pressure groups on its side, including the Insurance Agents Association of B.C. and the B.C. School Trustees. In its confrontation with Bill Bennett, the Solidarity movement was spearheaded by the B.C. Federation of Labour, which is relatively larger than in other provinces and generally supportive of the NDP. It was joined by a host of smaller groups—some individual unions such as the BC Teachers' Federation and the British Columbia Government Employees Union, and many social service organizations representing tenants, women, the handicapped, and the disadvantaged.

Other prominent groups include the B.C. Medical Association, the B.C. Federation of Agriculture, the Union of B.C. Municipalities, and the Business Council of B.C., the voice of all big business. Native groups, under the umbrella of the Native Brotherhood of B.C., have been active recently in pressing land claims. The right-wing think tank the Fraser Institute, although viewing itself as a national organization, seems to have most influence in the province where it is located.[42]

TABLE 11.7   **Leading British Columbia Pressure Groups**

Peak Business	British Columbia Chamber of Commerce
	British Columbia Manufacturers' Association
	Business Council of British Columbia
Industrial	Mining Association of British Columbia
	British Columbia and Yukon Chamber of Mines
	Insurance Brokers Association of British Columbia
	Council of Forest Industries of British Columbia
	British Columbia Forestry Association
	British Columbia Construction Association
	Fisheries Council of British Columbia
Labour	British Columbia Federation of Labour
	British Columbia Government Employees' Union
Agriculture	British Columbia Federation of Agriculture
	British Columbia Cattlemen's Association
Professional	British Columbia Medical Association
	British Columbia Teachers' Federation
Ethnic	Native Brotherhood of British Columbia
	Union of British Columbia Indian Chiefs
	Pacific Metis Association
Institutional	Union of British Columbia Municipalities
	British Columbia School Trustees Association
Environmental	British Columbia Environmental Network
	British Columbia Wildlife Federation
Public Interest	British Columbia Civil Liberties Association

The Media

The two major Vancouver newspapers, the *Sun* and the *Province*, are Southam News clones with much influence on political debate in the province. Southam has two other daily newspapers in the province, while Thomson Newspapers Ltd. owns five, most notably the *Victoria Times-Colonist*. British Columbia is the site of Conrad Black's largest Canadian newspaper holdings, eight dailies in total. The Canadian Broadcasting Corporation has English and French television stations in Vancouver and other English affiliates around the province, the CTV network has stations in Vancouver and Victoria, and one independent station exists, along with the educational service, the Knowledge Network. CBC also maintains English and French radio stations which compete with a multitude of private stations. British Columbia is probably the radio phone-in show capital of the country, with such well-known hosts as Jack Webster, Dave Barrett, and Rafe Mair, and, part-time, Bill Vander Zalm.

TABLE 11.8   Daily Newspapers in British Columbia, 1994

	Circulation	Chain Affiliation
Cranbrook Daily Townsman	4,304	Black
Dawson Creek-Peace River Block News	2,223	Black
Fort St. John-Alaska Highway News	3,072	Black
Kamloops Daily News	18,126	Southam
Kelowna Daily News	19,504	Thomson
Kimberley Daily Bulletin	2,088	Black
Nanaimo Daily Free Press	12,016	Thomson
Nelson Daily News	4,306	Black
Penticton Herald	9,833	Thomson
Port Alberni Valley Times	6,750	Black
Prince George Citizen	20,615	Southam
Prince Rupert Daily News	3,434	Black
Trail Times	5,553	Black
Vancouver Sun	193,846	Southam
Vancouver Province	159,687	Southam
Vernon Daily News	7,532	Thomson
Victoria Times-Colonist	80,424	Thomson

Source: *Canadian Advertising Rates and Data* (August 1994).

GOVERNMENT INSTITUTIONS[43]

In comparison with other provinces, British Columbia seemed to move rather slowly to modernize its political institutions. Many devices adopted elsewhere to enhance the status of the legislature or opposition, at the expense of the cabinet or the government, were delayed in this province. But so, too, were means of strengthening the executive branch.

Executive

The lieutenant-governor was kept busy in the early years dismissing governments and reserving bills.[44] Nowadays, in the insular environment of the B.C. government sitting in Victoria, the lieutenant-governor is probably more central to the social life of the capital than in many other provinces.

Premiers have usually been concerned with establishing a reasonable balance between the lower mainland and the interior, along with more subtle regional representation in the composition of their cabinets. In the case of Bill Bennett, especially in 1975, he also had to represent the different parties which had come together in his Social Credit coalition. Under W.A.C. Bennett, the cabinet operated on an informal, personalized basis without much staff or organization. The premier was dominant, especially because he doubled as finance minister and Treasury Board chairman.[45] The NDP government of Dave Barrett was even more informal and certainly more free-wheeling and creative, but lacked the dominant controlling and co-ordinating force of his predecessor. "Treasury Board was a kind of bazaar at which ministers would attempt to out-quip the premier in order to increase a departmental budget."[46] This style of "creative enthusiasm" was perhaps appropriate during Barrett's first year when revenues were ample but, as the economy slowed down and government operations and expenditures increased, it proved to be insufficient. Things were often done hastily and without much co-ordination, as ministers sought to transform laws and programs in their own fields as quickly as possible. This expansion of programs took place without accompanying changes in the processes of government administration, although the NDP did improve the situation somewhat in 1974 by recruiting Marc Eliesen as cabinet planning adviser.

Thus it was left to Bill Bennett to rationalize the operations of the cabinet in and after 1975, several years after such a reform occurred in most other provinces.[47] Bennett introduced a cabinet committee system, together with an expanded premier's office, and a more effective Treasury Board. The new cabinet committees have a fairly familiar sound: planning and priorities, chaired by the premier; Treasury Board, chaired by the finance minister; regional and economic development; social policy; legislation and regulations; and environment and land use. Bennett was advised by the cabinet secretariat and the premier's office, both headed by the deputy minister to the premier, where the bureaucratic and political apex met in one person. Bennett also created a Treasury Board secretariat located in the finance department, and transformed it into an effective management agency. All these devices added to the authority of the premier, and the combination of political and technical advisers filled the previous advisory vacuum around him. Vander Zalm added three other committees —cultural heritage, Native affairs, and drug abuse—to his cabinet, which eventually reached the size of 23, and created advisory councils on the economy, the disabled, Native affairs, and science and technology. Also, after an unhappy early experience, he split the premier's office into two divisions, one partisan, headed by the principal secretary, and the other bureaucratic, under the deputy minister. Mike Harcourt had a 19-member cabinet in 1994, with the following cabinet committees: planning board, Treasury Board, public issues, environment and land use, and regulations and orders-in-council. The planning board was the central committee chaired by the premier.

Legislature

In 1986 the B.C. legislature was increased to 69 members, and rose to 75 in 1991.[48] The legislature was of little consequence throughout the W.A.C. Bennett "legislation-by-exhaustion" period, and its sessions very short, but it was substantially modernized during the brief Barrett era. The Hansard, introduced in 1970 and which did not include committee of the whole or committee of supply proceedings (which combined took over half of the time of the session), was expanded to include all sittings of the House. This left P.E.I. as the only province without such a record of proceedings. In 1973 B.C. established a daily question period, the last province to do so. The legislative program was so heavy in these years that the work of an MLA became essentially a full-time job, and most now regard it as such. In 1994, the taxable indemnity was $32,812, the non-taxable allowance was $16,406, and facilities have been improved accordingly. An Opposition chair of the public accounts committee was appointed in this period and the NDP adjourned the legislature by 11 p.m., rather than have it occasionally run all night. All of these reforms helped the Opposition more than the government, making its criticism more effective, and while the reforms benefited the NDP after it reverted to Opposition, they were probably among the reasons for the party's return to that position.[49] The scrutiny of the estimates and the clause-by-clause examination of legislation are both performed in the committee of the whole (or supply) and of the two, the estimates take up much more of the chamber's time. Overall, the legislature sat for an average of 67 days between 1990 and 1993—not long for such a large province. The public accounts committee has long been in operation and, by 1994, the legislature had established a set of 12 other standing committees, generally corresponding to the structure of government departments. Television was introduced in 1991, just in time to catch the drama of the Vander Zalm resignation.

Bureaucracy

British Columbia employs 30,000 people in government ministries and agencies, another 23,500 in government business enterprises, and a further 83,000 in the wider public sector. It created the first civil service commission of any province in 1917, but it was not immediately effective and was itself subject to patronage and political influence. The commission was enlarged in 1945, and again charged with the enforcement of a merit system, after which a career-oriented system of public service developed. Many positions remained outside the commission's jurisdiction, however, and it had an unhealthy proximity to the premier's office in the W.A.C. Bennett era. That period was characterized by a rigid separation of politics and administration; and, with an authoritarian premier and ministers serving long terms in a single post, not much scope existed for bureaucratic creativity.[50] As far as other kinds of patronage are concerned, B.C. political history is replete with politicians seeking to gain personal advantage from their position.[51] The distribution of contracts and public works to companies or constituencies favouring the government has also been a common practice.

Under the NDP in the 1970s, the public service increased enormously, new departments were established, and the right of collective bargaining was extended to civil servants along with political rights and the right to strike. Several outside appointments to the higher bureaucratic levels took place, justified by the new government's intention to embark on a program of radical social change, but the same argument was used to justify a large turnover three years later when Bill Bennett had rather different priorities. By 1980, the senior levels of the public service had been significantly politicized.[52] The Barrett government also increased the number of state-owned enterprises. Bill Bennett began with a more effective financial management system, appointing a comptroller general, an auditor general, and a proper Treasury Board. The collective bargaining system was changed, with the Treasury Board replacing the public service commission as bargaining agent for the government, and was assisted in this capacity by the government employee relations bureau. Bennett also appointed the province's first ombudsman in 1979. This office was engaged in more conflict with the government than almost anywhere else, and led to a court decision that confirmed the ombudsman's right to examine the documents of Crown corporations. Immediately after the 1983 election, when the economy was particularly bad, Bennett introduced a package of severe restraint measures including wage controls, layoffs, abolition of certain programs, and restrictions on the right to strike. This resulted in increased militancy on the part of the B.C. Government Employees' Union and other public service unions.

TABLE 11.9   British Columbia Government Departments, 1994

Aboriginal Affairs
Agriculture, Fisheries and Food
Attorney General
Education
Employment and Investment
Energy, Mines and Petroleum Resources
Environment, Lands and Parks
Finance and Corporate Relations
Forests
Government Services
Health
Housing, Recreation and Consumer Services
Municipal Affairs
Skills, Training and Labour
Small Business, Tourism and Culture
Social Services
Transportation and Highways
Women's Equality

British Columbia developed a number of semi-independent agencies over the years, such as the Workmen's Compensation Board and several pioneering agricultural marketing boards. It also established several Crown

TABLE 11.10   Leading British Columbia Agencies, Boards, Commissions and Crown Corporations

Crown Corporations	British Columbia Hydro
	British Columbia Railway Company
	Insurance Corporation of British Columbia
	Liquor Distribution Branch
	British Columbia Lottery Corporation
	British Columbia Ferry Corporation
	British Columbia Transit
	British Columbia Trade Development Corporation
	Okanagan Valley Tree Fruit Authority
	British Columbia Pavilion Corporation
	British Columbia Buildings Corporation
	Provincial Rental Housing Corporation
	British Columbia Housing Management Commission
	Provincial Capital Commission
Agencies, Boards, and Commissions	British Columbia Council of Human Rights
	Agricultural Land Commission
	British Columbia Assessment Authority
	Workers' Compensation Board
	Labour Relations Board
	British Columbia Utilities Commission
	Environmental Appeal Board

corporations including the Pacific and Great Eastern Railway in 1918 (now B.C. Rail).[53] Other significant agencies include the B.C. Power Commission (created in 1945) and the B.C. Ferry Corporation (established in 1960). Of great surprise was the nationalization of the privately owned B.C. Electric in 1961, which was merged a year later with the Power Commission to form B.C. Hydro. This Crown corporation generates, transmits, and distributes 90 percent of the electricity in the province, and underwent a massive reorganization in the 1990s. The Barrett government nationalized the automobile insurance industry, creating the Insurance Corporation of British Columbia (ICBC) in 1973. Barrett also became involved directly in resource ownership in a variety of forms, including B.C. Cellulose, but Bill Bennett later transferred these initiatives over to the British Columbia Resources Investment Corporation (BCRIC). The B.C. Petroleum Corporation was wound up in 1994. Bill Bennett created several new Crown agencies, such as B.C. Place, to redevelop the False Creek area in Vancouver, and the B.C. Buildings and B.C. Systems Corporations, to administer government accommodation and data processing respectively. In addition, the province is involved directly or indirectly in providing urban transit via B.C. Transit. The Vander Zalm government then embarked on an ambitious privatization program, including parts of B.C. Hydro, B.C. Systems, and highway signs and maintenance, but as Table 11.10 reveals, the province continues to own a large number of Crown corporations.

Judiciary

The British Columbia judicial system consists of the Court of Appeal, the Supreme Court, county courts, and various provincial courts. The Court of Appeal normally sits in banks of three to five judges at the Law Courts in Vancouver. The Supreme Court is the province's superior trial court which sits in eight judicial districts, while provincial courts are located in numerous locations throughout the province and include small claims and family courts.

Municipal Government

The municipal government system was rather slow to develop in B.C. and much of the province was unorganized for municipal purposes as late as 1966. The system now includes cities, towns, and villages, as well as more than 300 local improvement districts. Twenty-nine regional districts have been superimposed on these lower tiers since the mid-1960s; they cover almost all of the province, including otherwise unorganized territory. These districts originally had two mandatory functions—regional and hospital planning—in addition to which they could be assigned other responsibilities by the lower tier municipalities of which they were composed. In fact, the regional districts double as regional hospital districts, something other provinces are establishing many years later. There is a certain resemblance between the regional districts and the regional governments of Ontario, but the limited powers of the Greater Vancouver Regional District make it a pale imitation of the municipal structure of Metro Toronto, although some might find that advantageous. The NDP relieved municipalities of several responsibilities in the 1970s, as the province took over the administration of justice, property assessment, much of public transit, and most of the welfare delivery system, while in 1983 Bill Bennett removed the planning powers of all districts. All of this centralized the provincial-municipal system, and the Harcourt government sought ways to reinstate the planning function.[54] The province also has 75 local school districts.

POLITICAL EVOLUTION

1870-1970

After many centuries of aboriginal occupation, the British established a colony on Vancouver Island in 1849, while the mainland, owned by the Hudson's Bay Company, was generally the preserve of fur traders. The discovery of gold on the Fraser River in 1858 led to an expansion of the mainland settlement and prompted the Crown to take it over as a separate colony. Against local sentiment, the British authorities combined the two colonies as British Columbia in 1866, with Victoria winning out as the new capital. There was little talk of joining Canada in 1867, although the promise of a railway to Canada, federal subsidies, and the assumption of the provincial debt were enough to persuade the colony to join Confederation four years later. Railway construction was to begin within two years and be completed within 10. The new province was simultaneously granted representative and responsible government in 1871, with a new 25-member Assembly replacing the previous legislative council. Although most members of the new Assembly called themselves Conservatives, the government was administered by shifting combinations of factions, and individual members were motivated primarily by considerations of patronage.

The 1871-85 period was preoccupied with the railway issue. Fierce disputes within the province broke out over the route across the province, the location of the terminus, and whether a line between Esquimalt and Nanaimo should be built. Moreover, the whole enterprise was hampered by the national depression and the new federal Liberal government's lack of enthusiasm for the project after John A. Macdonald's Conservatives had been defeated. This inaction resulted in a 1876 petition threatening to secede from Confederation if the province's grievances were not resolved. It was not until Macdonald was re-elected in 1878 that momentum was restored, and the Canadian Pacific Railway contract was finally signed in 1881. Construction then progressed at an incredible rate, considering the difficult mountain terrain. The company brought in large numbers of Chinese labourers to work on the project, and the last spike was pounded in November 1885, just four years behind the original schedule.

The completion of the CPR was a major boost to the economy of the province, and politics became dominated by "acquisitive merchants, lawyers, industrial and landed proprietors, whose wealth derived chiefly from investment in land, transportation, mines, lumbering, salmon canneries and flour mills."[55] The distribution of timber and mining rights and railway charters was the stuff of political activity. Immigration was high, and Vancouver developed as an important port, especially in the export of lumber. The employment of Chinese labourers, who would work for long hours at low wages, became a controversial issue and prompted the establishment of labour organizations to protect the interests of non-Oriental workers in the 1880s. The first labour representatives were elected to the Assembly in 1890, joining the majority in the legislature who were businessmen and large property owners.

Between 1871 and 1889 the province experienced a series of undistinguished premiers and governments. John Robson (1889-1892) was a marked contrast to his predecessors, and he introduced a comprehensive education program, reformed many of the province's laws and practices, and halted "the reckless expropriation of natural resources."[56] The palatial provincial legislature was constructed in the mid-1890s, a mining boom started in 1896, and by 1900, B.C.

had become a "company province,"[57] with many industries such as fishing, lumber, and electricity characterized by concentrated ownership.

The turn of the century was a period of social tension and unrest marked by continued labour organization, considerable strike activity in the fishing and mining industries, and much anti-Oriental sentiment. The province was a hotbed of militant unionism, and laws were passed prohibiting the employment of Orientals in the mines and denying them the franchise, while federal action was demanded to restrict Chinese and Japanese immigration.

This era of political instability set the stage for the introduction of strict party lines in the province in 1903. Several factors contributed to such a development, including the need for some political cohesion in the province, which was a growing collection of isolated communities, and the demand for legislative consistency. Dominant firms within the province were upset at the manner in which laws had been passed and amended, and charters and contracts made and broken by the fast succession of factional governments; the business community wanted a "stable investment climate."[58] Pressure also came from federal parties to operate provincial branches, and the obvious place for the emerging labour interest was in a party of its own.

As party lines solidified, Richard McBride, an "affable, poised, self-assured and polished" lawyer of Irish background,[59] became Conservative leader, and was called upon to form a government in 1903. Thus began an unprecedented 12-year rule based largely on his irresistible charm and the economic well-being of the province. Three central thrusts of his government were railway development, exclusion of Asians, and demanding "better terms" from Ottawa. It was also in 1903 that a British-American commission established the boundary between the province and Alaska, limiting B.C.'s direct access to the sea to the southern half of the province. This raised future problems over fishing rights because northern provincial salmon rivers had their outlets in American territory. The first decade of the century was a period of growth and optimism which witnessed more railway construction, McBride's survival of a railway scandal, and the creation of the Consolidated Mining and Smelting Co. McBride became an even more popular hero when he walked out of a 1906 federal-provincial conference on revising federal subsidies and then persuaded Winston Churchill to make minor adjustments to the amendment to the British North America Act which Laurier had sent over for passage.

Racial tension was one of the few negative features of this period. The federal government was pursuing expanded ties with the Orient and even persuaded Japan to limit emigration to Canada voluntarily, but McBride's government persisted in passing anti-Oriental legislation, most of it reserved by the lieutenant-governor or disallowed by Ottawa. In September 1907, after a particularly large group of immigrants arrived, an armed clash occurred in Vancouver between the forces of the Asiatic Exclusion League and the Japanese of the city.

The 1909 election was primarily concerned with a Mackenzie and Mann railway project from the Yellowhead pass through Kamloops to Vancouver. McBride sprang the railway announcement on his cabinet, causing two ministers to resign because of its guarantees regarding interest rates and the exclusion of Asiatic labour. This victory was followed by another three years of prosperity, based primarily on American and European investment in the province, and during which time more railways were constructed and the pulp and paper industry was established.

Although generally encouraging rampant development of the province's resources, the McBride government passed legislation to conserve timber and water power, to improve the lot of labour, and to protect public health. It built new schools along with a provincial library and archives, and established the University of British Columbia. An election in 1912 left only two Socialists in Opposition to the 40 Conservatives in the legislature.

The post-1912 period was a troubled one, marked by charges of government arrogance, patronage, and corruption, as well as economic recession. A riot in Nanaimo in 1913, precipitated by the hiring of Chinese and Japanese strike breakers in the coal mines, resulted in police and military intervention. A year later, B.C. enthusiastically joined in the war effort. Several ministers were accused of impropriety in 1915, and the government did not take seriously the various emerging reform groups: temperance, women's franchise, prison reform, direct legislation, and other new causes, although both Prohibition and the vote for women were to be referred to the people in a plebiscite. Then, in December 1915, McBride resigned suddenly and became the province's agent general in London.[60]

McBride was succeeded as Conservative leader by his right-hand man, William Bowser, who was an able administrator but lacked his predecessor's flair. The election that followed was fought mainly on government wrongdoing and was accompanied by the two reform plebiscites. The Socialists might have attracted more of the support of those dissatisfied with the government, but they were extremists fighting among themselves. Thus the Liberals became the beneficiaries of the reform movement composed of new progressive urban forces. They came out of nowhere to elect 37 members and form the government for the first time since party lines had been introduced. The women's suffrage plebiscite was carried two-to-one, and the Prohibition vote passed by a smaller margin.

The Liberal leader and new premier was H.C. Brewster, who formed a strong cabinet and adopted several significant reforms. In addition to introducing Prohibition and women's suffrage, Brewster sought to abolish patronage by introducing civil service reform against the wishes of many in his own party. He also tried to accommodate labour demands with a new Department of Labour and minimum wage legislation. Despite his efforts, a coal strike occurred in the Crow's Nest, and the continued labour militancy was based partly on disgust at the corruption in provincial politics as revealed, for example, in the investigation of the Pacific and Great Eastern Railway.

Brewster died in 1918 and was succeeded by John Oliver, a hard-working, common-sensical farmer, who served as premier for nine years. Although the economy began to improve, he faced several problems including continued strikes and difficulties caused by the return of soldiers from the war. The United Farmers of British Columbia was organized in 1917, but never matched the significance of its Prairie counterparts. Meanwhile, Oliver decided to rely on highway development as a route to re-election. Between 1920 and 1924, he was reasonably successful in challenging the federal government over the issue of railway freight rates, and enacted new liquor legislation after a 1920 plebiscite indicated a preference for government control rather than Prohibition. A number of dissident Conservatives joined forces with an assortment of businessmen, farmers, and others upset with the corruption in both major parties to form the Provincial Party in 1923, the same year in which the giant Kimberley mine opened.

The economy boomed in the late 1920s and Oliver introduced several pieces of social legislation including an extension of the minimum wage law and workmen's compensation and an industrial disputes act. He also spent money on roads, bridges, and university buildings, and one of his principal innovations was the creation of a series of agricultural marketing boards. He also allowed beer to be sold by the glass, even though this privilege had not been approved in the 1924 plebiscite. He died of cancer in August 1927, and his successor John MacLean called an election a year later, facing a new attractive Conservative leader, Simon Fraser Tolmie, a genial veterinarian who had served as a federal MP. As in several other provinces about the same time—just before the Great Depression—the Conservatives had the bad luck to win.

When the Depression struck in 1929 and every industry in the province collapsed, Tolmie proved to be unequal to the task of rebuilding the economy. Due to its mild climate, B.C. attracted the unemployed of other provinces, and had to establish many relief camps. Charges of corruption concerning the administration of relief funds surfaced, as well as allegations of patronage and waste in other government operations. Tolmie proposed a coalition government to the new Liberal leader, T.D. "Duff" Pattullo, but the latter was not interested, having been busy building a strong party organization of his own. Not surprisingly, Tolmie waited until the last possible moment to call the next election.

In addition to the well-organized Liberals, the 1933 election also featured the first appearance of the Co-operative Commonwealth Federation party, which attempted to unite the disparate factions on the left. The governing Conservatives were in such disarray that the executive of the provincial association decided not to participate in the campaign. Tolmie's caucus eventually supported the coalition idea as its official party position, but former leader Bowser came forward to lead a "non-partisan movement," while other dissident Conservatives ran as Independent-Conservatives or as Independents. The results showed a strong Liberal majority, with a CCF Opposition; Tolmie was defeated, and only three Conservatives of any variety were elected.

Pattullo was a 60-year-old former newspaper editor and public servant, who had sat in the legislature since 1916 and in the cabinet between 1916 and 1928. Dapper and somewhat vain, kindly and yet remote, Pattullo had campaigned on the basis of the slogan "work and wages" and had presented a comprehensive reform program which was sometimes called the "Little New Deal." He contrasted the "practical idealism" of his proposals with the "visionary socialism" of the CCF. He was the "first of the radical premiers of the 1930s to emerge, and the first significant figure in the modern Liberal party to sense the appeal of progressive Liberalism."[61] Pattullo had a well-considered philosophy of "socialized capitalism" which involved "the representation of the interests of both workingmen and businessmen within a political party dedicated to curbing the abuses of capitalism without fundamentally altering the system."[62] He was a pioneer practitioner of Keynesian economics, an admirer of F.D. Roosevelt, and "helped to move Canada forward on the path of state-planning for economic and social betterment."[63] Rather than cut public expenditures in time of the Depression, he believed that government should increase purchasing power by creating jobs and priming the pump of the private sector. When the anticipated federal financial support for such endeavours failed to materialize, even under the Mackenzie King Liberals after 1935, Pattullo also gained a reputation as a strong advocate of provincialism.

Owing to widespread strikes, unemployment, debts, and unrest, Pattullo acted on his economic theory by increasing levels of relief, raising the minimum wage, limiting the hours of work, and trying to distribute jobs through a work and wages act. He set up an economic council, passed collective marketing legislation, and offered financial aid to the mining and fish processing industries. In addition, a special powers act gave the cabinet emergency powers for which he was forever labelled autocratic. Other accomplishments were an industrial relations board, a reformed school system, and a major public works project, a bridge across the Fraser River at New Westminster. Those in the relief camps went on strike in April 1935 and converged on Vancouver in a protest that led to violence, with only the CCF supporting the strikers.

The economic situation began to improve in 1936, and Pattullo turned to the prospect of northern development, searching for oil and hoping to annex the Yukon, while he also unveiled a comprehensive health insurance scheme. This aroused so much public opposition, however, that he decided to submit it to a plebiscite, held simultaneously with the 1937 provincial election. The government was returned; the Conservatives had reunited and managed to regain second place; the CCF dropped to third, largely because of divisions within the party; and the insurance plan was approved.

From 1937 to 1941 Pattullo embarked on a second phase of "socialized capitalism," less concerned with economic redistribution and more centred on government regulation. He shelved the health insurance plan and became obsessed with the question of provincial rights. A public utilities act gave new regulatory powers to the cabinet in 1938, and powers over gas prices given to the coal and petroleum control board in 1939 were severely criticized by the oil industry. In response to the improved economy, the federal government closed the relief camps in 1938, and the province decided to cut off relief to unemployed men from the Prairies. As in 1935, this government action resulted in demonstrations and sit-ins in Vancouver, and property damage and injury occurred when the police forced protesters to evacuate public buildings. Pattullo was criticized for not intervening sooner and for carrying his quarrel with Ottawa too far. He then joined William Aberhart and Mitch Hepburn in opposing the recommendations of the Rowell-Sirois report, and behaved in a rather petulant, obstructionist manner at the 1941 federal-provincial conference convened to discuss that report.

The strategy of provincialism found little favour in B.C. after the outbreak of the Second World War, and both Pattullo's party and the electorate became increasingly dissatisfied with his leadership. The Depression had increased class polarization and the premier's middle course was unpopular with both left and right. In the October 1941 election the Liberals were reduced to 21 seats, compared with 14 for the CCF and 12 for the Conservatives. The CCF had mended its wounds and actually won the largest proportion of popular vote. In a minority situation, in wartime, much sentiment was naturally expressed in favour of a coalition government, either between the Liberals and the Conservatives or among all parties, but Pattullo rejected the idea. He perceived basic differences among liberalism, conservatism, and socialism, and saw no ideological basis for inter-party co-operation.[64] Pressure from businessmen and Liberal and Conservative politicians for a coalition government to establish a stable and anti-CCF majority was becoming too strong to resist, however, and ministers began to resign. In December 1941 the Liberal party called a convention which approved a resolution favouring the creation of a coalition government. This forced Pattullo out, and the party chose John Hart as its new leader.

After some negotiation, a Liberal-Conservative coalition government was formed containing five Liberals with Hart as premier, and four Tories, whose leader, R.L. Maitland, became attorney general. The next four years were dominated by national and international events, and the domestic scene was rather tranquil except for the uprooting and internment of the Japanese-Canadian community. The federal government removed some 20,000 Japanese-Canadians from the west coast, even though not one was ever charged with being disloyal to Canada. After being interned in camps in the B.C. interior during the war, and after their property had been confiscated and sold, they were dispersed across the country or deported. For other citizens of the province, however, it was a period of great economic prosperity as industries expanded in response to wartime demands and generated high government revenues. The Hart government was friendly to business, and provided a sympathetic environment in which to operate.

The period of the war also witnessed considerable growth in the province's union movement, which now included the International Woodworkers of

America, and, in 1944, the British Columbia Federation of Labour. This was of some benefit to the CCF, but would have been more helpful if Communists had not been so prominent in the movement. Their presence gave other parties and corporate forces much ammunition to use against the CCF, which actually shunned Communist support. On the other hand, the coalition government introduced a number of measures in response to the increased labour power, including amendments to the Workmen's Compensation Act and changes in the Industrial Conciliation Act. Other progressive legislation included mothers' allowance amendments, the creation of family courts, and sympathetic treatment of teachers, farmers, and veterans.

Even though a 1945 election approached and the wartime emergency was no longer a basis for coalition, little action was taken towards disbanding the alliance. The CCF threat remained, and the arrangement between the Liberals and the Conservatives was working well; indeed, the coalition government was widely felt to be the best the province ever had. Within the coalition itself, specific electoral arrangements had been made so that incumbent coalitionists would not be opposed by candidates from their partner's party. They further agreed that only one candidate would run against the CCF incumbents, so as not to split the non-CCF vote. The results in October 1945 saw the election of 37 coalition members to 10 for the CCF.

The next three years were even more prosperous, but reorganizing the government after both parties changed leaders proved to be difficult. The new Conservative leader, Herbert Anscomb, was made minister of Finance, but some Conservatives thought Anscomb should have become premier when Hart resigned. The new Liberal leader, Byron Johnson, was installed instead, and the Johnson-Anscomb coalition never worked as well as the Hart-Maitland partnership. Some of the legislative highlights of this period included the provincial enfranchisement of the Chinese and Native peoples, a reorganization of municipal finances, a new system of forest management licences, a bill to encourage Alcan to establish a complex in the province, and a controversial industrial conciliation and arbitration act. The government's development program included major highway, railway, and hydro projects, rural electrification, and the construction of schools and other public buildings. Spending for these projects had been so generous that new revenues were required by 1948. These were raised through increased timber royalties, mining taxes, a three percent retail sales tax, and premiums for the new compulsory hospital insurance plan.

The CCF continued to arouse suspicions because of occasional extremist statements or actions which departed from the party's generally moderate line. Such suspicions were magnified because of the international Cold War tensions prevalent during this period. In fact, during 1948 the Communist control of several unions as well as the B.C. Federation of Labour was broken, and this removed a considerable burden from the CCF. Meanwhile, the Social Credit party was beginning to come to life in the province, with a total of 27 official and affiliated candidates in the 1949 election.[65] The coalition was returned with 39 seats, while CCF was reduced to seven seats.

The 1950-52 period witnessed the disintegration of the coalition, as well as the growth of the Social Credit organization in the province. The catalyst of the coalition's demise was the new hospital insurance scheme which went into effect in 1949. Anscomb insisted on relatively high premiums and daily user fees (co-insurance), while the Liberals wanted to operate the plan out of general revenues. In an atmosphere of increasing tension, Johnson finally demanded Anscomb's resignation in January 1952, ostensibly for not consulting his cabinet colleagues about a new federal-provincial arrangement. The other Conservative ministers left along with Anscomb, and the Tories went into Opposition to the Johnson Liberals, who carried on until the end of the spring session.

Johnson called the election, which coincided with two plebiscite questions (liquor and daylight-saving time), for June 1952, at a time of booming prosperity. In anticipation of the breakup of the coalition, he introduced a new electoral system—the preferential system. Instead of voting with a single "X," candidates could be ranked first, second, third, etc., in order of preference. The logic of this innovation was that, even though the Liberals and Conservatives were no longer partners, they still preferred each other to anyone else, especially the CCF. Liberals could rank Conservative candidates second and vice versa, so that their combined vote would elect one or the other and keep the CCF out. This proved to be a mistaken assumption; supporters of each coalition party, now antagonistic to the other, opted for Social Credit as their second choice, a fresh but safe private-enterprise alternative that would continue the effort to block the CCF. Many CCF voters also ranked Social Credit candidates second, in defiance of orders from their leadership, to demonstrate their hostility to the coalition parties. Under the old non-preferential system, the results would have been as follows: CCF 21; Social Credit, 14; Liberals, nine; and Conservatives, three. When the votes were tabulated under the new system, Social Credit won 19 seats to 18 for the CCF, six for the Liberals, and four for the Conservatives.

To understand the development of Social Credit in British Columbia, it is necessary to follow the peregrinations of W.A.C. (Cecil) Bennett. Denied a provincial cabinet post, he resigned as an MLA to become a Conservative candidate in the 1948 federal by-election, but lost. He regained his provincial seat in 1949 and, after challenging Anscomb for the provincial Conservative leadership in March 1951, decided to sit as an Independent. Meanwhile, the Social Credit party was rapidly expanding, especially in the interior. It appealed to ex-Albertans, religious fundamentalists, small businesspeople, and other conservatives who were tired of the coalition government and frustrated in their own economic or political ambitions.[66] Several Alberta Social Credit cabinet ministers and organizers toured the region during this period and made much of the prosperity and political stability enjoyed by their province. As the election approached, the Socreds named Rev. Ernest Hansell, an Alberta MLA, as temporary campaign leader, while Bennett began to tour the province on his own as a Social Credit candidate. After their dramatic and unexpected victory, the Social Credit caucus chose Bennett as leader and therefore premier, probably on the strength of his legislative experience. Thus began his unprecedented 20-year rule.[67]

W.A.C. Bennett had moved to Kelowna during the Depression to establish a hardware store. Although lacking in formal education and embarrassingly inarticulate, Bennett was honest and affable, a bundle of energy, an avid reader, a hard worker, and a good organizer. He disavowed the original theory behind Social Credit, and had a moderately conservative political outlook. Bennett was obsessed with growth and development and the province's abundant natural resources gave him ample scope to indulge his passion. He became a great builder—of dams and roads in particular—and was especially sensitive to the needs of the interior communities. Although more in tune with small business-people than with the economic elite, his development policies were conceived in concert with the province's large companies, and he soon forged a close relationship with them. Bennett used the natural wealth of the province, as well as his own dominant leadership and his knack for reading public opinion, to provide British Columbians with the kind of stable government they appeared to want. The result was a string of majority Social Credit victories, with elections being held at three-year intervals. The Liberals maintained about 20 percent of the vote throughout this period and averaged five seats per election, while the Conservatives were virtually non-existent. Thus each election was essentially a contest between Social Credit and "the socialists" (the CCF/NDP), with remarkably little variation in the outcome, and the inter-election periods were characterized by much animosity between the government and organized labour.

The first few years of the Bennett era saw the completion of the Alcan project and Trans-Mountain oil pipeline, high investment in the mining and forestry industries, new resource taxes, and tremendous levels of public revenue. Bennett spent this money on improved health programs and developing the interior with a variety of projects including power, schools, and transportation. The Pacific and Great Eastern Railway was extended northward from Prince George and southward to North Vancouver, and some of the new highways and bridges were part of the federally assisted Trans-Canada Highway.[68] These roads, built under the authority of "Flying Phil" Gaglardi, the Pentecostal preacher and highways minister, were of much benefit to the logging, mining, and tourist industries, as well as to construction firms and their workers. Deliberately seeking defeat in the legislature on an educational finance package, Bennett was able to call another election for June 1953. In that election the preferential voting system was still in place and continued to benefit the Social Credit party.

Bennett was somewhat troubled by labour opposition to a new labour relations act in 1954 and the Sommers scandal in 1956. Robert Sommers, the lands, forests and mines minister, had received considerable sums of money from a small timber operator in return for preferential treatment in the allotment of forest management licences, and was eventually convicted of bribery and conspiracy and sentenced to five years in jail. These problems had little effect on the 1956 election, however, which was based on the slogan "progress—not politics." The electoral system had returned to an orthodox non-preferential one, and Social Credit was easily re-elected. The Socreds had proved "acceptable, at one and the same time, to the establishment and the anti-establishment, the companies and workingmen, and above all, to the middle classes, salesmen and merchants."[69]

To divert attention from the subsequent economic downturn, Bennett unveiled a proposal for a Peace River dam. He was impatient with ongoing Ottawa-U.S. negotiations on the construction of power dams on the Columbia River and wanted to have a parallel project entirely within his own control. He thus pursued a policy which called for the simultaneous development of both rivers, even though many felt there was no need for so much power. In a second diversionary tactic, he transferred provincial government debts to semi-independent agencies. Bennett thus claimed that the government was debt-free, and held a ceremony to burn the cancelled bonds in his home town. He also took aim against labour leaders in the process of founding the NDP, and in 1959 the passage of restrictive labour legislation led to a brief strike of civil servants. Labour problems also propelled the government into the ferry business.

After the 1960 election, Bennett was almost totally obsessed with hydroelectricity. The Americans wanted storage dams on the Canadian portion of the Columbia River to maximize the production of hydro power south of the border. The federal position had been to make Canadian dams the primary generating site, which left control of the waters in Canadian hands, rather than integrating management with the U.S. Bennett, determined to build a Peace River dam, favoured the American plan because power production from the Canadian portion of the Columbia would have rendered the Peace project unnecessary. Bennett also disliked the privately owned B.C. Electric, so in August 1961 he suddenly nationalized the company. Of all Bennett's unpredictable, maverick actions, this was the most striking and controversial, and particularly upset the major corporations in the province which had come to regard him as a reliable friend. Although the premier's primary motive was to acquire a company which could develop the Peace River, the takeover had secondary benefits: as a provincial Crown corporation, the company would not have to pay federal income tax and could be used as an agent of provincial development. Like the Lesage decision to nationalize electricity in Quebec, Bennett's actions could be considered an instance of "province building," but "without the clear moral purpose and rational debate which preceded the Quebec take-over."[70] Although his act undercut traditional CCF/NDP policy, it worsened his reputation for being arbitrary and autocratic, especially given the clause in the bill which forbade any appeal to the courts by aggrieved shareholders. While by most accounts the compensation paid to shareholders had been adequate, they challenged the nationalization action and the price in the courts in spite of the no-appeal clause, and the entire takeover was declared unconstitutional. A final out-of-court settlement in 1963 left intact the new Crown corporation, now called British Columbia Hydro.

Meanwhile, negotiations dragged on over the Columbia River treaty. The federal justice minister and B.C. representative in the cabinet, Davie Fulton, along with General A.G.L. McNaughton, Canadian representative on the International Joint Commission, stood by the original Canadian proposal: no mere Columbia storage dams and no Peace River dam. But in 1961 Prime Minister John Diefenbaker fired McNaughton, took the matter out of Fulton's hands, and signed a treaty with U.S. President Dwight Eisenhower, more or less as the Americans wanted. After Diefenbaker's parliamentary defeat and the election of the Liberals, a revised Columbia agreement emerged in September 1964. Prime Minister Lester B. Pearson came to terms with both President John F. Kennedy and Bennett so that Canada would build three reservoirs (the Mica, Duncan Lake, and Arrow Lakes dams). Money raised from the sale of Canada's downstream power entitlements over a 30-year period would be used to finance construction. McNaughton and other Canadian nationalists called the agreement "servitude in perpetuity of our vital rights and interests," but at least the Americans and Bennett were happy with the results. Bennett now had a new Crown corporation in control of hydroelectric power, his Peace River dam, and U.S. cash to build the Columbia River dams—exactly what he wanted.

Overshadowed by this excitement was the founding of the provincial New Democratic Party in 1961. It carried on where the CCF left off, already closely attached to the labour movement and having as a central plank in its platform the nationalization of major utilities in the province. In response to this new threat, Bennett introduced a bill which prohibited unions from using a check-off procedure for political purposes, so that unions could not collect dues at source to finance political activity.

Other developments at the turn of the decade included charges that Highways Minister Gaglardi was engaged in a variety of questionable activities, in addition to being fined $1,000 for contempt of court and ticketed for speeding. Davie Fulton, out of favour with Diefenbaker, returned to B.C. to unsuccessfully lead the provincial Conservative party in the 1963 election, the same year that Simon Fraser University was founded and a system of junior colleges established.

The mid-1960s saw more economic growth in the province, partly as a result of dam construction and receipt of the first U.S. payment for Columbia downstream benefits. Growth was especially strong in the pulp and paper industry. In 1964 Bennett staged another bond-burning display and abolished bridge and road tolls. The government introduced a partial medicare plan, and fought with Ottawa over its reluctance to establish the Bank of British Columbia. An independent redistribution commission was established, but the government ignored many of its recommendations in making changes to the electoral map. The September 1966 election thus failed to generate much excitement or change in party standings. The Conservatives could find no replacement for Davie Fulton and were barely able to participate, while three newly elected women were subsequently appointed ministers without portfolio in the Social Credit cabinet.

Economic problems increased in the last half of the decade, and in 1966 the government was forced to introduce an austerity program. Layoffs and strikes of various kinds occurred, as did more confrontation between the government and organized labour over injunctions and a ban on overtime. Ottawa finally approved the Bank of British Columbia on the condition that there be no provincial government involvement. In 1967 and 1968, it was revealed that the construction of the two power projects was more expensive than had been anticipated, and exceeded American contributions to the Columbia development. The Opposition charged that education, health, and municipalities were being starved to pay the additional cost of the dams. The completion of these projects also meant more unemployment, as did a decline in the international market for pulp and paper and forestry products. In 1967 the Supreme Court of Canada ruled that off-shore mineral rights belonged to the federal government rather than to the province, but this defeat was more than offset by the opening of the Peace River dam. A major new economic project was the strip mining of coal by Kaiser Resources, to be transported to Japan via the new "superport" at Roberts Bank. This aroused opposition, especially from environmentalists, who were not satisfied by reclamation legislation in 1969. Gaglardi admitted to using the government Lear jet to fly family members on personal business, and Bennett himself had to pay $15,000 damages in a slander suit. A new education finance formula in 1968 aroused strong opposition from the Teachers' Federation and although labour was outraged with a new mediation act, it was more satisfied with a revamping of Workmen's Compensation. The Liberals chose Pat McGeer as their new leader in 1968; and, after challenging incumbent Robert Strachan in 1967, labour lawyer Tom Berger was elected the new NDP chief in 1969. In response to a royal commission on automobile insurance, the government introduced a new compulsory no-fault plan, although the industry remained in private hands. With fewer accomplishments and more adversity than usual, Bennett called an election for August 1969. The new NDP leader was defeated, and replaced as House leader by Dave Barrett, who was confirmed as provincial NDP leader in 1970.[71]

The 1970s

The 1970s were a tumultuous decade in British Columbia politics. They would see the final collapse of the W.A.C. Bennett regime, the first election of an NDP government in the province, and a quick return to a new Social Credit coalition headed by Bennett's son, Bill.

The aging Social Credit party had its share of both success and failure during the 1970-72 period. New legislation reduced the age of majority, restricted the purchase of Crown land, established a municipal finance authority, provided increased protection through legislation for tenants and the environment, and increased social spending. The government also raised the homeowner grant annually, introduced a partial Hansard, and eliminated Grade 13. On the other hand, unemployment was generally higher than usual, inflation was rampant, and labour relations hit an all-time low. Phil Gaglardi, now minister of rehabilitation and social improvement, frequently outraged the Opposition; the Americans proposed to flood the Skagit Valley and allow oil tankers in the Strait of Juan de Fuca; several Social Credit members and friends of the party appeared to be benefiting financially from land speculation; and controversy erupted over the banning of all forms of tobacco and liquor advertising. Several serious disputes with the teaching and medical professions occurred, and limits were placed on provincial contributions to local school districts and hospitals. Bennett was accused by Prime Minister Pierre Trudeau of being a bigot in his opposition to equalization payments, especially those given to Quebec; and the premier later renamed the provincial portion of the Trans-Canada Highway as B.C. 1.[72] Two Social Credit members, including Scott Wallace, crossed the floor to become Conservatives, while other ambitious Socred members became impatient with Bennett who showed no signs of stepping down.

The August 1972 election ended W.A.C. Bennett's 20-year term and gave the NDP its first chance to govern B.C. In the midst of innumerable labour problems, Bennett unveiled an attractive "Kelowna charter," which promised to increase social spending in a variety of ways. But the NDP, under Dave Barrett, introduced an even more comprehensive manifesto, which also emphasized "people" issues. The Liberals changed leaders rather suddenly just before the campaign, choosing David Anderson to replace Pat McGeer. While the B.C. Teachers' Federation opposed the government and the B.C. Federation of Labour endorsed the NDP, insurance companies took out advertising against public automobile insurance. In spite of Bennett's warning that "the socialist hordes are at the gates," the public was apparently ready for a change; the NDP raised its share of the vote to 40 percent while Social Credit dropped to 31 percent, largely the result of a concerted Tory campaign which netted 13 percent of the popular vote. This left the NDP with 38 seats to 10 for Social Credit, five for the Liberals, and two for the Conservatives. Eleven senior cabinet ministers were defeated.

Dave Barrett was born in east Vancouver of moderate-income Jewish parents, and was educated at Seattle University and the Jesuit St. Louis University, where he earned a master's degree. He worked as a social worker for the provincial prison service, but was fired in 1960 after publicly criticizing the correctional system and helping to organize an employees' union. He was elected to the legislature that year and assumed the party leadership a decade later. With a keen sense of the theatrical side of politics, Barrett developed a folksy, populist, and entertaining style. He had a natural social worker's mentality with a strong emphasis on social policy and a pragmatic approach to public ownership, and was never close to organized labour. Making no secret of his belief that to get elected the NDP needed more support than that provided by the B.C. Federation of Labour, he saw the NDP as a "people's" party rather than a labour party.

The Barrett government lost no time in getting down to business in September 1972, and the legislature was in almost continuous session for the next three-and-one-half years.[73] The NDP had been preparing for office for so long, and Bennett's traditional approach had left so many aspects of provincial life open to reform, that the new government moved with great haste, and significant innovations were made in almost every aspect of provincial operations. Government revenues were plentiful, as the economy remained strong until the end of 1974, although unemployment persisted, partly because of high migration into the province.

One of the government's first priorities was to improve the condition of the sick, the aged, the handicapped, and the poor, and one of its first acts was the introduction of Mincome, a kind of guaranteed annual income of $200 per month for senior citizens. It also established a pharmacare plan making free prescription drugs available to this group. The government increased welfare rates substantially, expanded the day-care system, constructed new hospitals and nursing homes, and organized a province-wide ambulance service. These and other programs led to a significant increase in the expenditures of the Department of Human Resources, which overspent its budget by $100 million in 1974. Although the money was put to good use, the overspending gave the appearance of lax administration.

Other social policy developments included a new human rights code, consumer protection legislation and minor reforms in the education field. A new Department of Housing attempted to ease the acute shortage in this area with land-banking, low-income housing, rent controls, the appointment of a rentalsman, and increases in the annual grants to renters. Public parks and public transit were other social priorities.

The Barrett government was also very active in the economic sphere. One benefit to business was the B.C. Development Corporation, a Crown corporation designed to help small and medium firms. The government's taxation of resource companies, however, aroused heated protest from the corporate sector. The NDP increased corporate taxes and petroleum royalty rates, but the most controversial measure was the Mineral Royalties Act of 1974. This legislation was influenced by the Kierans report in Manitoba and, through its super-royalties, the government intended to skim revenue from high company profits. The industry reacted with a powerful campaign against the various government initiatives in the mining sector, and gradually forced the NDP to retreat.[74] In general, Barrett preferred to slow the exploitation of the province's minerals and engage in more prudent resource management, remarking that resources would not rot if left in the ground. He also wanted to increase the degree of mineral processing in the province and simultaneously reduce the environmental damage which often accompanied this activity. Natural gas prices were raised to provide additional public tax revenue, and new and increased stumpage rates produced more government revenue from the forestry industry, while the Timber Products Stabilization Act and other measures sought to introduce orderly production and marketing.

The government was also involved in industry ownership. It took over several companies in the forest sector, and combined them to form a Crown corporation, B.C. Cellulose. Even more dramatic was the $1-million purchase of the pulp mill and townsite at Ocean Falls, which was being phased out by Crown Zellerbach. Several other firms were purchased, such as B.C. Steamships, and in some cases the government bought shares without taking control, as with B.C. Telephone. It created the B.C. Petroleum Corporation to buy natural gas from producers and sell it to the distributor, Westcoast Transmission, in which the government also bought a few shares.

Two particularly controversial moves were the nationalization of the automobile insurance industry and the creation of the land commission. In the first case, the government set up the Insurance Corporation of British Columbia (ICBC) to administer the public autoplan. It took this action primarily as a means of reducing abnormally high premiums and of keeping premium monies in the province. ICBC became the sole supplier of motor vehicle insurance after March 1974, although private agents could become company representatives. It was also authorized to sell general insurance in competition with the private sector. By removing the profit margin from the industry, the government reduced insurance premiums, but for a variety of reasons the plan ran a deficit. It had a particularly difficult time at first, faced by a strike of its own employees and a war with the autobody shop operators, but worked reasonably well after the start-up problems were overcome.[75] In the matter of land, the government first imposed a virtual freeze on the subdivision of farm land and later introduced the land commission. This board had the power to issue regulations with the objective of keeping farmland in production rather than allowing it to be sold for urban development, as was occurring at an alarming rate, especially in the rich Fraser Valley. The commission's rulings overrode municipal by-laws, and its creation produced howls of protest from the "property industry," and from farmers who had hoped to make a fortune by selling their land for real estate development. Amendments were later introduced to allow for hearings and appeals.

Barrett did try to improve the lot of the farmers in other ways; indeed 14 bills in 1973 dealing with such items as insurance, credit, and income stabilization had the effect of reconstructing the provincial agricultural industry. Similarly, he introduced considerable labour legislation; the minimum wage was raised regularly, and the new labour code was "undoubtedly the most innovative in Canada."[76] The authority of the cabinet and the courts was removed from much of the labour-management process, although the new labour relations board could, in certain circumstances, impose agreements during the union's first year of operation. Labour unrest generally declined during this period, although the government had to use the Essential Services Act to order workers back to their jobs on three occasions before 1975.

In intergovernmental relations, the province assumed certain municipal responsibilities such as the administration of justice and many welfare services, and also increased the size of municipal grants. Relations with Ottawa improved, symbolized in the restoration of the Trans-Canada Highway signs. Although considered to be a pragmatic federalist, Barrett was frequently disposed to lay the blame for the province's problems on the federal government. He also tried to persuade René Lévesque to work for social and economic reform within the Canadian context.

Barrett made significant changes in the operation of the provincial government. The legislature saw its first question period, first complete Hansard, and first Opposition chair of the public accounts committee, which began to receive the annual reports of Crown corporations. Barrett attempted to strengthen the Opposition by ending "legislation by exhaustion" and bringing order to the schedule of the legislature, but faced an uproar when he tried to limit debate on departmental estimates. A greatly increased legislative workload was accompanied by enlarged indemnities and better services. The government amended the Constitution Act to enlarge the size of the cabinet, and expanded the secretariat to the environment and land use committee. Despite its record of innovation, there was a lack of co-ordination in the government's approach, an absence of general economic planning, and an inadequacy in financial administration. The premier acted as finance minister and Treasury Board president, as had his predecessor, but he was not as successful.[77] After 20 years of Social Credit rule, the NDP's relationship with the civil service was rather cool. While it dismissed only one deputy minister, it later demoted several others to associate deputy ministers, and brought in new people as ministerial assistants and consultants. Barrett introduced a full-scale collective bargaining system which protected the existing service, but might have been better off to dismiss a larger number of senior officials, given his government's radically different approach. The NDP caucus did not play a significant role in the policy-making process and, in spite of the record of innovation, the party organization passed a motion in 1973 calling on the government to abide by party policy.

While the NDP was thus preoccupied with trying to transform almost every aspect of the province in a single legislative term, significant developments were occurring in the Opposition. Scott Wallace had become the new Tory leader in 1973, and W.A.C. Bennett stepped down from the legislature and the Social Credit party leadership. His son, Bill, who had run the family hardware business and had shown no prior interest in politics, surprisingly sought and won his father's seat in a September 1973 by-election. Even more startling, he won the

Social Credit party leadership two months later. Meanwhile, much talk circulated of uniting opposition forces, and a gradual movement of Liberals and Conservatives to the Social Credit party took place at this time, including Hugh Curtis, a Conservative MLA, and three Liberal members, including Pat McGeer. Not surprisingly, David Anderson resigned as Liberal leader after this desertion and was replaced by Gordon Gibson, but the defections continued. Bill Bennett was engaged in an active and well-financed organization drive across the province, and attracted more and more supporters from the Liberal and Conservative camps.

In early 1975, after two-and-one-half years of controversial rule, the NDP government appeared to be in trouble. The federal party had lost support in B.C. in the 1974 election, and the provincial economy slowed substantially as exports fell. Unemployment and inflation increased. There was less legislation in 1975 as the government postponed other reforms such as the long-promised takeover of the American-owned B.C. Telephone and tougher environmental legislation until the party's anticipated second term. The 1975 budget reduced property taxes in support of education and small business income taxes, but increased the levies on large corporations. The Treasury Board was forced to freeze new civil service appointments and to limit grants to post-secondary education. Later in the year the province experienced a number of serious labour disputes, and a new mining minister was appointed to pacify the industry. The government also established a study committee to examine all aspects of mining legislation, including the questions of royalties and taxation. In September Barrett embarked on a province-wide campaign to improve the government's standing and, on Thanksgiving, Prime Minister Pierre Trudeau announced his wage-and-price control program. Barrett followed this federal action with his own, imposing a freeze on the price of food, drugs, and other essential goods and services, along with an increase in Mincome and the minimum wage. Next, the government brought in back-to-work legislation to end four strikes in the propane and forest industries, supermarkets, and B.C. Rail, an action popular with everyone but labour leaders. Then, with an independent redistribution of legislative seats just days away from implementation, Barrett called a snap December election.

The campaign witnessed the greatest polarization that the province had ever seen, as voters aligned either with the NDP or Social Credit. As the non-socialist alternative, the latter was inundated with corporate contributions. Many former Liberal and Conservative MLAs were now Social Credit candidates, and neither of those two parties fielded a full slate of candidates. Besides the two vigorous party efforts, many interest groups were active in the campaign, mostly opposed to the NDP. Bennett promised to revitalize the economy, and while his performance was shaky, his party organization was strong. Barrett attempted to focus the campaign on himself—lovable, fat, little Dave—in a one-man show across the province. But it was not enough: Social Credit won 35 seats, the NDP 18, and only the leaders of the Liberal and Conservative parties were successful.

Barrett lost his riding to a car dealer, an occupation shared by many Socred candidates.

In retrospect, several factors accounted for defeat. Most important was the combined Liberal and Conservative loss of 18 percent of the popular vote, the exact amount by which Social Credit increased over 1972. In fact, the NDP received more votes and only a half percentage point less support than in the preceding contest, but the "free-enterprise vote" had polarized against it. The NDP would have benefited somewhat from the pending redistribution and from a better system of enumerating voters. It should also have implemented its election finances legislation before calling the vote because it was greatly outspent by the Social Credit campaign. The NDP government had generally failed to explain its actions and to extol its real achievements, and suffered from a rather troubled relationship with the province's press. Barrett had also neglected the party in both policy and organization, and antagonized the B.C. Federation of Labour just before the vote. The government may have moved too far too fast, as each minister "had so many things he had long been desperate to do."[78] At the very least, there should have been more overall planning and co-ordination in the government's operations.

Bill Bennett's easy election as Socred leader in 1973 was an indication of the attrition in the ranks of his father's once powerful party. The coalition nature of the new Social Credit party was reflected in the composition of his new cabinet. No less than eight of 14 ministers—including Pat McGeer, Hugh Curtis, Jack Davis, and Bill Vander Zalm—were former Liberals or Conservatives. The new government's first task was to reveal the extent of their predecessor's financial mismanagement. Bennett accused the NDP of running up a deficit of $540 million, then appointed the accounting firm of Clarkson Gordon to investigate the finances of all government departments, agencies, and Crown corporations. The firm predicted a deficit of $400 million due to overspending and overestimation of revenues on the part of the NDP. The actual figure at the end of the fiscal year was more like $123 million, which would not substantiate the charge of fiscal irresponsibility, but the myth perpetuated by Bill Bennett served him well in the years ahead.[79] Restraint and fiscal responsibility—"pay as you go"—were the new order of the day. In consequence, Bennett raised the sales tax from five percent to seven percent, doubled Autoplan premiums, medicare premiums, and ferry rates, quadrupled the hospital per diem rate to $4, and also increased personal and corporate income taxes and a variety of other taxes and charges such as gas and electricity rates. The sales tax and ferry rate increases were rescinded just before the next election. Another aspect of the new government's takeover was the firing of several leading officials and the replacement of a large number of political appointments on government boards. It abolished many smaller NDP creations, and there appeared to be a "systematic scrapping of programs for women."[80]

Many other obvious departures from the NDP years were evident. In the area of labour law, Social Credit made it more difficult for workers to organize and continually broadened the definition of essential services, limiting the scope for strikes and often ending them by legislation. This caused the forging of a closer alliance between organized labour and the NDP after their strained relations in 1975-76. Other policy changes related to a dilution of land commission powers, the replacement of mining royalties with a profits tax, aid to independent schools, the abolition of the gift tax and succession duties, and a new forest act which seemed to please only the large, integrated companies. Other changes were not so ideologically oriented. They included more assistance for home purchases, increases in senior citizen homeowner and renter grants, a revised system of municipal finance, a new family relations act, an expanded pharmacare plan, and a new urban transit authority. Bennett also began to play a constructive role in federal-provincial relations, and introduced a number of structural changes in government itself. These included the appointment of an auditor general and an ombudsman, a reorganization of government departments which would now be called ministries, and a more effective executive decision-making system. A separate legislative committee would take over the responsibility of examining Crown corporation reports from the public accounts committee.

Bennett faced many problems and embarrassments over this period. At one point, 16 government inquiries of one kind or another were appointed to investigate such things as questionable land and stock market deals and nepotism among his officials. One of the main sources of controversy was Bill Vander Zalm, who started out as human resources minister. In assuming all costs of welfare administration from municipalities, and replacing Mincome with the Guaranteed Annual Income for Need (GAIN), he narrowed the definition of various categories of eligibility and strengthened means and assets tests. As a result, over 1975-76 Vander Zalm underspent his departmental budget by $100 million. After threatening to issue shovels to all employable welfare recipients, he introduced a Provincial Rehabilitation and Employment Program (PREP) designed to put them to work, relied increasingly on private welfare agencies, and made disparaging remarks about Native peoples and Quebec. When a *Victoria Times* cartoon likened his attitude towards his clients to pulling the wings off a fly, he sued for libel (losing on appeal), and Bennett moved him to another portfolio. The government's tarnished image was not helped when the long overdue redistribution of seats was gerrymandered by dividing several Socred seats into two-member ridings and abolishing a number of NDP constituencies.

Perhaps the most innovative of the government's proposals was the creation of the British Columbia Resources Investment Corporation (BCRIC, pronounced "brick"). This was a scheme to privatize most of the forestry holdings acquired by the NDP, as well as the government shares in Westcoast Transmission and its oil and gas exploration rights. The original plan was to offer shares to the public so that the government would own less than 50 percent. Later Bennett promised to give five free shares to each Canadian citizen resident in the province as an experiment in "people's capitalism," and to encourage them to buy others at $5 each. Eventually the government share in these ventures disappeared. The NDP ridiculed the BCRIC operation, arguing these assets were already owned by the people of the province, but Bennett tried to distinguish between individual and collective ownership.

Armed with BCRIC, a throne speech which proposed a denticare plan, and a budget which offered tax cuts and grants for almost everyone, Bennett called an election for May 1979. A federal campaign was already in progress, but the premier hoped that it would stretch NDP resources more than those of his own party. Again he had the assistance of the resource industries, typified by Crown Zellerbach's announcement that it would reassess its investment plans if the NDP won. The NDP presented itself as a more responsible party than that which had governed between 1972 and 1975, and Dave Barrett, re-elected to the legislature in a 1976 by-election, appeared quite statesmanlike. The results indicated that voters were still unprepared to forgive Barrett for his earlier performance, as Bennett's Social Credit government was returned to office by the slim margin of 31 seats to 26 for the NDP. The Liberal vote seemed to go mainly to the NDP, which raised its level of popular support to 46 percent, while most erstwhile Conservatives continued to support Social Credit, which gained 48 percent of the popular vote. For the first time since 1903, only two parties would be represented in the B.C. legislature, neither of them Liberal or Conservative.

The 1980s

The 1980s were rough for Bill Bennett and his government both economically and politically, and even rougher for many B.C. residents after actions were taken to cope with the problems. By 1982, the provincial economy was in its most depressed state since the Second World War, leaving a high rate of unemployment and reduced government revenues. In addition to federal-provincial conflicts, the 1979-83 period was marked by a never-ending series of strikes, including 1982's precedent-setting strike of public employees upset by the government's restraint program.

More positively, at least in the short run, the government promoted a number of public works projects including a second Peace River dam and another at Revelstoke, and two new megaprojects, Northeast Coal and B.C. Place. Northeast Coal was a joint federal-provincial, Canadian-Japanese scheme to mine coal and export it through Prince Rupert. It entailed the construction of railways, highways, power lines, and a new townsite with a cost to the province of at least $1 billion, for a probable return in government revenues of about half that amount.[81] B.C. Place was a redevelopment project in downtown Vancouver which would include Canada's first domed stadium, convention centres, a bridge, and Expo 86, a world transportation fair. Bennett persuaded Canadian Pacific Investments to withdraw its offer to buy MacMillan Bloedel, the premier declaring that "B.C. is not for sale," although the company was later sold to another outsider, Noranda Mines. He also announced a new forest management program, a federal-provincial salmon enhancement program on the Fraser River, and tougher pollution regulations under the Environmental Management Act. The government also introduced a new family and child service act, a reduced dental care package, a home mortgage plan, and a civil rights protection act in response to Ku Klux Klan activity, and outlawed extra-billing by doctors. The government's controversial Heroin Treatment Act, which provided for compulsory treatment, was ultimately upheld by the Supreme Court. By 1981 Bennett's position as party leader was less shaky, as he consolidated his leadership with the help of his chief of staff, Patrick Kinsella, and other officials imported from the Ontario Conservative big blue machine.

As in his earlier term, however, Bennett suffered many embarrassments. The Social Credit party had engaged in a number of "dirty tricks" in the 1979 campaign including writing phoney "letters to the editor" which criticized the NDP, and not reporting election expenditures paid from the party's "slush fund." It also became evident that the 1978 redistribution had been manipulated even more than first perceived. Another controversial redistribution proposal was abandoned after charges of more gerrymandering were raised. Quite a variety of court cases evolved out of one political situation or another.[82]

Given this mixed review, Bennett hoped to divert attention from domestic problems by stepping up his attacks on the federal government over the National Energy Program and the Constitution. B.C. finally signed an energy agreement with Ottawa in September 1981, and developed its own constitutional proposals which it promoted with an expensive public relations campaign. Neither these nor their author was a significant part of the final constitutional accord.

The economic situation became so bad in 1982 that the government ran a deficit for the first time, and introduced severe spending restraints in its February budget. Bennett limited public service salaries by a compensation stabilization act and announced that he would reduce the size of the service by 25 percent. The government cut back grants to school boards and universities; placed limits on hospital budgets, leading to a withdrawal of beds and staff reductions; restricted pharmacare; and abandoned denticare. Then, in the May 1983 election campaign, Bennett emphasized government restraint and fiscal responsibility, and portrayed Social Credit as a government that would inspire investor confidence. Considering the widespread discontent with the government's record, the NDP expected to topple the Socreds, but Barrett's statement that he would scrap the wage restraint program made his party vulnerable to renewed charges of fiscal irresponsibility. Thus, in another fairly close race, Bennett beat Barrett for the third time.

Over the next four years British Columbia experienced an unanticipated, unprecedented excursion into neo-conservatism, far beyond what had been promised in the campaign and generally more extreme than that practised by U.S. president Ronald Reagan or British Prime Minister Margaret Thatcher.[83]

The government's first objective was to institute a firm policy of restraint because of recession-reduced government revenues. This aim of balancing the budget could be achieved through limits on bureaucratic salaries and through reducing the size of the public service, a process begun in 1982. Its second goal was to limit the role of the government in the economy, and to reorder government spending to stimulate the growth of private enterprise. Because many of the restraint measures had little effect on the government deficit, they could only be justified as a means of creating business confidence and enhancing private investment and accumulation. Deregulation, the removal of protective processes of appeal and redress, and a transfer of funds from social to economic sectors were central to meeting this objective. But many observers felt that this was primarily a smoke-screen to take action against liberal or radical causes. Thus, the government could claim that economic necessity forced it to roll back such things as "excessive" human rights protection, and to centralize power in the hands of the cabinet and its agencies. The inspiration for much of the resulting program was the Fraser Institute, a right-wing think tank based in Vancouver. Others argued that the size of the deficit was anything but alarming, and that recovery would depend on increases in international prices and demand for B.C. exports, not on government fiscal policy within the province.

The new Bennett program was introduced by means of the July 1983 budget and the accompanying 26 pieces of legislation. The program naturally received a hostile reception from a large segment of the population and the NDP Opposition in the legislature. The government waited until September to introduce most of its bills, using closure 20 times and frequently resorting to all-night sittings. The Speaker made several questionable rulings, particularly the one that ejected Opposition leader Dave Barrett and barred him from re-entry for the remainder of the session. Most of the bills were passed in October, which simply did not allow for adequate scrutiny for such a comprehensive legislative program. A year later, the 1984 budget raised taxes and chopped spending in almost every field except health.

On the labour side several pieces of legislation were introduced. One reduced the maximum amount of public sector wage increases; another statute substantially enlarged the grounds for terminating public employees and abolished the principle of seniority; a third affected public sector pension plans; and Bill 2 removed government employees' rights to negotiate job security, promotion, transfer, hours and other working conditions. As for private sector workers, the government abolished the Employment Standards Board, reduced labour standards in many areas, and significantly amended the labour code to limit or abolish many previous rights. In that year, too, a lengthy labour dispute in the pulp and paper industry was ended by special legislation, and the International Labour Organization reported that several of the bills violated Canadian treaties.[84]

Among the many cutbacks on the social side were the removal of rent controls and the position of rentalsman; the abolition of the alcoholism and drug commission, the human rights branch, and the human rights commission; the elimination of a key "reasonable cause" clause in the human rights code; an increase in medicare premiums and hospital user fees; the appointment of a new businessman head of the Workers' Compensation Board and the elimination of 40 positions there; reductions in legal aid; and massive staff cuts at the Ministry of Human Resources, accompanied by the elimination, reduction, or transfer of many programs to voluntary or private agencies, and a tightening of eligibility requirements.

Increased ministerial control over the medical profession, post-secondary educational institutions, and local school board spending were examples of attempts to centralize power in the cabinet. Deregulation could be seen in the repealing of all regional plans and the abolition of the planning function of the regional districts, as well as in a loosening of the municipal property tax regulations and a dilution of the powers of land use control. Spending in health, education, and social services was downgraded in favour of infrastructure development, which was expected to facilitate long-run economic growth through the private sector. B.C. Rail, Northeast Coal, B.C. Place, Expo 86, and the Vancouver light rapid transit line Skytrain were all amply funded, while federal contributions to health and post-secondary education were not always used for their intended purposes.

The public reaction to the program in the latter half of 1983 was intense. A variety of groups staged protests of one kind or another, including the B.C. Government Employees' Union and the B.C. Federation of Labour, which formed a labour-oriented Operation Solidarity. It was also part of a wider Solidarity Coalition of all protesting groups.[85] A rally of 40,000 protesters took place at Empire Stadium in August and another of 60,000 at the Social Credit convention in October. The BCGEU struck on November 1, and was joined by teachers and other education workers on November 8. This walkout of nearly 100,000 people, which for a two-week period threatened to evolve into a general strike, was resolved to a degree by the "Kelowna Accord" negotiated by Premier Bennett and Solidarity representative Jack Munro of the International Woodworkers of America. The government would withdraw Bill 2 and exempt the BCGEU and B.C. Teachers' Federation from another of the labour bills. The accord, later considered a sell-out by many in the labour movement, thus settled the immediate public sector labour crisis. Collective bargaining in the public sector remained intact, but the vague government commitments about human rights and other issues were not kept.[86] Both Solidarity groups found it necessary to continue to operate, but with a lower profile.

This whole affair resulted, about three years later, in a "new economic reality" in the province, a "fundamental restructuring" of the B.C. economy. Employers, landlords, businessmen, and corporations had been strengthened, while public employees, labour, tenants, consumers, and disadvantaged groups had been weakened. Whether any of this had helped the economy fundamentally was debatable, for by 1985 unemployment and the government deficit were higher than ever.[87]

For several years, the Bennett government essentially played a waiting game, hoping the economy would turn around. Instead, it continued to face much opposition as its restraint policies took hold. Demonstrations against education cuts were staged as teachers were laid off and schools began to close; universities were forced to raise their fees by as much as 33 percent, at the same time as student grants were eliminated; and food banks were overwhelmed by demands made upon them. A clash occurred between unionized and non-unionized tradesmen at the Expo 86 site, and the dispute threatened the cancellation of the fair until Bennett ruled that the two groups would have to work alongside each other. Serious questions were also raised about the viability of the Quintette coal mine, and after the investment of $1.5 billion in federal and provincial funds in infrastructure, the Japanese buyers demanded price and volume cuts. Other problems at Northeast Coal included equipment failures, unexpectedly high ash contents, managerial and financial woes, and reports that the main pit was in the wrong place. Tech Corp. eventually took over the Denison share of Quintette and managed the mine, but the whole indebted project had to be restructured with the co-operation of the banks and B.C. Rail. The government and the medical profession came out even in their two court cases in this period. The Supreme Court of Canada upheld the provincial ban on extra-billing (called balance billing in B.C.), but the provincial Supreme Court ruled that the government could not regulate where doctors practised by rationing billing numbers. The issue of Native land claims also arose, especially in relation to Meares Island. The courts ruled that Macmillan Bloedel must stop logging until land claims were resolved. In regard to the South Moresby region of the Queen Charlotte Islands, the courts ruled against the Haida protesters. Meanwhile, when they would not surrender to his cost-cutting edicts, the education minister dismissed the Vancouver and Cowichan school boards and replaced them with a provincial trustee.

The government changed direction to some extent at the beginning of 1985. A premier's television address, the throne speech, and the budget all had the same basic thrust: restraint would continue but, having gained control of the situation, the government could now cut nearly $1 billion in a variety of corporate taxes over three years to revive the moribund economy, and a commissioner of critical industries was appointed to offer various kinds of corporate assistance. Later in the year, the government tried to increase petroleum exploration and development by offering a four-year royalty holiday for companies drilling for oil. Also of an optimistic flavour, an agreement was reached with the Americans to save the Skagit Valley; the terms of the Pacific Salmon Treaty with the U.S. were also agreed upon; and a $650-million Economic and Regional Development Agreement, which included funds for a large reforestation plan, was signed with the federal government. The most hopeful signs for the Bennett government were that the corporate tax reductions and oil drilling royalty holiday would have their anticipated effect, that new megaprojects—a $600-million fertilizer plant, the Coquihalla Highway, the New Westminster rapid transit line, and a new bridge across the Fraser River in south Vancouver—would benefit the economy, and that political benefits would flow from a successful Expo 86.

Dave Barrett resigned as NDP leader in 1984, and the party chose Bob Skelly as his successor. A former teacher, Skelly lacked the flair of his predecessor, and embarked on a low-key campaign to rebuild the party and gain control over the caucus. He predicted that dullness would enable him to win the next election. Yet another controversial redistribution proposal was adopted for the next election; it would add 12 seats, 11 of these creating dual-member ridings of which 10 were in seats held previously by Social Credit. Then, just when observers expected Bennett to call an election in mid-1986, he abruptly announced his resignation. At the July 1986 Social Credit convention, there were four main contenders for the party leadership—Grace McCarthy, Bud Smith, Bill Vander Zalm, and Brian Smith. Vander Zalm and his wife Lillian were proprietors of Fantasy Garden World, a garden centre and biblical theme park. He had resigned from Bennett's cabinet in 1983, was the most colourful and controversial of the candidates, and was selected as the new leader.

The handsome new premier's unbounded energy and enthusiasm gave the embattled government party a new lease on life.[88] He immediately settled the long-standing dispute between the government and its public servants, and helped end the four-month IWA loggers' strike. These incidents seemed to support his declared intention to end the climate of confrontation in the province and prolonged his post-convention honeymoon with the media and with the public. Lacking a seat in the legislature, Vander Zalm decided to capitalize on his personal popularity and the afterglow of Expo 86 by calling an election for October 1986.

The charismatic Vander Zalm, for whom everything was "fantastic," completely dominated the campaign. Party standings in the polls were quickly reversed, and the new premier romped to victory. Social Credit took all but one of the newly created two-member ridings, and in total the party won 47 seats to 22 for the NDP. The Liberals ran 55 candidates and picked up a total of 6.7 percent of the vote. Skelly resigned after the election, and the NDP leadership convention in April 1987 anointed former Vancouver mayor Mike Harcourt, who had entered provincial politics in the 1986 election.

Bill Vander Zalm was embroiled in almost daily controversy in the 1986-88 period. During his first year in office, for example, no less than four cabinet ministers resigned over conflict of interest charges, and questions were raised about the land zoning of Fantasy Gardens. Towards the end of the second year, two of his senior ministers, Brian Smith and Grace McCarthy, resigned because of the premier's interference in their departments and the centralization of power in his office, especially in the hands of his assistant, David Poole. When the government invited tenders for the sale and development of the Expo 86 site, Peter Toigo, a close friend of the premier, attempted to win the contract in private meetings arranged by Poole. The site was eventually awarded to Hong Kong billionaire Li Ka-shing (of Husky Oil fame), but the Toigo-Vander Zalm relationship became the subject of an RCMP investigation, and when Poole resigned, his severance package provoked an uproar. In June 1989 the Expo land deal was subject to an intensive investigation by the *Globe and Mail,* which revealed that Vander Zalm had intervened ineffectively to try to win the deal for Toigo.

Other controversies developed from Vander Zalm's penchant for off-the-cuff remarks, his impulsive, impromptu style of policy making, and his failure to consult cabinet and caucus. After the Supreme Court of Canada's ruling on abortion, for example, Vander Zalm spontaneously announced that medicare funding for abortion would be halted. This declaration brought forth accusations that he was imposing his fundamentalist convictions as public policy, but the decision was soon overturned by the B.C. Supreme Court. Later, as well as paying spies to infiltrate a pro-choice group which opened an abortion clinic in 1988, the government announced a new program to discourage abortion and encourage family life. The clinic was picketed regularly by anti-abortionists, but protesters were jailed for violating an injunction against such harassment.

On other policy questions, Vander Zalm set out a generally consistent right-wing agenda which mainly involved labour legislation, privatization, and the regionalization of government operations. Bills 19 and 20 reformed the provincial labour code, and, while public-sector wage restraints were abolished and teachers granted the right to strike, the legislation also invested a new industrial relations council with unprecedented powers to intervene in labour disputes, and placed many restrictions on strikes and picketing. The premier later introduced minor amendments, but on June 1, 1987, the province witnessed a one-day general strike of about 300,000 hostile unionized workers. This set the stage for a four-year boycott of the industrial relations council by the province's unions.

In the area of privatization, the similarities to Saskatchewan were striking: the British adviser, the new department to oversee the process, and the combination of ideological and budgetary motives. B.C. had an accumulated provincial debt of about $6 billion to which it was adding about $1 billion annually. Almost every Crown corporation and government operation and service was a potential candidate for privatization, but the first to be selected were the natural gas, rail, and research divisions of BC Hydro; the maintenance operations and sign manufacturing plant of the highways department; three government labs; nine forest nurseries; and parts of the Queen's Printer. It was hoped that the sale of these firms would produce about $3 billion, but the privatization program was partly responsible for another week-long government employees' strike in the fall of 1988. After a generally hostile reaction, both the privatization and decentralization schemes were diluted and delayed to some extent. On a more positive note, the Sechelt Indian Band became the first in Canada to be given the power of self-government.

In financial matters, a "populist" 1987 budget contrasted with a more neo-conservative one a year later. Of Bill Bennett's legacies, the Coquihalla highway was over-budget, the final balance sheet on Expo 86 was not entirely clear, and BCRIC, an earlier attempt at privatization, generally did not do well. In 1988 it changed its name to Westar Group Ltd., opened itself up to non-Canadian ownership, and eventually split into several, largely insolvent, parts. In federal-provincial relations, Vander Zalm supported the Mulroney Meech Lake and free trade initiatives and, after much federal pressure, Vander Zalm finally agreed to establish a national park on South Moresby Island. Just before the 1988 federal election, Ottawa promised to assist in constructing a controversial natural gas pipeline to Vancouver Island.

By August 1988, Vander Zalm had the largest cabinet in B.C. history, but it included only one woman and no representative from the City of Vancouver. Social Credit lost a series of by-elections to the NDP during this period. The premier himself became more subdued, but certain ministers continued to assail environmentalists, welfare recipients, and AIDS patients, although a late-1989 shuffle removed most of the offenders.

Over the 1986-90 period, the B.C. economy remained generally strong, even though unemployment was relatively high compared with other provinces. A New Zealand firm, Fletcher Challenge, took over and merged B.C. Forest Products and Crown Forest Industries into one of the largest forestry companies in the province, and Cominco and Lornex combined forces to develop the Highland Valley copper mine and mill, the second largest operation of its kind in the world. Despite criticism by environmentalists and aboriginal residents, Alcan began to expand its hydro facilities at Kemano in 1987 as part of a project to divert the Nechako River to increase the production of electricity at Kitimat. As in Saskatchewan and Alberta, a series of court cases followed on the question of an environmental review. A great deal of Hong Kong and other Asian capital entered the province, taking over the Bank of British Columbia, hotels, and condominiums among other things, and contributing to the escalating real estate values in Vancouver. When a dispute with Japanese buyers over price and volume reductions of Quintette coal was sent to arbitration, the Japanese steel mills won $46 million in a May 1990 arbitration award, but a later court ruling denied that they were preferred creditors in the financially troubled operation. Strikes in the province were common, most notably a 17-day nurses' strike in June 1989. Less controversial was the merging of County and Supreme Courts and the final acceptance of a royal commission report setting out 75 single-member ridings for the 1991 provincial election.

B.C. also experienced its usual complement of unusual political events over the 1986-90 period. Annual fall conventions of the Social Credit party, for example, provided considerable excitement. After much caucus squabbling over the premier's leadership, dissidents tried to hold a secret ballot on a motion of non-confidence in the leader in 1988. They secured 30 percent of the delegates, but Vander Zalm carried the resulting open vote. After charges of anti-semitism arose the next year, the 1990 convention removed the party's "Christianity clause" that articulated the objective of fostering Christian principles. Attorney General Bud Smith resigned after the release of taped telephone calls in which he was apparently trying to discredit the NDP, while other ministers found themselves in hot water for excessive use of government jets. Questions were increasingly raised about Vander Zalm's sale of Fantasy Gardens, and former premier Bill Bennett and business colleagues were charged with illegal share trading, that is, taking advantage of an inside tip in the stock market to sell their shares to avoid a loss before the price fell.

The 1990s

The 1990s saw Vander Zalm resign in disgrace, to be replaced by the first female premier in the country, and the NDP were elected for the second time in the province's history. Both before and after the change in government, the political agenda was dominated by forestry and aboriginal issues.

Social Credit environmental policy was generally weak, and the cabinet's tough guidelines for dioxin discharges from pulp mills were vetoed by Premier Vander Zalm. One particularly controversial project was the Canfor pulp and paper mill on Howe Sound; another was MacMillan Bloedel's logging in the Carmanah Valley on Vancouver Island. This latter area, with a stand of old growth Sitka spruce, was somewhat parallel to the Temagami district of Ontario. The Vander Zalm government tried to compromise by setting up a park where no timber harvesting or mining would be allowed and by compensating the company for the park area. As in Temagami, the conflict between the logging industry and the environmentalists was complicated by a Native land claim.

With very few historic Native treaties and a relatively large proportion of aboriginal peoples, B.C. provides the focal point for Canada's land claim problems. The Social Credit government originally refused to participate in land claim negotiations, but established a ministry of Native Affairs in 1988. The government changed its non-negotiation policy in 1990 on the recommendation of the Premier's Council on Native Affairs and amid demonstrations and road and train blockades inspired by the Mohawk standoff in Oka, Quebec. Vander Zalm agreed to establish the B.C. Claims Task Force, which reported in June 1991, three months after Mr. Justice Allan McEachern of the province's Supreme Court ruled with respect to the Gitksen Wet'suwet'en claim that aboriginal title had been extinguished. The land claim issue remains more complicated in B.C. than elsewhere given federal-provincial conflicts, divisions among Natives, the huge areas and sums of money in question, and the opposition of corporate forestry, mining, and fishing interests.

In addition to federal-provincial discord over Native land claims, B.C. took Ottawa to court over cuts to the Canada Assistance Plan and the federal government's stacking of the Senate in order to pass the goods and services tax. A controversial and California-inspired referendum act was passed permitting the government to consult the people on any matter and requiring a referendum on constitutional amendments. But his low standing in the polls dissuaded Vander Zalm from calling a provincial election.

In February 1991, mounting controversy over his $16-million sale of Fantasy Gardens to (non-Christian) Taiwanese billionaire Tan Yu led Vander Zalm to ask the conflict of interest commissioner to rule in the case. In March increasing public and party pressure forced the premier to announce his impending resignation. In April the commissioner issued a scathing report, saying Vander Zalm had promoted his private company while conducting government business. Contrary to earlier claims, Vander Zalm—not his wife—still owned 83 percent of the shares and was actively involved in negotiations. Many aspects of the sale, including the premier receiving a $20,000 cash payment from his real estate agent, Faye Leung, were also criticized. The report forced Vander Zalm to leave office ahead of schedule, joining the seven former cabinet ministers who had already resigned over allegations of improper conduct,[89] and without waiting for a Social Credit leadership convention. Rita Johnston took over as premier in April 1991 and apologized for Vander Zalm's betrayal of the province, but he had trouble recognizing what he had done wrong. He was later charged with breach of trust by a public official, but in 1992, when Tan Yu refused to testify, the courts ruled there was not enough evidence to convict.

Rita Johnston, the first female premier in Canadian history, formed a cabinet, introduced a speech from the throne, and brought in a budget predicting a small deficit. After acquiring a motherly image through the media, she won the party leadership at a convention in July, defeating Grace McCarthy on the second ballot. In September she called an election for October 17th. The Social Credit campaign was plagued with charges of past scandal and new difficulties with several candidates. The NDP took a moderate approach, talked about the value of a mixed economy and fiscal responsibility, and issued a 48-point platform. To change the party's image, Harcourt had been courting the business community for several years. The surprise of the election campaign was the rise of the Liberal party, which had not been represented in the legislature since 1979. In addition to benefiting from the demise of Social Credit and the negative advertising of the two main protagonists, the Liberals were given a boost by leader Gordon Wilson's strong performance in the televised leaders' debate. Lacking grassroots organization, however, the party could advance only so far. Thus, Mike Harcourt's New Democrats won 51 seats, the Liberals, 17, and Social Credit, seven, not including Rita Johnson. The NDP picked up seats in unexpected places, while the Liberals generally did best in former Socred constituencies. Social Credit had hoped to benefit from adding to the ballot two referendum questions, on the desirability of the recall and referendum devices. But, while the voters were overwhelmingly in favour of these measures, they were not persuaded to vote for their sponsors.

Mike Harcourt selected a 19-member cabinet including seven women, and created a Ministry of Women's Equality.[90] He immediately set off to seek Asian investment by visiting Tokyo, Hong Kong, and China. As Bill Bennett had done after his party replaced the NDP in 1975, the Harcourt government brought in accounting firms to review the province's finances. They were found to be in dismal shape, largely due to bad Social Credit business deals and expensive ministerial mistakes. Only one deputy minister and one Crown corporation chief executive officer were fired, but over the next year several deputy ministers left their positions.[91]

When the legislature met in March 1992, the throne speech emphasized conflict of interest and freedom of information legislation, and programs for women, including pay equity, child care, and improved access to and public funding of abortion. (A Vancouver doctor who performed abortions was later shot at his home.) The budget raised taxes on those with higher incomes, put a cap on doctors' fees, and abolished the doctors' pension plan, while the ICBC increased car insurance premiums by 19 percent. As in 1972, the 1991 NDP government felt almost every public policy needed fixing. Harcourt set up task forces, committees, and commissions in a variety of policy areas, and began to implement their recommendations later in his term. As mentioned, forestry and aboriginal issues were predominant.

In the first place, Harcourt faced the localized forestry dispute in Clayoquot (pronouced Clakwut) Sound.[92] This conflict over the last major stand of old growth rain forest on Vancouver Island pitched forestry companies and their workers against environmentalists and First Nations residents. In December 1991, the government made a deal with the First Nations to establish an interim joint-management plan and finance the training of First Nations people in all aspects of forestry management. Two hundred Clayoquot protesters halted the reading of the March 1993 throne speech, causing personal and property damage in the legislature. In the same month, the government outlined its forestry policy, which was to preserve 12 percent of the province from logging and other development. In April Harcourt announced that one-third of the Clayoquot area would be permanently preserved, with 45 percent designated as working forest and a ban on large clearcuts and the construction of logging roads. However, controversy surrounded the government's purchase of additional MacMillan Bloedel shares, because that company owned most of the logging rights in the area. During the summer of 1993, environmentalists maintained almost daily road blockades, and some 800 were arrested for violating a court injunction against interfering with logging operations. Among those arrested was Svend Robinson, an NDP MP, who later served a short jail term over the charge. A scientific panel recommended in 1995 that a system retaining single and clumps of trees should replace clearcutting.

The government created a Commission on Resources and Environment (CORE), headed by the highly respected former ombudsman Stephen Owen, to help resolve subsequent disputes over forest land use. Its first major task was to devise a general plan for Vancouver Island, which it issued in February 1994. CORE recommended 13 percent of the island be set aside for parks, and another eight percent be partially protected from logging. This report prompted a furious protest from loggers, and in March some 20,000 protested on the lawn of the legislature. Delegates to the annual NDP convention also demanded changes to the plan, and in June Harcourt announced his decision. The government accepted CORE's recommendation of 13 percent parkland, and announced the creation of 23 new parks on the island. But it rejected the second part of the CORE plan, making 81 percent of the island available for logging, six percent being set aside for farm and urban use. The government estimated that this plan would eliminate 900 logging jobs over five years, but promised alternative employment to those affected.

While trying to find a peaceful solution to specific forestry conflicts, the Harcourt government worked on a new general forestry policy. After much consultation with interested groups, it issued a series of related policy announcements in mid-1994. Harcourt claimed that the April Forest Renewal Plan represented an unprecedented partnership between the forest industry and its workers, environmentalists, First Nations, communities, and government. It concentrated on improving reforestation and silviculture, cleaning up environmental damage, increasing the jobs and value from the trees harvested, providing high-value skills training to forest workers, and enhancing First Nations' participation. Increased stumpage fees paid by forestry companies would add some $2 billion to the budget for forest renewal, and investments would be managed by the new agency, Forest Renewal B.C. Workers who lost their jobs would be retrained and rehired in silviculture. In May, the government unveiled a new forest practices code which established a comprehensive framework for legally enforceable forest practices, together with a new forest practices board. Massive clearcutting was banned, smaller clearcutting would not be allowed where alternative harvesting methods were more appropriate, and even cutblocks, areas to be clearcut, would be much smaller—40 hectares in the south and 60 hectares in the north. The policy also protected community watersheds, wildlife habitat areas, visually sensitive landscapes, and old growth stands. Heavy fines were provided for violations of the code. In June, the government announced a new forest land reserve including both Crown lands and privately managed forest lands. A forest land commission would rule on whether private lands could be removed from the reserve and recommend Crown lands to be so removed. Other aspects of the government plan included a timber supply review, designed to gather information, and a protected areas strategy working to protect 12 percent of B.C.'s land base.

Harcourt reminded loggers that they could not ignore the international pressure beginning to result in boycotts of B.C. forest products. In February

1994 he had made a two-week European tour to answer critics aroused by Greenpeace protesters. The European Parliament was concerned about clearcuts, Scott Paper in Britain announced that it would not buy pulp produced by companies cutting old growth trees, and U.S. Senator Tom Hayden promoted a law to this effect in California.

Other forestry industry issues were also prominent in the early 1990s. In spite of the Free Trade Agreement, the United States continued to take action against Canadian softwood lumber exports, 80 percent of which came from B.C. In 1992 the U.S. claimed that Canadian stumpage fees for lumber production on Crown land were too low, and imposed a 6.5 percent duty. The government brought in tough new standards for the most toxic of pulp mill pollutants, later backtracking on its ban of chlorine.

Only one aboriginal land claim was being negotiated before the Harcourt government came to office, that of the Nisga'a nation, a claim which began in 1976. In June 1993, however, the B.C. Court of Appeal gave a mixed decision in the *Delgamuukw* case, ruling that aboriginal title had not been extinguished as earlier determined, sending a strong message to the province to proceed. Harcourt responded by creating the B.C. Treaty Commission to oversee the negotiation of modern treaties. The process begins with a First Nation filing a statement of intent to negotiate a treaty, describing the geographic area involved. The treaties are expected to spell out the rights, responsibiliities and relationships of First Nations and the two levels of government, as well as deal with such issues as land ownership, self-government, wildlife and environmental management, sharing resources, financial benefits, and taxation. By 1995, some 43 such submissions had been made, the federal and provincial governments had agreed to share the cost of settlements, and the province had brought municipalities into the negotiations. Since some claims overlapped, they totalled 110 percent of the province's land mass, while the government said it would only cede 5 percent. Given this discrepancy, the number of governments involved, and the opposition of commercial logging, fishing, mining, and other interests, prospects for settlement were not encouraging. The public was becoming impatient with even the single Nisga'a claim, and the government issued a deadline for resolution of the problem. Harcourt also conducted a review of how aboriginal people were affected by the legal system, with the usual depressing results.

As in other provinces in this period, health care was a major concern in B.C., and the NDP adopted a "new directions" strategy in February 1993. The government planned to transfer as much acute care as possible to outpatient clinics and home care, and regional health boards and community health councils had the responsibility of carrying out the transfer. The government estimated that 4,800 acute-care jobs would be lost over the following three years, and negotiated a delicate agreement with unions in the health-care field to minimize layoffs, although it was more difficult to sell the agreement to the employer side.

Relations with doctors, who staged rotating walkouts, were also difficult. Federal Health Minister Diane Marleau penalized the province for allowing a small group of doctors to extra-bill, until Harcourt ended this privilege. The province also eliminated or reduced medicare premiums for over half a million lower-income residents.

On the social services front, the government focused on relieving child poverty, unveiling a selective school lunch program and providing more child-care spaces. It also took action on family violence and spousal support payments. Many observers were surprised by the government's hard line on social assistance, and Harcourt was not above complaining about abuses of the welfare system. He cracked down on welfare fraud, and took measures forcing over 50,000 social assistance recipients to seek employment or training, providing $200 million over two years for this purpose.

Although Harcourt made it clear that his government was not a captive of the labour movement, in late 1992 it introduced legislation which restored rights removed in 1987, and then went further by banning the use of replacement workers and making it easier to certify a new union. It adopted a "fair wage" policy in 1994 with the object of paying non-union workers on government projects the same wages as unionized workers. Meanwhile, the Labour Relations Board ruled that bargaining in the forestry industry should be done company by company, rather than on an industry-wide basis. Harcourt also introduced a venture capital fund owned by seven unions and modeled on the Solidarity Fund of the Quebec Federation of Labour. The fund provided tax credits for investment in small businesses to maintain employment. Civil servants were not happy with a two-percent pay increase in 1992, but the minimun wage rose in 1995.

The government also took considerable action in the broader environmental field and the Commission on Resources and Environment was to play a major role in developing an effective land-use planning system for the province. A controversial environmental assessment act gave stronger powers to the minister, the government killed Royal Oak Mines copper-gold mine project at Windy Craggy Mountain, and created several large new provincial parks, including the Juan de Fuca Marine Trail on Vancouver Island, and the Khutzeymateen Valley Park to protect grizzly bears. It announced that the Kitlope Valley would be preserved intact and adopted a plan for the Cariboo-Chilcotin area, which covered one-tenth of the province, to balance the concerns over forestry, mining, ranching, tourism, job security, and the environment. It also took action to stop the widespread proliferation of golf courses on agricultural land (which Vander Zalm had encouraged by lifting a land freeze). In 1995, Harcourt killed Alcan Aluminum's $1.3 billion Kemano Completion project to save dwindling salmon stocks, and the government altered the mandate of B.C. Hydro, with a new program called Power Smart, emphasizing conservation and the environment.

Harcourt was naturally involved in the 1992 Charlottetown Accord. While he was prepared to defend the concept of Quebec as a distinct society, he did not accept granting special powers to the province. Harcourt's poor defence of the part of the Accord which guaranteed Quebec 25 percent of the seats in the House of Commons did nothing to help sell the agreement in the B.C. referendum campaign.

On the budgetary front, Harcourt originally promised a balanced budget over five years. Although Social Credit had balanced its budget over the 1989-91 period, the NDP inherited a 1991-92 deficit of about $2 billion rather than the $400 million estimated by Rita Johnston. The provincial economy remained the best in the country over 1992 and 1993, but the government complained that federal funding of health, post-secondary education, and the Canada Assistance Plan had dropped to 33 percent from the original 50 percent. A 1993 surtax on expensive houses was withdrawn after protest, timber royalties were not raised as much as planned, but the sales tax rose to seven percent. On the other hand, Harcourt rejected Las Vegas-style government-run gambling casinos. He reduced the deficit to an anticipated balance for 1995–96, but was not as obsessed with the issue as many other provincial governments.

TABLE 11.11   Government of British Columbia Finances, 1990/91–1994/95 ($ millions)

	1990/91	1991/92	1992/93	1993/94	1994/95
Total revenues	$17,024	$17,530	$18,531	$20,138	$21,228
Debt charges	1,565	1,723	1,886	2,316	2,386
Total expenditures	17,259	19,473	20,217	21,476	22,726
Deficit	234	1,943	1,686	1,338	1,498

Source: Reproduced by authority of the Minister of Industry, 1995, Statistics Canada, *Public Sector Finance, 1994–95,* Financial Management System, cat. no. 68-212 (March 1995). Adapted by author.

In 1993, the government introduced BC21, a plan to expand and diversify the provincial economy to lay a solid foundation for the 21st century.[93] Under this rubric, the government announced a $840-million expansion of the ferry system over a 10-year period, and a $1 billion Vancouver Island highway. On the other hand, the fate of the Esquimalt and Nanaimo railway came into question.

Other NDP initiatives in the 1991-95 period included creating the University of Northern British Columbia in Prince George, educational and curriculum reform, adding discrimination on the basis of sexual orientation to the human rights code, and allowing Sikhs who were municipal police officers to wear turbans on duty. It raised the legal smoking age to 19, introduced restrictions on cigarette vending machines, and made a deal with Cominco to begin to operate its new lead smelter and expand its zinc operations. The government took action to clean up the scandal-ridden Vancouver Stock Exchange, and unenthusiastically passed the Recall and Initiative law. Based on the 1991 referendum, it allowed voters to recall their MLA and force the government to initiate new laws by means of petitions. A number of teachers' strikes occurred, some of which were settled by back-to-work legislation. In September 1993 a cabinet shuffle, partly designed to demonstrate that Harcourt was in control, gave the province its first female finance minister. U.S. salmon fishermen invaded B.C. salmon runs after their own expired due to the construction of dams, and the government demanded a renegotiation of the Canada-U.S. salmon treaty. The provincial treasury would benefit to the tune of $200 million per year for 30 years from a renegotiation of the Columbia River Treaty, although initial talks did not go well. In general, Premier Harcourt tried to steer a middle course, but the business community increasingly viewed the government as left of centre.

On the opposition side of the legislature, the Social Credit party gradually withered away. In 1993, Grace McCarthy was elected party leader but lost the by-election by which she hoped to enter the house. McCarthy later resigned the leadership, and most of the six Socred MLAs adopted the B.C. Reform Party label. After doing so well in the 1991 election, Liberal party leader Gordon Wilson came under attack from caucus members when he appointed Judy Tyabji as Liberal house leader. Amid growing caucus unrest and increasing media interest in his personal relationship with Tyabji, Wilson decided to step aside as Opposition leader but remain leader of the party.[94] After a caucus revolt, however, he called for a leadership convention which the party happily scheduled for September 1993. In the one member, one vote telephone tally, Wilson ran a distant third to photogenic and newly minted Liberal, Gordon Campbell, mayor of Vancouver, while ex-Liberal leader Gordon Gibson finished second. Wilson and Tyabji, now admitting their romantic attachment, decided to leave the Liberal caucus and sit as Independents, ultimately forming their own political party. In spite of these upheavals, the Liberal party maintained a strong showing in the polls, and Campbell won a by-election in February 1994. With a variety of NDP problems, including patronage appointments, questionable contracts, cabinet registrations, and budget and other leaks, Campbell felt that he had a good chance to win the 1996 election. Harcourt only hoped that Reform would serve to split the right-wing vote.

CONCLUSION

British Columbia politics, usually more colourful than anywhere else in the country, often attracts greater national attention than those of any other province except perhaps Quebec. Partly due to unfavourable economic circumstances, in the 1980s the polarization between left and right was more marked than ever, and British Columbians will not soon forget the Social Credit government's adoption of neo-conservatism. Bill Vander Zalm's unique performance only enhanced the distinctiveness of B.C. politics, although his star burned out rather quickly. Even though Mike Harcourt tried to move the new NDP government to the middle of the ideological road, opponents increasingly coalesced around the new Liberal party which replaced Social Credit on the right. Harcourt's failure seems to confirm the enduring distinctiveness of class consciousness and ideological polarization in British Columbia.

TABLE 11.12   British Columbia Provincial Election Results Since 1920

Year	Liberal		Conservative		Labour/CCF		Other	
	Seats	Popular Vote	Seats	Popular Vote	Seats	Popular Vote	Seats	Popular Vote
1920	26	(38%)	14	(32%)	3	(13%)	4	(18%)
1924	27	(32%)	16	(30%)	3	(13%)	2	(27%)
1928	12	(40%)	35	(53%)	1	(5%)	–	(2%)
1933	34	(42%)	–	–	7	(32%)	6	(27%)
1937	31	(37%)	8	(29%)	7	(29%)	2	(5%)
1941	21	(33%)	12	(31%)	14	(33%)	1	(3%)

Year	Coalition		CCF		Other	
	Seats	Popular Vote	Seats	Popular Vote	Seats	Popular Vote
1945	37	(56%)	10	(38%)	1	(5%)
1949	39	(61%)	7	(35%)	2	(2%)

Year	Social Credit		CCF/NDP		Liberal		Conservative		Other	
	Seats	Popular Vote	Seats	Popular Vote	Seats	Popular Vote	Seats	Popular Vote	Seats	Popular Vote
1952	19	(27%)	18	(31%)	6	(23%)	4	(17%)	1	(2%)
1953	28	(38%)	14	(31%)	4	(24%)	1	(6%)	1	(2%)
1956	39	(46%)	10	(28%)	2	(22%)	–	(3%)	1	(1%)
1960	32	(39%)	16	(33%)	4	(21%)	–	(7%)	–	–
1963	33	(41%)	14	(28%)	5	(20%)	–	(11%)	–	–
1966	33	(46%)	16	(34%)	6	(20%)	–	–	–	–
1969	38	(47%)	12	(34%)	5	(19%)	–	–	–	–

TABLE 11.12 continued

Year	Social Credit		CCF/NDP		Liberal		Conservative		Other	
	Seats	Popular Vote	Seats	Popular Vote	Seats	Popular Vote	Seats	Popular Vote	Seats	Popular Vote
1972	10	(31%)	38	(40%)	5	(16%)	2	(13%)	–	–
1975	35	(49%)	18	(39%)	1	(7%)	1	(4%)	–	–
1979	31	(48%)	26	(46%)	–	–	–	(5%)	–	–
1983	35	(50%)	22	(45%)	–	(3%)	–	(1%)	1	(1%)
1986	47	(49%)	22	(43%)	–	(7%)	–	(1%)	–	–
1991	7	(24%)	51	(41%)	17	(33%)	–	–	–	(2%)

TABLE 11.13 Premiers of British Columbia

Premier	Party	Year Elected
John McCreight		1871
Amor De Cosmos (William Alexander Smith)		1872
George Walkem		1874
Andrew Elliot		1876
George Walkem		1878
Robert Beaven		1882
William Smithe		1883
A.E.B. Davie		1887
John Robson		1889
Theodore Davie		1892
J.H. Turner		1895
C.A. Semlin		1898
Joseph Martin		1900
James Dunsmuir		1900
E.G. Prior		1902
Richard McBride	Conservative	1903
William Bowser	Conservative	1915
H.C. Brewster	Liberal	1916
John Oliver	Liberal	1918
J.D. MacLean	Liberal	1927
S.F. Tolmie	Conservative	1928
T.D. Pattullo	Liberal	1933
John Hart	Coalition	1941
Byron Johnson	Coalition	1947
W.A.C. Bennett	Social Credit	1952
Dave Barrett	New Democratic Party	1972
Bill Bennett	Social Credit	1975
Bill Vander Zalm	Social Credit	1986
Rita Johnston	Social Credit	1991
Mike Harcourt	New Democratic Party	1991

ENDNOTES

1. The province of British Columbia puts out an annual publication, *British Columbia Economic and Statistical Review* (Ministry of Finance and Corporate Relations), which is an excellent resource. The author only wishes other provinces did the same.

2. On the forest industry, see Patricia Marchak, *Green Gold: The Forest Industry in British Columbia* (Vancouver: University of British Columbia Press, 1983). On resources in general, see her article, "British Columbia: 'New Right' Politics and a New Geography," in Michael Whittington and Glen Williams, eds., *Canadian Politics in the 1990s* (Scarborough: Nelson Canada, 1989).

3. Martin Robin, "British Columbia, The Company Province," in Martin Robin, ed., *Canadian Provincial Politics* (Scarborough: Prentice Hall Canada, 1978), p. 31.

4. Michael Howlett and Keith Brownsey, "British Columbia: Public Sector Politics in a Rentier Resource Economy," in their book *The Provincial State* (Mississauga: Copp Clark Pitman, 1992).

5. Norman Ruff, "British Columbia and Canadian Federalism," in Terence Morley et al., eds., *The Reins of Power: Governing British Columbia* (Vancouver: Douglas and McIntyre, 1983), pp. 290-1.

6. Ibid., p. 275. The same three-sided relationship between resource companies and the two levels of government could be cited in Alberta or Ontario.

7. Robin, "British Columbia," in Robin, ed., *Canadian Provincial Politics;* Gordon Galbraith, "British Columbia," in David Bellamy et al., eds., *The Provincial Political Systems* (Toronto: Methuen, 1976); Edwin Black, "British Columbia: The Politics of Exploitation," in Hugh G. Thorburn, ed., *Party Politics in Canada* (Scarborough: Prentice Hall Canada, 4th ed., 1979); J.T. Morley, "British Columbia's Political Culture: Healing a Compound Fracture," an address to the Canadian Political Science Association (June 1983); Donald Blake, "Managing the Periphery: British Columbia and the National Political Community," an address to the Canadian Political Science Association (June 1983); R.M. Burns, "British Columbia and the Canadian Federation," in R.M. Burns, ed., *One Country or Two?* (Montreal: McGill-Queen's University Press, 1971); R.M. Burns, "British Columbia: Perceptions of a Split Personality," in R. Simeon, ed., *Must Canada Fail?* (Montreal: McGill-Queen's University Press, 1977); Tim Page, "Perceptions from the West: British Columbia in the Evolving Pattern of Canadian Federalism," *Occasional Papers,* Institute of Canadian Studies, (Ottawa: Carleton University, 1982); Donald Blake, "Western Alienation: A British Columbia Perspective," in A.W. Rasporich, ed., *The Making of the Modern West: Western Canada Since 1945* (Calgary: University of Calgary Press, 1984); and David Elkins, "British Columbia as a State of Mind," in Donald Blake, *Two Political Worlds: Parties and Voting in British Columbia* (Vancouver: University of British Columbia Press, 1985).

8. Black, "British Columbia: The Politics of Exploitation," pp. 226-9. The city of Victoria has a strong British heritage and observes certain traditions, such as tea and crumpets at the Empress Hotel.

9. Martin Robin, "British Columbia," *The Rush for Spoils, 1871-1933,* (Toronto: McClelland and Stewart, 1972), and *Pillars of Profit, 1934-1972* (Toronto: McClelland and Stewart, 1973).

10. Burns, "British Columbia and the Canadian Federation" and "British Columbia: Perceptions of a Split Personality." See also Norman Ruff, "Leadership Autonomy and Federal-Provincial Relations: British Columbia's Approaches to Federalism in the 1970s," an address to the Canadian Political Science Association (May 1981); Blake, "Managing the Periphery," points out that the alienation in B.C. is not universal, and is felt more by blue-collar voters than the attitude-forming elite, p. 17.

11. David Elkins, "The Sense of Place," in David Elkins and Richard Simeon, eds., *Small Worlds* (Toronto: Methuen, 1980), p. 21; Ruff, "Leadership Autonomy and Federal-Provincial Relations," makes the point that in B.C. "a premier's own conception of the federal system will be a principal determinant of a province's stance," p. 26.

12. On clientelism, see S.J.R. Noel, "Leadership and Clientelism," in David Bellamy et al., *The Provincial Political Systems.*

13. Jeffrey Simpson, *Spoils of Power* (Toronto: Collins, 1988), ch. 15.

14. Simeon and Elkins, "Provincial Political Cultures in Canada," in Elkins and Simeon, eds., *Small Worlds,* p. 51. On the question of trust, see David Elkins, Donald Blake, and Richard Johnston, "Who Trusts Whom to do What?" an address to the Canadian Political Science Association (June 1980). In brief, while respondents thought politicians were often crooked and civil servants frequently wasteful, trust remained high because both were regarded as competent.

15. John Wilson, "The Canadian Political Cultures," in *Canadian Journal of Political Science* (September 1974), pp. 468-9.

16. Black, "British Columbia: The Politics of Exploitation."

17. Zenon Kulchyckyj, "Subfragmentation and the Political Culture of the Canadian West," an address to the Canadian Political Science Association (May 1981), p.23.

18. Galbraith, "British Columbia," p. 70.

19. Alan Cairns and Daniel Wong, "Socialism, Federalism and the B.C. Party Systems 1933-1983," in Hugh G. Thorburn, *Party Politics in Canada* (Scarborough: Prentice Hall Canada, 6th ed., 1991); Donald Blake, *Two Political Worlds: Parties and Voting in British Columbia.*

20. The Liberal relationship is dealt with in R. Whitaker, *The Government Party* (Toronto: University of Toronto Press, 1977), and J. Wearing, *The L-Shaped Party* (Toronto: McGraw-Hill Ryerson, 1981).

21. Edwin R. Black, "Federal Strains Within A Canadian Party," in Thorburn, *Party Politics in Canada,* 5th ed.

22. Several interesting federal Conservative-provincial Socred relationships are discussed in Rand Dyck, "Relations Between Federal and Provincial Parties," in A.G. Gagnon and A.B. Tanguay, eds., *Canadian Parties in Transition* (Scarborough: Nelson Canada, 1989).

23. Neil Swainson, "Governing Amid Division: The Premiership in British Columbia," in Leslie Pal and David Taras, eds., *Prime Ministers and Premiers* (Scarborough: Prentice Hall Canada, 1988).

24. Robin, *Pillars of Profit,* p. 114, 248. The nickname "Wacky" could be used either in scorn or as a term of endearment.

25. Walter Young and J.T. Morley, "The Premier and the Cabinet," in Terence Morley et al., *The Reins of Power*, p. 68.

26. Ibid., p. 69.

27. "The NDP government under Dave Barrett was characterized by the populist oratory of the Premier and a blizzard of legislation which, regardless of its individual merits, did little to support the traditional claim that the left was wedded to and capable of coherent planning. The B.C. NDP was far removed from the cool, technical competence of the Blakeney regime in Saskatchewan, or the restrained, cautious administration of the Schreyer regime in Manitoba. Neither did it combine populist appeals with technical competence, as had the Douglas/Lloyd governments in Saskatchewan from 1944 to 1964." Cairns and Wong, "Socialism, Federalism and the B.C. Party Systems," pp. 295-6.

28. Allan Garr, *Tough Guy: Bill Bennett and the Taking of British Columbia* (Toronto: Key Porter Books, 1985).

29. Gary Mason and Keith Baldrey, *Fantasyland: Inside the Reign of Bill Vander Zalm* (Toronto: McGraw-Hill Ryerson, 1989); Stan Persky, *Fantasy Government: Bill Vander Zalm and the Future of Social Credit* (Vancouver: New Star Books, 1989).

30. Donald Blake and Kenneth Carty, "Televoting for the Leader of the British Columbia Liberal Party," an address to the Canadian Political Science Association (June 1994). See also Blake, Carty and Lynda Erickson, *Grassroots Politicians: Party Activists in British Columbia* (Vancouver: UBC Press, 1991), and their article, "Leaders, Parties, and Polarized Politics: The Case of British Columbia," in their *Leaders and Parties in Canadian Politics: Experiences of the Provinces* (Toronto: Harcourt Brace Jovanovich, 1992).

31. Robin, *Pillars of Profit*, p. 263.

32. In a study of provincial innovations from the early 1950s to the early 1970s, W.A.C. Bennett is credited with pioneering legislation in the following areas: condominiums, environment, unsolicited credit cards and lowering the age of majority. Unfortunately the study did not include the entire Barrett period. Dale Poel, "The Diffusion of Legislation among the Canadian Provinces: A Statistical Analysis," in *Canadian Journal of Political Science* (December 1976).

33. Marsha A. Chandler, "The Politics of Provincial Resource Policy," in Michael M. Atkinson and Marsha A. Chandler, eds., *The Politics of Canadian Public Policy* (Toronto: University of Toronto Press, 1983), pp. 53-6.

34. Kathryn Harrison and W.T. Stanbury, "Privatization in British Columbia: Lessons from the Sale of Government Laboratories," *Canadian Public Administration* (Summer 1990).

35. Norman Ruff, "The Right to Vote and Inequality of Voting Power in British Columbia: The Jurisprudence and Politics of the Dixon Case," in John Courtney et al., eds., *Drawing Boundaries* (Saskatoon: Fifth House Publishers, 1992).

36. *Dixon v. British Columbia* (Attorney General), [1989] 35 B.C.L.R. (2nd) 273, 59 D.L.R. (4th) 247, 4 W.W.R. 393 (C.A.).

37. *Canadian Annual Review*, 1965, p. 170. On elections in general, see T.P. Boyle, *Elections British Columbia* (Vancouver: Lion's Gate Press, 1982).

38. Blake, *Two Political Worlds,* pp. 79-80.

39. A study of NDP activists as opposed to supporters revealed that nearly one-third were labour and another one-third were professional in occupational background, with a high proportion rejecting traditional religious beliefs. This relates to their general "radical, deviant, dissident" behaviour, as well as to their lack of involvement in other organizations. W.D. Young, "A Profile of Activists in the British Columbia NDP," in *Journal of Canadian Studies* (February 1971).

40. R.J. Wilson, "The Impact of Communications Developments on British Columbia Electoral Patterns, 1903-1975," in *Canadian Journal of Economics and Political Science* (September 1980), and R.J. Wilson, "Geography, Politics, and Culture: Electoral Insularity in British Columbia," in *Canadian Journal of Political Science* (December 1980).

41. Their campaign is well documented in Raymond Payne, "Corporate Power, Interest Group Activity and Mining Policy in British Columbia, 1972-77," an address to the Canadian Political Science Association (June 1980), and contrasted with that of the insurance industry in Nukhet Kardam, "Interest Group Power and Government Regulation," in *B.C. Studies* (Winter 1983-84).

42. Andrea Demchuk, "B.C. Hydro and the Stikine-Iskut Basin: A Case of Internal Colonialism," an address to the Canadian Political Science Association (June 1985); Laurent Dobuzinskis, "A Critical Analysis of the Fraser Institute's Approach to Political Economy," an address to the Canadian Political Science Association (June 1985); and Jeremy Wilson, "Resolution of Wilderness vs. Logging Conflicts in British Columbia," an address to the Canadian Political Science Association (June 1987).

43. Campbell Sharmon, "The Strange Case of a Provincial Constitution: The British Columbia Constitution Act," in *Canadian Journal of Political Science* (March 1984).

44. John Saywell, *The Office of Lieutenant-Governor* (Toronto: University of Toronto Press, 1957), pp. 130-43.

45. Ruff, "Managing the Public Service," p. 164.

46. Walter Young and J.T. Morley, "The Premier and the Cabinet," p. 68.

47. Ibid., p. 78.

48. The growth in the size of the legislature was as follows:

1871-1886:	25	1933-1937:	47
1886-1890:	27	1937-1956:	48
1890-1898:	33	1956-1966:	52
1898-1903:	38	1966-1979:	55
1903-1916:	42	1979-1986:	57
1916-1924:	47	1986:	69
1924-1933:	48	1991-present:	75

On this subject, see Jeremy Wilson, "British Columbia: A Unique Blend of the Traditional and the Modern," in Gary Levy and Graham White, eds., *Provincial and Territorial Legislatures in Canada* (Toronto: University of Toronto Press, 1989).

49. R.J. Wilson, "The Legislature," in Terence Morley et al., eds., *The Reins of Power,* p. 33.

50. Interviews with B.C. officials; Ruff, "Managing the Public Service," 162; and Black, "The Politics of Exploitation," p. 232.

51. Simpson, *Spoils of Power.*

52. Neil A. Swainson, "The Public Service," in Morley et al., *The Reins of Power,* p. 127.

53. Neil A. Swainson, "The Crown Corporation in the Governance of British Columbia," an address to the Canadian Political Science Association (May 1981). On this subject, see also John Langford, "The Question of Quangos: Quasi-public Service Agencies in British Columbia," *Canadian Public Administration* (Winter 1983); and John Langford and Neil A. Swainson, "Public and Quasi-Public Corporations in British Columbia," in O.P. Dwivedi, ed., *The Administrative State in Canada* (Toronto: University of Toronto Press, 1982).

54. On municipal issues in B.C., see P.J. Smith, "Planning at Cross Purposes: Provincial-Municipal Relations in Greater Vancouver," an address to the Canadian Political Science Association (June 1983); and P.J. Smith, "Regional Government in British Columbia: Recent Changes and Prospects," an address to the Canadian Political Science Association (June 1985).

55. Robin, "British Columbia," in Robin, *Canadian Provincial Politics,* p. 41; Robin, *The Rush for Spoils* and *Pillars of Profit;* Margaret Ormsby, *British Columbia, a History* (Toronto: Macmillan, 1958), p. 304-5.

56. Ormsby, *British Columbia,* p. 311.

57. The subtitle of Robin's two books.

58. Robin, "British Columbia," in Robin, *Canadian Provincial Politics,* p. 42.

59. Ormsby, *British Columbia,* p. 330.

60. The apparent reasons were poor health, personal debts, damaged prestige, and diminished personal strength, ibid., p. 383. Simpson emphasizes the many patronage charges in *Spoils of Power.*

61. Margaret Ormsby, "T. Dufferin Pattullo and the Little New Deal," in H.J. Schultz et al. eds., *Politics of Discontent* (Toronto: University of Toronto Press, 1967), p. 46; Robin Fisher, *Duff Pattullo of British Columbia* (Toronto: University of Toronto Press, 1991); Fisher, "The Decline of Reform: British Columbia Politics in the 1930s," *Journal of Canadian Studies* (August 1990).

62. Robin, *Pillars of Profit,* p. 52.

63. Ormsby, "The Little New Deal," p. 47.

64. Robin, *Pillars of Profit,* p. 59.

65. Robin describes Social Credit supporters as "the drab collection of monetary fetishists, British Israelites, naturopaths, chiropractors, preachers, pleaders and anti-Semites," ibid., p. 84. On the CCF, see Christina Nicol, "In Pursuit of the Voter: The British Columbia CCF, 1945-1950," in William Brennan, ed., *Building the Co-operative Commonwealth* (Regina: Canadian Plains Research Centre, 1984).

66. Robin, *Pillars of Profit,* p. 127.

67. Among the sources on this period are Martin Robin's works; David Mitchell, *W.A.C. Bennett and the Rise of British Columbia* (Vancouver: Douglas and McIntyre, 1983); Ronald B. Worley, *The Wonderful World of W.A.C. Bennett* (Toronto: McClelland and Stewart, 1971); Paddy Sherman, *Bennett* (Toronto: McClelland and Stewart, 1966); R. Keene and D.C. Humphreys, *Conversations with W.A.C. Bennett* (Toronto: Methuen,

1980); and, since 1960, annual accounts of British Columbia in the *Canadian Annual Review*. On the 1952 election, see H.F. Angus, "The British Columbia Election, June, 1952" in *Canadian Journal of Economics and Political Science* (November 1952).

68. Stephen Tomblin, "W.A.C. Bennett and Province-Building in British Columbia," *BC Studies* (Spring 1990).

69. Robin, *Pillars of Profit,* p. 202.

70. Ibid., p. 234. On the Columbia River question in general see Neil Swainson, *Conflict over the Columbia* (Montreal: McGill-Queen's University Press, 1979); John Krutilla, *The Columbia River Treaty* (Baltimore: Johns Hopkins Press, 1967); A.R. Vining, "Provincial Hydro-Utilities," in Allan Tupper and Bruce Doern, eds., *Public Corporations and Public Policy in Canada* (Montreal: Institute for Research on Public Policy, 1981); and Raymond Payne, "Electric Power, Crown Corporations and the Evolution of an Energy Policy Process in British Columbia: 1960-1980," an address to the Canadian Political Science Association (May 1981).

71. Berger was later appointed to the B.C. Supreme Court and then asked to head the federal inquiry into the proposed Mackenzie Valley Gas Pipeline, a position which elevated him to national prominence. Later still, he was pressured to resign from the bench due to comments he made on the Constitution and Native rights.

72. Bennett had a "personalized and erratic" and "introverted" approach to federal-provincial relations: he limited the contact of ministers and civil servants not only with Ottawa but also with other provinces, restricting travel and long-distance phone calls. He argued for a high degree of political autonomy, and was the most persistent opponent of equalization payments. Norman Ruff, "Leadership Autonomy and Federal-Provincial Relations," an address to the Canadian Political Science Association (May 1981).

73. Sources on this period include Lorne Kavic and G.B. Nixon, *The 1200 Days, A Shattered Dream, Dave Barrett and the NDP in B.C. 1972-75* (Coquitlam: Kaen Publishers, 1978), and annual accounts on B.C. in the *Canadian Annual Review of Politics and Public Affairs.*

74. Raymond Payne, "Corporate Power, Interest Group Activity and Mining Policy in British Columbia, 1972-77."

75. Kavic and Nixon, *The 1200 Days,* p. 141. Nukhet Kardam explains why the mining industry was succesful in its confrontation with the NDP government but the insurance industry was not. See Kardam, "Interest Group Power and Government Regulation: The Case of the Mining and Insurance Industries During the Period of New Democratic Party Government in British Columbia, 1971-1975," in *B.C. Studies* (Winter 1983-84).

76. Kavic and Nixon, *The 1200 Days,* p. 151.

77. Kavic and Nixon, *The 1200 Days,* p. 85. "Lacking formal or informal training in the fields of economics and finance, Barrett had neither the upbringing nor the inclination to use the positions of Finance Minister and chairmanship of the Treasury Board for purposes of economic planning."

78. Kavic and Nixon, *The 1200 Days,* p. 250; Paul Tennant, "The NDP Government in British Columbia: Unaided Politicians in an Unaided Cabinet," in *Canadian Public Policy* (Autumn 1977).

79. That there had been any such evidence was enough to allow the construction of the rest of the fiscal credibility argument, Stan Persky, *Son of Socred* (Vancouver: New Star Books, 1979), p. 29; "... the intended damage had been done and few people were interested in knowing that the actual NDP deficit was most likely well within the province's $150 million cash reserves, that it was in line with deficits of other provincial governments, and had been caused by the severity of the recession rather than incompetence," Stan Persky, *Bennett II* (Vancouver: New Star Books, 1983), p. 35.

80. Persky, *Son of Socred,* p. 110.

81. Persky, *Bennett II,* p. 155.

82. Although the courts threw out a libel suit concerning a Canadian Broadcasting Corp. report that the deputy attorney general had improperly intervened in three criminal cases, the premier successfully sued the NDP's David Stupich for $10,000 over statements about "cornflakes and scotch." When Bennett wanted to have morning sessions of the legislature rather than night sittings, he suggested that MLAs wouldn't drink scotch with their cornflakes. Stupich took exception to this remark and declared that there were times when Bennett himself seemed in no state to attend legislative sessions in the evening, Persky, ibid., p. 96.

83. On this episode see Warren Magnusson et al., *The New Reality, the Politics of Restraint in British Columbia* (Vancouver: New Star Books, 1984); Patricia Marchak, "The Rise and Fall of the Peripheral State: The Case of British Columbia," in R.J. Brym, ed., *Regionalism in Canada* (Toronto: Irwin, 1986); and Marchak's "British Columbia: 'New Right' Politics and a New Geography." For the view that these events represented a continuity in B.C. political economy, see Michael Howlett and Keith Brownsey, "The Old Reality and the New Reality: Party Politics and Public Policy in British Columbia," *Studies in Political Economy* (Spring 1988).

84. Marchak argues that the "restraint program" was designed to diminish the power of unions, not to deal with the deficit, and to cope with the impact of global economic changes on a provincial society dependent on resource exports.

85. Bryan Palmer, *Solidarity: The Rise and Fall of an Opposition in British Columbia* (Vancouver: New Star Books, 1987); Art Kube et al., *British Columbia's Operation Solidarity: What Can We Learn?* (Ottawa: Canadian Centre for Policy Alternatives, 1984).

86. Warren Carroll, "The Solidarity Coalition," in Magnusson et al., *The New Reality,* p. 104.

87. Every article in *The New Reality* expresses doubts. The government's case was later made in "The Economy in a Changing World," March 1985.

88. On this period see David J. Mitchell, *Succession* (Vancouver: Douglas and McIntyre, 1987); Mason and Baldrey, *Fantasyland;* Persky, *Fantasy Government;* Blake et. al., "Ratification or Repudiation: The Social Credit Leadership Selection in British Columbia," *Canadian Journal of Political Science* (September 1988); and Patrick Smith, "Perestroika and Policy Gambling in Fantasyland," an address to the Canadian Political Science Association (June 1988).

89. Graham Leslie, *Breach of Promise: Socred Ethics under Vander Zalm* (Medeira Park: Harbour Publishing, 1991).

90. Terry Morley, "From Bill Vander Zalm to Mike Harcourt: Government Transition in British Columbia," in Donald Savoie, ed., *Taking Power: Managing Government Transitions* (Toronto: Institute of Public Administration of Canada, 1993).

91. Ibid.

92. T. Berman et al., *Clayoquot and Dissent* (Vancouver: Ronsdale Press, 1994).

93. Marjorie Cohen, "British Columbia: Playing Safe is a Dangerous Game," *Studies in Political Economy* (Spring 1994).

94. Kenneth Whyte, "I Got You, Babe," *Saturday Night* (December 1993); Judi Tyabji, *Political Affairs* (Victoria: Horsdal and Schubart, 1994).

READINGS

Berman, T. et al. *Clayoquot and Dissent.* Vancouver: Ronsdale Press, 1994.

British Columbia Ministry of Finance and Corporate Relations. *British Columbia Economic and Statistical Review.*

Canadian Annual Review of Politics and Public Affairs. Toronto: University of Toronto Press, annual.

Carty, R.K., Lynda Erickson, and Donald Blake. *Grassroots Politicians: Party Activists in British Columbia.* Vancouver: University of British Columbia Press, 1991.

Carty, R.K., et al., eds. "Leaders, Parties, and Polarized Politics: The Case of British Columbia." R.K. Carty et al., eds. *Leaders and Parties in Canadian Politics: Experiences of the Provinces.* Toronto: Harcourt Brace Jovanovich, 1992.

Howlett, Michael, and Keith Brownsey. "Public Sector Politics in a Rentier Resource Economy." Keith Brownsey and Michael Howlett, eds. *The Provincial State.* Mississauga: Copp Clark Pitman, 1992.

Morley, Terence. "From Bill Vander Zalm to Mike Harcourt: Government Transition in British Columbia." Donald Savoie, ed. *Taking Power: Managing Government Transitions.* Toronto: Institute of Public Administration of Canada, 1993.

Morley, Terence, et al. *The Reins of Power, Governing British Columbia.* Vancouver: Douglas and McIntyre, 1983.

CONCLUSION

The preceding chapters have examined the provinces on an individual basis to reveal their unique political characteristics and patterns of political development. Only occasional interprovincial similarities or differences were mentioned. To conclude the analysis a more deliberate comparative approach is taken, although a comprehensive comparison is beyond the scope of this study. Here the provinces are contrasted under the headings of setting, political culture, party and electoral systems, and government institutions, culminating in an outline of features they have in common.

SETTING

There is a fairly consistent ranking of provinces on most economic measures, although it is too much to expect all such indicators to show exactly the same pattern. The various aspects of the basic economic strength of the provinces can be seen in Tables 13.15 (Provincial Gross Domestic Product), 13.17 (Personal Income per Person), 13.18 (Proportion of Families with Incomes Less than $20,000 and over $70,000), 13.21 (Educational Attainment), 13.22 (Annual Unemployment Rate), and 13.29 and 13.30 (Federal Transfers to Provincial Governments) in the Appendix. Alberta, Ontario, and B.C. consistently rank at the top; Quebec, Manitoba, and Saskatchewan are intermediate; and the four Atlantic provinces bring up the rear. Many other indicators of general prosperity could be used, but most would yield a similar distribution. The most significant anomalies in the mid-1990s were that Saskatchewan fell below Nova Scotia in terms of per capita income, and that, within the Atlantic region, New Brunswick fared better than Nova Scotia when it came to unemployment.

The degree of industrialization can be measured by Tables 13.3 (Rate of Urbanization), 13.14 (Selected Manufacturing Statistics), 13.16 (Distribution of Labour Force by Sector), and 13.19 (Rate of Unionization). These sets of figures show surprisingly little correlation with each other, with the exception of the generally reverse relationship between primary and manufacturing employment. While the Atlantic provinces are the least urbanized, for example, the prairie provinces have relatively least manufacturing. Nevertheless, Ontario and Quebec could be identified as the two most industrialized provinces.

On the social side, the provinces can be grouped according to mother tongue, home language, language transfer rate, birthplace and religion, as in Tables 13.23, 13.24, 13.25, 13.27, and 13.28 in the Appendix. Newfoundland, Prince Edward Island, and Nova Scotia have the highest percentage of population with English mother tongue and home language, six others are in the intermediate range in this respect, and Quebec is at the bottom. Quebec and New Brunswick are the only two with sizeable francophone populations. The five most westerly provinces (including Ontario) have the largest proportion of residents with "other" mother tongue. It could therefore be said that progressing from east to west there are three English provinces, one English-French province (New Brunswick), one French province, and five English-ethnic provinces. The figures on birthplace reveal the stability of the Atlantic provinces' populations, the immobility of Quebecers, and both the interprovincial migration and heavy immigration into Ontario, Alberta and British Columbia.

With the exception of Catholic Quebec, the provinces have a fairly uniform proportion of Protestants. The percentage of Roman Catholics declines as one moves westward, while the proportion of those with other religions, or no religion, increases in the West. Thus, in general, the five most easterly provinces have a higher number of Catholics and the five most westerly provinces are more unorthodox in their religious beliefs.

POLITICAL CULTURE

Since the late 1960s and early 1970s when Simeon and Elkins did their research based on national election surveys, few data have been available that are relevant to variations in provincial political cultures. In the absence of recent information on such measures as degree of trust and efficacy, commitment to principles of democracy, and general patterns of political participation, there are two indicators which can be cited with confidence: provincial voter turn-out rate for federal and provincial elections, and relative support for both levels of government. The provincial averages for voter turn-out in the most recent six federal and provincial elections are given in Table 12.1.

These figures reveal that the highest rates at both levels are in Prince Edward Island, while Saskatchewan is also consistently high. New Brunswick, Nova Scotia, Manitoba, and British Columbia are moderate in both federal and provincial turn-out, and Alberta is uniformly low. However, Quebec and Newfoundland are much higher at the provincial level than in federal elections, and Ontario demonstrates the opposite characteristic. Such statistics suggest that residents of Quebec and Newfoundland are more provincially than federally oriented, that Ontarians are the reverse, and that Albertans lack a participatory mentality.

TABLE 12.1   Average Voter Turn-out in Six Federal and Provincial Elections to the end of 1994

Federal Elections		Provincial Elections	
Prince Edward Island	80.5%	Prince Edward Island	83.0%
Saskatchewan	74.5%	Saskatchewan	81.8%
Ontario	73.8%	Quebec	81.2%
British Columbia	73.8%	New Brunswick	79.7%
Quebec	73.2%	Newfoundland	78.0%
New Brunswick	73.2%	Nova Scotia	74.8%
Manitoba	72.8%	British Columbia	73.0%
Nova Scotia	72.7%	Manitoba	71.8%
Alberta	67.5%	Ontario	62.6%
Newfoundland	60.5%	Alberta	57.6%

Reports of federal and provincial Chief Electoral Officers, calculations by author.

The other quantifiable question was the subject of Table 1.1, on the differential federal and provincial orientation of the residents of each province. It generally confirmed these observations about Ontario, Quebec, and Newfoundland. Other comparative dimensions of provincial political cultures must await further research.

PARTY AND ELECTORAL SYSTEMS

With respect to provincial party systems, several questions can be examined on a comparative statistical basis. These include a comparison of which parties formed the government in each province since 1920 (Figure 12.1), the longest tenure of provincial governments and premiers (Tables 12.2 and 12.3), patterns of one-party dominance or two-party systems (Tables 12.4 and 12.5), and the success of the NDP (Table 12.6). Provinces can also be ranked according to the fairness of their electoral systems (Table 12.7), that is, in terms of disparities in the size of constituencies.

Figure 12.1 illustrates the Liberal-Conservative monopoly of power in the Atlantic region and relatively uniform changes from one party to another in the government of those provinces. It also shows the variety of other parties which came to office in Quebec and the four Western provinces, and, over the post-1970 period, the demise of Liberal governments in the West, the success of

Conservatives in that region, and recent disruptions in this pattern. As mentioned previously, there were turn-overs in almost all provinces in the early 1920s, mid-1930s, and around 1970.

FIGURE 12.1   Provincial Governments by Party 1920-1995

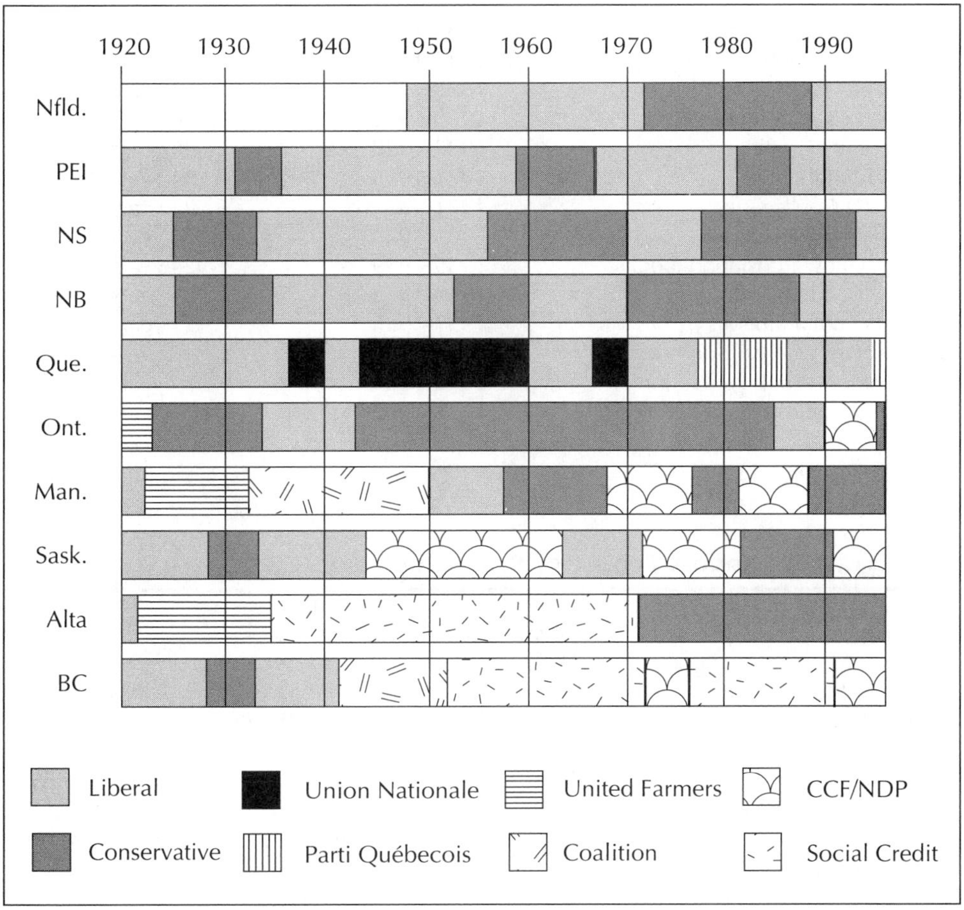

Table 12.2 lists the 13 provincial regimes since 1867 which lasted at least 20 consecutive years in office. The demise of the Conservative regime in Ontario after 42 years in office ended the threat it posed to the Nova Scotia Liberal record of 43 years between 1882 and 1925. As of 1995, the most enduring incumbent regimes were in Alberta (24 years), P.E.I. (nine years), and New Brunswick (eight years). Table 12.3 demonstrates the 16 most durable provincial premiers since 1867, with six serving at least 20 consecutive years: George

Murray, Ernest Manning, Oliver Mowat, Joey Smallwood, John Bracken, and W.A.C. Bennett. In 1995, the most enduring premiers were Frank McKenna (since 1987), Gary Filmon (since 1988), and Clyde Wells (since 1989).

TABLE 12.2   Longest Tenure of Provincial Governments

1.	Nova Scotia Liberals	1882-1925	43 years
2.	Ontario Conservatives	1943-1985	42 years
3.	Quebec Liberals	1897-1936	39 years
4.	Alberta Social Credit	1935-1971	36 years
5.	Manitoba Coalition	1922-1958	36 years
6.	Ontario Liberals	1871-1905	34 years
7.	Alberta Conservatives	1971-present	24 years
8.	Saskatchewan Liberals	1905-1929	24 years
9.	Prince Edward Island Liberals	1935-1959	24 years
10.	Newfoundland Liberals	1949-1972	23 years
11.	Nova Scotia Liberals	1933-1956	23 years
12.	Saskatchewan Co-operative Commonwealth Federation	1944-1964	20 years
13.	British Columbia Social Credit	1952-1972	20 years

Source: Compiled by the author.

TABLE 12.3   Longest Tenure of Provincial Premiers

1.	George Murray	Nova Scotia	1896-1923	27 years
2.	Ernest Manning	Alberta	1943-1968	25 years
3.	Oliver Mowat	Ontario	1872-1896	24 years
4.	Joey Smallwood	Newfoundland	1949-1972	23 years
5.	John Bracken	Manitoba	1922-1943	21 years
6.	W.A.C. Bennett	British Columbia	1952-1972	20 years
7.	Maurice Duplessis	Quebec	1936-40; 1944-59	19 years
8.	T.C. Douglas	Saskatchewan	1944-1961	17 years
9.	Richard Hatfield	New Brunswick	1970-1987	17 years
10.	Louis-Alexandre Taschereau	Quebec	1920-1936	16 years
11.	Angus Macdonald	Nova Scotia	1933-40; 1945-54	16 years
12.	Lomer Gouin	Quebec	1905-1920	15 years
13.	Rodmond Roblin	Manitoba	1900-1915	15 years
14.	Peter Lougheed	Alberta	1971-1985	14 years
15.	Bill Davis	Ontario	1971-1985	14 years
16.	Robert Bourassa	Quebec	1970-76; 1985-93	14 years

Source: Compiled by the author.

Tables 12.4 and 12.5 seek to discover, by various means, patterns of one-party dominance or two- or three-party systems since 1970. The tables examine the average percentage of popular vote and average percentage of legislative seats won by the leading party, as well as the difference between the first and second parties in percentage of popular vote and the absolute difference in their number of seats. Alberta ranks as the leader of the one-party dominant provinces in both percentage of popular vote and of seats. On the other hand, there is no evidence of one-party dominance in Manitoba, Ontario, British Columbia, or Nova Scotia.

Two parties dominate the political scene in Prince Edward Island, Newfoundland, Quebec, and New Brunswick—that is, there is little support for third parties. Nova Scotia and British Columbia occupy a middle position on this measure, while Saskatchewan, Manitoba, Ontario and Alberta all have more evidence of third party success.

Since 1960 Ontario has remained the only real three-party system as third-party support in that province has averaged 25 percent, minority governments have been common, and all three parties have formed a majority government during the past decade. Manitoba has also moved in that direction.

TABLE 12.4   One-Party Dominance, 1970-1994: First Party's Average Percentage of Popular Vote and Seats, and Difference between First and Second Party in Percentage of Vote and Number of Seats

First Party Percentage of Vote		First–Second Difference in Percentage of Vote		First Party Percentage of Seats		First–Second Difference in Percentage of Seats	
Alta.	52.6	Alta.	34.7	Alta.	78.6	Alta.	70.7
P.E.I.	52.3	Sask.	14.0	Que.	72.3	Que.	49.6
Nfld.	50.1	Que.	12.1	P.E.I.	68.0	P.E.I.	36.0
Que.	48.7	Nfld.	9.1	Nfld.	58.6	Sask.	26.9
N.B.	48.0	N.B.	8.8	N.B.	58.0	Nfld.	20.3
Sask.	46.2	P.E.I.	7.8	Sask.	57.7	N.B.	18.9
N.S.	43.4	Man.	4.7	N.S.	52.0	N.S.	7.8
B.C.	42.3	N.S.	3.4	B.C.	48.1	Ont.	4.8
Man.	41.7	Ont.	0.9	Man.	46.2	B.C.	3.3
Ont.	35.9	B.C.	0.5	Ont.	39.3	Man.	3.2

Source: Compiled by the author. These figures exclude elections after 1994.

TABLE 12.5 Two-Party Dominance 1970-1994: First Two Parties' Average Percentage of Popular Vote and of Seats and Government Turn-overs (with most recent in parentheses)

Two-Party Percentage of Vote		Two-Party Percentage of Seats		Turn-overs		
P.E.I.	96.8	P.E.I.	100.0	Que.	4	(1994)
Nfld.	91.1	N.B.	97.1	Man.	4	(1988)
N.B.	87.2	Nfld.	96.9	Sask.	4	(1991)
Que.	85.3	N.S.	96.2	N.B.	3	(1987)
B.C.	84.0	Que.	95.0	P.E.I.	3	(1986)
N.S.	83.8	B.C.	92.9	B.C.	3	(1991)
Man.	78.7	Sask.	91.5	N.S.	3	(1993)
Sask.	78.4	Man.	89.2	Nfld.	2	(1989)
Ont.	70.9	Alta.	86.5	Ont.	2	(1990)*
Alta.	70.5	Ont.	73.8	Alta.	1	(1971)

Source: Compiled by the author.
*Power changed hands in Ontario in 1995.

In addition to classifying party systems in terms of the number of participating parties, one should also consider the interesting question of whether the various systems have any significant difference in ideology. Although an over-simplification, it would not be inaccurate to argue that where the Liberals and Conservatives coexist as major parties there is no significant ideological difference between them, while the NDP presents an alternative. Thus Table 12.6 indicates the comparative strength of the NDP to illustrate ideologically polarized provincial party systems. The NDP has had greatest success in Saskatchewan, Manitoba, British Columbia, and Ontario, where it has formed governments, and in Alberta, where it rose to official Opposition status on more than one occasion. It has some presence in Nova Scotia and has occasionally elected members in New Brunswick and Newfoundland.

Because ideological polarization is to some extent related to class politics, Table 12.6 might also be used to indicate the relative ranking of the degree of class politics in the various provinces in the same sequence listed above. The absence of the NDP in Quebec and the ambiguous ideological position of the Parti Québécois make it difficult to place that province in either the class or ideological ranking. By other means of measurement, however, Quebec would probably be ranked with Ontario as far as the extent of class politics in the post-1960 period is concerned. This would mean that class and ideological politics are least developed in the Atlantic region, and most developed in the West, with the two central provinces occupying an intermediate position.

TABLE 12.6   New Democratic Party Success: Percentage of Popular Vote and Percentage of Seats Won in General Elections, 1970-1994

Percentage of NDP Vote, 1970-1994		Percentage of NDP Seats, 1970-1994	
Sask.	46.2	Sask.	57.7
B.C.	42.3	B.C.	48.1
Man.	37.0	Man.	43.0
Ont.	27.6	Ont.	26.1
Alta.	17.9	Alta.	6.6
N.S.	14.7	N.S.	5.2
N.B.	7.3	N.B.	0.6
Nfld.	4.4	Nfld.	0.5

Source: Compiled by the author.

Table 12.7 examines provincial redistribution systems. It indicates the mean number of voters per constituency in each province, the variation between the largest and smallest constituencies, and the average variation from the provincial mean. The table reveals that almost all provinces contain major discrepancies between largest and smallest constituencies, although in isolated cases this can be justified. When the overall average variation is examined, the situation is marginally better, but only Manitoba has an average difference below 10 percent; most of the provinces fall between 10 and 20 percent; and the worst discrepancies exist in Prince Edward Island, New Brunswick, and Newfoundland. Some of these discrepancies will be improved by the time of the next elections.

TABLE 12.7   Provincial Redistribution Statistics

	Election	Mean number of voters per constituency	Largest constituency	Smallest constituency	Average variation from mean
Nfld.	1993	8,660	13,108	1,468	21.6%
P.E.I.	1993	5,759	12,681	1,995	54.0%
N.S.	1993	12,582	16,230	5,910	13.2%
N.B.	1991	8,924	19,930	4,064	31.7%
Que.	1994	39,148	54,351	10,682	13.5%
Ont.	1990	48,584	101,558	21,437	16.5%
Man.	1990	12,504	16,009	8,450	7.7%
Sask.	1991	9,882	13,224	5,635	12.7%
Alta.	1993	19,840	28,498	9,043	15.7%
B.C.	1991	26,521	38,523	15,407	17.6%

Source: Compiled by the author from *Reports* of provincial Chief Electoral Officers.

GOVERNMENT INSTITUTIONS

There are many ways to rank the provinces in terms of the sophistication of their political institutions. Legislatures, for example, can be compared with respect to the number of sitting days and the amount of members' indemnities, as revealed in Tables 13.34 and 13.35.

Legislators in Ontario and Quebec, representing the largest number of constituents and belonging to the largest and most active law-making institutions, are most inclined to view their positions as full-time and have remunerated themselves accordingly. Alberta MLAs and Newfoundland MHAs spend many days in the legislature and are also well paid. Manitoba MLAs seem to be underpaid for the length of the legislative sessions, while there is a consistency between the shorter sessions and the low salary level in Prince Edward Island. Of course, these figures do not take into account the variation among provinces in the degree of committee activity between sessions.

Provincial executives could also be compared, although the numerical measures are more variable and not as easy to come by. There was a general tendency in the early 1990s to reduce the size of provincial cabinets, but the ratio of cabinet size to the legislature is probably more significant. With a high proportion of the legislators in the cabinet, there can be little pretence of independent legislative influence on the executive.

TABLE 12.8   **Federal, Provincial and Municipal Employees Per 1000 Population, and Provincial and Municipal Employees Per 1000 Population (divided by 1991 population) by Province, 1992**

	Federal Employees	Provincial Employees	Municipal Employees	Provincial and Municipal Employees	Provincial and Municipal Employees
Newfoundland	2.3	5.0	0.6	31,973	5.6
Prince Edward Island	2.8	5.9	2.2	10,568	8.1
Nova Scotia	3.7	3.9	3.5	66,416	7.4
New Brunswick	2.8	7.0	0.7	56,102	7.7
Quebec	1.6	4.9	3.2	554,123	8.0
Ontario	2.1	3.3	4.2	765,068	7.6
Manitoba	2.7	4.5	4.1	93,798	8.6
Saskatchewan	1.6	3.9	4.6	84,508	8.5
Alberta	1.7	3.2	5.3	216,971	8.5
British Columbia	1.6	4.1	2.9	231,100	7.0

Source: Reproduced by authority of the Minister of Industry, 1995, Statistics Canada, *Public Sector Employment and Remuneration,* 1992, cat. no. 72-209 (October 1993), calculations by author.

Provincial bureaucracies can be compared by absolute size and by number of public servants per 1000 population, figures provided in Table 12.8. While number of provincial public servants per 1000 population may seem to be a meaningful measure, it is not; certain functions are performed in some provinces at the provincial level and in others at the municipal level. Taking combined provincial and municipal employees per 1000 population is perhaps a better indicator—but is it a measure of ideology, patronage, government revenues, or efficiency?

The analysis of provincial institutions thus reveals the following very general conclusions: there are two large central provinces (Ontario and Quebec) with large governmental establishments and active, full-time, and well-paid legislatures, cabinets, and bureaucracies; at the other extreme is tiny Prince Edward Island. The other provinces rank in between, with the size of political institutions generally related to population size but with considerable differences on a per-capita basis.

While it is fascinating to compare and contrast the 10 provinces in these and other ways, two general conclusions emerge: regional distinctions continue to be significant but, at the same time, there is an increasing similarity among all the provinces. In the case of regional similarities, of course, the Atlantic and Western groupings stand out.

Whether one speaks of the "Atlantic" provinces (including Newfoundland) or the "Maritime" provinces (Prince Edward Island, Nova Scotia, and New Brunswick), many similarities are evident. They are smaller and economically distressed with marginal economies, especially with the closure of the ground-fish industry, desperate for economic development, and heavily dependent on Ottawa. They are more traditional in political culture and, while religion still plays a larger role in society and government than in other provinces, it is on the decline. This can be seen particularly in changes to the Newfoundland educational system and the P.E.I. electoral system. Political patronage is still evident but is also declining, as all four provinces feel the need to operate with an expert bureaucracy. In addition, these provinces have distinctive non-polarized, two-party systems with minimal support for the NDP. Certain government institutions may be more traditional, but many are in the process of changing. One of the other striking features of the Atlantic and Maritime provinces is their inclination to interprovincial co-operation. Standing out among many organizations of this nature are the Atlantic Provinces Economic Council, as well as the Council of Maritime Premiers and the array of authorities that operate under its umbrella: the Maritime Provinces Higher Education Commission, the Maritime Provinces Education Foundation, the Land Registration and Information Service, the Maritime Municipal Training and Development Board, and the Maritime Geomatics Board.

The pace of regional co-operation accelerated in the early 1990s, partly as a result of Charles McMillan's 1989 study for the premier's council, *Standing Up to the Future: The Maritimes in the 1990s.* Incumbent premiers agreed that the provinces should aim for economic integration and policy harmonization rather than political union. Thus, 1991 and 1992 saw the signing of the Atlantic Accord on Environmental Cooperation and the Atlantic Procurement Agreement; forums of cabinets from all three provinces; and an explosion of interprovincial committees in various policy fields. In 1992, all three provinces passed the Maritime Economic Cooperation Act, which contained their commitment to remove barriers to the mobility of goods, services, people and capital, as well as to improved and shared infrastructure.

Quebec is large and ethnically distinctive, industrialized but still in economic difficulty. Its political culture and governmental institutions have undergone a remarkable transformation since 1960 and in many respects are now more advanced than the rest of the country. Its two-party system is polarized on nationalist if not ideological questions, after a period of intense debate on such issues.

Ontario is the largest, strongest, and most industrialized province but, with its fate tied so closely to the fortunes of the automobile industry and manufacturing in general, it has not been immune from economic hardship. It is, or at least was, "progressive conservative" in political culture, generally advanced in its governmental institutions, and is the possessor of a distinctive three-party system resulting in recurrent minority governments. Ontario is unique in electing majority governments of three different parties within a single decade. The party system is partially polarized, placing it, along with Quebec, in an intermediate position between the Atlantic and Western blocs. While they constitute separate and distinct regions, Ontario and Quebec also "tend to stand as a single cohesive Central Canadian entity" to some extent, especially when viewed from the eastern and western ends of the country.[1]

The West (whether it is seen as one region or divided into two comprised of the prairie provinces and British Columbia) has become increasingly affluent because of petroleum and other natural resources, although it is still vulnerable to changes in international developments and domestic policies. Even the Atlantic provinces have a higher proportion of their labour force engaged in manufacturing. The West is ethnically diverse and somewhat unsympathetic to the central Canadian concepts of French-English duality and official bilingualism. Given their common frontier experience, the prairie provinces developed a regional political consciousness, partly based on alienation from central Canada and partly on their own populist spirit, whether "crypto-liberal," "radical democratic," "social democratic," or "plebiscitarian."[2] They are marked by a penchant for direct democracy, co-operatives, and expansion of government, and developed a reputation for pioneering progressive social policies. Another aspect of central Canada which the West rejected was the national party system. In its place, the west has relied on coalition and non-party governments, distinctive third parties, or giving greater support to national third parties, especially the

Co-operative Commonwealth Federation and New Democratic Party. Much more than central and eastern Canada, the West has been characterized by polarized, class-based, ideological politics, often within a two-party format. In the 1990s, however, this may be changing, as the provincial Liberal party makes a comeback in all four provinces.

Despite their many similarities, co-operation among the three prairie provinces has not been as marked or as institutionalized as in the Maritimes. But it has increased, especially since 1965, with an annual premiers' meeting, the Prairie Economic Council. British Columbia joined the Economic Council in 1973, and the group's name eventually changed to the Western Premiers' Conference. It meets annually and often establishes ministerial task forces on specific issues.[3]

In the mid-1990s, however, what stand out even more than regional similarities are the features common to all provinces. They are increasingly alike in both policy and institutional terms. With regard to government policy, regardless of party in power, ideology, or region, all provinces are

1. Obsessed with debts and deficits, and are therefore trying to balance budgets.
2. Reducing expenditures.
3. Seeking new sources of revenue, such as lotteries and casinos.
4. Freezing or reducing public sector wages.
5. Cutting back on social assistance and trying to get welfare recipients into employment or training programs.
6. Cutting back on health-care expenditures.

In institutional terms, all provinces are

1. Reducing the size of the cabinet.
2. Freezing legislators' remuneration, sometimes reducing benefits or even the size of the legislature.
3. Moving closer to the principle of representation by population in the distribution of legislative seats.
4. Regulating election finance.
5. Implementing official language minority school boards, but otherwise amalgamating and reducing the powers of the school boards.
6. Establishing regional health authorities with wide jurisdiction over the delivery of health care.

Table 13.3 compares the provinces in terms of size of net debt, debt as a percentage of Gross Domestic Product, and per capita debt. In absolute size, of course, the Ontario and Quebec debts are largest, and it is also true that their governments, at least until mid-1995, were least concerned about balancing their budgets. But when expressed as a percentage of GDP, the Newfoundland and Nova Scotia debts are more serious, although Quebec's is still high, and, on a per capita basis, Quebec and Nova Scotia lead the way. In terms of all three measures, the Alberta and British Columbia debts are relatively smaller than those of other provinces.

How can one explain the fact that the provinces have never been more similar in their policies and operations? Several factors have affected them all on the economic front: the early 1990s recession, cut-backs in federal transfers, and the suddenly dominant view that government debts must be reduced. To some extent, all provinces were forced to take similar action, whether by public opinion, economic necessity, international competitiveness, or the edicts of lending institutions and credit-rating agencies. Non-economic forces are also at work in promoting an increasing similarity among provincial government policies. These include increasing interprovincial co-operation; judicial edicts on such matters as official minority language school boards and redistribution procedures; and public attitudes (whether well founded or not) on such issues as politicians' pay and welfare abuse.

We are left to conclude that, in their geographic, economic, class, and demographic settings, the 10 Canadian provinces remain distinct political systems, and in certain respects can be grouped into regions. The same is true with regard to many aspects of their political cultures and party systems, and they remain delightfully idiosyncratic in their political leadership. On the other hand, in terms of such political institutions as electoral systems, cabinets, legislatures, and bureaucracies, they are increasingly similar. As they approach the turn of the century, however, it is in the realm of policy, primarily determined by a common shortage of funds, where the similarities among the provinces are most striking.

ENDNOTES

1.   See the *Journal of Canadian Studies* (Spring 1983), which illustrates an intriguing mix of commonality and difference, p. 3.

2.   David Laycock, *Populism and Democratic Thought in the Canadian Prairies, 1910-1945* (Toronto: University of Toronto Press, 1989).

3.   David Smith, *Regional Decline of a National Party: Liberals on the Prairies* (Toronto: University of Toronto Press, 1981), p. 19; Hugh G. Thorburn, *Planning and the Economy* (Toronto: Canadian Institute for Economic Policy, 1984), pp. 121-22; and Norman Ruff, "Leadership Autonomy and Federal-Provincial Relations: British Columbia's Approaches to Federalism in the 1970s," an address to the Canadian Political Science Association (May 1981), pp. 10-11.

APPENDIX

Geography

TABLE 13.1 Size of Provincial Population, 1991 Census and January 1995

	1991 Census		January 1995	
Ontario	10,084,885	36.9%	11,004,800	37.4%
Quebec	6,895,963	25.3%	7,300,000	24.8%
British Columbia	3,282,061	12.0%	3,719,400	12.6%
Alberta	2,545,553	9.3%	2,726,900	9.3%
Manitoba	1,091,942	4.0%	1,132,800	3.9%
Saskatchewan	988,928	3.6%	1,017,200	3.5%
Nova Scotia	899,942	3.3%	938,300	3.2%
New Brunswick	723,900	2.7%	760,600	2.6%
Newfoundland	568,474	2.1%	579,500	2.0%
Prince Edward Island	129,765	0.5%	135,500	0.5%
Northwest Territories	57,649	0.2%	65,000	0.2%
Yukon	27,797	0.1%	30,100	0.1%
Canada	27,296,859		29,409,900	

Source: Reproduced by authority of the Ministry of Industry, 1995, Statistics Canada, *1991 Census, A National Overview - Population and Dwelling Counts,* cat. no. 93-301, and *Quarterly Demographic Statistics,* cat. no. 91-002 (April 1995).

TABLE 13.2   Census Metropolitan Areas over 100,000, 1991 Census

	1991 Census
Toronto	3,893,046
Montreal	3,127,242
Vancouver	1,602,502
Ottawa-Hull	920,857
Edmonton	839,924
Calgary	754,033
Winnipeg	652,354
Quebec	645,550
Hamilton	599,760
London	381,522
St. Catharines-Niagara	364,552
Kitchener	356,421
Halifax	320,501
Victoria	287,897
Windsor	262,075
Oshawa	240,104
Saskatoon	210,023
Regina	191,692
St. John's	171,859
Chicoutimi-Jonquière	160,928
Sudbury	157,613
Sherbrooke	139,194
Kingston	136,401
Trois-Rivieres	136,303
Thunder Bay	124,427
Saint John	124,981
Sydney	116,100
Matsqui	113,562
Kelowna	111,846
Moncton	106,503

Source: Reproduced by authority of the Minister of Industry, 1995, Statistics Canada, *1991 Census, Census Metropolitan Areas and Census Agglomerations,* cat. no. 93-303.

TABLE 13.3   Rate of Urbanization by Province, 1991 Census

Ontario	81.8%	Saskatchewan	63.0%
British Columbia	80.4%	Newfoundland	53.6%
Alberta	79.8%	Nova Scotia	53.5%
Quebec	77.6%	New Brunswick	47.7%
Manitoba	72.1%	Prince Edward Island	39.9%
	Canada	76.6%	

Source: Reproduced by authority of the Minister of Industry, 1995, Statistics Canada, *1991 Census, Profile of Urban and Rural Areas - Part A,* cat. no. 93-339, adapted by author.

TABLE 13.4   Busiest Airports, 1992—Passengers and Cargo

	Thousands of Passengers		Tonnes of Cargo
Pearson, Toronto	19,119	Pearson, Toronto	299,939
Vancouver International	9,443	Vancouver International	131,389
Montreal Dorval	5,563	Montreal Mirabel	87,868
Calgary International	4,675	Calgary International	41,747
Ottawa International	2,496	Winnipeg International	28,352
Montreal Mirabel	2,424	Montreal Dorval	25,882
Halifax International	2,310	Halifax International	21,545
Winnipeg International	2,142	Edmonton International	18,123
Edmonton International	1,791	Ottawa International	6,676
Edmonton Municipal	872	St. John's	4,190

Source: Reproduced by authority of the Minister of Industry, 1995, Statistics Canada, *Aviation in Canada,* cat. no. 51-501E (October 1993).

TABLE 13.5   Busiest Ports, 1992—Cargo loaded and unloaded, domestic and international (tonnes)

Vancouver	61,315,000
Port Cartier	21,313,000
Sept Iles	19,195,000
Montreal	16,577,000
Quebec	15,660,000
Saint John	15,598,000
Halifax	13,775,000
Thunder Bay	12,743,000
Prince Rupert	12,649,000
Hamilton	12,626,000

Source: Reproduced by authority of the Minister of Industry, 1995, Statistics Canada, *Shipping in Canada,* cat. no. 54-205, 1992 (February 1994).

Economy

TABLE 13.6   Farm Cash Receipts, 1992

A. Crops ($ thousands)

	Wheat	Oats and Barley	Canola	Soybeans	Corn	Potatoes
Nfld.	–	–	–	–	–	1,076
P.E.I.	1,153	5,026	–	852	–	98,654
N.S.	620	386	–	–	207	7,258
N.B.	393	2,468	–	–	–	66,589
Que.	11,658	26,821	–	19,060	148,130	57,734
Ont.	80,298	18,221	8,755	418,247	266,008	48,661
Man.	496,273	90,071	252,404	–	2,774	55,555
Sask.	1,591,441	215,546	532,207	–	–	12,145
Alta.	601,910	236,447	434,604	–	–	57,529
B.C.	11,850	7,015	8,522	–	–	40,770
Total	2,795,596	601,941	1,236,492	438,159	417,119	445,971

	Vegetables	Fruit and Berries	Nursery	Tobacco	Other Crops	Total Crops
Nfld.	3,537	1,079	4,334	–	970	10,993
P.E.I.	6,543	2,169	1,115	5,610	2,287	123,409
N.S.	16,032	26,037	24,728	845	14,848	90,901
N.B.	6,787	9,105	15,156	385	15,205	116,088
Que.	182,447	54,658	140,952	24,318	127,274	793,052
Ont.	362,502	118,114	438,163	259,232	135,060	2,153,321
Man.	19,531	3,845	20,553	–	129,398	1,070,404
Sask.	1,224	–	13,640	–	283,180	2,649,383
Alta.	36,253	3,201	71,710	–	135,512	1,577,166
B.C.	105,152	136,326	212,239	–	64,996	586,870
Total	740,008	354,534	942,590	290,390	908,727	9,171,587

TABLE 13.6 continued

B. Livestock ($ thousands)

	Cattle and Calves	Hogs	Dairy	Poultry and Eggs	Other Livestock	Total Livestock
Nfld.	1,704	2,920	20,803	23,012	768	49,207
P.E.I.	33,736	21,564	38,897	6,815	1,367	102,379
N.S.	31,335	26,363	83,790	60,103	10,106	211,697
N.B.	25,863	16,049	56,651	51,141	2,695	152,399
Que.	389,807	610,750	1,141,456	439,408	44,722	2,626,143
Ont.	979,005	563,014	1,072,547	626,643	109,969	3,351,178
Man.	356,499	276,718	115,125	103,075	71,573	922,990
Sask.	708,649	155,282	88,452	58,416	45,164	1,055,963
Alta.	2,147,768	322,536	244,663	151,114	69,215	2,935,296
B.C.	312,108	40,721	268,109	234,494	30,422	885,854
Total	4,986,474	2,035,917	3,130,493	1,754,221	386,001	12,293,106

C. Totals ($ thousands)

	Total Crops	Total Livestock	Support Payments	Total Receipts
Nfld.	10,993	49,207	3,463	63,663
P.E.I.	123,409	102,379	12,782	238,570
N.S.	90,901	211,697	8,065	310,663
N.B.	116,088	152,399	17,065	285,552
Que.	793,052	2,626,143	505,803	3,924,998
Ont.	2,153,321	3,351,178	449,855	5,954,354
Man.	1,070,404	922,990	382,771	2,376,165
Sask.	2,649,383	1,055,963	825,515	4,530,861
Alta.	1,577,166	2,935,296	515,221	5,027,683
B.C.	586,870	885,854	41,273	1,513,997
Total	9,171,587	12,293,106	2,761,813	24,226,506

Source: Reproduced by authority of the Minister of Industry, 1995, Statistics Canada, *Farm Cash Receipts from Farming Operations—1993,* cat. no. 21-603E (May, 1994).

TABLE 13.7   Census Farms, Total and Average Acreage, 1991

	No. of Farms	Total Acreage	Average Acreage
Saskatchewan	60,840	66,386,100	1,091
Alberta	57,245	51,425,100	898
Manitoba	25,706	19,088,900	743
Ontario	68,633	13,470,700	196
Quebec	38,076	8,474,800	223
British Columbia	19,225	5,911,600	307
Nova Scotia	3,980	981,100	247
New Brunswick	3,252	928,200	285
Prince Edward Island	2,361	639,700	271
Newfoundland	725	117,000	161
Canada	280,043	167,423,100	598

Source: Reproduced by authority of the Minister of Industry, 1995, Statistics Canada, *1991 Census*, cat. no. 93-348, adapted by author.

TABLE 13.8   Production of Selected Minerals by Province, by Volume and Value, 1992

	Volume	Value
Asbestos		
Quebec	567,000 t	$224,549,000
Newfoundland	14,000 t	3,531,000
British Columbia	6,000 t	2,939,000
Coal		
Alberta	33,526,000 t	$564,200,000
British Columbia	17,174,000 t	706,300,000
Saskatchewan	10,027,000 t	101,700,000
Nova Scotia	4,486,000 t	264,900,000
New Brunswick	399,000 t	32,200,000
Copper		
British Columbia	323,781,000 kg	$908,412,000
Ontario	272,242,000 kg	763,814,000
Quebec	91,950,000 kg	257,979,000
Manitoba	60,024,000 kg	168,405,000
New Brunswick	13,697,000 kg	38,428,000

TABLE 13.8 continued

	Volume	Value
Gold		
Ontario	74,343 kg	$992,705,000
Quebec	44,589 kg	595,400,000
British Columbia	16,773 kg	224,966,000
Northwest Territories	13,518 kg	180,501,000
Yukon	3,737 kg	49,898,000
Manitoba	3,106 kg	41,471,000
New Brunswick	490 kg	6,541,000
Alberta	34 kg	452,000
Iron Ore		
Newfoundland	17,692,000 t	$645,333,000
Quebec	13,350,000 t	not available
Ontario	482,000 t	not available
British Columbia	59,000 t	1,353,000
Lead		
Yukon	135,688,000 kg	$99,595,000
British Columbia	81,591,000 kg	59,888,000
New Brunswick	78,137,000 kg	57,352,000
Northwest Territories	39,141,000 kg	28,729,000
Manitoba	1,487,000 kg	1,091,000
Nova Scotia	834,000 kg	612,000
Natural Gas		
Alberta	95,180,000,000 cu. m	$4,736,172,000
British Columbia	14,293,000,000 cu. m	588,006,000
Saskatchewan	6,182,000,000 cu. m	327,466,000
Ontario	427,000,000 cu. m	40,079,000
Natural Gas By-products		
Alberta	25,798,000 cu. m	$2,346,446,000
British Columbia	772,000 cu. m	72,544,000
Saskatchewan	129,000 cu. m	12,416,000
Manitoba	6,000 cu. m	561,000
Nickel		
Ontario	118,860,000 kg	$1,005,556,000
Manitoba	58,695,000 kg	496,556,000

TABLE 13.8 continued

	Volume	Value
Peat		
New Brunswick	323,000 t	$38,053,000
Quebec	271,000 t	36,944,000
Alberta	94,000 t	20,500,000
Newfoundland	5,000 t	725,000
Petroleum (Crude)		
Alberta	74,505,000 cu. m	$8,823,901,000
Saskatchewan	13,355,000 cu. m	1,415,908,000
British Columbia	2,060,000 cu. m	262,772,000
Manitoba	656,000 cu. m	86,289,000
Nova Scotia	577,000 cu. m	96,097,000
Ontario	224,000 cu. m	35,175,000
Silver		
British Columbia	345,000 kg	$56,312,000
New Brunswick	254,000 kg	38,800,000
Ontario	247,000 kg	37,725,000
Quebec	143,000 kg	21,798,000
Yukon	124,000 kg	19,014,000
Manitoba	41,000 kg	6,246,000
Northwest Territories	16,000 kg	2,397,000
Uranium		
Saskatchewan	8,125,000 kg	$400,148,000
Ontario	989,000 kg	166,204,000
Zinc		
New Brunswick	301,020,000 kg	$450,928,000
Yukon	292,304,000 kg	303,051,000
Ontario	190,523,000 kg	285,403,000
Northwest Territories	171,481,000 kg	256,878,000
British Columbia	133,149,000 kg	199,458,000
Quebec	107,466,000 kg	160,984,000
Manitoba	89,211,000 kg	133,638,000
Nova Scotia	582,000 kg	871,000

Source: Reproduced by authority of the Minister of Industry, 1995, Statistics Canada, *Canada's Mineral Production (Preliminary Estimates 1993),* cat. no. 26-202 (March 1994).

TABLE 13.9   Total Value of Mineral Production by Province, 1992 ($ thousands)

	Metals	Non-Metals	Structural	Fuels	Total
Nfld.	$ 664,767	$ 8,255	$ 32,650	$ –	$ 705,673
P.E.I.	–	–	1,699	–	1,699
N.S.	1,925	85,910	74,201	360,997	523,033
N.B.	594,174	243,745	38,002	32,200	908,121
Que.	1,663,010	541,415	489,982	–	2,694,407
Ont.	3,505,366	250,001	938,957	75,254	4,769,578
Man.	905,808	17,072	72,314	86,850	1,082,044
Sask.	424,379	848,633	27,249	1,857,490	3,157,751
Alta.	452	149,414	264,789	16,470,719	16,885,374
B.C.	1,501,697	62,644	305,241	1,629,622	3,499,204

Source: Reproduced by authority of the Minister of Industry, 1995, Statistics Canada, *Canada's Mineral Production (Preliminary Estimates 1993)*, cat. no. 26-202 (March 1994).

TABLE 13.10   Forest Production, 1991—Value of Shipments* ($ millions)

	Logging	Saw-mills	Other Wood	Total Wood	Pulp and Paper	Other Paper	Total Paper	Total
Nfld.	132.6	14.5	23.1	37.6	x	x	x	x
P.E.I.	3.3	4.8	6.4	11.2	–	–	–	x
N.S.	198.2	66.1	55.5	121.6	428.0	76.6	504.6	824.4
N.B.	492.2	243.3	181.8	425.1	1238.4	59.8	1298.2	2,215.5
Que.	1520.6	1562.2	1543.3	3105.5	5206.4	1652.1	6858.5	11,524.6
Ont.	1092.6	695.9	1596.7	2292.6	3491.8	3105.5	6597.3	9,982.5
Man.	61.7	36.4	149.2	185.6	x	x	245.7	493.0
Sask.	78.3	43.7	57.9	101.6	x	x	x	x
Alta.	273.4	446.3	409.4	855.7	674.0	260.0	934.0	2,063.1
B.C.	3848.5	4615.0	1414.2	6029.2	3756.4	268.7	4025.1	13,902.8
Total	7702	7728	5437	13166	15446	5557	21003	41,871.1

Source: Reproduced by authority of the Minister of Industry, 1995, Statistics Canada, *Forestry Statistics 1991*, cat. no. 25-202 (October 1993).

*Dashes represent negligible or zero figures; Xs represent confidential figures.

TABLE 13.11 Canadian Sea Fisheries Landings, 1993

Province	Quantity (tonnes)	Value ($ thousands)
Nova Scotia	400,930	$470,362
British Columbia	227,832	341,639
Newfoundland	226,688	171,935
New Brunswick	115,483	103,118
Quebec	58,308	91,256
Prince Edward Island	32,986	65,414

Source: Department of Fisheries and Oceans, *Canadian Fisheries Landings,* December 1994, Vol. 16, No. 4, used with permission.

TABLE 13.12 Production of Electricity, 1992 (MW.H)

	Hydro	Steam	Nuclear	Other	Total
Que.	141,351,862	867,537	4,599,950	257,877	147,077,226
Ont.	39,718,625	30,508,487	66,586,451	1,703,945	138,517,508
B.C.	60,554,982	3,522,980	–	87,371	64,165,333
Alta.	1,584,788	43,665,987	–	2,269,566	47,520,341
Nfld.	34,880,434	1,730,477	–	69,798	36,680,709
Man.	26,433,551	303,360	–	26,236	26,763,147
N.B.	2,972,072	8,134,815	4,834,622	20,831	15,962,331
Sask.	3,054,567	10,927,832	–	144,440	14,126,839
N.S.	896,036	8,821,759	–	4,546	9,722,341
P.E.I.	–	33,544	–	586	34,130

Source: Reproduced by authority of the Minister of Industry, 1995, Statistics Canada, *Electric Power Statistics,* December 1993, cat. no. 57-001 (March 1994), adapted by author.

TABLE 13.13 Export and Import of Electricity, 1992 (MW.H)

| | Export | | | | Import | | |
To other Province(s)			To U.S.	From other Province(s)			From U.S.
Nfld.	25,985,123	B.C.	9,205,499	Que.	29,526,816	Ont.	4,166,201
Que.	4,509,382	Que.	8,877,283	N.B.	3,925,299	Que.	1,387,728
N.B.	4,345,294	Man.	6,249,897	Ont.	2,203,436	B.C.	692,439
Man.	3,113,343	Ont.	5,303,001	B.C.	1,992,880	N.B.	116,433
Alta.	2,016,498	N.B.	1,775,499	Sask.	1,584,532	Sask.	99,840
Sask.	1,083,146	Sask.	138,110	Man.	965,053	Man.	11,305
B.C.	267,344	Alta.	–	P.E.I.	737,663	Alta.	2,332
Ont.	200,758	Nfld.	–	Alta.	399,363	Nfld.	–
N.S.	66,924	N.S.	–	N.S.	252,770	N.S.	–
P.E.I.	–	P.E.I.	–	Nfld.	–	P.E.I.	–
Total	41,587,812		31,549,289		41,587,812		6,476,278

Source: Reproduced by authority of the Minister of Industry, 1995, Statistics Canada, *Electric Power Statistics,* December 1993, cat. no. 57-001 (March 1994), adapted by author.

TABLE 13.14 Selected Manufacturing Statistics, 1990

	No. of Esta-blishments	No. of Employees	Salaries and Wages	Value of Shipments	Percentage of Total Value
			($ millions)		
Ont.	15,563	945,930	$31,346	$188,583.2	54.8
Que.	13,362	512,541	15,427	80,831.1	23.5
B.C.	4,126	154,468	5,637	27,243.6	7.9
Alta.	2,827	91,404	2,947	21,293.9	6.1
Man.	1,167	52,863	1,461	7,293.9	2.1
N.B.	714	34,007	1,000	6,297.7	1.8
N.S.	760	37,264	1,070	5,910.3	1.7
Sask.	809	20,234	605	4,084.2	1.2
Nfld.	341	16,343	413	1,961.4	0.6
P.E.I.	141	3,486	74	457.6	0.1
Total	39,864	1,868,983	$59,992	$344,033.3	

Source: Reproduced by authority of the Minister of Industry, 1995, Statistics Canada, *Manufacturing Industries of Canada,* cat. no. 31-203 (March 1994), adapted by author.

TABLE 13.15 Provincial Gross Domestic Product, 1991 and 1992

	1991		1992	
	$ millions	**Percentage**	**$ millions**	**Percentage**
Newfoundland	9,312	1.4	9,232	1.3
Prince Edward Island	2,078	0.3	2,151	0.3
Nova Scotia	17,605	2.6	17,987	2.6
New Brunswick	13,689	2.0	13,878	2.0
Quebec	155,864	23.1	157,067	22.8
Ontario	270,463	40.1	277,454	40.3
Manitoba	23,340	3.5	23,969	3.5
Saskatchewan	19,985	3.0	20,237	2.9
Alberta	72,168	10.7	72,942	10.6
British Columbia	84,088	12.7	86,669	12.6
Territories	3,076	0.5	3,125	0.5
Total	674,388		688,541	

Source: Reproduced by authority of the Minister of Industry, 1995, Statistics Canada, *Provincial Economic Accounts, Annual Estimates 1988-1992*, cat. no. 13-213 (March 1994).

TABLE 13.16 Distribution of Labour Force by Sector, 1991

	Primary	**Secondary**	**Tertiary**
Newfoundland	8.3%	20.5%	71.1%
Prince Edward Island	14.7%	17.0%	68.3%
Nova Scotia	6.9%	18.5%	74.7%
New Brunswick	7.4%	20.7%	71.8%
Quebec	4.0%	23.7%	72.2%
Ontario	3.5%	24.0%	72.5%
Manitoba	9.6%	16.3%	74.1%
Saskatchewan	21.0%	10.6%	68.5%
Alberta	12.8%	14.9%	72.2%
British Columbia	6.4%	18.7%	74.9%

Source: Reproduced by authority of the Minister of Industry, 1995, Statistics Canada, *1991 Census*, adapted by author.

Class

TABLE 13.17   Personal Income per Person, 1992

Ontario	$23,593
British Columbia	22,662
Alberta	22,389
Quebec	20,648
Manitoba	19,862
Nova Scotia	18,680
Saskatchewan	18,448
Prince Edward Island	17,915
New Brunswick	17,724
Newfoundland	17,227
Canada	21,687

Source: Reproduced by authority of the Minister of Industry, 1995, Statistics Canada, *Provincial Economic Accounts, Annual Estimates 1988-1992,* cat. no. 13-213 (March 1994).

TABLE 13.18   Proportion of Families with Incomes Less than $20,000 and Over $70,000, 1991 Census

	Under $20,000	Over $70,000	Median
Ontario	12.6%	26.8%	$50,046
Alberta	15.4%	22.8%	46,146
British Columbia	15.1%	22.0%	46,151
Quebec	18.1%	16.8%	41,051
Manitoba	18.3%	16.0%	40,671
Nova Scotia	19.4%	14.2%	38,997
Saskatchewan	20.4%	15.0%	38,531
Prince Edward Island	17.5%	12.2%	37,486
New Brunswick	20.9%	12.7%	37,152
Newfoundland	23.4%	12.0%	35,184

Source: Reproduced by authority of the Minister of Industry, 1995, Statistics Canada, *1991 Census,* adapted by author.

TABLE 13.19   Rate of Unionization by Province, 1991

Newfoundland	53.3%	Prince Edward Island	33.2%
Quebec	40.6%	Saskatchewan	32.9%
British Columbia	38.7%	Ontario	31.9%
Manitoba	37.1%	Nova Scotia	31.0%
New Brunswick	36.8%	Alberta	26.4%
	Canada	35.1%	

Source: Reproduced by authority of the Minister of Industry, 1995, Statistics Canada, *CALURA, Labour Unions,* 1991, cat. no. 71-202 (October 1993).

**TABLE 13.20   Membership in Different Types of Unions, 1991
(in thousands of members)**

	International	National	Government	Total
Nfld.	19.6 (21%)	50.5 (55%)	22.0 (24%)	92.1
P.E.I.	1.7 (13%)	5.8 (44%)	5.7 (43%)	13.2
N.S.	30.6 (29%)	49.7 (47%)	24.6 (23%)	104.9
N.B.	24.5 (26%)	55.2 (59%)	13.1 (14%)	92.8
Que.	240.3 (22%)	756.1 (69%)	99.1 (9%)	1,095.5
Ont.	520.9 (37%)	678.7 (49%)	193.3 (14%)	1,392.9
Man.	54.8 (35%)	68.6 (44%)	34.2 (22%)	157.6
Sask.	31.6 (28%)	61.0 (54%)	21.4 (19%)	114.0
Alta.	90.9 (31%)	144.2 (49%)	61.0 (21%)	296.1
B.C.	168.5 (32%)	287.0 (55%)	64.0 (12%)	519.5
Total	1,185.0 (30%)	2,158.5 (56%)	545.1 (14%)	3,888.6

Source: Reproduced by authority of the Minister of Industry, 1995, Statistics Canada, *CALURA, Labour Unions,* 1991, cat. no. 71-202 (October 1993).

TABLE 13.21   Educational Attainment, 15 Years of Age and Over, 1991

Less Than Grade Nine		University Degree		Average Years of School	
B.C.	9.1%	Ont.	13.0%	B.C.	12.5
Alta.	9.1%	Alta.	11.9%	Alta.	12.4
Ont.	11.9%	B.C.	11.2%	Ont.	12.4
N.S.	13.6%	N.S.	10.4%	N.S.	11.8
Man.	15.2%	Que.	10.3%	Que.	11.6
P.E.I.	15.7%	Man.	10.2%	Man.	11.6
Sask.	16.3%	Sask.	8.6%	Sask.	11.6
N.B.	20.1%	P.E.I.	8.5%	P.E.I.	11.6
Que.	20.6%	N.B.	8.4%	N.B.	11.3
Nfld.	20.8%	Nfld.	6.6%	Nfld.	10.8
Canada	14.3%	Canada	11.4%	Canada	12.1

Source: Reproduced by authority of the Minister of Industry, 1995, Statistics Canada, *1991 Census, Educational Attainment and School Attendance,* cat. no. 93-328.

TABLE 13.22   Annual Unemployment Rate, 1970-1994

	Nfld.	P.E.I.	N.S.	N.B.	Que.	Ont.	Man.	Sask.	Alta.	B.C.	Canada
1970	7.3	NA	5.3	6.3	7.0	4.4	5.3	4.2	5.1	7.7	5.7
1971	8.4	NA	7.0	6.1	7.3	5.4	5.7	3.5	5.7	7.2	6.2
1972	9.2	10.8	7.0	7.0	7.5	5.0	5.4	4.4	5.6	7.8	6.2
1973	10.0	NA	6.6	7.7	6.8	4.3	4.6	3.5	5.3	6.7	5.5
1974	13.0	NA	6.8	7.5	6.6	4.4	3.6	2.8	3.5	6.2	5.3
1975	14.0	8.0	7.7	9.8	8.1	6.3	4.5	2.9	4.1	8.5	6.9
1976	13.3	9.6	9.5	11.0	8.7	6.2	4.7	3.9	4.0	8.6	7.1
1977	15.5	9.8	10.6	13.2	10.3	7.0	5.9	4.5	4.5	8.5	8.1
1978	16.2	9.8	10.5	12.5	10.9	7.2	6.5	4.9	4.7	8.3	8.3
1979	15.1	11.2	10.1	11.1	9.6	6.5	5.3	4.2	3.9	7.6	7.4
1980	13.3	10.6	9.7	11.0	9.8	6.8	5.5	4.4	3.7	6.8	7.5
1981	13.9	11.2	10.1	11.5	10.3	6.6	5.9	4.6	3.8	6.7	7.5
1982	16.7	12.9	13.1	14.1	13.8	9.7	8.5	6.1	7.7	12.1	11.0
1983	18.7	12.2	13.2	14.8	13.9	10.3	9.4	7.3	10.6	13.8	11.8
1984	20.2	12.8	13.0	14.8	12.8	9.0	8.4	8.0	11.1	14.7	11.2
1985	20.8	13.3	13.6	15.1	11.8	8.0	8.2	8.1	10.0	14.1	10.5
1986	19.2	13.4	13.1	14.3	11.0	7.0	7.7	7.7	9.8	12.5	9.5
1987	17.9	13.2	12.3	13.1	10.3	6.1	7.4	7.4	9.6	11.9	8.8
1988	16.4	13.0	10.2	12.0	9.4	5.0	7.8	7.5	8.0	10.3	7.8
1989	15.8	14.1	9.9	12.5	9.3	5.1	7.5	7.4	7.2	9.1	7.5
1990	17.1	14.9	10.5	12.1	10.1	6.3	7.2	7.0	7.0	8.3	8.1

TABLE 13.22 continued

	Nfld.	P.E.I.	N.S.	N.B.	Que.	Ont.	Man.	Sask.	Alta.	B.C.	Canada
1991	18.4	16.8	12.0	12.7	11.9	9.6	8.8	7.4	8.2	9.9	10.3
1992	20.2	17.7	13.1	12.8	12.8	10.8	9.6	8.2	9.5	10.4	11.3
1993	20.2	17.7	14.6	12.6	13.1	10.6	9.2	8.0	9.6	9.7	11.2
1994	20.6	17.0	13.3	12.5	12.1	9.6	9.1	7.0	8.4	9.3	10.3

Source: Reproduced by authority of the Minister of Industry, 1995, Statistics Canada, *The Labour Force, 1993*, cat. no. 71-201 (February 1994 and December 1994).

Demography

TABLE 13.23   Mother Tongue by Province, 1991 Census

English		French		Other	
Newfoundland	98.6	Quebec	82.2	Manitoba	20.3
Prince Edward Island	94.2	New Brunswick	33.6	Ontario	18.4
Nova Scotia	93.6	Ontario	5.0	British Columbia	17.9
Saskatchewan	84.2	Manitoba	4.7	Alberta	15.2
Alberta	82.5	Prince Edward Island	4.5	Saskatchewan	13.5
British Columbia	80.5	Nova Scotia	4.1	Quebec	8.1
Ontario	76.6	Alberta	2.3	Nova Scotia	2.3
Manitoba	75.0	Saskatchewan	2.2	New Brunswick	1.3
New Brunswick	65.1	British Columbia	1.6	Prince Edward Island	1.2
Quebec	9.7	Newfoundland	0.5	Newfoundland	0.9
Territories	66.1	Territories	2.7	Territories	31.2
Canada	61.7	Canada	24.4	Canada	13.9

Source: Reproduced by authority of the Minister of Industry, 1995, Statistics Canada, *1991 Census, Home Language and Mother Tongue*, cat. no. 93-317, adapted by author.

TABLE 13.24   Home Language by Province, 1991 Census

English		French		Other	
Newfoundland	99.2	Quebec	83.0	Ontario	11.6
Prince Edward Island	97.3	New Brunswick	31.2	Manitoba	9.9
Nova Scotia	96.3	Ontario	3.2	British Columbia	9.9
Saskatchewan	94.4	Nova Scotia	2.5	Alberta	7.7
Alberta	91.5	Manitoba	2.3	Quebec	5.8
British Columbia	89.6	Prince Edward Island	2.3	Saskatchewan	4.9
Manitoba	87.7	Alberta	0.8	Nova Scotia	1.2
Ontario	85.2	Saskatchewan	0.7	New Brunswick	0.7
New Brunswick	68.2	British Columbia	0.4	Newfoundland	0.5
Quebec	11.2	Newfoundland	0.2	Prince Edward Island	0.3
Territories	76.5	Territories	1.3	Territories	22.2
Canada	68.3	Canada	23.3	Canada	8.4

Source: Reproduced by authority of the Minister of Industry, 1995, Statistics Canada, *1991 Census, Home Language and Mother Tongue*, cat. no. 93-317, adapted by author.

TABLE 13.25   Language Transfer Rate (Those with French Mother Tongue Who Have a Different Home Language), 1991 Census

British Columbia	72.8%	Prince Edward Island	46.8%
Saskatchewan	67.5%	Nova Scotia	41.7%
Alberta	64.5%	Ontario	36.9%
Newfoundland	54.9%	New Brunswick	9.7%
Manitoba	50.5%	Quebec	1.0%

Source: Reproduced by authority of the Minister of Industry, 1995, Statistics Canada, *1991 Census, Home Language and Mother Tongue*, cat. no. 93-317, adapted by author.

TABLE 13.26   Residents with Aboriginal Origins by Province and Territory, 1991 Census

Ontario	243,555	Manitoba	10.8%
British Columbia	169,035	Saskatchewan	9.9%
Quebec	137,615	Alberta	5.9%
Alberta	148,220	British Columbia	5.2%
Manitoba	116,200	Nova Scotia	2.5%
Saskatchewan	96,580	Ontario	2.4%
Northwest Territories	35,390	Newfoundland	2.3%
Nova Scotia	21,880	Quebec	2.0%
Newfoundland	13,110	New Brunswick	1.8%
New Brunswick	12,815	Prince Edward Island	1.5%
Yukon	6,385		
Prince Edward Island	1,880		
Total	1,002,670	Total	3.7%

Source: Reproduced by authority of the Minister of Industry, 1995, Statistics Canada, *1991 Census, Canada's Aboriginal Population*, cat. no. 94-326, adapted by author.

TABLE 13.27   Place of Birth, 1991 (percentages)

Born in Province		Born in Canada		Immigrant	
Nfld.	93.3	Nfld.	98.5	Ont.	24.1
Que.	87.3	P.E.I.	96.7	B.C.	22.4
N.B.	82.8	N.B.	96.6	Alta.	15.2
Sask.	81.3	N.S.	95.6	Man.	12.9
N.S.	79.8	Sask.	94.1	Que.	8.7
P.E.I.	79.7	Que.	91.3	Sask.	5.9
Man.	73.1	Man.	87.1	N.S.	4.4
Ont.	65.5	Alta.	84.8	N.B.	3.4
Alta.	57.6	B.C.	77.5	P.E.I.	3.2
B.C.	48.9	Ont.	75.9	Nfld.	1.5

Source: Reproduced by authority of the Minister of Industry, 1995, Statistics Canada, *1991 Census, Immigration and Citizenship*, cat. no. 93-316, adapted by author.

TABLE 13.28   Religion, 1991 (percentages)

Protestant		Roman Catholic		Other		None	
Nfld.	61.0	Que.	86.1	Ont.	7.6	B.C.	30.4
N.S.	54.1	N.B.	54.0	B.C.	6.5	Alta.	19.7
Sask.	53.4	P.E.I.	47.3	Alta.	5.4	Man.	13.7
Man.	50.8	N.S.	37.2	Man.	4.9	Ont.	12.5
P.E.I.	48.4	Nfld.	37.0	Que.	4.2	Sask.	11.0
Alta.	48.4	Ont.	35.5	Sask.	3.1	N.S.	7.6
B.C.	44.5	Sask.	32.5	N.S.	1.1	N.B.	5.4
Ont.	44.4	Man.	30.3	N.B.	0.5	Que.	3.9
N.B.	40.1	Alta.	26.5	P.E.I.	0.5	P.E.I.	3.8
Que.	5.9	B.C.	18.6	Nfld.	0.3	Nfld.	1.6

Source: Reproduced by authority of the Minister of Industry, 1995, Statistics Canada, *1991 Census, Religions in Canada,* cat. no. 93-319, adapted by author.

Intergovernmental Relations

TABLE 13.29   Transfers from Federal Government as Percentage of Provincial Government Revenue, 1992 ($ millions)

	Total Provincial Government Revenue	Federal Transfers to Provincial Government	Percentage of Provincial Government Revenue Received from Ottawa
Nfld.	$3,346	$1,496	44.7%
P.E.I.	734	299	40.7%
N.S.	4,376	1,637	37.4%
N.B.	3,955	1,405	35.5%
Man.	6,417	1,899	30.0%
Sask.	5,879	1,663	28.3%
Que.	40,010	7,548	18.9%
Ont.	43,789	6,812	15.6%
Alta.	14,979	2,269	15.1%
B.C.	17,987	2,330	13.0%

Source: Reproduced by authority of the Minister of Industry, 1995, Statistics Canada, *Provincial Economic Accounts, Annual Estimates 1988-1992,* cat. no. 13-213 (March 1994).

TABLE 13.30 Federal Transfers to Provincial Governments, Municipalities, Persons, and Businesses, 1992 ($ millions)

	Province	Municipalities	Persons	Businesses
Newfoundland	$1,496	$ 35	$ 1,940	$ 285
Prince Edward Island	299	4	433	73
Nova Scotia	1,637	90	2,337	181
New Brunswick	1,405	47	1,975	226
Quebec	7,548	156	13,708	1,227
Ontario	6,812	357	17,134	2,055
Manitoba	1,899	51	2,298	477
Saskatchewan	1,663	7	2,082	944
Alberta	2,269	58	4,027	824
British Columbia	2,330	107	6,635	405

Source: Reproduced by authority of the Minister of Industry, 1995, Statistics Canada, *Provincial Economic Accounts, Annual Estimates 1988-1992*, cat. no. 13-213 (March 1994), adapted by author.

TABLE 13.31 Provincial Employees, 1992

	Departments, Ministries and Agencies	Government Business Enterprises	Wider Public Sector	Total
Newfoundland	12,450	2,617	13,420	28,487
Prince Edward Island	3,190	293	3,794	7,277
Nova Scotia	11,606	2,033	19,246	32,885
New Brunswick	11,175	4,918	33,863	49,956
Quebec	69,446	36,631	225,488	331,565
Ontario	88,353	42,919	199,271	330,543
Manitoba	12,742	12,337	23,636	48,175
Saskatchewan	9,834	11,419	16,624	37,877
Alberta	34,990	5,149	39,865	80,004
British Columbia	30,128	23,583	82,950	136,661

Source: Reproduced by authority of the Minister of Industry, 1995, Statistics Canada, *Public Sector Employment and Remuneration 1992*, cat. no. 72-209 (October 1993), adapted by author.

Note: Statistics Canada warns that these figures should not be used for inter-provincial comparisons. The wider public sector is difficult to define, and not all provinces will include the same types of employees in this category. Moreover, the division of responsibility between provincial and municipal governments varies from province to province. For the author, the two first columns are of most interest.

TABLE 13.32   Federal, Provincial and Municipal Employees, 1992

	Federal	Provincial	Municipal	Total
Newfoundland	13,249	28,510	3,463	45,222
Prince Edward Island	3,660	7,700	2,868	14,228
Nova Scotia	37,070	34,979	31,437	103,486
New Brunswick	20,080	50,677	5,425	76,182
Quebec	112,699	335,285	218,838	666,822
Ontario	211,299	338,017	427,051	976,367
Manitoba	29,422	48,886	44,912	123,220
Saskatchewan	15,758	38,908	45,600	100,266
Alberta	43,138	82,157	134,814	260,109
British Columbia	54,108	135,837	95,263	285,208

Source: Reproduced by authority of the Minister of Industry, 1995, Statistics Canada, *Public Sector Employment and Remuneration 1992*, cat. no. 72-209 (October 1993), adapted by author.

TABLE 13.33   Net Provincial Debts, Debt as a Percentage of GDP, and Debt Per Capita, May 31, 1995

	Net Debt ($ millions)	Debt as % of GDP	Debt Per Capita
Newfoundland	$ 4,458	62.9	$7,693
Prince Edward Island	467	42.4	3,590
Nova Scotia	7,749	59.0	8,259
New Brunswick	3,949	38.2	5,192
Quebec	60,527	50.7	8,291
Ontario	79,747	37.0	7,218
Manitoba	6,885	38.1	6,078
Saskatchewan	6,754	35.7	6,640
Alberta	3,725	5.1	1,366
British Columbia	7,733	11.1	2,079

Source: Reproduced by authority of the Minister of Industry, 1995, Statistics Canada, *Public Sector Finance, 1994–95*, Financial Management System, cat. no. 68-212 (March 1995). Adapted by author.

Note: Column two divides column one by GDP figures used throughout this text (Conference Board of Canada), and column three divides column one by Statistics Canada population estimates for January 1995.

TABLE 13.34   Number of Days in Legislative Session, 1990-93

	1990	1991	1992	1993	Average	Rank
Alta.	135	98	94	117	111	1
Man.	98	103	97	95	98.25	2
Ont.	72	101	94	98	91.25	3
Nfld.	94	89	90	37	77.5	4
Que.	83	80	69	78	77.5	4
Sask.	67	64	76	81	72	6
B.C.	26	38	112	91	66.75	7
N.S.	77	40	51	52	55	8
N.B.	37	25	48	31	35.25	9
P.E.I.	28	27	26	17	24.5	10

Source: Calculations by author, based on legislative documents and the kind assistance of legislative clerks.

TABLE 13.35   Remuneration for Provincial Legislators, 1994

	Indemnity (taxable)	Expense Allowance (non-taxable)	Total	Total in taxable terms*
Quebec	$63,469	$11,203	$74,672	$85,875
Alberta	38,335	19,167	57,502	76,669
Ontario	44,675	14,984	59,659	74,643
Newfoundland	36,316	18,158	54,474	72,632
British Columbia	32,812	16,406	49,218	65,624
New Brunswick	35,807	14,323	50,130	64,453
Nova Scotia	30,130	15,065	45,195	60,260
Manitoba	28,780	14,390	43,170	57,560
Saskatchewan	38,546	7,622	46,168	53,790
Prince Edward Island	32,000	9,700	41,700	51,400

* Calculated by doubling the non-taxable allowance, assuming a tax rate of 50 percent on this marginal increase.

Source: Calculations by author, based on legislative documents and the kind assistance of legislative clerks.

Index